Brilliant

Adobe®

InDesign® CC

Steve Johnson

Perspection, Inc.

Harlow, England • London • New York • Boston • San Francisco • Toronto • Sydney • Auckland • Singapore • Hong Kong
Tokyo • Seoul • Taipei • New Delhi • Cape Town • São Paulo • Mexico City • Madrid • Amsterdam • Munich • Paris • Milan

Pearson Education Limited
Edinburgh Gate
Harlow
Essex CM20 2JE
England

and Associated Companies throughout the world

Visit us on the World Wide Web at:
www.pearson.com/uk

Original edition, entitled ADOBE® INDESIGN® CC ON DEMAND, 9780789751638 by JOHNSON, STEVE; PERSPECTION, INC., published by Pearson Education, Inc., publishing as Que, Copyright © 2013 Perspection, Inc.

This UK edition published by PEARSON EDUCATION LTD, Copyright © 2013

This edition is manufactured in the USA and available for sale only in the United Kingdom, Europe, the Middle East, and Africa.

ISBN: 978-0-7897-5230-7

British Library Cataloguing-in-Publication Data
A catalogue record for this book is available from the British Library

10 9 8 7 6 5 4 3 2 1
17 16 15 14 13

Printed and bound in the United States of America

Brilliant Guides

What you need to know and how to do it

When you're working on your computer and come up against a problem that you're unsure how to solve, or want to accomplish something in an application that you aren't sure how to do, where do you look?? Manuals and traditional training guides are usually too big and unwieldy and are intended to be used as an end-to-end training resource, making it hard to get to the info you need right away without having to wade through pages of background information that you just don't need at that moment – and helplines are rarely that helpful!

Brilliant guides have been developed to allow you to find the info you need easily and without fuss and guide you through the task using a highly visual, step-by-step approach – providing exactly what you need to know when you need it!!

Brilliant guides provide the quick easy-to-access information that you need, using a detailed index and troubleshooting guide to help you find exactly what you need to know, and then presenting each task on one or two pages. Numbered steps then guide you through each task or problem, using numerous screenshots to illustrate each step. Added features include "See Also…" boxes that point you to related tasks and information in the book, whilst "Did you know?…" sections alert you to relevant expert tips, tricks and advice to further expand your skills and knowledge.

In addition to covering all major office applications, and related computing subjects, the *Brilliant* series also contains titles that will help you in every aspect of your working life, such as writing the perfect CV, answering the toughest interview questions and moving on in your career.

Brilliant guides are the light at the end of the tunnel when you are faced with any minor or major task!

Acknowledgments

Perspection, Inc.

Brilliant Adobe InDesign CC has been created by the professional trainers and writers at Perspection, Inc. to the standards you've come to expect from Que publishing. Together, we are pleased to present this training book.

Perspection, Inc. is a software training company committed to providing information and training to help people use software more effectively in order to communicate, make decisions, and solve problems. Perspection writes and produces software training books, and develops multimedia and web-based training. Since 1991, we have written more than 120 computer books, with several bestsellers to our credit, and sold over 5 million books.

This book incorporates Perspection's training expertise to ensure that you'll receive the maximum return on your time. You'll focus on the tasks and skills that increase productivity while working at your own pace and convenience.

We invite you to visit the Perspection web site at:

www.perspection.com

Acknowledgments

The task of creating any book requires the talents of many hard-working people pulling together to meet impossible deadlines and untold stresses. We'd like to thank the outstanding team responsible for making this book possible: writer, Steve Johnson; production editor, James Teyler; proofreader, Beth Teyler; and indexer, Katherine Stimson.

At Que publishing, we'd like to thank Greg Wiegand and Laura Norman for the opportunity to undertake this project, Cindy Teeters for administrative support, and Sandra Schroeder for your production expertise and support.

Perspection

About the Author

Steve Johnson has written more than 80 books on a variety of computer software, including Adobe Edge Animate, Adobe Photoshop CS6, Adobe Dreamweaver CS6, Adobe InDesign CS6, Adobe Illustrator CS6, Adobe Flash Professional CS5, Microsoft Windows 8, Microsoft Office 2013 and 2010, Microsoft Office 2008 for the Macintosh, and Apple OS X Mountain Lion. In 1991, after working for Apple Computer and Microsoft, Steve founded Perspection, Inc., which writes and produces software training. When he is not staying up late writing, he enjoys coaching baseball, playing golf, gardening, and spending time with his wife, Holly, and three children, JP, Brett, and Hannah. Steve and his family live in Northern California, but can also be found visiting family all over the western United States.

Contents

Introduction   *xvii*

1 Getting Started with InDesign CC   1

    Installing InDesign   2 **New!**
    Getting Started   4 **New!**
    Viewing the InDesign Window   6 **New!**
    Showing and Hiding Panels   7
    Working with Panels   8
    Using the Tools and Control Panel   10
    Opening a Document   12 **New!**
    Opening a Document with Adobe Bridge   14
    Inserting Images or Text in a Document   16
    Using the Status Bar   17
    Working with Document Windows   18
    Checking for Updates Online   20 **New!**
    Getting Help While You Work   22
    Saving a Document   24 **New!**
    Finishing Up   26

2 Creating and Viewing a Document   27

    Creating a New Document   28 **New!**
    Creating a New Document from a Template   30
    Creating a New Document Using Presets   32 **New!**
    Setting Up a Document   34 **New!**
    Changing the Display View   36
    Changing the View with the Zoom Tool   38
    Viewing and Using Rulers   40
    Using Guides   42
    Changing Guides & Pasteboard Options   44 **New!**
    Using Smart Guides   46
    Using the Grid   48
    Moving Around with the Hand Tool   50
    Working with the Info Panel   51

Creating and Displaying Workspaces 52
Using Undo and Redo 54

3 Managing Pages and Books 55

Using the Pages Panel 56
Inserting Pages 58
Navigating Pages 60
Changing the Page Size 62
Deleting Pages 65
Moving Pages 66
Working with Page Spreads 68
Rotating Page Spreads 69
Creating Master Pages 70
Working with Master Pages 72
Working with Page Numbers and Sections 74
Working with Chapter Numbers 76
Creating and Using Text Variables 78
Creating a Book 80
Managing Books 82
Creating a Table of Contents 84
Starting an Index 86
Creating an Index Entry 88
Creating an Index 90
Managing an Index 92

4 Working with Text 95

Using Type Tools 96
Creating Type in a Text Frame 97
Creating Type Using Frame Tools 98
Creating Path Type 100
Importing Text 102
Flowing Imported Text 104
Working with Overflow Text 106
Using Smart Text Reflow 108
Typing and Selecting Text 110
Editing Text with Autocorrect 112
Copying and Moving Text 113
Changing Fonts 114 **New!**
Changing Font Size 116
Changing Text Leading 117
Changing Text Kerning 118

Changing Text Tracking   119
Scaling or Skewing Text   120
Aligning Paragraphs   121
Indenting and Spacing Paragraphs   122
Creating a Drop Cap   123
Applying a Paragraph Rule   124
Adding Bullets and Numbering   126
Setting Tabs   128
Working with Glyphs   129
Inserting Special Text Characters   130
Working with Hidden Text   131
Setting Text Frame Options   132
Creating Columns   134
Wrapping Text Around an Object   136
Creating Type Outlines   138
Adding Page Numbers to Continued Text   139
Working with Different Languages   140

5 Placing and Working with Graphics   141

Placing Graphics   142
Placing Graphics with Options   143
Setting Place Import Options   144
Placing Multiple Graphics   146
Placing Graphics from Adobe Bridge   148
Adding Captions to Graphics   150
Copying or Moving Graphics   152
Using the Links Panel   153
Managing Linked Graphics   154
Editing a Linked Graphic   156
Displaying XMP Graphic Information   157
Creating Specialty Frames for Graphics   158
Selecting and Moving Frames and Graphics   160
Fitting Graphics in Frames   162
Nesting Graphics in Frames   164
Formatting Graphics in Frames   165
Controlling Graphics Display Performance   166
Adding Alt Text to Graphics   168

6 Working with Objects and Layers   169

Creating Shapes   170
Creating Lines   172

Creating Multiple Objects in a Grid   173
Using the Selection Tool   174
Using the Direct Selection Tool   176
Resizing Objects   178
Moving Objects   179
Duplicating Objects   180
Grouping and Combining Objects   182
Aligning Objects   184
Distributing Objects   186
Arranging Object Stack Order   188
Transforming Objects   189
Repeating Object Transformations   190
Using the Free Transform Tool   191
Scaling Objects   192
Shearing Objects   193
Rotating Objects   194
Locking and Unlocking Objects   196
Creating Inline Objects   197
Creating Anchored Objects   198
Creating and Deleting Object Layers   200
Setting Layer Options   202
Showing and Hiding Layers and Objects   203
Locking Layers and Objects   204
Merging Layers and Groups   205
Working with Objects on Layers   206
Using the Measure Tool   207
Using Live Screen Drawing   208

7 Applying and Managing Color   209

Changing Color Settings   210
Changing Color Profiles   212
Working with Color Modes   214
Applying Colors   215
Using the Eyedropper Tool   216
Working with the Color Panel   218
Working with the Swatches Panel   220
Managing Color Swatches   222
Working with Swatch Libraries   224
Creating Tint Swatches   225
Creating Gradient Swatches   226
Creating Mixed Inks   228

Using Colors from the Kuler Panel	230	
Overprinting Colors	232	
Proofing Colors on the Screen	233	
Changing the Interface Color Theme	234	**New!**

8 Applying Fills, Strokes, and Effects — 235

Applying Fill and Stroke Colors	236
Changing Stroke Attributes	238
Creating Stroke Styles	240
Applying Gradients	242
Using the Gradient Tool	244
Using the Gradient Feather Tool	245
Creating Blends and Effects	246
Applying Shadow Effects	248
Applying Glow Effects	249
Applying Bevel and Emboss Effects	250
Applying Feather Effects	251
Applying Corner Object Effects	252
Converting Shape Objects	254
Setting Object Defaults	255

9 Working with Points and Paths — 257

Drawing with the Pen Tool	258
Selecting and Moving Points and Segments	260
Converting Points	262
Adding and Deleting Anchor Points	264
Splitting Paths	266
Joining Anchor Points	268
Using the Smooth Tool	269
Using the Pencil Tool	270
Erasing to Reshape Paths	272
Working with Pathfinder	273
Creating a Compound Path	274
Working with Clipping Paths	276

10 Working with Tables — 279

Creating Tables	280
Importing Text into Tables	282
Entering and Editing Text in a Table	284
Modifying a Table	286

Adjusting Table Rows and Columns 288
Adjusting Table Cells 290
Aligning Content in Table Cells 291
Creating Table Headers and Footers 292
Adding Strokes and Fills 294
Alternating Fills and Strokes 296
Adding Diagonal Lines in Cells 298
Adding a Border to a Table 299
Adjusting Tables in the Text Frame 300

11 Working with Styles 301

Using the Paragraph Styles or Character Styles Panel 302
Changing the Basic Paragraph Style 303
Creating Paragraph Styles 304
Creating Character Styles 306
Creating GREP Styles 308
Creating Style Groups 309
Loading and Importing Styles 310
Applying and Overriding Styles 312
Creating Nested Styles 314
Creating Object Styles 316 **New!**
Creating Table and Cell Styles 318
Using Quick Apply 320
Mapping Styles to Export Tags 322 **New!**

12 Finalizing a Document 323

Using Spell Check 324
Using Custom Dictionaries 326
Finding and Changing Fonts 327
Using Find and Change 328
Searching for Text 330
Searching Using GREP 332
Searching for Glyphs 333
Searching for Objects 334
Working with Hyphenation 335
Keeping Lines Together 336
Changing Justification Options 337
Using the Story Editor 338
Adding Footnotes 340
Changing Case 342

13 Creating an Interactive Document   343

Defining Hyperlink Destinations   344
Creating Hyperlinks   346
Converting and Stylizing Hyperlinks   348
Using the Hyperlinks Panel   350
Creating Cross-References   352
Creating Bookmarks   354
Adding Media   356
Setting Media Options   358
Adding Animation with Motion Presets   360
Working with Animations   362
Changing Animation Order   364
Adding Page Transitions   365
Using the Buttons and Forms Panel   366
Creating Buttons   368
Creating Forms   370
Working with Events and Actions   372
Working with Button States   374
Setting Tab Order   375
Creating Multi-State Objects   376
Inserting HTML Content   378
Creating QR Codes   379 **New!**
Using the SWF Preview Panel   380

14 Creating a Digital Publication   381

Creating Liquid Layouts   382
Creating Alternate Layouts   384
Working with Alternate Layouts   386
Adjusting Layouts   387
Getting Started with Digital Publishing Suite   388
Creating a Folio Overlay   390
Creating a Folio Publication   392
Importing Articles into a Folio Publication   394
Setting Folio and Article Properties   395
Previewing a Folio Publication   396

15 Automating the Way You Work   397

Creating a Library   398
Using and Updating a Library   400
Changing Library Item Information   401

Searching and Sorting Libraries 402
Creating and Using Snippets 404
Creating Conditional Text 406
Collecting and Placing Content 408
Creating Linked Content 410
Linking Content Across Documents 412
Managing Linked Content 413
Using and Running Scripts 414
Using Data Merge 416
Working with XML 418
Exporting XML or IDML 420

16 Exporting a Document **421**

Exporting a Document 422
Understanding Export File Formats 423
Exporting as a Print PDF 424
Setting PDF General Options 426
Setting PDF Compression Options 428
Setting PDF Marks and Bleeds Options 429
Setting PDF Output Options 430
Setting PDF Advanced Options 431
Setting PDF Security Options 432
Exporting with PDF Presets 433
Exporting PDF Files in the Background 434
Setting PDF Media Options 435
Exporting as an Interactive PDF 436
Exporting as an EPS 438
Exporting as a JPEG or PNG 440
Exporting as a Flash Movie 442
Exporting as a Flash File 444
Ordering Content in the Articles Panel 446
Exporting as an Accessible PDF 448
Applying Tags to a PDF 450
Exporting Tags for EPUB and HTML 451 **New!**
Exporting as an EPUB eBook 452 **New!**
Exporting as an HTML 454 **New!**
Setting EPUB and HTML Options 456 **New!**

17 Printing and Outputting a Document **457**

Printing a Document 458
Printing with Presets 459

Setting General and Setup Print Options   460
Setting Marks and Bleed Options   462
Setting Graphics Options   464
Previewing Color Separations   465
Setting Output Options   466
Setting Trapping Options   468
Setting Advanced Options   470
Setting Color Management Options   472
Creating a Print Summary   473
Printing Spreads in a Booklet   474
Using Live Preflight   476
Inserting File Information   478
Creating a Package   480
Using Document Fonts   482

18   Customizing the Way You Work   483

Setting General Preferences   484
Setting Interface Preferences   485   **New!**
Setting Type Preferences   486
Setting Advanced Type Preferences   488   **New!**
Setting Composition Preferences   489
Setting Units & Increments Preferences   490
Setting Dictionary Preferences   492
Setting Spelling Preferences   494
Setting Notes Preferences   496
Working with Appearance of Black Preferences   497
Setting Story Editor Display Preferences   498
Setting File Handling Preferences   500
Setting Clipboard Handling Preferences   502
Defining Shortcut Keys   503
Customizing Menus   504
Configuring Plug-In and Extensions   505   **New!**
Customizing the Control Panel   506

19   Collaborating with Others   507

Creating and Working with Notes   508
Tracking Text Changes   510
Sharing Content with Adobe InCopy   512
Setting Up User Identification   513
Exporting Content from InDesign   514
Using the Assignments Panel   515

Creating an Assignment 516
Checking Content Out and In 518
Updating Content 519
Working with InCopy 520

20 Working Together with Adobe Programs 521

Exploring Adobe Programs 522 **New!**
Exploring Adobe Bridge 523
Getting Started with Adobe Bridge 524
Getting Photos from a Digital Camera 525
Working with Raw Images from a Digital Camera 526 **New!**
Modifying Images in Camera Raw 528 **New!**
Working with Images Using Adobe Bridge 530
Setting Preferences in Adobe Bridge 532
Applying Image Adjustments 534
Automating Tasks in Adobe Bridge 535
Using Mini-Bridge 536
Scripting with Adobe ExtendScript Toolkit 537
Working with Adobe Media Encoder 538
Working with Adobe Extension Manager 540 **New!**
Using the Adobe Exchange Panel 541 **New!**
Accessing Adobe Creative Cloud 542 **New!**

New Features 543 **New!**
Adobe Certification 549
Index 555

Introduction

Welcome to *Brilliant Adobe InDesign CC*, a visual quick reference book that shows you how to work efficiently with InDesign. This book provides complete coverage of basic to advanced InDesign skills.

How This Book Works

You don't have to read this book in any particular order. We've designed the book so that you can jump in, get the information you need, and jump out. However, the book does follow a logical progression from simple tasks to more complex ones. Each task is presented on no more than two facing pages, which lets you focus on a single task without having to turn the page. To find the information that you need, just look up the task in the table of contents or index, and turn to the page listed. Read the task introduction, follow the step-by-step instructions in the left column along with screen illustrations in the right column, and you're done.

What's New

If you're searching for what's new in InDesign CC, just look for the icon: **New!**. The new icon appears in the table of contents and throughout this book so you can quickly and easily identify a new or improved feature in InDesign. A complete description of each new feature appears in the New Features guide in the back of this book.

Keyboard Shortcuts

Most menu commands have a keyboard equivalent, such as Ctrl+P (Win) or ⌘+P (Mac), as a quicker alternative to using the mouse. A complete list of keyboard shortcuts is available on the web at *www.perspection.com*.

How You'll Learn

How This Book Works

What's New

Keyboard Shortcuts

Step-by-Step Instructions

Real World Examples

Workshops

Adobe Certification

Get More on the Web

Step-by-Step Instructions

This book provides concise step-by-step instructions that show you "how" to accomplish a task. Each set of instructions includes illustrations that directly correspond to the easy-to-read steps. Also included in the text are time-savers, tables, and sidebars to help you work more efficiently or to teach you more in-depth information. A "Did You Know?" provides tips and techniques to help you work smarter, while a "See Also" leads you to other parts of the book containing related information about the task.

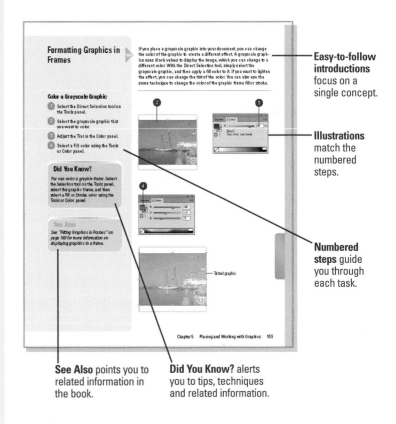

Easy-to-follow **introductions** focus on a single concept.

Illustrations match the numbered steps.

Numbered steps guide you through each task.

See Also points you to related information in the book.

Did You Know? alerts you to tips, techniques and related information.

Real World Examples

This book uses real world example files to give you a context in which to use the task. By using the example files, you won't waste time looking for or creating sample files. You get a start file and a result file, so you can compare your work. Not every topic needs an example file, such as changing options, so we provide a complete list of the example files used throughout the book. The example files that you need for project tasks along with a complete file list are available on the web at *www.perspection.com*.

Real world examples help you apply what you've learned to other tasks.

Workshops

This book shows you how to put together the individual step-by-step tasks into in-depth projects with the Workshops. You start each project with a sample file, work through the steps, and then compare your results with a project results file at the end. The Workshop projects and associated files are available on the web at *www.perspection.com*.

The **Workshops** walk you through in-depth projects to help you put InDesign to work.

Adobe Certification

This book prepares you fully for the Adobe Certified Expert (ACE) exam for Adobe InDesign CC. Each Adobe Certified Expert certification level has a set of objectives, which are organized into broader skill sets. To prepare for the certification exam, you should review and perform each task identified with an ACE objective to confirm that you can meet the requirements for the exam. Information about the ACE program is available in the back of this book. The Adobe Certified Expert objectives and the specific pages that cover them are available on the web at *www.perspection.com*.

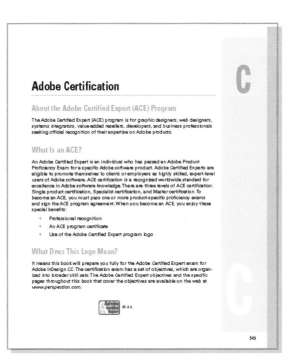

Get More on the Web

In addition to the information in this book, you can also get more information on the web to help you get up-to-speed faster with InDesign CC. Some of the information includes:

Transition Helpers

◆ **Only New Features.** Download and print the new feature tasks as a quick and easy guide.

Productivity Tools

◆ **Keyboard Shortcuts.** Download a list of keyboard shortcuts to learn faster ways to get the job done.

More Content

◆ **Photographs.** Download photographs and other graphics to use in your InDesign documents.

◆ **More Content.** Download new content developed after publication.

You can access these additional resources on the web at *www.perspection.com*.

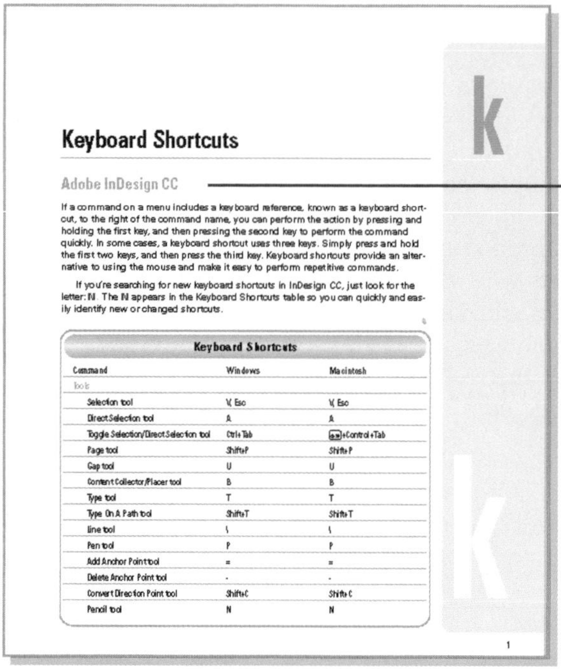

Keyboard Shortcuts

Adobe InDesign CC ——————————————————— Additional content is available on the web.

If a command on a menu includes a keyboard reference, known as a keyboard short-cut, to the right of the command name, you can perform the action by pressing and holding the first key, and then pressing the second key to perform the command quickly. In some cases, a keyboard shortcut uses three keys. Simply press and hold the first two keys, and then press the third key. Keyboard shortcuts provide an alternative to using the mouse and make it easy to perform repetitive commands.

If you're searching for new keyboard shortcuts in InDesign CC, just look for the letter: N. The N appears in the Keyboard Shortcuts table so you can quickly and easily identify new or changed shortcuts.

Keyboard Shortcuts		
Command	Windows	Macintosh
Tools		
Selection tool	V, Esc	V, Esc
Direct Selection tool	A	A
Toggle Selection/Direct Selection tool	Ctrl+Tab	⌘+Control+Tab
Page tool	Shift+P	Shift+P
Gap tool	U	U
Content Collector/Placer tool	B	B
Type tool	T	T
Type On A Path tool	Shift+T	Shift+T
Line tool	\	\
Pen tool	P	P
Add Anchor Point tool	=	=
Delete Anchor Point tool	-	-
Convert Direction Point tool	Shift+C	Shift+C
Pencil tool	N	N

1

Getting Started with InDesign CC

Introduction

Adobe InDesign CC is a desktop publishing and layout program that runs seamlessly on both Windows and Macintosh platforms. InDesign CC is a stand-alone program, but it's also part of Adobe's Creative Cloud of professional programs that work together to help you create designs in print, on the web, or on mobile devices. Adobe Creative Cloud also includes additional Adobe services and tools—such as Bridge, Camera Raw plug-in, Media Encoder, Extension Manager, Exchange, and ExtendScript Toolkit—to help you manage and work with files. With InDesign CC, you can sign in to Adobe Creative Cloud and Adobe.com with your Adobe ID to access online cloud services. If you don't have an account, you can create one. Creative Cloud is a membership-based cloud solution that allows you to access and download Adobe software programs, personal files, tutorial videos, and sync program settings online from any computer or device. A free membership is available with entry level features. A monthly cost-based membership adds downloads and more features. You can go to *www.creativecloud.com* for more details.

With InDesign, you can create books, brochures, catalogs, manuals, labels, certificates, newsletters, flyers, forms, label sheets, and even interactive presentations. As a page layout program, you can create a one page flyer, a 500 or more page book, or something in between. InDesign provides all the tools you need to create a page layout design, import or enter text, insert images, add drawings, create tables, and finalize the document. When you're done, you can print the document to a local desktop or commercial printer, create a template, so you can reuse the document again later, or export the document as an Adobe PDF or digital ebook for use online, over a network or on mobile and tablet devices, or for use in other programs, such as Adobe Flash (FLA or SWF) or Adobe Dreamweaver (HTML) and web browsers.

What You'll Do

Install and Start InDesign

View the InDesign Window

Show and Hide Panels

Work with Panels

Use the Tools and Control Panel

Open a Document

Open a Document with Adobe Bridge

Insert Images or Text in a Document

Use the Status Bar

Work with Document Windows

Check for Updates Online

Get Help While You Work

Save a Document

Finish Up

Installing InDesign

The process of installing the InDesign program, either 32- or 64-bit (**New!**) edition, is fairly straightforward; you download the InDesign CC software from Adobe Creative Cloud (**New!**) to your computer and double-click the setup program, and then follow the on-screen instructions. If you meet the minimum system requirements, the installer will guide you through the steps to complete the installation. Remember to have your serial number handy, because you will have to type it in during the installation process. In order to access online content on Adobe Creative Cloud (**New!**) and Adobe.com, you'll need to sign in with your Adobe ID, which you can do within the installer or program. Creative Cloud is a membership-based cloud solution that allows you to access and download Adobe software, personal files, and sync program settings online from any computer or device. Go to *www.creativecloud.com* or *www.adobe.com* for more details.

Install InDesign CC in Windows

1 Download the InDesign CC software online from Adobe Creative Cloud to your hard disk.

2 Open the folder with the downloaded software, and then double-click the setup icon.

3 Follow the on-screen instructions to install the product; the installer asks you to enter a serial number or enter or create an Adobe ID for Creative Cloud and Adobe.com to sign in (required) (**New!**) and register the product, read and accept a licensing agreement, select program options, indicate the language you want, and specify where you want to install the software.

See Also

See "Accessing Adobe Creative Cloud" on page 542 for more information on signing in and out of Creative Cloud.

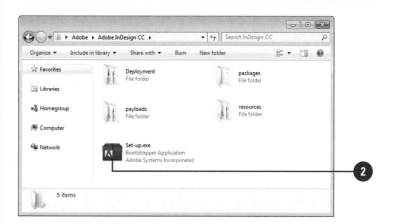

Install InDesign CC in Macintosh

1 Download the InDesign CC software online from Adobe Creative Cloud to your hard disk.

2 Open the folder with the downloaded software, and then double-click the setup icon.

3 Follow the on-screen instructions to install the product; the installer asks you to enter a serial number or enter or create an Adobe ID for Creative Cloud and Adobe.com to sign in (required) (**New!**) and register the product, read and accept a licensing agreement, select program options, indicate the language you want, and specify where you want to install the software.

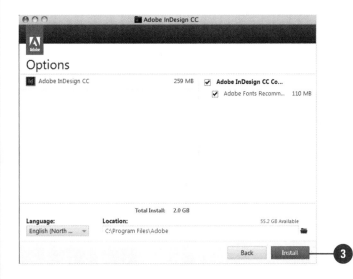

Did You Know?

Adobe applications can be down-loaded. It's all very simple; go to *www.creativecloud.com*, sign-in, and then follow links to download, or go to *www.adobe.com*, click Products, click the application you want, and then fol-low links to purchase and download.

You can get resources and content. Many Adobe CC products include bonus content and files in the Goodies or Cool Extras folder. Check it out! For additional online resources, go to *www.adobe.com* and visit Adobe Exchange. In InDesign, you can use the Adobe Exchange panel (**New!**). Click the Window menu, point to Extensions, and then click Adobe Exchange. *See "Using the Adobe Exchange Panel" on page 541 for more information on using the panel.*

InDesign CC System Requirements

Hardware/Software	Minimum (Recommended)
WINDOWS	
Computer Processor	Intel Pentium 4 or AMD Athlon 64 or compatible
Operating System	Microsoft Windows 7 SP1 or Windows 8
Hard Drive Free Space	1.6 GB for InDesign; 1.3 GB for InCopy
Available RAM	2 GB (8 GB recommended)
Video Card	16-bit
Monitor Resolution	1024 x 768 (1280 x 800 recommended)
DVD-ROM drive	Any type
Internet connection	Broadband required for online services
MACINTOSH	
Computer Processor	Multicore Intel-based Macs
Operating System	Macintosh OS X 10.6.8 & 10.7 or higher
Hard Drive Free Space	2.6 GB for InDesign; 2.0 GB for InCopy Not supported on UFS or HFS
Available RAM	1 GB MB (2 GB recommended)
Video Card	16-bit
Monitor Resolution	1024 x 768 (1280 x 800 recommended)
DVD-ROM drive	Any type
Internet connection	Broadband required for online services

Getting Started

You can start InDesign in several ways, depending on the platform and version you are using. When you start InDesign, the program displays the InDesign window. The program also checks for updates to InDesign and related CC software using the Adobe Application Manager. In order to access online content on Adobe Creative Cloud (**New!**) and Adobe.com, you'll need to sign in to the service with your Adobe ID. If you're not signed in when you start InDesign, you'll be asked to sign in, which you can also do or sign out from the Help menu (**New!**). After you start InDesign, the program window opens with an updated user interface (**New!**) to match other Adobe apps, such as Illustrator, Photoshop, and Premier Pro. The user interface also includes HiDPI (**New!**), which enables the rendering process for an improved display on high resolution devices, such as a Macbook Pro with Retina display, where artwork, graphics, text, content, and UI elements appear crisper.

Start InDesign CC in Windows

1. Start Windows, if necessary, and then use the method for your Windows version.

   ◆ **Windows 8.** Display the Start screen; click or tap the **Start** button on the Charm bar.

   ◆ **Windows 7.** Click **Start** on the taskbar, and then point to **All Programs** (which changes to Back).

2. Click **Adobe InDesign CC**.

3. If prompted, specify the following:

   ◆ Enter or create an Adobe ID to sign in to register the product and use Creative Cloud.

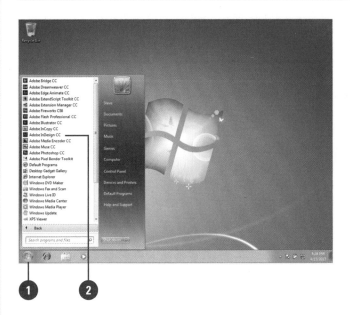

Did You Know?

You can create a shortcut icon on your desktop to start InDesign (Win). In Win 8, right-click the Adobe InDesign CC tile, and then click Pin to Start or Pin to taskbar. In Win 7, right-click Adobe InDesign CC on the Start menu, point to Send To, and then click Desktop (Create Shortcut).

Start InDesign CC in Macintosh

1 Open the **Applications** folder (located on the main hard drive).

◆ For Mac OS X Lion or later, you can also click the **Launchpad** icon on the Dock, and then click the **Adobe InDesign CC** icon.

2 Double-click the **Adobe InDesign CC** folder.

3 Double-click the **Adobe InDesign CC** program icon.

4 If prompted, specify the following:

◆ Enter or create an Adobe ID to sign in to register the product and use Creative Cloud.

Did You Know?

You can create a shortcut on the Macintosh. Drag and drop the InDesign application to the bottom of the screen, and then add it to the dock.

You can create and use a keyboard shortcut to start InDesign (Win 7). In Win 7, click Start on the taskbar, point to All Programs, right-click Adobe InDesign CC, and then click Properties. In the Shortcut Key box, type or press any letter, number, or function key, such as P, to which Windows adds Ctrl+Alt, and then click OK. To start InDesign, press the keyboard shortcut you defined (Ctrl+Alt+P).

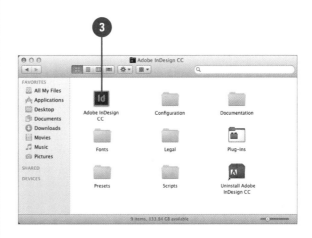

Shortcut for Adobe InDesign CC

Launchpad icon in Mac OS X Lion or later

For Your Information

Using InDesign in 32-bit and 64-bit Mode

The terms 32-bit and 64-bit refer to the way a computer CPU processes information. A 64-bit system handles large amounts of RAM more effectively than 32-bit systems. InDesign in 64-bit mode takes advantage of more than 4 GB of RAM when needed, instead of swapping out to the hard drive, which increases performance. When you install a 64-bit version of InDesign (**New!**) on a 64-bit system and version of Windows 7 or 8, you can use InDesign in 32-bit or 64-bit modes. When you install a 32-bit version of InDesign, you can only use it in 32-bit mode. For Windows on a 64-bit system, InDesign CC installs 32-bit and 64-bit versions with shortcuts on the Start menu, where you can start either one. Any 32-bit plug-ins will no longer work in the 64-bit version. For the Mac (10.6.8, 10.7, 10.8, or higher), InDesign CC only installs one version in 64-bit mode.

Viewing the InDesign Window

When you start InDesign, an updated program window (**New!**) displays several windows of varying types you can use to work with documents. In InDesign, windows appear in the workspace in panels. A **panel** is a window you can collapse, expand, and group with other panels, known as a **panel group**, to improve accessibility and workflow. A panel group consists of either individual panels stacked one on top of the other or related panels organized together with tabs.

The **Tools panel** contains a set of tools you can use to create shapes, such as lines, rectangles, and ellipses. You can fill and stroke shapes and text with different colors and stroke widths. When you select a tool, additional options appear on the **Control panel**.

A **menu** is a list of commands that you use to accomplish specific tasks. A **command** is a directive that accesses a feature of a program. InDesign has its own set of menus. The **Application bar** provides easy access to commonly used features, such as choosing zoom levels, view options, screen mode, document arrangement, workspaces, and online Help.

The **Document window** displays open InDesign documents. It includes tabs to make it easier to switch back and forth between documents and a close button to quickly close a document. In Interface preferences, you change the interface color theme (**New!**) from a dark gray (default) to a light gray, as well as choose to match the **pasteboard** area outside the document in the Document window.

Application bar
Displays buttons and menus to change the document layout.

Document window
Displays open InDesign documents.

Control panel
Displays options for the currently selected tool.

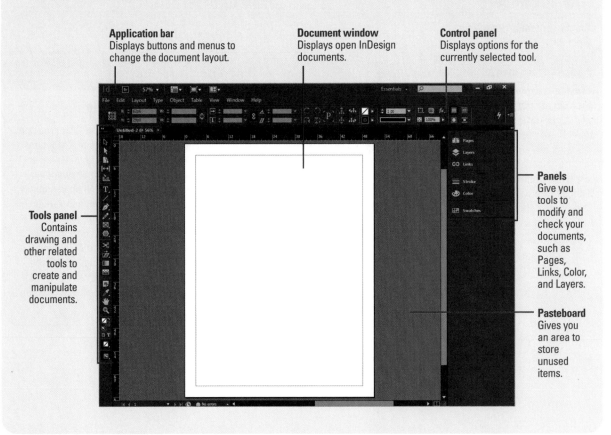

Tools panel
Contains drawing and other related tools to create and manipulate documents.

Panels
Give you tools to modify and check your documents, such as Pages, Links, Color, and Layers.

Pasteboard
Gives you an area to store unused items.

Showing and Hiding Panels

Panels give you easy access to many task-specific commands and operations from color control to vector path information. By default, the main panel display is located along the right side of your window. You can use the Window menu or click a panel tab within a group to display it, and then select options on the panel or choose panel-specific commands from the panel Options menu to perform actions. Instead of continually moving, resizing, or opening and closing windows, you can use the header bar with the panel tabs to collapse or expand individual panels within a window to save space.

Open and Close a Panel

1. Click the **Window** menu.

2. Point to a submenu (if needed), such as Color, Editorial, Extensions, Interactive, Object & Layout, or Type & Tables.

3. Click a panel name, such as Animation, Color, Layers, or Swatches.

   TIMESAVER *To close a panel, or a single tab, right-click (Win) or control-click (Mac) a panel tab, and then click Close Tab Group or Close (for a single tab). On the Mac, you can also click the Close button on the panel.*

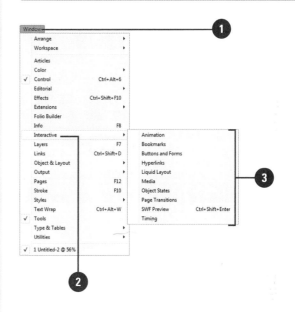

Collapse or Expand a Panel

1. To collapse or expand an open panel, click the dark gray area or double-click a title tab on the header bar of the panel.

   If the panel is in icon mode, click on the icon to expand or collapse it. To reduce the panel back to icon mode, click on the double right-facing arrows in the dark gray area. To expand from icons to panels, click on the double left facing arrows.

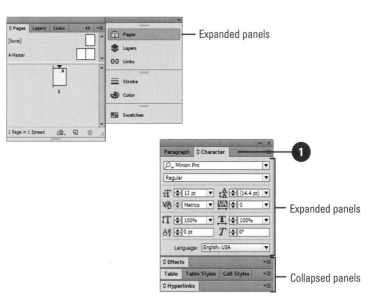

Expanded panels

Expanded panels

Collapsed panels

Working with Panels

The movable panels are organized into groups, such as Stroke/Color and Pages/Links, to save screen space and help with workflow. You can also dock (add) or undock (subtract) specific panels within a group to customize your workspace. A panel appears with a header, which includes the tab titles and three options: the Collapse To Icons or Expand Panels button, the Close button, and the Options button. The Options menu provides you with panel commands. The entire set of panels includes a double arrow at the top you can use to collapse and expand the entire panel back and forth between icons and full panels.

Dock a Panel

1 Select a panel; click on a named panel, or click the **Window** menu, and then click a panel name.

2 Drag the panel away from the group to another panel.

◆ **Add to Panel Group.** Drag to a panel group until a blue rectangle appears around the panel.

◆ **Append to Panel.** Drag to a panel until a blue line appears along the side of the panel.

Undock a Panel

1 Select a panel; click on a named panel, or click the **Window** menu, and then click a panel name.

2 Drag the panel out of the group.

3 Drop it onto the InDesign window.

Did You Know?

You can dock and undock panels to a docking channel. You can dock and undock, panels or panel groups in docking channels. A docking channel is a region located on the left and right side of the InDesign window to which you can attach and detach panels. When you drag a panel over a dockable area, a blue line appears.

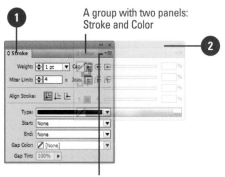

A group with two panels: Stroke and Color

Click to choose commands from the panel Options menu

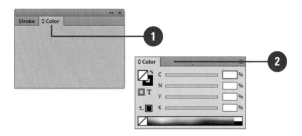

For Your Information

Hiding Panels While You Work

If InDesign's panels get in the way, just press the Tab key to temporarily hide all the panels. Or, you can hold down the Shift key, and then press the Tab key to hide the panels, but leave the Toolbox and Control panel. Press the Tab key again to restore all the panels to their most recent positions.

Collapse and Expand the Panel Set Between Icons and Panels

◆ To collapse the panel set to icons with text, click the double arrow pointing right (Collapse to Icons) at the top of the panels.

◆ To expand the panel set from icons with text to full panels, click the double arrow pointing left (Expand Panels) at the top of the panels.

◆ To have an expanded panel icon automatically collapse or hide when you click away, right-click (Win) or Control-click (Mac) a panel, and then click **Auto-Collapse Iconic Panels** or **Auto-Show Hidden Panels**.

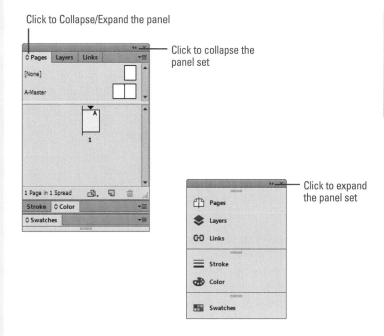

Click to Collapse/Expand the panel

Click to collapse the panel set

Click to expand the panel set

Use the Panel Options Menu

1 Open or expand a panel.

2 Click the **Options** button on the right side of the panel header bar.

3 Click a command from the list (commands vary).

Did You Know?

You can temporarily hide all of InDesign's panels and Tools panel. Press the Tab key to hide the panels. Press the Tab key a second time to display the hidden panels. Hold down the Shift key, and then press the Tab key to hide the panels, but not the Tools and Control panels.

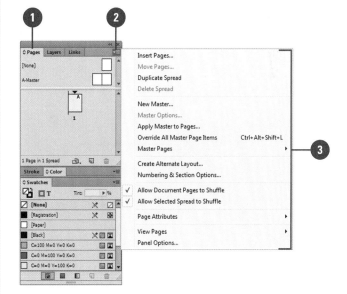

Using the Tools and Control Panel

InDesign has an abundance of tools that give an InDesign designer tremendous control over any creative designing problems that may crop up. For example, the InDesign toolbox contains a variety of different tools: selection tools (you can never have enough selection tools), drawing or shape tools, type tools, and other tools dedicated to creating documents, transforming objects, and working with pages. Add viewing tools and you have everything you need to do any job.

When you work on a document, it's important to know what tools are available, and how they can help in achieving your design goals. InDesign likes to save space, so it consolidates similar tools under one button. To access multiple tools, click and hold on any Tools panel button that contains a small black triangle, located in the lower right corner of the tool button. Take a moment to explore the InDesign toolbox and get to know the tools.

The InDesign Tools panel contains the tools needed to work through any InDesign job, but it's not necessary to click on a tool to access it. Simply using a letter of the alphabet can access all of InDesign's tools. For example, pressing the P key switches to the Pen tool, and pressing the T key switches to the Type tool. If you're not sure what letter to press, you can use the Tools Hints panel, which lists all the hidden modifier keys available for the currently selected tool. Click the Window menu, point to Utilities, and then click Tool Hints. If you prefer a complete list of letter assignments for all the tools, you can refer to Adobe InDesign CC Keyboard Shortcuts (available for download on the web at *www.perspection.com*). You can temporar-

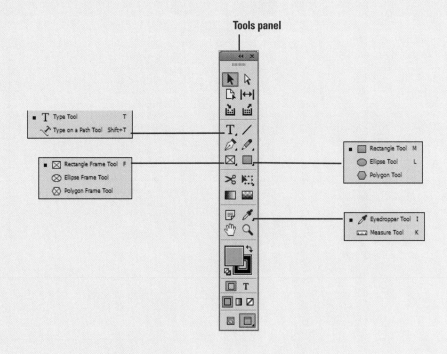

Tools panel

ily switch from the current tool to any other tool by holding down the appropriate letter key. As you hold down the key, your current tool changes to the new tool, and when you release it, you return to the previous tool. To really get efficient in InDesign, you need to learn to use both hands. Use one hand for your mouse or drawing tablet, and the other on the keyboard to make quick changes of tools and options. Think of using InDesign like playing a piano—you need to use both hands.

Using the Control Panel

The Control panel displays the options for the currently selected tool. For most tools, your options include X and Y Location, W and H dimensions, Scale X and Y, Rotation and Shear Angle, Rotate and Flip, Fill and Stroke Color, Stroke Weight and Style, Apply Effect, Opacity, Drop Shadow, Quick Apply, and Options button. The important thing to remember is that the Control panel is customized based on the tool you have selected, so options will vary.

Control panel

Quick Apply button

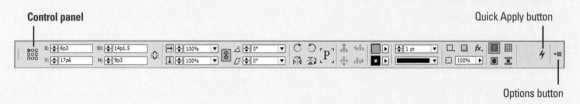

Options button

Tools panel

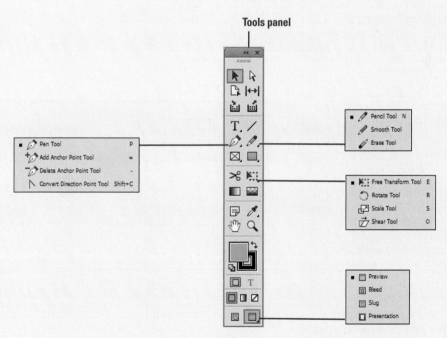

Opening a Document

InDesign lets you open document files created in different formats, such as InDesign (INDD), InDesign CS3 Interchange (INX), InDesign Markup (IDML), and QuarkXPress (3.3-4.1x). If you want to simply open an InDesign document, the Open Recent or Open commands are the most efficient ways. However, if you need to manage, organize, or process files, Adobe Bridge is the way to go. You open an existing InDesign document file the same way you open documents in other programs. In Windows Explorer (Win) or Finder (Mac), you can double-click an InDesign document to open the InDesign program and the document. When you open a document, a tab appears across the top of the Document window, with the document title. When you open an InDesign CS6 document, the document tab includes "[Converted]," which you can save to update it to InDesign CC (**New!**). You can click the tab at any time to display that particular document.

Open an Existing Document

1. Click the **File** menu, and then click **Open** to display all file types in the file list of the Open dialog box.

2. Click the **Files of Type** (Win) or **Enable** (Mac) list arrow, and then select a format.

   Select **All Readable Files** to display all files that can be opened in InDesign or select **InDesign** to display only InDesign files.

3. Navigate to the location with the document you want to open.

4. Click the file you want to open.

   TIMESAVER *Press and hold the Shift key to select multiple contiguous files to open while in the Open dialog box.*

5. Click the (Open) **Normal** (original document or copy of a template), (Open) **Original** (original document or template), or (Open) **Copy** (copy of a document or template) option.

6. Click **Open**.

7. If an alert appears for missing fonts or links, select an option, and then click **OK** or another button.

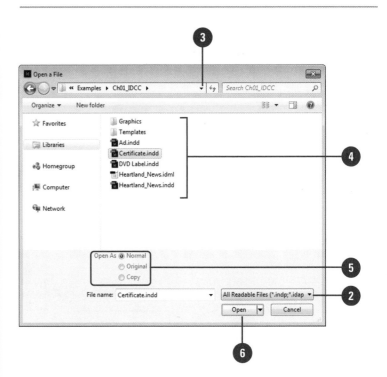

Open a Recently Opened Document

1. Click the **File** menu, and then point to **Open Recent**.

2. Click the document you want to open.

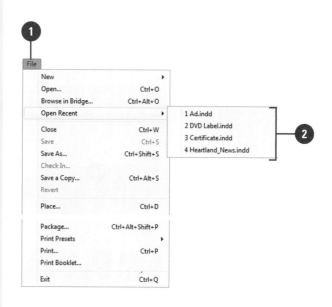

InDesign Open File Formats

File Format	Description
InDesign	Opens INDP (Package file), IDAP, INNDD (InDesign file), INDT (InDesign Template file), INDL (InDesign Object Library) files.
InDesign CS3 Interchange	Opens InDesign CS3 INX files; a older file format.
InDesign Markup	Opens older CS3/CS4 InDesign files saved in the InDesign Markup Language (IDML).
QuarkXPress	Opens older QuarkXPress 3.3-4.1x files.
InDesign Book	Opens InDesign Book INDB files.
Adobe PDF Creations Settings Files	Opens PDF settings files in the JOBOPTIONS file format.

Opening a Document with Adobe Bridge

With Adobe Bridge CC, available for download from Creative Cloud, you can drag assets into your layouts as needed, preview them, and add metadata to them. Bridge allows you to search, sort, filter, manage, and process files one at a time or in batches. You can also use Bridge to create new folders; rename, move, delete and group files (known as stacking); edit metadata; rotate images; and run batch commands. You can also view information about files and data imported from your digital camera.

Browse and Open Documents with Adobe Bridge

1. Click the **Go to Bridge** button on the Application bar or click the **File** menu, and then click **Browse in Bridge**.

   ◆ If prompted, install or update from Adobe Application Manager.

2. In Bridge, select a specific workspace to view your files the way you want.

3. Navigate to the location with the file you want to open.

4. To open an image in InDesign, use any of the following:

   ◆ Double-click on a thumbnail to open it in the default program.

   ◆ Drag the thumbnail from the Bridge into an open Adobe application.

   ◆ Select a thumbnail, click the **File** menu, point to **Open With**, and then click **Adobe InDesign CC**.

   ◆ Select a thumbnail, click the **File** menu, point to **Place**, and then click **In InDesign**.

5. To return to InDesign, click the **File** menu, and then click **Return to Adobe InDesign**.

Work with Files Using Bridge

1 Click the **Go to Bridge** button on the Application bar or click the **File** menu, and then click **Browse in Bridge**.

◆ If prompted, install or update from Adobe Application Manager.

2 Click the **Folders** tab and choose a folder from the scrolling list.

3 Click the **Favorites** tab to choose from a listing of user-defined items, such as Pictures.

4 To narrow down the list of images using a filter, click the criteria you want to use in the Filter panel.

5 Click an image within the preview window to select it.

6 Click the **Preview** tab to view a larger thumbnail of the selected image. Multiple images appear when you select them.

7 Drag the **Zoom** slider to increase or decrease the thumbnail views.

8 Use the file management buttons to rotate or delete images, or create a new folder.

9 Double-click on a thumbnail to open it in the default program, or drag the thumbnail from the Bridge into an open Adobe application.

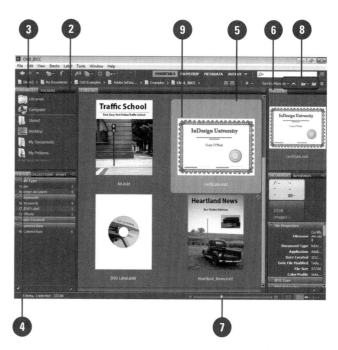

Did You Know?

You can reveal a document in Adobe Bridge from InDesign. Open a document in InDesign, click the Open icon (looks like a piece of paper with edge folded over) on the Status Bar, and then click Reveal In Bridge.

For Your Information

Viewing InDesign Documents in Adobe Bridge

If you save multiple page previews of InDesign documents, you can preview them in Adobe Bridge. In File Handling preferences, select the Always Save Preview Images With Documents check box, click the Pages list arrow, select the number of pages you want to save as a preview, and then click OK. Save the document in InDesign. In Bridge, you can view the thumbnails for the set number of pages from the document in the Preview pane. If you forget the linked location of an image in an InDesign document while in Bridge, you can display thumbnails of all the placed files contained in the document. In Bridge, navigate to and select the InDesign document, and then view the linked locations of images in the Metadata panel.

Inserting Images or Text in a Document

You can use InDesign's Place command to insert artwork into an open document. To increase your control of the new image, InDesign allows you to use the place cursor to create a frame with the size you want on the active layer. InDesign lets you place files saved in InDesign, Media Files, Images, Adobe PDF, EPS, MS Excel or Word, and TXT formats to name a few. When you place a vector-based image, you have the ability to modify the width, height, and rotation while retaining the vector format. When you insert an image, you can also create a caption.

Insert an Image or Text in a Document

1. Open an InDesign document.

2. Click the **File** menu, and then click **Place**.

3. Navigate to the location with the image, and then select the image you want to place into the active document.

4. Select any of the following options:

   ◆ **Show Import Options.** Select to specify import options for the imported item.

   ◆ **Replace Selected Item.** Select to replace the currently selected item on the page.

   ◆ **Create Static Captions.** Select to create a static text caption using the title of the file.

5. Click **Open**.

6. If you selected the Show Import Options check box, specify the Import options that you want, and then click **OK**. If not, click or drag the place cursor to insert the image. If you selected the Create Static Captions check box, click or drag to create a text box.

   InDesign places the image in the active layer, and then encloses it within a frame.

7. Adjust the Scale X and Scale Y values on the Control panel to resize the placed image.

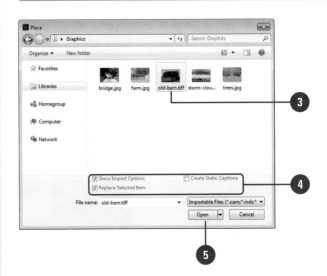

Using the Status Bar

To work efficiently in InDesign you need information about the active document. Details about the document's preflight profile can help in the design and preparation of the final document. You can quickly enable the current or all open documents as preflight documents. In addition, you can open the Preflight panel or Preflight Profile dialog box to view and set preflight options. From the Status Bar, you can also switch between pages.

Use the Status Bar

1. Click the **triangle** (Preflight menu) near the Status bar info box, and then select from the following options:

   ◆ **Preflight Panel.** Opens the Preflight panel.

   ◆ **Define Profiles.** Opens the Preflight Profiles dialog box.

   ◆ **Preflight Document.** Enables or disables the current document as a preflight document.

   ◆ **Enable Preflight for All Documents.** Enables or disables all open documents as preflight documents.

2. To locate the current document in Explorer, Finder, or Bridge, click the **Open** menu, and then click **Reveal in Explorer** (Win) or **Reveal in Finder** (Mac), or **Reveal in Bridge**.

3. To switch between pages, use any of the following:

   ◆ **First or Last.** Displays the first or last page.

   ◆ **Previous or Next.** Displays the previous or next page.

   ◆ **Page Navigation.** Displays the specified page.

Working with Document Windows

When you open multiple documents, you can use the Arrange Documents or Window menu or tabs at the top of the Document window to switch between them. You can click a tab name to switch to and activate the document. By default, tabs are displayed in the order in which you open or create documents. When you want to move or copy information between documents, it's easier to display several document windows on the screen at the same time and move them around. However, you must make the window active to work in it. Each tab also includes a Close button to quickly close a document. If the document view is too small or large, you can change it to suit your needs. If you want to compare multiple documents, you can also split the layout view.

Work with Multiple Documents

1. Open more than one document.

2. Click a tab name to switch to the document.

   TIMESAVER *Press Ctrl+Tab or Ctrl+Shift+Tab to cycle to the tab you want.*

   ◆ You can also click the **Window** menu, and then click a document name at the bottom of the menu.

3. To move a document window around, do any of the following:

   ◆ To rearrange the order of tabbed documents, drag a window's tab to a new location.

   ◆ To switch to another document when dragging a selection, drag the selection over the document's tab.

   ◆ To remove a document from the tabbed documents group, drag a window's tab away from the tabbed group.

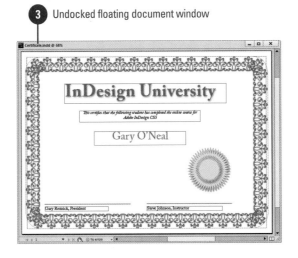

③ Undocked floating document window

Arrange Multiple Documents

1. Open more than one document.

2. Click the **Arrange Documents** menu on the Application bar.

   ◆ You can also click the **Window** menu, point to **Arrange**, and then select an arrangement command.

      ◆ **Split Window.** Creates a new window and displays a split window. You can also click the **Split Layout View** button to turn the view on and off.

      ◆ **Bring All to Front.** Displays all open document to the front screen (Mac).

3. On the menu, select an arrangement button icon:

   ◆ **Consolidate All.** Displays all active documents as tabs.

   ◆ **Tile All In Grid.** Displays all open documents in a grid pattern on the screen.

   ◆ **Tile All Vertically.** Displays all open documents vertically on the screen.

   ◆ **Tile All Horizontally.** Displays all open documents horizontally on the screen.

   ◆ **2-Up, 3-Up, 4-Up, 5-Up, or 6-Up.** Displays the number of documents in the selected pattern (in the menu icon) on the screen.

   ◆ **Float All in Windows.** Displays all open windows in separate undocked floating windows.

   ◆ **New Window.** Creates a new window with the contents of the active window.

4. To dock or undock a document window, drag the window's tab out of the group or into the group.

Arranged documents

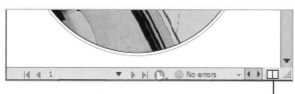

Click to open and close Split Layout View

Window menu

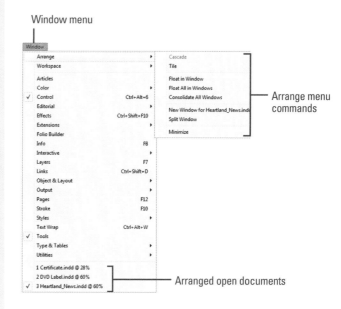

Arrange menu commands

Arranged open documents

Checking for Updates Online

As time passes, InDesign—like any other program—will change. There are two types of changes to a program: updates and patches. Updates are improvements to a program such as a new feature, option, or command. Patches are software fixes for problems discovered after the public release of the program. The good news is that both updates and patches are free, and once downloaded, are self-installing. Adobe gives you two ways to check for changes. You can check manually by going to the Adobe web site, or automatically through the Adobe Application Manager by using the Updates command on the Help menu. When you access a related program, such as Adobe Bridge on the Application bar, that is not installed, the Adobe Application Manager (**New!**) opens, where you can install or update Adobe programs. The Adobe Application Manager Preferences dialog box allows you to set update options for InDesign and other installed Adobe products, such as Bridge. You can choose to be notified of new updates on the menu bar and you can also choose to allow Adobe to verify the success or failure of an update by sending a failure status to you.

Check for Updates Directly from the Internet

1. Open your Internet browser.

2. Go to the following web address: *www.adobe.com/downloads/updates/*

3. Click the list arrow, and then click **InDesign - Macintosh** or **InDesign - Windows**.

4. Click **Go**.

   Any updates or patches appear in a list.

5. Based on your operating system, follow the onscreen instructions to download and install the software.

   IMPORTANT *Checking on your own requires a computer with a connection to the Internet. Since some of the updates can be rather large, it's recommended you have high-speed access.*

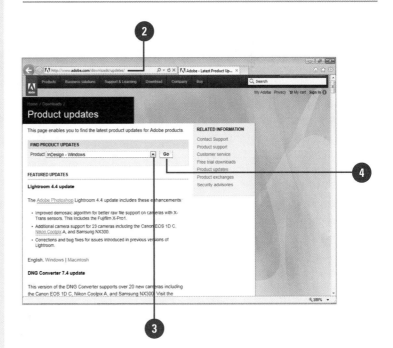

Check for Updates from the InDesign Help Menu

1 Click the **Help** menu, and then click **Updates**.

Adobe checks your software with the latest available version.

2 To manually check, click the **Check For New Updates** button.

3 To change preferences, click **Preferences**, select the update options you want, and then click **OK**.

4 Select the check boxes with the updates you want to install, and then click **Update**.

◆ Click the **Expand/Collapse** arrow to show or hide updates.

5 When you're done, click the **Close** button.

Did You Know?

You can sign in or sign out to Creative Cloud with your Adobe ID. You can sign in to your Creative Cloud (**New!**) with your Adobe ID to access online services for use with InDesign. If you don't have an account, you can create one. Click the Help menu, click Sign In, Sign In Now in the Creative Cloud dialog box, enter your Adobe ID and password, click Sign In, and then click Continue. To sign out, click the Help menu, click Sign Out (user account e-mail), and then click Sign out. Signing out allows you to activate your Adobe products on another device.

You can complete or update your Adobe ID profile. An Adobe ID allows you to access Adobe online services. To complete or update your Adobe ID profiles, click the Help menu, click Complete/Update Adobe ID Profile, and then follow the online instructions.

Getting Help While You Work

At some time, everyone has a question or two about using a program. When you start InDesign Help, your default web browser window opens, displaying online Community Help categories and topics for InDesign. Along with help text, some help topics include links to text and video tutorials. You can start a help search from InDesign on the Application bar. When you perform a search using keywords or phrases, a list of possible answers is shown from the search location with the most likely responses at the top. You can search product help from Adobe.com, Support, or Community Help by using keywords or phrases or browsing through a list of categories and topics to locate specific information. Adobe.com accesses related help information on Adobe.com, Support accesses Adobe support related help information, while Community Help accesses product help online. In addition to help content, comments and ratings from users are available to help guide you to an answer. You can add feedback and suggestions by signing in to Adobe.com using an Adobe ID.

Get Help Information

1. Click the **Help** menu, and then click **InDesign Help**.

   TIMESAVER *Press F1 (Win) or* ⌘+*/ (Mac).*

   Your default web browser opens, displaying online help and tutorials for InDesign.

2. Click the topic link you want.

   - ◆ What's New. Click the **What's New in CC** link.

   - ◆ PDF Manual. Click the **InDesign CC manual** link to open the PDF document, which you can save to your local device.

3. Read the topic, and if you want, click any links to get information on related topics or definitions.

4. To search for a topic, type one or more keywords in the Search box, and then press Enter (Win) or Return (Mac).

5. When you're done, click the **Close** button to exit your web browser.

Click to go to home help   Click to open help in a PDF

Click to find out what's new

Search for Help Information

1 In InDesign, on the Application bar, type one or more keywords in the Search box, and then press Enter (Win) or Return (Mac).

◆ You can also click the **Help** menu, and then click **InDesign Help** to open Help and use the Search box.

Your default web browser opens, displaying Adobe Community Help with a list of topics that match the keywords you entered in the Search box for InDesign.

2 To search another Adobe product, click the **Select Product** list arrow, and then select a product.

3 To change the search, select any of the following options, and then re-enter the search keywords:

◆ **Adobe.com.** Click to display results from Adobe.com.

◆ **Support.** Click to display results from Adobe.com.

◆ **Community Help.** Click to display results from Community Help for the Adobe program.

4 Click the link to the topic you want from the search list of results.

5 Read the topic, and if you want, click any links to get information on related topics or definitions.

◆ **Navigate Topics.** Click a navigation link at the top of the page. Click **InDesign** to go back to the help home page.

6 When you're done, click the **Close** button to exit your web browser.

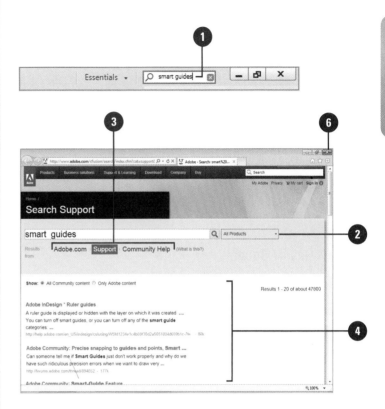

For Your Information

Participating in Adobe Product Improvement

You can participate in the Adobe Product Improvement Program. Click the Help menu, click Adobe Product Improvement Program, and then follow the on-screen instructions. This is an opt-in program that allows you to test Adobe products and make suggestions for future products. This program enables Adobe to collect product usage data from customers while maintaining their privacy.

Saving a Document

When you finish working on your InDesign document, you need to save it before you close the document or exit InDesign. You can save an InDesign CC document in the programs default file format (INDD) or as a template in the default template format (INDT). A template is a special document that makes it easier to create a new document. You might want to change the type if you're creating a custom template or sharing files with someone who doesn't have the Adobe InDesign program. When you open an InDesign CS5-CS6 document, the document tab includes "[Converted]." A converted document in InDesign CC acts like an untitled document, which you need to save to update it (**New!**). You cannot save the CC document in the CS6 or CS5 document format (INDD). However, you can save it to IDML (InDesign Markup Language), which you can open in InDesign CS4 or later (make sure software is updated).

Save an InDesign Document

1. Click the **File** menu, and then click **Save** (for an untitled or converted document) or **Save As**.

   ◆ When you click Save for an InDesign CC document, the file is saved with its current name and in the same location.

   TIMESAVER *Press Ctrl+S (Win) or ⌘+S (Mac) for a Save. Press Ctrl+Shift+S (Win) or ⌘+Shift+S (Mac) for a Save As.*

2. Enter a name for the file.

3. Click the **Save as Type** list arrow (Win) or **Format** popup (Mac), and then click **InDesign CC document**.

4. Navigate to the location where you want to save the document.

5. Select the **Always Save Preview Images with Documents** check box to save a preview image with the document for use in dialog boxes and thumbnails as a preview.

6. Click **Save**.

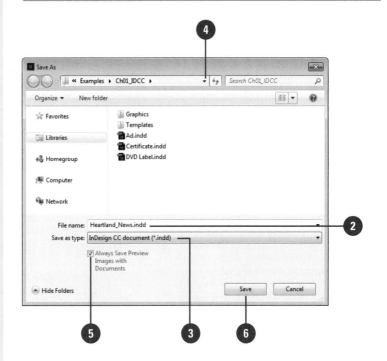

Save a Document for InDesign CS4 or Later

1 Click the **File** menu, and then click **Save As**.

2 Enter a name for the file.

3 Click the **Save as Type** list arrow (Win) or **Format** popup (Mac), and then click **InDesign CS4 or later (IDML)**.

4 Navigate to the location where you want to save the document.

5 Click **Save**.

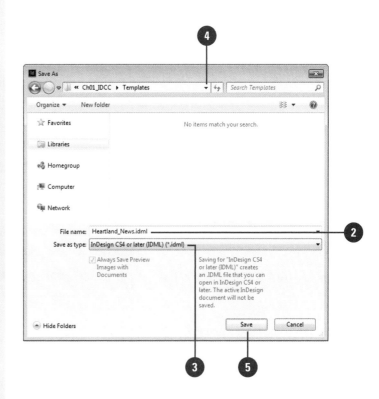

Did You Know?

You can save a copy of an InDesign document. Click the File menu, click Save a Copy or press Ctrl+Alt+S (Win) or ⌘+Option+S (Mac), click the Save As Type (Win) or Format (Mac) popup, click InDesign CC document, enter a name, specify a location, select the Always Save Preview Images with Documents check box to save a preview image with the document for use in dialog boxes and other thumbnails as a preview, and then click Save.

You can save a document as a template. Click the File menu, click Save As, click the Save As Type (Win) or Format (Mac) popup, click InDesign CC Template, enter a name, specify a location, and then click Save.

You can revert to the last saved version. Click the File menu, and then click Revert.

You can save all open documents. Press Ctrl+Alt+Shift+S (Win) or ⌘+Option+Shift+S (Mac) to save all open documents to their existing locations and filenames.

For Your Information

Understanding the IDML File Format

IDML (InDesign Markup Language) files provide an interchangable format for Adobe InDesign documents, as well as a way for third-party tools to modify and assemble InDesign documents. An IDML file is actually a compressed package using Zip compression. It contains a collection of XML files in a hierarchy of folders. The entire set of files represent a complete InDesign document. If you have a document in the InDesign CC Document file format (INDD), and you want to open it in InDesign CS4, CS5, CS5.5, or CS6, you can save it in the IDML file format from InDesign CC, and then open it from the InDesign software version you want. It's important to make sure the InDesign software is up-to-date before you open the IDML file; click the Help menu, and then click Updates.

Finishing Up

After you work on a document, you can finish up by closing the document or by exiting InDesign. You should save the document before closing it. Exiting InDesign closes the current document and the InDesign program and returns you to the desktop. You can use the Exit command on the File menu (Win) or Quit InDesign command on the InDesign menu (Mac) to close a document and exit InDesign, or you can use the Close button on the InDesign Document tab. If you try to close a document without saving your final changes, a dialog box opens, asking if you want to do so.

Close a Document

1. Click the **Close** button on the Document tab, or click the **File** menu, and then click **Close**.

   TIMESAVER *Press Ctrl+W (Win) or ⌘+W (Mac) to close a document.*

2. If necessary, click **Yes** to save any changes you made to your open documents before the program quits.

Document tab Close button

Exit InDesign

1. Choose one of the following:

   ◆ Click the **Close** button, or click the **File** menu, and then click **Exit** (Win).

   ◆ Click the **InDesign** menu, and then click **Quit InDesign** (Mac).

   TIMESAVER *Press Ctrl+Q (Win) or ⌘+Q (Mac) to exit InDesign.*

2. If necessary, click **Yes** to save any changes you made to your open documents before the program quits.

Exit (Win)   Click to exit (Win)

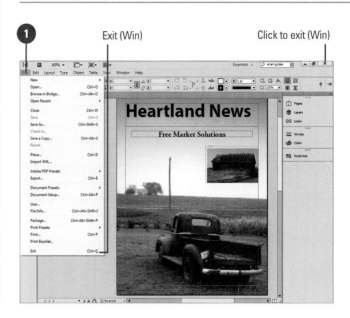

Creating and Viewing a Document

2

Introduction

You can either open an existing document or create a new one to work on in InDesign. When you create a new document, you can create one from scratch or use one of the built-in types, such as document, book or library. The built-in document presets make it easy to create documents for specific purposes without the hassle of specifying individual settings. However, if you know the individual settings you want, you can create a new document from scratch.

InDesign uses two main Screen Modes: Normal and Preview. Normal mode displays the area inside document pages, guides, pasteboard, bleed, and slug areas, while Preview mode simply displays the area inside document pages. There are two additional Screen Modes: Bleed and Slug. The bleed is an area outside the trim of the page where objects still print, while slug is an area outside the page trim that may or may not print. If you want to view pages as a slide show, you can use Presentation mode, which hides the Application bar and all panels.

Having problems squinting at the small details of a document? Using the Zoom tool is a great way to get you focused where you need to be. Zooming into a specific section of a document makes touching up the fine details just that much easier.

InDesign's navigation and measurement systems—rulers, grid, guides, smart guides—are more than just information; they represent control of the document and control of the creative process. In addition, the Info panel gives you up-to-date information on the exact position of the cursor inside the document, as well as detailed color space and profile information that can be indispensable in preparing your designs.

What You'll Do

Create a New Document

Create a New Document from a Template

Create a New Document Using Document Presets

Set Up a Document

Change the Display View

Change the View with the Zoom Tool

View and Use Rulers

Use Guides

Change Guides & Pasteboard Options

Use Smart Guides

Use the Grid

Move Around with the Hand Tool

Work with the Info Panel

Create and Display Workspaces

Use Undo and Redo

Creating a New Document

Creating a new InDesign document requires more thought than creating a new word processing document. For example, there are the intended output type, either print, web, or digital publishing for tablets, number of pages, start page number, page size (preset or custom), columns, and margins considerations to keep in mind. The page size option include US business card and compact disc for print, monitor sizes for web and tablet and mobile device types for digital publishing and allows you to create and name multiple custom page sizes within a single document. You can also set options for the bleed and slug. The **bleed** is an area outside the trim of the page where objects still print, while **slug** is an area outside the page trim that may or may not print. The slug is typically used to add non-printing information to a document. As you specify new document settings, you can preview (**New!**) them in the Document window as well as save your settings as a preset for future use.

Create a New Document

1. Click the **File** menu, point to **New**, and then click **Document**.

2. Click the **Document Preset** list arrow, and then select a preset, or choose your own options to create a custom document.

3. Click the **Intent** list arrow, and then select a output type: **Print**, **Web**, or **Digital Publishing**.

4. Select from the following options:

   ◆ **Number of Pages.** Specify the number of document pages.

   ◆ **Start Page #.** Specify the start page number for the document.

   ◆ **Facing Pages.** Select to use facing pages (left and right), like a book. Deselect to use single pages in order.

   ◆ **Primary Text Frame.** Select to use a common text frame for a document.

5. Select from the following options:

   ◆ **Page Size.** Select a preset size or click Custom Page Size. For Custom Page Size, enter a name, width and height, and then click **Add**. To remove, select a name, and then click **Delete**.

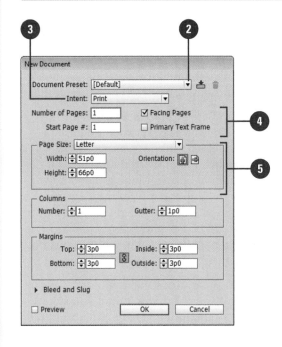

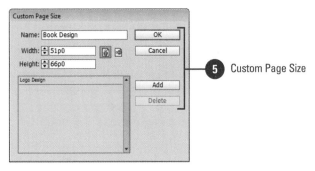

Custom Page Size

- ◆ **Width and Height.** Specify a custom width and height for a custom document size.
- ◆ **Orientation.** Select the Portrait or Landscape button.

6 Select from the following Columns options:

- ◆ **Number.** Specify the number of columns for the pages.
- ◆ **Gutter.** Specify the space between the columns.

7 Select from the following Margins options:

- ◆ **Top and Bottom.** Specify the top and bottom margin size at the top and bottom page edges.
- ◆ **Inside and Outside.** If Facing Pages is selected, specify Inside margins for the space between pages (e.g. binding) and Outside margins for page edges.
- ◆ **Make All Settings the Same.** Click the chain icon to make all settings the same or allow selection of different settings.

8 Click the **Expand** icon (triangle) (if needed), and then select the advanced options you want:

- ◆ **Bleed.** Specify the bleed values for top, bottom, inside and outside.
- ◆ **Slug.** Specify the slug values for top, bottom, inside and outside.
- ◆ **Make All Settings the Same.** Click the chain icon to make all settings the same or allow selection of different settings.

9 To preview the settings in the Document window, select the **Preview** check box (**New!**).

10 To save custom settings as a preset, click **Save Preset**, type a name, and then click **OK**.

11 Click **OK**.

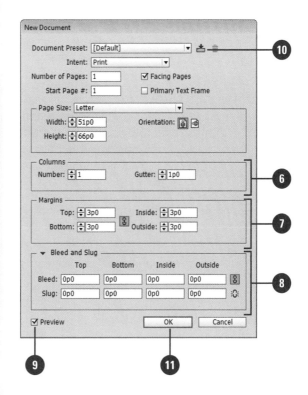

Document Page Sizes

Page Type	Page Size
Letter	8.5 by 11 inches
Legal	8.5 by 14 inches
Tabloid	11 by 17 inches
Letter-Half	8.5 by 5.5 inches
Legal-Half	8.5 by 7 inches
A4	21 by 29.7 centimeters
A3	29.7 by 42 centimeters
A5	14.8 by 21 centimeters
B5	25 by 17.6 centimeters
US Business Card	3.5 by 2 inches
Compact Disc	4.7222 by 4.75 inches
Monitor	600 x 300, 640 x 480, 760 x 420, 800 x 600, 984 x 588, 1024 x 768, 1240 x 620, 1280 x 800
Tablet	iPhone, iPad, Kindle Fire/Nook, Android 10"
Custom Page Size	User-defined; add multiple custom page sizes

Creating a New Document from a Template

A template is a special document that makes it easier to create a new document. If you frequently use an existing document, such as Books or Brochures, to start a new document, then you should create a template, which uses the InDesign Template (INDT) file format. You can create your own template or use one already done. When you create a new document from a template, the document appears with the template extension (INDT), which you can then save as a normal InDesign document with the INDD extension. You can use the Open dialog box from within InDesign to select a template or use Adobe Bridge to access and select a template for use back in InDesign.

Create a New Document from a Template

1. Click the **File** menu, and then click **Open**.

2. Click the **Files of Type** (Win) or **Enable** (Mac) list arrow, and then click **All Readable Files**.

3. Navigate to the folder location where the template is stored.

4. Click the template file you want to use.

5. Click **Open**.

   The template file opens back in InDesign as an untitled document.

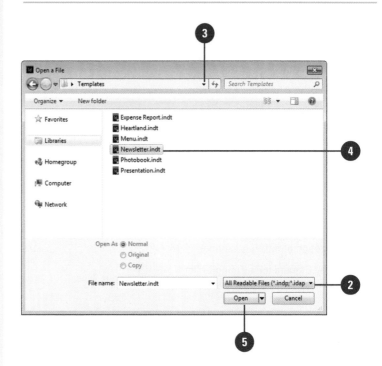

Did You Know?

You can open a template from Adobe Bridge. Click the Go To Bridge button on the Applications bar, navigate to the folder location where the template you want to use is stored, and then double-click the template file you want to use. The template file opens back in InDesign as an untitled document.

Create a Template Document

1. Open a new or existing document.

2. Create a custom document.

3. Click the **File** menu, and then click **Save As**.

4. Type a name for the new template.

5. Click the **Save as Type** (Win) or **Format** (Mac) list arrow, and then click **InDesign CC template (*.indt)**.

6. Navigate to the location where you want to store the template.

7. Select the **Always Save Preview Images with Documents** check box to save a preview image with the document for use in dialog boxes and other thumbnails as a preview.

8. Click **Save**.

Creating a New Document Using Presets

If you frequently use custom settings to create an InDesign document, you can save time by creating a preset. You can create or delete (**New!**) a preset when you create a new document in the New Document dialog box or you can create and manage presets in the Document Presets dialog box. After you create a preset, you can export and share it with others, which they can import with the Load button in the Document Presets dialog box. When you no longer need a preset, you can delete it. However, you can't delete the [Default] preset.

Create a New Document Using Presets

① Click the **File** menu, point to **Document Presets**, and then select a preset.

◆ You can also click the **File** menu, point to **New**, click **Document**, and then select a preset.

The New Document dialog box appears, displaying the selected preset.

② Click **OK**.

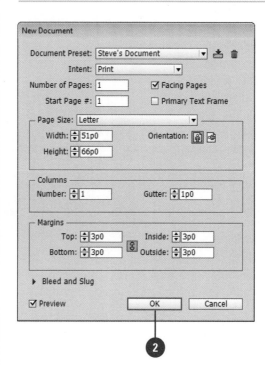

Did You Know?

You can save or delete a preset in the New Document dialog box. Click the File menu, point to New, click Document, specify the settings you want, click the Save Preset button, type a name, and then click OK. To delete a preset, select it, click the Delete Preset button (**New!**), and then click OK. When you're done, click OK.

See Also

See "Creating a New Document" on page 28 for more information on saving a preset in the New Document dialog box.

Work with Presets for New Documents

1. Click the **File** menu, point to **Document Presets**, and then click **Define**.

2. Perform any of the following:

   ◆ New. Click **New**, specify the options that you want, and then click **OK**.

   ◆ Edit. Select a custom preset (not a predefined one), click **Edit**, change the options, and then click **OK**.

   ◆ Delete. Select a custom preset (not a predefined one), and then click **Delete**.

   ◆ Import. Click **Load**, navigate to the preset file, select it, and then click **Open**.

   ◆ Export. Select a preset, click **Save**, specify a location and name, and then click **Save**.

3. Click **OK**.

Did You Know?

You can perform calculations in edit boxes. In an edit field box or dialog box, you can perform simple calculations, such as 1+3, as well as more complex ones, such as 12.5p / 2x3.

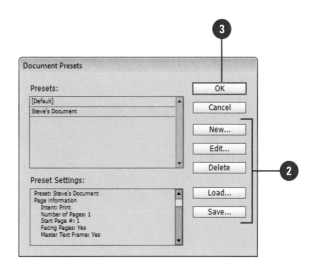

New preset

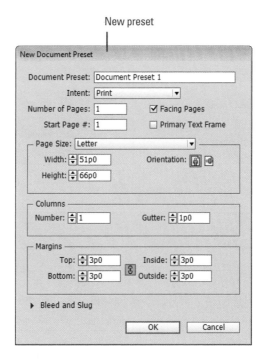

Setting Up a Document

After you create a document, you can use the Document Setup command on the File menu and the Margins and Columns command on the Layout menu to change document settings. In the Document Setup dialog box, you can specify the intended output type, either print, web, or digital publishing for tablets (including iPhone, iPad, Kindle Fire/Nook, and Android (**New!**)), number of pages, start page number, page size (preset or custom), orientation, and advanced settings for bleed and slug as well as preview (**New!**) them in the document window. You can create and name multiple custom page sizes within a single document, which is useful keeping different sized designs, such as a business card and letter head, in the same document. In the Margins and Columns dialog box, you can specify margin, column, and gutter settings, which are only applied to the current page or two page spread and not the entire document. If you want to change the entire document, you need to change the master page.

Change Margins and Column Options

1. Click the **Layout** menu, and then click **Margins and Columns**.

2. Select from the following Columns options:

   ◆ **Number.** Specify the number of columns for the pages.

   ◆ **Gutter.** Specify the space between the columns.

3. Select from the following Margins options:

   ◆ **Top and Bottom.** Specify the top and bottom margin size at the top and bottom page edges.

   ◆ **Inside and Outside.** If Facing Pages is selected, set Inside margins for the space between pages (e.g. binding) and Outside margins for page edges.

   ◆ **Make All Settings the Same.** Click the chain icon to make all settings the same or allow selection of different settings.

4. Select the **Enable Layout Adjustment** check box to adjust the current layout.

5. Click **OK**.

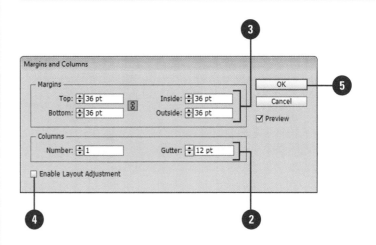

Common Tablet Sizes

Device	Resolution Size	OS
iPhone	480 x 320 px	iOS
iPad/iPad Mini	1024 x 768 px	iOS
iPad with Retina	2048 x 1536 px	iOS
Kindle Fire	1024 x 600 px, 1920 x1200 px (HD)	Android
Barnes & Noble Nook	1024 x 600 px, 1440 x 900 px (HD)	Android
Android 10"	1280 x 800 px	Android
Surface RT, Pro	1366 x 768 px, 1920 x 1080 px	Win 8
Tablet PC	1366 x 768 px	Win 8

Change Document Options

1. Click the **File** menu, and then click **Document Setup**.

2. Click the **Intent** list arrow, and then select a output type: **Print**, **Web**, or **Digital Publishing**.

3. Select from the following options:

   ◆ **Number of Pages.** Specify the number of document pages.

   ◆ **Start Page #.** Specify the start page number for the document.

   ◆ **Facing Pages.** Select to use facing pages (left and right), like a book. Deselect to use single pages in order.

   ◆ **Primary Text Frame.** Select to use a common text frame for a document.

4. Select from the following Page Size options:

   ◆ **Page Size.** Select a preset size or click Custom Page Size. For Custom Page Size, do any of the following:

      ◆ Add. Enter a name, width and height, and then click **Add**.

      ◆ Remove. Select a name, and then click **Delete**.

      ◆ Edit. Select a name, and then click **Change**.

   ◆ **Width and Height.** Specify a custom width and height for a custom document size.

   ◆ **Orientation.** Select the Portrait or Landscape button.

5. Click the **Expand** icon (triangle) to set Bleed and Slug values.

6. To preview the settings in the Document window, select the **Preview** check box (**New!**).

7. Click **OK**.

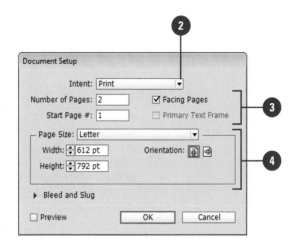

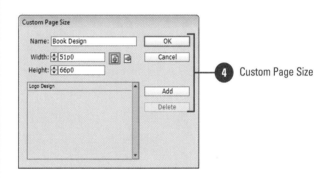

Custom Page Size

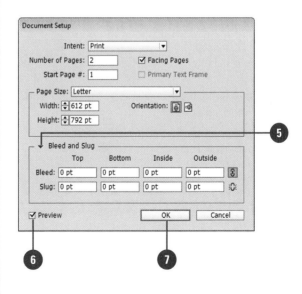

Changing the Display View

InDesign uses two main modes: Normal and Preview. Normal mode displays document pages, guides, pasteboard, bleed, and slug areas, while Preview mode displays the area inside the page boundaries. There are two additional modes: Bleed and Slug. The bleed is an area outside the trim of the page where objects still print, while slug is an area outside the page trim that may or may not print. Bleed mode displays the bleed area and document pages, while Slug mode displays the slug area and document pages. If you want to view pages as a slide show, you can use Presentation mode, which hides the Application bar and all panels. You can use keystrokes and mouse clicks to move forward or backwards through the document one spread at a time. In addition to the display modes, you can also preview aspects of your output, such as overprinting, color proofs and separations, and flattened artwork.

Change the Display View

1. Click the **Screen Mode** button on the Application bar or on the bottom of the Tools panel, and then select one of the following modes:

   ◆ **Normal.** Shows the guides, pasteboard, bleed, and slug areas.

   ◆ **Preview.** Shows the area inside the page boundaries.

   The pasteboard is replaced by a colored background, which you can change in Guides & Pasteboard preferences.

   ◆ **Bleed.** Shows the area inside the page boundaries and the bleed area.

   ◆ **Slug.** Shows the area inside the page boundaries and the slug area.

   ◆ **Presentation.** Shows document spreads as a slide show. Hides the Application bar and all panels. Use Arrow keys and mouse clicks to move forward or backward through the document one spread at a time. Press Esc to exit.

Preview view

Normal button

Display Output Views

◆ **Overprint Preview Mode.** Displays an ink preview with blending, transparency, and overprinting in color separated output. Click the **View** menu, and then click **Overprint Preview**.

◆ **Separations Preview Mode.** Displays separations as they print. Click the **Window** menu, point to **Output**, and then click **Separations Preview**.

◆ **Flattener Preview Mode.** Displays and highlights artwork areas that are flattened when saved or printed. Click the **Window** menu, point to **Output**, and then click **Flattener Preview**.

◆ **Soft Proofs.** Displays your artwork as it will appear on a monitor or output device. Click the **View** menu, point to **Proof Setup**, and then select a proof type.

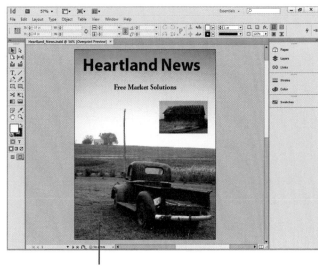

Overprint preview

Separations Preview panel

Separations preview

Did You Know?

You can rotate the Spread view and edit content. Display the two page spread you want to rotate, click the View menu, point to Rotate Spread, and then choose 90° CW (clockwise), 90° CCW (counter clockwise), or 180°. Edit the content you want. To restore the view, click Clear Rotation.

You can temporarily hide all of InDesign's panels and Tools panel. Press the Tab key to hide the panels. Press the Tab key a second time to display the hidden panels. Hold down the Shift key, and then press the Tab key to hide the panels, but not the Tools and Control panels.

Changing the View with the Zoom Tool

Working with the Zoom tool gives you one more way to control exactly what you see in InDesign. The Zoom tool does not change the active image, but allows you to view the image at different magnifications. The Zoom tool is located towards the bottom of InDesign's Tools panel, and resembles a magnifying glass. The maximum magnification of an InDesign document is 4000%, and the minimum size is 5.0%. Large documents are difficult to work with and difficult to view. Many large documents, when viewed at 100%, are larger than the maximum size of the document window, requiring you to reduce the zoom in order to view the entire image. In addition to the Zoom tool, you can also select view options to fit the page or spread to the window, show the actual size, or show the entire pasteboard.

Zoom In the View of an Image

① Select the **Zoom** tool on the Tools panel.

② Use one of the following methods:

- ◆ **Click on the document.** The image increases in magnification centered on where you clicked.

- ◆ **Drag to define an area with the Zoom tool.** The image increases in magnification based on the boundaries of the area you dragged.

- ◆ **Set a specific view size.** Click the **Zoom Level** button on the Application bar, and then select a specific percentage size magnification.

- ◆ **Fit Page in Window.** Click the **View** menu, and then click **Fit Page In Window**.

- ◆ **Fit Spread in Window.** Click the **View** menu, and then click **Fit Spread In Window**.

- ◆ **Actual Size.** Click the **View** menu, and then click **Actual Size**.

- ◆ **Show Entire Pasteboard.** Click the **View** menu, and then click **Entire Pasteboard**.

② Click and drag method

Zoom in

Zoom Out the View of an Image

1. Select the **Zoom** tool on the Tools panel.

2. Hold down the Alt (Win) or Option (Mac) key, and then click on the screen to reduce the magnification of the active document.

   TIMESAVER *Press Ctrl+= (Win) or ⌘+= (Mac) for Zoom In and press Ctrl+- (Win) or ⌘+- (Mac) for Zoom Out. The shortcuts work when you have a dialog box open.*

   The zoom reduction centers at the spot where you click on the active document.

   IMPORTANT *The best way to really see what the printed results of your artwork will look like is to view the image (even if it is too big for the screen) at 100%.*

Did You Know?

You can zoom in or out using shortcut keys regardless of what tool you're currently using. To zoom in, press Ctrl+Spacebar (Win) or ⌘+Spacebar (Mac) and click or drag to define an area. To zoom out, press Ctrl+Spacebar+Alt (Win) or ⌘+Spacebar+Option (Mac) and click or drag to define an area.

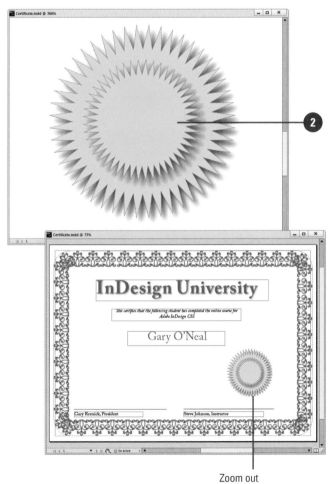

Zoom out

Viewing and Using Rulers

Carpenters know that precise measurements are essential to making things fit, so they have a rule: Measure Twice, Cut Once. The designers of InDesign also know that measurements are essential and give you several measuring systems—among them are the rulers. Rulers are located on the top and left sides of the active document window, and serve several purposes. Rulers start numbering at the top left corner of the page. You can move this point, known as the zero point, to another position. Rulers let you measure the width and height of the active image, they let you place guides on the screen to control placement of other image elements, and they create markers that follow your cursor as you move. As you can see, rulers are critical in the design of a document by helping you correctly align image design elements. The default measurement is in picas, which you can change in Preferences. You can also change the origin, which allows you to use rulers across spreads and spines.

Change Ruler Options

1 Click the **Edit** (Win) or **InDesign** (Mac) menu, point to **Preferences**, and then click **Units & Increments**.

2 Click the **Origin** list arrow, and then select an option:

◆ **Spread.** Displays rulers for two pages at a time, as in a book or magazine.

◆ **Page.** Displays rulers for one page at a time.

◆ **Spine.** Displays rulers for the area where two page spreads are bound together.

3 Click the **Horizontal** and **Vertical** list arrows, and then select a measurement from the available options.

◆ If you selected **Custom**, enter the number of points for each unit on the ruler.

4 Click **OK**.

IMPORTANT *If the Rulers are not visible in the active document, click the View menu, and then click Show Rulers.*

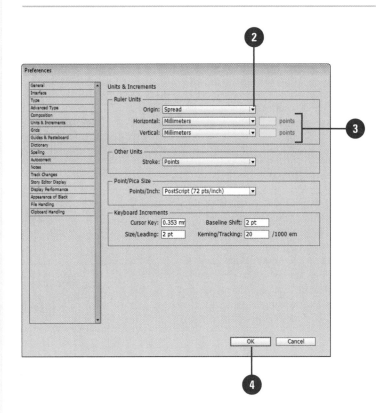

Work with Rulers

◆ **Show or Hide Rulers.** Click the **View** menu, and then click **Show Rulers** or **Hide Rulers**.

> **TIMESAVER** *Press Ctrl+R (Win) or ⌘R (Mac).*

  ◆ You can also click the **View Options** button on the Application bar, and then click **Rulers**.

◆ **Change Measurement Units.** Right-click (Win) or Option-click (Mac) a ruler, and then select a unit of measure.

◆ **Change Ruler Origin.** Point to the upper-left corner where the rulers intersect, and then drag the pointer to where you want the new ruler origin.

When you change the ruler origin on a spine with facing pages, the X values are positive for right-sided pages and negative for left-sided pages.

◆ **Reset Ruler Origin.** Double-click the upper-left corner where the rulers intersect.

Horizontal Ruler bar

Vertical Ruler bar

Did You Know?

You can change the number of points per inch in InDesign. Points are used to measure font characters. In the Units & Increments Preferences dialog box, you can change the points per inch. Click the Edit (Win) or InDesign (Mac) menu, point to Preferences, click Units & Increments, specify an option, and then click OK.

For Your Information

Using Pixels as the Unit of Measure

If you prefer working in pixels instead of points or inches, you can specify Pixels as the unit of measure in Units & Increments preferences. Click the Edit (Win) or InDesign (Mac) menu, point to Preferences, and then click Units & Increments. In addition, you can specify pixels as the unit of measure by adding px to your values in the Control panel, dialog boxes, and other panels. When you use pixels as the unit of measure, objects and x/y coordinates snap to whole pixel values and the line weights displayed in the Stroke panel change to pixels.

Using Guides

A guide is a nonprinting vertical or horizontal line that helps you align text and graphic objects. You can quickly show and hide guides, lock them in place, and align objects to them. With the Snap to Guides command, you can align an object to a guide. When the object's edge comes within a specified distance in pixels of a guide, it snaps to the guide point. When you no longer need one or all of the guides, you can quickly select and remove them.

Create and Move Guides

1. Click the **View** menu, and then click **Show Rulers** to display the ruler bars within the document window.

2. Move to the vertical or horizontal Ruler bar, and then click and drag into the document.

3. Return to the Ruler bar and continue to drag until you have all your guides properly set.

4. To lock the existing guides in place, click the **View** menu, point to **Grids & Guides**, and then click **Lock Guides**.

5. Click the **Selection** tool on the Tools panel to drag existing guides to a new position (make sure Lock Guides is not selected).

Did You Know?

InDesign snaps to values. When you snap an object to a guide or grid, InDesign snaps to logical values based on the current unit of measure. If you're using inches, values snap to the nearest eighth of an inch (.125). If you're using picas, values snap to the nearest whole point.

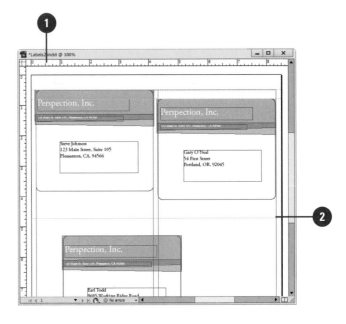

Work with Guides

◆ **Show or Hide Guides.** Click the
View menu, point to **Grids &
Guides**, and then click **Show
Guides** or **Hide Guides**.

TIMESAVER *Press Ctrl+; (Win)
or* ⌘+; *(Mac).*

 ◆ You can also click the **View
Options** button on the
Application bar, and then click
Guides.

◆ **Lock/Unlock Guides.** Click the
View menu, point to **Grids &
Guides**, and then click **Lock
Guides**.

TIMESAVER *Press Alt+Ctrl+;
(Win) or Option+*⌘+; *(Mac).*

◆ **Lock/Unlock Column Guides.** Click
the **View** menu, point to **Grids &
Guides**, and then click **Lock
Column Guides**.

◆ **Snap Objects to Guides.** Click the
View menu, point to **Grids &
Guides**, and then click **Snap To
Guides**.

When you drag an object near a
guide, the object snaps to it.

TIMESAVER *Press Shift+Ctrl+;
(Win) or Shift+*⌘+; *(Mac).*

◆ **Delete Guides.** Click the ruler
guide with one of the Selection
tools, and then press the Delete or
Backspace key.

◆ **Delete All Guides.** Right-click
(Win) or Ctrl-click (Mac) a ruler,
and then click **Delete All Guides**,
or click the **View** menu, point to
Grids & Guides, and then click
Delete All Guides On Spread.

Guide   Snap to guide

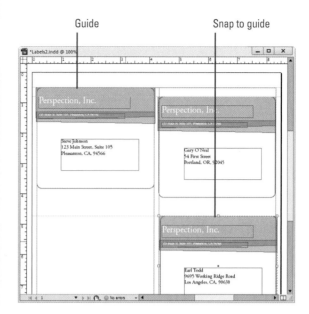

Changing Guides & Pasteboard Options

InDesign uses several different types of guides to show different areas of a document. Ruler guides are user-defined guides for moving and aligning objects. Margin guides show the current margins in the document. Column guides show current column settings for a page or master page. Bleed and Slug guides show the bleed and slug areas in a document. You can use Guides & Pasteboard preferences to set guide settings, such as color and display options, and pasteboard settings, such as color in Preview view and size above and below the document. You can also specify a snap to distance to align an object to a guide.

Change Guides & Pasteboard Preferences

1. Click the **Edit** (Win) or **InDesign** (Mac) menu, point to **Preferences**, and then click **Guides & Pasteboard**.

2. Select from the following Guides & Pasteboard options:

   ◆ **Margins.** Specify a guide color for margins.

   ◆ **Columns.** Specify a guide color for columns.

   ◆ **Bleed.** Specify a guide color for the bleed area.

   ◆ **Slug.** Specify a guide color for the slug area.

   ◆ **Preview Background.** Select the **Match to Theme Color** check box (**New!**). If not, specify a color for the pasteboard background in Preview view.

   ◆ **Snap to Zone.** Enter a value to specify the distance in pixels when an object snaps to a guide.

   ◆ **Guides in Back.** Select to show guides in the background of text and objects.

   ◆ **Horizontal and Vertical Margins.** Enter a size to change the margins of the pasteboard area above and below the document.

3. Click **OK**.

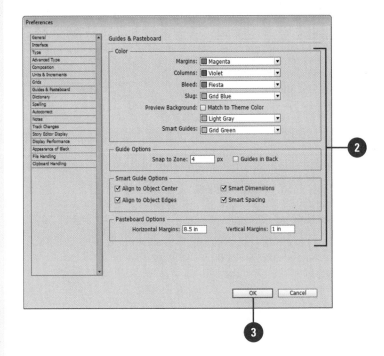

Change the Appearance of Ruler Guides

1. Click the **Layout** menu, and then click **Ruler Guides**.

2. Click the **Color** list arrow, and then select a color.

3. Click the **View Threshold** list arrow, and then select the lowest view percentage at which the ruler guides will be visible.

    When you increase the threshold, guides are hidden at low magnifications and are visible at high magnifications.

4. Click **OK**.

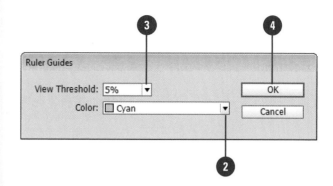

Did You Know?

You can turn on or off the Smart Cursor. Smart cursors display the X and Y values of objects you create, resize, or move them. To turn on or off smart cursors, click the Edit (Win) or InDesign (Mac) menu, point to Preferences, click Interface, select or deselect the Show Transformation Values check box, and then click OK.

Using Smart Guides

InDesign gives you the ability to use Smart Guides to help align shapes and objects as you draw or drag to move, rotate, or resize. They appear automatically as you draw or move an element, and then disappear after the element is drawn or moved. They enable you to visually align one object to another with a minimum of effort. Smart Guides also display alignment and measurement information, known as Smart Dimensions, such as distances between objects, angles of rotation, and whether an object matches the size of nearby objects, to make drawing and alignment even easier. You can also use Smart Spacing to evenly space multiple elements by snapping objects into position. Smart Guides are automatically turned on by default. You can use Guides & Pasteboard preferences to set color and information display options to customize your Smart Guides.

Use Smart Guides

1 Open or create a multi-layered document.

2 To turn Smart Guides on and off, click the **View** menu, point to **Grids & Guides**, and then click **Smart Guides**.

  ◆ You can also click the **View Options** button on the Application bar, and then click **Smart Guides**.

3 To draw a shape and use Smart Guides, select a shape tool from the Tools panel, and then drag to draw the shape.

  As you draw the shape, Smart Guides appear to help you create shapes that match and align to other objects.

4 Select the **Selection** tool on the Tools panel, and then select and drag the objects you want to move and align.

  As you move the object, Smart Guides appear to help you align it with other objects.

5 Release the mouse and the guides disappear.

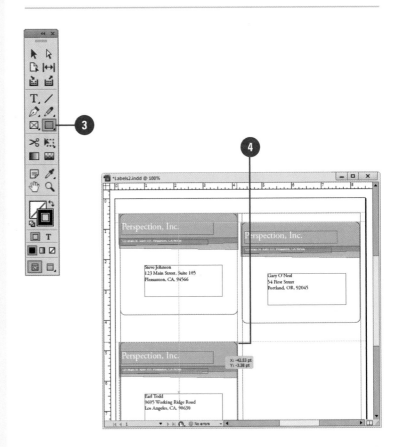

Change Smart Guide Preferences

1. Click the **Edit** (Win) or **InDesign** (Mac) menu, point to **Preferences**, and then click **Guides & Pasteboard**.

2. Click the **Smart Guides** list arrow, and then select a guide color.

3. Select from the following options:

   ◆ **Align to Object Center.** Select to display guides along the center of objects, art, and bleeds.

   ◆ **Align to Object Edges.** Select to display guides along edges of objects, artboard, and bleeds.

   ◆ **Smart Dimensions.** Select to enable the Smart Dimensions feature, which allows you to show width, height or rotation of an object, and indicate when the size or rotation matches nearby objects.

   ◆ **Smart Spacing.** Select to enable the Smart Spacing feature, which allows you to evenly space multiple items by snapping objects into position.

   ◆ **Snap to Zone.** Enter a value to specify the distance in pixels when an object snaps to a guide.

   ◆ **Guides in Back.** Select to show guides in the background of text and objects.

4. Click **OK**.

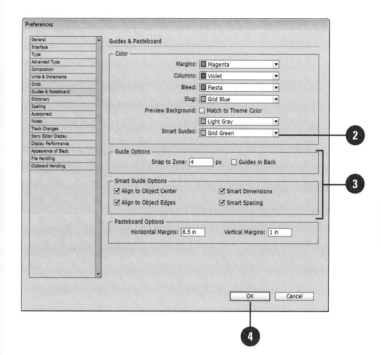

Using the Grid

A grid is a checkerboard display that you can use to help you align text and graphic objects. There are two types of grids: Document and Baseline. The document grid displays a checkerboard pattern, which is helpful for aligning objects, while the baseline grid displays horizontal lines, which is helpful for aligning text. The grid appears behind your text and artwork, so it doesn't get in the way. With the Snap to Document Grid command, you can align an object to a gridline. When the object's edge comes within a specified number of pixels of a gridline, it snaps to the gridline point. You can use Grids preferences to set grid settings, such as color and spacing.

Work with the Grid

◆ **Show or Hide Document Grid.** Click the **View** menu, point to **Grids & Guides**, and then click **Show Document Grid** or **Hide Document Grid**.

TIMESAVER *Press Ctrl+' (Win) or* ⌘+' *(Mac).*

◆ **Show or Hide Baseline Grid.** Click the **View** menu, point to **Grids & Guides**, and then click **Show Baseline Grid** or **Hide Baseline Grid**.

TIMESAVER *Press Alt+Ctrl+' (Win) or Option+*⌘+' *(Mac).*

   ◆ You can also click the **View Options** button on the Application bar, and then click **Baseline Grid**.

   ◆ When you use a measurement system other than points, baseline grid values still use points to match text size and leading.

◆ **Snap Objects to Gridline.** Click the **View** menu, point to **Grids & Guides**, and then click **Snap To Document Grid**.

TIMESAVER *Press Shift+Ctrl+' (Win) or Shift+*⌘+' *(Mac).*

When you drag an object near a gridline, it snaps to the gridline.

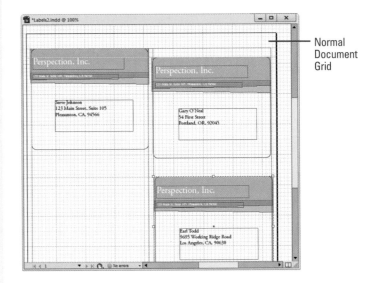

Normal Document Grid

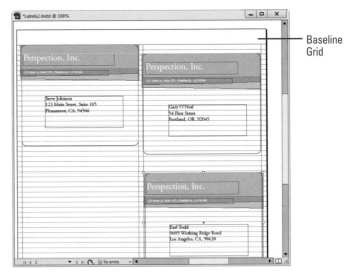

Baseline Grid

Change Grid Preferences

1. Click the **Edit** (Win) or **InDesign** (Mac) menu, point to **Preferences**, and then click **Grids**.

2. Select from the following Baseline Grid options:

   ◆ **Color.** Specify a grid color.

   ◆ **Start.** Specify a start value for the baseline.

   ◆ **Relative To.** Specify the location of the start value relative to the page or margin.

   ◆ **Increment Every.** Specify a measurement for the interval of gridlines. The default is 12 points.

   ◆ **View Threshold.** Specify the lowest view percentage at which the grid is visible.

3. Select from the following Document Grid options:

   ◆ **Color.** Specify a grid color.

   ◆ **Gridline Every (Horizontal and Vertical).** Specify a measurement for the interval of gridlines.

   ◆ **Subdivisions (Horizontal and Vertical).** Specify the number of grid subdivisions.

   ◆ **Grids in Back.** Select to show grids in the background of text and objects.

4. Click **OK**.

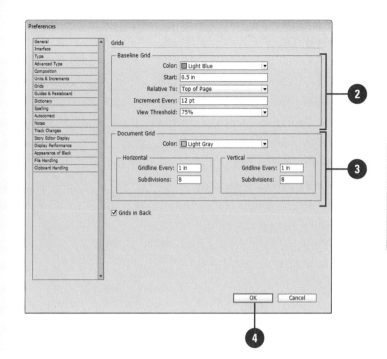

Moving Around with the Hand Tool

One of those little used, but handy, tools is InDesign's Hand tool. The Hand tool (so named because it resembles an open hand) lets you quickly move the active image within the document window without ever using the scroll bars. For example, you've zoomed the image beyond the size that fits within the document window and you need to change the visible portion of the document. It's a simple operation, but a handy one to know.

Move a Page Around in the Document Window

1. Select the **Hand** tool on the Tools panel.

2. Drag in the active document to move it.

3. Click and hold to zoom in. Release the mouse to return to the previous magnification.

Did You Know?

You can quickly access the Hand tool whenever you need it. Hold down the Spacebar to temporarily change to the Hand tool. Drag in the active document to the desired position, and then release the Spacebar. You're instantly returned to the last-used tool. It's important to note that you cannot use the Spacebar to access the Hand tool if you are currently using the Type tool.

See Also

See "Changing the View with the Zoom Tool" on pages 38-39 for more information on increasing and decreasing the view magnification.

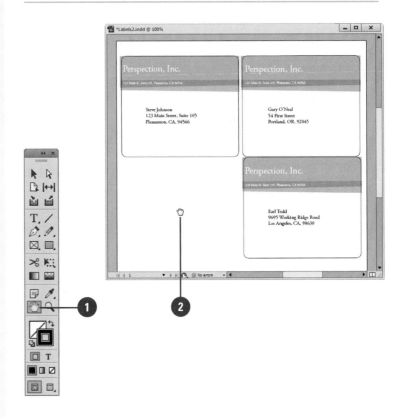

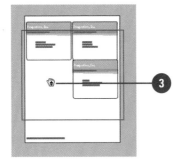

Working with the Info Panel

InDesign's Info panel gives you a wealth of data on the current document. The Info panel displays information on the x and y (horizontal/vertical) position of your mouse cursor within the active document window. In addition, when you're using one of InDesign's drawing, measuring, or transformation tools, the Info panel gives you up-to-date information on the size of the object you're creating. When an object is selected, the Info panel display the x and y position, width (w) and height (h). If you select multiple objects, only information that is the same for all selected objects appears in the Info panel. When you're using the Zoom tool, the Info panel displays the magnification factor and the x and y position. The Info panel also displays color information when you choose to show options.

Create a Specific Size Object

1. Select the **Info** panel.

2. Select a drawing tool on the Tools panel, and then drag to create a shape.

3. Release the mouse when the Info panel displays the desired dimensions.

4. To display color fill and stroke information for a selected object, click the **Options** button, and then click **Show Options**.

5. To change cursor, fill or stroke information, click the related icon (with a small black triangle), and then select an option.

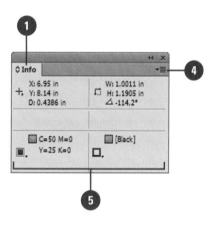

Did You Know?

You can measure the distance between objects. Select the Measure tool in the Tools panel, and then click two points, or click the first point and drag to the second point. Use Shift-drag to constrain the tool to multiples of 45 degrees. The Info panel displays the distances from the x and y axes, the absolute horizontal and vertical distances, the total distances, and the angle measured.

Creating and Displaying Workspaces

As you work with InDesign, you'll open, close, and move around windows and panels to meet your individual needs. After you customize the InDesign workspace, you can save the location of windows and panels as a workspace, which you can display by using the Workspace menu on the Application bar or the Workspaces submenu on the Window menu. You can create custom workspaces, or use one of the workspaces provided by InDesign, which are designed for space and workflow efficiency. The built-in workspaces include Advanced, Book, Digital Publishing, Essentials, Interactivity for PDF, Printing and Proofing, and Typography. If you no longer use a custom workspace, you can remove it at any time.

Create a Workspace

1. Open and position the panels and add the custom menus you want to include in the workspace.

2. Click the **Workspace** menu on the Application bar (the menu name displays the current workspace), and then click **New Workspace**.

   ◆ You can also click the **Window** menu, point to **Workspace**, and then click **New Workspace**.

   The New Workspace dialog box appears.

3. Type a name in the Name box.

4. Select or deselect check boxes to include **Panel Locations** and **Menu Customization**.

5. Click **OK**.

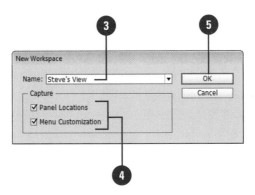

Display a Workspace

1. Click the **Workspace** menu on the Application bar (the menu name displays the current workspace), and then select a panel option:

   ◆ **Custom panel name.** Displays a custom panel layout that you created.

   ◆ **Advanced, Book, Digital Publishing, Essentials, Interactive for PDF, Printing and Proofing, or Typography.** Displays panel layouts created by Adobe for specific purposes in InDesign.

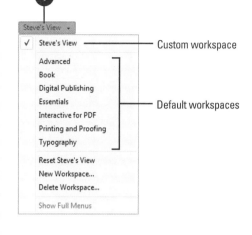

Custom workspace

Default workspaces

Delete a Workspace

1. Click the **Workspace** menu on the Application bar, and then click **Delete Workspace**.

   ◆ You can also click the **Window** menu, point to **Workspace**, and then click **Delete Workspace**.

   The Delete Workspace dialog box appears.

2. Select the workspace you want to delete.

3. Click **Delete**.

   The workspace is now deleted.

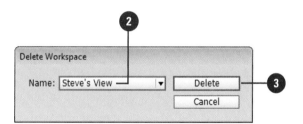

Using Undo and Redo

Probably one of the greatest inventions of the computer industry is the ability to Undo, and Redo. Now, if we could just figure out how to give real life an undo feature... that would be something. InDesign gives us the ability to undo our past mistakes, and redo something we wished we had not undone. However, you can no longer view actions, such as Set Preview and Show Guides with the undo feature.

Undo or Redo One Action at a Time

◆ Click the **Edit** menu, and then click **Undo** to reverse your most recent action, such as typing a word or formatting a paragraph.

  TIMESAVER *Press Ctrl+Z (Win) or ⌘+Z (Mac) to undo.*

◆ Click the **Edit** menu, and then click **Redo** to restore the last action you reversed.

  TIMESAVER *Press Shift+Ctrl+Z (Win) or Shift+⌘+Z (Mac) to redo your undo.*

Click to Undo or Redo the previous command or action.

Managing Pages and Books

3

Introduction

Most documents are more than one page, so inserting new pages is a common practice in InDesign. You can quickly add a new blank page to a document using the Pages panel. The Pages panel allows you to visually display and navigate through all the pages in your document. When you work with multiple page documents, moving pages around is inevitable. You can simply drag pages in the Pages panel to rearrange them within a document or use the Move Page command on the panel Options menu to move them between documents. When you no longer need a page, you can quickly delete it from your document using the Pages panel.

A master page is one of the most important parts of creating an InDesign document. A master page holds and displays all the elements that you want to appear on every page in a document, such as headers, logos, page numbers, and footers. The master is like a background layer to a page. Everything on the background layer appears on the page in front of it. When you make a change to a master page, the change appears in all document pages unless you override the change.

Instead of creating long documents, you can break them up into smaller documents, like chapters, and then add them to a book. In InDesign, a book is not a single document. It simply keeps track of all the documents in the book and coordinates document page numbers, colors, and styles. When you create a book, you can synchronize page numbers, colors, and styles for all the documents in the book. Each book uses a file called the *style source* to control the style sheets, swatches, and master pages for all the documents in the book. When you make changes to the style source file, all the documents in the book are synchronized to the file.

What You'll Do

Use the Pages Panel

Insert Pages

Navigate Pages

Change the Page Size

Delete or Move Pages

Work with Page Spreads

Rotate Page Spreads

Create Master Pages

Work with Master Pages

Work with Page Numbers and Sections

Work with Chapter Numbers

Create and Use Text Variables

Create and Manage Books

Create a Table of Contents

Start an Index

Create an Index Entry

Create an Index

Manage an Index

Using the Pages Panel

The Pages panel allows you to visually display all the pages in your document. The Pages panel shows thumbnails for each page. At the top of the panel are the master pages for the document. A master page contains elements that are repeated on every page. When you're working with a multi-page document with or without multi-layouts, the Pages panel is an essential part of working with pages. You can add and remove pages as well as navigate to and from pages. The Pages panel, like all panels, provides an Options menu where you can select page-related commands and Pages panel view and display options. The view options allow you to view page icons horizontally, vertically, or by alternate layouts (for different size mobile devices). The display options allow you to change page icons size, position, and location. In addition, you can also set options to show or hide icons for page transparency, transition, and spread rotation.

Change the Pages Panel View

1. Select the **Pages** panel.

   ◆ Click the **Window** menu, and then click **Pages**.

2. Click the **Options** button on the panel, point to **View Pages**, and then select an option:

   ◆ **Horizontally.** View page icons horizontally.

   ◆ **Vertically.** View page icons vertically.

   ◆ **By Alternate Layout.** View page icons in multiple layouts.

3. For the By Alternate Layout view, use any of the following:

   ◆ **Layout Options.** Click the **Layout Options** menu to create or delete alternate layouts, delete pages, set HTML5 pagination options, and split window to compare layouts.

   ◆ **Rename Layouts.** Double-click the layout name, edit the name, and then press Enter (Win) or Return (Mac).

   ◆ **Switch Layout Columns.** Drag the layout names to the other side.

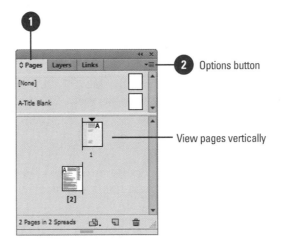

2 Options button

View pages vertically

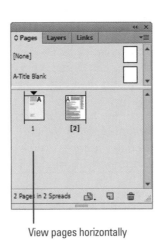

View pages horizontally

Layout name   Layout Options menu

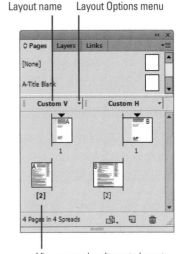

View pages by alternate layout; two layouts appear here.

Change the Pages Panel Display

1. Select the **Pages** panel.
   - ◆ Click the **Window** menu, and then click **Pages**.
2. Click the **Options** button on the panel, and then click **Panel Options**.
3. Select from the following Pages panel options:
   - ◆ **Size.** Specify an icon size for Pages and Masters.
   - ◆ **Show Vertically.** Select to show master page icons vertically.
   - ◆ **Show Thumbnails.** Select to show page or master page icons as thumbnails.
4. Select from the following options for icon display:
   - ◆ **Transparency.** Select to display icons when transparency is applied to a page or spread.
   - ◆ **Spread Rotation.** Select to display icons when the spread view is rotated.
   - ◆ **Page Transitions.** Select to display icons when page transitions are applied to a page or spread.
5. Click the **Pages on Top** or **Masters on Top** option.
6. Click the **Resize** list arrow, and then select an option when you resize the Pages panel.
7. Click **OK**.

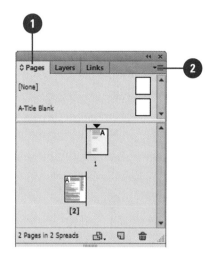

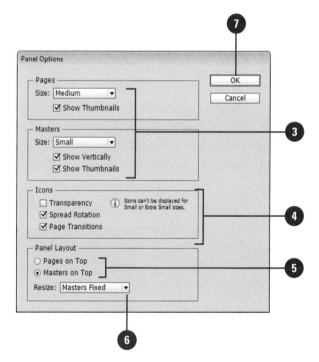

Inserting Pages

Most documents will be more than one page, so inserting new pages is a common practice in InDesign. You can quickly add a new blank page to a document using the Pages panel. You have several different methods to complete the task. You can use the New Page button on the page, drag a master page to the document area in the Pages panel, or use the Insert Pages command on the Options menu. If you're inserting only one or two pages, the first two methods work the best. If you want to insert multiple pages, the Insert Pages command is your best option, where you can use the Insert Pages dialog box to set additional options.

Insert Pages Using the Pages Panel

1. Select the **Pages** panel.
   - ◆ Click the **Window** menu, and then click **Pages**.
2. Use any of the following methods to insert a page:
   - ◆ Insert Page. Click the **Create New Page** button on the panel.
   - ◆ Insert from Master Pages. Drag a master page or a nonmaster page from the master page area to the document page area of the panel.
3. Continue to insert pages as needed.

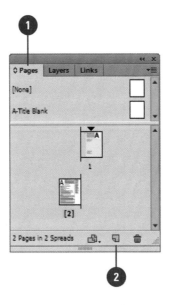

Did You Know?

You can duplicate a page. Select the Pages panel, select the pages or spreads you want to duplicate, and then drag the selected pages to the Create New Page button on the panel or use the Duplicate Spread command on the Options menu.

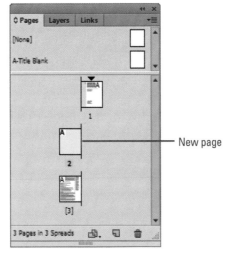

New page

Insert Multiple Pages Using the Insert Pages Dialog Box

1. Select the **Pages** panel.

   ◆ Click the **Window** menu, and then click **Pages**.

2. Click the **Options** button, and then click **Insert Pages**.

3. Enter the number of pages that you want to insert.

4. Click the **Insert** list arrow, and then specify how you want to insert the pages:

   ◆ **After Page.** Inserts new pages after a specific page.

   ◆ **Before Page.** Inserts new pages before a specific page.

   ◆ **At Start of Document.** Inserts new pages at the start of the document.

   ◆ **At End of Document.** Inserts new pages at the end of the document.

5. Specify the specific page to use when you choose After Page or Before Page as your Insert option.

6. Click the **Master** list arrow, and then select a master or nonmaster page to use as the basis for the new pages.

7. Click **OK**.

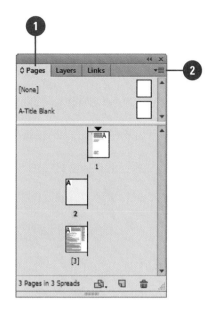

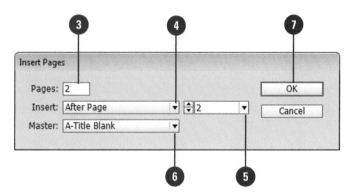

Navigating Pages

After you insert new pages into a document, you can use the Pages panel, Layout menu commands, and Status bar to navigate between them. As you work with pages in the Pages panel, there are two types of page selections. One targets a page and the other activates a page. A targeted page is a page selected in the Pages panel, while an activated page is a working page in the document window. When you target a page, you can apply a command in the Pages panel even though it may not be the current working page in the document window.

Target or Activate on a Page

1. Select the **Pages** panel.

   ◆ Click the **Window** menu, and then click **Pages**.

2. Use any of the following methods to select a page:

   ◆ Target a Page. Click a page in the Pages panel.

   The thumbnail is highlighted.

   ◆ Work on (Activate) a Page. Double-click a page in the Pages panel.

   The thumbnail is highlighted and the page number or name below it is highlighted in black.

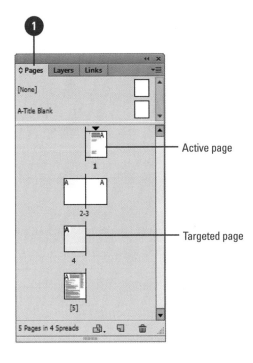

Active page

Targeted page

Navigate to Pages

◆ **Pages Panel.** Select the **Pages** panel, and then double-click the page in the panel that you want to work on.

◆ **Status Bar.** Use the navigation buttons on the Status bar to browse through pages or click the list arrow to select a specific page.

◆ **Layout Menu.** Click the **Layout** menu, and then select any of the following commands:

    ◆ **First Page.** Displays the first page in the document.

    ◆ **Previous Page.** Displays the previous page in the document.

    ◆ **Next Page.** Displays the next page in the document.

    ◆ **Last Page.** Displays the last page in the document.

    ◆ **Next Spread.** Displays the next spread of pages in the document.

    ◆ **Previous Spread.** Displays the previous spread of pages in the document.

    ◆ **Go To Page.** Displays the specified page in the document.

    ◆ **Go Back.** Displays the previously active page in the document.

    ◆ **Go Forward.** Displays the previously active page before the use of the Go Back command.

Pages panel

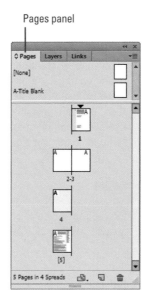

Status bar with page navigation

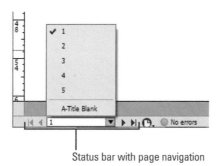

Layout menu with page navigation

Changing the Page Size

If you need to change the size of a page in a document, you can use the Page tool on the Tools panel along with the Control panel or the Edit Page Size button on the Pages panel. You can use a pre-defined page size based on the document intent, either print, web, or digital publishing, or create and name custom page sizes. When you manually change a page size using the Page tool, you can specify how you want InDesign to adjust objects on the resized page with the Liquid Page Rule. You can have different pages within a single document, which is useful keeping different sized designs, such as a business card and letterhead, in the same document.

Change the Page Size Using the Page Tool

1. Select the **Page** tool on the Tools panel.

2. Select the master page or layout page you want to resize in the layout, not in the Pages panel.

   Resize handles appear around the edge of the page.

3. Specify any of the following settings in the Control panel:

   ◆ **X and Y Values.** Specify X and Y values to set the position of the page in relation to other pages in the spread.

   ◆ **W and H Values, Preset, or Custom.** Specify the Width and Height for the selected page or select a preset from the Preset Size list; click Custom to create or delete a custom size.

      ◆ The available preset page sizes are based on the document intent.

   ◆ **Orientation.** Click the Portrait or Landscape button.

   ◆ **Liquid Page Rule.** Select an option to specify how to adjust objects when the page size changes.

      ◆ **Off.** Disables the option.

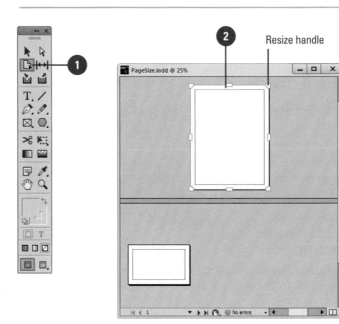
Resize handle

- **Scale.** All objects work as a group and scale proportional. For different aspect ratios, a black band may appear on top and bottom or left and right.

- **Re-center.** Objects are centered no matter the width; not resized.

- **Object-based.** Object edges are defined as fixed or fluid relative to the corresponding page edge. Select an object and click pins to toggle settings. A filled circle pins objects as fixed; an unfilled circle pins as fluid.

- **Guide-based.** Similar to the concept of 3 & 9 slice scaling. Slice guides define a straight line across the page where elements can resize. You add slide guides by dragging from the ruler.

- **Controlled by Master.** Let the master determine it.

- **Show Master Page Overlay.** Select to show a shaded box over the selected page. You can move the master page overlay so items appear correctly.

- **Objects Move with Page.** Select to move objects on the page when the page size changes.

④ To manually change the page size with the liquid layout rules:

- **Preview Manual Changes.** Drag a resize handle. When you release it, the page returns to the original size.

- **Manually Change Page Size.** Press Alt (Win) or Option (Mac), and drag a resize handle to resize the page.

   Continue Topic Next Page

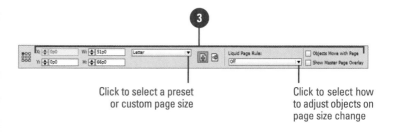

Click to select a preset or custom page size

Click to select how to adjust objects on page size change

Object-based Liquid Page Rule

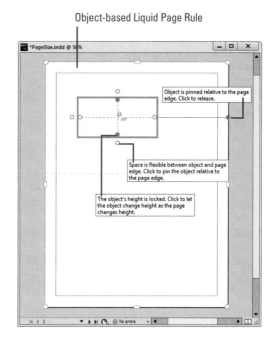

Object is pinned relative to the page edge. Click to release.

Space is flexible between object and page edge. Click to pin the object relative to the page edge.

The object's height is locked. Click to let the object change height as the page changes height.

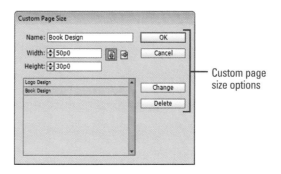

Custom page size options

Continued Topic from Previous Page

Change the Page Size

1. Select the **Pages** panel.

   ◆ Click the **Window** menu, and then click **Pages**.

2. Select the pages you want to change in the Pages panel.

3. Click the **Edit Page Size** button.

4. Select from the following on the menu:

   ◆ **Preset Size.** Changes the selected pages to the preset page size. The available preset page sizes are based on the document intent—Print, Web, or Digital Publishing.

   ◆ **Custom.** Creates and names custom page sizes. In the Custom Page Size dialog box, do any of the following, and then click **OK**.

   ◆ Add. Enter a name, width and height, and then click **Add**.

   ◆ Remove. Select a name, and then click **Delete**.

   ◆ Edit. Select a name, and then click **Change**.

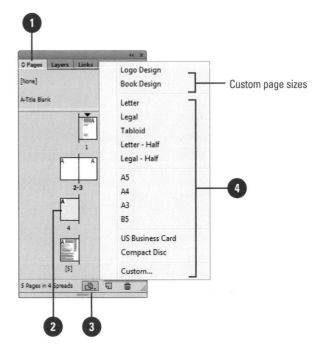

Custom page sizes

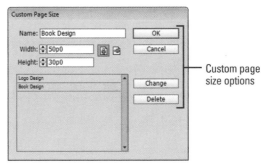

Custom page size options

Deleting Pages

When you no longer need a page, you can delete it from your document using the Pages panel. You can use the Delete Page or Delete Spread button on the panel or the same command on the Options menu. When you select a single page, InDesign uses the Delete Page button or command. When you select a spread of pages, InDesign uses the Delete Spread button command.

Delete Pages

1. Select the **Pages** panel.

   ◆ Click the **Window** menu, and then click **Pages**.

2. Select the pages that you want to delete.

   ◆ You can use the Shift key to select contiguous pages or the Ctrl (Win) or ⌘ (Mac) to select noncontiguous pages.

3. Click the **Delete Page** or **Delete Spread** button on the panel.

   ◆ You can also click the **Options** button, and then click **Delete Pages** or **Delete Spread**.

   IMPORTANT *When you have a spread of pages selected, the button and command changes to Delete Spreads.*

4. Click **OK** to confirm the deletion.

   TIMESAVER *Hold down the Alt (Win) or Option (Mac) key, when you select the Delete Pages button or command to bypass the confirmation dialog box.*

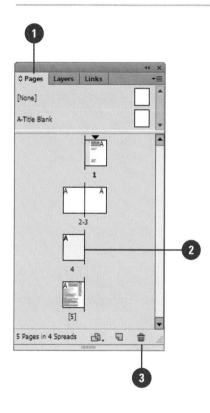

Moving Pages

Moving and arranging pages is a common part of working with multiple page documents. You can simply drag pages in the Pages panel or use the Move Page command on the Options menu. When you drag pages, the cursor indicates new page location. With the Move Page command, you can move pages within the current document or to another open document. When you move the pages, objects in the slug and bleed areas are also moved. Page numbers in the slug area display a number rather than the pasteboard index entry.

Move Pages by Dragging

1. Select the **Pages** panel.

2. Click the **Options** button, and then select a move related option:

    ◆ **Allow Document Pages to Shuffle.** Enables or disables the shuffling of document pages.

    ◆ **Allow Selected Spread to Shuffle.** Enables or disables the shuffling of selected spread pages.

3. Drag a page next to or between spread pages.

    A straight black line indicates the move location with a shuffle. A bracket black line indicates the move location with attachment.

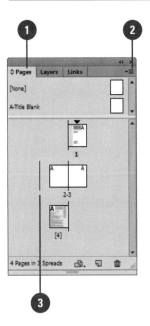
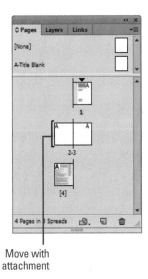

Move with attachment

Move Pages

① Select the **Pages** panel.

◆ Click the **Window** menu, and then click **Pages**.

② Click the **Options** button, and then click **Move Pages**.

③ Specify the pages that you want to move. Use a hyphen to designate a range, such as 1-4.

④ Click the **Destination** list arrow, select an option, and then enter a page number, if necessary.

⑤ Click the **Move To** list arrow, and then select a document location.

⑥ If you are moving the page(s) to a separate open file, select the **Delete Pages After Moving** check box if you want to delete the pages from the current document.

⑦ Click **OK**.

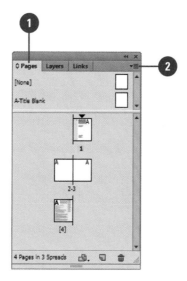

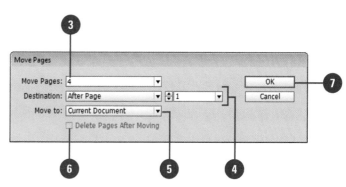

Working with Page Spreads

Most documents are either one or two page spreads. A single-page spread displays pages one at a time (top to bottom), while a two-page spread displays pages as facing pages (left and right). If you want to create a larger spread for a magazine foldout or a brochure, you can add more pages to a one or two page spread. These multiple-page spreads are also called **island spreads**. When you no longer want a larger spread, you can remove pages from the spread.

Add and Remove Pages from a Spread

1. Select the **Pages** panel.

2. Click the **Options** button on the panel, and then click **Allow Document Pages to Shuffle** to deselect it.

3. To add pages, drag a page from the pages area, or a master page next to the spread where you want to add the page.

4. To remove pages, drag a page from the spread to outside of the spread, and then click **No**, if necessary.

Did You Know?

You can keep pages in a spread together. Select the Pages panel, select the spread you want to protect, click the Options button, and then click Allow Selected Spread To Shuffle to deselect it.

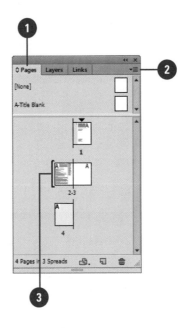

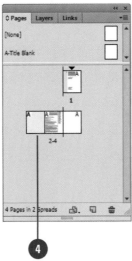

Rotating Page Spreads

If you need to work on non-horizontal design elements, such as a calendar, you can rotate the current spread in 90 degree increments to make it easier to work on. When you rotate the current spread view, you have full editing capabilities. When you're done, you can quickly clear the rotation to return to a normal view.

Rotate Page Spreads

1 Select the **Pages** panel.

 ◆ Click the **Window** menu, and then click **Pages**.

2 Double-click the page numbers of the page spread you want to rotate.

3 Click the **Options** button on the panel, point to **Page Attributes**, point to **Rotate Spread View**, and then click **90° CW**, **90° CCW**, or **180°**.

 ◆ You can also click the **View** menu, point to **Rotate Spread**, and then click **90° CW**, **90° CCW**, or **180°**.

A rotation icon appears next to the page indicating the spread is rotated.

4 Edit and modify the page spread the way you want.

5 Click the **Options** button on the panel, point to **Page Attributes**, point to **Rotate Spread View**, and then click **Clear Rotation**.

 ◆ You can also right-click (Win) or Control-click (Mac) the rotation icon to select a rotation spread command.

See Also

See "Using the Pages Panel" on pages 56 for more information on showing the spread rotation icon in the Pages panel.

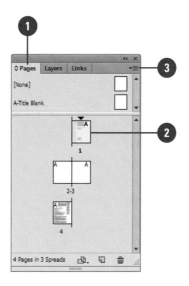

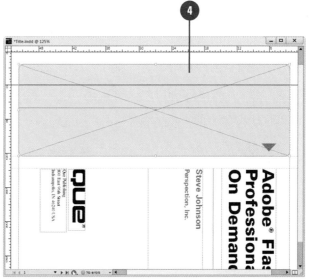

Creating Master Pages

A master page holds and displays all the elements that you want to appear on every page in a document, such as headers, logos, page numbers, and footers. The master is like a background layer to a page. Everything on the background layer appears on the page above it. Master elements appear on document pages surrounded by a dotted border to make them easy to identify. When you create a new document, you also create a master page. If you want to create additional master pages, you can create them from scratch with a custom page size (**New!**) or from an existing page or spread.

Add Objects to an Existing Master Page

1 Select the **Pages** panel.

- ◆ Click the **Window** menu, and then click **Pages**.

2 Double-click the master page in the master page area of the Pages panel.

The master page or two page spread appears in the document window.

3 Add text boxes, graphics, or any other elements you want on the page.

4 Double-click a page in the document page area of the Pages panel.

The elements added to the master page or spread appear on the document page.

Did You Know?

You can load master pages from another document. Select the Pages panel, click the Options button, click Load Master Pages, select the file, and then click Open.

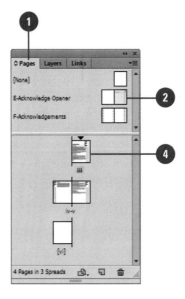

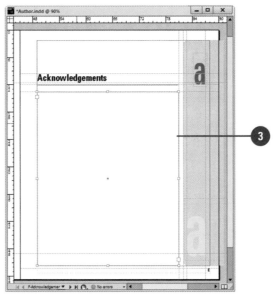

Create a Master Page from an Existing Page

1. Select the **Pages** panel.

   ◆ Click the **Window** menu, and then click **Pages**.

2. Drag a page or a spread from the document page area to the master page area.

   ◆ You can also select a page or spread, click the **Options** button, point to **Master Pages**, and then click **Save As Master**.

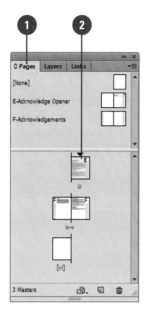
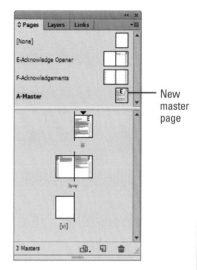

New master page

Create a New Master Page

1. Select the **Pages** panel.

   ◆ Click the **Window** menu, and then click **Pages**.

2. Click the **Options** button on the panel, and then click **New Master**.

3. Select from the following Pages panel options:

   ◆ **Prefix.** Enter a prefix up to four characters. This identifies the applied master for each page.

   ◆ **Name.** Enter a name for the master page.

   ◆ **Based on Master.** Select an existing master on which to base the new master.

   ◆ **Number of Pages.** Enter the number of master pages (1-10).

   ◆ **Page Size.** Select a preset page size or specify a custom size and orientation.

4. Click **OK**.

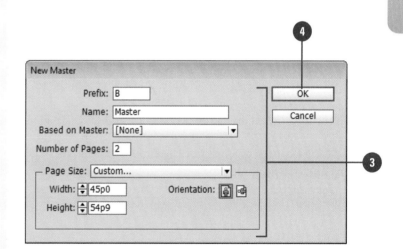

Working with Master Pages

When you apply a master page to a document page, all the elements on the master page are attached and displayed on the document page. A master page can also contain a single (only one) primary text frame, which you can use to flow or type your text on all document pages. When you only want a selected number of elements from the master page on a document page, you can override or detach the elements you want. Overriding a master puts a copy of the master element on the document page and keeps the link, where you can make changes to it. The changes made on the document page don't affect the master; however, any changes to the same element on the master (separate from the document page) still appear from the master on the document page. Detaching a master overrides a master element and removes the link. Instead of overriding or detaching master elements, you have the option of hiding them.

Apply a Master Page to a Document Page

1. Select the **Pages** panel.
   - ◆ Click the **Window** menu, and then click **Pages**.

2. Drag a master page or spread from the master page area to a page or spread in the document page area.

3. To apply a master to multiple pages, select the pages in the document page area, and then Alt (Win) or Option (Mac) the master page you want to apply.
   - ◆ You can also click the **Options** button, click **Apply Master To Pages**, specify the options you want, and then click **OK**.

Did You Know?

You can change master page options. Select the Pages panel, select the master page, click the Options button, click Master Options for *master page name*, specify the options you want, and then click OK.

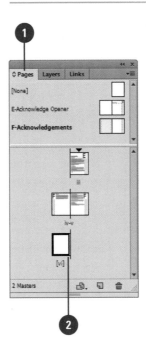

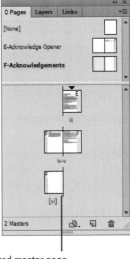

Selected master page
applied to page

Work with Master Pages

- **Delete Masters.** In the Pages panel, drag the master page to the **Delete Selected Pages** button on the panel.

- **Copy Masters.** In the Pages panel, drag the master page to the **Create New Page** button on the panel.

- **Create Primary Text Frame.** In the Pages panel, double-click a master page, create and select a text frame, and then click the **Text** icon on the text frame. Click the icon again to disable it.

- **Hide Master Elements.** In the Pages panel, select the document page, click the **Options** button, point to **Master Pages**, and then click **Hide Master Items**.

- **Override a Master Element.** In the Pages panel, click the **Options** button, point to **Master Pages**, and then click **Allow Master Item Overrides On Selection** to select it. On a document page, Ctrl+Shift+click (Win) or ⌘+Shift+click (Mac) an element.

  - You can also click the document page in the Pages panel, click the **Options** button, and then click **Override All Master Page Items**.

- **Remove All Local Overrides.** In the Pages panel, click the **Options** button, point to **Master Pages**, and then click **Remove All Local Overrides**.

- **Detach All Objects From Master.** In the Pages panel, click the **Options** button, and then click **Detach All Objects From Master**.

- **Unassign Master.** In the Pages panel, drag the **[None]** master from the master page area to a page in the document page area.

  All master elements are no longer attached to the document page.

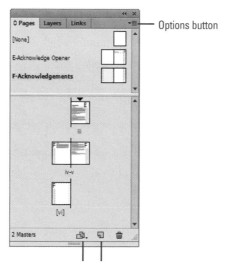

Options button

Create New Page   Delete Selected Pages

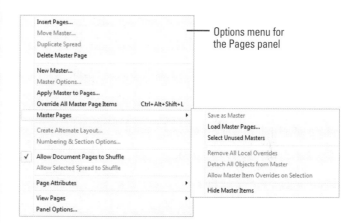

Options menu for the Pages panel

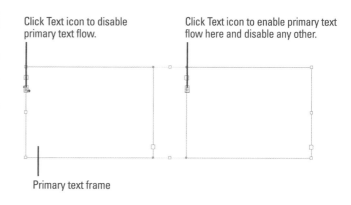

Click Text icon to disable primary text flow.

Click Text icon to enable primary text flow here and disable any other.

Primary text frame

Working with Page Numbers and Sections

One of the most common elements added to a master page is a page number. InDesign uses a special character to designate page numbers. On a master page, simply create a text box, place the insertion point in the box, and then insert the current page number marker. You can also insert and format additional text and variables in the text box to create a header or footer across the top or bottom of the page. You can also use the Numbering & Section Options dialog box to change the format of page numbers or the starting page number. If you want to insert text before the page number, you can specify a section prefix. In addition to page numbers, you can also define a section within a document with separate numbering. A section indicator icon (black triangle) appears above the page thumbnail in the Pages panel.

Add a Page or Section Number to a Page Master

1 Select the **Pages** panel.

◆ Click the **Window** menu, and then click **Pages**.

2 Double-click the master page in the master page area of the Pages panel.

The master page or two page spread appears in the document window.

3 Select the **Type** tool on the Tools panel.

4 Click where you want to create a text box for the page or section number.

5 Click the **Type** menu, point to **Insert Special Character**, point to **Markers**, and then click **Current Page Number** or **Section Marker**.

A special character marker appears in the text box. The current page or section number is the prefix for the master page.

6 For facing pages, repeat steps 3-5 for the other page.

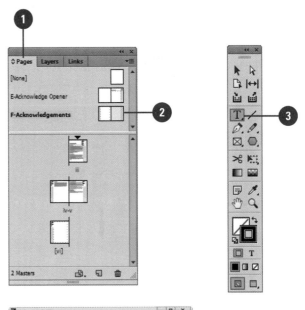

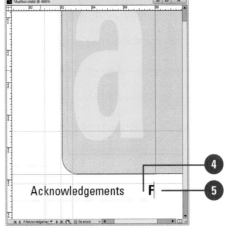

Set Page Numbering and Section Options

1. Select the **Pages** panel.

   ◆ Click the **Window** menu, and then click **Pages**.

2. Double-click the page where you want to start the page numbering or section to start.

3. Click the **Layout** menu, and then click **Numbering & Section Options**.

4. Select the **Start Section** check box to start a new section.

5. Click the **Automatic Page Numbering** or **Start Page Numbering At** option.

6. If you selected the Start Page Numbering At option, specify the following options:

   ◆ **Section Prefix.** Enter a prefix that will appear before the page number, if desired.

   ◆ **Style.** Select a style for the page number.

   ◆ **Section Marker.** Enter text, such as *Section*, for a section within a document.

   ◆ **Include Prefix When Numbering Pages.** Select this option if you want to add the section prefix to the page number.

7. Click **OK**.

   A section indicator icon (black triangle) appears above the page thumbnail in the Pages panel.

8. Double-click the page where you want the section to end, and then repeat steps 3-7 for section numbering (except, in this case, you will need to deselect the **Start Section** check box).

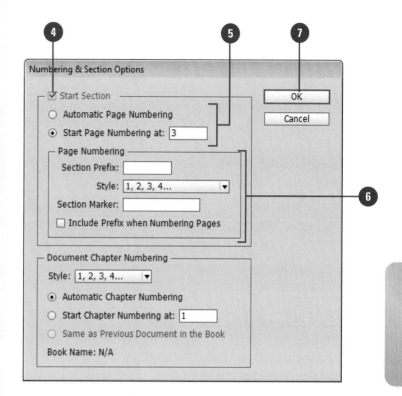

Working with Chapter Numbers

Like page numbers, you can insert chapter numbers into documents that will be part of a book. Unlike a page number, a chapter number is a predefined text variable. The chapter number variable can be updated automatically and formatted as text. To insert a chapter number variable, create a text box, place the insertion point in the box, and then insert the variable using the Text Variable submenu on the Type menu. You can use the Numbering & Section Options dialog box to change updating options for chapter numbers.

Add a Chapter Number to a Document

1. Select the **Pages** panel.
   - ◆ Click the **Window** menu, and then click **Pages**.
2. Double-click the page or master page where you want to place a chapter number.
3. Select the **Type** tool on the Tools panel.
4. Click where you want to create a text box for the chapter number.
5. Click the **Type** menu, point to **Text Variables**, point to **Insert Variable**, and then click **Chapter Number**.

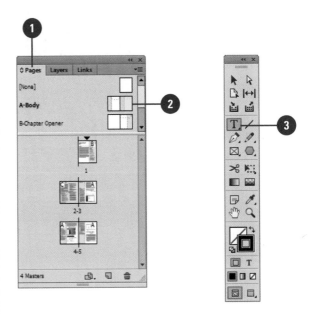

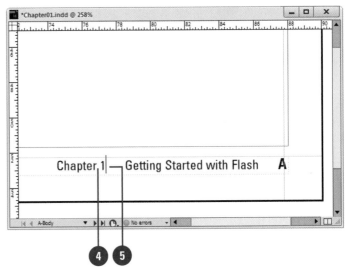

Set Chapter Numbering Options

1. Select the **Pages** panel.

   ◆ Click the **Window** menu, and then click **Pages**.

2. Double-click the page where you want to start the chapter numbering.

3. Click the **Layout** menu, and then click **Numbering & Section Options**.

4. Click the **Style** list arrow, and then select a chapter numbering style.

5. Select one of the following options:

   ◆ **Automatic Chapter Numbering.**

   ◆ **Start Chapter Numbering At.** Enter a starting chapter number.

   ◆ **Same as Previous Document in the Book.**

6. Click **OK**.

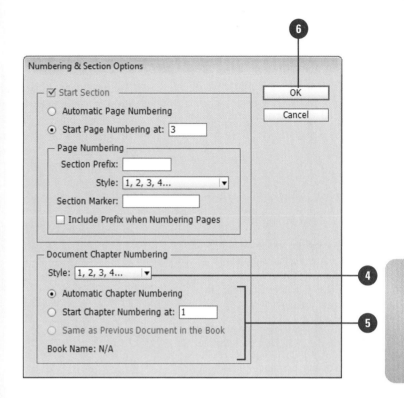

Creating and Using Text Variables

A text variable is an element that varies based on circumstances in the document. You can use one of the preset text variables that comes with InDesign or you can create your own. Some of the preset variables include Running Header and Chapter Number. These are useful for adding information to master pages. Other variables, such as Creation Date, Modification Date, Output Date, and File Name, are useful for adding file information to the slug area for printing. To use a text variable, simply create a text box, place the insertion point in the box, and then insert the variable using the Text Variable submenu on the Type menu. You can also insert and format additional text along with the Running Header variable in the text box to create a header or footer across the top or bottom of the page on a document or master page.

Define a Text Variable

1. To define text variables for all documents, close all open documents. Otherwise, the text variable is only available for the current document.

2. Click the **Type** menu, point to **Text Variables**, and then click **Define**.

3. Click **New**, or select an existing variable, and then click **Edit**.

4. Type a name for the variable.

5. Click the **Type** list arrow, and then select a variable type.

6. Specify the options you want for the selected variable type.

   Options vary; some of the common options include:

   ◆ **Text Before or Text After**. Insert text to add before or after the text variable.

   ◆ **Style**. Select a style for the selected variable type.

7. Click **OK**.

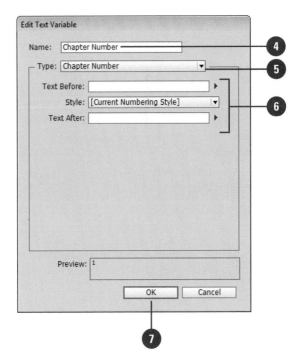

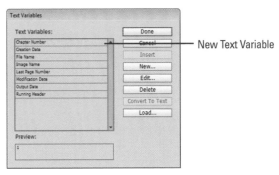

New Text Variable

Work with Text Variables

◆ **Insert Text Variables.** Click to place the insertion point where you want the text variable (on a document or master page), click the **Type** menu, point to **Text Variables**, point to **Insert Variable**, and then select a variable.

◆ **Delete Text Variables.** Click the **Type** menu, point to **Text Variables**, click **Define**, select the variable, and then click **Delete**.

◆ **Convert Text Variables to Text.** Select the text variable in the document, click the **Type** menu, point to **Text Variables**, and then click **Convert Variable To Text**.

◆ To convert all instances of the text variable, click the **Type** menu, point to **Text Variables**, click **Define**, select the variable, and then click **Convert To Text**.

◆ **Import Text Variables from Another Document.** Click the **Type** menu, point to **Text Variables**, click **Define**, click **Load**, double-click the document with the variables, select the variables that you want in the Load Text Variables dialog box, and then click **OK**.

Text variables

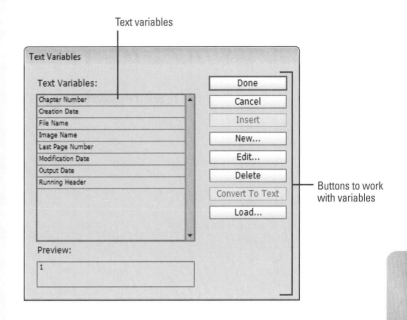

Buttons to work with variables

Type menu

Variables

Creating a Book

Instead of creating long InDesign documents, you can break them up into smaller documents, like chapters, and then create a book to bring them all together. A book is not a document. It simply keeps track of all the documents in the book and coordinates document page numbers, colors, and styles. When you create a new book or open an existing book, the Book panel appears, displaying the book name in the title tab. In the Book panel, you can add, remove, move, or open documents.

Create a New Book

1. Click the **File** menu, point to **New**, and then click **Book**.

2. Enter a name for the book file.

3. Navigate to the location where you want to save the book.

4. Click **Save**.

   The tab for the Book panel displays the name of the book.

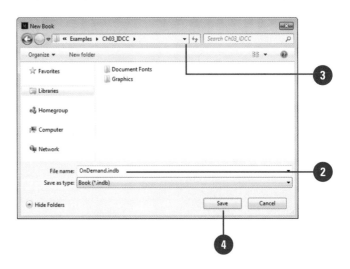

Open an Existing Book

1. Click the **File** menu, and then click **Open**.

2. Navigate to the location where the book you want to open is stored.

3. Select the book you want to open.

4. Click **Open**.

   The Book panel opens.

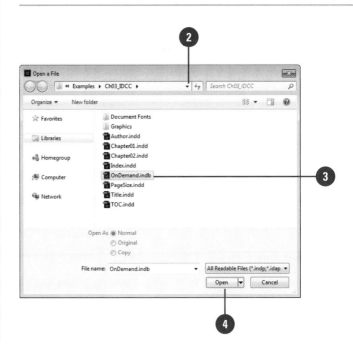

Add, Remove, Move, or Open Documents in a Book

1. Open the book you want to edit.

2. Do any of the following:

   ◆ **Add a Document.** Click the **Add Document** button on the panel, locate the document you want to add, and then click **Open**.

   ◆ **Remove a Document.** Select a document in the Book panel, and then click the **Remove Document** button at the bottom of the panel.

   ◆ **Move a Document.** Drag a document to a new position in the Book panel.

   ◆ **Open a Document.** Double-click a document in the Book panel. An open book icon appears, indicating the book is open.

   ◆ **View a Document in Explorer or Finder.** Select a document in the Book panel, click the **Options** button, and then click **Reveal in Explorer** (Win) or **Finder** (Mac).

3. Click the **Save Book** button on the panel.

4. Click the **Close** button to close the book.

Did You Know?

You can replace a document in a book. Open the book, select the document that you want to replace, click the Options button, click Replace Document, select the replacement file, and then click Open.

You can print an entire book. Open the book, and then click the Print Book button on the panel.

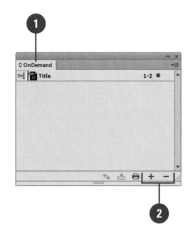

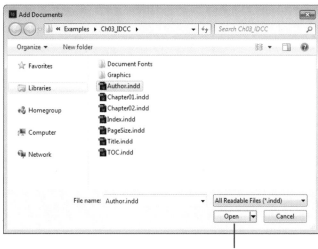

Open a document

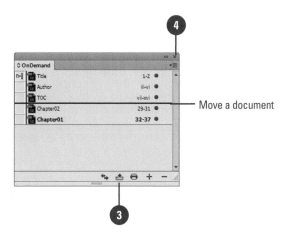

Move a document

Managing Books

When you create a book, you can synchronize page numbers, colors, and styles for all the documents in the book. Each book uses a file called the *style source* to control the style sheets (including character, paragraph, table, and object styles), swatches, conditional text, numbered lists, text variables, and master pages for all the documents in the book. When you make changes to the style source file, all or selected documents in the book are synchronized to the file. You can set synchronizing options to specify the features that you want to keep up-to-date in the Synchronize Options dialog box. With the Smart Match Style Groups synchronize option, you can synchronize a book without creating duplicate styles.

Synchronize Books

◆ **Synchronize Options.** Open the book, click the **Options** button, click **Synchronize Options**, select the options you want to synchronize, and then click **OK**.

◆ **Set Style Source.** Open the book, and then click the **Style Source** box next to the name of the document.

◆ **Synchronize Style Source for a Book.** Open the book, and then click the **Synchronize Book** button on the panel.

◆ **Synchronize Style Source for a Document.** Open the book, select the document, click the **Options** button, and then click **Synchronize Selected Documents**.

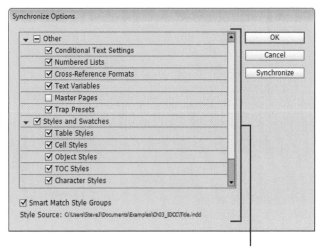

Synchronize options

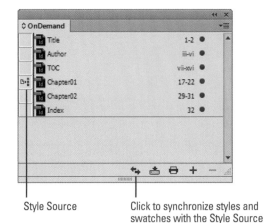

Style Source

Click to synchronize styles and swatches with the Style Source

Did You Know?

You can set page numbers for each document in a book. Open the book, click the Options button, click Document Numbering Options, specify the options you want, and then click OK. *See "Working with Page Numbers and Sections," on page 74 for details about the page numbering options.*

Set Page Numbering Options in a Book

1. Open the book you want to change.

2. Click the **Options** button, and then click **Book Page Numbering Options**.

3. Select one of the following Page Order options:

   ◆ **Continue from previous document.** Starts new pages in sequence.

   ◆ **Continue on next odd page.** Starts new pages on an odd number.

   ◆ **Continue on next even page.** Starts new pages on an even number.

4. Select any of the following options:

   ◆ **Insert Blank Page.** Select to insert a blank page when using odd or even page numbers.

   ◆ **Automatically Update Page & Section Numbers.** Select to automatically adjust page numbers in book documents.

5. Click **OK**.

6. To update numbering in a book, click the **Options** button, choose **Update Numbering**, and then click any of the following:

   ◆ **Update Page & Section Numbers.**

   ◆ **Update Chapter & Paragraph Numbers.**

   ◆ **Update All Numbers.**

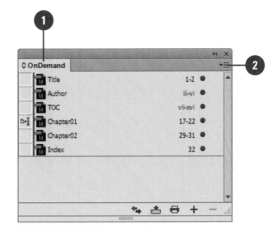

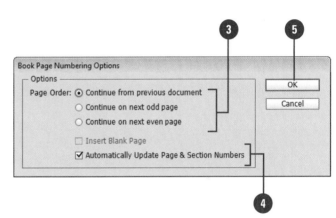

Creating a Table of Contents

A table of contents (TOC) appears at the beginning of a document, typically a long one, with page numbers associated with the beginning of main sections of the document. InDesign creates a table of contents based on the styles applied to paragraphs in the document. The table of content displays the text and page number associated with the paragraph styles. For example, when you apply different styles for chapter and topic titles in this book, you create a table of contents based on chapters and topics. So, before you can create a table of contents, you need to apply paragraph styles to text in your document.

Prepare for and Create a Table of Contents

1. To prepare for creating a table of contents, do the following:

   ◆ **Add Page for TOC.** Add a page for the table of contents.

   ◆ **Add Paragraph Styles.** Apply different paragraph styles to the text that you want to use in the table of contents.

2. Click the **Layout** menu, and then click **Table of Contents**.

3. Enter text for the title of the table of contents, and then use the Styles menu to select a style for the title text.

4. Select the paragraph styles that are applied to text in your document (under Other Styles), and then click **Add** to include them in the other list (under Include Paragraph Styles).

   ◆ To remove a style, select it (under Include Paragraph Styles), and then click **Remove**.

5. To format an entry in the table of contents, select the entry (under Include Paragraph Styles), click the **Entry Style** list arrow, and then select a style.

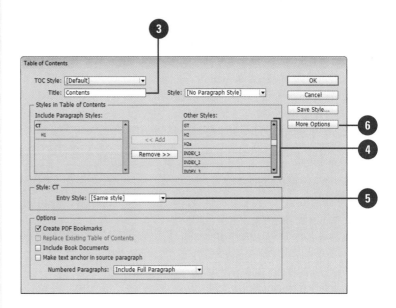

6 Click **More Options** to display additional options.

7 Select any of the following advanced options:

◆ **Page Number.** Select a position for the entry's page number.

◆ **Between Entry and Number.** Select a separator character between the entry and the number.

◆ **Sort Entries in Alphabetical Order.** Select to alphabetize the table of contents.

◆ **Level.** Select an indent level for each entry in the table of contents.

8 Select any of the following options:

◆ **Create PDF Bookmarks.** Select to add bookmarks to the PDF created from the table of contents.

◆ **Replace Existing Table of Contents.** Select to update or change the table of contents.

◆ **Include Book Documents.** Select to create a table of contents of all the documents in a book.

◆ **Numbered Paragraphs.** Select to format how paragraphs with auto numbering are formatted.

◆ **Run-In.** Select to create a single paragraph table of contents with each entry separated by a semicolon (;) and a space.

◆ **Include Text on Hidden Layers.** Select to use hidden text on layers.

9 Click **OK**.

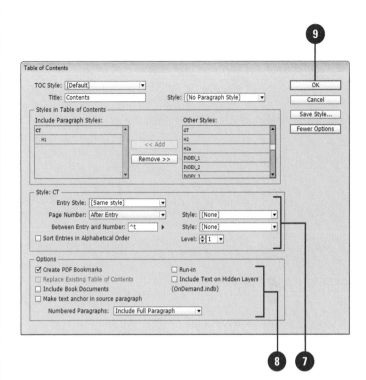

Starting an Index

An index is a table of entries in alphabetical order that reference topics, names, and other information in a book. The entries usually provide the page on which a particular word or topic is located in the book. The index is typically located in the back of a book. In InDesign, you can create only one index for a document or book. The single index can be a simple or comprehensive one to the information in a document or book. To create an index, you create a topic list (optional), create index entries (assign index markers to topics), generate the index, and then flow the index into a story. You create, edit, and preview an index in the Index panel, which displays index information using the Reference and Topic modes. The Reference mode displays complete index entries, while the Topic mode displays only topic (no page references and cross-references—"See" or " See also"). Instead of typing each topic when you create an index entry, you can create or import a list of topics to save time and create consistency.

Create or Edit a List of Index Topics

1. Open the document or book you want to index.

2. Select the **Index** panel.

   ◆ Click the **Window** menu, point to **Type & Tables**, and then click **Pages**.

3. Click the **Topic** option.

4. To view index entries from any open documents in a book, select the **Book** check box.

5. Click the **Create New Index Entry** button to create a new topic or double-click a topic to edit it.

6. Type the topic name in the first box under Topic Levels. To create subtopics, type a name in the boxes below. Each item is indented a level.

   ◆ To change an existing topic, double-click it, and then make the changes you want.

7. To change the order, click the **Up Arrow** and **Down Arrow** button.

8. Click **Add** to apply it, and then click **Done** or **OK**.

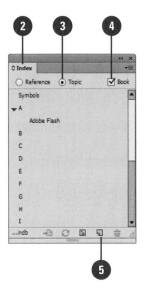

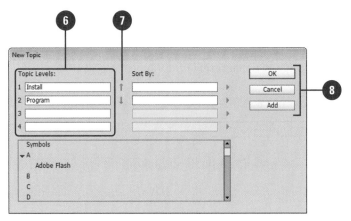

Create an Index Entry Using Keyboard Shortcuts

1 Open the document or book you want to index.

2 Select the **Type** tool on the Tools panel.

3 Select the word or words in the document you want to index.

4 Use any of the following keyboard shortcuts:

- **Standard Words.** Press Shift+Alt+Ctrl+[(Win) or Shift+Option+Command+[(Mac). A standard word consists of any word.

- **Proper Names.** Press Shift+Alt+Ctrl+] (Win) or Shift+Option+Command+] (Mac). A proper name consists of a name, such as Gary O'Neal, which are indexed in reverse order. The name Gary O'Neal is indexed by O'Neal.

  The index entry is added to the index using default settings.

Did You Know?

You can create a new entry from an existing one. Click an insertion point in the document or select text, click the Reference option in the Index panel, and then drag the existing entry to the New Entry button, make any changes, and then click Add or OK.

You can import a topic list. In the Index panel, click the Options button, click Import Topics, select the document with the topic list (where each topic entry is separated by a Enter (Win)/Return (Mac), tab, semicolon, or a comma), and then click Open.

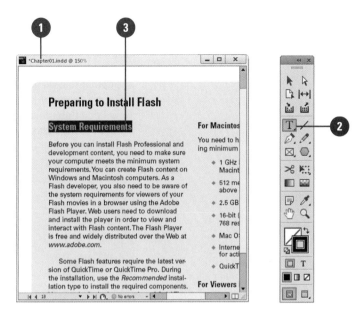

For Your Information

Tips for Creating an Index

When you create an index, it's important to be well-planned and consistent. During the planning process you need to think about what type of index you want to create, either a simple index or a complex one with cross-references and equivalent terms. You also need to think about a topic list to ensure coverage of the material and consistency in the index. Readers look for content in different ways, so you need to think about how a reader might look up information in order to make it easier for them to find what they want. Some consistency problems can occur when you fluxuate between the use of uppercase and lowercase letters and plurals and non plurals. For example, the words *Book*, *book*, and *books* are treated as separate entries in InDesign, which can cause confusion for readers.

Creating an Index Entry

An index entry consists of a topic and a reference. You can create or import topics ahead of time or provide them when you create an index entry. A reference is a page number, page range, or cross-reference. Instead of indexing to a page number or range, you can index to a cross-reference, which refers to equivalent terms (denoted by "See") or another related entry (denoted by "See also") in the index. You can add an index entry several different ways in InDesign. You can use the New Page Reference dialog box, shortcut keys (see previous page for details), or the Index panel. If you want to index all occurrences of a word in a document or book, you can use the Add All button in the New Page Reference dialog box.

Create an Index Entry

1 Open the document or book you want to index.

2 Select the **Type** tool on the Tools panel, and then click to place the insertion point where you want to put the index marker or select in the document to use as the entry.

3 Select the **Index** panel.

◆ Click the **Window** menu, point to **Type & Tables**, and then click **Pages**.

4 Click the **Reference** option.

5 To view index entries from any open documents in a book, select the **Book** check box.

6 Click the **Create New Index Entry** button to create a new topic or double-click a topic to edit it.

7 Type the topic name in the first box under Topic Levels. To create subtopics, type a name in the boxes below. Each item is indented a level.

◆ To change an existing topic, double-click it, and then make the changes you want.

8 To change the order, click the **Up Arrow** and **Down Arrow** button.

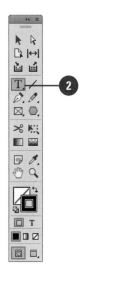

9 To sort the entry in the index, type the word you want to sort by in the Sort By box.

◆ You can also select the sort order of number, symbols, and languages.

10 Click the **Type** list arrow, and then select any of the following:

◆ Page Range. Select a type relating to a range (top of menu), such as **Current Page**, or those options starting with **To Next**, **To End**, or **For Next**, which extend from the index marker to the specified place.

◆ No Pages. Click **Suppress page Range**.

◆ Cross-reference. Select a type relating to references (bottom of menu), those options starting with **See**, and then type a topic or drag an existing topic from the bottom list to the Referenced box.

11 To add emphasis to an index entry, select the **Number Style Override** check box, and then select a character style.

12 To add an index entry, do any of the following:

◆ **Add.** Adds current entry to the index and leaves the dialog box open.

◆ **Add All.** Locates all instances of the selected text and adds entries for each one to the index. InDesign considers only whole words, and searches are case-sensitive. You might end up with some duplicate entries.

◆ **OK.** Adds current entry to the index and closes the dialog box.

13 When you're finished, click **Done** or **OK**.

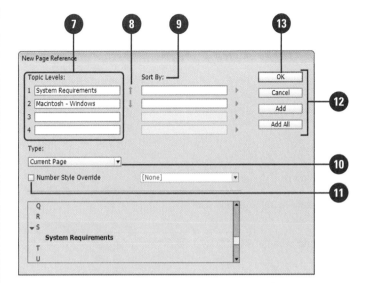

Creating an Index

After you add index entries and preview them in the Index panel, you can create an index. When you create an index, InDesign compiles all of the index entries in the Index panel and page numbers in a document or across a book to generate an index story, which you can place within the existing document or in a separate document. If you make changes to any of the index entries or page numbering in your document or book, you need to update the index. In addition to generating an index, you can also select paragraph and character styles to format the appearance of the index the way you want.

Create an Index

1. Open the document or book you want to index.

2. Select one of the following:

   ◆ **Document.** Create an empty page at the end.

   ◆ **Book.** Create or open the document you want in the book.

3. Select the **Index** panel.

4. Click the **Generate Index** button.

5. Select the following options:

   ◆ **Title.** Enter the text that appears at the top of the index.

   ◆ **Title Style.** Select a style for the title text.

   ◆ **Replace Existing Index.** Select to update an existing index.

   ◆ **Include Book Documents.** Select to create a single index for all documents in the book. Deselect to create an index for the current document.

   ◆ **Include Entries On Hidden Layers.** Select to index entries on hidden layers.

6. To add formatting, click the **More Options** button, and then specify any of the following options:

   ◆ **Nested or Run-in.** Nested formats in the default indented paragraph style, while Run-in formats in the non-indented paragraph style.

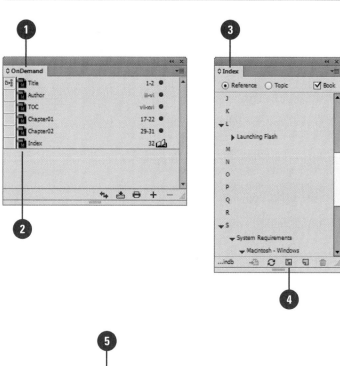

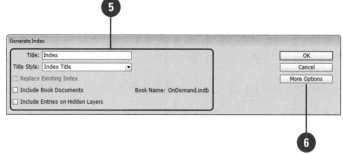

- ◆ **Include Index Section Headings.** Select to create section headings (A, B, C, etc.).

- ◆ **Include Empty Index Sections.** Select to create sections headings for all letters even if an entry doesn't exist for one.

- ◆ **Level Style.** Select a paragraph style for the different levels.

- ◆ **Section Heading.** Select a paragraph style for the headings.

- ◆ **Page Number.** Select a character style for the page numbers.

- ◆ **Cross-reference.** Select a character style for "See" or "See also."

- ◆ **Cross-referenced Topic.** Select a character style for the related cross-reference topic.

- ◆ **Following Topic.** Specify a special character to separate the entry and page number.

- ◆ **Between Page Numbers.** Select to index entries on hidden layers.

- ◆ **Between Entries.** Specify a special character to separate an entry and subentry (for Run-in) or two cross-references under a single entry (for Nested).

- ◆ **Before Cross-reference.** Specify a special character to separate a reference and cross reference.

- ◆ **Page Range.** Specify a special character to separate a page range.

- ◆ **Entry End.** Specify a special character to appear at the end of entries.

7️⃣ Click **OK**.

8️⃣ With the place cursor, click where you want to insert the index.

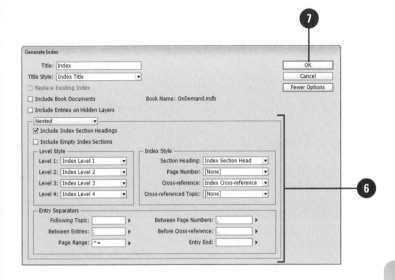

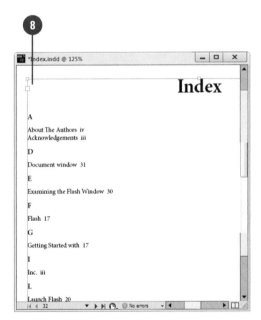

Managing an Index

After you create an index, you can perform several common index management tasks, such as view all topics in a book, removing unused topics, find entries, edit entries, and delete entries. When you make changes to index entries or page numbering in your document or book, you need to update the index (generate a new one). If you just want to update the preview area in the Index panel, you can use the Update preview button on the panel.

Manage an Index

◆ **View All Index Topics in a Book.** Open the book file and all of its documents, open the Index panel, and then select the **Book** check box.

◆ **Show Unused Topics from the Topic List.** In the Index panel, click the **Options** button, and then click **Show Unused Topics**.

◆ **Remove Unused Topics from the Topic List.** In the Index panel, click the **Options** button, and then click **Remove Unused Topics**.

◆ **Edit an Index Entry.** In the Index panel, click the **Topic** option to edit a topic and update all entries using the topic or click the **Reference** option to edit an individual entry. Double-click an index entry or page reference, edit the entry, and then click **OK**.

◆ **Delete an Index Entry.** In the Index panel, select the entry or topic you want to remove, click the **Delete Selected Entry** button, and then click **Yes**.

◆ **Find an Index Entry.** In the Index panel, click the **Options** button, click **Show Find Field**, type the name of the entry you want to locate, and then click the Up Arrow or Down Arrow.

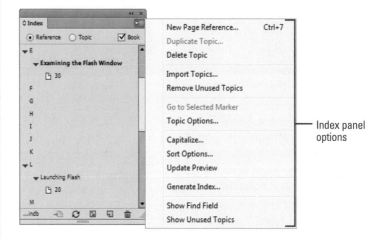

Index panel options

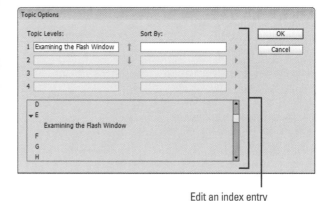

Edit an index entry

- **Locate Index Markers in a Document.** Click the **Type** menu, click **Show Hidden Characters**, open the Index panel, click the **Reference** option, select the entry you want to locate, and then click the **Go To Selected Marker** button on the Index panel.

- **Capitalize Index Entries.** In the Index panel, select the entry you want to change, click the **Options** button, click **Capitalize**, select an option to capitalize what you want, and then click **OK**.

- **Update the Index Preview.** In the Index panel, click the **Update Preview** button on the Index panel to update the preview area in the Index panel after a change in the document.

- **Change Language Sort.** In the Index panel, select the entry you want to change, click the **Options** button, click **Sort Options**, select the check boxes for the languages you want, use the Up Arrow and Down Arrow buttons to move items in the order you want, and then click **OK**.

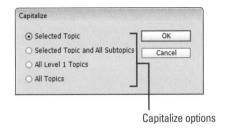

Capitalize options

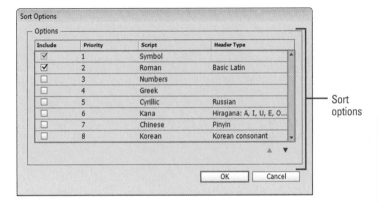

Sort options

Did You Know?

You might see codes in the Index panel. Before the index is generated, codes appear in place of page references in Reference mode. The codes include: PB (on pasteboard), HL (on a hidden layer), HT (in a hidden condition), PN (in overset text), and Master (on a master page). Click the Update Preview button in the Index panel to view them.

Working with Text

4

Introduction

InDesign comes with two main type tools: Type and Type on a Path. The Type tool allows you to create a rectangle text frame where you can store text in your document, while the Type on a Path tool allows you to add text along the inner or outer edge of a path.

Before you can work with text in InDesign, you need to select it. You can select the entire text frame or the characters in the text frame. You can use the type tools to select only the characters in the text frame, not the text frame itself, or use the Selection and Direct Selection tools to select both characters and the text frame. If you type, paste, or import more text than a text frame can hold, an overflow symbol (a tiny red plus sign in a square) appears on the edge of the text frame. You can reshape the text frame to accommodate the extra text or create a thread (link) to another text frame. You can thread overflow text from one text frame to a new or existing text frame.

InDesign provides two panels to modify characters and paragraphs. With the Character panel, you can change the font family (for example, Arial or Times New Roman) and style (Italic, Bold, or Condensed), as well as change other text attributes, such as size, kerning, scale, tracking, leading, and language. With the Paragraphs panel, you can change text alignment, indenting, and before and after spacing.

When integrating artwork and graphics with your text, you can wrap the text in a text frame around another object, such as a graphic. Another type effect, Create Outlines, allows you to convert characters in a text frame into a separate object with a path.

What You'll Do

Use Type Tools

Create Type and Path Type

Import and Flow Text

Work with Overflow Text

Use Smart Text Reflow

Type and Select Text

Edit Text with Autocorrect

Copy and Move Text

Change Fonts and Font Size

Change Text Leading, Kerning, and Tracking

Scale and Skew Text

Align, Indent, and Space Paragraphs

Create a Drop Cap

Apply a Paragraph Rule

Set Tabs

Work with Glyphs

Insert Special Text Characters

Set Text Frame Options

Create Columns

Wrap Text Around an Object

Create Type Outlines

Add Page Numbers to Continued Text

Work with Different Languages

Using Type Tools

InDesign comes with two main type tools: Type and Type on a Path. The Type tool allows you to create a rectangle text frame where you can store text in your document, while the Type on a Path tool allows you to add text along the inner or outer edge of a path. In addition to the type tools, you can also use the Frame tools—Rectangle, Ellipse, and Polygon—to add text to your document. The default font is now the cross-platform Open Type version of Minion Pro Regular instead of Times (Mac) and Times New Roman (Win).

Use Type Tools

1 Click the Type tool slot on the Tools panel.

◆ Click the arrow on the right of the Type tools menu to create a detachable panel.

2 Click one of the following Type tools:

◆ **Type.** Creates a text frame box.

◆ **Type on a Path.** Creates text along the outer edge of an open or closed path.

3 For the Type tool, drag to draw a text box. For the Type on a Path tool, click on a path.

4 Type some text.

Did You Know?

You can make fonts available for a document. If you store any fonts in a Document Fonts folder in the same location as an InDesign document, the fonts in the folder are available in the opened InDesign document.

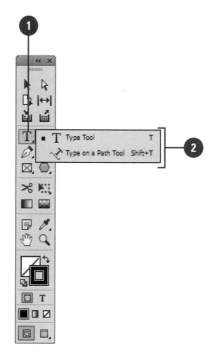

Adobe InDesign Type Tool — 4

Creating Type in a Text Frame

With the Type tool, you can create a rectangle text box any size that you want. Simply, select the Type tool on the Tools pane, drag to create a text frame and then start typing. When you type text in a text frame, it automatically wraps to the size of the frame. If you type more text than the frame can hold, an overflow symbol (a tiny red plus sign in a square) appears on the edge of the rectangle box. You can reshape the text frame object to display the text or create a thread (link) to another text frame.

Create Type in a Text Frame

1. Select the **Type** tool on the Tools panel.

2. Drag to create a rectangle text box the size that you want.

   A flashing insertion point appears in the text frame.

3. Type some text. The text automatically wraps to the shape of the text frame. Press Enter (Win) or Return (Mac) if you want to start a new line.

   ◆ If the overflow symbol appears, deselect the text frame, select the **Selection** tool on the Tools panel, and then drag a corner to reshape the text frame.

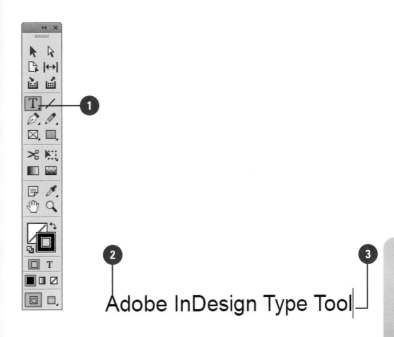

Adobe InDesign Type Tool

Creating Type Using Frame Tools

In addition to the Type tool, you can also use the Frame tools—Rectangle, Ellipse, and Polygon—to add text to your document. Instead of a rectangle shape for type, you can create irregular shapes to store text in your document. In addition to creating a polygon shape, you can also use the Polygon Frame tool to create a star shape for type. You can drag to create a frame box to the size that you want. If you need a frame box to be an exact size, you can click a blank area with the Rectangle and Ellipse tools or set width and height settings on the Control panel.

Create a Rectangle or Elliptical Frame for Type

1. Select the **Rectangle Frame** or **Ellipse Frame** tool on the Tools panel.

2. Drag to create a rectangle or elliptical frame the size that you want.

   ◆ To create a frame to an exact size, click a blank area, specify the width and height you want, and then click **OK**.

3. Select the **Type** tool on the Tools panel.

4. Click in the frame, and then type some text. The text automatically wraps to the shape of the text frame. Press Enter (Win) or Return (Mac) if you want to start a new line.

   ◆ If the overflow symbol appears, deselect the text frame, select the **Selection** tool on the Tools panel, and then drag a corner to reshape the text frame.

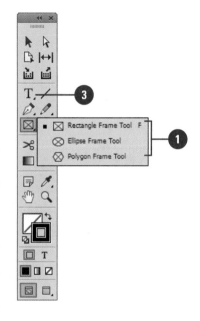

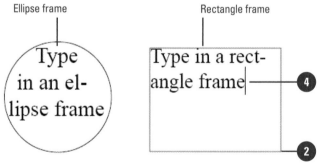

Ellipse frame

Type in an el- lipse frame

Rectangle frame

Type in a rect- angle frame

Create a Polygon Frame for Type

1. Double-click the **Polygon Frame** tool on the Tools panel.

2. Enter a **Number of Sides** value for the polygon.

3. Leave the **Star Inset** value at 0% to create a polygon.

4. Click **OK**.

5. Drag to create a polygon frame box the size that you want.

   ◆ As you drag, press the Up or Down arrow keys to increase or decrease the number of sides.

6. Click in the frame with the **Type** tool, and then type some text. The text automatically wraps to the shape of the text frame. Press Enter (Win) or Return (Mac) if you want to start a new line.

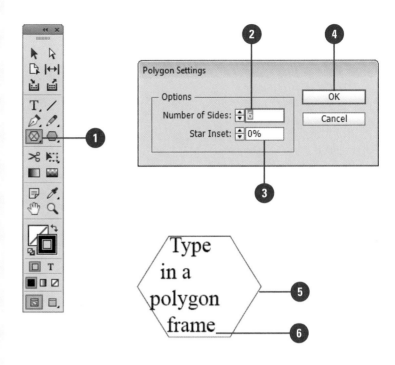

Create a Star Frame for Type

1. Double-click the **Polygon Frame** tool on the Tools panel.

2. Enter a **Number of Sides** value for the star.

3. Enter a **Star Inset** value. The higher the amount, the sharper the points.

4. Click **OK**.

5. Drag to create a star frame box the size that you want.

   ◆ As you drag, press the Up or Down arrow keys to increase or decrease the number of sides.

6. Click in the frame with the **Type** tool, and then type some text. The text automatically wraps to the shape of the text frame. Press Enter (Win) or Return (Mac) if you want to start a new line.

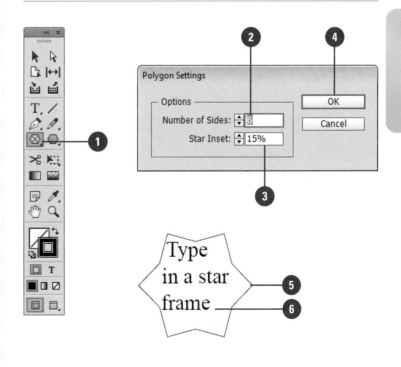

Creating Path Type

With the Type on a Path tool, you can add type along the inner or outer edge of a path. You can place the text on either side of the path, but not on both. If you initially place it on the inner part of the path, you can always move it to the outer part of the path later. When you select text on a path, brackets appear that you can drag to adjust the position and placement of the text.

Create Type on a Path

1. Select the **Type on a Path** tool on the Tools panel.

2. Click on the edge of the path (closed or open) to which you want to add type.

   A flashing insertion point appears in the text frame. Any fill or stroke on the object is removed.

3. Type some text. The text automatically wraps to the shape of the text frame. Don't press Enter (Win) or Return (Mac).

   The type appears along the edge of the object, conforms to its shape, and removes the fill and stroke.

   ◆ If the overflow symbol appears, deselect the text frame, select the **Direct Selection** tool on the Tools panel, and then drag a corner to reshape the text frame.

4. Select a selection tool or select the type tool again.

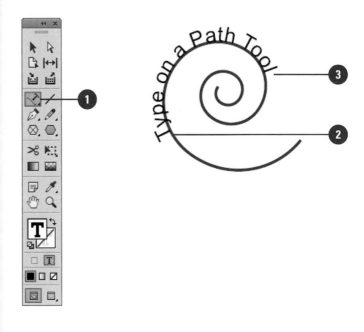

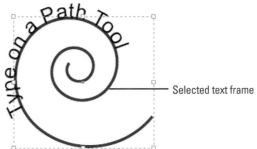

Selected text frame

Did You Know?

You can delete the text on a path. With a selection tool, select the text path frame, click the Type menu, point to Type On A Path, and then click Delete Type From Path.

Modify Type on a Path

1. Select the **Direct Selection** tool on the Tools panel.

2. Click on the type.

   Center, left, and right brackets appear around the type.

3. Drag the bracket (not the square) to adjust the position of the type on a path.

   ◆ **Swap Sides.** Drag the Center bracket to the other side to change the inner/outer position of the type along the path.

   ◆ **Left.** Drag to position the left side (or starting point) of the type along the path.

   ◆ **Center.** Drag left or right to position the type along the path.

   ◆ **Right.** Drag to position the right side (or ending point) of the type along the path.

   If the overflow symbol appears, deselect the text frame, select the **Direct Selection** tool on the Tools panel, and then drag a corner to reshape the text frame.

4. To change type on path options, click the **Type** menu, point to **Type on a Path**, and then click **Options**.

   ◆ Select the **Preview** check box to view your changes as you make them.

5. Specify the options (Effect, Flip, Align, To Path, and Spacing) you want, and then click **OK**.

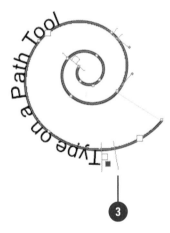

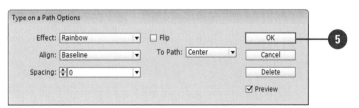

Importing Text

If you have text from another document that you want to use in your InDesign document, you can use the Place command to import it. You can import text from the following text formats: plain text (TXT), Rich Text Format (RTF), Microsoft Word (DOC or DOCX), or Microsoft Excel (XLS or XLSX). When you import text using the Place command on the File menu, InDesign allows you to place the text in a new text frame or an existing one.

Import Text

1. Click the **File** menu, and then click **Place**.

2. Click the **Files of Type** (Win) or **Enable** (Mac) list arrow, and then click **Importable Files** or select a text format:

    ◆ **Text Import.** Plain text.

    ◆ **Microsoft Word.** Microsoft Word 2003 (DOC) or earlier.

    ◆ **Microsoft Word 2007.** Microsoft Word 2007 (DOCX) or later.

    ◆ **RTF.** Rich Text Format (RTF).

    ◆ **Microsoft Excel.** Microsoft Excel 2003 (XLS) or earlier.

    ◆ **Microsoft Excel 2007.** Microsoft Excel 2007 (XLSX) or later.

3. Navigate to the location with the text file you want to import.

4. Select the text file you want to place.

5. Select the **Replace Selected Item** check box to replace the selected item with the imported text.

6. Click **Open**.

    The imported text is placed in a loaded text cursor.

7. Click or drag a text frame with the loaded text cursor to place the text where you want it in your document.

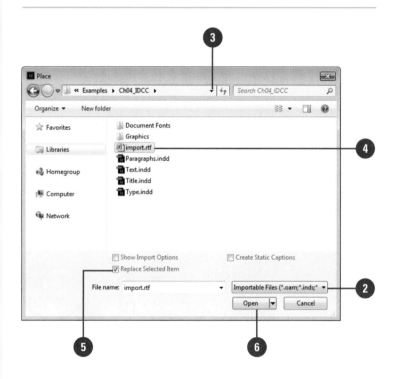

Imported text

Import Text with Options

1. Click the **File** menu, and then click **Place**.

2. Click the **Files of Type** (Win) or **Enable** (Mac) list arrow, and then click **Importable Files**.

3. Navigate to the location with the text file you want to import.

4. Select the text file you want to place.

5. Select the **Show Import Options** check box to select import options.

6. Click **Open**.

7. Select the options you want. Options vary depending on the imported file format.

8. Click **OK**.

   The imported text is placed in a loaded text cursor.

9. Click or drag a text frame with the loaded text cursor to place the text where you want it in your document.

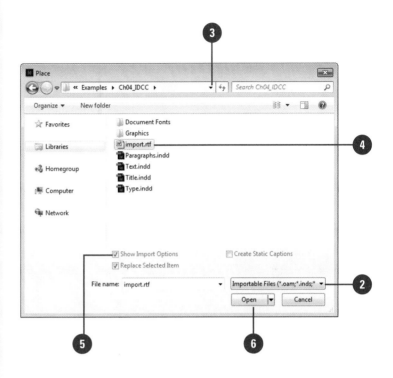

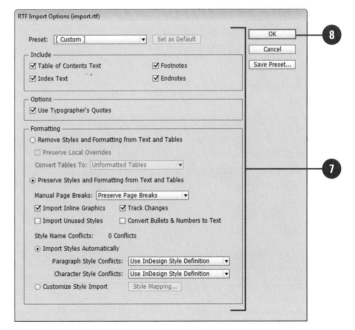

Flowing Imported Text

When you import text into your document, InDesign imports the text into a loaded text cursor with a small text icon and the first part of the text. When the text is loaded, you have several options to place the text into your document. You can create a new text frame or add the text to an existing text frame in a document or master page. When the loaded text cursor displays straight lines, the text will be placed in a new text frame. When the loaded text cursor displays curved lines, the text will be placed in an existing text frame. After you import the text, you can reflow the text manually with the overflow symbol (a tiny red plus sign in a square), or automatically with keyboard options.

Import and Flow Text

1. Click the **File** menu, and then click **Place**.

2. Navigate to and select the text file you want to place.

3. Click **Open**.

   The imported text is placed in a loaded text cursor.

4. Use any of the following to place the imported text in your document:

   ◆ **New Text Frame.** Drag to create a text frame the size you want.

   ◆ **New Text Frame within Margins.** Click to create a text frame the width of the margins.

   ◆ **Existing Text or Master Text Frame.** With the text or master text frame not selected, click inside the text frame.

Did You Know?

You can create a master text frame when you create a new document. Click the File menu, point to New, click Document, select the Master Text Frame check box, and then click OK.

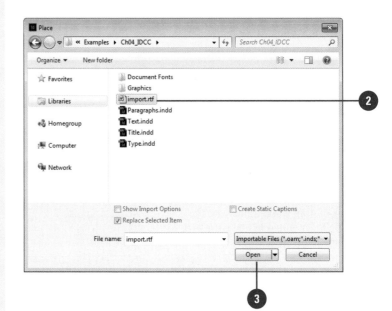

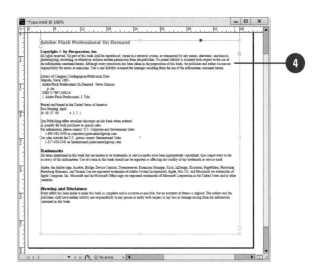

Import and Autoflow Text

① Click the **File** menu, and then click **Place**.

② Navigate to and select the text file you want to place.

③ Click **Open**.

The imported text is placed in a loaded text cursor.

④ Use any of the following to place the imported text in your document:

◆ **Semi-Autoflow.** Hold down Alt (Win) or Option (Mac), and then click in an existing frame or drag a new frame. Continue to hold down Alt (Win) or Option (Mac), and then click or drag to create another text frame that is linked to the first.

◆ **Autoflow.** Hold down Shift, and then point to an existing frame or master frame (unselected) or click at the top-left corner of the margins, click to flow the text on the page and create as many additional pages as needed.

◆ **Autoflow on Fixed Pages.** Hold down Shift+Alt (Win) or Shift+Option (Mac), and then click in the master text frame or the margins of the page to flow text on the number of pages in the document.

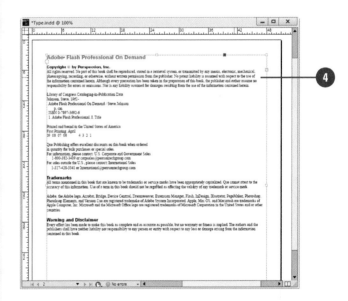

Working with Overflow Text

If you type, paste, or import more text than a text frame can hold, an overflow symbol (a tiny red plus sign in a square) appears on the edge of the text frame. You can reshape the text frame to display the text or create a thread (link) to another text frame. You can thread overflow text from one text frame to a new or existing text frame. After you create a thread between two or more text frames, you can use the Show Text Threads command on the Extras submenu (on View menu) to display the thread connection. If you no longer want to thread two or more text frames, you can unthread or disconnect them. When you unthread text frames, the text in the text frame remains in the first text frame (it may still overflow). When you disconnect text frames, the text in the text frames remains where it is.

Thread Overflow Text and Show Text Threads

1. Select the **Selection** tool on the Tools panel.

2. Select the text frame with the overflow text.

3. Click the **Out Port** icon on the selected object.

   TIMESAVER *Double-click an Out Port icon with the Selection tool to create a linked copy of the text frame.*

   The pointer changes to the Loaded Text cursor.

4. To create a new text frame for the overflow text, click a blank area or drag to create a text frame.

   To use an existing text frame, click in an existing text frame.

   Overflow text from the first text frame threads to the second text frame.

5. To display a text thread between text frames, select a threaded text frame, click the **View** menu, point to **Extras**, and then click **Show Text Threads**.

Library of Congress Cataloging-in-Publication Data
Johnson, Steve, 1961-
   Adobe Flash Professional On Demand / Steve Johnson
      p. cm.
   ISBN 0-7897-3692-6
   1. Adobe Flash Professional. I. Title

Printed and bound in the United States of America
First Printing: April
09 08 07 06   4 3 2 1

Unthread Text Frames

1. Select the **Selection** tool on the Tools panel.

2. Select a threaded text frame.

3. Double-click the **In Port** or **Out Port** icon on the selected object.

Did You Know?

You can show or hide text threads. Click the View menu, point to Extras, and then click Show Text Threads or Hide Text Threads.

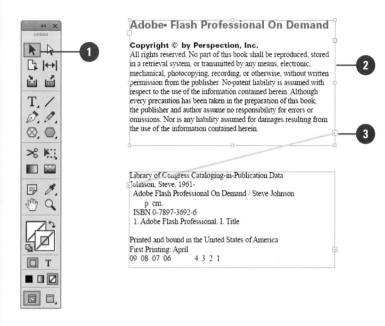

Change the Thread Between Frames

1. Select the **Selection** tool on the Tools panel.

2. Select a threaded text frame.

3. Click the **In Port** or **Out Port** icon on the selected object.

4. To create a new text frame for the overflow text, click a blank area or drag to create a text frame.

   To use an existing text frame, click in an existing text frame.

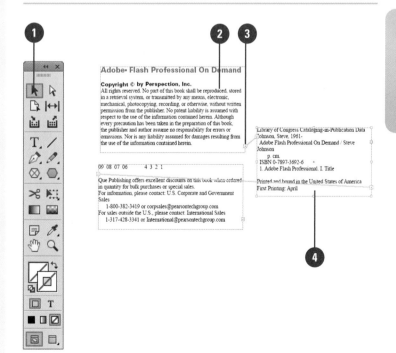

Using Smart Text Reflow

Smart Text Reflow allows you to automatically add or remove pages when you are typing and editing text. You can use Smart Text Reflow on master text frames (the default) and document text frames. When you want to reflow text in document text frames, the text frame needs to be threaded (linked) to another text frame on a different page. Before you reflow text, you can set Smart Text Reflow options in the Type preferences dialog box.

Set Smart Text Reflow Options

1. Click the **Edit** (Win) or **InDesign** (Mac) menu, point to **Preferences**, and then click **Type**.

2. Select the **Smart Text Reflow** check box to enable the feature.

3. Select from the following Smart Text Reflow options:

   ◆ **Add Pages To.** Specify where you want to add overflow pages.

   ◆ **Limit To Master Text Frames.** Select to only reflow text to master text frames. Deselect to reflow text in a threaded text frame from one page to another.

   ◆ **Preserve Facing-Page Spreads.** Select to add two page spreads for text reflow. Deselect to add a single page for text reflow and shuffle pages.

   ◆ **Delete Empty Pages.** Select to delete pages when an empty text frame is the only object on the page.

4. Click **OK**.

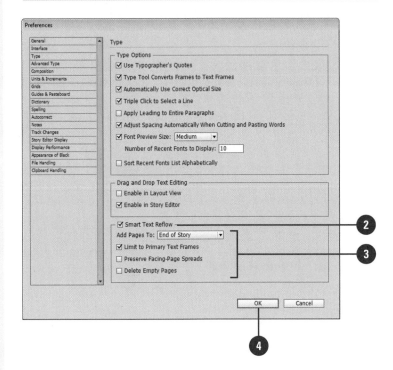

Use Smart Text Reflow

1. In Type preferences, select the **Smart Text Reflow** and **Delete Empty Pages** check boxes.

   ◆ **Type preferences.** Click the **Edit** (Win) or **InDesign** (Mac) menu, point to **Preferences**, and then click **Type**.

2. Hold down Ctrl+Shift (Win) or ⌘+Shift (Mac), and then click the master text frame to override it.

3. Type text until you fill the text frame to automatically add a page, or delete enough text to automatically delete a page.

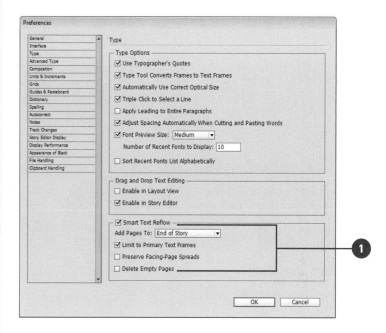

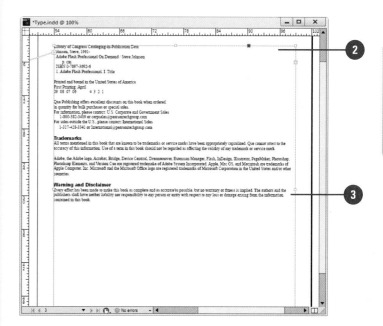

Typing and Selecting Text

Before you can work with text in InDesign, you need to select it. You can select the entire text frame or the characters in the text frame. The selection tools (Selection and Direct Selection) allow you to select both characters and its object. You can use the type tools to select only the characters in the text frame, but not the object. When you add text to a text frame, pressing Enter (Win) or Return (Mac) creates a new paragraph. If you want to force a line break, known as a soft return, instead of a new paragraph, you can press Shift+Enter (Win) or Shift+Return (Mac).

Select Type and its Object

1. Select the **Selection** or **Direct Selection** tool on the Tools panel.

2. Use the appropriate selection method:

   ◆ **Type.** Click on the text.

   ◆ **Path Type.** Click on the path or text.

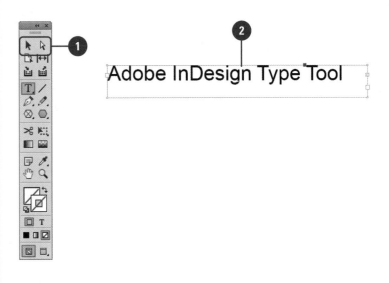

Type Text

1. Select the **Type** tool on the Tools panel.

   TIMESAVER *With a selection tool, double-click text to place the insertion point.*

2. Click to place the insertion point where you want to insert text.

3. Type some text. The text automatically wraps to the shape of the text frame.

4. Press Enter (Win) or Return (Mac) to create a new paragraph or press Shift+Enter (Win) or Shift+Return (Mac) to create a new line and not a new paragraph.

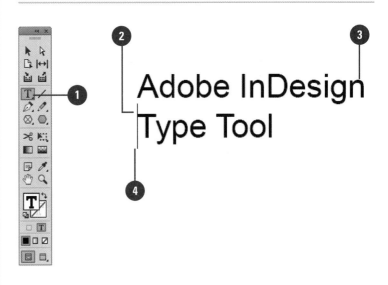

Select and Deselect Type Text

1. Select the **Type** tool on the Tools panel.

2. Do any of the following to select:

   ◆ **Text.** Drag the I-beam cursor to select and highlight a word or line of text.

   ◆ **Text Range.** Click to place the insertion point at the beginning of the text range, press Shift, and then click at the end of the text range.

   ◆ **Word.** Double-click a word of text.

   ◆ **Paragraph.** Triple-click a paragraph of text.

   ◆ **All Text.** Click to place the insertion point, click the **Edit** menu, and then click **Select All**.

   TIMESAVER *Click in a text frame, press Ctrl+A (Win) or ⌘+A (Mac) to select all the text.*

3. To deselect the text, click outside the text frame.

   ◆ You can also click the **Edit** menu, and then click **Deselect All**.

   TIMESAVER *Press Esc to return the text frame from text editing mode.*

Did You Know?

You can change what triple-clicking does. Click the Edit (Win) or InDesign (Mac) menu, point to Preferences, click Type, select the Triple Click To Select A Line check box, and then click OK.

Adobe InDesign Type Tool

Select All

Adobe InDesign Type Tool

Editing Text with Autocorrect

InDesign's Autocorrect feature automatically corrects common capitalization and spelling errors as you type. Autocorrect comes with hundreds of text and symbol entries you can edit or remove. You can add words and phrases to the Autocorrect dictionary that you tend to misspell, or add often-typed words and save time by just typing their initials. You can use Autocorrect to quickly insert symbols. For example, you can type (c) to insert ©. You can enable Autocorrect and customize settings in the Autocorrect preferences dialog box.

Set Autocorrect Options

1. Click the **Edit** (Win) or **InDesign** (Mac) menu, point to **Preferences**, and then click **Autocorrect**.

2. Select the **Enable Autocorrect** check box to enable the feature.

3. Select from the following Autocorrect options:

   ◆ **Autocorrect Capitalization Errors.** Select to have InDesign automatically correct capitalization errors.

   ◆ **Language.** Choose the language dictionary you want InDesign to use when checking your text.

4. Do one of the following:

   ◆ **Add.** Type a misspelled word or an abbreviation to add it to the list of words that will be autocorrected.

   ◆ **Edit.** Select any words you want to change.

   ◆ **Remove.** Select any words you want to delete.

5. Click **OK**.

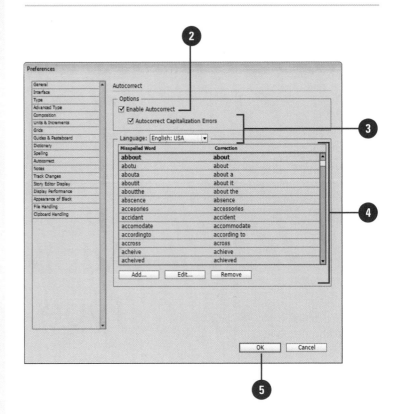

Copying and Moving Text

Like most programs, you can copy and move text by using the Copy or Cut and Paste commands or drag-and-drop techniques. InDesign is no different. There are a couple of differences. When you paste text, you can paste it without formatting. Another difference is that InDesign allows you to inherit formatting from the destination text when you drag and drop text. You can use the Type preferences dialog box to enable drag and drop editing in Layout view and Story Editor.

Copy or Cut and Paste Text

1. Select the **Type** tool on the Tools panel, and then select the text you want to copy or cut (move).

2. Click the **Edit** menu, and then click **Cut** or **Copy**.

3. Click to place the insertion point where you want to place the text.

4. Click the **Edit** menu, and then click **Paste** or **Paste Without Formatting**.

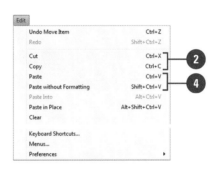

Drag Text

1. Select the **Type** tool on the Tools panel, and then select the text you want to move or copy. The cursor changes to an arrow with a T.

2. Use any of the following methods:

   ◆ **Move.** Drag the selected text to a new text frame location.

   ◆ **Copy.** Press Alt (Win) or Option (Mac) and drag the selected text to a new text frame location.

   ◆ **Inherit Formatting.** Press Shift and drag the selected text to a new text frame location. The text inherits the formatting of the text destination frame.

Changing Fonts

A **font** is a collection of alphanumeric characters that share the same typeface, or design, and have similar characteristics. With the Character panel, you can change the font family (Arial or Times New Roman) and style (Italic, Bold, or Condensed), as well as change other type attributes, such as size, kerning, scale, tracking, leading, and language. You can also change these and other attributes by using the Type menu and Control panel. On Font menus, a font sample appears for easy recognition, and you can search for fonts (**New!**) as well as set and show favorite fonts (**New!**) for easy access. After you select the text that you want to change, you can change font attributes directly on the Control panel. For example, you can style text using All Caps, Small Caps, Underline, Strikethrough, Subscript and Superscript. As you can see, there are several ways to change font attributes.

Change Font Family and Style

1. Select the **Type** tool on the Tools panel, and then select the text that you want to change.

   ◆ You can also select the **Selection** tool, and then click the text frame to change all text in the frame.

2. Select the **Character** panel.

   ◆ Click the **Type** menu, and then click **Character**.

3. To search for a font (**New!**), click in the Font Family box, and then type a font name. Matching fonts appear in a list. To cancel, click the **Close** button in the box.

   ◆ **Options.** Click the **Magnifying Glass** icon (**New!**), and then click **Search Entire Font Name** or **Search First Word Only**.

4. Click the **Font Family** list arrow, click an **Expand** icon (triangle) to display styles (**New!**), and then select a font. Recently used fonts appear at the top of the list. You can also browse with Arrow keys.

5. To set and show favorite fonts (**New!**), click the **Font Family** list arrow, click a **Star** icon to set/unset a font favorite, and then select the **Show Favorite Fonts Only** check box.

Click to cancel search

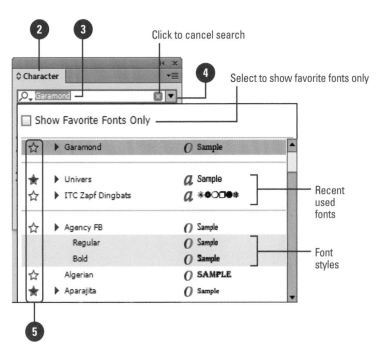

Select to show favorite fonts only

Recent used fonts

Font styles

Type results

Adobe InDesign Type Tool

Apply Additional Font Styles

1. Select the **Type** tool on the Tools panel, and then select the text that you want to change.

   - You can also select the **Selection** tool, and then click the text frame to change all text in the frame.

2. Select the **Character** panel.

   - Click the **Type** menu, and then click **Character**.

   - You can quickly access the following styles on the Options menu or the Control panel.

3. Click the **Options** button, and then select the style you want:

   - **All Caps.** Changes lowercase letters to all capitals.

   - **Small Caps.** Changes lowercase letters to reduced capitals.

   - **Superscript.** Reduces and raises the text above the baseline.

   - **Subscript.** Reduces and lowers the text below the baseline.

   - **Underline.** Underlines the text.

   - **Strikethrough.** Adds a line through the text.

   - **Underline Options.** Opens a dialog box, where you can change underline options.

   - **Strikethrough Options.** Opens a dialog box, where you can change strikethrough options.

4. To change the font color, click the **Fill** or **Stroke** box on the Control panel, and then select a color from the Swatch menu.

   - Click the **Character Formatting Controls** button to display character related options.

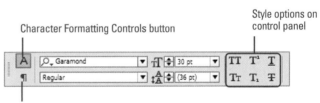

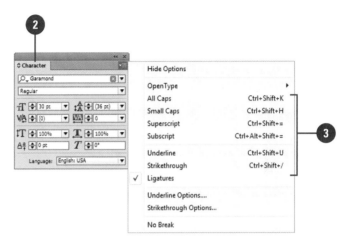

Character Formatting Controls button

Style options on control panel

Paragraph Formatting Controls button

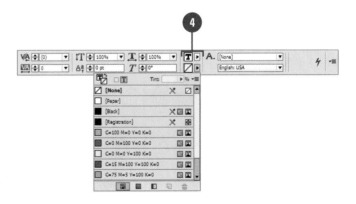

Changing Font Size

After setting the font family and style, the next attribute to set is the font size. The font size can range from 6 points to 72 points and beyond depending on the font. Open or TrueType fonts can be scaled to any size and still look and print well. Bitmap (screen fonts) fonts, on the other hand, cannot be scaled and you need to use the available sizes to print well. However, bitmap fonts are the best choice for commercial print jobs. An "O" appears next to an OpenType font, a "TT" appears next to a TrueType font, and an "a" appears next to a bitmap font on the Font submenu.

Change Font Size

1. Select the **Type** tool on the Tools panel, and then select the text that you want to change.

   ◆ You can also select the **Selection** tool, and then click the text frame to change all text in the frame.

2. Select the **Character** panel.

   ◆ Click the **Type** menu, and then click **Character**.

3. Enter a point size, or click the **Font Size** list arrow, and then select a font size. Press Enter (Win) or Return (Mac) to apply the value.

   ◆ You can also hold down Ctrl+Shift (Win) or ⌘+Shift (Mac), and then press > to increase the point size or press < to decrease the point size.

   Use Ctrl+Alt-Shift (Win) or ⌘+Option+Shift to change the point size 5 sizes at a time.

   ◆ You can also click the **Type** menu, point to **Size**, and then select a point size or Other.

Did You Know?

What is a point? The size of each font character is measured in points (a point is approximately 1/72 of an inch). The default is 12-point Times New Roman.

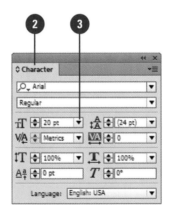

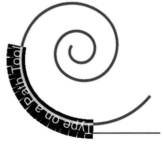

Type results

Changing Text Leading

Leading is the distance from the baseline of one line to the baseline of the next line and is measured in points. Each line of text can have a different leading size. You can specify a specific setting or use Auto, which is a percentage of the largest text size on each line. Leading is applied to horizontal text. If you want to change vertical spacing in text, you need to adjust horizontal tracking.

Change Text Leading

1. Select the **Type** tool on the Tools panel, and then select the text that you want to change.

   ◆ You can also select the **Selection** tool, and then click the text frame to change all text in the frame.

2. Select the **Character** panel.

   ◆ Click the **Type** menu, and then click **Character**.

3. Enter a leading point size, or click the **Leading** arrows, and then select a leading size. Press Enter (Win) or Return (Mac) to apply the value.

   ◆ You can also hold down Alt (Win) or Option (Mac), and then press the **down arrow** to increase the point size or press the **up arrow** to decrease the point size.

   The text increases or decreases by the Size/Leading value set in the Type preferences.

4. To shift characters up or down from the baseline, enter a baseline value, or click the **Baseline Shift** arrows, and then select a baseline value. A positive size adds space while a negative number removes space. Press Enter (Win) or Return (Mac) to apply the value.

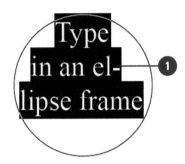

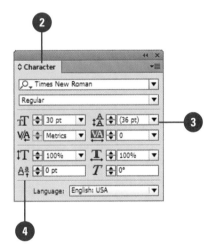

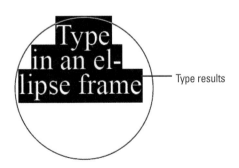

Type results

Changing Text Kerning

Kerning is adding or removing space between pairs of characters in your text. Sometimes the space between two characters is larger than others, which makes the word look uneven. You can use the Character panel to change the kerning setting for selected characters. You can expand or condense character spacing to create a special effect for a title, or realign the position of characters to the bottom edge of the text—this is helpful for positioning copyright or trademark symbols.

Change Text Kerning

1. Select the **Type** tool on the Tools panel, and then click between the two characters of text you want to change.

2. Select the **Character** panel.

   ◆ Click the **Type** menu, and then click **Character**.

3. Enter a kerning size, or click the **Kerning** arrows, and then select a kerning size. A positive size adds space while a negative number removes space. Press Enter (Win) or Return (Mac) to apply the value.

   ◆ You can also hold down Alt (Win) or Option (Mac), and then press the **right arrow** to increase the point size or press the **left arrow** to decrease the point size.

   The text increases or decreases by the Tracking value set in the Type preferences.

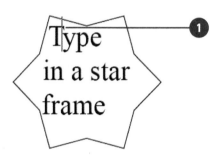

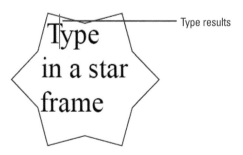

Type results

Changing Text Tracking

Tracking is the adjustment of space between three or more characters. Typically, you'll track a line of text or a few words depending on the length and design application. This is useful for creating specialize text for a caption or short heading. To adjust space between two characters, kerning is the best choice. To track characters, you need to select them first and then set the Tracking option in the Character panel.

Change Text Tracking

1. Select the **Type** tool on the Tools panel, and then select the text that you want to change.

   ◆ You can also select the **Selection** tool, and then click the text frame to change all text in the frame.

2. Select the **Character** panel.

   ◆ Click the **Type** menu, and then click **Character**.

3. Enter a tracking size, or click the **Tracking** arrows, and then select a tracking size. A positive size adds space while a negative number removes space. Press Enter (Win) or Return (Mac) to apply the value.

   ◆ You can also hold down Alt (Win) or Option (Mac), and then press the **right arrow** to increase the point size or press the **left arrow** to decrease the point size.

   The text increases or decreases by the Tracking value set in the Type preferences.

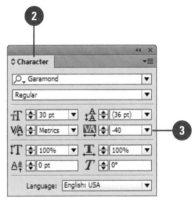

Type results

Scaling or Skewing Text

Scaling allows you to make text wider or narrower for horizontal text and taller or shorter for vertical text. You can use the Horizontal Scale and Vertical Scale options in the Character panel to modify text. **Skewing** allows you to distort the text at an angle to give it perspective. If the scaling or skewing doesn't look quite right, you can always use the Undo command to reverse the modification.

Scale and Skew Text

1. Select the text that you want to change.

   ◆ You can also select the **Selection** tool, and then click the text frame to change all text in the frame.

2. Select the **Character** panel.

   ◆ Click the **Type** menu, and then click **Character**.

3. To scale text, enter a horizontal or vertical percentage, or click the **Vertical Scale** or **Horizontal Scale** arrows. Press Enter (Win) or Return (Mac) to apply the value. Other ways of scaling text include:

   ◆ To scale a text frame, select the object, double-click the **Scale** tool on the Tools panel, specify a **Horizontal** and **Vertical** percentage, and then click **OK**.

   ◆ To scale a text frame, select the object, select the **Free Transform** tool on the Tools panel, and then drag a side handle on the bounding box.

4. To skew text, enter a degree value, or click the **Skew** arrows. Press Enter (Win) or Return (Mac) to apply the value.

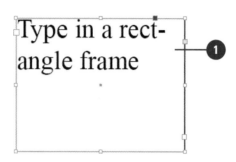

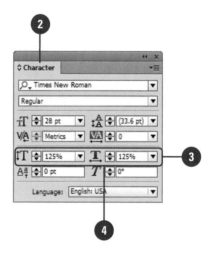

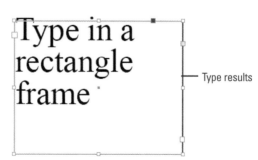

Type results

Aligning Paragraphs

When you press the Enter (Win) or Return (Mac) in a text frame, InDesign creates a paragraph. You can use the Paragraph panel to align and indent paragraphs in your document. At the top and bottom of the Paragraph panel is a set of buttons that you can use to align text in one or more paragraphs. The panel includes the typical options to align: left, center, right and justify. However, it also includes options to justify text with only the last line aligned left, center, or right.

Align Paragraphs

1. Select the **Type** tool on the Tools panel, and then click in a paragraph or select multiple paragraphs you want to align.

2. Select the **Paragraph** panel.

    ◆ Click the **Type** menu, and then click **Paragraph**.

3. Use any of the following alignment buttons on the panel:

    ◆ **Align Left**, **Align Center**, or **Align Right**. Click these buttons to align paragraph text left, center, or right.

    ◆ **Justify Left, Center, or Right.** Click these buttons to justify the paragraph text with only the last line aligned left, center, or right.

    ◆ **Justify.** Click to justify all lines.

    ◆ **Align Towards Spine.** Click to align the paragraph text towards the spine.

    ◆ **Align Away From Spine.** Click to align the paragraph text away from the spine.

    ◆ **Do Not Align To Baseline Grid.** Click to keep the paragraph text from aligning to the baseline grid.

    ◆ **Align To Baseline Grid.** Click to align the paragraph text to the baseline grid.

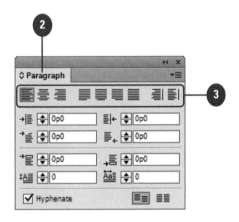

Left aligned

Dionsendiam nim augiam del ut at iustrud digna ad dolor at. Ut velit irit aliquis dolobore exero ero ex elendrer augait, con henim iliquam nibh et, quat vent ex exercing ea feumsan enim vel ut iure tat lore magniam, volore ver irit venit augiat. Sed tin ver iliquametum ipsustie consenibh er autetum

Dionsendiam nim augiam del ut at iustrud digna ad dolor at. Ut velit irit aliquis dolobore exero ero ex elendrer augait, con henim iliquam nibh et, quat vent ex exercing ea feumsan enim vel ut iure tat lore magniam, volore ver irit venit augiat. Sed tin ver iliquametum ipsustie consenibh er autetum

Center aligned

Right aligned

Dionsendiam nim augiam del ut at iustrud digna ad dolor at. Ut velit irit aliquis dolobore exero ero ex elendrer augait, con henim iliquam nibh et, quat vent ex exercing ea feumsan enim vel ut iure tat lore magniam, volore ver irit venit augiat. Sed tin ver iliquametum ipsustie consenibh er autetum

Dionsendiam nim augiam del ut at iustrud digna ad dolor at. Ut velit irit aliquis dolobore exero ero ex elendrer augait, con henim iliquam nibh et, quat vent ex exercing ea feumsan enim vel ut iure tat lore magniam, volore ver irit venit augiat. Sed tin ver iliquametum ipsustie consenibh er autetum quat

Justified

Indenting and Spacing Paragraphs

Quickly indent lines of text to precise locations from the left or right margin with the horizontal ruler. Indent the first or last line of a paragraph (called a **first-line** or **last-line indent**) as books do to distinguish paragraphs. Indent the second and subsequent lines of a paragraph from the left margin (called a **hanging indent**) to create a properly formatted bibliography. Indent the entire paragraph any amount from the left and right margins (called **left indents** and **right indents**) to separate quoted passages. In addition to indenting paragraphs, you can also set the spacing you want before or after a paragraph.

Indent and Space Paragraphs

1. Select the **Type** tool on the Tools panel, and then click in a paragraph or select multiple paragraphs you want to change.

2. Select the **Paragraph** panel.

   ◆ Click the **Type** menu, and then click **Paragraph**.

3. Enter a **Left Indent** and/or **Right Indent** value or use the up and down arrows to specify one. Press Enter (Win) or Return (Mac) to apply the value.

4. To create a first-line or last-line indent, enter a **First-Line Indent** or **Last-Line Indent** value or use the up and down arrows to specify one. Press Enter (Win) or Return (Mac) to apply the value.

   ◆ To create a hanging indent, enter a negative value in the First-line Left Indent box.

   ◆ To insert a manual indent, place the insertion point, click the **Type** menu, point to **Insert Special Character**, point to **Other**, and then click **Indent To Here**.

5. To add spacing between paragraphs, enter a **Space Before Paragraph** and/or **Space After Paragraph** value or use the up and down arrows to specify one. Press Enter (Win) or Return (Mac) to apply the value.

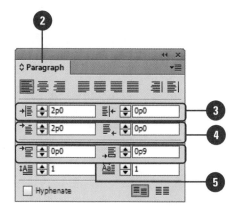

Left Indent

First-Line Indent

Dionsendiam nim augiam del ut at iustrud digna ad dolor at. Ut velit irit aliquis dolobore exero ero ex elendrer augait, con henim iliquam nibh et, quat vent ex exercing ea feumsan enim vel ut iure tat lore magniam, volore ver irit venit augiat. Sed tin ver iliquametum ipsustie consenibh er autetum quat lute modit dunt pratem veliquamet, quamet, veliquat in ute erat. Tat.

To od tat, consenit, cortinisi blaore tem zzrilis autpat. Ut niam, se conulla consequat. Ut inci blaor sit, susto core

Right Indent

Creating a Drop Cap

A few simple elements—drop caps, borders, and shading—make your newsletters and brochures look like a professional produced them. A **drop cap** is the enlarged first letter of a paragraph that provides instant style to a document. You can quickly achieve this effect in the Paragraph panel. You can change the drop cap position, font, and height, and then enter the distance between the drop cap and paragraph.

Create a Drop Cap

1. Select the **Type** tool on the Tools panel, and then click in a paragraph or select multiple paragraphs you want to change.

2. Select the **Paragraph** panel.

   ◆ Click the **Type** menu, and then click **Paragraph**.

3. Enter a **Drop Cap Number of Lines** value or use the up and down arrows to specify one. Press Enter (Win) or Return (Mac) to apply the value.

4. Enter a **Drop Cap One or More Characters** value or use the up and down arrows to specify one. Press Enter (Win) or Return (Mac) to apply the value.

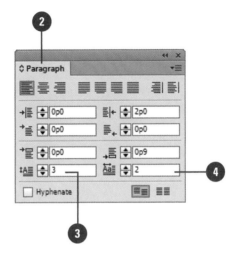

Drop cap

Tod tat, consenit, cortinisi blaore tem zzrilis autpat. Ut niam, se conulla consequat. Ut inci blaor sit, susto core magna faciliscipit adignim nos ad tinibh et la consequi ex elit wisi.

Applying a Paragraph Rule

If you want a line above or below a paragraph, you can apply it to a paragraph, so the line stays with the paragraph as you add or delete text. A paragraph rule can also be applied as part of a style sheet. In the Paragraph Rules dialog box, you can set the weight, style type, color, width, and position of the paragraph rule line.

Apply a Paragraph Rule

1. Select the paragraph to which you want to apply a rule.

2. Select the **Paragraph** panel.

3. Click the **Options** button, and then click **Paragraph Rules**.

4. Select the **Preview** check box to see changes as you make them.

5. Select **Rule Above** or **Rule Below** from the list arrow, and then select the **Rule On** check box.

   ◆ To set paragraph rules for both Rule Above and Rule Below, repeat Step 5.

6. Select any of the following appearance options:

   ◆ **Weight.** Specify the thickness of the line rule.

   ◆ **Type.** Specify the style of the line rule.

   ◆ **Color.** Specify the color of the line rule.

   ◆ **Tint.** Specify a tint for the line color.

   ◆ **Gap Color.** If you selected a type with a gap, specify a gap color for the line rule.

   ◆ **Gap Tint.** Specify a tint for the line gap color.

   ◆ **Overprint Gap.** Select to set the gap ink to overprint.

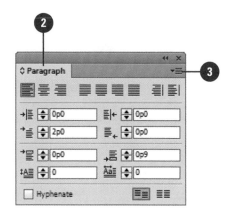

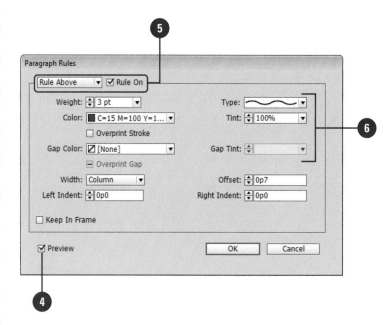

7 Select any of the following appearance options:

- ◆ **Width.** Select the rule line length equivalent to the column or the text.

- ◆ **Offset.** Specify the position above or below the baseline.

  By default, the paragraph rule is positioned on the baseline of the text.

- ◆ **Left and Right Indent.** Specify an indent value from the column or text margin.

8 To keep the rule in the text frame, select the **Keep In Frame** check box.

9 Click **OK**.

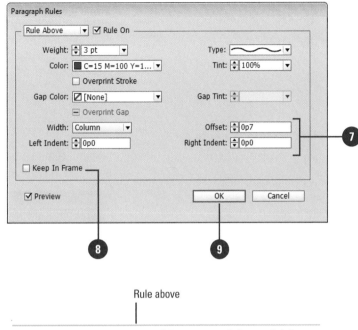

Rule above

Dionsendiam nim augiam del ut at iustrud digna ad dolor at. Ut velit irit aliquis dolobore exero ero ex elendrer augait, con henim iliquam nibh et, quat vent ex exercing ea feumsan enim vel ut iure tat lore magniam, volore ver irit venit augiat. Sed tin ver iliquametum ipsustie consenibh er autetum quat lute modit dunt pratem veliquamet, quamet, veliquat in ute erat. Tat.

Rule below

Did You Know?

The Preview box in any dialog box is retained. When you select a Preview check box in any dialog box, InDesign remembers the selection after you exit and restart InDesign.

See Also

See "Setting Advanced Type Preferences" on page 488 for more information on setting options for language usage with Adobe Composers.

For Your Information

Using Single-line or Paragraph Composer

As you type or edit a paragraph, InDesign adjusts word spacing, hyphenation, and line breaks a paragraph at a time with Adobe Paragraph Composer or a single-line at a time with Adobe Single-line Composer. This explains why you may notice text reflowing above the line you are editing. For headings and other short text boxes, Adobe Single-line Composer looks better, while for long text boxes, Adobe Paragraph Composer (default setting) looks better. For international uses, Adobe includes options for World-Ready Single-line or Paragraph Composer. To set a composer option, select the Paragraph panel, click the Options button, and then click the option you want.

Adding Bullets and Numbering

The best way to draw attention to a list is to format the items with bullets or numbers. For different emphasis, change any bullet or number style to one of InDesign's many predefined formats. For example, switch round bullets to check boxes or Roman numerals to lowercase letters. You can also customize the list style. If you move, insert, or delete items in a numbered list, InDesign sequentially renumbers the list for you.

Add Bullets or Numbering to a Paragraph

1. Select the paragraphs to which you want to add bullets or numbers.

2. Click the **Paragraph Formatting Controls** button to display paragraph related options.

3. Click the **Bulleted List** or **Numbered List** button on the Control panel.

   ◆ You can also click the **Type** menu, point to **Bulleted & Numbered Lists**, and then click **Apply Bullets** or **Apply Numbers**.

   The last used settings in the Bullets and Numbering dialog box are applied to the text.

Did You Know?

You can convert bullets or numbers to text. Select the text, click the Type menu, point to Bulleted & Numbered Lists, and then click Convert Bullets To Text or Convert Numbering To Text.

Format Bullets and Numbers

1. Select the **Paragraph** panel.

2. Click the **Options** button, and then click **Bullets and Numbering**.

3. Select the **Preview** check box to see changes as you make them.

4. Click the **List Type** list arrow, and then select **Bullets** or **Numbers**.

5. For Bullets, select from the following options:

   ◆ **Bullet Character.** Select a bullet character. Add or remove specific characters from the list.

   ◆ **Text After.** Specify characters to separate the bullet and text.

   ◆ **Character Style.** Specify a bullet style.

6. For Numbers, select from the following options:

   ◆ **Format.** Specify a number format style.

   ◆ **Number.** Specify characters to separate the number and text.

   ◆ **Character Style.** Specify a number style.

   ◆ **Mode.** Specify a start number or sequence.

7. Select any of the following Bullet or Number Position options:

   ◆ **Alignment.** Specify an alignment.

   ◆ **Left Indent.** Specify an indent value.

   ◆ **First Line Indent.** Specify a first line indent value.

   ◆ **Tab Position.** Specify the position of the first character after the bullet or number.

8. Click **OK**.

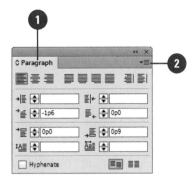

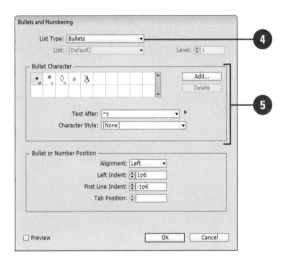

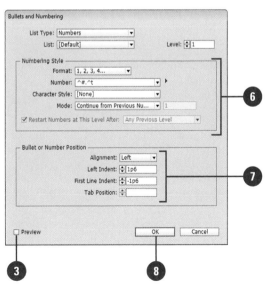

Setting Tabs

In your document, **tabs** determines how text or numerical data is aligned in relation to the document margins. A **tab stop** is a predefined stopping point along the document's typing line. Default tab stops are set every half-inch, but you can set multiple tabs per paragraph at any location. Choose from four types of text tab stops: left, right, center, and decimal (for numerical data). In the Tabs panel, you can view a ruler with the current tab setting for the selected text and add, move, or delete tab stops. When you press the Tab key with the insertion point active, the text shifts to the next tab stop.

Set Tabs

1. Select the **Type** tool on the Tools panel, and then click to place the insertion point in a text frame.

2. Select the **Tabs** panel.

   ◆ Click the **Type** menu, and then click **Tabs**.

   ◆ To use the default tabs, press the tab key to shift the text to the next default tab stop.

3. To move the panel next to the text, click the **Position Panel Above Text Frame** button on the panel.

4. Do any of the following:

   ◆ **Insert.** Click one of the tab stop buttons, and then click in the ruler where you want to place it. You can also enter a number in the X box to insert a tab at an exact position.

   ◆ **Move.** Drag the tab stop left or right or enter an exact position in the X box.

   ◆ **Delete.** Drag a tab stop down off the ruler.

   ◆ **Leader.** Enter a character that repeats in the tabbed space, such as a period.

   ◆ **Align On.** Enter a character that is used with the Decimal tab, such as a decimal point.

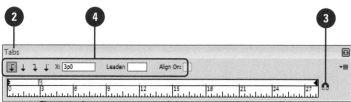

Dionsendiam nim augiam del ut at iustrud digna ad dolor at. Ut velit irit aliquis dolobore exero ero ex elendrer augait, con henim iliquam nibh et, quat vent ex exercing ea feumsan enim vel ut iure tat lore magniam, volore ver irit venit augiat. Sed tin ver iliquametum ipsustie consenibh er autetum quat lute modit dunt pratem veliquamet, quamet, veliquat in ute erat. Tat.

To od tat, consenit, cortinisi blaore tem zzrilis autpat. Ut niam, se conulla consequat. Ut inci blaor sit, susto core magna faciliscipit adignim nos ad tinibh et la consequi ex elit wisi.

Working with Glyphs

A glyph is a style variation—such as ligatures, ordinals, swashes, and fractions—for a given character in an OpenType font. OpenType fonts appear with an "O" next to the font name on the Font submenu. OpenType fonts are designed to work well on both Windows and Macintosh operating systems, which reduces font substitution problems when going back and forth between platforms. However, you can always add more character styles to extend the font format. For example, you can change fractions with numerals and slashes to properly formatted fractions. You can automatically insert alternate glyphs with the OpenType panel or insert them manually with the Glyphs panel to extend the font format.

Replace or Insert a Glyph

1. Select the **Type** tool on the Tools panel, and then select a character (to replace a glyph) or click in text (to insert a glyph).

2. Select the **Glyphs** panel.

   ◆ Click the **Type** menu, and then click **Glyphs**.

3. Select a different font and font style.

4. Click the **Show** list arrow, and then select a glyphs category.

   Alternates for Selection or **Entire Font** are common choices.

5. Double-click the glyph that you want to replace or insert.

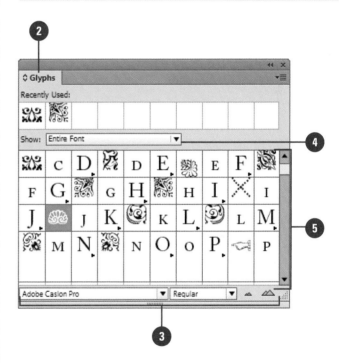

Inserting Special Text Characters

In addition to inserting normal alphanumeric text, you can also insert special text characters, such as symbols, markers, hyphens, dashes, white space, and breaks. For example, you can insert text breaks to force a break between lines, or add white space, such as an Em or En space, between characters. If you want to keep two words together on the same line, you can insert a nonbreaking space. You can insert special characters, white space, and break characters by using submenus on the Type menu.

Insert Special Text Characters

1. Select the **Type** tool on the Tools panel.

2. Click to place the insertion point where you want to place the text.

3. To insert a break, click the **Type** menu, point to **Insert Break Character**, and then select a text break.

    ◆ Includes column, frame, page, paragraph return, and forced line break.

4. To insert special characters, click the **Type** menu, point to **Insert Special Character**, point to any of the following, and then select a special character:

    ◆ **Symbols.** Includes copyright and trademark.

    ◆ **Markers.** Includes page numbers and section markers.

    ◆ **Hyphens and Dashes.** Includes Em and En dashes.

    ◆ **Quotation Marks.** Includes double and single quotation marks.

    ◆ **Other.** Includes tabs and indents.

5. To insert a space, click the **Type** menu, point to **Insert White Space**, and then select a text break.

    ◆ Includes Em and En space, Hair, Thin, Punctuation, and Figure.

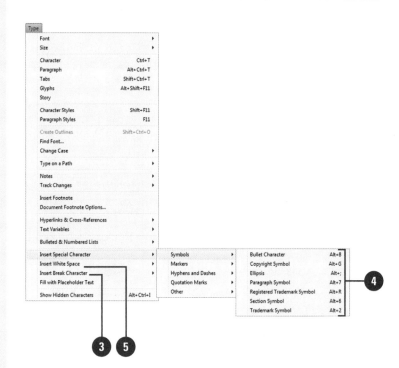

Working with Hidden Text

When you edit a document, sometimes it's hard to see the number of spaces between words. To make this job easier, you can show hidden characters, such as the Spacebar, Tab key, and Enter (Win) or Return (Mac) key. If you're still having trouble viewing the text, you can change the color of the hidden text by changing the color of the layer in the Layers panel. Hidden text is also hidden in Preview or Overprint Preview mode.

Show and Hide Text

◆ **Show Hidden Text.** Click the **Type** menu, and then click **Show Hidden Characters**.

   TIMESAVER *Press Alt+Ctrl+I (Win) or Option+⌘+I (Mac).*

◆ **Hide Hidden Text.** Click the **Type** menu, and then click **Hide Hidden Characters**.

Figure space

#

Adobe· Flash Professional On Demand¶
¶
Copyright © by Perspection, Inc.¶
All rights reserved. No part of this book shall be reproduced, stored in a retrieval system, or transmitted by any means, electronic, mechanical, photocopying, recording, or otherwise, without written permission from the publisher. No patent liability is assumed with respect to the use of the information contained herein. Although every precaution has been taken in the preparation of this book, the publisher and author assume no responsibility for errors or omissions. Nor is any liability assumed for damages resulting from the use of the information contained herein.¶
¶

Paragraph   Space

Setting Text Frame Options

If you need to make adjustments to all the text in a text frame, you can use the Text Frame Options dialog box to make all your changes in one place. You can create columns with fixed or flexible widths, balance text in columns, adjust inset spacing and vertical justification, specify a first baseline offset, add a baseline grid for a text frame, and set auto-sizing text frames reflow and constraints. Inset spacing is the space between the text and the frame. Vertical justification controls the alignment of text and paragraph spacing limits in rectangle and non-rectangle text frames from the top to the bottom. If you're working with wrapped text in a text frame, you can set an option to ignore it.

Set Text Frame Options

1. Select the text frame you want to change.

2. Click the **Object** menu, and then click **Text Frame Options**.

3. Select the **Preview** check box to see changes as you make them.

4. Click the **General** tab.

5. Select any of the following Columns options:

   ◆ **Columns.** Select to keep a fixed column width or number, or allow a flexible width.

   ◆ **Number.** Specify the number of columns you want to create.

   ◆ **Width.** Specify the column width you want.

   ◆ **Gutter.** Specify the gutter space between the columns you want.

   ◆ **Maximum.** For Flexible Width, specify the maximum size before adding a column.

   ◆ **Balance Columns.** Select to automatically balance text across columns in a multiple column text frame.

6. Specify inset spacing values for **Top**, **Bottom**, **Left** and **Right**.

7. Select any of the following Vertical Justification options:

   ◆ **Align.** Specify an alignment option for a text frame.

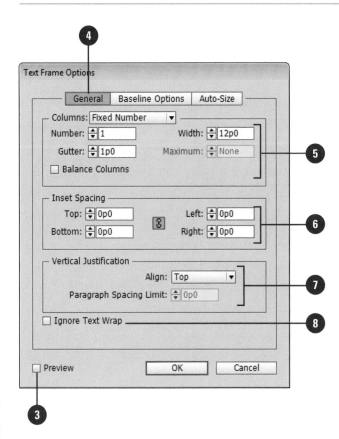

◆ **Paragraph Spacing Limit.**
When you select the Justify alignment option, specify a paragraph spacing limit.

8 To ignore text wrapping for the selected text frame, select the **Ignore Text Wrap** check box.

9 Click the **Baseline Options** tab.

10 Click the **Offset** list arrow, select an option, and then specify a minimum offset space.

11 Select any of the following Baseline Grid options:

◆ **Use Custom Baseline Grid.**
Select to create a baseline grid for the selected text frame.

◆ **Start.** Specify a start location for the baseline grid.

◆ **Relative To.** Specify a relative location where you want the baseline grid.

◆ **Increment Every.** Specify an interval for the baseline grid.

◆ **Color.** Select a color for the baseline grid.

12 Click the **Auto-Size** tab.

13 Click the **Auto-Sizing** list arrow, select an option: **Off**, **Height Only**, **Width Only**, **Height and Width**, and **Height and Width (Keep Proportions)**.

14 Select an auto size reflow option.

15 Select from the following available Auto-Sizing Constraints options:

◆ **Minimum Height** or **Width.**
Select to set the minimum height or width for auto-sizing.

◆ **No Line Breaks.** Select to specify no line breaks during auto-sizing.

16 Click **OK**.

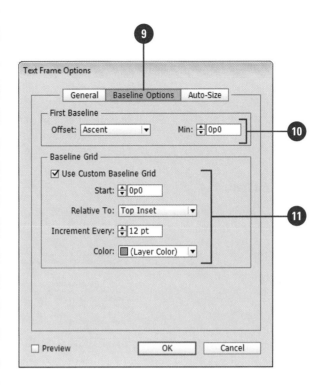

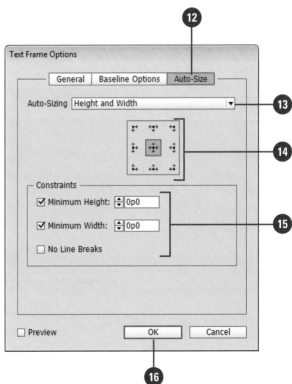

Creating Columns

You can create columns with fixed or flexible widths and automatically balance text in the same text box. You can span a paragraph across multiple columns or split a paragraph into multiple columns within the same text frame. When you have a paragraph span across multiple columns, InDesign balances the text before the spanning paragraph. Vertical justification controls the alignment of text in rectangle and non-rectangle text frames from the top to the bottom. When you set vertical justification to Justify, you can set paragraph spacing limits. Keep options are applied to paragraphs that span or split columns.

Create Multiple Columns

1. Click to place the insertion point in the paragraph you want to change.

2. Select the **Paragraph** panel.

3. Click the **Options** button, and then click **Span Columns**.

4. To span columns, click the **Paragraph Layout** list arrow, click **Span Columns**, and then specify the following options:

   ◆ **Span.** Specify the number of columns you want the paragraph to straddle.

   ◆ **Space Before Span** or **Space After Span.** Specify the space before or after the span.

5. To split columns, click the **Paragraph Layout** list arrow, click **Split Columns**, and then specify the following options:

   ◆ **Sub-columns.** Specify the number of columns you want to divide the paragraph into.

   ◆ **Space Before Split** or **Space After Split.** Specify the space before or after the split.

   ◆ **Inside Gutter or Outside Gutter.** Specify the gutter space between (inside) columns or outside the columns.

6. To remove split or span, click the **Paragraph Layout** list arrow, and then click **Single Column**.

7. Click **OK**.

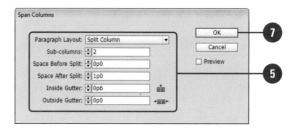

Split columns

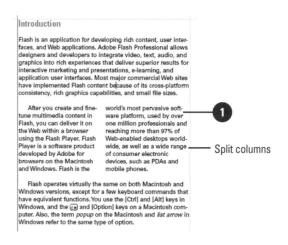

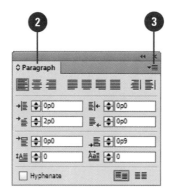

Set Column and Vertical Justification Options

1 Select the text frame you want to change.

2 Click the **Object** menu, and then click **Text Frame Options**.

3 Select the **Preview** check box to see changes as you make them.

4 Click the **General** tab.

5 Select any of the following Columns options:

◆ **Column.** Select to keep a fixed column width or number, or allow a flexible width.

◆ **Number.** Specify the number of columns you want to create.

◆ **Width.** Specify the column width you want.

◆ **Gutter.** Specify the gutter space between the columns you want.

◆ **Maximum.** For Flexible Width, specify the maximum size before adding a column.

◆ **Balance Columns.** Select to automatically balance text across columns in a multiple column text frame.

6 Select any of the following Vertical Justification options:

◆ **Align.** Specify an alignment option for a rectangle text frame.

◆ **Paragraph Spacing Limit.** When you select the Justify alignment option, specify a paragraph spacing limit.

7 Click **OK**.

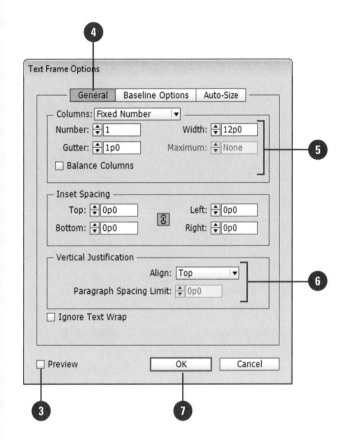

Wrapping Text Around an Object

When integrating graphics with your text, you can wrap the text around objects to create the results that you want. You can use the Text Wrap panel to quickly select button options to wrap text around an object. Some of the text wrapping options include No Wrap, Bounding Box, Object Shape, Jump Object, and Jump to Next Column. When you select Object Shape, you can select additional options to customize text wrapping around the object.

Wrap and Unwrap Text Around an Object

1. Arrange the object to be wrapped in front of the text frame. The objects should be overlapping.

2. Select the object to be wrapped.

3. Select the **Text Wrap** panel.

   ◆ Click the **Window** menu, and then click **Text Wrap**.

4. Select one of the following buttons:

   ◆ **No Text Wrap.** Text flows through the object.

   ◆ **Bounding Box.** Text wraps around the bounding box.

   ◆ **Object Shape.** Text wraps around the shape.

   ◆ **Jump Object.** Text wraps to the space under the object.

   ◆ **Jump to Next Column.** Text wraps to the next column or text frame.

5. Select the **Invert** check box to flow the text inside the object.

6. Enter offset values to specify the distance between the text and the object.

   ◆ Click the **Make All Settings the Same** button (chain icon) to set all the offset values to be the same. Click it again (broken chain icon) if you want to set different values.

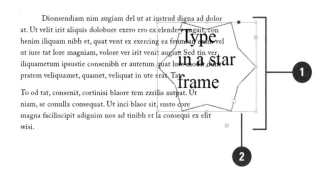

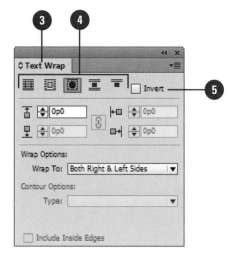

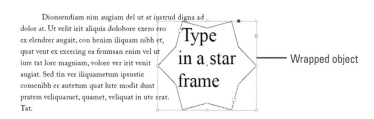

Wrapped object

Set Object Shape Wrap Options

1 Select the object to be wrapped.

2 Select the **Text Wrap** panel.

3 Click the **Object Shape** button.

4 Click the **Wrap To** list arrow, and then select an option:

- ◆ **Right Side.** Wraps around the right side.

- ◆ **Left Side.** Wraps around the left side.

- ◆ **Both Right & Left Sides.** Wraps to both sides.

- ◆ **Side Towards Spine.** Wraps to the left or right side towards the spine.

- ◆ **Side Away From Spine.** Wraps to the left or right side away from the spine.

- ◆ **Largest Area.** Wraps to the side with the most space.

5 Click the **Type** list arrow, and then select an option to control the shape of the wrap:

- ◆ **Bounding Box.** Uses the bounding box rectangle.

- ◆ **Detect Edges.** Uses the difference between the image pixels and the background.

- ◆ **Alpha Channel.** Uses an embedded alpha channel.

- ◆ **Photoshop Path.** Uses an embedded path.

- ◆ **Graphic Frame.** Uses the frame of the graphic object.

- ◆ **Same As Clipping.** Uses the clipping path shape for the graphic.

6 Select the **Include Inside Edges** check box to wrap text inside holes in the graphic, path, or alpha channel.

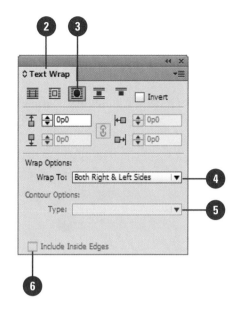

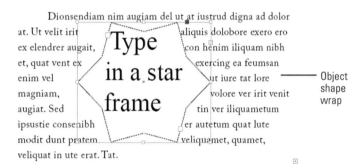

Object shape wrap

Creating Type Outlines

The Create Outlines command converts characters in a text frame into a separate object with a path. Some characters, such as "A" or "B," that contain an interior shape (known as a counter) are converted into compound objects. After you create an outline, you can reshape the path, use it as a mask object, fill it with a gradient or a mesh, or use it in a compound object. When you create outlines, the fill and stroke attributes and any appearances of the type are applied to the outlines. Before you use the Create Outlines command, it's a good idea to make a copy of the text frame or your document as a backup to preserve a copy of the original text frame.

Create Type Outlines

1. Select the **Selection** tool on the Tools panel.

2. Select the text frame or select characters.

3. Click the **Type** menu, and then click **Create Outlines**.

Type outlines

Adding Page Numbers to Continued Text

When you enter or import text for an article or story that you want to continue on another page, you can add a page number in a separate text frame to the bottom of the article or story as a jump line to where it continues. The continuation page number is typically put in a separate text frame, so the reflow of text doesn't move it. When you change pagination in a document, the continuation page numbers are automatically updated.

Add Page Numbers to Continued Text

1. Select the **Type** tool on the Tools panel.

2. Drag to create a text frame for the page number.

3. Select the **Selection** tool on the Tools panel, and then drag to move the text frame so that it touches or overlaps the frame containing the story you want to continue on another page.

4. Select the **Type** tool on the Tools panel, click in the text frame, and then type text you want to appear next to the page number, such as *Continued on* or *Continued from*.

5. Click the **Type** menu, point to **Insert Special Character**, point to **Marker**, and then click **Next Page Number** or **Previous Page number**.

6. Shift-click to select the text frame and the frame containing the story, click the **Object** menu, and then click **Group** to keep both together.

Adobe· Flash Professional On Demand

Copyright © by Perspection, Inc.
All rights reserved. No part of this book shall be reproduced, stored in a retrieval system, or transmitted by any means, electronic, mechanical, photocopying, recording, or otherwise, without written permission from the publisher. No patent liability is assumed with respect to the use of the information contained herein. Although every precaution has been taken in the preparation of this book, the publisher and author assume no responsibility for errors or omissions. Nor is any liability assumed for damages resulting from the use of the information contained herein.

Continued on 3

Adobe· Flash Professional On Demand

Copyright © by Perspection, Inc.
All rights reserved. No part of this book shall be reproduced, stored in a retrieval system, or transmitted by any means, electronic, mechanical, photocopying, recording, or otherwise, without written permission from the publisher. No patent liability is assumed with respect to the use of the information contained herein. Although every precaution has been taken in the preparation of this book, the publisher and author assume no responsibility for errors or omissions. Nor is any liability assumed for damages resulting from the use of the information contained herein.

Continued on 3

Working With Different Languages

If you work with languages, such as English, French, or Greek, you can specify a language for the document in the Character or Control panel. If you work with non-western languages, you can set options in Advanced Type preferences or on the Options menu in the Paragraph panel to use Adobe World-Ready Composer (WRC)—a GUI-less, scriptable methods—to display the correct word shaping and options. You can enable Single-line Composer or Every-line composer to base text justification on individual lines or paragraphs. WRC supports Indian languages as well as east asian languages, including Japanese, Chinese, and Korea, as well as mixed language use. Some languages require a language specific version of InDesign; see Adobe for details.

Change Text Language

1 Select the **Type** tool on the Tools panel, and then select the text that you want to change.

♦ You can also select the **Selection** tool, and then click the text frame to change all text in the frame.

2 Select the **Character** panel.

♦ Click the **Type** menu, and then click **Character**.

3 Click the **Language** list arrow, and then select the available language you want from the list.

♦ If the language you want is not available from the list, you need to download and install the font on your system. You can get fonts from Adobe Creative Cloud. See the Adobe Creative Cloud web site for details.

See Also

See "Setting Advanced Type Preferences" on page 488 for more information on setting options for language usage with Adobe Composers.

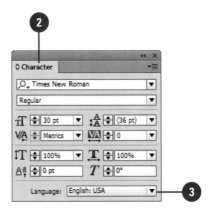

For Your Information

Getting Additional Language Support

Some language specific versions of InDesign, such as Arabic and Hebrew, support additional text features in the Paragraph and Character panels, such as text direction, story direction, and binding directions, as well as automatic Kashida insertion (for text justification), Diacritical marks (a glyph for consonant length or short vowels), and Diacritical coloring. If the options are not available in the panels or Options menu, you don't have the supported language edition.

Placing and Working with Graphics

Introduction

You can use InDesign's Place command to insert artwork into an open document. InDesign lets you place graphic files saved in Illustrator AI, Photoshop PSD, JPEG, EPS, TIFF, PICT (Mac), and PDF (Portable Document Format) formats, to name a few. You can even place another InDesign INDD file into a document. With the Place command, you can place multiple graphics of different types at the same time. If you need more control over the import and placement of graphics in your document, you can display and use an import dialog box for the type of graphic that you want to place.

When you place graphics, InDesign loads them into a graphic preview cursor, which you can use to place them into a new or existing frame. When you place a graphic, InDesign creates a link to the original file. You can display and work with linked graphics in the Links panel.

Before you can work with the graphic in a frame, you need to select it first. You have several options depending on what you want to accomplish. You can select the frame and graphic, just the frame, or just the graphic. When you place a graphic into a frame, it doesn't always fit the way you want. You can automatically resize the graphic to fill the entire frame or proportionally fill the frame. In some cases you want to place a graphic on top of an existing graphic. This is called a nesting graphic. For example, you can place a graphic in a rectangle frame, and then place another graphic in a circle frame inside the rectangle frame.

When you place multiple graphics in a document, the display performance of your screen can slow down. You can change display resolution settings for the entire document or for individual graphics to improve performance.

What You'll Do

Place Graphics

Place Graphics with Options

Set Place Import Options

Place Multiple Graphics

Place Graphics from Adobe Bridge

Add Captions to Graphics

Copy or Move Graphics

Use the Links Panel

Manage Linked Graphics

Edit a Linked Graphic

Display XMP Graphic Information

Create Specialty Frames for Graphics

Select and Move Frames and Graphics

Fit Graphics in Frames

Nest Graphics in Frames

Format Graphics in Frames

Control Graphics Display Performance

Add Alt Text to Graphics

Placing Graphics

You can use InDesign's Place command to insert artwork into an open document. InDesign lets you place graphic files saved in Illustrator AI, Photoshop PSD, BMP, JPEG, EPS, PNG, TIFF, GIF, WMF, PICT (Mac), SCT, DCS, and PDF formats, to name a few. You can even place another InDesign INDD file into a document. You can place multiple graphics of different types at the same time. When you place graphics, InDesign loads them into a graphic preview cursor, which you can use to place them into a new or existing frame. When you draw a new frame, the frame constrains to the proportions of the graphic unless you hold down Shift. The scale is displayed as part of the loaded cursor.

Place a Graphic

1. To place a graphic into an existing frame (rectangle, elliptical, or polygon), select the frame using the **Selection** or **Direct Selection** tool on the Tools panel.

2. Click the **File** menu, and then click **Place**.

3. Click the **Files of Type** (Win) or **Enable** (Mac) list arrow, and then click **Importable Files**, or select a specific file format.

4. Navigate to the location with the file you want to import.

5. Select the graphic file you want to place.

6. Select the **Replace Selected Item** check box to replace the selected item with the imported graphic.

7. Click **Open**.

   The imported graphic is placed in a loaded preview cursor.

8. Click or drag a rectangle frame with the loaded cursor to place the graphic in a new frame, or click in an empty frame to place it in an existing frame.

   ◆ To place the graphic in an existing frame with a graphic, Alt (Win) or Option (Mac) click in the frame to add the graphic to it.

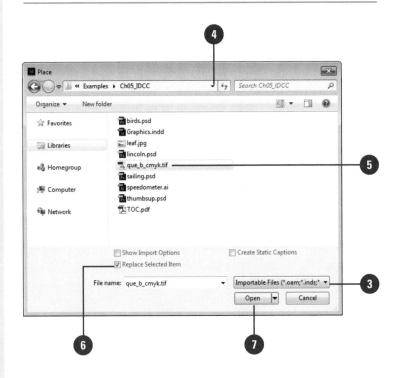

Placing Graphics with Options

If you need more control over the import and placement of graphics in your document, you can display and use an import dialog box for the type of graphic that you want to place. For example, when you import Illustrator artwork, you can specify import options to select individual artboards, layers, and a transparent background. When you import most images, such as TIFF and JPEG, you can specify import options to apply a clipping path along with an Alpha Channel and specify a color profile. For a Photoshop image, you can also select layers.

Place Graphics with Options

1. Click the **File** menu, and then click **Place**.

2. Click the **Files of Type** (Win) or **Enable** (Mac) list arrow, and then click **Importable Files**.

3. Navigate to the location with the file you want to import.

4. Select the file you want to place.

5. Select the **Show Import Options** check box to select import options.

6. Click **Open**.

   ◆ If you don't select the Show Import Options check box, you can press Shift as you click the Open button to show import options.

7. Select the options you want. Options vary depending on the imported file format.

8. Click **OK**.

   The imported graphic is placed in a loaded cursor.

9. Click or drag a rectangle frame with the loaded cursor to place the graphic where you want it in your document.

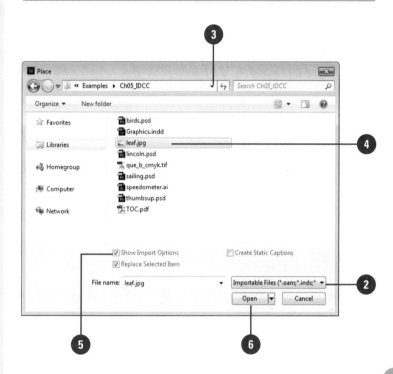

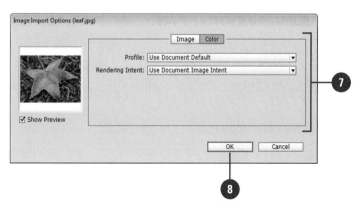

Setting Place Import Options

When you import graphics saved from Photoshop, Illustrator, or other compatible graphics programs, you can specify import options to use the same transparency as the original file, set the visibility of layers, and use clipping paths, which allows you to use only part of a graphic (the rest is transparent). If you save a Photoshop file with an Alpha Channel (white or shades of gray) as a PSD, TIFF or JPEG, or with a clipping path as a PSD, TIFF or EPS, you can import the graphic into your document and retain the Alpha Channel transparency or clipping path. For Photoshop, Illustrator, InDesign, and PDF files, you can specify which layers in the file you want to import into your document.

Import Layers or Transparency

1. Click the **File** menu, and then click **Place**.

2. Select the file (PSD, AI, INDD, or PDF) you want to place.

3. Select the **Show Import Options** check box to select import options.

4. Click **Open**.

   The Place PDF or Image Import Options dialog box appears.

5. To set transparency, click the **General** tab, and then select the **Transparent Background** check box.

6. To set layer visibility, click the **Layers** tab, and then do any of the following:

   ◆ Show or Hide Layers. Click the visibility icon.

   ◆ Update Links. Select options to reset/use or maintain layer visibility overrides.

7. Click **OK**.

8. Click or drag a rectangle frame with the loaded cursor to place the graphic.

9. To edit the layers options, click the **Object** menu, and then click **Object Layer Options**.

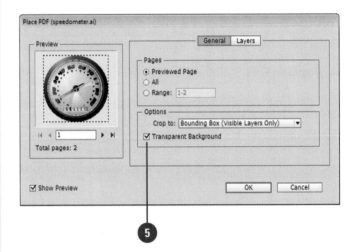

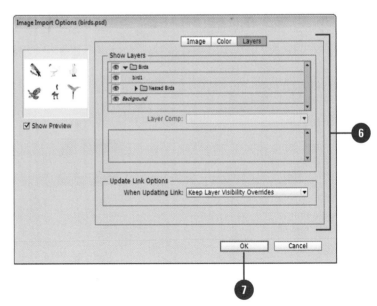

Import and Modify Clipping Paths or Alpha Channels

① Click the **File** menu, and then click **Place**.

② Select the file (PSD, TIFF, JPEG, or EPS) with the clipping path or Alpha Channel you want to place.

③ Select the **Show Import Options** check box to select import options.

④ Click **Open**.

The Image Import Options dialog box appears.

⑤ Click the **Image** tab.

⑥ To import clipping paths, select the **Apply Photoshop Clipping Path** check box.

⑦ To select an Alpha Channel, click the **Alpha Channel** list arrow, and then select the one you want or select **None**.

⑧ Click **OK**.

⑨ Click or drag a rectangle frame with the loaded cursor to place the graphic.

⑩ To edit the clipping path, do any of the following:

◆ **Modify Path Shape.** Click the **Selection** tool, select the path, and drag points and handles.

◆ **Convert Path to a Frame.** Select the path, click the **Object** menu, point to **Clipping Path**, and then click **Convert Clipping Path to Frame**.

◆ **Set Path Options.** Click the **Object** menu, point to **Clipping Path**, and then click **Options**.

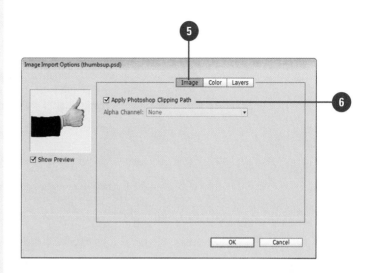

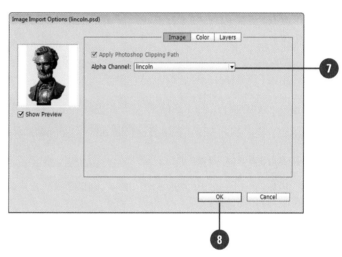

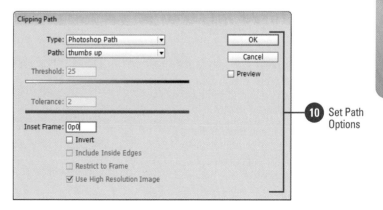

⑩ Set Path Options

Placing Multiple Graphics

With the Place command, you can place multiple graphics of different types at the same time. When you place graphics, InDesign loads them into a graphic preview cursor, which you can use to place them into a new or existing frame. A number appears in the loaded cursor indicating the number of loaded graphics. With the loaded cursor, you can also create a contact sheet to place multiple graphics in a grid arrangement with the number of rows, columns, and spacing you want.

Place Multiple Graphics

1. Click the **File** menu, and then click **Place**.

2. Click the **Files of Type** (Win) or **Enable** (Mac) list arrow, and then click **Importable Files**.

3. Navigate to the location with the files you want to import.

4. Select the graphic files you want to place.

   ◆ To select multiple files, use the Ctrl (Win) or ⌘ (Mac) key for individual files or the Shift key for a range of files.

5. Click **Open**.

   The imported graphic is placed in a loaded preview cursor. A number appears indicating the number of loaded graphics.

   ◆ Use the arrow keys to cycle through the graphic preview in the loaded cursor.

   ◆ Press Esc to delete the graphic in the preview of the loaded cursor.

   ◆ Use Alt (Win) or Option (Mac) to swap the element in the frame with the graphic in the loaded cursor.

6. Click or drag a rectangle frame with the loaded cursor to place each graphic in a new frame, or click in an empty frame to place the graphic in an existing frame.

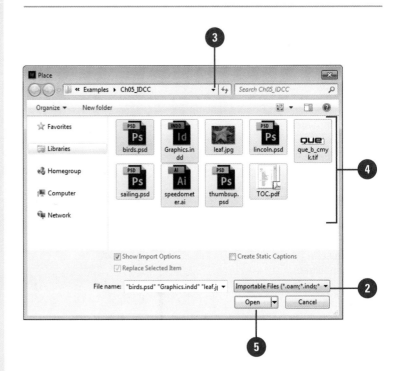

Place Multiple Graphics to Create a Contact Sheet

1. Click the **File** menu, and then click **Place**.

2. Click the **Files of Type** (Win) or **Enable** (Mac) list arrow, and then click **Importable Files**.

3. Navigate to the location with the file you want to import.

4. Select the graphic files you want to place.

   ◆ To select multiple files, use the Ctrl (Win) or ⌘ (Mac) key for individual files or the Shift key for a range of files.

5. Click **Open**.

   The imported graphic is placed in a loaded preview cursor. A number appears indicating the number of loaded graphics.

   ◆ Use the arrow keys to cycle through the graphic preview in the loaded cursor.

   ◆ Press Esc to delete the preview graphic in the loaded cursor.

   ◆ Use Alt (Win) or Option (Mac) to swap the element in the frame with the graphic in the loaded cursor.

6. Ctrl (Win) or ⌘ (Mac)+Shift+drag a rectangle frame with the loaded cursor to place the graphics.

   ◆ Grid. Before you release the mouse, use the arrow keys (Up and Down for rows or Right and Left for columns) to adjust the grid.

   ◆ Gutter. Before you release the mouse, use the Page Up or Page Down keys, or hold down Ctrl (Win) or ⌘ (Mac) and press the arrows keys to change the gutter space.

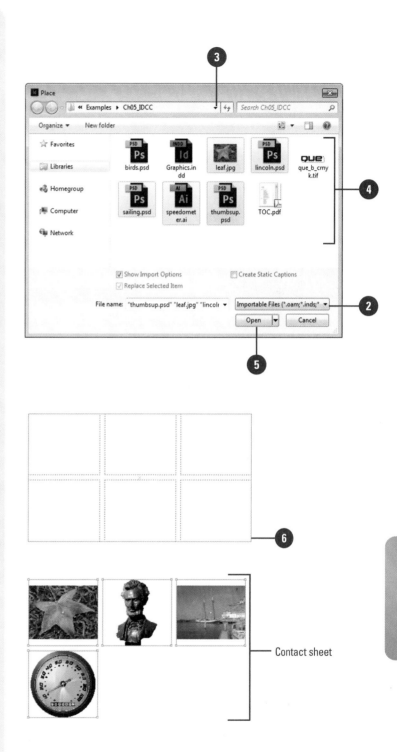

Contact sheet

Placing Graphics from Adobe Bridge

Adobe Bridge CC—available for download from Creative Cloud—allows you to search, sort, filter, manage, and process files one at a time or in batches. You can open or place graphics directly into InDesign by using the Open With (Adobe InDesign) or Place (In InDesign) commands in Bridge from the File menu. You can also drag thumbnails from Bridge into an open InDesign document window.

Browse and Open Graphics with Adobe Bridge

1 Click the **Go to Bridge** button on the Application bar or click the **File** menu, and then click **Browse in Bridge**.

◆ If prompted, install or update from Adobe Application Manager.

Adobe Bridge opens, displaying files and folders on your computer.

2 Navigate to the location with the file you want to place.

3 Select the graphic thumbnail representing the file that you want to open in your InDesign document.

4 Click the **File** menu, point to **Open With**, and then click **Adobe InDesign CC**.

Did You Know?

You can locate a linked graphic in Bridge from InDesign. In the Links panel, select the graphic name, click the Options button, and then click Reveal In Bridge.

Place Graphics with Adobe Bridge

1. Click the **Go to Bridge** button on the Application bar or click the **File** menu, and then click **Browse in Bridge**.

   ◆ If prompted, install or update from Adobe Application Manager.

   Adobe Bridge opens, displaying files and folders on your computer.

2. Navigate to the location with the file you want to place.

3. Select the graphic thumbnail that represents the file you want to place in your InDesign document.

4. Click the **File** menu, point to **Place**, and then click **In InDesign**.

   ◆ **Drag to InDesign.** Drag the graphic from Bridge to the InDesign icon on the taskbar (Win) or Dock (Mac), hold for a moment to display InDesign, release the mouse (loaded cursor), and then drag to create a frame for the graphic.

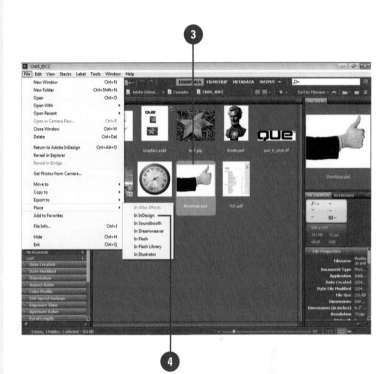

Did You Know?

You can change XMP data for a graphic. Click the Go to Bridge button on the Application bar, locate and select the image you want, select the Metadata panel, click the Edit button for a data item, enter data, and then click the Apply button (check mark) at the bottom of the panel.

Adding Captions to Graphics

A caption is a description that appears below a graphic. Within InDesign, you can create static or live caption. A static caption remains the same unless you manually modify it, while a live caption can change if the graphic is updated or the metadata changes. A caption is placed in a text frame. You can create a caption from an existing graphic or while placing a graphic. When you create a caption, InDesign creates the text—either static text or variable text—based on the current caption settings. A live caption displays a string of variable text. If you move a live caption text frame to another graphic, the caption display changes.

Setup and Create a Caption

1. Click the **Object** menu, point to **Captions**, and then click **Caption Setup**.

2. Click the **Metadata** list arrow, select the caption data you want, and then type the text you want before and after the metadata.

3. To add multiple rows of metadata, click the **Plus sign**, and then repeat Step 2.

   ◆ To remove a row of metadata, click the Minus sign next to it.

4. Specify any of the following:

   ◆ **Alignment.** Specify where to place the caption.

   ◆ **Offset.** Specify the spacing between the text frame and graphic.

   ◆ **Paragraph Style.** Specify a paragraph style for the text.

   ◆ **Layer.** Specify which layer to place the caption.

   ◆ **Group Caption With Image.** Select to group the caption with the graphic.

5. Click **OK**.

6. To add a caption, select the graphic, click the **Object** menu, point to **Captions**, and then click **Generate Static Caption**, or click **Generate Live Caption**.

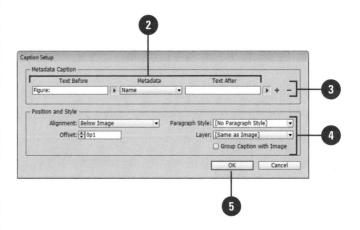

Define and Create a Caption Using Variables

1. Click the **Type** menu, point to **Text Variables**, and then click **Define**.

2. Click **New** to create a new variable or select a variable, and then click **Edit** to change an existing one.

3. Type or revise the name.

4. Click the **Type** list arrow, and then click **Metadata Caption**.

5. Click the **Metadata** list arrow, select the caption data you want, and then type the text you want before and after the metadata.

6. Click **OK**.

7. Click **Done**.

8. Create a text frame for the caption with the **Text** tool, and then click to place the insertion point in the text frame.

9. Click the **Type** menu, point to **Text Variables**, point to **Insert Variable**, and then click **Live Metadata Caption: Name** or another variable.

10. Move the caption text frame next to graphic frame or group the caption frame to the graphic frame.

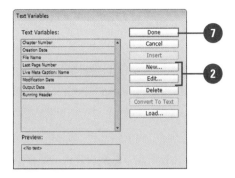

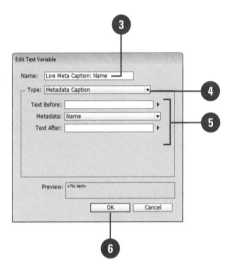

Did You Know?

You can create a static caption while placing a graphic. Click the File menu, click Place, select a graphic file, select the Generate Static Captions check box, and then click Open.

You can convert a live caption to a static caption. Select the live caption, click the Object menu, point to Captions, and then click Convert To Static Caption.

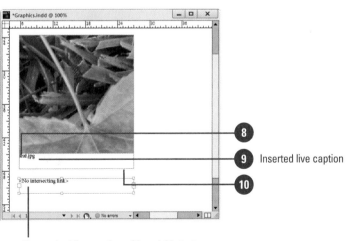

Inserted live caption

Unattached live caption with variable text

Copying or Moving Graphics

Instead of using the Place command, you can also copy and paste or drag-and-drop graphics from other programs directly into frames in your document. When you copy and paste graphics, InDesign converts the image to a compatible format during the transfer and embeds the graphic in your document at full resolution. **Embedding** inserts a copy from one document into another. An embedded graphic doesn't appear in the Links panel. When you drag-and-drop a graphic, InDesign creates a link just like when using the Place command.

Copy or Move Graphics

1. Open the program with the graphic that you want to copy or move into your InDesign document.

2. Select the graphic you want to use in InDesign.

3. Click the **Edit** menu, and then click **Copy** or **Cut**.

4. Close the program and switch back to InDesign.

5. Select the frame in which you want to place the graphic.

6. Click the **Edit** menu, and then click **Paste Into**.

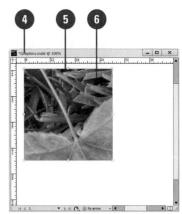

Drag and Drop Graphics

1. Open the program with the graphic that you want to copy into your InDesign document together with the InDesign program.

2. Select the graphic you want to use in InDesign.

3. Drag the graphic from the original program into your InDesign document.

Using the Links Panel

When you place a graphic, InDesign creates a link to the original file. **Linking** displays information stored in one document (the **source file**) in another (the **destination file**). You can edit the linked object from either file, although changes are stored in the source file. If you break the link between a linked object and its source file, the object becomes embedded. **Embedding** inserts a copy from one document into another. You can display and work with linked graphics in the Links panel. The Links panel allows you to relink a missing graphic, display a linked graphic, update a linked graphic, or edit a linked graphic in another program. Special icons appear next to linked graphics indicating a missing or modified link. You can also sort items and display information about a linked graphic, such as name, color space (mode), dimension (resolution), scale, format, and the path to the source in the Links panel.

Display Linked Graphic Information in the Links Panel

1. Select the **Links** panel.
   - Click the **Window** menu, and then click **Links**.

   TIMESAVER *Press Shift+Ctrl+D (Win) or Shift+⌘+D (Mac).*

2. Select the linked graphic for which you want to display information.

3. Click the **Show/Hide Link Information** triangle button on the panel.
   - You can click the **Next** and **Previous** button to view links.

4. Scroll down the list as needed to review the information for the selected linked graphic.

5. To sort items in the Links panel, click the **Name**, **Status** icon, **Page** icon, or **Type** icon at the top of the panel to sort items in the list. Click the icon again to change the sort order.

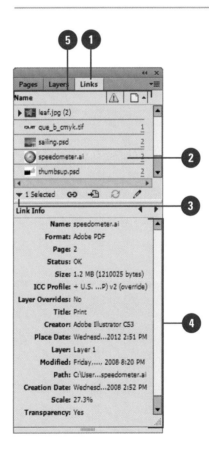

Managing Linked Graphics

After you link or embed a graphic image file into an InDesign document, you can use the Links panel in InDesign to manage and work with the files. The Links panel displays a list of all the linked or embedded (contained within the document) files in your document. You can use the Links panel to update, replace, or relink a graphic image file. If a linked file is moved from its original location, you need to repair the link the next time you open the document. If a linked file needs to be updated, a warning icon appears in the Links panel to let you know. If you place the same graphic in multiple locations, the link collapses into a single row in the Links panel, which you can expand using the triangle.

Replace a Linked Graphic

1. Select the **Links** panel.

   ◆ Click the **Window** menu, and then click **Links**.

2. Select the linked graphic that you want to relink.

3. Click the **Relink** button on the panel.

4. Select the graphic file that you want to use as the replacement in the active document.

5. Click **Open**.

   ◆ You can also select the image in the document window, click the **File** menu, click **Place**, select a replacement image, select the **Replace Selected Item** check box, and then click **Open**.

Did You Know?

You can change a linked graphic to an embedded graphic. Select the Links panel, select the linked graphic, click the Options button, and then click Embed Link. If you prefer the graphic to be linked, select the embedded graphic (with the embedded icon), click the Options button, click Unembed Link, and then click Yes.

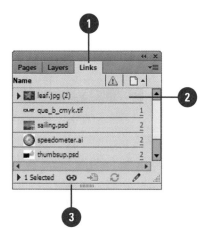

Work with Linked Graphics

1. Select the **Links** panel.
   - Click the **Window** menu, and then click **Links**.

2. Select the linked graphic that you want to change.
   - **Expand/Collapse Multiple Links to Same Source.** Click the **Expand/Collapse** triangle in the Links panel.

   To enable or disable this option, click the **Options** button, click **Panel Options**, select or deselect the **Collapse Multiple Links to Same Same Source** check box, and then click **OK**.

3. Do any of the following:
   - **Update a Link.** Click the **Update Link** button on the panel.
   - **Update All Links.** Click the **Options** button, and then click **Update All Links**.
   - **Locate a Placed Graph in a Document.** Click the **Go To Link** button on the panel.
   - **Edit Original.** Click the **Edit Original** button on the panel to open the program that created the file and edit it.
   - **View Information.** Double-click the graphic name, and then view the link information at the bottom of the panel.
   - **Change from Linked to Embedded.** Click the **Options** button, and then click **Embed Link**.

Warning icon

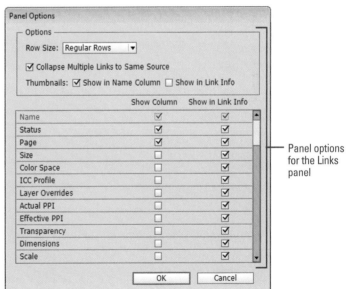

Panel options for the Links panel

Editing a Linked Graphic

When you link a graphic into an InDesign document, you need to edit the graphic in the source file using the original or a compatible program. You can open the program from Windows Explorer or the Finder and then open the graphic file, or you can have InDesign do it for you. You can use the Edit Original command to edit the file with the program associated with that particular file extension, or go to the Edit With submenu to select an editing program. If you select multiple graphics, the Edit Original command opens all the images in their respective editing programs.

Edit a Linked Graphic in the Source

1 Select the **Links** panel.

- Click the **Window** menu, and then click **Links**.

2 Select the linked graphic that you want to edit.

3 Do any of the following:

- **Edit Original.** Click the **Edit Original** button on the Links panel.

  If you selected multiple graphics, each graphic is opened in their respective editing program.

- **Edit With.** Click the **Options** button, point to **Edit With**, and then select an editing program.

  The editing program opens, displaying the linked graphic.

4 Make the changes you want to the linked graphic.

5 Click the **File** menu, and then click **Save**.

6 Click the **File** menu, and then click **Exit** or **Quit**.

  Your saved changes are updated in your document.

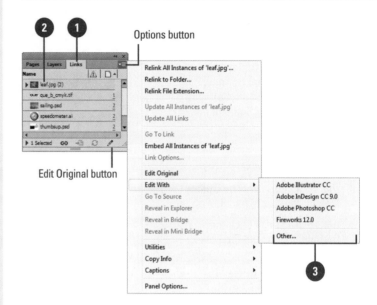

Options button

Edit Original button

Displaying XMP Graphic Information

When you place a graphic into an InDesign document, the graphic file includes information and data about itself. This data is saved with the file as metadata in the XMP format (Extensible Metadata Platform), and can be recognized and accessed by InDesign or any other application, such as Adobe Bridge, that reads and edits XMP metadata. For example, if an image is a photograph, the metadata includes the type of image, where the image was shot, the camera used, shutter speed, f-stop, and other information, such as author and copyright. You can do the same with video and audio data, too.

Display XMP Metadata for a Linked Image

1 Select the **Links** panel.

◆ Click the **Window** menu, and then click **Links**.

2 Select the linked graphic for which you want to display information.

3 Click the **Options** button, point to **Utilities**, and then click **XMP File Info**.

4 Click the different tabs to display information about the graphic.

5 Review the information and enter any new information (if available) you have related to the graphic.

6 Click **OK**.

See Also

See *"Inserting File Information"* on page 478 for more information on the types of information available in the File Information dialog box.

See *"Placing Graphics from Adobe Bridge"* on page 148 for information on changing metadata for a selected graphic in Adobe Bridge.

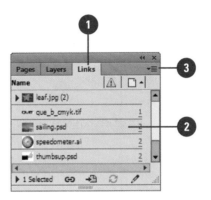

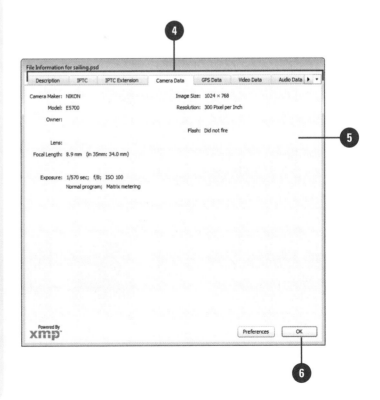

Creating Specialty Frames for Graphics

Instead of using the standard rectangle, ellipse, or polygon frames to place graphics, you can create and use specialty frames. A specialty frame is a vector-based compound path. You can create a compound path from one or more standard frames or text in InDesign, or you can import one from another vector-based program, such as Adobe Illustrator, that uses the AICB (Adobe Illustrator Clipboard). When you combine multiple frames into one compound path, the placed graphic appears across all the frames. You can create unique specialty frames from text characters. The Create Outlines command converts characters in a text frame into a compound path. If you no longer want to use a compound path, you can use the Release Compound Path command to split the compound path up into individual frames.

Create and Release a Compound Path as a Frame

1. Select the **Selection** or **Direct Selection** tool on the Tools panel.

2. Select the frames that you want to use in the compound path.

   ◆ If the frames overlap, a transparent hole appears where the frames overlap.

3. Click the **Object** menu, point to **Paths**, and then click **Make Compound Path**.

   A compound path displays diagonal lines across the entire set of frames instead of individual frames.

4. To release a compound path, select the compound path, click the **Object** menu, point to **Paths**, and then click **Release Compound Path**.

   If there is a graphic in the compound path, it will only appear in the first frame after you release the compound path. The other frames will be empty.

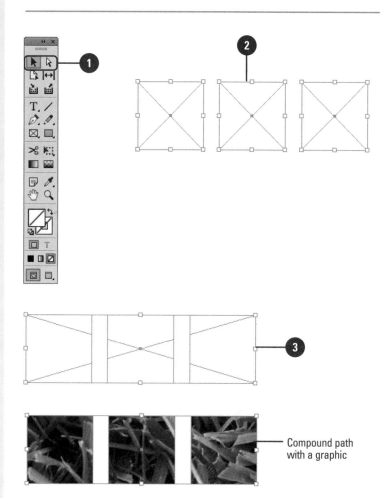

Compound path with a graphic

Create Type Outlines as Frames

1. Select the **Selection** tool on the Tools panel.

2. Select the text frame or double-click the text and then select characters.

3. Click the **Type** menu, and then click **Create Outlines**.

   InDesign creates a compound path from the text in the text frame.

   If you want to place different graphics in each of the letter frames, you need to ungroup (if needed) and release the compound path for the entire group first.

4. To release the compound path, click the **Object** menu, point to **Paths**, and then click **Release Compound Path**.

Import Paths as Frames

1. Open the program with the path that you want to copy into your InDesign document together with the InDesign program.

2. Drag the path from the original program into your InDesign document.

   When a black line appears around the boundaries of your document window, release the mouse to place the path.

Did You Know?

You can also use copy and paste.
Instead of using drag-and-drop, you can also use copy and paste to import a path from another vector-based program.

Outline with a graphic

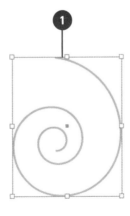

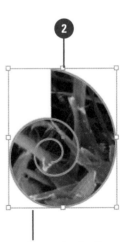

Imported path with a graphic

Selecting and Moving Frames and Graphics

Before you can work with the graphic in a frame, you need to select it first. There are two bounding boxes around the graphic. One for the frame (blue) and another for the graphic (brown). You have several options depending on what you want to accomplish. You can select the frame and graphic, just the frame, or just the graphic. If you want to resize the frame as well as the graphic inside, you can select them both or use the Auto-Fit option. With the Auto-Fit option enabled, when you resize the frame, the graphic inside automatically resizes too. If you want to keep the frame the current size and resize the graphic, you need to just select the graphic and not the frame. The Selection and Direct Selection tools allow you to select the parts you want. To reposition the graphic and not the frame, you can use the Selection tool and content grabber (which replaces the Position tool).

Select and Move Frames and Graphics

◆ **Select the Frame or Graphic.** Select the **Selection** tool on the Tools panel, double-click the frame or graphic to select the other (it no longer switches to the Direct Selection tool).

◆ **Select and Move the Frame and Graphic.** Select the **Selection** tool on the Tools panel, click the frame to show a bounding box, and then drag the selection.

◆ **Select and Move the Graphic within the Frame.** Select the **Direct Selection** tool on the Tools pane, point to the graphic inside the frame, point to the content grabber (a circle), and then drag the graphic with the Hand cursor, or select the **Direct Selection** tool on the Tools panel, click inside the frame to show a bounding box with the Hand cursor, and then drag the graphic.

◆ **Select and Move the Frame.** Select the **Direct Selection** tool on the Tools panel, click the edge of the frame to show the points on the frame, Alt+click (Win) or Option (Mac)+click the frame edge again to select all the points, release the keys, and then drag the frame.

Frame selected

Content grabber

Graphic selected

Graphic moved

Use the Auto-Fit Option to Resize Frames and Graphics

1. Click the **Object** menu, point to **Fitting**, and then click **Frame Fitting Options**.

2. Select the **Preview** check box to view your results in the document window.

3. Select the **Auto-Fit** check box to resize a graphic automatically when you resize frame.

   TIMESAVER *Click the Auto-Fit option in the Control panel.*

4. Click **OK**.

5. To clear frame fitting options, click the **Object** menu, point to **Fitting**, and then click **Clear Frame Fitting Options**.

Did You Know?

You can show or hide content grabber. Click the View menu, point to Extras, and then click Show Content Grabber or Hide Content Grabber.

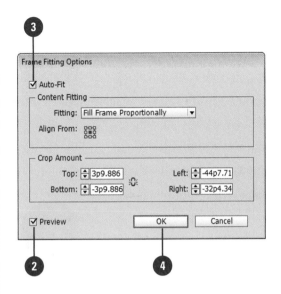

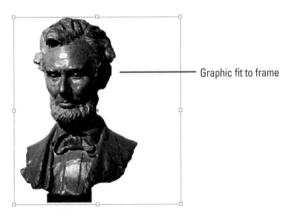

Graphic fit to frame

Fitting Graphics in Frames

When you place a graphic into a frame, it doesn't always fit the way you want. You can automatically resize the graphic to fill the entire frame or proportionally fill the frame. You can resize the graphic to fit the frame using commands on the Fitting submenu on the Object menu. If you want more control over how the graphic fits the frame, you can use the Frame Fitting Options dialog box. Instead of sizing frames and graphics separately, you can use the Auto-Fit option to resize them together. If you don't want to use the frame fitting options, you can clear them.

Fit Graphics in Frames

① Select the **Selection** or **Direct Selection** tool on the Tools panel.

② Select the frame or the graphic.

③ Click the **Object** menu, point to **Fitting**, and then use any of the following:

◆ Resize the Graphic to the Frame. Click **Fit Content to Frame**.

◆ Resize the Graphic Proportionally to the Frame. Click **Fit Content Proportionally**.

◆ Center the Graphic in the Frame. Click **Center Content**.

◆ Resize the Frame to the Graphic. Click **Fit Frame to Content**.

◆ You can also double-click a frame handle to resize it to the graphic; a corner for proportional; a top or bottom for vertical; a right or left for horizontal.

◆ Resize the Graphic to Fill the Frame. Click **Fill Frame Proportionally**.

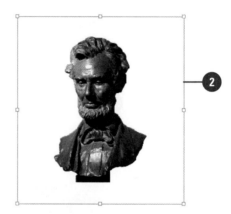

2

Resized graphic to fit frame

Fit Graphics in Frames Using Dialog Box Options

1. Select the **Selection** or **Direct Selection** tool on the Tools panel.

2. Select the frame or the graphic.

3. Click the **Object** menu, point to **Fitting**, and then click **Frame Fitting Options**.

4. Select the **Preview** check box to view your results in the document window.

5. Use any of the following methods:

   ◆ **Auto-Fit.** Select to resize a graphic automatically when you resize frame.

   TIMESAVER *Click the Auto-Fit option in the Control panel.*

   ◆ **Fitting.** Select a fitting option to fit content to the frame, fit content proportionally to the frame, or to fill the frame proportionally.

   ◆ **Align From Reference Point.** Click the square you want to use as the positioning point for graphic fitting adjustments.

   ◆ **Crop Amount.** Specify position values for Top, Bottom, Left, and Right to crop the graphic.

6. Click **OK**.

7. To clear frame fitting options, click the **Object** menu, point to **Fitting**, and then click **Clear Frame Fitting Options**.

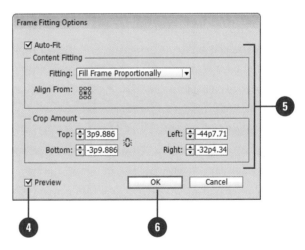

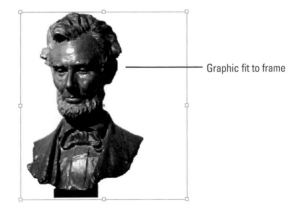

Graphic fit to frame

Nesting Graphics in Frames

In some cases you may want to place a graphic on top of an existing graphic. This is called a nesting graphic. For example, you can place a graphic in a rectangle frame, and then place another graphic in a circle frame inside the rectangle frame. You can also nest a text frame in a graphic frame. Frames can hold multiple levels of nested frames. After you nest graphics in a frame, you can use commands from the Select submenu on the Object menu to select the main container frame or nested frames.

Nest Graphics in a Frame

1. Select the **Selection** tool on the Tools panel.

2. Select the graphic or text frame that you want to place in a graphic frame.

3. Click the **Edit** menu, and then click **Cut** or **Copy**.

4. Select the graphic frame in which you want to place a graphic or text frame.

5. Click the **Edit** menu, and then click **Paste Into**.

6. To select frames, do any of the following:

   ◆ **Main Container.** Click the frame using the **Selection** tool on the Tools panel.

      ◆ You can drag the center point square (cursor changes to a black arrow) to move the object.

   ◆ **Nested Content.** Select the main container, click the **Object** menu, point to **Select**, and then click **Content**.

      ◆ To select other objects, click the **Object** menu, point to **Select**, and then click **Container**.

Formatting Graphics in Frames

If you place a grayscale graphic into your document, you can change the color of the graphic to create a different effect. A grayscale graphics uses black values to display the image, which you can change to a different color. With the Direct Selection tool, simply select the grayscale graphic, and then apply a fill color to it. If you want to lighten the effect, you can change the tint of the color. You can also use the same technique to change the color of the graphic frame fill or stroke.

Color a Grayscale Graphic

1. Select the **Direct Selection** tool on the Tools panel.

2. Select the grayscale graphic that you want to color.

3. Adjust the **Tint** in the Color panel.

4. Select a **Fill** color using the Tools or Color panel.

Did You Know?

You can color a graphic frame. Select the Selection tool on the Tools panel, select the graphic frame, and then select a Fill or Stroke color using the Tools or Color panel.

See Also

See "Fitting Graphics in Frames" on page 160 for more information on displaying graphics in a frame.

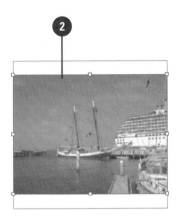

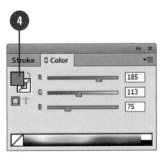

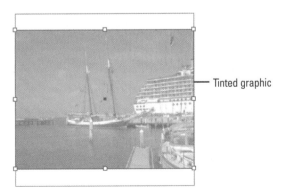

Tinted graphic

Controlling Graphics Display Performance

When you place multiple graphics in a document, the display performance of your screen can slow down. You can change display resolution settings for the entire document or for individual graphics to improve performance. You can set default display performance settings for all documents in the Display Performance preferences dialog box, for the current document on the Display Performance submenu on the View menu, or for individual graphics on the Display Performance submenu from the Object menu.

Change a Graphics Display Performance

1. Click the **View** menu, point to **Display Performance**, and then click **Allow Object-Level Display Settings** to select it.

2. Select the **Selection** or **Direct Selection** tool on the Tools panel.

3. Select the imported graphic.

4. Click the **Object** menu, point to **Display Performance**, and then select a performance option:

   ◆ **Fast Display.** Draws raster images or vector graphics as a gray box. Use to quickly page through documents with a lot of graphics. Best performance, lowest quality.

   ◆ **Typical Display.** Draws a low-resolution image (default). Use to quickly identify parts of a graphic.

   ◆ **High Quality Display.** Draws a high-resolution image. Use to view image details. Lowest performance, highest quality.

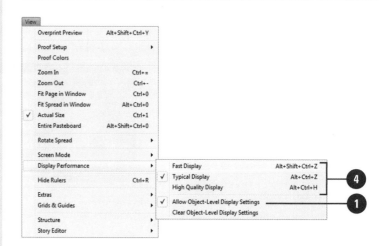

Set Default Display Performance Options

1. Click the **Edit** (Win) or **InDesign** (Mac) menu, point to **Preferences**, and then click **Display Performance**.

2. Click the **Default View** list arrow, and then select a performance option. See the previous page for details.

3. Select the **Preserve Object-Level Display Settings** check box to specify different display performance settings for individual objects.

4. Click the **Adjust View Settings** list arrow, and then select a performance option. See the previous page for details.

   If you want a custom setting, drag the sliders for **Raster Images**, **Vector Graphics**, and **Transparency**.

5. Click the **Interface** category.

6. To specify text and graphic display performance with the Hand tool, drag the **Hand Tool** slider to the setting you want between better performance and higher quality.

   Greeking refers to text or graphics not meant to be readable, such as placeholder text, "lorem ipsum."

7. To enable greeking when you drag vector graphics for improved performance, select the **Greek Vector Graphics on Drag** check box.

8. Click **OK**.

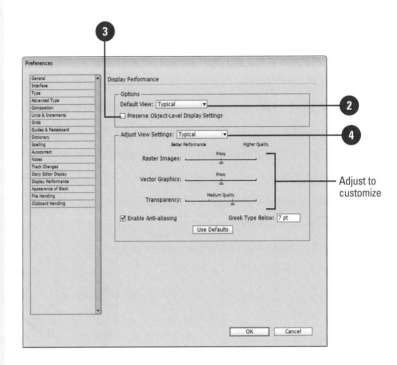

Adjust to customize

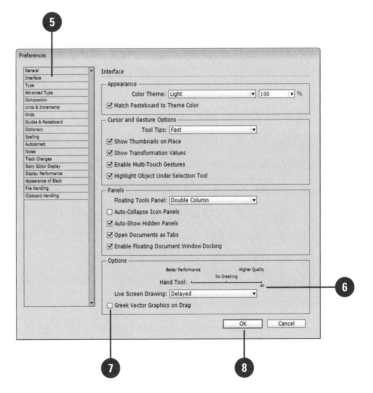

Adding Alt Text to Graphics

Alternative text, or alt text, is a brief text-based description of a graphic used to provide information to screen-readers or assistive devices, or to users when the graphic is not rendered. You can set alt text for a selected graphic by using the Object Export Options dialog box. You can enter alt text manually, use text specified in the document structure (elements marked with XML tags), or use text from metadata in the XMP format (Extensible Metadata Platform) applied to the graphic. You can view and change XMP data in applications like Adobe Bridge. When you import content from Microsoft, InDesign also imports alt text applied to graphics. In InDesign, you can view XMP data for a graphic in the Links panel; see "Displaying XMP Graphic Information," on page 157 for details.

Add Alt Text to Graphics

1. Select the **Selection** tool on the Tools panel.

2. Select the graphic frame or group that you want to add alt text.

3. Click the **Object** menu, and then click **Object Export Options**.

4. Click the **Alt Text** tab.

5. Click the **Alt Text Source** list arrow, and then select an option:

   - **Custom.** Enter text manually.

   - **From Structure.** Use text as specified in the Structure pane; items marked with XML tags.

   - **From XMP: Title, Description, or Headline.** Use data stored in XMP title, description, or headline fields. When XMP data is updated in another application, and the link is updated. When link is updated, the alt text is too.

   - **From Other XMP.** Use data stored in another XMP field. Enter the complete namespace and property name in <ns>:<property> format.

6. Select another object to apply settings; the dialog box stays open.

7. Click **Done**.

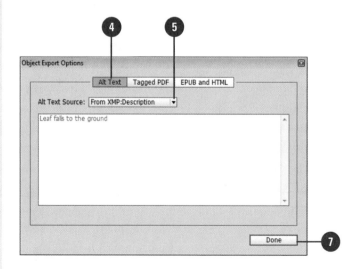

Working with Objects and Layers

Introduction

A frame is a container that holds graphics, text, and shapes. There are three types of frames: unassigned, graphic, and text. The unassigned frame is useful for adding fill and stroke color to a layout. You use the Rectangle, Ellipse, Polygon, and Line tools to create unassigned frames, while you use the Rectangle Frame, Ellipse Frame and Polygon Frame tools to create a graphic frame. A dot appears in the middle of an unassigned frame, while diagonal lines appear in a graphic frame. You can create shapes using unassigned or graphic shapes. You use the Type tool to create a text frame, which appears with small ports to thread text between frames.

With the transformation tools in InDesign, you can quickly move, scale (resize), shear (distort), and rotate an object. InDesign provides several ways to transform objects: tools (Rotate, Scale, and Shear) on the Tools panel, options on the Transform and Control panels, and commands on the Transform submenu on the Object menu.

Layers give you the ability to separate individual elements of your design, and then control how those elements appear. You can think of Layers as a group of transparent sheets stacked on top of each other, where each layer contains a separate aspect of the total design. Having multiple layers allows you to adjust and move each element independently.

What You'll Do

Create Shapes and Lines

Create Multiple Objects in a Grid

Use the Selection Tool

Use the Direct Selection Tool

Resize and Move Objects

Duplicate Objects

Group and Combine Objects

Align and Distribute Objects

Arrange Object Stack Order

Transform Objects

Repeat Object Transformations

Use the Free Transform Tool

Scale, Shear, and Rotate Objects

Lock and Unlock Objects

Hide and Show Objects

Create Inline Objects

Create Anchored Objects

Create and Delete Object Layers

Set Layer Options and Work with Layers

Use the Measure Tool

Creating Shapes

A frame is a container that holds graphics, text, and shapes. There are three types of frames: unassigned, graphic, and text. The unassigned frame is useful for adding fill and stroke color to a layout. You use the Rectangle, Ellipse, and Polygon tools to create unassigned frames, while you use the Rectangle Frame, Ellipse Frame and Polygon Frame tools to create a graphic frame. A dot appears in the middle of an unassigned frame, while diagonal lines appear in a graphic frame. You can create shapes using unassigned or graphic shapes. In addition to creating a polygon shape, you can also use the Polygon Frame tool to create a star shape for type. You can drag to create a frame box to the size you want using the tool tip which displays width and height. If you need a frame box to be an exact size, you can click a blank area with the Rectangle and Ellipse tools or set width and height settings on the Control panel.

Create a Rectangle or Elliptical Shape

1. Select the **Rectangle** or **Rectangle Frame** tool or select the **Ellipse** or **Ellipse Frame** tool on the Tools panel.

   ◆ To create a frame to an exact size, click a blank area, specify the width and height you want, and then click **OK**.

2. Drag to create a rectangle or elliptical frame the size you want using the tool tip width and height.

   ◆ **Draw from the center.** Hold down Alt (Win) or Option (Mac) as you drag.

   ◆ **Constrain to Square or Circle.** Hold down Shift as you drag.

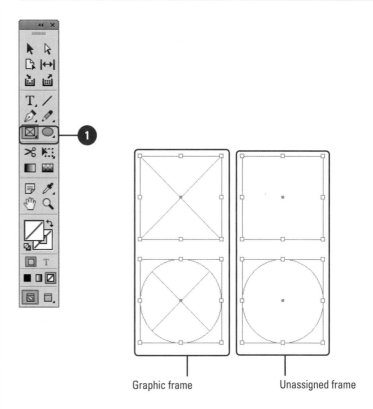

Graphic frame   Unassigned frame

Did You Know?

You can show or hide frame edges.
Click the View menu, point to Extras, and then click Show Frame Edges or Hide Frame Edges.

Create a Polygon Shape

1. Double-click the **Polygon** or **Polygon Frame** tool on the Tools panel.

2. Enter a **Number of Sides** value for the polygon.

3. Leave the **Star Inset** value at 0% to create a polygon.

4. Click **OK**.

5. Drag to create a polygon frame box the size you want using the tool tip width and height.

   ◆ As you drag, press the Up or Down arrow keys to increase or decrease the number of sides.

   ◆ Use the Alt (Win) or Option (Mac) key as you drag to draw from center, or the Shift key to draw a proportional shape.

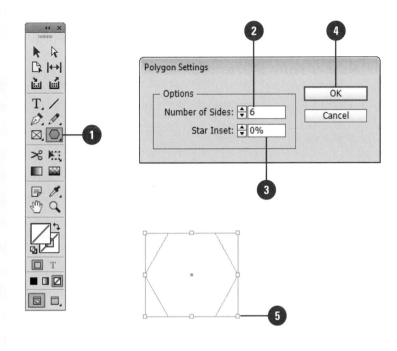

Create a Star Shape

1. Double-click the **Polygon** or **Polygon Frame** tool on the Tools panel.

2. Enter a **Number of Sides** value for the star.

3. Enter a **Star Inset** value. The higher the amount, the sharper the points.

4. Click **OK**.

5. Drag to create a star frame box the size that you want using the tool tip width and height.

   ◆ As you drag, press the Up or Down arrow keys to increase or decrease the number of sides.

   ◆ Use the Alt (Win) or Option (Mac) key as you drag to draw from center, or the Shift key to draw a proportional shape.

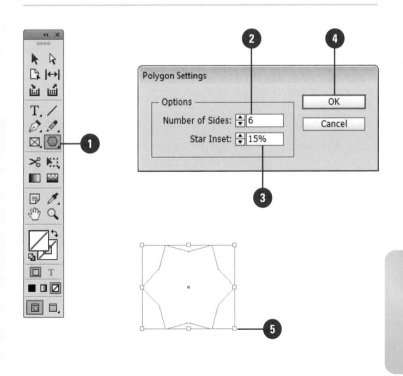

Creating Lines

The Line tool draws perfectly straight lines in any direction you drag your mouse. In InDesign, a line is called a stroke and there is a variety of thicknesses, styles, colors, and fills that can be applied to it using the Control, Stroke, and Color panels. You can also create your own line style for specific types of dashed, dotted or artistic lines. You can draw lines at precise 45- or 90-degree angles by holding down the Shift key as you drag.

Draw a Line

1. Click the **Line** tool on the Tools panel.

   The pointer becomes a crosshair that you can drag on the pasteboard.

2. Select a line **Weight** on the Control panel.

3. Drag to create a line the size you want using the tool tip length.

   ◆ As you drag, hold down the Shift key, and then drag to draw a 45-, 90-, or 180-degree line.

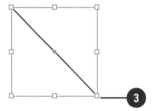

Creating Multiple Objects in a Grid

Instead of creating one shape at a time, you can create a grid of equally spaced frames or objects by using one or two shortcut keys while you drag. You can use any of the frame creation tools on the Tools panel, such as Rectangle, Rectangle Frame, Ellipse, Ellipse Frame, Polygon, Polygon Frame, Line, and Type, to create a grid. The arrow keys allow you to specify how many columns and rows of frames or objects you want to create. If you add the Ctrl (Win) or ⌘ (Mac) keys, you can adjust the spacing between the frames. If multiple column guides appear on the current spread, InDesign uses the gutter width as the spacing between frames. In addition to creating a grid of shapes from scratch, you can also duplicate existing objects into a grid using a similar technique.

Create Multiple Objects in a Grid

1. Select any of the frame creation tools on the Tools panel.

   ◆ The tools include Rectangle, Rectangle Frame, Ellipse, Ellipse Frame, Polygon, Polygon Frame, Line, and Type.

2. Drag to create a frame the size you want using the tool tip width and height.

   ◆ **Columns.** Press the Left and Right arrow keys to change the number of columns.

   ◆ **Rows.** Press the Up and Down arrow keys to change the number of rows.

   ◆ **Space Between Frames.** Hold down Ctrl (Win) or ⌘ (Mac) and press the arrow keys.

Did You Know?

You can duplicate objects in a grid.
Select the Selection tool, select an object, hold down Alt (Win) or Option (Mac) and start to drag, release the Alt or Option key. Press the arrow keys to change the columns and rows. Drag a rectangle to specify the size of the grid.

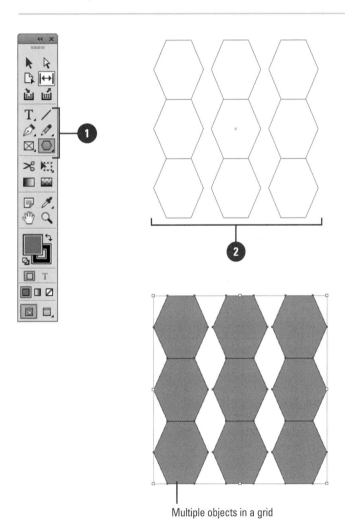

Multiple objects in a grid

Using the Selection Tool

There are several ways to select objects in InDesign. The Selection tool selects entire objects, while the Direct Selection tool selects a point on an object or images inside objects. With the Selection tool, you can select an object's stroke or fill. When you point to an object, InDesign displays the frame edge (or dashed line for a group) in the object's layer color to make it easier to find before you select it, which is useful in Preview mode or with hidden frame edges. After you select one or more objects, you can add or subtract objects to/from the selection. In addition, you can use the Selection tool and drag a marquee to select parts of the object or drag over a portion of it to create a selection rectangle. When you work with graphics, you can double-click the content or graphic frame to select the other (it no longer switches to the Direct Selection tool) or use the content grabber to position the content frame (which replaces the Position tool). If you don't want the content grabber to appear, you can hide it.

Select an Object with the Selection Tool

1. Click the **Selection** tool on the Tools panel.

   The pointer becomes a black arrow. When you point to a selectable object, a black dot appears on the bottom right.

2. Position the arrow on the edge or fill (if present) of the object and then click to select it.

   ◆ You can also drag a marquee across all or part of the object to select the entire object.

   Square resize handles appear on each corner and midpoint line of the object.

3. To add or subtract objects from the selection, hold down the Shift key, and then click unselected objects to add or click selected objects to subtract them from the selection.

   TIMESAVER *Click the Edit menu, and then click Select All or press Ctrl+A (Win) or ⌘+A (Mac) to select everything on the page.*

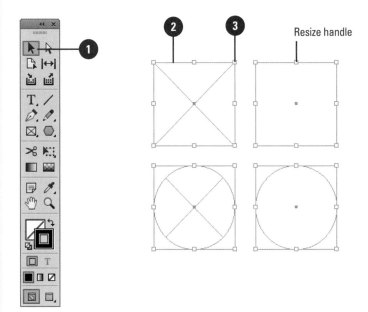

Resize handle

Select a Graphic with the Selection Tool

1. Click the **Selection** tool on the Tools panel.

   The pointer becomes a black arrow. When you point to a selectable graphic, a black dot appears on the bottom right, and a circle appears, known as the content grabber. For a group, the content grabber appears over each frame within it.

   ◆ To show or hide the content grabber, click the **View** menu, point to **Extras**, and then click **Show Content Grabber** or **Hide Content Grabber**.

2. Use any of the following methods:

   ◆ **Highlight Frame Edge.** Point to an object's edge to display it with the color of the object's layer (or a dashed line for a group).

   ◆ **Select and Move the Graphic within the Frame.** Point to the graphic inside the frame, point to the content grabber (a circle), and then drag the graphic with the Hand cursor.

   ◆ **Select the Frame or Graphic.** Double-click the frame or graphic to select the other. For a group, double-clicking an item selects it. Double-clicking the item again, re-selects the group.

Did You Know?

You can delete an object. Select the object that you want to delete, and then press Delete, or click the Edit menu, and then click Clear.

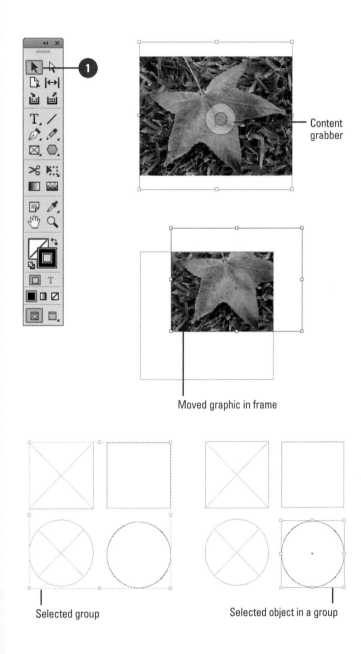

Content grabber

Moved graphic in frame

Selected group

Selected object in a group

Using the Direct Selection Tool

With the Direct Selection tool, you can select a point on an object or graphics inside an object. When you point to or select an object with the Direct Selection tool, path and anchor points appear on the corners of the frame to make it easier to identify and view. You no longer need to select an object to select an anchor point. You can hover over the object to show the anchor points and drag to change the shape of the frame. With the Direct Selection tool, you can also select a graphic. There are two bounding boxes around a graphic frame. One for the frame (blue) and another for the graphic (brown). You can select the frame or graphic. When you select the frame, anchor points appear. When you select the graphic, square resizing handles appear on each corner and midpoint line. When you select a graphic, the Direct Selection tool works like the Selection tool.

Select a Graphic with the Direct Selection Tool

1. Click the **Direct Selection** tool on the Tools panel.

   The cursor becomes a white arrow. When you point to a graphic, the cursor changes to a hand.

   TIMESAVER *Press A to select the Direct Selection tool.*

2. Position the hand cursor on the graphic, then click to select it.

   Square resizing handles appear on each corner and midpoint line of the object.

3. Use any of the following to work with the selected graphic:

   ◆ To move the graphic in the frame, drag the graphic.

   ◆ To resize the graphic, drag the resize handles.

See Also

See "Selecting and Moving Frames and Graphics" on pages 160 for more information on using the Position tool.

Frame selected

Select an Object and Anchor Points with the Direct Selection Tool

1. Click the **Direct Selection** tool on the Tools panel.

   The cursor becomes a white arrow. When you point to a selectable point, a black dot appears near the white arrow. When you point to a selectable edge, a small line appears near the white arrow.

   TIMESAVER *Press A to select the Direct Selection tool.*

2. Position the arrow on the edge or fill (if present) of the object and then point to (hover over) or click to select it.

   ◆ You can also drag a marquee across all or part of the object to select the entire object.

   Small square anchor points appear on each corner.

3. To move an anchor point, drag it to another location.

4. To select an anchor point, click the small square point to select it.

   The anchor point becomes solid.

5. To add or subtract anchor points or segments from the selection, hold down the Shift key, and then click unselected items to add them or selected items to subtract them from the selection.

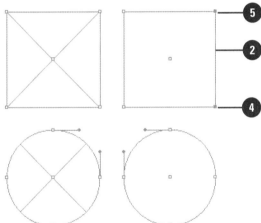

Did You Know?

Selecting graphics is different.
Double-clicking graphics with the Selection tool no longer switches to the Direct Selection tool; it selects the content frame.

Resizing Objects

When an object is too big or small for its location, you can resize the object to fit. When you select one or more objects with the Selection tool, square resizing handles appears on the corner and midpoint, which you can drag to change the size of the object. If you're working with multiple objects, you no longer have to group objects before you resize, scale, or rotate them with the Selection tool; a bounding box appears with resizing handles, which you can use to resize them all together. You can also use Live Distribute to resize the space between objects proportionally. Resizing an object is different than scaling an object. Resizing an object changes the width and height, but the scaling remains the same. Scaling an object changes the width and height by a percentage. If you need to resize an object to an exact size, you can select the object, and then enter specific values in the Control panel.

Resize Objects

1. Select the **Selection** tool on the Tools panel.

2. Select one or more objects that you want to resize.

3. Drag a resizing handle to adjust the size of the objects using the tool tip width and height:

   ◆ Drag a corner handle to resize both width and height. You can also use one or more of the following keys as you drag:

      ◆ **Resize from Center.** Press the Alt (Win) or Option (Mac) key.

      ◆ **Resize Proportionally.** Press the Shift key.

      ◆ **Scale.** Press the Ctrl (Win) or ⌘ (Mac) key.

      ◆ **Resize Space Between Selected Objects.** Press the Spacebar to resize the space between objects proportionally using Live Distribute.

   ◆ Drag a side handle to resize only the width or height.

4. Release the mouse to resize the object to the size you want.

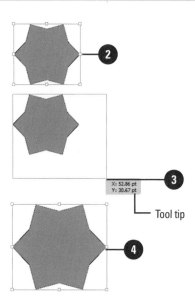

Tool tip

Moving Objects

Moving an object or group of objects is very easy. The simplest way is to drag the edge or fill (if present) of an object. If you want to constrain the movement of the object in multiples of 45 degrees, then use the Shift key as you drag. When you drag an object with Smart Guides enabled, Smart Guides appear automatically to make it easier for you to align objects with other objects. With the Smart Cursor enabled, the cursor displays the current X and Y coordinate values on the page.

Move an Object

1. Select the **Selection** tool on the Tools panel.

2. Select one or more objects that you want to move.

3. Drag the edge or fill (if present) of an object using the Smart Cursor X and Y coordinates.

   ◆ To constrain the movement of the object to multiples of 45 degrees, hold down the Shift key as you drag.

   ◆ If you drag one of several overlapping objects, the selected object remains selected. To select a different object, click a portion of that different object.

Did You Know?

You can enable Smart Guides. Click the View menu, point to Grids & Guides, and then click Smart Guides to select it (a check mark indicates the item is selected).

You can turn on or off the Smart Cursor. Smart cursors display the X and Y values of objects you create, resize, or move them. To turn on or off smart cursors, click the Edit (Win) or InDesign (Mac) menu, point to Preferences, click Interface, select or deselect the Show Transformation Values check box, and then click OK.

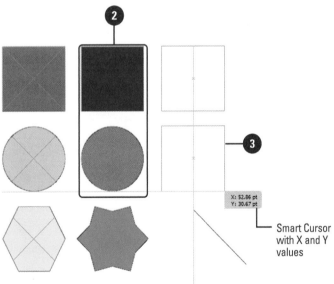

X: 52.86 pt
Y: 30.67 pt

Smart Cursor with X and Y values

Duplicating Objects

Duplicating objects can be a powerful way of creating geometrical art-work. You can duplicate one or more selected objects by dragging them, using keys, copying to and pasting from the Clipboard, or using the Step and Repeat command. While you drag, you can also duplicate existing objects into a grid using keyboard shortcuts. The Step and Repeat command duplicates copies of an object and positions them at specific horizontal and vertical intervals. For example, you can create a span of objects across the page, or a grid of objects.

Duplicate and Copy Objects

1. Select the **Selection** tool on the Tools panel.

    ◆ If the object is in a group, select the **Direct Selection** tool on the Tools panel.

2. Use any of the following methods:

    ◆ **Copy and Paste.** Select the object, click the **Edit** menu, and then click **Copy**. Click in the target document or area, click the **Edit** menu, and then click **Paste** or **Paste in Place**.

    ◆ **Duplicate.** Select the object, click the **Edit** menu, and then click **Duplicate**.

    ◆ **Duplicate Between Documents.** Open the documents side by side, and then drag the edge or fill of the object from one document to another.

    ◆ **Duplicate as you Drag.** Hold down Alt (Win) or Option (Mac), and then drag the edge or fill of the object.

    ◆ **Duplicate as you Drag in a Grid.** Hold down Alt (Win) or Option (Mac), start to drag the edge or fill of the object, release the Alt or Option key. Press the arrow keys to change the columns and rows. Drag a rectangle to specify the size of the grid.

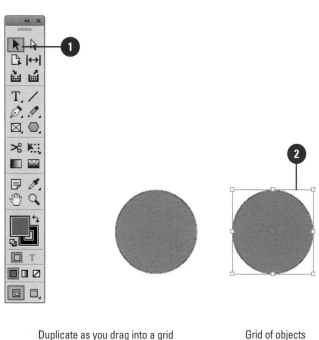

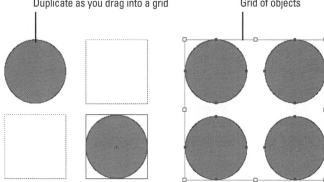

Duplicate as you drag into a grid   Grid of objects

Duplicate Multiple Objects

1. Select the **Selection** tool on the Tools panel.

2. Select the object that you want to duplicate using the step and repeat process.

3. Click the **Edit** menu, and then click **Step and Repeat**.

4. Select the **Preview** check box to view your results in the document window.

5. Select the **Create as a grid** check box to duplicate objects into a grid.

6. Enter a **Repeat Count** value with the number of duplicates you want to create in the top row.

7. Enter a **Horizontal Offset** value with the horizontal distance you want between the duplicate objects, and then enter a **Vertical Offset** value with the vertical distance you want between the duplicate objects.

8. Click **OK**.

Did You Know?

You can create a grid with the Step and Repeat command. Select an object, click the Edit menu, and then click Step And Repeat. Enter the number of duplicates for the Repeat Count, enter zero for the Horizontal Offset, and then click OK. Select the entire row of objects, click the Edit menu, and then click Step And Repeat. Enter the number of rows for the Repeat Count, enter zero for the Vertical Offset, and then click OK.

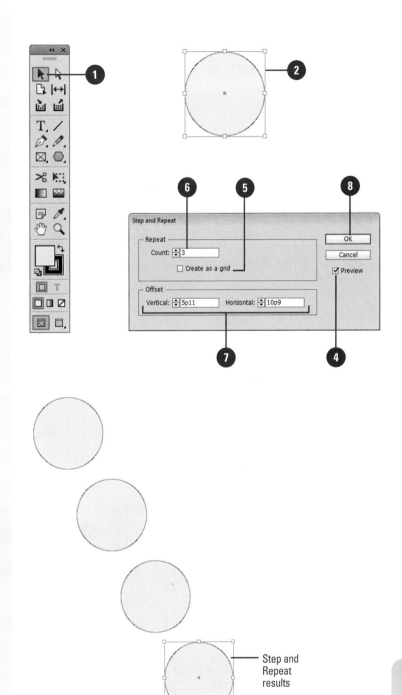

Step and Repeat results

Grouping and Combining Objects

Selecting and grouping objects makes it easier to work with multiple objects as if they were a single object. You can easily select, cut, copy, paste, move, recolor, and transform a grouped object. You can group all types of objects, yet still edit individual objects within the group as needed without having to ungroup them first by using the Direct Selection tool. You can double-click an object in a group to select it and then double-click the selected object to reselect the group again. If you no longer need to group objects, you can ungroup them. You can also use the Paste In command to combine objects.

Create a Group

1 Select the **Selection** tool on the Tools panel.

2 Use a selection method to select the objects that you want in the group.

3 Click the **Objects** menu, and then click **Group**.

◆ You can use the Group command again to group objects already in a group; this is known as a nested group.

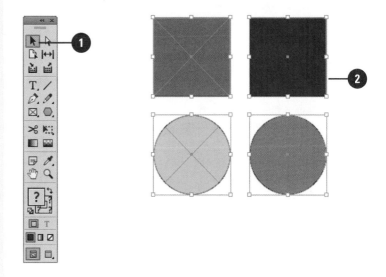

Ungroup Objects

1 Select the **Selection** tool on the Tools panel.

2 Select the grouped objects that you want to ungroup.

3 Click the **Objects** menu, and then click **Ungroup**.

◆ If you have nested groups within an object, you can use the Ungroup command again to ungroup them.

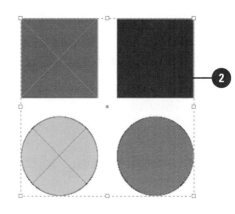

Select Objects in a Group

1. Select the **Selection** tool on the Tools panel.

2. Select the grouped object.

   TIMESAVER *Double-click to select an object in the group. Double-click the selected object to reselect the group.*

3. Click the **Object** menu, point to **Select**, and then click **Content**.

   The topmost object in the group is selected.

4. Click the **Object** menu, point to **Select**, and then click **Previous Object** or **Next Object**.

   The previous or next object in the group is selected.

5. To select the group again, click the **Object** menu, point to **Select**, and then click **Container**.

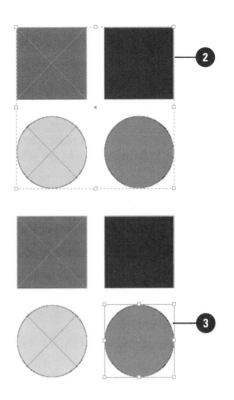

Combine Objects

1. Select the **Selection** tool on the Tools panel.

2. Select the object you want to combine into another object.

3. Click the **Edit** menu, and then click **Copy** or **Cut**.

4. Select the object with which you want to combine other objects.

5. Click the **Edit** menu, and then click **Paste Into**.

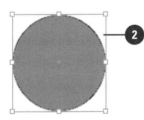

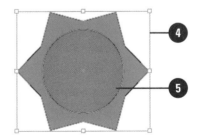

Did You Know?

You can remove a combined object. Select the Direct Selection tool, select the pasted-in object, and then press Delete.

Aligning Objects

In addition to using grids and guides to align objects to a specific point, you can align a group of objects to each other. The alignment buttons on the Align and Control panels make it easy to align two or more objects relative to each other or to the page. Before you select an align command, specify how you want InDesign to align the objects. You can align the objects in relation to the page, margins, spread, or selection. In addition to the alignment buttons, you can also use the Gap tool to align and adjust the size of a gap between two or more objects. You can resize objects with commonly aligned edges at the same time, while keeping the gaps between them fixed.

Align Objects

1. Select the **Selection** tool on the Tools panel.

2. Select two or more objects to align them.

3. Select the **Align** panel.

    ◆ Click the **Window** menu, point to **Object & Layout**, and then click **Align**.

4. Click the **Align To** list arrow, and then select an align option:

    ◆ **Align to Selection.** Aligns objects to themselves.

    ◆ **Align to Key Object.** Aligns objects to the key object.

    ◆ **Align to Margins.** Aligns objects to the margin size.

    ◆ **Align to Page.** Aligns objects to the page size.

    ◆ **Align to Spread.** Aligns objects to the spread size.

5. If you want to align objects to an object, click the **Object** menu, and then click **Lock** to lock the object.

6. Use the alignment buttons on the Align or Control panel.

    ◆ **Align Top or Bottom Edges.**

    ◆ **Align Left or Right Edges.**

    ◆ **Align Horizontal or Vertical Centers.**

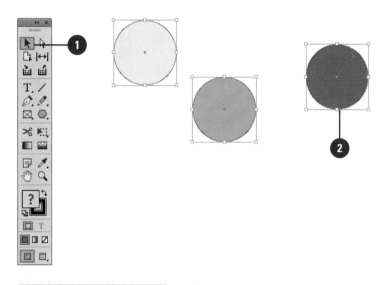

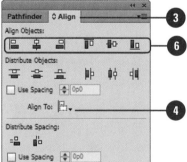

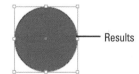

Results

Align Objects Using the Gap Tool

1. Select the **Gap** tool on the Tools panel.

2. Position the pointer between two objects.

3. Use any of the following actions:

   ◆ **Move Gap and Resize Objects.** Drag to move the gap and resize all objects aligned along the gap.

   ◆ **Move Gap Two Nearest Objects.** Hold down Shift and then drag to move the gap between only the two nearest objects.

   ◆ **Resize Gap and Not Move It.** Hold down Ctrl (Win) or ⌘ (Mac), and then drag to resize the gap instead of moving it. Hold down Shift to resize the gap between only the two nearest objects.

   ◆ **Move Gap and Objects.** Hold down Alt (Win) or Option (Mac), and then drag to move the gap and objects in the same direction. Hold down Shift to resize the gap between only the two nearest objects.

   ◆ **Resize Gap and Move Objects.** Hold down Ctrl+Alt (Win) or ⌘ +Option (Mac), and then drag to resize the gap and move the objects. Hold down Shift to resize the gap between only the two nearest objects.

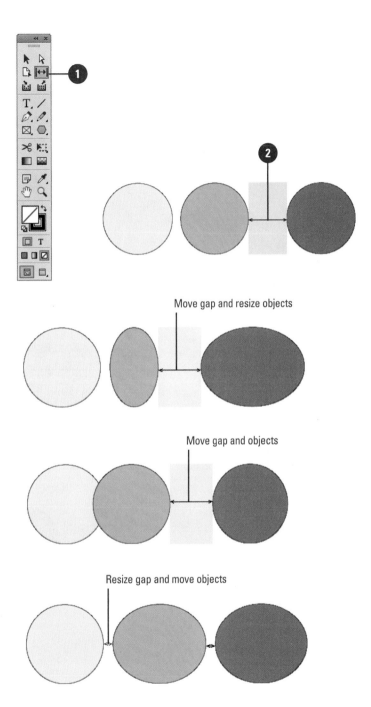

Move gap and resize objects

Move gap and objects

Resize gap and move objects

Distributing Objects

To evenly align several objects to each other across the document, either horizontally or vertically, select them and then choose a distribution option. For a quick alternative, you can use Live Distribute to evenly create space between objects proportionally. Resizing an object is different than scaling an object. Before you select an align command, specify how you want InDesign to align the objects. You can align the objects in relation to the page, margins, spread, or selection.

Distribute Objects

① Select the **Selection** tool on the Tools panel.

② Select three or more objects to distribute them.

③ Select the **Align** panel.

◆ Click the **Window** menu, point to **Object & Layout**, and then click **Align**.

④ To apply a spacing distance, select the **Use Spacing** check box, and then enter a spacing value for tops, centers, bottoms, or sides.

⑤ Use the distribution buttons on the Align panel.

◆ **Distribute Top or Bottom Edges.**

◆ **Distribute Left or Right Edges.**

◆ **Distribute Horizontal or Vertical Centers.**

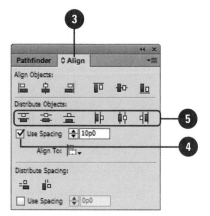

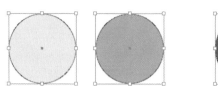

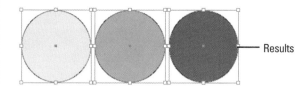

Results

Distribute Objects with Spacing

1. Select the **Selection** tool on the Tools panel.

2. Select two or more objects to distribute them.

   TIMESAVER *Start to drag a resize handle and hold down the Spacebar while dragging.*

3. Select the **Align** panel.

   ◆ Click the **Window** menu, point to **Object & Layout**, and then click **Align**.

4. To apply a spacing distance, select the **Use Spacing** check box, and then enter a spacing value.

5. Use the **Distribute Horizontal Space** or **Distribute Vertical Space** buttons on the Align panel.

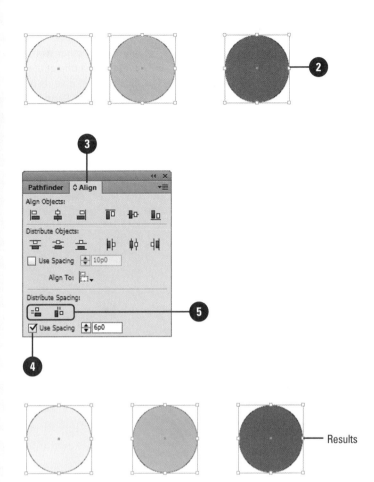

Results

Arranging Object Stack Order

Multiple objects on a document appear in a stacking order, like layers of transparencies. Stacking is the placement of objects one on top of another. In other words, the first object that you draw is on the bottom and the last object that you draw is on top. You can change the order of this stack of objects by using Bring to Front, Send to Back, Bring Forward, and Send Backward commands on the Arrange submenu from the Object menu.

Arrange a Stack of Objects

1. Select the **Selection** tool on the Tools panel.

2. Select the objects you want to arrange.

3. Click the stacking option you want.

   ◆ Click the **Object** menu, point to **Arrange**, and then click **Bring to Front** or **Bring Forward** to move an object to the top of the stack or up one location in the stack.

   ◆ Click the **Object** menu, point to **Arrange**, and then click **Send to Back** or **Send Backward** to move an object to the bottom of the stack or back one location in the stack.

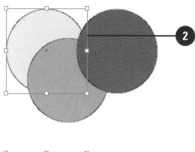

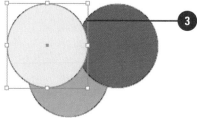

Transforming Objects

With the transformation tools in InDesign, you can quickly move, scale (resize), shear (distort), and rotate an object. InDesign provides several ways to transform objects: tools (Rotate, Scale, and Shear) on the Tools panel, options on the Transform and Control panels, and commands on the Transform submenu on the Object menu. All transformations are performed based on a reference point; center is the default, however, you can change it on the Control or Transform panel. When you perform a transformation on an object, InDesign remembers it, which allows you to repeat the last transformation by using commands on the Transform Again submenu on the Object menu. If you don't like a transformation, you can use the Clear Transformation command to remove it.

Transform Objects

1. Select the **Selection** tool on the Tools panel.

2. Select one or more objects to transform.

3. Use any of the following methods:

   ◆ **Transform Tools.** Select a transform tool (Rotate, Scale, and Shear) on the Tools panel, and then drag to apply the transformation.

   ◆ **Transform Panel.** Click the **Window** menu, point to **Object & Layout**, and then click **Transform**. Enter desired values to apply the transformation.

   ◆ **Transform Menu.** Click the **Object** menu, point to **Transform**, and then select a transform option.

       ◆ Click **Clear Transformations** to remove a transformation.

   ◆ **Transform Again.** Select a different object to apply the same transformation. Click the **Object** menu, point to **Transform Again**, and then select a transform again option.

   ◆ **Reference Point.** Select an object, and then click a square reference point on the Control or Transform panel.

Repeating Object Transformations

When you perform a transformation on an object, InDesign remembers your choices, which allows you to repeat the transformation again on another object. With the commands on the Transform Again submenu on the Object menu, you can repeat transformations individually or as a sequence. Experiment with the different options to create varied results. If you don't like a transformation, you can use the Clear Transformation command from the Transform submenu on the Object menu to remove it.

Repeat Object Transformations

1. Select the **Selection** tool on the Tools panel.

2. Select one or more objects to transform.

3. Use any of the transformation commands on an object.

4. Select a different object.

5. Click the **Object** menu, point to **Transform Again**, and then select one of the following commands:

   ◆ **Transform Again.** Applies the last single transform command to the selection as a whole.

   ◆ **Transform Again Individually.** Applies the last single transform command to each object in the selection.

   ◆ **Transform Sequence Again.** Applies the last set of transform commands to the selection as a whole.

   ◆ **Transform Sequence Again Individually.** Applies the last set of transform commands to each object in the selection.

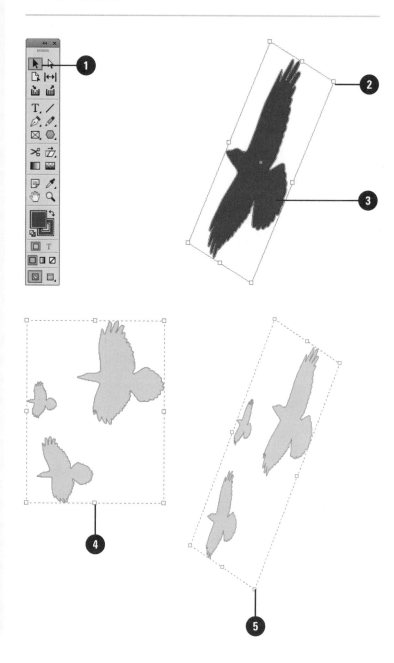

Using the Free Transform Tool

The Free Transform tool allows you to rotate, scale (resize), or shear (slant) an object. However, you cannot copy an object or move the reference point. As you drag to transform an object, you can use keyboard keys to alter the results of a transformation. Free Transform makes it easy to transform an object by using the mouse to visually get the results that you want. The Free Transform tool works just like the one in Illustrator and Photoshop. If you need to use exact values for a transformation, you can use the Control or Transform panel.

Transform an Object with the Free Transform Tool

1. Select the **Free Transform** tool on the Tools panel.

2. Select one or more objects to transform.

3. Use any of the following methods:

   ◆ Scale. Drag a corner handle to scale along two axes; drag a side handle to scale along one axis; Shift-drag to scale proportionally; hold down Alt (Win) or Option (Mac), and then drag to scale from the center. Or, hold down Shift to scale from the center proportionally.

   ◆ Rotate. Point slightly outside a corner handle (pointer changes to a double arrow), and then drag in a circular motion. To rotate in 45-degree increments, Shift-drag.

   To rotate an object 180 degrees, drag a corner handle diagonally all the way across the object.

   ◆ Shear. Drag a side handle and then hold down Ctrl (Win) or ⌘ (Mac) as you continue to drag. To constrain the movement, also press Shift. To shear from the center, add the Alt (Win) or Option (Mac) key.

Shear

Scale

Rotate

Scaling Objects

After you create an object, you can change its size by scaling it. To resize an object, either smaller or larger, you can use the Scale tool, which is under the Free Transform tool. In addition, you can scale and flip or scale and copy an object. You can transform the object from its center or the reference point. If you want to scale an object using exact percentages, you can use the Transform panel, which is available from the Object & Layout submenu on the Window menu.

Scale an Object

1. Select the **Selection** tool on the Tools panel.

2. Select one or more objects to transform.

3. Select the **Scale** tool on the Tools panel.

4. To move the reference point, click a new point.

5. Use any of the following methods:

   ◆ Scale. Drag away from or toward the object. Shift-drag to scale proportionally; hold down Alt (Win) or Option (Mac), and then drag to scale from the center. Or, hold down Shift to scale from the center proportionally.

   ◆ Scale and Flip. Drag across the entire object.

   ◆ Scale and Copy. Hold down Alt+Shift (Win) or Option+Shift (Mac), and then drag.

6. To scale an object using exact percentages, use the Control or Transform panel.

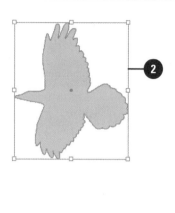

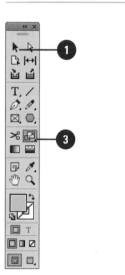

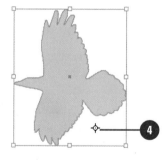

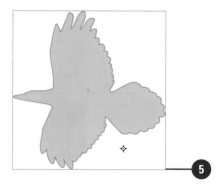

Shearing Objects

The Shear tool on the Tools panel allow you to be creative as you trans-form objects by creating a slanted version of that object. With the Shear tool, which is under the Free Transform tool, you can transform the object from its center or the reference point. If you want to shear an object using exact angle values, you can use the Control panel or the Transform panel, which is available on the Object & Layout sub-menu on the Window menu.

Shear an Object

1. Select the **Selection** tool on the Tools panel.

2. Select one or more objects to transform.

3. Select the **Shear** tool on the Tools panel.

4. To move the reference point, click a new point.

5. Drag away from the object.

6. To shear an object using exact angle values, use the Control or Transform panel.

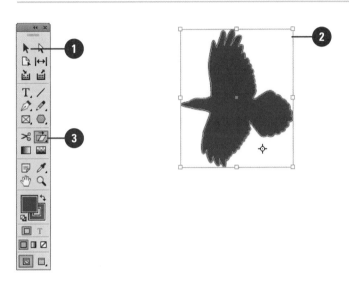

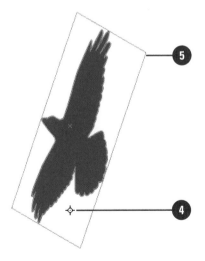

Rotating Objects

After you create an object, you can change its orientation by rotating it. For a freeform rotation, when you want to rotate the object in other than 90-degree increments, you can use the Selection or Rotate tool. You can transform the object from its center or the reference point. With the Selection tool, you can drag a corner handle just like in Illustrator to rotate around the center. With the Rotate tool, which is under the Free Transform tool, you drag the object to rotate around the reference point. As you drag a freeform rotation, rotation lines and a tool tip appear from the center or reference to indicate the rotation angle. To rotate an object in 90-degree increments or flip it horizontally or vertically, you can use easy access buttons on the Control panel. If you want to rotate an object with an exact angle value, you can use the Control or Transform panel, which is available on the Object & Layout submenu on the Window menu.

Free Rotate an Object Using the Selection Tool

1. Select the **Selection** tool on the Tools panel.

2. Select one or more objects to transform.

3. Position the pointer just outside a corner handle (cursors changes to an arc with arrows).

4. Drag in a circular motion. As you drag, rotation lines appears indicating the rotation angle.

   ◆ To rotate in 45-degree increments, Shift-drag.

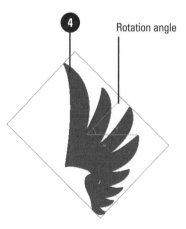

Rotation angle

Free Rotate an Object Using the Rotate Tool

1. Select the **Selection** tool on the Tools panel.

2. Select one or more objects to transform.

3. Select the **Rotate** tool on the Tools panel.

4. To move the reference point, click a new point.

5. Drag in a circular motion.

   ◆ To rotate in 45-degree increments, Shift-drag.

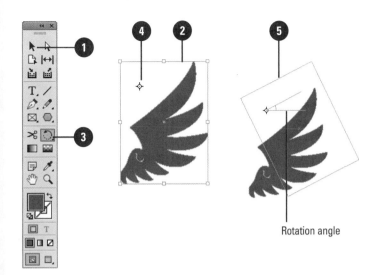

Rotation angle

Rotate or Flip an Object in Increments

1. Select the **Selection** tool on the Tools panel.

2. Select one or more objects to transform.

3. Use any of the following methods:

   ◆ Rotate Value. Enter a **Rotation Angle** on the Control or Transform panel.

   ◆ Rotate 90° Intervals. Click the **Rotate 90° Clockwise** or **Rotate 90° Counter-clockwise** button on the Control panel.

   ◆ Flip. Click the **Flip Horizontal** or **Flip Vertical** button on the Control panel.

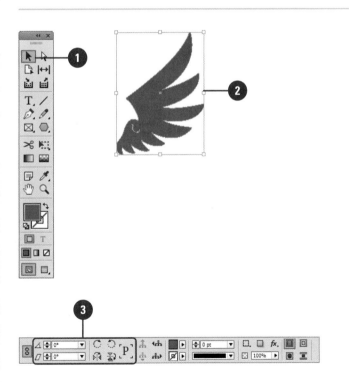

Locking and Unlocking Objects

After you've spent a lot of time laying out objects in your document, you may want to lock everything into place. The Lock command on the Object menu allows you to lock the position of one or more selected objects. When you lock an object, a lock icon appears on the edge of the object. With the Prevent Selection of Locked Objects option in General preferences, you can specify whether a locked object can still be selected and text or graphics inside the object can still be modified. However, the position of the object cannot be changed. If you want to move a locked object, you need to unlock it on the spread first.

Lock or Unlock Objects

1. Select the **Selection** tool on the Tools panel.

2. Select one or more objects to lock or locked objects to be unlocked.

3. Click the **Object** menu, and then click **Lock** or **Unlock All On Spread**.

   When you try to move the object, the cursor changes to a lock icon, and the object doesn't move.

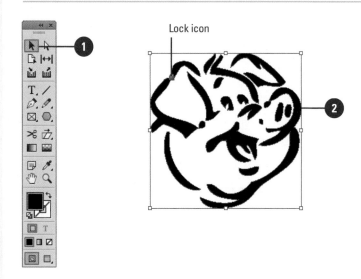

Lock icon

Set Lock Options

1. Click the **Edit** (Win) or **InDesign** (Mac) menu, point to **Preferences**, and then click **General**.

2. Select the **Prevent Selection of Locked Objects** check box to prevent locked objects from being changed, or deselect it to prevent it from being moved (yet you can still select it and modify text or graphics inside).

3. Click **OK**.

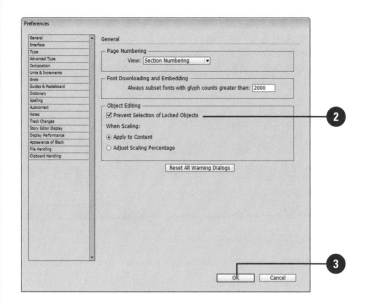

Creating Inline Objects

An inline object is a shape or graphic that is dragged or pasted as an anchored object within the text into a text frame. When you modify text, the anchored object adjusted as needed. When the object is placed in a text, you can adjust the object in the frame by using the Direct Selection tool or move the object in the text frame by using the Selection tool. You can also use any of the Text Wrap commands in the Text Wrap panel to wrap text around the object.

Create an Inline Object

1. Click the **View** menu, point to **Extras**, and then click **Show Anchored Object Control**.

2. Select the **Selection** tool on the Tools panel.

3. Select a text frame into which you want to paste a shape or graphic.

4. Hold down the Shift key, and then drag the blue square where you want to create an inline object.

   An anchor symbol icon appears in place of the blue square.

5. To move the anchored object, hold down the Shift key and drag the anchor symbol icon by using the **Selection** tool. To adjust the object in the text frame, drag the object by using the **Direct Selection** tool.

6. To change anchor options, Alt+click (Win) or Option+click the anchor symbol icon. See page 199 for details on dialog box options.

Did You Know?

You can paste an inline object. Copy the object, click to place the insertion point where you want the inline object, and then paste the object.

You can place an inline graphic object. Click to place the insertion point where you want the inline graphic, click the File menu, click Place, select the graphic file, and then click Open.

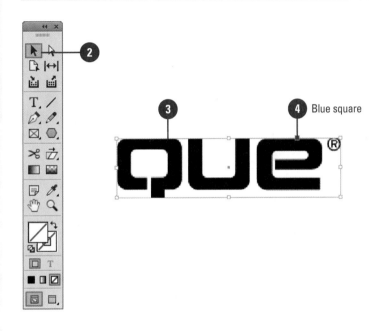

Blue square

Adobe· Flash Professional On Demand

Copyright © by Perspection, Inc.

All rights reserved. No part of this book shall be reproduced, stored in a retrieval system, or transmitted by any means, electronic, mechanical, photocopying, recording, or otherwise, without written permission from the publisher. No patent liability is assumed with respect to the use of the information contained herein. Although every precaution has been taken in the preparation of this book, the publisher and author assume no responsibility for errors or omissions. Nor is any liability assumed for damages resulting from the use of the information contained herein.

Anchor symbol

Inline object

Creating Anchored Objects

An anchored object is an object, such as images or text boxes, that is attached to a text frame. When you move the text frame, the anchored object moves too. You can create an anchored object by using drag and drop or the Insert Anchored Object dialog box, which allows you to control how, where, and what type an object is placed in a text frame. When you specify options, an anchored object frame with an anchor symbol appears next to the text frame. If you no longer want the anchored object, you can release it from the text frame.

Create an Anchored Object Using Drag and Drop

1. Click the **View** menu, point to **Extras**, and then click **Show Anchored Object Control**.

2. Select an object that you want to anchor using the **Selection** tool.

3. Drag the blue square where you want the object's anchor.

   ◆ **Specify Options.** Press Alt (Win) or Option (Mac) as you drag the blue square.

   An anchor symbol icon appears in place of the blue square and a dashed line connects the objects, and the objects remain in place.

4. To view anchor object markers:

   ◆ **View Anchor Markers.** Click the **Type** menu, and then click **Show Hidden Characters**.

   ◆ **View Anchor Symbol.** Click the **View** menu, point to **Extras**, and then click **Show Frame Edges**.

   ◆ **View Dashed Line.** Click the **View** menu, point to **Extras**, and then click **Show Text Threads**.

5. To select anchored objects, select only one anchor object using the **Selection** tool, or select a range of text with multiple anchor markers using the **Type** tool.

6. To release an anchored object from a text frame, select the object, click the **Object** menu, point to **Anchored Object**, and then click **Release**.

③ Blue square

Adobe⋅ Flash Professional On Demand

Copyright © by Perspection, Inc.
All rights reserved. No part of this book shall be reproduced, stored in a retrieval system, or transmitted by any means, electronic, mechanical, photocopying, recording, or otherwise, without written permission from the publisher. No patent liability is assumed with respect to the use of the information contained herein. Although every precaution has been taken in the preparation of this book, the publisher and author assume no responsibility for errors or omissions. Nor is any liability assumed for damages resulting from the use of the information contained herein.

Anchor marker

Anchor symbol

Dashed line

Anchored object

Create an Anchored Object with Specific Options

1 Click to place the insertion point in the text where you want to place the anchored object by using the **Type** tool. (You can change this location later if you want.)

2 Click the **Object** menu, point to **Anchored Object**, and then click **Insert**.

3 Specify the following options you want:

◆ **Object Options.** Specify options for content type, object and paragraph style, and height and width.

◆ **Position.** Select the **Custom** or **Inline or Above Line** option, and then specify options that relate to your choice.

◆ **Allow Drag Move.** Deselect the **Prevent Manual Positioning** check box.

4 Click **OK**.

An anchored object frame with an anchor symbol appears next to the text frame.

5 To move anchored objects, select the object using a selection tool, and then drag it to new position.

6 To change options for the anchored object, select it, click the **Object** menu, point to **Anchored Object**, and then click **Options**.

7 To release an anchored object from a text frame, select the object, click the **Object** menu, point to **Anchored Object**, and then click **Release**.

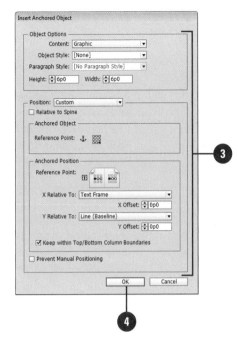

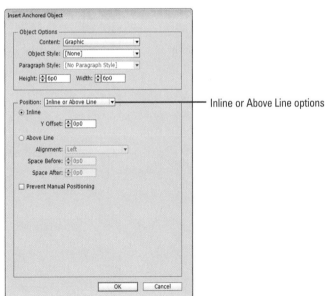

Inline or Above Line options

Creating and Deleting Object Layers

You can think of Layers as a group of transparent sheets stacked on top of each other, where each layer can contain a separate aspect of the total design. Layers give you control over the design elements of your document. When you open a document, a default layer is already there for you to work on. Everything you create in the document appears on the default layer until you create a new one. Each object is given a generic name, such as <rectangle>, until you change it. Each layer uses an Expand/Collapse triangle in the Layers panel to show/hide the objects on it and their stacking order. You can quickly create a new layer or duplicate an existing one using a button in the Layers panel or selecting options in a dialog box. When you create a new layer, it's given a generic name, such as Layer 1, and a color, which is used to highlight object frames and paths. When you duplicate a layer, any objects on the layer are also duplicated. When you no longer need a layer, you can quickly delete it. Remember that once you've deleted a layer and saved the document, there is no way to recover the deleted layer. However, while the document is open, you can use the Undo command to recover a deleted layer.

Create and Rename a New Layer

1. Select the **Layers** panel.
   - ◆ Click the **Window** menu, and then click **Layers**.
2. Click the **New Layer** button on the panel.
   - ◆ To create a new layer and specify the options you want, click the **Options** button, click **New Layer**, specify options, and then click **OK**.

   A new layer appears in the panel.
3. To rename the layer, double-click the layer, enter a name, and then click **OK**.

Did You Know?

You can create a new layer while you paste. Select the Layers panel, click the Options button, and then select Paste Remembers Layers. With this option selected, InDesign creates a new layer when you paste, or drag and drop objects from another document.

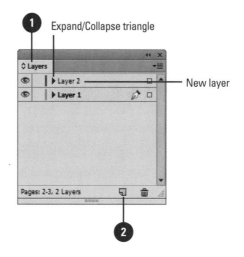

Expand/Collapse triangle

New layer

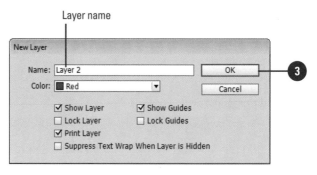

Layer name

Duplicate a Layer

1. Select the **Layers** panel.

   ◆ Click the **Window** menu, and then click **Layers**.

2. Drag the layer that you want to duplicate onto the **New Layer** button on the panel.

   InDesign creates an exact copy of the layer and appends the word *copy* at the end of the original layer name.

3. To rename the layer, double-click the layer, enter a name, and then click **OK**.

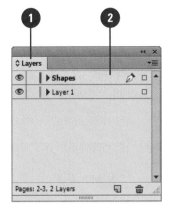
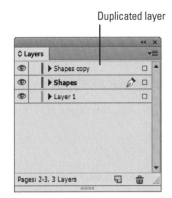

Duplicated layer

Delete Layers

1. Select the **Layers** panel.

   ◆ Click the **Window** menu, and then click **Layers**.

2. Select the layers that you want to delete.

   ◆ Hold down the Ctrl (Win) or ⌘ (Mac) key, and then click to select multiple items.

3. Click the **Delete Layer** button.

4. Click **OK** to delete any objects on the layer.

Layer deleted

Did You Know?

You can delete all unused layers. Select the Layers panel, click the Options button, and then click Delete Unused Layers.

Setting Layer Options

When you create a layer, it's given a generic name, (Layer 1, Layer 2, etc.) and a distinctive color. The color is used to highlight object frames and paths. To avoid confusion, it's a good idea to specify names for layers in a document. You can quickly rename and set layer options by double-clicking the layer you want to change. In the Layer Options dialog box, you can set options for color, showing and hiding layers, locking and unlocking layers, printing layers, showing and hiding guides, locking and unlocking guides, and suppressing text wraps when a layer is hidden.

Set Layer Options

1. Select the **Layers** panel.

   ◆ Click the **Window** menu, and then click **Layers**.

2. Double-click an existing layer or select a layer, click the **Options** button, and then click **Layer Options for**.

3. Select or deselect any of the following options:

   ◆ **Name.** Enter a name for the layer.

   ◆ **Color.** Specify a color for the layer. This color is used to highlight object frames and paths.

   ◆ **Show Layer.** Select to show the layer or deselect to hide it.

   ◆ **Lock Layer.** Select to lock the layer or deselect to unlock it.

   ◆ **Print Layer.** Select to print the layer or deselect to prevent printing.

   ◆ **Suppress Text Wrap When Layer is Hidden.** Select to prevent text wrapping on hidden layers.

   ◆ **Show Guides.** Select to show guides on the layer.

   ◆ **Lock Guides.** Select to lock guides on the layer.

4. Click **OK**.

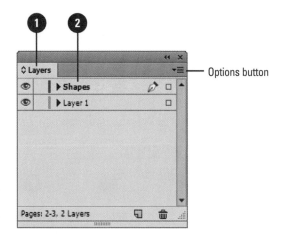

Options button

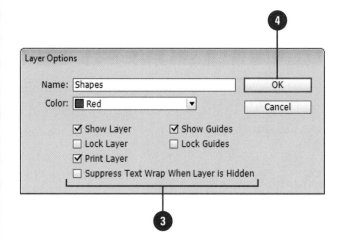

Showing and Hiding Layers and Objects

When you have a lot of objects in the document window, it can be hard to work with them. In the Layers panel, you can hide layers and objects to reduce the clutter and make it easier to work with the layers and objects that you want. Each layer uses an Expand/Collapse triangle in the Layers panel to show/hide the objects on it and their stacking order. When you click the visibility (first) column, an eye icon appears indicating the layer is visible. To hide a layer or object, you simply click the eye icon to remove visibility. When objects are hidden, they are not printed or exported, and cannot be selected. When you save, close, and reopen your document, any hidden objects remain hidden until you show them.

Show and Hide Layers and Objects in the Layers Panel

1. Select the **Layers** panel.

   ◆ Click the **Window** menu, and then click **Layers**.

2. Click the **Expand/Collapse** triangle to display the objects on the layer.

3. Use any of the following:

   ◆ **Show/Hide Individual.** Click the visibility (first) column for each layer or object that you want to show or hide.

   ◆ **Show/Hide Multiple.** Click and drag the visibility (first) column.

   ◆ **Show/Hide Except One.** Alt+click (Win) or Option+click (Mac) the visibility (first) column for a top-level layer to show/ hide all the other top-level layers except the one you clicked.

Did You Know?

You can hide or show objects using the Object menu. Select the Selection tool, select the objects you want to hide, click the Object menu, and then click Hide or press Ctrl+3 (Win) or ⌘+3 (Mac). To show objects, click Show All On Spread or press Alt+Ctrl+3 (Win) or Option+⌘+3 (Mac).

Expand/Collapse triangle

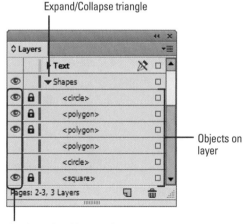

Objects on layer

Eye icons for objects on layer

Locking Layers and Objects

When you don't want an object to be moved or modified, you can lock it in the Layers panel. When you lock a layer or object, the objects remain visible in the document window. When you click the lock (second) column in the Layers, a padlock icon appears, indicating the layer is locked. When you lock a layer, all the objects on the layer are locked. You can also expand a layer in the Layers panel and lock/unlock individual objects. To unlock a layer or object, you simply click the padlock icon to remove it. You can lock/unlock individual layers and multiple layers.

Lock and Unlock Layers and Objects in the Layers Panel

1. Select the **Layers** panel.

   ◆ Click the **Window** menu, and then click **Layers**.

2. Click the **Expand/Collapse** triangle to display the objects on the layer.

3. Use any of the following:

   ◆ **Lock/Unlock Individual.** Click the lock (second) column for each layer that you want to lock or unlock.

   ◆ **Lock/Unlock Multiple.** Click and drag the lock (second) column.

   ◆ **Lock/Unlock Except One.** Alt+click (Win) or Option+click (Mac) the lock (second) column for a layer to lock/unlock all the other layers except the one you clicked.

See Also

See "Locking and Unlocking Objects" on page 196 for more information on locking and unlocking objects.

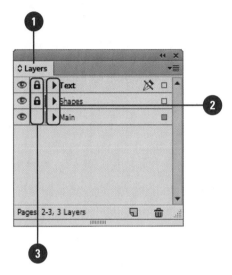

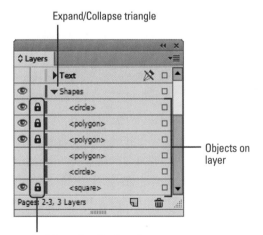

Expand/Collapse triangle

Objects on layer

Lock icons for objects on layer

Merging Layers and Groups

If you have objects on multiple layers and want to consolidate them onto one layer, you can merge them together. You can merge two or more layers. However, you can't merge an object with another object. If a layer is locked or hidden, you can still use it in a merge. Before you use the Merge Layers command, it's a good idea to make a copy of your document as a backup to preserve a copy of the separate layers.

Merge Layers in the Layers Panel

1. Select the **Layers** panel.

   ◆ Click the **Window** menu, and then click **Layers**.

2. Select two or more layers that you want to merge.

   ◆ Hold down the Ctrl (Win) or ⌘ (Mac) key, and then click to select multiple items.

3. Click the last layer into which you want to merge the selected layers.

4. Click the **Options** button, and then click **Merge Layers**.

Did You Know?

You can reorder layers. Select the Layers panel, and then drag one layer above or below another layer to the new position that you want. A thick black line appears, indicating the new position.

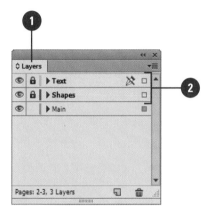

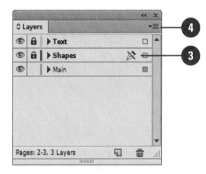

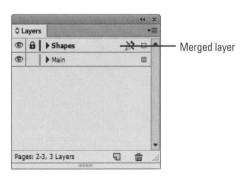

Merged layer

Working with Objects on Layers

After you have created more than one layer, you can create objects on the new layers or move objects from one layer to another. To work with a layer, all you need to do is select an object on the layer in the document window or select a layer or object in the Layers panel. Each layer in the Layers panel uses an Expand/Collapse triangle to show/hide the objects on it and their stacking order. The color of an object's frame indicates the layer on which it is located. Blue is the default color of the first layer when you create a new document. This makes it easy to identify objects and layers. When you select an object, a square object icon appears in the Layers panel. A quick way to move an object from one layer to another is to drag the object name or square object icon from one layer to another in the Layers panel.

Work with Objects on Layers

- ◆ **Select a Layer with Objects.** Select an object in the document window with the same color frame as the layer color.

- ◆ **Select a Layer in the Layers Panel.** Select the Layers panel, and then click a layer.

- ◆ **Expand/Collapse a Layer in the Layers Panel.** Select the Layers panel, and then click the Expand/Collapse triangle.

- ◆ **Move an Object Between Layers.** Select the Layers panel, select an object in the document window or Layers panel, and then drag the square object icon from the selected layer to another layer.

- ◆ **Copy an Object Between Layers.** Select an object in the document window, select the Layers panel, hold the Alt (Win) or Option (Mac) key, and then drag the object name or square object icon from the selected layer to another layer.

- ◆ **Reorder Layers or Objects.** Select the Layers panel, then drag a layer or object from one position to another. A thick black line appears, indicating the new position.

- ◆ **Rename an Object.** Select the layers panel, select the object, pause, and then click it again to highlight the name. Type a name, and then press Enter (Win) or Return (Mac).

Layer selected

Objects on Main layer

Objects selected on Main layer

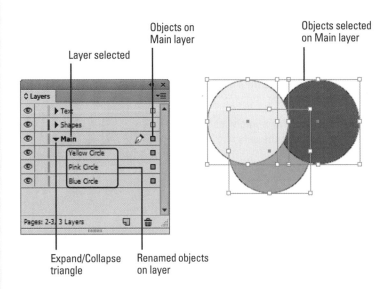

Expand/Collapse triangle

Renamed objects on layer

Objects moved to Shapes layer

Objects on a new layer

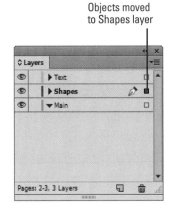
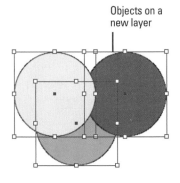

Using the Measure Tool

The Measure tool allows you to find out the size of items or measure the distance between objects. The Measure tool displays measurement information in the Info panel. The panel shows you the horizontal and vertical position, distance and angle of the measurement line, and width and height of the bounding box.

Measure Distances and Angles with the Measure Tool

1. Select the **Info** panel.

   ◆ Click the **Window** menu, and then click **Info**.

2. Click the **Measure** tool on the Tools panel.

3. Point to the start point of what you want to measure, and then drag to draw a line to the end point.

4. To create an angle, point to the start or end point, hold the Alt (Win) or Option (Mac) key, and then drag a new line to the angle you want.

5. To move a measurement line, drag the line (not the end points) to a new position.

6. To adjust the start and end points on the measurement line, drag the start or end point to a new position.

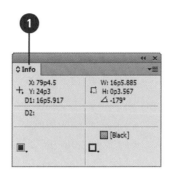

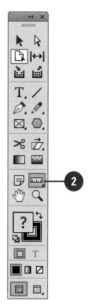

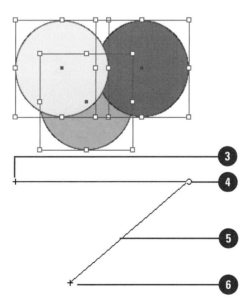

Using Live Screen Drawing

In previous versions of InDesign, you needed to pause before dragging to see the content as you draw. Now, you can see the content drawn as you drag without the pause using Live Screen Drawing. In the Interface preferences dialog box, you can can select the Live Screen Drawing option you want. If you prefer the old way, then you can select the Delayed option. If you want to see content as you draw, then select the Immediate option. If you don't want either, then select Never.

Set Live Screen Drawing Options

1. Click the **Edit** (Win) or **InDesign** (Mac) menu, point to **Preferences**, and then click **Interface**.

2. Click the **Live Screen Drawing** list arrow, and then select any of the following:

   ◆ **Never.** Select to never show content as you draw.

   ◆ **Immediate.** Select to show content immediately as you draw.

   ◆ **Delayed.** Select to pause before you show content as you draw (like the behavior in InDesign CS4).

3. Click **OK**.

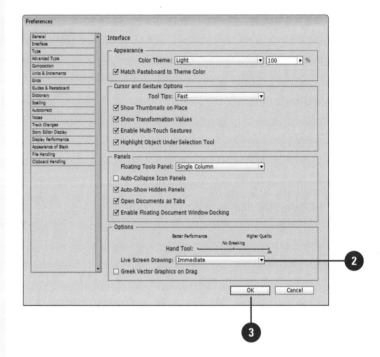

Applying and Managing Color

7

Introduction

Color management is an important part of working with InDesign. Setting up document and graphic image color settings in the right way will make it easier for a printer to produce the results that you want.

InDesign does its best to manage color for you. However, sometimes there are color conflicts or you have specific color requirements that you want to use. If a document's profile doesn't match the current working color space or is not assigned a color profile, you can use the Assign Profile dialog box to change or remove a profile to avoid conflicts. A working space is a temporary color space used to define and edit color in Adobe programs. Each color mode has a working space profile. InDesign's color modes are Lab, RGB (Red, Green, and Blue), and CMYK (Cyan, Magenta, Yellow, and Black). Color modes not only define the working color space of the active document, they also represent the color space of the output document. You can use the Color Settings dialog box to select a working space profile.

InDesign not only lets you select virtually any colors you desire in the Color panel, it also lets you store those colors for future use in the Swatches panel. You can also create swatches with color tints, gradients, and mixed inks. If you're not sure what colors to use, you can use the swatch libraries from color systems, such as Trumatch and Pantone, to select colors with predictable results.

After you create the colors and swatches you want, you can apply them to objects in your documents. The Tools panel provides color boxes to make it easy for you to apply fill and stroke colors and the Eyedropper tool on the Tools panel makes it easy to quickly pick up a color from one area of your artwork and apply it to another area.

What You'll Do

Change Color Settings

Change Color Profiles

Work with Color Modes

Apply Colors

Use the Eyedropper Tool

Work with the Color Panel

Work with the Swatches Panel

Manage Color Swatches

Work with Swatch Libraries

Create Tint Swatches

Create Gradient Swatches

Create Mixed Inks

Use Colors from the Kuler Panel

Overprint Colors

Proof Colors on the Screen

Change the Interface Color Theme

Changing Color Settings

InDesign does its best to manage color for you. However, sometimes there are color conflicts or you have specific color requirements that you want to use. When you create or open a document, InDesign creates or looks for a color profile, which specifies color usage in the document. The Color Settings dialog box allows you to specify color settings and select options to deal with conflicts. The two main color settings are Working Space and Color Management Policies. Working Space controls how RGB and CMYK colors are used in a document that doesn't have an embedded profile, while Color Management Policies controls how InDesign works with color when opening files that don't have a color profile or one that doesn't match your current color settings from the RGB and CMYK menus. If you need to convert colors between color spaces, use Advanced mode.

Change Color Settings

1. Click the **Edit** menu, and then click **Color Settings**.

2. Click the **Settings** list arrow, and then select from the following preset color settings:

   ◆ **Monitor Color.** Useful for video and onscreen content. Sets the RGB working space to your current monitor space.

   ◆ **North America General Purpose 2.** Useful for screen and print content in North America.

   ◆ **North America Prepress 2.** Useful for common printing conditions in North America. The default RGB color space is set to Adobe RGB.

   ◆ **North America Web/Internet.** Useful for non-print content on the web in North America.

3. Click **OK** to use the defined settings, or select your own custom settings:

   ◆ **Working Spaces.** Controls how RGB and CMYK colors are used in a document that doesn't have an embedded profile.

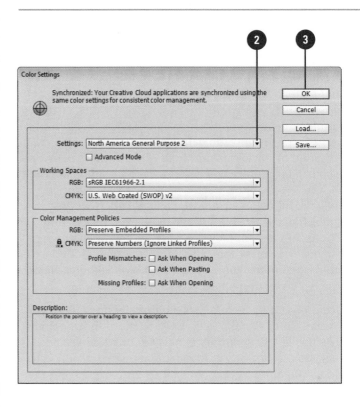

Select **Monitor RGB** for onscreen output; **Adobe RGB** for photo inkjet printers (converts RGB images to CMYK images); **ProPhoto RGB** for inkjet printers; and **sRGB IEC61966-2.1** for web output.

◆ **Color Management Policies.** Controls how InDesign works with color when opening files that don't have a color profile or one that doesn't match your current color settings from the RGB and CMYK menus.

Select **Off** to prevent the use of color management, **Preserve Numbers** to preserve the document color profile for CMYK documents, **Preserve Embedded Profiles** to preserve links to color profiles, or **Convert to Working Space** to use the working space color (useful for the web).

Select the appropriate check boxes to choose if and when InDesign will warn you of profile mismatches (no warning, when opening the file, or when pasting) or missing profiles (when opening a file or no warning).

④ To set additional options for conversion purposes and use Black Point compensation, select the **Advanced Mode** check box.

⑤ Click **OK**.

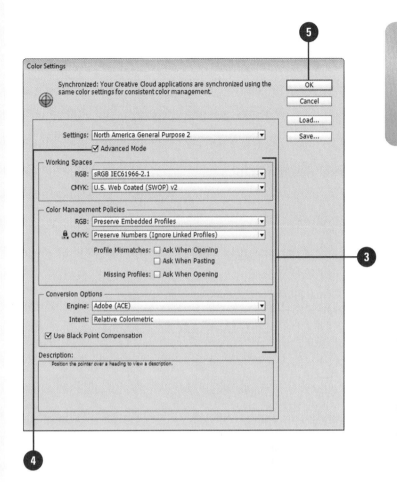

Changing Color Profiles

When you create or open a document, InDesign creates or looks for a color profile, which specifies color usage in the document. If a document's profile doesn't match the current working color space or is missing an assigned color profile, you can use the Assign Profiles dialog box to change or remove a profile to avoid conflicts. You can also specify rendering intent (object display or print) for the transition from one color space to another. When you change a color profile, color in your document may shift to match the new color profile.

Change or Remove Color Profiles

1. Click the **Edit** menu, and then click **Assign Profiles**.

2. Select one of the following RGB or CMYK Profile options:

   ◆ **Discard (use current working space).** Select to remove a color profile from your document and use the current working color settings.

   ◆ **Assign Current Working Space.** Select when your document doesn't have an assigned profile or its profile is different from the current working space.

   ◆ **Assign Profile.** Select to assign a different profile to your document.

3. Select any of the following options:

   ◆ **Solid Color Intent.** Specify a rendering intent for vector objects.

   ◆ **Default Image Intent.** Specify a rendering intent for bitmap images.

   ◆ **After-Blending Intent.** Specify a rendering intent for the proofing or final color space for colors (from transparency interactions).

4. Click **OK**.

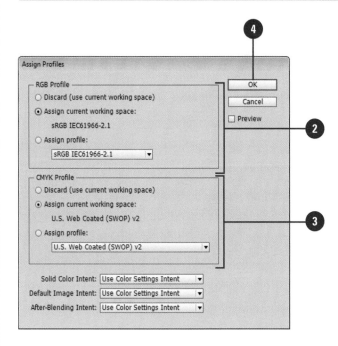

Convert Document Colors to Another Profile

1. Click the **Object** menu, and then click **Convert to Profile**.

2. Click the **RGB Profile** and **CMYK Profile** list arrow, and then select a profile.

3. Select the Conversion Options you want:

   ◆ **Engine.** Specify the color management module used to map the gamut of one color space to the gamut of another.

   ◆ **Intent.** Specify rendering intent (object display or print) for the transition from one color space to another.

   ◆ **Perceptual.** Use to preserve the visual look of colors; useful for photographs. The standard in Japan.

   ◆ **Saturation.** Use to create vivid color in an image; useful for graphics and charts.

   ◆ **Relative Colorimetric.** Use to shift out-of-gamut colors to the closest color in the destination color space. The standard in North America and Europe.

   ◆ **Absolute Colorimetric.** Use to leave out-of-gamut colors unchanged in the destination color space.

   ◆ **Use Black Point Compensation.** Select to preserve shadow detail in images. Use when printing to ensure the detail.

4. Click **OK**.

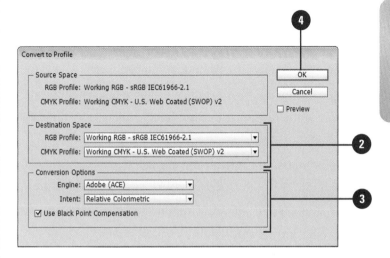

For Your Information

Changing Profiles for Imported Bitmap Images

If you import a bitmap image into your document, you can view, override, or disable profiles assigned to it. For cases when an image doesn't have a profile, you can assign one. Select the imported bitmap image, click the Object menu, click Image Color Settings, select a Profile option, select a Rendering Intent option (optional), and then click OK.

Working with Color Modes

Color modes define the colors represented in the active document. Although you can change the color mode of a document, it is best to select the correct color mode at the start of the project. InDesign's color modes are Lab, RGB (Red, Green, and Blue), and CMYK (Cyan, Magenta, Yellow, and Black). Color modes not only define the working color space of the active document, they also represent the color space of the output document. It's the document output (print, press, or monitor) that ultimately determines the correct document color mode. Color modes do not just determine what colors the eye sees; they represent how the colors are mixed, and that's very important because different output devices use different color mixes.

Lab Mode

The Lab color mode is an old color measuring system. Created in France, its purpose was to measure color based on visual perception. Since personal computers had not been created at that time, the Lab mode is not based on a particular computer or operating system, and so Lab color is device independent. The Lab mode measures color using a lightness channel, an "a" channel (red to green), and a "b" channel (blue to yellow). Lab color works well for moving images between operating systems (Mac to Win), and for printing color images to PostScript Level 2 or 3 devices. Because of its ability to separate the gray tones of an image into an individual channel (lightness), the Lab color mode is excellent for sharpening, or increasing the contrast of an image without changing its colors.

RGB Mode

The RGB color mode is probably the most widely used of all the color modes. RGB gen-

erates color using three 8-bit channels: 1 red, 1 green, and 1 blue. Since each channel is capable of generating 256 steps of color, mathematically, that translates into 16,777,216 possible colors per image pixel. The RGB color mode (sometimes referred to as Additive RGB) is the color space of computer monitors, televisions, and any electronic display. This also includes PDAs (Personal Digital Assistants), and cellular phones. RGB is considered a device-dependent color mode. Device independent means that the colors in images created in the RGB color mode will appear differently on various devices. In the world of computer monitors and the web, what you see is very seldom what someone else sees; however, understanding how InDesign manages color information goes a long way to gaining consistency over color.

CMYK Mode

The CMYK color mode is the color mode of paper and press. Printing presses (sometimes referred to as 4-color presses) convert an image's colors into percentages of CMYK (Cyan, Magenta, Yellow, and Black), which eventually become the color plates on the press. One at a time, the plates apply color to a sheet of paper, and when all 4 colors have been applied, the paper contains an image similar to the CMYK image created in InDesign. The CMYK color mode can take an image from a computer monitor to a printed document. Before converting an image into the CMYK mode, however, it's important to understand that you will lose some color saturation during the conversion. The colors that will not print are defined as being out of gamut. **Out of gamut** means that the current RGB or Lab color doesn't have a CMYK equivalent, which means you can't use it on a commercial project unless you select a substitute color close to a CMYK equivalent.

Applying Colors

The Tools panel provides color boxes to make it easy for you to apply fill and stroke colors. The color box in the foreground is the Fill box and the outlined box in the background is the Stroke box. When you select an object, fill, or stroke, the color boxes (also known as thumbnails), on the Tools and Control panel display the current colors. To change the fill or stroke color, select an object, fill or stroke, select the Fill or Stroke box, and then select a color from the Color or Swatches panel. You can also drag the current color swatch and apply it to an object.

Apply Colors to an Object, Fill or Stroke

1. Select an object, fill, or stroke using a selection tool.

2. Click the **Fill** or **Stroke** color box on the Tools panel to choose the color's destination.

3. Click the **Apply Color** button on the Tools panel to apply a color or click **Apply None** to apply no color.

4. Use any of the following methods to change the active fill or stroke colors:

   ◆ Select the **Swatches** panel, and then click a color swatch to change the color.

   ◆ Click the **Fill** or **Stroke** color box on the Control panel, and then click a color swatch to change the color.

   ◆ Select the **Color** panel, and then specify a color using the sliders or the color spectrum.

   ◆ Double-click the **Fill** or **Stroke** color box to open the Color Picker dialog box, select a color or enter color values, and then click **OK**.

   ◆ To set the default colors of black and white, click the **Default Fill and Stroke** icon on the Tools panel.

   ◆ To switch the current fill and stroke color, click the **Swap Fill and Stroke** icon on the Tools panel.

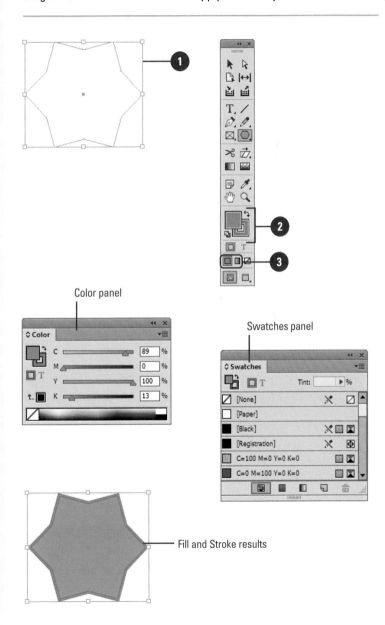

Color panel

Swatches panel

Fill and Stroke results

Using the Eyedropper Tool

The Eyedropper tool on the Tools panel makes it easy to quickly pick up a color from one area of your artwork and apply it to another area. When you click an object with the Eyedropper tool, it picks up the object's color and stroke attributes and displays them in the Tools, Color, and Stroke panels. You can pick up attributes from any type of object, even a graphic image, and the object doesn't even need to be selected. If an object is selected, the color and stroke attributes are applied to the selected object. The Eyedropper tool also provides options for you to customize the attributes—such as Stroke, Fill, Character, Paragraph, and Object—that you want to pick up with the tool.

Apply Colors and Attributes with the Eyedropper Tool

1 If you want to apply the acquired color and attributes to one or more objects, then select them first.

2 Select the **Eyedropper** tool on the Tools panel.

The eyedropper appears white, ready to sample object attributes.

3 Click an object that contains the color and attributes that you want to pick up and apply.

The eyedropper appears black, filled with object attributes. If an object is selected, the attributes are applied to the object.

4 Click an object to apply the attributes.

◆ To pick up different object attributes, Alt+click (Win) or Option+click (Mac) another object.

◆ To have the Eyedropper tool only pick up an object's color and not other attributes, click the Fill or Stroke box on the Tools or Color panel, and then Shift+click the color to be picked up.

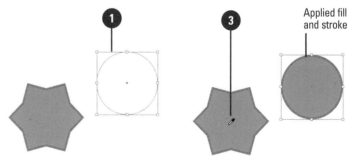

Applied fill and stroke

Change Eyedropper Options

1 Double-click the **Eyedropper** tool on the Tools panel.

2 Click the **Expand** arrow to display individual options for the main settings (Stroke, Fill, Character, Paragraph, or Object).

3 Select the check boxes for the options that you want the Eyedropper to pick up and deselect the ones you don't.

4 Click **OK**.

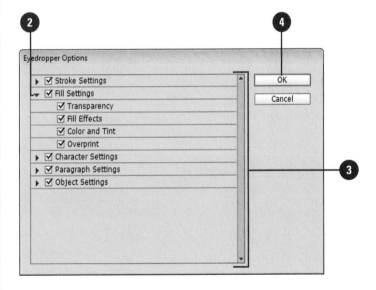

Working with the Color Panel

The Color panel gives you access to InDesign's color-generation tools. This single panel lets you select a color mode (Lab, RGB, or CMYK), create colors using different sliders, spectrum color selectors, and an option that lets you create a color ramp for the current fill and stroke colors. For example, the CMYK spectrum displays a rainbow of colors in the CMYK color gamut. Moving the eyedropper into the spectrum box and clicking lets you select any color and gives you a visual representation of the relationships between various colors.

Select Color Modes with the Color Panel

1. Select the **Color** panel.

   ◆ Click the **Window** menu, point to **Color**, and then click **Color**.

2. Click the **Options** button on the panel.

3. Select from the following type of Color Sliders:

   ◆ **Lab.** Creates three sliders (L, a, and b). The L slider has a possible value from 0 to 100, and the a and b sliders have a possible value from-128 to 127.

   ◆ **CMYK.** Creates four subtractive sliders (cyan, magenta, yellow, and black). Each slider has a possible value from 0 to 100. The values for CMYK are rounded to the nearest whole number. Converts the lower portion of the Color panel to the CMYK spectrum. Clicking anywhere in the spectrum changes the active color.

   ◆ **RGB.** Creates three sliders (red, green, and blue). Each slider has a possible value from 0 to 255. Converts the lower portion of the Color panel to the RGB spectrum. Clicking anywhere in the spectrum changes the active color.

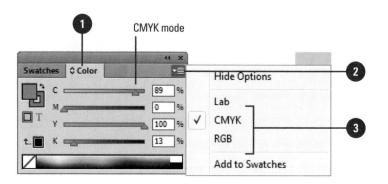

CMYK mode

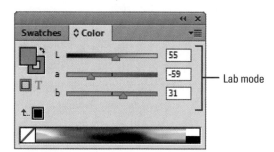

Lab mode

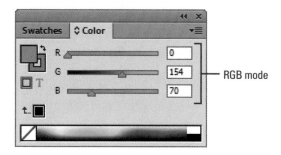

RGB mode

Work with the Color Panel

1 Select the **Color** panel.

◆ Click the **Window** menu, point to **Color**, and then click **Color**.

2 To change a color, click a color box, use a slider, enter specific color values, or click a color in the spectrum. The box with the red diagonal line is the None color.

◆ Hold the Shift key while you drag a slider to have all the other sliders move too.

◆ You can also drag a color directly from the Color panel onto objects.

3 To change a color using the Color Picker, double-click a color box, select a color using the color range or color mode options, and then click **OK**.

4 To add the current color to the Swatches panel, drag it to the Swatches panel, or click the **Options** button, and then click **Add To Swatches**.

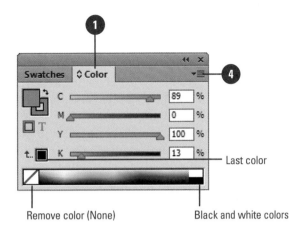

Last color

Remove color (None)   Black and white colors

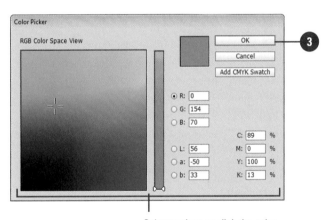

Select options or click the color range to select a color.

Did You Know?

You can identify out-of-gamut colors. If an out-of-gamut warning icon (a triangle with an exclamation point) appears below the color boxes on the Color panel, it indicates that the current RGB or Lab color doesn't have a CMYK equivalent, which means you can't use it in a commercial project.

You can convert out-of-gamut colors. If an out-of-gamut warning icon (a triangle with an exclamation point) appears below the color boxes on the Color panel, click the small square next to the out-of-gamut symbol to convert the color to the closest process-color equivalent.

Working with the Swatches Panel

InDesign not only lets you select virtually any colors you desire, it also lets you store those colors for future use in the Swatches panel. Where the Color panel lets you select virtually any color you need, the Swatches panel lets you save and re-use specific colors that you use often. In the Swatches panel, you can point to a color box to display a tooltip indicating the color's settings. If you want to view more information, you can change the Swatches panel display to make it easier to view and work with colors. To help you find the swatches you need, you can display them by type or you can adjust the size of the swatch.

Change the Swatches Panel Display

1. Select the **Swatches** panel.

   ◆ Click the **Window** menu, point to **Color**, and then click **Swatches**.

2. To display different types of swatches, click one of the following buttons: **Show All Swatches**, **Show Color Swatches**, or **Show Gradient Swatches**.

3. To display swatches by size, click the **Options** button, and then choose from the following options: **Name**, **Small Name**, **Small Swatch**, or **Large Swatch**.

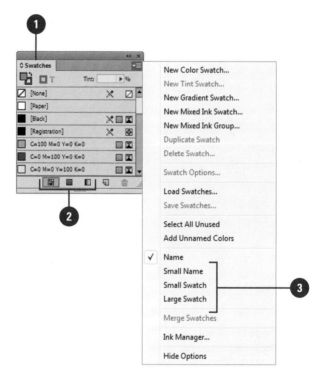

Did You Know?

You can duplicate a color swatch from the Swatches panel. Select the Swatches panel, select a color swatch, and then click the New Swatch button on the panel. The duplicate color swatch appears at the bottom of the list with the word *copy* at the end of the name.

Add or Edit a Color Swatch

1 Select the **Swatches** panel.

◆ Click the **Window** menu, point to **Color**, and then click **Swatches**.

2 Click the **Options** button, and then click **New Color Swatch** to add a new color swatch, or double-click the swatch to edit it.

TIMESAVER *Alt+click (Win) or Option+click (Mac) the New Swatch button on the panel to add a color swatch.*

◆ To add a color, you can also drag a color from the color boxes on the Tools or Color panel to the Swatches panel.

3 To enter a color swatch name, deselect the **Name with Color Value** check box, and then enter a name.

4 Click the **Color Type** list arrow, and then click one of the following:

◆ **Process.** Colors printed using small dots of the CMYK inks to create color combinations.

◆ **Spot.** Colors printed using color-specific inks.

5 Click the **Color Mode** list arrow, and then select a color mode.

6 Adjust the color sliders to create the color you want.

7 Click **OK**.

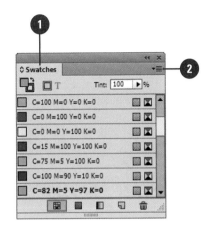

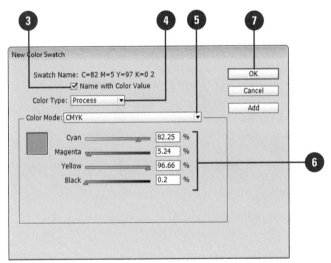

Did You Know?

You can delete a color swatch from the Swatches panel. Select the Swatches panel, display and select the color you want to delete, and then click the Delete Swatch button.

Managing Color Swatches

In addition to adding and editing swatches, you can also move, delete, duplicate, merge, save, load, rename, and name unnamed color swatches in the Swatches panel. Unnamed colors are colors that are applied to objects using the Color panel or Color Picker, while named colors are applied from the Swatches panel. If you no longer use a color or you want to change the use of a color, you can use the Delete Swatches button on the Swatches panel. If a color is not in use, InDesign simply deletes it. If the color is in use, InDesign gives you an opportunity to delete the color and use another one or specify the color as unnamed. The default swatches for None, Paper, Black, and Registration cannot be edited or deleted.

Delete Color Swatches

1. Select the **Swatches** panel.

   ◆ Click the **Window** menu, point to **Color**, and then click **Swatches**.

2. Select the swatches you want to delete.

   ◆ To select multiple swatches, hold the Shift key to select the first and last swatch in a contiguous range, or hold the Ctrl (Win) or ⌘ (Mac) key to select noncontiguous swatches.

3. Click the **Delete Swatch** button on the panel.

   If the swatch is being used, an alert dialog box appears.

4. Click the **Defined Swatch** option, and then select a color, or click the **Unnamed Swatch** option.

5. Click **OK**.

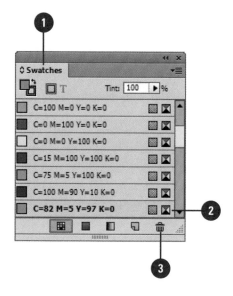

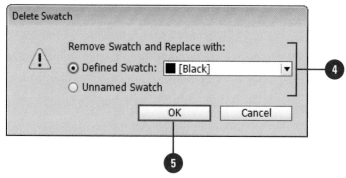

Did You Know?

You can delete all unused color swatches. Select the Swatches panel, click the Options button, click Select All Unused, and then click the Delete Swatch button on the panel.

Work with Swatches

◆ **Select Swatches.** Hold the Shift key to select the first and last swatch in a contiguous range, or hold the Ctrl (Win) or ⌘ (Mac) key to select noncontiguous swatches.

◆ **Move Swatches.** Select a swatch in the **Swatches** panel, and then drag the swatch to a new position. A thick black line appears, indicating the new position.

◆ **Duplicate Swatches.** Select a swatch in the **Swatches** panel, and then click the **New Swatch** button on the panel.

◆ **Merge Swatches.** Select the **Swatches** panel, click the first color (which is the merge into color), hold the Ctrl (Win) or ⌘ (Mac) key, and then click to select other swatches for the merge. Click the **Options** button, and then click **Merge Swatches**.

◆ **Save Swatches.** Select the swatches you want to save in the **Swatches** panel, click the **Options** button, click **Save Swatches**, specify a name and location, and then click **Save**. Swatches are saved with the Adobe Swatch Exchange (ASE) file format.

◆ **Load Swatches.** Select the **Swatches** panel, click the **Options** button, click **Load Swatches**, select the ASE swatches file, and then click **Open**.

◆ **Add All Unnamed Colors to the Swatches Panel.** Unnamed colors are colors that are applied to objects using the Color panel or Color Picker. Select the **Swatches** panel, click the **Options** button, and then click **Add Unnamed Colors**. The unnamed colors are named with color percentage values.

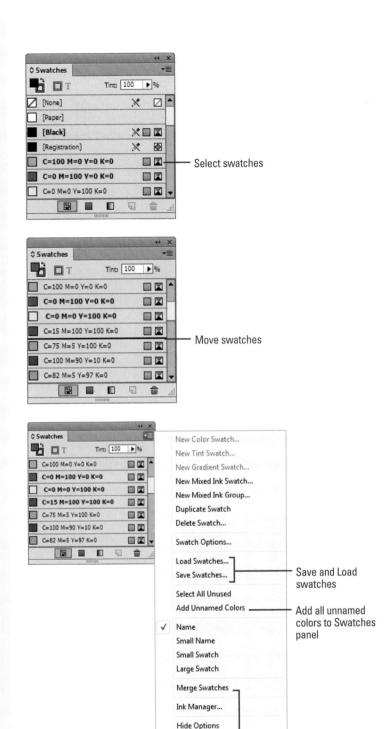

Select swatches

Move swatches

Save and Load swatches

Add all unnamed colors to Swatches panel

Merge swatches

Working with Swatch Libraries

Instead of creating your own color swatches, you can use the swatch libraries from color systems, such as Trumatch and Pantone. Trumatch and Pantone are common color libraries in North America for prepress and desktop color printing. These color systems are universally used by printers, so you can produce consistent results. Other color libraries include ANPA (commonly used for newspapers), DIC (commonly used in Japan), Focoltone (commonly used in France and Great Britain), HKS (commonly used in Europe), System (Macintosh), System (Windows), Toyo (commonly used in Japan), and Web. Web is a common color library of 216 web-safe colors for use on the web by both the Macintosh and Windows operating systems.

Add Colors from Swatch Libraries

1. Select the **Swatches** panel.

   ◆ Click the **Window** menu, point to **Color**, and then click **Swatches**.

2. Click the **Options** button, and then click **New Color Swatch** to add a new color swatch, or double-click the swatch to edit it.

3. Click the **Color Mode** list arrow, and then select a swatch library.

4. Select a color in the library.

5. Click **OK**.

Did You Know?

You can import swatches from other documents. Select the Swatches panel, click the Options button, click Load Swatches, navigate to and select the InDesign or Illustrator document, and then click Open.

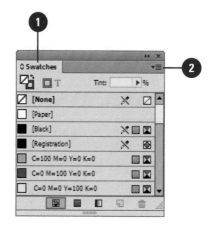

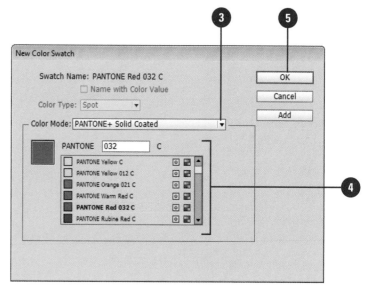

Creating Tint Swatches

A tint is a shade of a base color. The base color is a 100% tint. You can adjust the tint of a color by lowering the percentage from 1% to 99%. You can create a new tint swatch by using a dialog box or the Tint option at the top of the Swatches panel. I like the dialog box method better. After you create a new tint color swatch, it appears in the Swatches panel list with the new tint percentage in the name. If you need to edit a tint swatch, simply double-click the swatch to open the Swatch Options dialog box to make the changes you want.

Create and Edit a Tint Swatch

1. Select the **Swatches** panel.

   ◆ Click the **Window** menu, point to **Color**, and then click **Swatches**.

2. Do either of the following:

   ◆ **New.** Select a base color in the Swatches panel as the basis for the color tint, click the **Options** button, and then click **New Tint Swatch**.

   ◆ **Edit.** Double-click the tint swatch.

3. Enter a **Tint** percentage value or drag the slider to create a tint screen of the color.

4. Click **OK**.

   The new tint swatch appears in the Swatches panel list with the new tint percentage.

Did You Know?

You can create a tint swatch without the dialog box. Select the Swatches panel, select a color as the basis, enter a tint percentage in the Tint control at the top of the Swatches panel, and then click the New Swatch button on the panel.

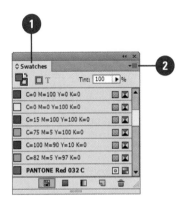

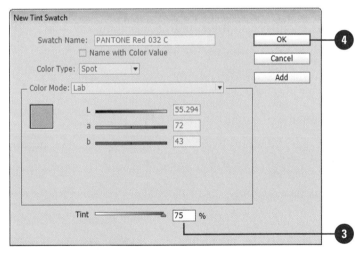

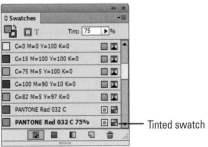

Tinted swatch

Creating Gradient Swatches

A gradient is a smooth transition between two or more colors in an object. You can create and save a gradient of your own by using the Swatches panel. You can create a gradient with two or more colors. There are two types of gradients: Radial (circular) and Linear (horizontal). You can adjust the number and blend of gradient colors by adding or changing color stops. After you create a gradient, you can apply it to objects just like any other swatch in the Swatches panel. In addition to the Swatches panel, you can also create a gradient by using the Gradient panel. The gradient is unnamed and not saved unless you store it as a swatch.

Create a Gradient Swatch

1. Select the **Swatches** panel.

   ◆ Click the **Window** menu, point to **Color**, and then click **Swatches**.

2. Click the **Options** button, and then click **New Gradient Swatch**.

3. Enter a name for the gradient swatch.

4. Click the **Type** list arrow, and then select a gradient type: **Radial** or **Linear**.

5. Click the left color stop.

6. Click the **Stop Color** list arrow, select a color type, and then use the sliders to create the color you want.

7. Repeat the previous step for the right color stop.

8. To add color stops, click below the gradient spectrum in a blank area. To remove a color stop, drag it down and away from the gradient spectrum.

9. To adjust the amount of each color in the gradient, drag the diamond above the gradient spectrum.

10. Click **Add** to add the gradient to the Swatches panel and continue to add gradients, or click **OK**.

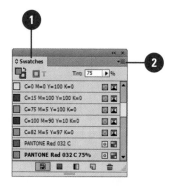

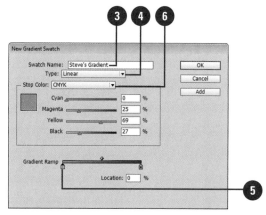

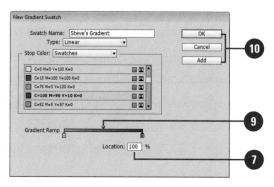

Create a Gradient with the Gradient Panel

1. Select the **Gradient** panel.
   - ◆ Click the **Window** menu, point to **Color**, and then click **Gradient**.

2. Click the **Type** list arrow, and then select a gradient type: **Radial** or **Linear**.

3. Click the left color stop.

4. Use the color spectrum and sliders in the Color panel to create the color you want.

5. Repeat the previous step for the right color stop.

6. To add color stops, click below the gradient spectrum in a blank area. To remove a color stop, drag it down and away from the gradient spectrum.

7. To adjust the amount of each color in the gradient, drag the diamond above the gradient spectrum.

8. Enter an **Angle** value to set the angle of the gradient.

9. To reverse the position of the color stops, click the **Reverse** button.

10. To save the gradient, drag the gradient preview box to the Swatches panel or click the **New Swatch** button on the Swatches panel.

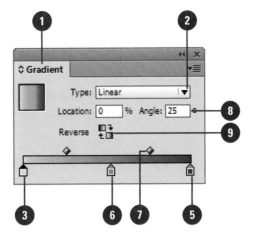

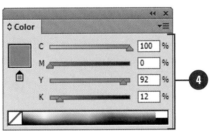

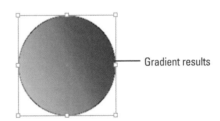

Gradient results

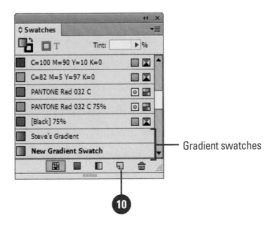

Gradient swatches

Creating Mixed Inks

Mixed inks combine a spot color with other spot colors or process colors to give you more color options for your custom designs. Mixed inks can be useful when you want a darker shade of a color to make it stand out in your design or to create a new spot color from two other existing spot colors. You can even use a mixed ink group to create a collection of mixed inks. This is useful when you want to create a series of color mixes.

Create a Mixed Ink

1. Select the **Swatches** panel.

   ◆ Click the **Window** menu, point to **Color**, and then click **Swatches**.

2. Click the **Options** button, and then click **New Mixed Ink Swatch**.

3. Enter a name for the mixed ink swatch.

4. Click two or more ink controls to select the colors you want to use in the mixed ink swatch.

5. Drag the sliders to adjust the inks to achieve the color you want.

6. Click **OK**.

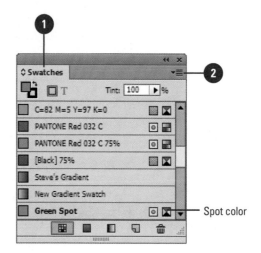

Spot color

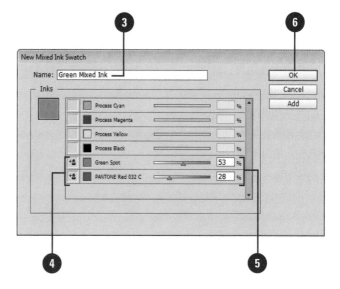

Create a Mixed Ink Group

1. Select the **Swatches** panel.

   ◆ Click the **Window** menu, point to **Color**, and then click **Swatches**.

2. Click the **Options** button, and then click **New Mixed Ink Group**.

3. Enter a name for the mixed ink group.

4. Click two or more ink controls to select the colors you want to use in the mixed ink group.

5. Enter an **Initial** value to define the color amount for the first instance of an ink.

6. Enter a **Repeat** value to set the number of mixed inks in the new color.

7. Enter an **Increment** value to set the increment value for each new mixed ink.

8. Click **Preview Swatches** to see the results of the grouping.

9. Click **OK**.

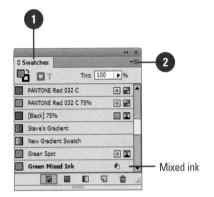

Mixed ink

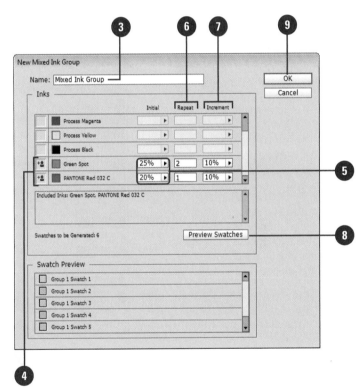

Did You Know?

You can edit a mixed ink group. Select the Swatches panel, and then double-click the mixed ink group. Select the ink controls to remove colors, or use the list arrows to change colors. Choose Swatch Options from the Options button and then select the Convert Mixed Ink Swatches To Process check box to change all the colors in the mixed ink swatches to their process color equivalents. When you're done, click OK.

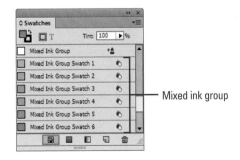

Mixed ink group

Using Colors from the Kuler Panel

The Kuler panel is an extension to InDesign that allows you to use groups of color, or themes in your projects. You can use the panel to browse thousands of color themes, create your own using the complementary harmony rules, and share them with others in the Kuler community. After you find or create the theme you want, you can add it to the Swatches panel for use in your project. You can access the Kuler panel by using the Extensions submenu on the Window menu. The Kuler panel is also available in Photoshop, Flash, Illustrator, and Fireworks.

Browse Themes and Add to the Swatches Panel

1. Click the **Window** menu, point to **Extensions**, and then click **Kuler**.

2. Click the **Browse** tab.

3. To search for a theme, click in the Search box, enter the name of the theme, a tag, or a creator, and then press Enter (Win) or Return (Mac).

   IMPORTANT *In a search, use only alphanumerical characters (Aa-Zz, 0-9).*

4. To narrow down the browse list, click the list arrows, and then select the filter options you want. Some include Highest Rated, Most Popular, Newest.

   ◆ To save a search, click the first list arrow, click **Custom**, enter your search criteria, and then click **Save**.

5. To browse for a theme, click the **View Previous Set Of Themes** or **View Next Set Of Themes** button.

6. Select a theme in the panel.

7. To add the theme to the Swatches panel, click the **Add Selected Theme To Swatches** button.

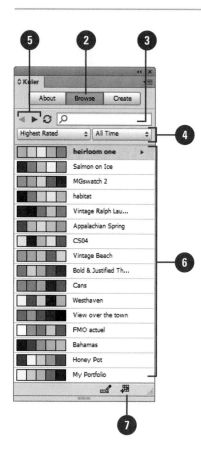

Create or Edit a Theme

① Click the **Window** menu, point to **Extensions**, and then click **Kuler**.

② To create or edit a theme, do either of the following:

- ◆ **Create a theme.** Click the **Create** tab.

- ◆ **Edit a theme.** Click the **Browse** tab, select the theme you want to edit, and then click **Edit Theme in Create Panel.**

③ Click the **Select Rule** list arrow, and then select a harmony rule or **Custom**.

The harmony rule uses the base color as the basis for generating the colors in the color group, so you can create a theme with complementary colors.

④ Select a color box, and then use the sliders and the color wheel to display the color you want.

⑤ Use the buttons below the color boxes to add/remove the theme color, add the current stroke/fill color as the base color, or adjust the other colors.

- ◆ Double-click a color box to set the active color in InDesign.

⑥ Upon completion, do any of the following:

- ◆ **Save theme.** Click **Save Theme**, name the theme, and then click **Save** to create a new one.

- ◆ **Add to Swatches Panel.** Click the **Add This Theme To Swatches** button.

- ◆ **Upload to Kuler.** Click the **Upload Theme To Kuler** button.

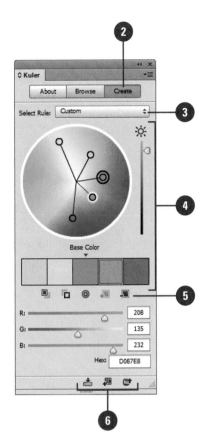

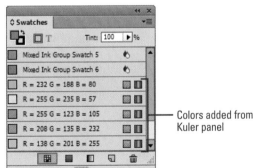

Colors added from Kuler panel

Overprinting Colors

Overprinting allows you to set the color of one object to mix with any colors underneath. For example, when you have a red object overlapping a blue object, the red object knocks out the overlapped area underneath in the blue object. When you set the red object to overprint, the red object mixes with the blue object underneath to create another color. You can individually set fill, stroke, and gap colors to overprint. After you set overprint options for an object, you can preview your results by using Overprint Preview.

Set a Fill or Stroke to Overprint and Preview the Results

1. Select the object.

2. Select the **Attributes** panel.

   ◆ Click the **Window** menu, point to **Output**, and then click **Attributes**.

3. Select from the following options:

   ◆ **Overprint Fill.** Select to set the object's fill color to overprint.

   ◆ **Overprint Stroke.** Select to set the object's stroke color to overprint.

   ◆ **Overprint Gap.** Select to set the gap color applied to stroke effects to overprint.

   ◆ **Nonprinting.** Select to not print the object.

4. To preview overprinting, click the **View** menu, and then click **Overprint Preview**.

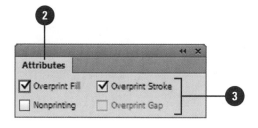

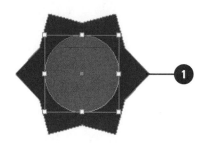

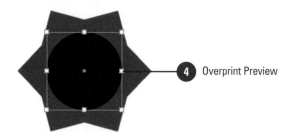

Overprint Preview

Proofing Colors on the Screen

As you start to use color in your document, it's important to see how your color or grayscale settings appear. It would be nice to see a printed copy in color to see the actual colors. However, that is not always possible. Instead, you can view a soft proof on your screen to quickly see how your colors or grayscale will appear. A soft proof simulates the output of your actual device and media, such as a printer with a specific type of paper.

Display a Soft Proof

1. Click the **View** menu, and then point to **Proof Setup**.

2. Select from one of the available output devices to simulate, or click **Custom** to set up your own.

3. For a custom soft proof setup, select from the following options:

   ◆ **Device to Simulate.** Select a target device to simulate.

   This includes additional targets: grayscale Dot Gain (10%, 15%, 20%, 25%, 30%) Gray Gamma 1.8 or 2.2, Black & White, and sGray.

   ◆ **Preserve CMYK Numbers.** Select to use colors as they are and not convert them to the color space. Deselect to use a rending intent to display colors.

   ◆ **Simulate Paper Color.** Select to simulate white paper.

   ◆ **Simulate Black Ink.** Select to simulate dark gray instead of black.

4. Click **OK**.

5. Click the **View** menu, and then click **Proof Colors**.

See Also

See "Setting PDF Output Options" on page 430 for more information on exporting a grayscale PDF using grayscale profiles.

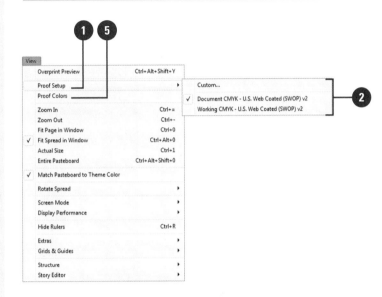

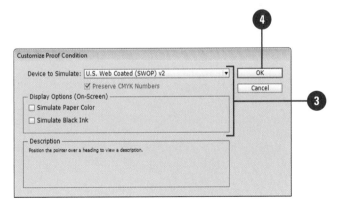

Changing the Interface Color Theme

InDesign allows you to change the color theme of the user interface from a dark gray (default) (**New!**) to a light gray (similar to InDesign CS6). You can change the interface color theme in Interface preferences with a specified color theme or a custom one. In addition, you can select an option match the pasteboard color area around the document in the Document window with the color theme (**New!**).

Set the Interface Color Theme

1. Click the **Edit** (Win) or **InDesign** (Mac) menu, and then point to **Preferences**.

2. Click **Interface**.

3. Click the **Color Theme** list arrow (**New!**), and then select an option:

   - **Light.** Selects a color theme shade with 100%.

   - **Medium Light.** Selects a color theme shade with 67%.

   - **Medium Dark.** Selects a color theme shade with 33%.

   - **Dark.** Selects a color theme shade with 0%.

   - **Custom.** Enter a shade percentage (0-100%), or lick the Color Theme arrow, and then drag the slider.

4. To match the pasteboard in the Document window to the color theme, select the **Match Pasteboard to Theme Color** check box (**New!**).

5. Click **OK**.

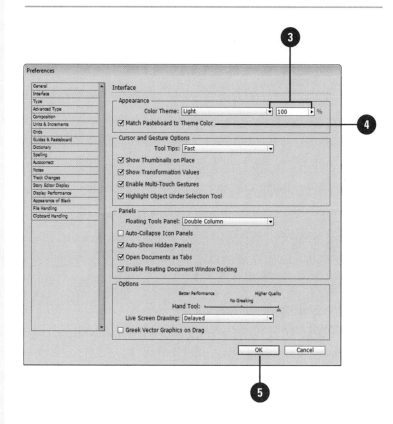

Applying Fills, Strokes, and Effects

Introduction

After you draw an object, you can apply fills, strokes, gradients, and other effects to enhance your documents. The Tools panel provides color boxes to make it easy for you to apply fill and stroke colors to objects. The Stroke panel provides additional options to quickly change stroke attributes, such as weight (width), position on the path, and stroke style. In addition to the typical stroke styles found in the Stroke panel, you can create and use custom stroke styles with stripes, dashes, and dots. For example, you can create a custom dashed stroke where you can specify the length of the dashes and gaps.

A gradient is a smooth transition between two or more colors in an object. You can apply a gradient from the Swatches or Gradient panel. The Gradient and Gradient Feather tools on the Tools panel allows you to change how a gradient appear for an object. You can specify how gradient colors blend, the angle of a linear gradient, and the location of the center for a radial gradient with a drag of the mouse over the gradient fill.

If you want to create a cool effect, you can apply blending modes, transparency, and other effects—shadow, glow, bevel and emboss, satin, and feather—to objects. A blend mode allows you to apply colors and shades to one object and have the effect interact with the objects underneath. InDesign comes with a variety of blend modes, including Overlay, Soft Light, Hard Light, Darken, Lighten, and Color. Transparency allows you to create see-through objects. Other special effects allow you to be creative without even knowing how to draw.

If you always create an object with a certain fill or stroke attribute, you can make those settings the default. InDesign has its own default fill and stroke settings of a black stroke and no fill. These are separate from any defaults that you may set.

What You'll Do

Apply Fill and Stroke Colors

Change Stroke Attributes

Create Stroke Styles

Apply Gradients

Use the Gradient Tool

Use the Gradient Feather Tool

Create Blends and Effects

Apply Shadow Effects

Apply Glow Effects

Apply Bevel and Emboss Effects

Apply Feather Effects

Apply Corner Object Effects

Convert Shape Objects

Set Object Defaults

Applying Fill and Stroke Colors

The Tools panel provides color boxes to make it easy for you to apply fill and stroke colors. The color box in the foreground is the Fill box and the outlined box in the background is the Stroke box. When you select an object, fill, or stroke, the color boxes (also known as thumbnails), on the Tools panel display the current colors. To change the fill or stroke color, select an object, fill or stroke, select the Fill or Stroke box on the Tools or Control panel, and then select a color from the Color and Swatches panel, or use the Eyedropper to apply a color from the active document.

Apply Colors to an Object, Fill or Stroke

1. Select an object, fill, or stroke using a selection tool.

2. Click the **Fill** or **Stroke** color box on the Tools or Color panel to choose the color's destination.

3. Click the **Color** button on the Tools panel to apply a color or click **None** to apply no color.

   ◆ A fill or stroke of None makes the object item transparent.

4. Use any of the following methods to change the active fill or stroke colors:

   ◆ Select the **Swatches** panel, and then click a color swatch to change the color.

   ◆ Select the **Color** panel, and then specify a color using the controls.

   ◆ Select the **Eyedropper** tool on the Tools panel, and then click anywhere in the active document to change the color.

   ◆ Double-click the **Fill** or **Stroke** color box to open the Color Picker dialog box, select a color or enter color values, and then click **OK**.

   ◆ Click the **Fill** or **Stroke** color box on the Control panel, and then click a color swatch to change the color.

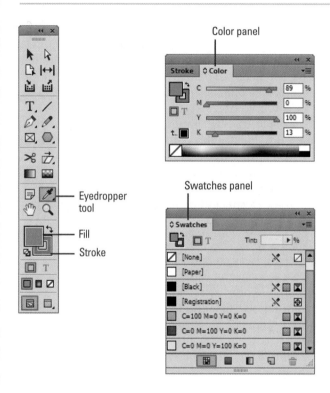

Color panel

Swatches panel

Eyedropper tool

Fill

Stroke

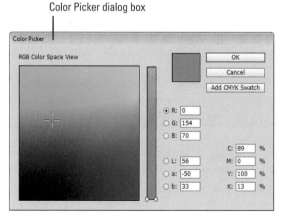

Color Picker dialog box

Use Default Colors and Switch the Fill and Stroke Colors

1 Click the **Default Fill and Stroke** button to revert the fill and stroke colors to their default values of no fill and a black stroke.

2 Click the **Swap Fill and Stroke Colors** button to switch current colors.

TIMESAVER *Press D to change the fill and stroke colors to their default values of no fill and a black stroke, and press X to switch the current colors.*

Did You Know?

You can add colors from the Color Picker to the Swatches panel. Open the Color Picker dialog box, select the color you want to add to the Swatches panel, click Add To Swatches, type a name for the color, and then click OK.

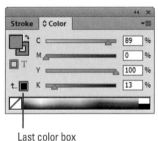

Last color box

Changing Stroke Attributes

The Stroke panel makes it easy to change stroke attributes, such as weight (width), position on the path, and stroke style. The weight of a stroke represents the thickness of the line. A weight smaller than .25 may not print and a weight of 0 completely removes the stroke. In addition to the width of a stroke, you can also specify the position (known as alignment) of the stroke on the path (either center, inside, or outside) as well as specify the stroke cap, end join, and miter limit. You can apply these options to any object, even a text object. Style is what stands out on the page. You can change the stroke style by applying dashes and endpoints, such as arrows, circles, and squares.

Change the Weight of a Stroke

1. Select one or more objects.

2. Select the **Stroke** panel.

3. Specify or enter a weight in the Stroke or Control panel.

   ◆ Click the up or down arrow, or Shift+click to change the weight by a larger interval.

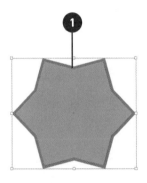
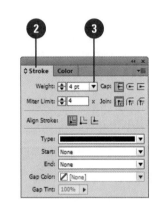

Change the Alignment of a Stroke on the Path

1. Select one or more closed objects.

2. Select the **Stroke** panel.

3. Click one of the following alignment buttons:

   ◆ **Align Stroke to Center.**

   ◆ **Align Stroke to Inside.**

   ◆ **Align Stroke to Outside.**

Center

Outside

Inside

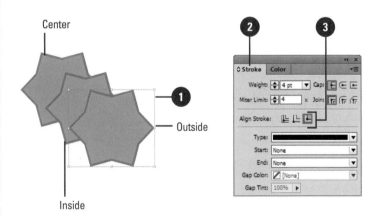

Change Stroke Caps or Joins

1 Select one or more objects.

2 Select the **Stroke** panel.

3 To change the endpoints, click one of the following buttons:

- **Butt Cap.** Creates a square-edged end.

- **Round Cap.** Creates a rounded end.

- **Projecting Cap.** Creates a square-edged end that extends past the endpoint.

4 To change the bends on corner points, click one of the following:

- **Miter Join.** Creates a pointed join point.

- **Round Join.** Creates a rounded join point.

- **Bevel Join.** Creates a beveled (cut off) join point.

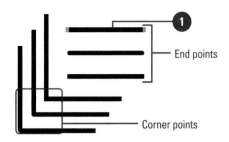

End points

Corner points

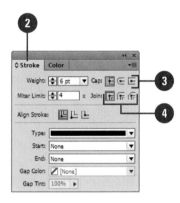

Style a Stroke

1 Select one or more objects.

2 Select the **Stroke** panel.

3 Specify any of the following:

- **Type.** Select a line style.

- **Start.** Select a style for the start point of the line.

- **End.** Select a style for the end point of the line.

- **Gap Color.** Select a color for the gap in dashed or dotted lines.

- **Gap Tint.** Select a tint percentage for the gap color.

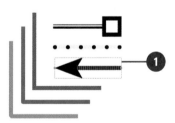

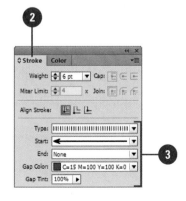

Creating Stroke Styles

In addition to the typical stroke styles found in the Stroke panel, you can create and use custom stroke styles with stripes, dashes, and dots. For example, you can create a custom dashed stroke where you can specify the length of the dashes and gaps. In the Stroke Styles dialog box, you can create, edit, delete, save, and load stroke styles. After you create a custom stroke style, the saved stroke style appears in the Stroke panel for use in the future.

Apply a Custom Dashed Stroke

1. Select one or more objects.

2. Select the **Stroke** panel.

3. Click the **Type** list arrow, and then click **Dashed** (at the bottom).

   The Stroke panel expands to display options for corners, dashes, and gaps.

4. Enter a value in the first Dash box.

   If you don't enter any more values, the value in the first box is used for the rest of the boxes.

5. Enter a value in the first Gap box.

6. Fill in the remaining boxes.

7. To adjust the dashes and gaps, click the **Corners** list arrow, and then select an option:

   ◆ **None.** No changes.

   ◆ **Adjust Dashes.** Adjusts corner dashes to be equal.

   ◆ **Adjust Gaps.** Adjusts gap lengths to be equal.

   ◆ **Adjust Dashes and Gaps.** Adjusts corner dashes and gap lengths to be equal.

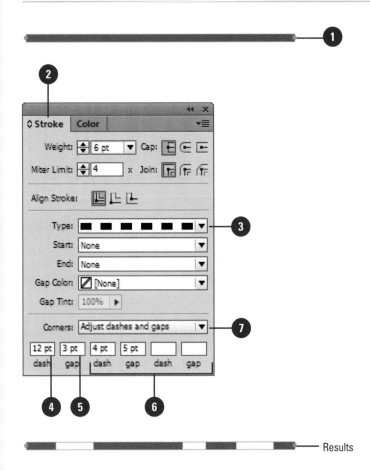

Results

Create a Custom Stroke Style

1. Select the **Stroke** panel.

2. Click the **Options** menu, and then click **Stroke Styles**.

   The Stroke Styles dialog box appears, where you can create, edit, save, and load stroke styles.

3. To use an existing style as the base for a new style, select it.

4. Click **New**.

   The New Stroke Style dialog box appears, where you can create a stroke style.

5. Enter a name for the stroke style.

6. Click the **Type** list arrow, and then select a stroke type: **Stripe**, **Dotted**, or **Dash**.

   The dialog box varies depending on the stroke type that you choose.

7. Adjust the options to create the style that you want.

8. View the preview at the bottom of the dialog box and adjust the **Preview Weight** to view the custom stroke style.

9. Click **OK**.

   ◆ To continue adding stroke styles, click **Add**.

10. To delete a custom stroke style, select it, and then click **Delete**.

11. To save stroke styles to a file, or load stroke styles from a file, click **Save** or **Load**.

12. Click **OK**.

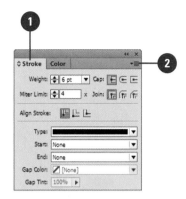

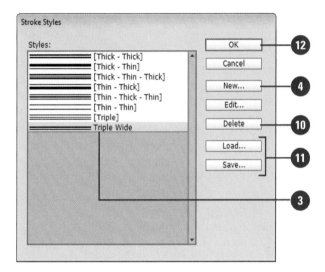

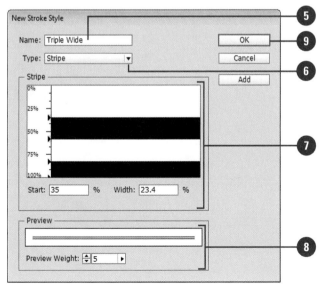

Applying Gradients

A gradient is a smooth transition between two or more colors in an object. You can apply a gradient from the Swatches or Gradient panel. After you apply a gradient, you can edit it. You can edit a gradient in an object and keep the gradient in the Swatches panel unchanged or you can edit the gradient in the Swatches panel and keep the gradient in an object unchanged. Editing a gradient is similar to creating one. The techniques are the same. All you need to do is select the element that you want to edit.

Apply a Gradient to an Object

1. Select an object.

   ◆ For a fill, click the **Fill** box on the Tools panel.

   ◆ For a stroke, click the **Stroke** box on the Tools panel.

   ◆ For type, convert it to outlines (click the Type menu, and then click Create Outlines), and then apply a gradient Fill or Stroke.

2. Click the **Apply Gradient** button on the Tools panel.

3. Or, do one of the following to apply a gradient:

   ◆ **Swatches Panel.** Select the **Swatches** panel, and then click a gradient on the panel.

   ◆ **Gradient Panel.** Select the **Gradient** panel, select a color stop, and then use the color spectrum and sliders in the Color panel to create a color gradient.

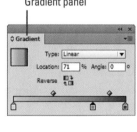

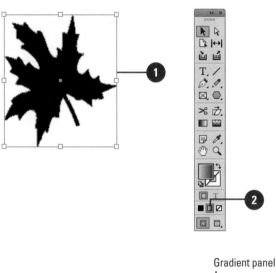

Gradient panel

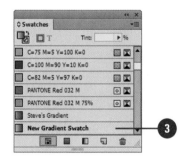

See Also

See "Creating Gradient Swatches" on pages 226-227 for more information on creating gradients using the Swatches and Gradient panels.

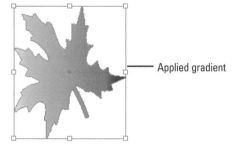

Applied gradient

Edit a Gradient

① Select an object with a gradient.

② Select the **Gradient** panel.

   ◆ To edit a gradient in the Swatches panel, select the **Swatches** panel, double-click a gradient swatch, edit the options as shown below, and then click **OK**.

③ To change the gradient type, click the **Type** list arrow, and then select a gradient type: **Radial** or **Linear**.

④ Do any of the following:

   ◆ **Add color stops.** Click below the gradient spectrum in a blank area.

   ◆ **Remove color stops.** Drag the stop down and away from the gradient spectrum.

   ◆ **Move color stops.** Drag the stop or enter a **Location** value.

   ◆ **Duplicate color stops.** Alt+drag (Win) or Option+drag (Mac) a color stop.

   ◆ **Adjust color amount.** Drag the diamond above the gradient spectrum.

   ◆ **Reverse color stops.** Click the Reverse button on the Gradients panel.

⑤ To save the edited gradient, click the **New Swatch** button on the Swatches panel.

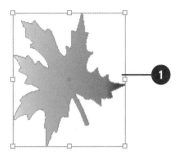

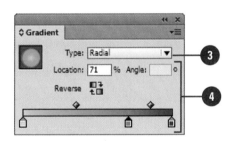

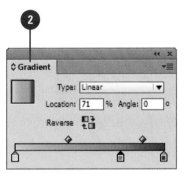

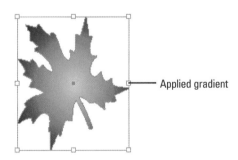

Applied gradient

Using the Gradient Tool

The Gradient tool on the Tools panel allows you to change how a gradient appears for an object. You can change how gradient colors blend, the angle of a linear gradient, and the location of the center for a radial gradient with a drag of the mouse over the gradient fill. You can double-click the Gradient tool to display the Gradient panel and create a gradient, or drag across an existing gradient to adjust the gradient fill.

Use the Gradient Tool to Change a Gradient

1. Select an object with a gradient that you want to change.

2. Click the **Gradient** tool on the Tools panel.

3. To manually apply or adjust a gradient, double-click the **Gradient** tool on the Tools panel, and then specify any of the following options in the Gradient panel.

   ◆ Type. Specify the type: **Radial** or **Linear**.

   ◆ Angle. Specify the gradient angle.

   ◆ Add color stops. Click below the gradient spectrum in a blank area.

   ◆ Remove color stops. Drag stops down and away from the gradient spectrum.

   ◆ Duplicate color stops. Alt+drag (Win) or Option+drag (Mac) a color stop.

   ◆ Reverse color stops. Click the **Reverse** button on the Gradients panel.

4. To adjust the gradient angle and color stops, drag across the gradient in the object.

   The first drag point is the first color stop and the last drag point is the last color stop.

5. To save the edited gradient, click the **New Swatch** button on the Swatches panel.

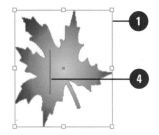

Applied gradient

Using the Gradient Feather Tool

The Gradient Feather tool on the Tools panel allows you to add an opacity, or transparency, to a gradient for an object. The Gradient Feather tool works just like the Gradient tool. You can change how gradient colors blend, the angle of a linear gradient, and the location of the center for a radial gradient with a drag of the mouse over the gradient fill. You can double-click the Gradient Feather tool to display the Effects dialog box, where you can adjust gradient feather options.

Use the Gradient Feather Tool to Change a Gradient

1. Select an object with a gradient that you want to change.

2. Click the **Gradient Feather** tool on the Tools panel.

3. To manually apply or adjust a gradient feather, double-click the **Gradient Feather** tool on the Tools panel, specify any of the following options in the Effects dialog box, and then click **OK**.

   ◆ Type. Specify the type: **Radial** or **Linear**.

   ◆ Angle. Specify the gradient angle.

   ◆ Add color stops. Click below the gradient spectrum in a blank area.

   ◆ Remove color stops. Drag stops down and away from the gradient spectrum.

   ◆ Reverse color stops. Click the **Reverse** button on the Gradients panel.

4. To apply or adjust a gradient feather, drag across the gradient in the object.

   The first drag point is the first color stop and the last drag point is the last color stop.

5. To save the edited gradient, click the **New Swatch** button on the Swatches panel.

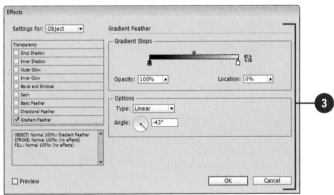

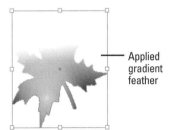

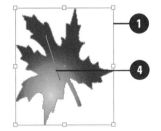

Applied gradient feather

Creating Blends and Effects

Blend mode allows you to apply colors and shades to one object and have the effect interact with the objects underneath. InDesign comes with a variety of blend modes, including Overlay, Soft Light, Hard Light, Darken, Lighten, and Color. Experiment with them to find out what works best for you. When you work with groups of objects, you can set options to apply blending modes and opacity settings with the objects in the group or not. The Knockout Group option doesn't apply settings to object groups, but it does to objects not in the group, while the Isolate Blending option does apply settings to object groups. You can set options in the Effects panel or Effects dialog box for Transparency.

Create a Blend Effect

1. Select an object that appears on top of another object.

2. Select the **Effects** panel.

   ◆ Click the **Window** menu, and then click **Effects**.

3. Click the **Blend Mode** list arrow, and then select a blend mode.

4. To add object transparency, enter an **Opacity** percentage or drag the slider to adjust it.

5. Choose any of the following:

   ◆ Isolate Blending. Objects in a group display their blending mode and transparency with each other. Group and select the objects that you want to use, and then select the **Isolate Blending** check box.

   ◆ Knockout Group. Objects in a group display their blending mode and transparency with other objects, but not each other. Group and select the objects that you want to use, and then select the **Knockout Group** check box.

   ◆ Add an Effect. Click the **fx** button to specify effect options for the selected object.

   ◆ Clear All Effects. Click the **Clears All Effects** button on the panel to clear all effects for the selected object.

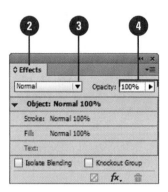

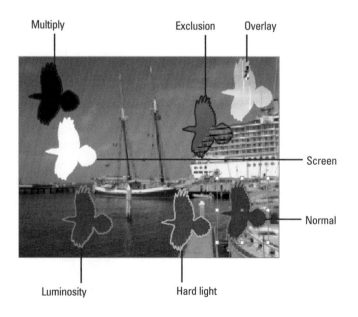

Multiply   Exclusion   Overlay

Screen

Normal

Luminosity   Hard light

Create a Transparency Effect

1. Select one or more objects.

2. Select the **Effects** panel.

   ◆ Click the **Window** menu, and then click **Effects**.

   ◆ You can also click the **Object** menu, point to **Effects**, and then click **Transparency** to use a dialog box.

3. Enter an **Opacity** percentage or drag the slider to adjust it.

See Also

See "Controlling Graphics Display Performance" on pages 166-167 for more information on setting transparency preferences for the onscreen quality of transparent objects in a new document.

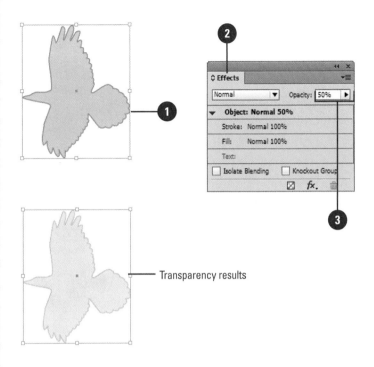

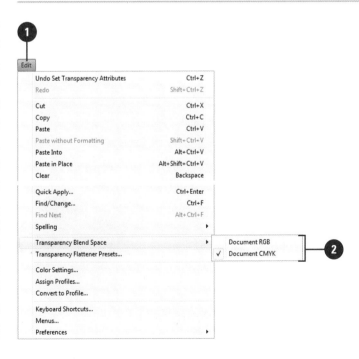

Transparency results

Select a Color Space for Blending Transparent Objects

1. Click the **Edit** menu, and then point to **Transparency Blend Space**.

2. Select a document's color space, such as Document RGB or Document CMYK.

   This converts the colors of all objects to a common color space (RGB or CMYK) for blending. This avoids color mismatches between objects in different color spaces.

Applying Shadow Effects

The Drop Shadow style is probably the most common effect used (next to Bevel and Emboss). The Inner Shadow style applies a shadow to the inside of an object. When you apply the Inner Shadow style, the shadow effect appears on the inside edges—like a reverse drop shadow. In addition to the distance and angle of the drop shadow, you can apply a blending mode and transparency. Other options include Global Light, Choke (inner), Spread (outer), and Noise. The Use Global Light option allows you to simulate the same light source on objects. The Spread and Choke options determine the amount of transparency used for the outer or inner part of the shadow. The Noise option introduces a random shift to the colors of the drop shadow.

Apply a Shadow Effect

1. Select one or more objects.

2. Click the **Object** menu, point to **Effects**, and then click **Drop Shadow** or **Inner Shadow**.

3. Do any of the following:

   ◆ **Blending options.** Select a blending mode and opacity for the shadow effect.

   ◆ **Position options.** Specify **Distance**, **Angle**, and **Offset** (X and Y) values to position the shadow in relation to the object.

   Select the **Use Global Light** check box to simulate the same lighting angle for all effects.

   ◆ **Other options.** Specify size and other options for the shadow; options vary depending on the type of shadow.

   The **Spread** and **Choke** options determine the amount of transparency used for the outer or inner part of the shadow. The **Noise** option introduces a random shift to the colors of the drop shadow.

4. Click **OK**.

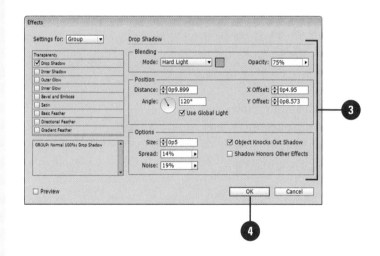

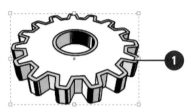

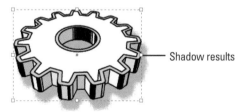

Shadow results

Applying Glow Effects

Outer Glow applies a glow in any color you choose to all selected objects. The Outer Glow style is an excellent way to create a neon effect for text. The Inner Glow style applies a glow to the inside of an object. When you apply the Inner Glow style, the effect appears on the inside edges—like a reverse outer glow. In addition to the technique (softer or precise) of the glow, you can apply specific blending modes and transparency. Other options include choke (inner), spread (outer), and Noise. The Spread and Choke options determine the amount of transparency used for the outer or inner part of the glow. The Noise option introduces a random shift to the colors of the glow.

Apply a Glow Effect

1. Select one or more objects.

2. Click the **Object** menu, point to **Effects**, and then click **Outer Glow** or **Inner Glow**.

3. Do any of the following:

   ◆ **Blending options.** Select a blending mode and opacity for the glow effect.

   ◆ **Other options.** Specify a **Technique** (softer or more precise glow) and **Size** of the glow; options vary depending on the type of glow.

   The **Spread** and **Choke** options determine the amount of transparency used for the outer or inner part of the glow. The **Noise** option introduces a random shift to the colors of the glow.

4. Click **OK**.

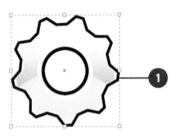

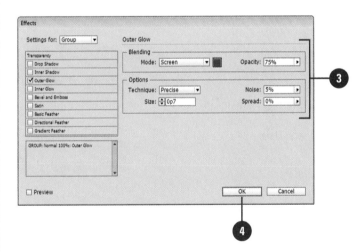

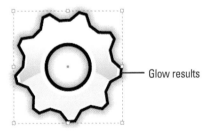

Glow results

Did You Know?

You can apply the satin effect. The satin effect applies a textured appearance to an object. Select one or more objects, click the Object menu, point to Effects, click Satin, specify angle, distance, size, and invert options, and then click OK.

Applying Bevel and Emboss Effects

The Bevel and Emboss style, second only to Drop Shadow in popularity, creates a 3D illusion of roundness to a flat surface. You can apply the Bevel effect to outline text to get the impression of 3D text. If the object you're applying the Bevel and Emboss has no transparent areas, the style will be applied to the outer edge of the image, and if you want to experiment beyond the standard rounded bevel, you can use a Chisel Hard option that makes text appear as if it's carved out of stone.

Apply a Bevel and Emboss Effect

1️⃣ Select one or more objects.

2️⃣ Click the **Object** menu, point to **Effects**, and then click **Bevel and Emboss**.

3️⃣ Do any of the following:

- ◆ **Structure options.** Specify a **Style** (inner or outer bevel, emboss or pillow emboss), **Technique** (smooth, chisel hard, chisel soft), **Direction**, and **Size** for the effect.

- ◆ **Shading options.** Specify the **Angle** and **Altitude** values to position the effect in relation to the object.

   Select the **Use Global Light** check box to simulate the same lighting angle for all effects.

   Select a blending mode for **Highlight** and **Shadow**.

4️⃣ Click **OK**.

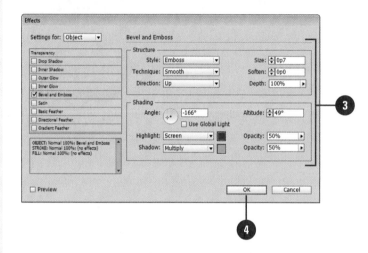

Bevel and Emboss results

Did You Know?

You can set the global light. The global light allows you to simulate the same lighting angle for all effects. You can set the angle and altitude options to create shadows. Click the Object menu, point to Effects, and then click Global Light.

Applying Feather Effects

A feather effect softens the edges of an object to appear transparent. InDesign provides three different feather effects: Basic, Directional, and Gradient. The Basic Feather effect creates a soft edge around the outside of objects. The Directional Feather effect creates soft edges for the top, bottom, left, or right sides of objects. The Gradient Feather effect creates soft edges in a gradient. Instead of making a transition from one color to another, a gradient feather makes a transition from a color to a transparent fade. Some common feather options include Choke (inner) and Noise. The Choke option determines the amount of transparency used for the inner part of the feather. The Noise option introduces a random shift to the colors of the feather.

Apply a Feather Effect

1. Select one or more objects.

2. Click the **Object** menu, point to **Effects**, and then click **Basic Feather**, **Directional Feather**, or **Gradient Feather**.

3. Specify the options for the type of feather effect you selected:

   ◆ **Basic Feather.** Specify a **Feather Width**, **Choke**, **Corners** (sharp, rounded, or diffused), and **Noise** for the effect.

   ◆ **Directional Feather.** Specify a **Feather Width** for top, bottom, left, or right, **Noise**, **Choke**, **Shape**, and **Angle** for the effect.

   ◆ **Gradient Feather.** Specify **Opacity** and **Location** for color stops, and **Type** and **Angle** for the gradient.

4. Click **OK**.

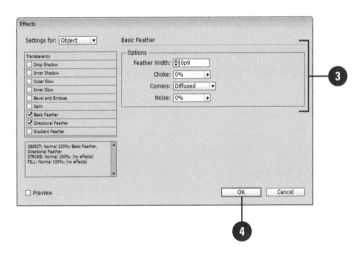

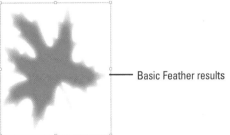

Basic Feather results

Applying Corner Object Effects

If you have an object with corners, you can change the shape of the object by applying corner object effects in the Corner Options dialog box. The effects include Fancy, Bevel, Inset, Inverse Rounded, and Rounded. In addition to specifying a corner effect, you can also specify a size for the effect. If you're not satisfied with the end result, you can always open the dialog box and adjust the corner effect and size. In addition to the Corner Options dialog box, you can also use Live Corners to apply corner effects to rectangular frames. When you show Live Corners, a yellow box appears on the frame, which you can select and adjust (with yellow diamond handles) to change the corner radius and apply different corner effects.

Apply Corner Object Effects

1. Select an object that you want to change.

2. Click the **Object** menu, and then click **Corner Options**.

3. Select the **Preview** check box to view your results in the document window.

4. To apply the corner effects to all four corners of a rectangle, click the **Make All The Settings The Same** icon to select it.

5. Click a corner **Effect** list arrow, and then select an effect.

   ◆ **Fancy.**

   ◆ **Bevel.**

   ◆ **Inset.**

   ◆ **Inverse Rounded.**

   ◆ **Rounded.**

6. Specify a **Size** value for the effect.

7. Click **OK**.

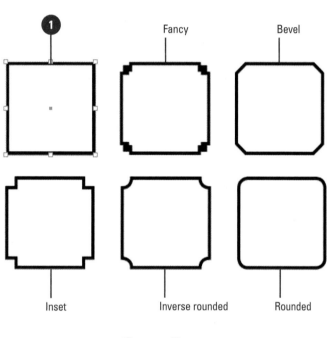

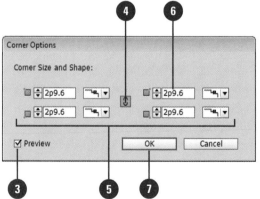

Use Live Corners

1. Click the **View** menu, point to **Extras**, and then click **Show Live Corners**.

2. Select an object that you want to change.

3. Click the yellow box on the frame edge.

   Four yellow diamonds appear on the selected frame.

4. To add corner effects, do any of the following:

   ◆ **All Four Corners.** Drag one of the yellow diamonds.

   ◆ **Single Corner.** Hold down Shift, and then drag a yellow diamond.

   ◆ **Apply Effects.** Alt (Win) or Option (Mac) click a yellow diamond to cycle through the effects.

   ◆ **Change Effect Radius.** Drag a yellow diamond toward the center of the frame.

5. To stop editing, click anywhere outside the selected frame.

6. To remove corner effects, click the **Object** menu, point to **Corner Options**, select **None** from an Effects list arrow, and then click **OK**.

7. Click the **View** menu, point to **Extras**, and then click **Hide Live Corners**.

Did You Know?

You can set corner effects on all of a path's corner points. Corner effects do not appear on smooth points. When you move a path's corner points, the effects automatically change angles.

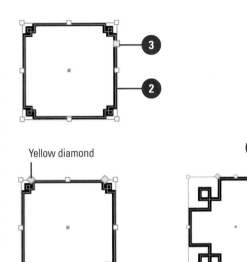

Yellow diamond

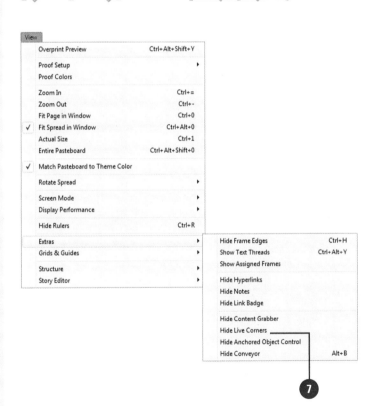

Converting Shape Objects

Sometimes when you create a shape with a certain look you just need to change the shape. Instead of creating a new shape, you can convert the shape to another shape by using Convert Shape buttons in the Pathfinder panel. The Pathfinder panel provides several different types of shapes: rectangle, rounded rectangle, beveled rectangle, inverted rounded rectangle, ellipse, triangle, polygon, and line. Some of the rectangle shapes use the radius value in the Corner Options dialog box to complete the conversion, so you can customize the shape.

Convert Shape Objects

① Select one or more objects.

② Select the **Pathfinder** panel.

◆ Click the **Window** menu, point to **Object & Layout**, and then click **Pathfinder**.

③ Select from the following Pathfinder Convert Shape buttons:

◆ **Rectangle.** Converts selection to a rectangle.

◆ **Rounded Rectangle.** Converts selection to a rounded rectangle using the radius from the Corner Options dialog box.

◆ **Beveled Rectangle.** Converts selection to a beveled rectangle using the radius from the Corner Options dialog box.

◆ **Inverted Rounded Rectangle.** Converts selection to an inverted rounded rectangle using the radius from the Corner Options dialog box.

◆ **Ellipse.** Converts selection to an ellipse.

◆ **Triangle.** Converts selection to a triangle.

◆ **Polygon.** Converts selection to a polygon.

◆ **Line.** Converts selection to a line.

◆ **Vertical or Horizontal Line.** Converts selection to a vertical or horizontal line.

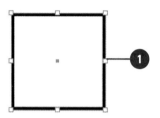

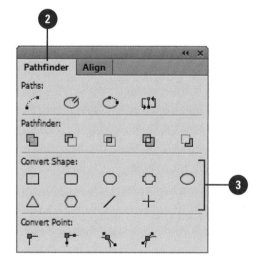

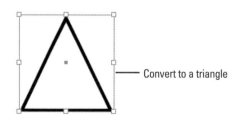

Convert to a triangle

Setting Object Defaults

If you always create an object with a certain fill or stroke attribute, you can make those settings the default. I find it useful to set the stroke weight to 1 point. Then I don't have to do it every time I create a new object. You can set the object defaults for the current document or for all new documents. InDesign has its own default fill and stroke settings of no fill and a black stroke. These program defaults are separate from the defaults you set.

Set Object Defaults

◆ **Document Defaults.** Open a document, deselect all objects, and then specify the defaults you want in the Stroke or other panels.

◆ **All New Document Defaults.** Close all documents, and then specify the defaults you want in the Stroke or other panels.

◆ **Apply InDesign Defaults.** Click the **Default Fill and Stroke** button on the Tools panel.

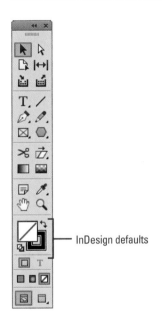

— InDesign defaults

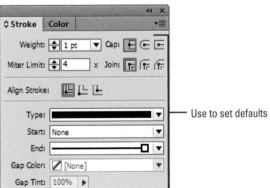

— Use to set defaults

Working with Points and Paths

Introduction

When you use InDesign's vector drawing or pen tools, InDesign creates a path to store that information. Paths are defined mathematically using anchor points and segments. Once created, they can be precisely modified to fit any design situation.

Working with the various Pen tools, it's possible to create precise paths, and even create complicated selections around virtually any shape. Once the path is created, it's a simple matter to subtract anchor points, and add new or modify existing anchor points to produce complex paths. It's even possible to convert straight segments (the visible line that connects two anchor points together) into elegantly curved segments, or you can remove the curve from a segment with a single click.

Paths can be used to precisely guide a brush stroke, or the interior of a path can be filled with any color or gradient available in InDesign using the Color, Stroke and Gradient panels. Paths can even be used as a clipping mask, which is an object whose shape masks out everything except the contents behind the shape.

What You'll Do

Draw with the Pen Tool

Select and Move Points and Segments

Convert Points

Add and Delete Anchor Points

Split Paths

Join Anchor Points

Use the Smooth Tool

Use the Pencil Tool

Erase to Reshape Paths

Work with Pathfinder

Create a Compound Path

Work with Clipping Paths

Drawing with the Pen Tool

When you work with InDesign's Pen tool, you're creating a path. The path consists of curved and straight segments connected by anchor points. When you click with the Pen tool, you create corner points and straight segments. When you drag with the Pen tool, you can create smooth points and curve segments, which have direction handles you can use to change the curved segment. The shape of the curve segment is defined by the length and direction of the direction handles. As you create drawings with the Pen tool, you can turn on Smart Guides to help you align the segments.

Draw a Polygon with the Pen Tool

1. Click the **Fill** box on the Tools panel, and then click the **Color** or **None** button to specify whether you want to fill the object or not.

2. Select the **Pen** tool on the Tools panel.

3. Click to create the first anchor point.

    ◆ To draw segments constrained to 45 degrees, hold down Shift while you click.

4. Click to create the second anchor point at another location.

    A line segment appears between the two anchor points.

5. Continue to add anchor points.

6. Do any of the following to complete the shape as a:

    ◆ **Open Path.** Click the Pen tool or any other tool on the Tools panel, or Ctrl+click (Win) or ⌘+click (Mac) outside the new shape to deselect it.

    ◆ **Closed Path.** Point to the starting anchor point, and then click it.

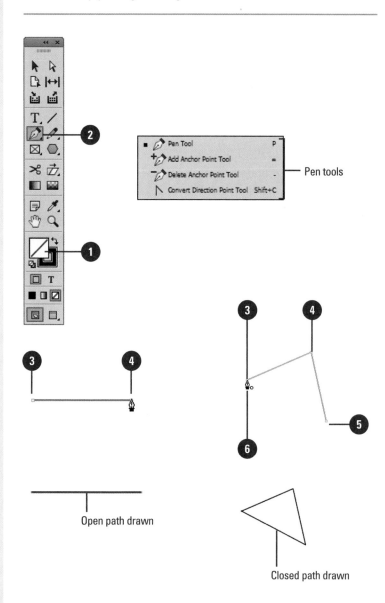

Pen tools

Open path drawn

Closed path drawn

Draw Curves with the Pen Tool

1. Click the **Fill** box on the Tools panel and then click the **Color** or **None** button to specify whether you want to fill the object or not.

2. Select the **Pen** tool on the Tools panel.

3. Click and drag to create the first anchor point.

   As you drag, the direction handles move.

4. Release the mouse, and then move to where you want the second point.

5. Click and drag to create the second anchor point and a smooth curve.

   ◆ To create the second anchor point and corner curves, hold the Alt (Win) or Option (Mac) key as you drag.

   A curve segment appears between the two anchor points. As you drag, the direction handles move, which changes the curve segment.

   The shape of the curve segment is defined by the length and direction of the direction handles.

6. Continue to add anchor points and direction handles.

7. Do any of the following to complete the shape as a:

   ◆ **Open Path.** Click the Pen tool or any other tool on the Tools panel, or Ctrl+click (Win) or ⌘+click (Mac) outside the new shape to deselect it.

   ◆ **Closed Path.** Point to the starting anchor point, and then click it.

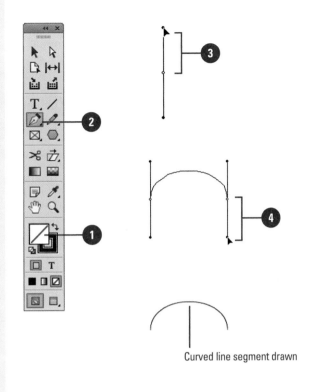

Curved line segment drawn

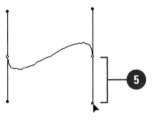

S-Curve drawn

Selecting and Moving Points and Segments

It's hard to draw a segment right the first time. Moving anchor points and segments is all part of the process of creating artwork. When you move an anchor point, the segments that are connected to it change. When you move a straight segment, the anchor points on the segment move with it. If an anchor point connects two segments, moving the anchor point changes both segments. When you move a curve segment, the curve changes, but the connecting anchors remain the same. You can also change a curve segment by adjusting a direction point on the direction handle.

Select, Move, and Reshape Anchor Points or Segments

1. Select the **Direct Selection** tool on the Tools panel.

2. Click a blank area to deselect all points.

   ◆ To select and move multiple anchor points and segments, hold the Shift key, and then click the anchor points or segments you want, or drag a rectangle marquee around the ones you want.

3. Drag an anchor point or drag the middle of a segment.

   ◆ For a smaller move, click the anchor point or segment, and then press an arrow key.

   ◆ To constrain the movement of anchor points or segments to 45 degrees, hold down Shift while dragging.

4. To reshape a curve segment, click an anchor point or a curve segment, and then drag a direction point at the end of the direction handle.

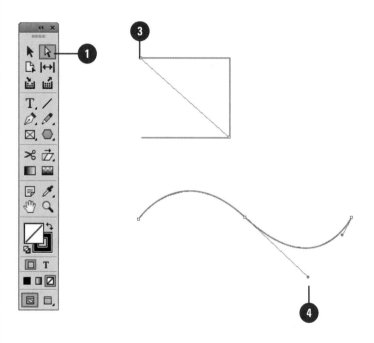

Work with Anchor Points or Segments

1. Select the **Direct Selection** tool on the Tools panel.

2. Do any of the following:

   ◆ **Move Straight Segments.** Select the segment, and then drag it.

   ◆ **Adjust Length or Angle of Straighten Segments.** Select an anchor point on the segment, and then drag the anchor point.

   ◆ **Adjust Position or Shape of Curved Segments.** Select a curved segment or an anchor point on the end, and then drag the segment.

   ◆ **Move or Nudge Anchor Points or Segments.** Select an anchor point or segment, click or hold down any of the arrow keys to move 1 pixel at a time in the direction of the arrow. To move 10 pixels at a time, hold down the Shift key.

   ◆ **Copy a Path or Segment.** Select a path or segment, hold down Alt (Win) or Option (Mac), and then drag the path or segment to another location.

   TIMESAVER *Hold down Shift while dragging to constrain the movement of anchor points or segments to 45 degrees.*

Did You Know?

You can quickly edit segments. When drawing with the Pen tool, you can temporarily use the Direct Selection tool to adjust existing segments by pressing Ctrl (Win) or ⌘ (Mac) while drawing.

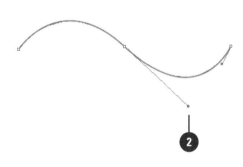

Converting Points

When you create a curve with the Pen tool, the curve segment after the second anchor point appears on the opposite side as the first curve segment. If you want the second curve segment to appear on the same side as the first, you need to convert the anchor point from a smooth point to a corner point. You can make this conversion as you create the curve segment with the Pen tool or you can do it later with commands on the Convert Point submenu, with buttons on the Pathfinder panel, or with the Convert Direction Point tool.

Convert Points on a Path

1. Select the **Direct Selection** tool on the Tools panel.

2. Select one or more points on a path to convert.

3. Select the **Pathfinder** panel.

   ◆ Click the **Window** menu, point to **Object & Layout**, and then click **Pathfinder**.

   ◆ You can also click the **Object** menu, point to **Convert Point**, and then select a convert command.

4. Click the button with the convert command you want:

   ◆ **Plain.** Changes points to have no direction points or lines.

   ◆ **Corner.** Changes points to have independent direction lines.

   ◆ **Smooth.** Changes points to be a continuous curve with connected direction lines.

   ◆ **Symmetrical.** Changes point to smooth points with equal length direction lines.

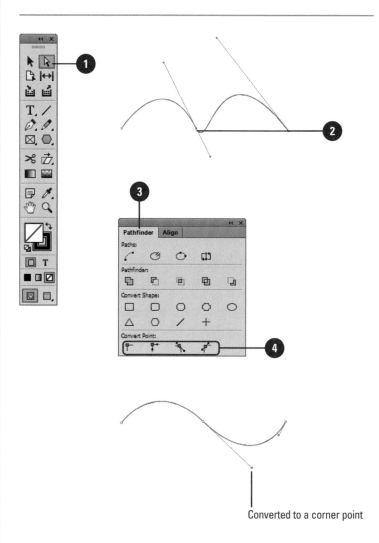

Converted to a corner point

Convert Points on a Path Using the Convert Direction Point Tool

1. Select the **Direct Selection** tool on the Tools panel, and then select a path to convert points.

2. Select the **Convert Direction Point** tool on the Tools panel.

3. Do any of the following to convert a point on a path:

   ◆ Drag a corner point to create a smooth point with no handles.

   ◆ Click a smooth curve point to create a corner point with no handles.

   ◆ Drag one of the handles of a smooth curve point to create a corner curve.

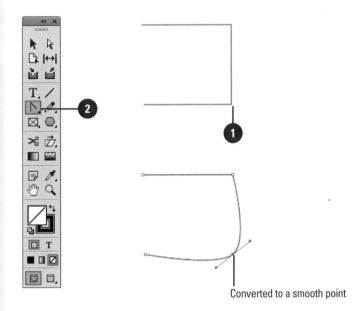

Converted to a smooth point

Adding and Deleting Anchor Points

Creating a path is not necessarily the end of the job; in fact, there are many ways you can modify a path once it's been created. For example, you can add, subtract, or delete anchor points on an existing path. You can also modify those points to conform to any desired shape. In addition, existing anchor points can be modified to change the segments connecting the points. Just like anything else in InDesign, paths are flexible. They can be modified to meet whatever design considerations are needed to make the job successful.

Add Anchor Points

1. Select the **Direct Selection** tool on the Tools panel.

2. Select the object to which you want to add an anchor point.

3. Select the **Add Anchor Point** tool on the Tools panel.

4. Click once on the path to add a new anchor point.

   When you add an anchor point to a curve segment, a smooth point appears on the path. When you add an anchor point to a straight segment, a corner point appears.

5. Click and drag on the path to add to and modify the segment.

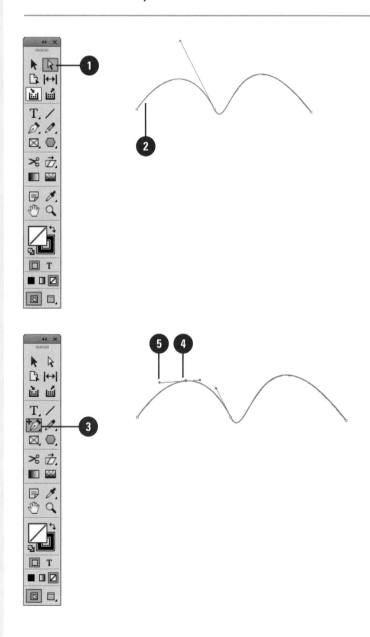

Add Anchor Points to an Open Path

1. Select the **Pen** tool on the Tools panel.

2. Point to the endpoint to which you want to add an anchor point.

   A slash appears next to the Pen pointer.

3. Click the endpoint to make it a corner point or drag it to make a smooth point.

4. Click once on the path to add a new anchor point.

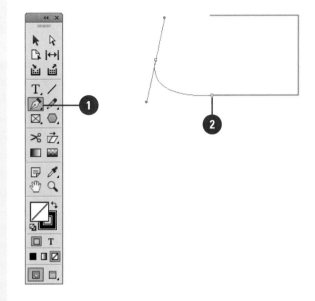

Delete Anchor Points

1. Select the **Direct Selection** tool on the Tools panel.

2. Select the object from which you want to delete an anchor point.

3. Select the **Delete Anchor Point** tool on the Tools panel.

4. Click once on an existing anchor point to remove it from the path.

   The anchor points on either side of the deleted point are now used to define the segment.

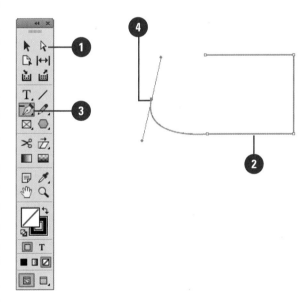

Did You Know?

You can delete a segment. Select the Direct Selection tool, click to select the segment, and then press the Delete key or click the Edit menu, and then click Clear.

Splitting Paths

The Scissors tool on the Tools panel allows you to split an open path into two paths or open a closed path. If you just want to open a closed path, you can also use the Open Path button on the Pathfinder panel or the same command on the Paths submenu. You can split a path at an anchor point or in the middle of a segment. The Scissors tool creates two points, one on top of the other. You can use the Direct Selection tool to move one point away from the other. If a path contains text, you cannot split it into two segments.

Split a Path

1 Select the **Direct Selection** tool on the Tools panel.

2 Select the object with the path that you want to split.

3 Select the **Scissors** tool on the Tools panel.

4 Click the object's path where you want to split it.

If you click on a closed path, it turns into an open path. If you click on an open path, it splits it into two paths.

If you click a line segment, two endpoints appear, one on top of the other.

5 To move the endpoints, select the **Direct Selection** tool, and then drag the selected endpoint to display the endpoint below it.

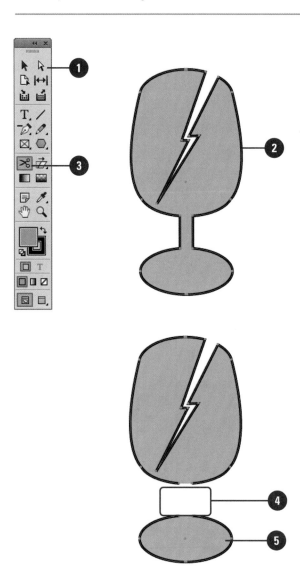

Open a Closed Path

1. Select the **Direct Selection** tool on the Tools panel.

2. Select the anchor point or segment where you want to open a closed path.

3. Select the **Pathfinder** panel.

   ◆ Click the **Window** menu, point to **Object & Layout**, and then click **Pathfinder**.

4. Click the **Open Path** button on the panel.

   The closed path turns into an open path.

5. To move the endpoints, select the **Direct Selection** tool, and then drag the selected endpoint to display the endpoint below it.

Did You Know?

You can reverse the direction of a path. Select the Direct Selection tool, select the path you want to reverse, and then click the Reverse button on the Pathfinder panel, or click the Object menu, point to Paths, and then click Reverse Path.

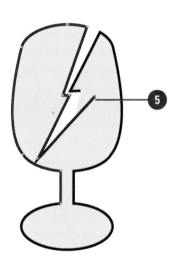

Joining Anchor Points

If you have an open path with two endpoints that you want to connect, you can use the Join or Close Path buttons on the Pathfinder panel to connect them with a straight line. You can also use the Join or Open Path commands from the Paths submenu on the Object menu. With the Join command, you need to select the two anchor points that you want to connect. With the Close Path command, all you need to do is select the open path.

Join Anchor Points

1. Select the **Direct Selection** tool on the Tools panel.

2. Select the two anchor points on a path you want to join.

3. Select the **Pathfinder** panel.

   ◆ Click the **Window** menu, point to **Object & Layout**, and then click **Pathfinder**.

4. Click the **Join Path** button on the panel.

   The anchor points are joined together.

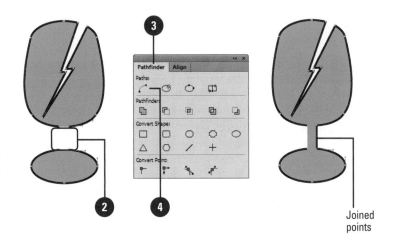

Joined points

Close an Open Path

1. Select the **Direct Selection** tool on the Tools panel.

2. Select the open path you want to close.

3. Select the **Pathfinder** panel.

   ◆ Click the **Window** menu, point to **Object & Layout**, and then click **Pathfinder**.

4. Click the **Close Path** button on the panel.

   The open path becomes closed.

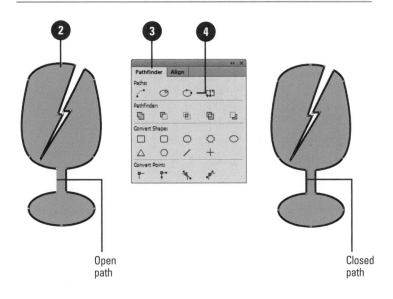

Open path

Closed path

Using the Smooth Tool

If you create a path with some jagged edges, you can use the Smooth tool to remove extra anchor points to smooth it out. Simply select the Smooth tool on the Tools panel, and then drag along a selected path. You can customize the way the Smooth tool works by setting preferences in the Smooth Tool Preferences dialog box.

Use the Smooth Tool

1. Select the **Direct Selection** tool on the Tools panel.

2. Select the path you want to smooth out.

3. Select the **Smooth** tool on the Tools panel.

4. Drag along the path to smooth it out.

   The path is reshaped with fewer points.

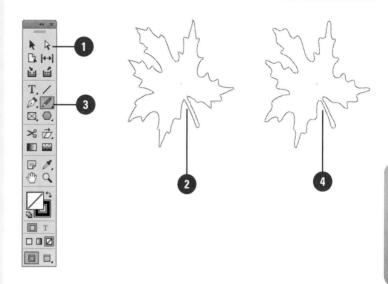

Set Smooth Tool Options

1. Double-click the **Smooth** tool on the Tools panel.

2. Drag the slider or enter a **Fidelity** value (.5-20). Fidelity determines how far the mouse must move before an anchor point is added. A higher value creates fewer anchor points and a smoother path while a lower value creates more anchor points and a rougher path.

3. Drag the slider or enter a **Smoothness** value (0-100). A high value creates a smoother curve, while a low value creates bends.

4. Select the **Keep Selected** check box to keep paths selected after you draw them.

5. Click **OK**.

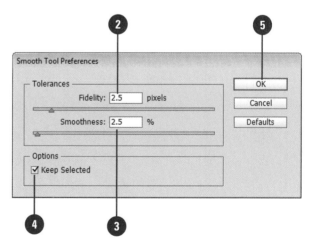

Using the Pencil Tool

The Pencil tool is exactly what its name implies…a pencil. If you like to draw freehand or sketch objects, especially with a drawing tablet, the Pencil tool is right for you. You can use the Pencil tool in several ways. You can draw new line segments to create a path, reshape a path, or add to a path. You can customize the way the Pencil tool works by setting preferences in the Pencil Tool Preferences dialog box.

Use the Pencil Tool

1. Select the **Pencil** tool on the Tools panel.

2. Select a stroke color and weight and a fill of **None** on the Tools or Stroke panels.

3. Use any of the following methods:

   ◆ **New Path.** Drag in a blank area to create an open or closed path. To create a closed path, hold down Alt (Win) or Option (Mac) while you finish drawing.

   ◆ **Reshape Path.** Drag along the edge of a selected open or closed path.

   ◆ **Add to Path.** Drag from an endpoint of an open path.

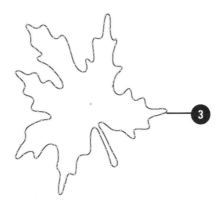

Set Pencil Tool Options

1. Double-click the **Pencil** tool on the Tools panel.

2. Drag the slider or enter a **Fidelity** value (.5-20). Fidelity determines how far the mouse must move before an anchor point is added. A higher value creates fewer anchor points and a smoother path while a lower value creates more anchor points and a rougher path.

3. Drag the slider or enter a **Smoothness** percentage value (0%-100%). A high value creates a smoother curve, while a low value creates bends.

4. Select or deselect any of the following check boxes:

   ◆ **Keep Selected.** Select to keep pencil paths selected after you draw them.

   ◆ **Edit Selected Paths.** Select to enable Reshaping for the Pencil tool within the specified pixel range (2-20).

5. To revert settings back to the defaults, click **Defaults**.

6. Click **OK**.

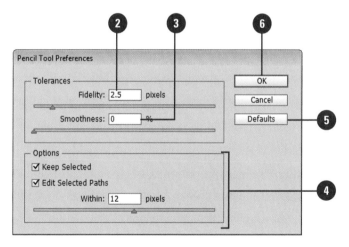

Erasing to Reshape Paths

Instead of selecting and deleting individual anchor points to reshape a path, you can use the Eraser tool on the Tools panel to delete parts of a path. When you use the Eraser tool to remove parts of a closed path, InDesign creates an open path. If you remove parts of an open path, InDesign creates two separate open paths. When you erase inside of a filled path, InDesign creates a compound path. This is useful when you want to simplify a complex drawing or remove a background.

Erase Parts of Paths

1. Select the objects that you want to reshape with the Eraser tool.

2. Select the **Eraser** tool on the Tools panel.

3. Drag across the parts of the object that you want to erase.

   The remaining parts of the path reconnect to close the path.

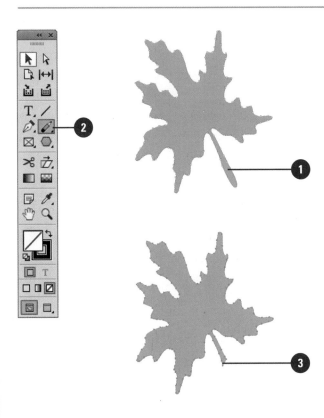

Working with Pathfinder

If you have overlapping objects, you can use buttons on the Pathfinder panel to create compound shapes, which are editable and releasable (restoring original attributes). You can use Pathfinder buttons (Add, Subtract, Intersect, Exclude Overlap, or Minus Back) on almost any object, except placed or rasterized images, mesh objects, or a single group.

Apply a Pathfinder Command

1. Select two or more overlapping objects.

2. Select the **Pathfinder** panel.

   ◆ Click the **Window** menu, point to **Object & Layout**, and then click **Pathfinder**.

3. Select from the following Pathfinder buttons:

   ◆ **Add.** Use to join the outer edges of selected objects into a compound shape.

   ◆ **Subtract.** Use to remove objects in front of other objects and still preserve paint attributes.

   ◆ **Intersect.** Use to preserve object areas that intersect.

   ◆ **Exclude Overlap.** Use to change overlapping areas to transparency.

   ◆ **Minus Back.** Use to remove objects in the back, leaving only part of the frontmost object.

Did You Know?

You can release a compound shape to restore object attributes. Select the Selection tool on the Tools panel, select the compound shape, click the Object menu, point to Paths, and then click Release Compound Path.

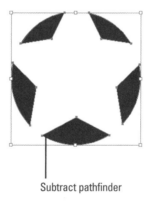

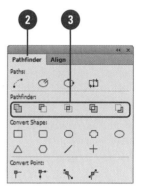

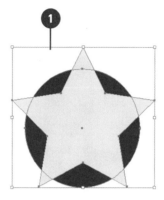

Subtract pathfinder

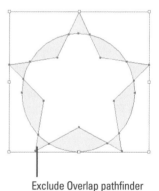

Exclude Overlap pathfinder

Creating a Compound Path

A compound path is a single object made up from two or more objects. In overlapping areas, a compound path removes the overlapping space displaying the attributes of the backmost object behind it. Think of it like a cookie cutter. After you create a compound path, you can release (restore) it at any time. However, the results are not exact. If you want to add another object to the compound path, you need to arrange the object in front or back of the compound object, select them both, and then reuse the Make Compound Path command.

Create a Compound Path

1. Arrange your objects so that the frontmost object will be cut out to reveal the attributes of the backmost object.

2. Select all the objects that you want to include in the compound path.

3. Click the **Object** menu, point to **Paths**, and then click **Make Compound Path**.

4. To add another object to the compound path, arrange the object in front or back of the compound object, select them both, and then click the **Object** menu, point to **Paths**, and then click **Make Compound Path**.

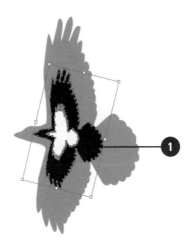

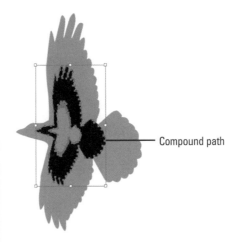

Compound path

Did You Know?

You can convert a clipping path into a frame. Select the clipping path, click the Object menu, point to Clipping Path, and then click Convert Clipping Path To Frame.

See Also

See "Working with Pathfinder" on pages 273 for more information on additional ways to work with overlapping objects.

Reverse an Object's Fill in a Compound Path

1. Click in a blank area to deselect the compound path.

2. Select the **Direct Selection** tool on the Tools panel.

3. Click the edge of the object for which you want to reverse the fill.

4. Select the **Pathfinder** panel.

   ◆ Click the **Window** menu, point to **Object & Layout**, and then click **Pathfinder**.

5. Click the **Reverse Path** button on the panel.

Reverse an object's fill

Release a Compound Path

1. Select the compound path.

2. Click the **Object** menu, point to **Paths**, and then click **Release Compound Path**.

   The single object reverts back to individual objects. All the objects are selected and painted with the attributes from the compound path, not their original attributes.

Released compound path

Working with Clipping Paths

A clipping path, or clipping mask, is a path whose shape masks out everything except the image contents behind the shape. You can create one in Adobe Photoshop and then place it into your InDesign document with the Apply Photoshop Clipping Path option in the Import Options dialog box, or you can have InDesign try to create a clipping path from the edges of an image. Once you have a clipping path, you can select and modify it like any other path using the Direct Selection tool and change options using the Clipping Path dialog box.

Modify a Clipping Path from a Graphic Image

1. Select the clipping path.

2. Click the **Object** menu, point to **Clipping Path**, and then click **Options**.

3. Select the **Preview** check box to view your results in the document window.

4. Click the **Type** list arrow, and then click **Detect Edges**.

5. Specify a **Threshold** value to define the color used as the area outside the clipping path and **Tolerance** value to apply small color variations and smooth out the path.

6. Click **OK**.

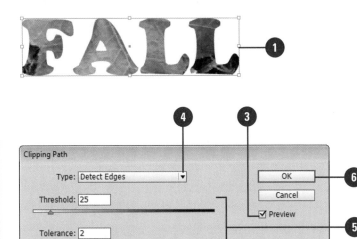

Did You Know?

You can convert a clipping path into a frame. Select the clipping path, click the Object menu, point to Clipping Path, and then click Convert Clipping Path To Frame.

See Also

See "Setting Place Import Options" on pages 144 for more information on importing and modifying clipping paths or alpha channels.

Select a Path or Alpha Channel as the Clipping Path

① Select the clipping path.

② Click the **Object** menu, point to **Clipping Path**, and then click **Options**.

③ Select the **Preview** check box to view your results in the document window.

④ Click the **Type** list arrow, and then click **Photoshop Path** or **Alpha Channel**.

The list arrow below it changes to Path for Photoshop Path or Alpha for Alpha Channel.

⑤ Specify a **Threshold** value to define the color used as the area outside the clipping path and a **Tolerance** value to apply small color variations and smooth out the path.

⑥ Specify any of the following:

◆ **Inset Frame.** Use to enlarge (negative values) or shrink (positive values) the path in the image.

◆ **Invert.** Select to switch the visible and non-visible areas.

◆ **Include Inside Edges.** Select to add areas to the clipping path in the image.

◆ **Restrict to Frame.** Select to prevent the clipping path frame from displaying areas outside the frame.

◆ **Use High Resolution Image.** Select to create the path from the high resolution version of the image.

⑦ Click **OK**.

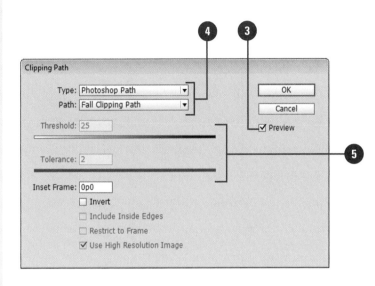

Alpha Channel

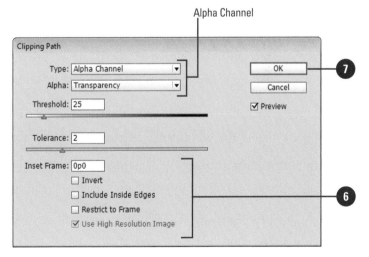

Working with Tables

Introduction

There are times when typing a paragraph will not do your text justice. Creating a bulleted or numbered list might better show your information. Another way to organize items in a document is with a table. A **table** is an object that is inserted into the document that displays text in rows and columns. You can set up your table with existing or imported text, or create a blank table and enter in new text. Once created, you can adjust the cells (where the text is contained in the rows and columns). You can also adjust the table to insert or delete rows, columns or individual cells, or change the alignment of text or graphics in cells.

In InDesign, a table is placed in a text frame, which might be larger or smaller than the table. You can drag the corner of the text frame to adjust the frame. If the text frame is smaller than the table, an overflow symbol appears in the bottom right corner. The overflow symbol works the same for tables as it does for normal text. When a table overflows, you can repeat the first (header) and last (footer) rows of a table when it appears in a different text frame on the same or different page. The information you enter in the header and footer automatically appears in the repeated headers and footers.

When you create a table, InDesign automatically creates strokes around cells to format it. You can remove or customize the strokes or add fills by using the Strokes and Fills tab on the Cell Options dialog box. If that is not enough, you can apply a border to the table. If you want to take formatting to the next level, you can add an alternating pattern to rows or columns to make it easier to read information in a table.

What You'll Do

Create Tables

Import Text into Tables

Enter and Edit Text in a Table

Modify a Table

Adjust Table Rows and Columns

Adjust Table Cells

Align Content in Table Cells

Create Table Headers and Footers

Add Strokes and Fills

Alternate Fills and Strokes

Add Diagonal Lines in Cells

Add a Border to a Table

Adjust Tables in the Text Frame

Creating Tables

A table organizes your information into rows and columns. The intersection of a row and column is called a **cell**. You can create a blank table, and then enter text, or make a table from existing text separated by paragraphs, tabs, or commas. The first row in the table is good for column headings, whereas the leftmost column is good for row labels. Knowing how to select the rows and columns of a table is also essential to working with the table itself. If you want create a table within a table, you can create **nested tables**. If you decide a particular table is not really necessary after all, you can convert it to text.

Create a New Table

1. Click to place the insertion point in a text box where you want to create a new table.

   ◆ To insert a table within a table, click to place the new table insertion point in a table cell.

2. Click the **Table** menu, and then click **Insert Table**.

3. Specify the following dimensions:

   ◆ **Body Rows.** Enter a number to specify the number of rows you want in the table.

   ◆ **Columns.** Enter a number to specify the number of columns you want in the table.

   ◆ **Header Rows.** Enter a number to set the number of header rows at the top of the table.

   ◆ **Footer Rows.** Enter a number to set the number of footer rows at the bottom of the table.

4. Click the **Table Style** list arrow, and then select a table style.

5. Click **OK**.

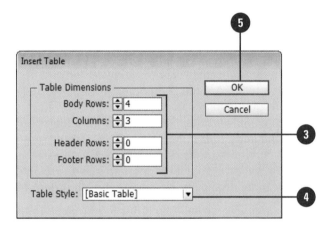

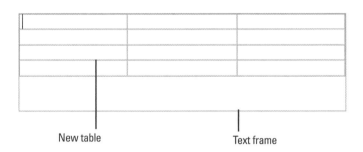

New table   Text frame

Did You Know?

You can delete a table. Click inside the table you want to delete, click the Table menu, point to Delete, and then click Table.

Convert Text to a Table

1. Select the text that you want to convert into a table.

2. Click the **Table** menu, and then click **Convert Text to Table**.

3. Click the **Column Separator** list arrow, and then select a separator: **Tab**, **Comma**, or **Paragraph**.

4. Click the **Row Separator** list arrow, and then select a separator: **Tab**, **Comma**, or **Paragraph**.

5. Enter a **Column** number to set the number of columns in the table.

6. Click the **Table Style** list arrow, and then select a table style.

7. Click **OK**.

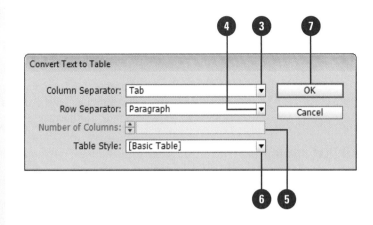

Convert a Table into Text

1. Click to place the insertion point inside any cell in the table.

2. Click the **Table** menu, and then click **Convert Table to Text**.

3. Click the **Column Separator** list arrow, and then select a separator: **Tab**, **Comma**, or **Paragraph**.

4. Click the **Row Separator** list arrow, and then select a separator: **Tab**, **Comma**, or **Paragraph**.

5. Click **OK**.

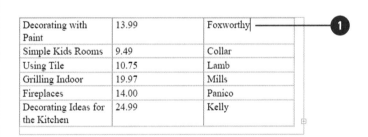

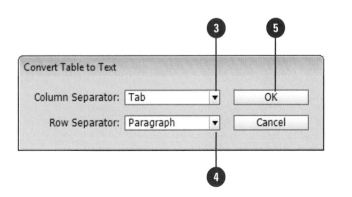

Importing Text into Tables

In addition to creating a table from text in an InDesign document, you can copy tabbed text from other programs and paste it into a table in your document. If you have a table in Microsoft Word or a spreadsheet in Microsoft Excel that you want to use in a document, you can import the table by using the Place command on the File menu. During the import process, you can specify import options to place the information you want in the way you want. A red dot inside a table cell indicates there is overflow text.

Import Text into a Table

1. Open the program where you want to copy text for a table.

   ◆ You can also copy text from another table to paste into an InDesign table.

2. Select and copy text that has tab separators.

3. Switch back to InDesign.

4. Select the cells in the table where you want to paste text.

5. Click the **Edit** menu, and then click **Paste**.

   The text appears in the selected cells. Any additional text appears in new cells.

Did You Know?

You can import a graphic into a table cell. Click to place the insertion point in the cell where you want the graphic, click the File menu, click Place, select the graphic file, and then click OK. The graphic is linked to the document in the table cell. You can use the Links panel to update or relink the graphic. See Chapter 5, "Placing and Working with Graphics" for details.

You can adjust table options. Click inside the table, click the Table menu, point to Table Options, click Table Setup, specify the options you want, and then click OK.

Decorating with Paint	13.99	Foxworthy
Simple Kids Rooms	9.49	Collar
Using Tile	10.75	Lamb
Grilling Indoor	19.97	Mills
Fireplaces	14.00	Panico
Decorating Ideas for the Kitchen	24.99	Kelly
Decorating Garden Style	32.48	Burley
Home Sense's Complete Home Decorating Book	45.50	Pearl
Using Color at Home	12.99	Law
Rooms for Little Ones	7.39	Miller
Kid's Rooms made Simple	8.88	Poulson
Express Yourself with Color	4.99	Cartwright
Painting Techniques	29.97	Heyn
Great Bathrooms Ideas	17.96	Woodring
Window Décor made Simple	10.83	Wallis
Great Kitchens Ideas	17.96	Allen

Import a Table from Word or Excel

1. Click the **File** menu, and then click **Place**.

2. Navigate to the location with the file you want to import.

3. Select the file you want to place.

4. Select the **Show Import Options** check box to select import options.

5. Click **Open**.

6. Specify the following options:

   - **For Word.** Select options from the Microsoft Word Import Options dialog box.

     - **Preset and Include.** Select an import preset and select check boxes to include Word elements.

     - **Formatting.** Select formatting options to Remove or Preserve Styles and Formatting from Text and Tables, or Import Styles Automatically.

   - **For Excel.** Select options from the Microsoft Excel Import Options dialog box.

     - **Sheet, View, and Cell Range.** Select an Excel sheet, view, and cell range. You can also import hidden cells not saved in view.

     - **Formatting.** Select formatting options for table, style, cell alignment, the number of decimal places to use, and typographer's quotes.

7. Click **OK**.

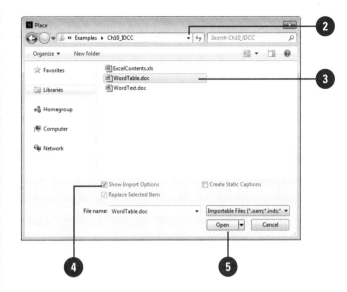

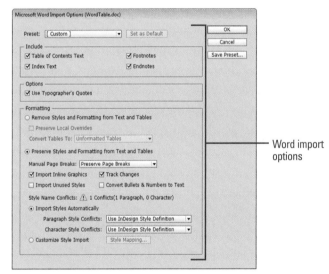

Word import options

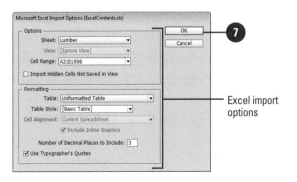

Excel import options

Entering and Editing Text in a Table

Once you create your table, you enter text into cells just as you would in a paragraph, except in a table, pressing Tab moves you from cell to cell. As you type in a cell, text wraps to the next line, and the height of a row expands as you enter text that extends beyond the column width. Before you can edit text directly in a table, you need to know how to select the rows and columns of a table. If you want to focus solely on table text, you can use the Story Editor, which displays text in sequential columns and rows for easy editing.

Enter Text and Navigate a Table

1. The insertion point shows where text that you type will appear in a table. After you type text in a cell:

   ◆ Press Enter (Win) or Return (Mac) to start a new paragraph within that cell.

   ◆ Press Tab or Shift+Tab to move the insertion point to the next or previous cell (or to the first cell in the next or last row).

   ◆ Press the arrow keys or click in a cell to move the insertion point to a new location.

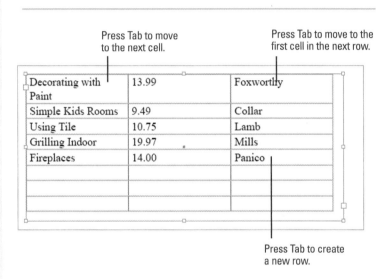

Press Tab to move to the next cell.

Press Tab to move to the first cell in the next row.

Press Tab to create a new row.

Select Table Elements

Refer to this table for methods of selecting table elements, including:

   ◆ The entire table

   ◆ One or more rows and columns

   ◆ One or more cells

Did You Know?

You can delete contents within a cell. Select the contents of the cell you want to delete, and then press Delete.

Selecting Table Elements

To Select	Do This
The table	Click the top left corner of the table and then click ➡ or click in the table, click the Table menu, point to Select, and then click Table.
One or more columns	Click just above the first column you want to select, and then drag with ⬇ to select the columns you want.
The column or row with the insertion point	Click in the column or row, click the Table menu, point to Select, and then click Column or Row.
A single cell	Drag a cell or click the cell with ➡. , or click the Table menu, point to Select, and then click Cell.
More than one cell	Drag with ➡ to select a group of cells.

Select and Edit Text

1. Move the I-beam pointer to the left or right of the text you want to select.

2. Drag the pointer to highlight the text, or click in the document to place the insertion point where you want to make a change.

3. Perform one of the following editing commands:

   ◆ To replace text, type your text.

   ◆ To delete text, press the Backspace key or the Delete key.

   ◆ Drag the selection to the new location.

Edit Table Elements in the Story Editor

1. Click in the table you want to edit using Story Editor.

2. Click the **Edit** menu, and then click **Edit in Story Editor**.

3. Drag the pointer to highlight the text, or click in the document to place the insertion point where you want to make a change.

4. Perform one of the following editing commands:

   ◆ To replace text, type your text.

   ◆ To delete text, press the Backspace key or the Delete key.

   ◆ Drag the selection to the new location.

5. Click the **Close** button.

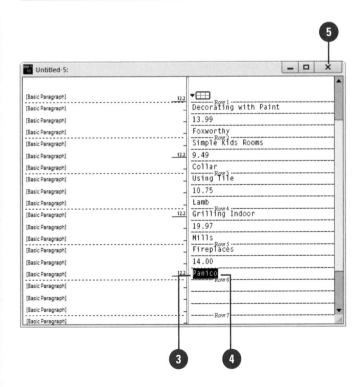

Modifying a Table

As you begin to work on a table, you might need to modify table contents by using options available on the Control and Table panels and Table menu. You can modify the table's structure by adding more rows, columns, or cells to accommodate new text, graphics, or other tables. The table realigns as needed to accommodate the new structure. When you insert rows or columns, the existing rows shift down and the existing columns shift right. Similarly, when you delete unnecessary rows or columns from a table, the table automatically realigns.

Modify Tables Using the Control or Table Panels

① Select the cells, rows, or columns you want to modify.

The Control panel displays options for the current selection.

② Select the **Table** panel.

③ Use the following Control and Table panel options:

◆ **Number of Rows or Columns.** Specify a number.

◆ **Row Height or Column Width.** Specify a number.

◆ **Align Top, Center, Bottom, and Justify.** Click a button.

◆ **Rotate 0°, 90°, 180°, 270°.** Click a button.

◆ **Cell Inset Top, Bottom, Right or Left.** Specify a number for spacing between cell edge and cell contents.

Additional Control panel options include:

◆ **Merge and Unmerge.** Click a button to combine or uncombine cells.

◆ **Stroke Weight.** Enter a line thickness.

◆ **Stroke Style.** Select a line style.

◆ **Proxy Cell Line Preview.** Select which lines to which you want to apply settings.

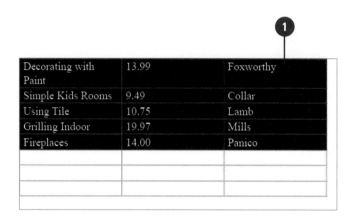

Decorating with Paint	13.99	Foxworthy
Simple Kids Rooms	9.49	Collar
Using Tile	10.75	Lamb
Grilling Indoor	19.97	Mills
Fireplaces	14.00	Panico

Table options

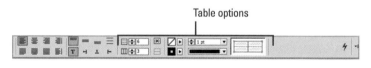

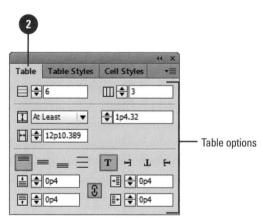

Table options

Insert Additional Rows or Columns

1. Select the row or column next to where you want the new ones.

   TIMESAVER *Drag the last row or column, and then press Alt (Win) or Option (Mac) as you drag to insert new rows or columns.*

2. Drag to select the number of rows or columns you want to insert.

3. Click the **Table** menu, point to **Insert**, and then click **Rows** or **Columns**.

4. Specify the number of rows or columns, and then select an option for the position.

5. Click **OK**.

Insert rows

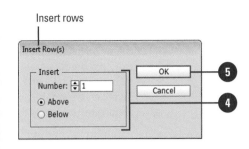

Insert columns

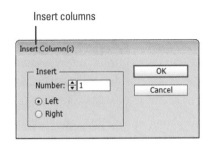

Delete Rows and Columns

1. Select the rows or columns you want to delete.

2. Click the **Table** menu, point to **Delete**, and then click **Row** or **Column**.

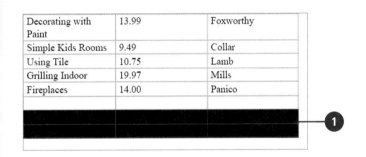

Deleted rows

Adjusting Table Rows and Columns

After you insert and delete rows and columns in a table, you can adjust them to any size you want. If you want to create evenly sized rows and columns, you can use the Distribute Rows Evenly or Distribute Columns Evenly command to quickly do the job. If you want custom sizes, you can drag the row or column borders to the size you want or set exact sizing in the Rows and Columns tab in the Cell Options dialog box. Sometimes a long table doesn't fit in a text frame. You can also set cell options to keep rows together.

Distribute Row or Column Spacing Evenly

1. Specify the content position of the rightmost column or bottommost row that you want to use as the model for the row or column spacing.

2. Select the columns or rows in which you want the content distributed to match the model row or column.

3. Click the **Table** menu, and then click **Distribute Rows Evenly** or **Distribute Columns Evenly**.

Decorating with Paint	13.99	Foxworthy
Simple Kids Rooms	9.49	Collar
Using Tile	10.75	Lamb
Grilling Indoor	19.97	Mills
Fireplaces	14.00	Panico

Decorating with Paint	13.99	Foxworthy
Simple Kids Rooms	9.49	Collar
Using Tile	10.75	Lamb
Grilling Indoor	19.97	Mills
Fireplaces	14.00	Panico

Evenly distributed columns

Adjust Row Heights and Column Widths

- ◆ **Adjust Rows.** Point to a row border (cursor changes to a double-arrow), and then drag to adjust the height of the row.

- ◆ **Adjust All Rows.** Point to the bottom row border (cursor changes to a double-arrow), and then drag to adjust the height of all rows.

- ◆ **Adjust Columns.** Point to a column border (cursor changes to a double-arrow), and then drag to adjust the width of the column.

Drag to adjust columns

Decorating with Paint	13.99	Foxworthy	
Simple Kids Rooms	9.49	Collar	
Using Tile	10.75	Lamb	
Grilling Indoor	19.97	Mills	
Fireplaces	14.00	Panico	

Adjust Row and Column Options

1. Select the cells you want to adjust.

2. Click the **Table** menu, point to **Cell Options**, and then click **Rows and Columns**.

3. Specify the following row and column options.

    - ◆ **Row Height.** Enter a row height value for the **At Least** or **Exactly** option.

    - ◆ **Column Width.** Enter a column width.

    - ◆ **Start Row.** Select an option to control when and how the rows of a table break across text frames.

    - ◆ **Keep with Next Row.** Select to keep the selected row with the one following it across text frames.

4. Click **OK**.

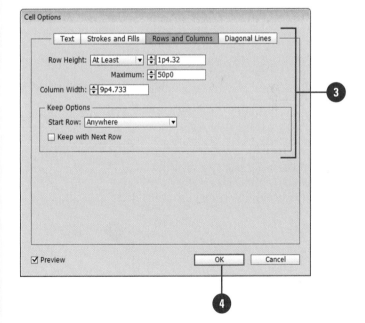

Adjusting Table Cells

Often, there is more to modifying a table than adding or deleting rows or columns; you need to make cells just the right size to accommodate the text or graphics you are entering in the table. For example, a title in the first row of a table might be longer than the first cell in that row. To spread the title across the top of the table, you can merge (combine) the cells to form one long cell. Sometimes, to indicate a division in a topic, you need to split (or divide) a cell into two. You can also split one table into two at any row. Moreover, you can modify the width of any column and height of any row to better present your data.

Merge Table Cells

1. Select the two or more cells you want to merge into a single cell.

2. Drag to select the number of rows you want to insert.

3. Click the **Table** menu, and then click **Merge Cells**.

4. To unmerge table cells, click in the single merged cell, click the **Table** menu, and then click **Unmerge Cells**.

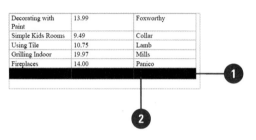

Merged cells

Split Table Cells

1. Click the cell you want to split into two cells.

2. Click the **Table** menu, and then click **Split Cell Horizontally** or **Split Cell Vertically**.

Split cells

Aligning Content in Table Cells

After you enter or insert text and graphics into cells in a table, you can adjust the spacing of the content to position it where you want in a cell. You can control how text is positioned vertically or horizontally in the cell as well as the text baseline. A graphic appears in a table as an inline graphic, so you can adjust its position like you would text. If the graphic is larger than the cell, you can set the Clip Content to Cell option to crop the image to the cell boundaries.

Adjust the Spacing of Text and Graphics in a Cell

1. Select the cells you want to adjust.

2. Click the **Table** menu, point to **Cell Options**, and then click **Text**.

3. Select the **Preview** check box to view your results in the document window.

4. Specify any of the following options:

   ◆ **Cell Insets.** Enter the spacing sizes for the top, bottom, left and right inside areas of the cell.

   ◆ **Vertical Justification.** Specify an alignment position for vertical text in the cell.

   ◆ **Paragraph.** Enter an amount for the space between the lines or paragraphs in the cell.

   ◆ **First Baseline.** Specify an option to control where the first text baseline appears in the cell.

   ◆ **Clipping for Graphics.** Select the **Clip Contents to Cell** check box to restrain the graphic content to the size of the cell. Deselect it to allow the graphic to appear outside of cell boundaries.

   ◆ **Text Rotation.** Specify a rotation angle for the contents of the cell.

5. Click **OK**.

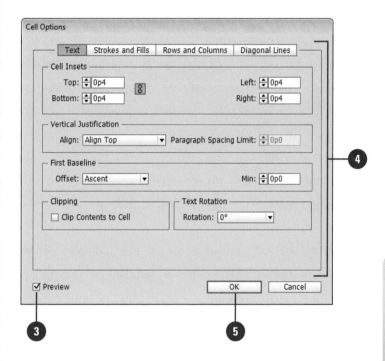

Creating Table Headers and Footers

Table headers are the first row in a table and footers are the last row. Sometimes a long table doesn't fit in a text frame. You can repeat the first and last rows of a table when they appear in a different text frame on the same or a different page. The information you enter in the header and footer automatically appears in the repeated headers and footers. If you already have text in the table that you want to use as a header or footer, you can convert the rows into a table header or footer. On the flip side, you can also convert header or footer rows into normal rows.

Insert a Header or Footer in a Table

1. Click in the table you want to add a header or footer.

2. Click the **Table** menu, point to **Table Options**, and then click **Headers and Footers**.

3. Select the **Preview** check box to view your results in the document window.

4. Enter a **Header Rows** value to set a number for header rows.

   - To disable header rows, set the value to zero.

5. Enter a **Footer Rows** value to set a number for footer rows.

   - To disable footer rows, set the value to zero.

6. Click the **Repeat Header** or **Repeat Footer** list arrow, and then specify a repeat option.

   - **Every Text Column.** Repeat everywhere in the table.

   - **Once Per Frame.** Repeat only once in the same frame.

   - **Once Per Page.** Repeat only once in the same page.

7. Select the **Skip First** or **Skip Last** check box to display the header or footer only after the first or last use.

8. Click **OK**.

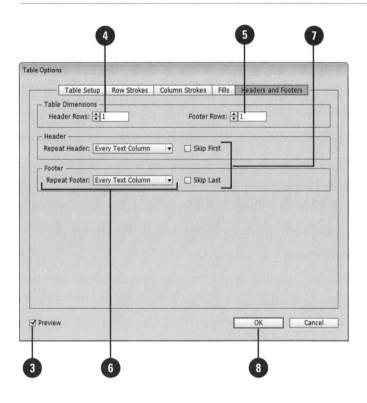

Convert Cells into a Table Header or Footer

1 Select the rows that you want to convert into a header or footer.

2 Click the **Table** menu, point to **Convert Rows**, and then click **To Header** or **To Footer**.

If you already have text in a header or footer, the new header or footer text is added to the bottom (for a header) or top (for a footer) of the existing cells.

Book	Price	Author	
Decorating with Paint	13.99	Foxworthy	**1**
Simple Kids Rooms	9.49	Collar	
Using Tile	10.75	Lamb	
Grilling Indoor	19.97	Mills	
Fireplaces	14.00	Panico	
	Average		

Convert a Header or Footer into Cells

1 Select the header or footer row that you want to convert into normal body rows of table cells.

2 Click the **Table** menu, point to **Convert Rows**, and then click **To Body**.

Book	Price	Author
Decorating with Paint	13.99	Foxworthy
Simple Kids Rooms	9.49	Collar
Using Tile	10.75	Lamb
Grilling Indoor	19.97	Mills
Fireplaces	14.00	Panico
	Average	

1

Did You Know?

You can use menu commands to edit headers or footers. Click in the table you want to edit, click the Table menu, and then click Edit Header or Edit Footer. The first header or footer cell is selected and ready for edits. You can also click in the header or footer cell to edit it.

Adding Strokes and Fills

When you create a table, InDesign automatically creates strokes around cells. You can remove or customize the strokes, and even add custom fills by using the Strokes and Fills tab on the Cell Options dialog box. In the dialog box, you select cell lines in a proxy preview to specify to which actual lines in the cell you want to apply formatting. When you mix and match stroke colors and styles in a table, you also need to specify stroke drawing order to determine how the table should be drawn. After you apply formatting once, you don't need to reselect the proxy preview lines the next time you want to apply formatting changes to the same cells.

Set Stroke Drawing Order

1. Select the cells in the table you want to format.

2. Click the **Table** menu, point to **Table Options**, and then click **Table Setup**.

3. Select the **Preview** check box to view your results in the document window.

4. Click the **Draw** list arrow, and then select a stroke drawing order option:

   ◆ **Best Joins.** Allows InDesign to choose the best way to display strokes.

   ◆ **Row Strokes in Front.** Displays the strokes from rows in front of strokes from columns.

   ◆ **Column Strokes in Front.** Displays strokes from columns in front of strokes from rows.

   ◆ **InDesign 2.0 Compatibility.** Uses a combination of Best Joins for the table border and Row Strokes for interior cells.

5. Click **OK**.

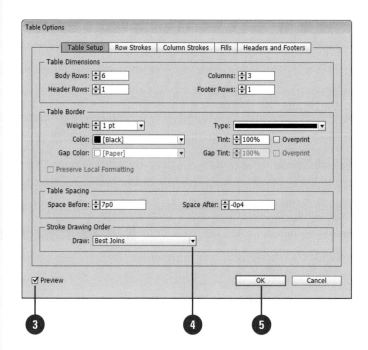

Add Strokes or Fills to Cells

1. Select the cells in the table you want to format.

2. Click the **Table** menu, point to **Cell Options**, and then click **Strokes and Fills**.

3. Select the **Preview** check box to view your results in the document window.

4. Click the lines in the cell proxy preview to select (they will turn blue) the edges that you want to format.

5. Specify the following Cell Stroke and Fill options:

   ◆ **Weight.** Enter a value to set the thickness of the stroke.

   ◆ **Type.** Specify a style for the stroke.

   ◆ **Color and Tint.** Specify a color and tint for the stroke. Select the Overprint Stroke check box to apply it.

   ◆ **Gap Color and Tint.** If you selected a stroke type with dashes or dots, specify a gap color (for the space between the lines) and tint for the stroke. Select the Overprint Gap check box to apply it.

   ◆ **Color and Tint for Fill.** Specify a color and tint for the fill. Select the Overprint Fill check box to apply it.

6. Click **OK**.

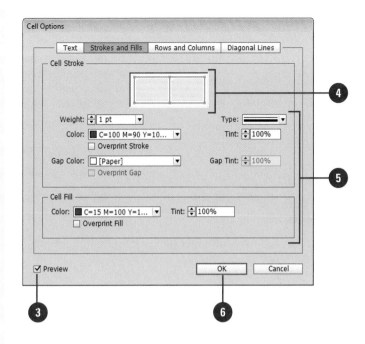

Book	Price	Author
Decorating with Paint	13.99	Foxworthy
Simple Kids Rooms	9.49	Collar
Using Tile	10.75	Lamb
Grilling Indoor	19.97	Mills
Fireplaces	14.00	Panico
	Average	

Applied fills

Alternating Fills and Strokes

Alternating rows or columns with a color or a pattern can make it easier to read information in a table. With this thought in mind, InDesign allows you to format a table with repeating alternating fills and strokes. The alternating fills and strokes remain in place until you change the alternating option to None. If you insert or delete a row or column, the alternating pattern reapplies to the table. You can create alternating patterns with fills in a table and strokes in a row or column.

Alternate Fills in Table Cells

1. Click in the table to which you want to add alternating fills.

2. Click the **Table** menu, point to **Table Options**, and then click **Alternating Fills**.

3. Select the **Preview** check box to view your results in the document window.

4. Click the **Alternating Pattern** list arrow, and then select a pattern option.

5. Specify the following options on the left for the first set of columns or rows, and on the right for the second set of columns or rows:

   ◆ **First** or **Next**. Enter a value to set the number of rows in the alternating pattern.

   ◆ **Color and Tint**. Specify a color and tint for the fill. Select the Overprint check box to apply it.

   ◆ **Skip First** or **Skip Last**. Enter a value to omit the number of rows or columns at the start or end of the alternating fills.

   ◆ **Preserve Local Formatting.** Select to use the cell formatting instead of the border formatting. Deselect to use the border formatting.

6. Click **OK**.

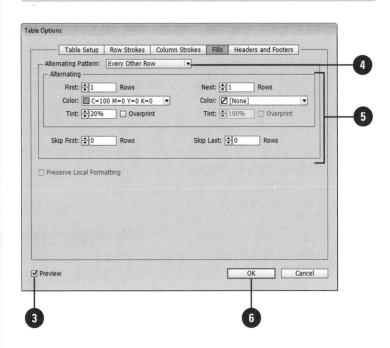

Book	Price	Author	
Decorating with Paint	13.99	Foxworthy	Alternating fills
Simple Kids Rooms	9.49	Collar	
Using Tile	10.75	Lamb	
Grilling Indoor	19.97	Mills	
Fireplaces	14.00	Panico	
	Average		

Alternate Strokes for Rows or Columns in Table Cells

1. Click in the table to which you want to add alternating fills.

2. Click the **Table** menu, point to **Table Options**, and then click **Alternating Row Strokes** or **Alternating Column Strokes**.

3. Select the **Preview** check box to view your results in the document window.

4. Click the **Alternating Pattern** list arrow, and then select a pattern option.

5. Specify the following options on the left for the first set of columns or rows, and on the right for the second set of columns or rows:

   ◆ **First** or **Next**. Enter a value to set the number of rows in the alternating pattern.

   ◆ **Weight**. Enter a value to set the thickness of the stroke.

   ◆ **Type**. Specify a style for the stroke.

   ◆ **Color and Tint**. Specify a color and tint for the stroke. Select the Overprint check box to apply it.

   ◆ **Gap Color and Tint**. If you selected a stroke type with dashes or dots, specify a gap color (for the space between the lines) and tint for the stroke. Select the Overprint check box to apply it.

   ◆ **Skip First** or **Skip Last**. Enter a value to omit the number of rows or columns at the start or end of the alternating strokes.

6. Click **OK**.

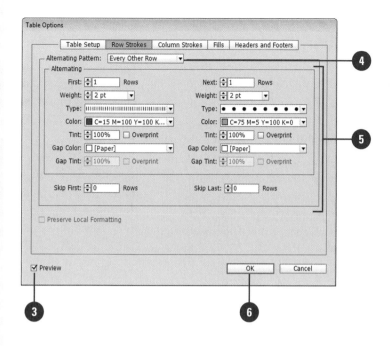

Book	Price	Author
Decorating with Paint	13.99	Foxworthy
Simple Kids Rooms	9.49	Collar
Using Tile	10.75	Lamb
Grilling Indoor	19.97	Mills
Fireplaces	14.00	Panico
	Average	

Alternating strokes

Adding Diagonal Lines in Cells

Diagonal lines or X's in a table cell can be an effective formatting tool to indicate no data is available or the data in the cell needs to reviewed or changed. You can use the Diagonal Lines tab in the Cell Options dialog box to quickly add a diagonal line to one cell or a range of cells in a table. You can specify the color, weight (width), and style you want. Even after you add a diagonal line to a cell, you can still add information to it and specify which item appears in front.

Add Diagonal Lines in Cells

1. Select the cells in the table to which you want to add diagonal lines.

2. Click the **Table** menu, point to **Cell Options**, and then click **Diagonal Lines**.

3. Select the **Preview** check box to view your results in the document window.

4. Click a button to select the type of diagonal line you want to apply.

5. Specify the following Line Stroke options:

   ◆ **Weight.** Enter a value to set the thickness of the line.

   ◆ **Type.** Specify a style for the line.

   ◆ **Color and Tint.** Specify a color and tint for the line. Select the Overprint Stroke check box to apply it.

   ◆ **Gap Color and Tint.** If you selected a line type with dashes or dots, specify a gap color (for the space between the lines) and tint for the line. Select the Overprint Gap check box to apply it.

   ◆ **Draw.** Specify how you want to show the line: Content in Front or Diagonal in Front.

6. Click **OK**.

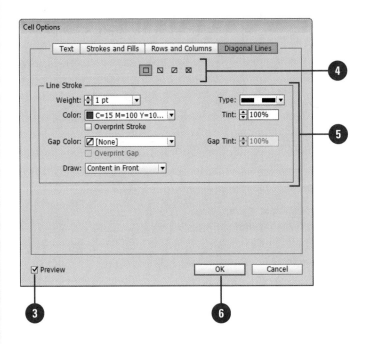

Book	Price	Author
Decorating with Paint	13.99	Foxworthy
Simple Kids Rooms	9.49	Collar
Using Tile	10.75	Lamb
Grilling Indoor	19.97	Mills
Fireplaces	14.00	Panico
	Average	

Diagonal lines

Adding a Border to a Table

A border is the line around a table. A border is a good way to add definition to the outside of a table and make it stand out. You can use the Table Setup tab in the Table Options dialog box to to quickly add a border and specify the color, weight (width), and style you want. If you applied a stroke to a cell that is also a border edge, you can select an option to preserve the formatting already applied to the cell.

Add a Border to a Table

1. Click in the table to which you want to add a border.

2. Click the **Table** menu, point to **Table Options**, and then click **Table Setup**.

3. Select the **Preview** check box to view your results in the document window.

4. Specify the following Table Border options:

    ◆ **Weight.** Enter a value to set the thickness of the border line.

    ◆ **Type.** Specify a style for the border line.

    ◆ **Color and Tint.** Specify a color and tint for the border line. Select the Overprint check box to apply it.

    ◆ **Gap Color and Tint.** If you selected a border type with dashes or dots, specify a gap color (for the space between the lines) and tint for the border line. Select the Overprint check box to apply it.

    ◆ **Preserve Local Formatting.** Select to use the cell formatting instead of the border formatting. Deselect to use the border formatting.

5. Click **OK**.

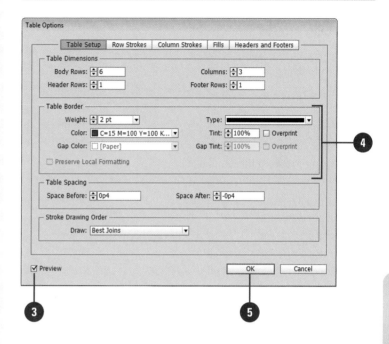

Book	Price	Author
Decorating with Paint	13.99	Foxworthy
Simple Kids Rooms	9.49	Collar
Using Tile	10.75	Lamb
Grilling Indoor	19.97	Mills
Fireplaces	14.00	Panico

Applied border

Adjusting Tables in the Text Frame

A table is placed in a text frame, which might be larger or smaller than the table. You can drag the corner of the text frame to adjust the frame. If the text frame is smaller than the table, an overflow symbol appears in the bottom right corner. The overflow symbol works the same for tables as it does for normal text. You can adjust the space around the table in the text frame by setting options in the Table Setup tab in the Table Options dialog box.

Set Spacing Around a Table

1. Click to place the insertion point somewhere in the table.

2. Click the **Table** menu, point to **Table Options**, and then click **Table Setup**.

3. Select the **Preview** check box to view your results in the document window.

4. Specify the following Table Spacing options:

   ◆ **Space Before.** Enter a value to set the distance that appears before the table.

   ◆ **Space After.** Enter a value to set the distance that appears after the table.

5. Click **OK**.

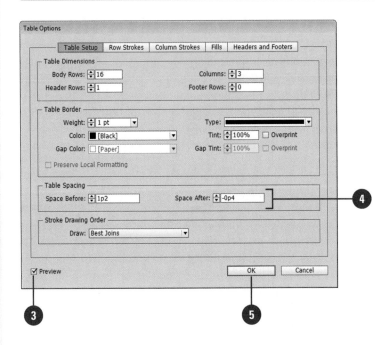

Applied spacing between text and table

Featured Books		
Book	Price	Author
Decorating with Paint	13.99	Foxworthy
Simple Kids Rooms	9.49	Collar
Using Tile	10.75	Lamb

Book	Price	Author
Grilling Indoor	19.97	Mills
Fireplaces	14.00	Panico
Decorating Ideas for the Kitchen	24.99	Kelly
Decorating Garden Style	32.48	Burley

Table in two text frames

Working with Styles

Introduction

A style is a group of format settings that you can create or modify to get the exact look you want. In InDesign, you can create two types of styles, character and paragraph. Character styles apply formatting to only character attributes, while paragraph styles apply formatting for both characters and paragraphs attributes.

The styles panels for paragraphs, characters, objects, tables, and cells are centralized places to work with the different types of styles in InDesign. The panels display the current styles in the InDesign document. You can use buttons on the bottom of the panel to quickly create a new style group, clear overrides in a selection, create a new style, and delete styles. If you have styles in one InDesign document that you want to use in another, you can transfer them from one document into another. If you have styles in a word processing document, such as Microsoft Word, you can import them into an InDesign document, too.

After you create styles, you can use any of the style panels or keyboard shortcuts to apply them. However, you can also use the Quick Apply button. The Quick Apply button provides an easy way to apply any style in your InDesign document. You can even use keyboard shortcuts to speed up the process. After you apply a style, you can still apply additional formatting, known as local or override formatting, by using the Control, Paragraph, or Character panels. Instead of applying individual character styles for a line of text, you can create and apply a nested style to do it for you. A nested style is useful for a list of predictable elements on a line, such as a name, address, and phone number.

What You'll Do

Use the Paragraph Styles or Character Styles Panel

Change the Basic Paragraph Style

Create Paragraph Styles

Create Character Styles

Create GREP Styles

Create Style Groups

Load and Import Styles

Apply and Override Styles

Create Nested Styles

Create Object Styles

Create Table and Cell Styles

Use Quick Apply

Map Styles to Export Tags

Using the Paragraph Styles or Character Styles Panel

The Paragraph Styles and Character Styles panels are centralized places to work with paragraph and character styles in InDesign. The panels display the current paragraph and character styles in the InDesign document. You can use buttons on the bottom of the panel to quickly create a new style group, clear overrides in a selection (Paragraph only), create a new style, and delete styles. You can also use the Options menu to duplicate and edit styles, as well as sort styles in the panel by name.

Use the Paragraph Styles or Character Styles Panel

1. Select the **Paragraph Styles** or **Character Styles** panel.

   ◆ Click the **Type** menu, and then click **Paragraph Styles** or **Character Styles**.

2. Use any of the following buttons or commands to perform an operation:

   ◆ **Create a New Style Group.** Click the **Create New Style Group** button to create a folder to organize styles. Double-click the style group, enter a name, and then click **OK**.

   ◆ **Clear Style Overrides.** Select the style, and then click the **Clear Overrides** button.

   ◆ **Create a New Style.** Click the **Options** button, click **New Paragraph** or **Character Style**, make changes to the style, and then click **OK**.

   ◆ **Delete a Style or Group.** Select the style or group, and then click the **Delete Selected Style/Groups** button.

   ◆ **Edit a Style.** Select the style, click the **Options** button, click **Style Options**, make changes to the style, and then click **OK**.

   ◆ **Duplicate a Style.** Select the style, click the **Options** button, click **Duplicate Style**, enter a name, and then click **OK**.

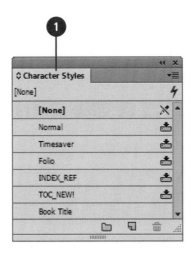

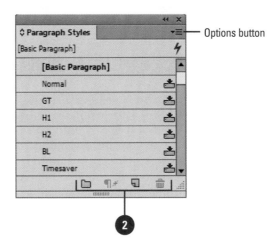

Options button

Changing the Basic Paragraph Style

The **Basic Paragraph** style is the default style for the document and all new text uses this style. You can modify the Basic Paragraph style, or create a new style. To modify the Basic Paragraph style or any style for that matter, adjust the formatting settings for the existing style. When you see a plus (+) sign after the name, it means that the text with the applied style also contains other formatting, which you can redefine.

Redefine the Basic Paragraph Style

1 Select the **Type** tool on the Tools panel, and then select text that uses the Basic Paragraph style.

◆ You can use the same method to redefine any style.

2 Use the Control, Character, and Paragraph panels to change text attributes.

3 Select the **Paragraph Styles** panel.

◆ Click the **Type** menu, and then click **Paragraph Styles**.

A plus (+) sign appears next to the style name.

4 Click the **Options** button, and then click **Redefine Style**.

The plus (+) sign disappears.

5 To manually change style attributes, select the Basic Paragraph style, and then do the following:

◆ Click the **Options** button, and then click **Style Options**.

◆ View the current settings and make any changes that you want.

◆ Click **OK**.

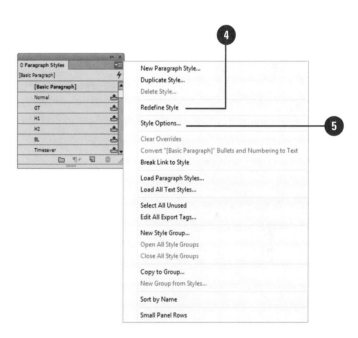

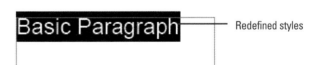

Redefined styles

Creating Paragraph Styles

A paragraph style is a group of paragraph and character format settings that can be applied to text. You can create a new paragraph style from the formatting of existing text or use the New Paragraph Styles dialog box to specify the formatting and other attributes you want. When you create a new paragraph style with the New Paragraph Styles dialog box, you can create a new style from scratch or base the new style on an existing style and then modify it. You can also select a style for the next paragraph. When you press Enter (Win) or Return (Mac), InDesign automatically switches from the current style to the next style. If you like using keyboard shortcuts, you can attach a shortcut to the style to make it easy to apply.

Create a Paragraph Style from Existing Text

1. Select the **Type** tool on the Tools panel, and then select the text that you want to use as the style.

   ◆ You can use the Control, Character, and Paragraph panels to change text attributes.

2. Select the **Paragraph Styles** panel.

   ◆ Click the **Type** menu, and then click **Paragraph Styles**.

3. Click the **Create New Style** button on the panel.

4. To rename the style, double-click the style, enter a name, and then click **OK**.

Creating Graphics

Changing Drawing Settings
Drawing with the Line Tool
Drawing with the Pencil Tool
Drawing Shapes with the Rectangle and Oval Tools
Using the Polystar Tool

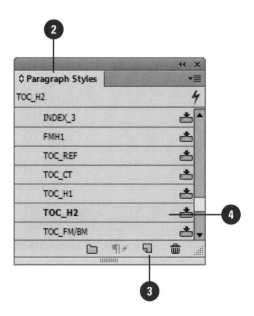

> ## Did You Know?
>
> *You can delete paragraph styles.*
> Select the Paragraph Styles panel, select the styles you want to delete, and then click the Delete Selected Style button on the panel. If the style is in use, select a replacement style, and then click OK. To select all unused styles to delete, click the Options button, and then click Select All Unused.

Create a Paragraph Style

1. Select the **Paragraph Styles** panel.

   ◆ Click the **Type** menu, and then click **Paragraph Styles**.

2. Click the **Options** button, and then click **New Paragraph Style**.

3. Enter a name for the style.

4. Select the **General** category, and then specify the following:

   ◆ **Based On.** Select a style to use as the base for the new style.

   ◆ **Next Style.** Select a style to use as the style for the next paragraph when you press Enter (Win) or Return (Mac).

   ◆ **Shortcut.** Press a keyboard combination to create a shortcut for the style.

5. Select each category to set text attributes.

   ◆ **Basic Character Formats.**
   ◆ **Advanced Character Formats.**
   ◆ **Indents and Spacing.**
   ◆ **Tabs.**
   ◆ **Paragraph Rules.**
   ◆ **Keep Options.**
   ◆ **Hyphenation.**
   ◆ **Justification.**
   ◆ **Span Columns.**
   ◆ **Drop Caps and Nested Styles.**
   ◆ **GREP Style.**
   ◆ **Bullets and Numbering.**
   ◆ **Character Color.**
   ◆ **OpenType Features.**
   ◆ **Underline Options.**
   ◆ **Strikethrough Options.**
   ◆ **Export Tagging.**

6. View the current settings and make any changes that you want.

7. Click **OK**.

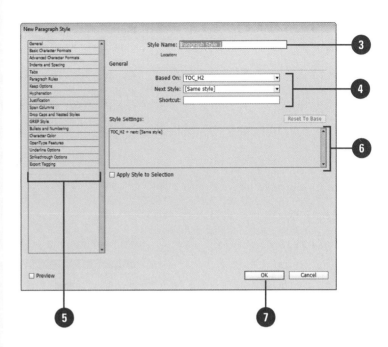

For Your Information

Exporting Tags to EPUB, HTML, or PDF

In order to prepare your document styles for export in EPUB, HTML, or PDF output, you need to map styles to export tags. Mapping styles to export tags specifies how you want to translate your current document paragraph and character styles into HTML and PDF tags. By mapping styles to tags, you'll ensure the best possible results for export to EPUB, HTML, or PDF output. For example, you can map an InDesign body text style to an HTML <p> tag, and then add a class named paragraph1 to differentiate between a typical paragraph and the first paragraph. For EPUB, you can also specify whether you want to split the document after a style. You can define individual mapping styles using the paragraph or character Style Options dialog box. See "Mapping Styles to Export Tags," on page 322 for more details.

Creating Character Styles

A character style is a group of format settings that is applied to any block of text. Rather than formatting text from the Control or Character panels, using the character styles features allows you to quickly make changes later. You can create a new character style from the formatting of existing text or use the New Character Style dialog box to specify the formatting and other attributes you want. When you create a new character style with the New Character Style dialog box, you can create a new style from scratch or base the new style on an existing style and then modify it. If you like using keyboard shortcuts, you can attach a shortcut to the style to make it easy to apply.

Create a Character Style

1. Select the **Type** tool on the Tools panel, and then select the text that you want to use as the style.

   ◆ You can use the Control, Character, and Paragraph panels to change text attributes.

2. Select the **Character Styles** panel.

   ◆ Click the **Type** menu, and then click **Character Styles**.

3. Click the **Create New Style** button on the panel.

4. To rename the style, double-click the style, enter a name, and then click **OK**.

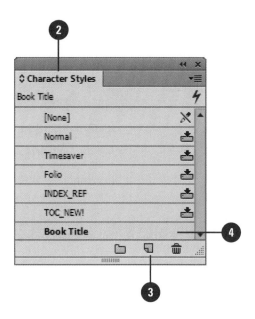

Did You Know?

You can delete character styles.
Select the Characters Styles panel, select the styles you want to delete, and then click the Delete Selected Style button on the panel. If the style is in use, select a replacement style, select the Preserve Formatting check box to convert the style into local formatting, and then click OK. To select all unused styles to delete, click the Options button, and then click Select All Unused.

Create a Character Style

1. Select the **Character Styles** panel.

   ◆ Click the **Type** menu, and then click **Character Styles**.

2. Click the **Options** button, and then click **New Character Style**.

3. Enter a name for the style.

4. Select the **General** category, and then specify the following:

   ◆ **Based On.** Select a style to use as the base for the new style.

   ◆ **Shortcut.** Press a keyboard combination to create a shortcut for the style.

5. Select each category to set text attributes.

   ◆ **Basic Character Formats.**

   ◆ **Advanced Character Formats.**

   ◆ **Character Color.**

   ◆ **OpenType Features.**

   ◆ **Underline Options.**

   ◆ **Strikethrough Options.**

   ◆ **Export Tagging.**

6. View the current settings and make any changes that you want.

7. Click **OK**.

See Also

See "Mapping Styles to Export Tags" on page 322 for more information on ways to map styles.

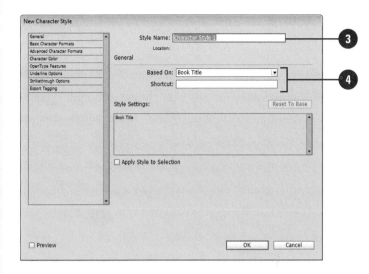

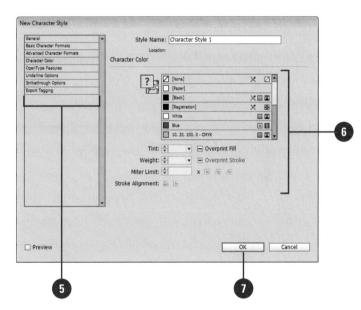

Creating GREP Styles

A **GREP expression** is an advanced method for locating text and special characters in a document. GREP (Global Regular Expression Print) is used by the Find/Change dialog box to find and replace text and special characters, such as tabs, ends of paragraphs, white space, variables, and wildcards. You can create a style to apply a character style to text that conforms to a GREP expression. A GREP style is a Character style with a GREP expression. When text matches the GREP expression, the character style is applied to the text. In the GREP Styles and Find/Change dialog boxes (where you can select a character or paragraph style), you can create a style without having to exit the dialog box.

Create a GREP Style

1. Select the **Paragraph Styles** panel.

   ◆ Click the **Type** menu, and then click **Paragraph Styles**.

2. Click the **Options** button, and then click **New Paragraph Style**.

   ◆ To add a GREP expression to an existing style, select the style, click the **Options** button, and then click **Style Options**.

3. Enter a name for the style.

4. Select each category to set text attributes.

5. Select the **GREP Style** category.

6. Click **New GREP Style**.

7. Click to the right of *Apply Style*, and then select a character style or click **New Character Style** to create one.

8. Click to the right of *To Text*, and then enter a search expression or click the **Special Character For Search** icon to the right to display a menu. Choose options from the **Locations**, **Repeat**, **Match**, **Modifiers**, and **Posix** submenus to help construct the GREP expression.

9. Click **OK**.

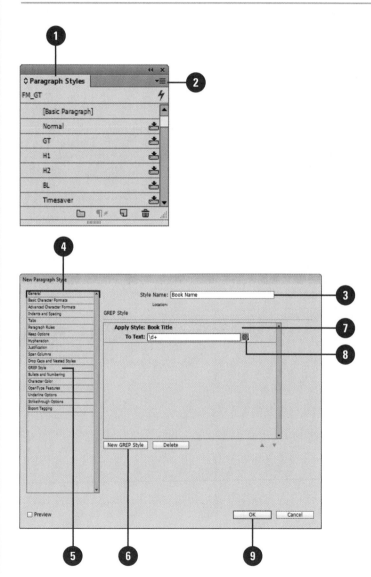

Creating Style Groups

As you continue to create styles, the list in the Paragraph and Character panels can become long and difficult to use. A style group is a folder you can use to organize styles in the Paragraph or Character panels. This can help you reduce the clutter in the panels and make it easier to find and work with the styles you want. After you create a style group, you can drag styles into it, just like you drag files into a folder in Windows Explorer (Win) or Finder (Mac).

Create a Style Group and Move Styles into the Group

1 Select the **Paragraph Styles** or **Character Styles** panel.

◆ Click the **Type** menu, and then click **Paragraph Styles** or **Character Styles**.

2 Click the **Create New Style Group** button on the panel.

◆ You can also select styles, click the **Options** button, and then click **New Group from Styles**.

◆ You can also Alt+click (Win) or Option+click (Mac) the **Create New Style Group** to display the New Style Group dialog box.

3 Double-click the new style group.

◆ You can also click the style group name to select it, click it again to edit it, and then press Enter (Win) or Return (Mac).

4 Enter a name for the style group.

5 Click **OK**.

6 To move styles into the group, select a style, and then drag it into the new style group.

7 To copy styles into the group, select a style, click the **Options** button, click **Copy to Group**, select the group, and then click **OK**.

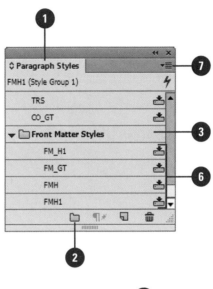

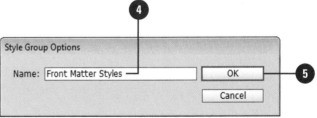

Loading and Importing Styles

If you have styles in one InDesign document that you want to use in another, you can transfer (or load) them from one document into another. If you have styles in a word processing document, such as a Microsoft Word file, you can import them into an InDesign document, too. When you place text from a word processing document, the styles associated with the text are added to the Paragraph or Character panels in the InDesign document. When you add styles to an InDesign document, there may be times when style names are the same. In this case, you need to resolve the conflict between the styles. Style names are case-sensitive, so the name *Header text* is different than *header text*. If you want text with an imported style to be used by a current style, you can map the incoming style to the current style. This way, you don't have to reapply the text style.

Load Styles from an InDesign Document

1. Select the **Paragraph Styles** or **Character Styles** panel.

   ◆ Click the **Type** menu, and then click **Paragraph Styles** or **Character Styles**.

2. Click the **Options** button, and then click **Load Character Styles**, **Load Paragraph Styles**, or **Load All Text Styles**.

3. Navigate to the document with text styles that you want to open.

4. Click the file you want to open.

5. Click **Open**. If a conflict occurs, the Load Styles dialog box appears.

6. Select the check boxes for the styles you want to load and deselect the check boxes for the styles you don't want to load.

7. For each checked style, click the **Conflict With Existing Style** list arrow, and then select an option:

   ◆ **Auto-Rename.** Add a suffix to create a new style name.

   ◆ **Use Incoming Definition**. Changes the existing style to match the imported style.

8. Click **OK**.

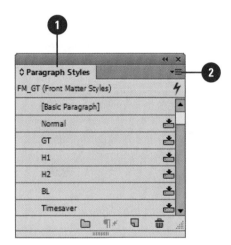

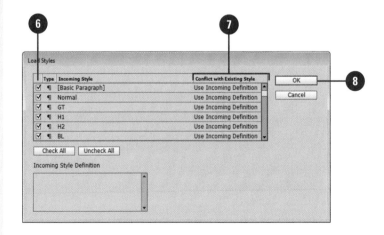

Import Styles from a Word Processing Document

1. Click the **File** menu, and then click **Place**.

2. Navigate to the document with text styles that you want to open.

3. Click the file you want to open.

4. Select the **Show Import Options** check box.

5. Click **Open**.

6. Click the **Preserve Styles and Formatting from Text and Tables** option.

7. To resolve style conflicts automatically, click the **Import Styles Automatically** option, and then select conflict options:

   ◆ **Use InDesign Style Definition.** Select to have InDesign styles override incoming styles.

   ◆ **Redefine InDesign Style.** Select to have incoming styles override InDesign styles.

   ◆ **Auto Rename.** Select to add incoming styles to the list of InDesign styles.

8. To map styles, click the **Customize Style Import** option, click **Style Mapping**, select a style under the InDesign Style column for each incoming Word style, and then click **OK**.

9. Click **OK**.

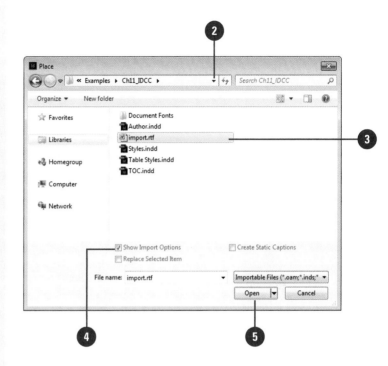

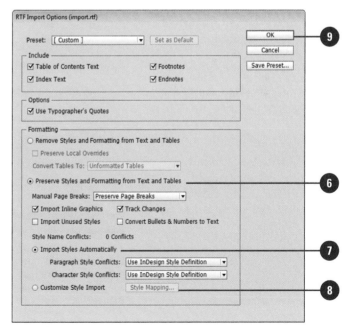

Applying and Overriding Styles

After you create paragraph and character styles, you can use the Paragraph Styles and Character Styles panels or keyboard shortcuts to apply styles to text. For a GREP style, you can use the GREP styles dialog box to apply styles to selected paragraphs. After you apply a style, you can still apply additional formatting, known as **local** or **override formatting**, by using the Control, Paragraph, or Character panels. When the applied style also contains other formatting, a plus sign (+) appears after the style name, which you can remove to redefine the style. You can use the Clear Override button on the Paragraph Styles panel to remove formatting overrides in a text selection.

Apply Styles

1. Select the **Type** tool on the Tools panel, and then select the text that you want to change.

   For paragraph styling, select a text frame or select paragraphs. For character styling, select specific text, not a text frame.

   ◆ You can also select the **Selection** tool, and then click the text frame to change all text in the frame.

2. Select the **Character Styles** or **Paragraph Styles** panel.

3. Click a style name in one of the panels, or press the keyboard shortcut defined for the style.

Did You Know?

You can apply the next style. Select the text to which you want to apply the next style, select the Paragraph Styles panel, right-click (Win) or Control-click (Mac) the next style, click Apply *name of style* then Next Style.

You can break the link to a style. Click to place an insertion point in the paragraph in which you want to break, click the Options button in the Paragraph Styles or Character Styles panel, and then click Break Link To Style.

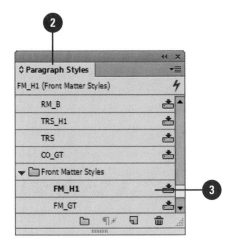

Acknowledgements

The task of creating any book requ pulling together to meet impossibl thank the outstanding team respor Steve Johnson; the technical editor Teyler and Beth Teyler; the proofer Stimson.

Acknowledgements —— Applied style

The task of creating any book re together to meet impossible de outstanding team responsible f son; the technical editor Nathar Beth Teyler; the proofer reader,

Apply GREP Styles

1. Select the **Type** tool on the Tools panel, and then select the paragraphs for which you want to change styles.

   For paragraph styling, select a text frame or select paragraphs.

2. Click the **Control panel** menu, and then click **GREP Styles**.

3. Select a GREP style.

4. Click **OK** to apply the style.

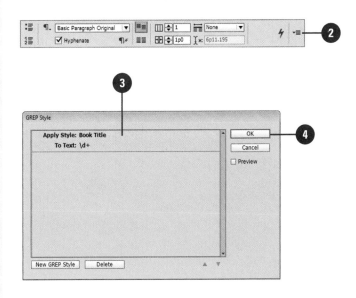

Clear Style Overrides

1. Select the **Type** tool on the Tools panel, and then select the text that you want to clear.

2. Select the **Paragraph Styles** panel.

3. Use any of the following:

   ◆ **Clear Local Formatting in a Selection.** Click the **Clear Overrides** button on the panel.

   ◆ **Clear Local Character Formatting in a Selection.** Ctrl+click (Win) or ⌘+click (Mac) the **Clear Overrides** button on the panel.

   ◆ **Clear Local Paragraph Formatting in a Selection.** Ctrl+Shift+click (Win) or ⌘+Shift+click (Mac) the **Clear Overrides** button on the panel.

We invite you to visit the Perspection Web site at:

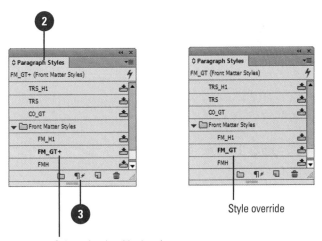

Selected style with plus sign

Style override

Creating Nested Styles

Instead of applying individual character styles for a line of text, you can create and apply a nested style to do it for you. A nested style is useful for a list of predictable elements, such as a name, address, and phone number, on a line. You can also create and use nested inline styles to apply complex character formatting through the end of a line. Before you create a nested style, you need to create the individual characters that you want to make up the nested style. If you want a nested style to end at a certain place in the text, you can insert the End Nested Style Here special character.

Create a Nested Line Style

1. Select the **Paragraph Styles** panel.

    ◆ Click the **Type** menu, and then click **Paragraph Styles**.

2. Click the **Options** button, and then click **New Paragraph Style**.

3. Enter a name for the style.

4. Select the **Drop Caps and Nested Styles** category.

5. Click **New Line Style**.

6. Click the **Nested Line Styles** list arrow for each line style, and then select a line style or click **New Line Style** to create one.

    ◆ To loop two or more nested styles, select **Repeat** from the list arrow.

7. Enter a value for the number of repeating lines for each line style.

8. To move a style up or down the list, click the **Up** or **Down** arrow.

9. To remove a style, select it, and then click **Delete**.

10. Click **OK**.

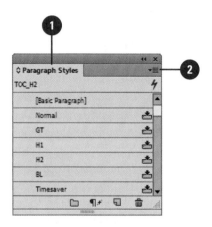

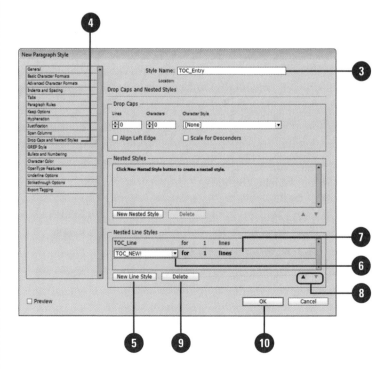

Create a Nested Style

1. Select the **Paragraph Styles** panel.

   ◆ Click the **Type** menu, and then click **Paragraph Styles**.

2. Click the **Options** button, and then click **New Paragraph Style**.

3. Enter a name for the style.

4. Select the **Drop Caps and Nested Styles** category.

5. Click **New Nested Style**.

6. Click the **Nested Styles** list arrow for each nested style, and then select a nested style or click **New Nested Style** to create one.

   ◆ To loop two or more nested styles, select **Repeat** from the list arrow.

7. Click the **Duration** list arrow for each nested style, and then click **Through** to include the repeating elements or **Up to** to not include the repeating elements.

8. Enter a value for the number of repeating elements for each nested style.

9. Click the **Repeating Element** list arrow for each nested style, and then select which element controls the nested style.

10. To move a style up or down the list, click the **Up** or **Down** arrow.

11. To remove a style, select it, and then click **Delete**.

12. Click **OK**.

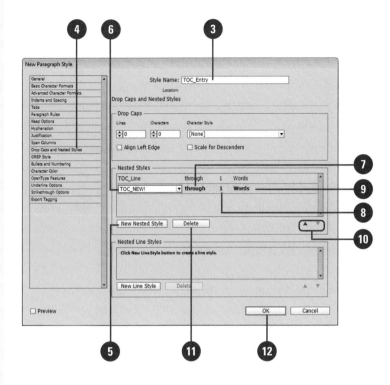

For Your Information

Inserting the End Nested Style Here Character

The End Nested Style Here special character allows you to control where a nested style ends. To insert the special character, click to place the insertion point where you want the nested style to end, click the Type menu, point to Insert Special Character, point to Other, and then click End Nested Style Here. This special character is a hidden character. Click the Type menu, and then click Show Hidden Characters to show hidden characters.

Creating Object Styles

In the same way you create paragraph and character styles, you can also create and modify styles for objects. InDesign comes with two default objects styles, one for a graphics frame and another for a text frame. There is also a style for None, which removes all formatting from an object. You can create and modify object styles in the Object Styles panel and Object Style Option dialog box, which includes exporting options (**New!**) for alt text, tagging, and EPUB and HTML; for option details, see the topic on page 452. Just as when using text styles, when the applied style also contains other formatting, a plus sign (+) appears after the style name, which you can remove, redefine, or clear.

View and Apply Object Styles

1 Select the object to which you want to apply a style.

2 Select the **Object Styles** panel.

◆ Click the **Window** menu, point to **Styles**, and then click **Object Styles**.

3 Click one of the built-in styles: **[Basic Graphics Frame]**, **[Basic Text Frame]**, or **[None]** or a custom style.

Modify the Default Object Styles

1 Select the object to which you want to apply a style.

2 Select the **Object Styles** panel.

◆ Click the **Window** menu, point to **Styles**, and then click **Object Styles**.

3 Double-click **[Basic Graphics Frame]** or **[Basic Text Frame]**.

4 Select each main category (**New!**) to set individual object style options.

5 Select the **General** category, and then view Style Settings to see a description of the completed style.

6 Click **OK**.

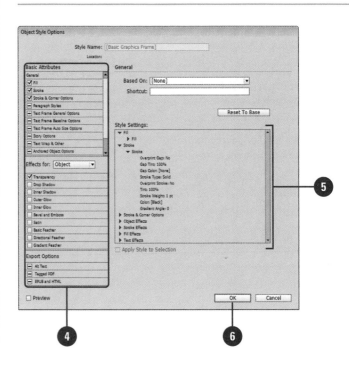

Create an Object Style

1. To create an object style by using an object, select the object.

2. Select the **Object Styles** panel.

   ◆ Click the **Window** menu, point to **Styles**, and then click **Object Styles**.

3. Click the **Options** button, and then click **New Object Style**.

   ◆ You can also Alt+click (Win) or Option+click (Mac) the **New Object Style** button on the panel.

4. Enter a name for the style.

5. If you didn't select an object or if you want add more options, select each main category (**New!**) to set individual object style options.

6. Select the **General** category, and then view Style Settings to see a description of the completed style.

7. Click **OK**.

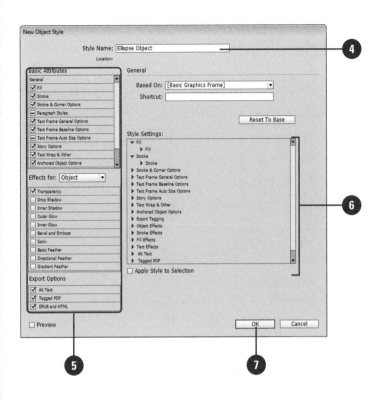

Clear Object Style Overrides

1. Select the object that local formatting applied.

2. Select the **Object Styles** panel.

   ◆ Click the **Window** menu, point to **Styles**, and then click **Object Styles**.

3. Use any of the following:

   ◆ Clear Local Formatting Not Defined in the Style. Click the **Clear Attributes Not Defined by Style** button on the panel.

   ◆ Clear Local Formatting in a Selection. Click the **Clear Overrides** button on the panel.

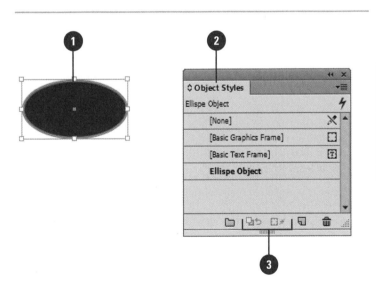

Creating Table and Cell Styles

You can use the Table Styles or Cell Styles panels to create, apply, import, modify, and organize table and cell styles. In the Table Styles and Cell Styles panels, you can perform the same operations as in other style panels, including creating a style group, clearing overrides, creating a new style, and deleting styles. You can also use the Options menu to duplicate and edit styles, select all unused styles, as well as sort styles in the panel by name. When you create a table style, you can use cell styles, so you should create your cell styles before you create table styles.

Create Cell Styles

1. Select the **Cell Styles** panel.
   - Click the **Window** menu, point to **Styles**, and then click **Cell Styles**.
2. Click the **Options** button, and then click **New Cell Style**.
   - You can also Alt+click (Win) or Option+click (Mac) the **Create New Style** button on the panel.
3. Enter a name for the style.
4. Select the **General** category, and then specify the following:
   - **Based On.** Select a style to use as the base for the new style.
   - **Shortcut.** Press a keyboard combination to create a shortcut for the style.
   - **Paragraph Styles.** Select a default paragraph style for the table cells.
5. Select each main category (**Text**, **Strokes and Fills**, and **Diagonal Lines**) to set individual cell attributes.
6. Select the **General** category, and then view Style Settings to see a description of the completed style.
7. Click **OK**.

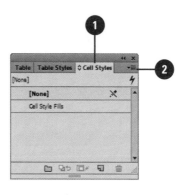

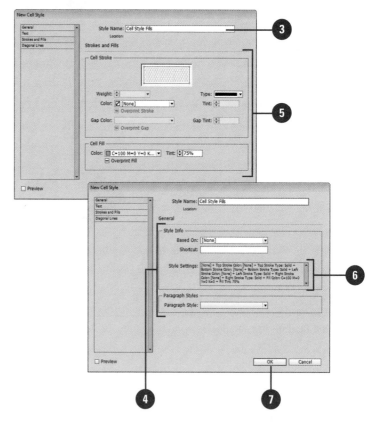

Create Table Styles

1. Select the **Table Styles** panel.

   ◆ Click the **Window** menu, point to **Styles**, and then click **Table Styles**.

2. Click the **Options** button, and then click **New Table Style**.

   ◆ You can also Alt+click (Win) or Option+click (Mac) the **Create New Style** button on the panel.

3. Enter a name for the style.

4. Select the **General** category, and then specify the following:

   ◆ **Based On.** Select a style to use as the base for the new style.

   ◆ **Shortcut.** Press a keyboard combination to create a shortcut for the style.

   ◆ **Cell Styles.** Select a default cell style for the table cells.

5. Select each main category (**Table Setup**, **Row Strokes**, **Column Strokes**, and **Fills**) to set individual table attributes.

6. Select the **General** category, and then view Style Settings to see a description of the completed style.

7. Click **OK**.

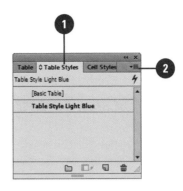

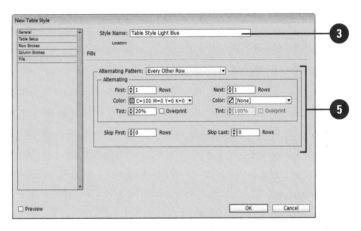

Did You Know?

You can delete and clear table and cell styles. In the Table Styles or Cell Styles panel, select the styles, and then click the Delete Selected Style/Groups or Clear Overrides button on the panel.

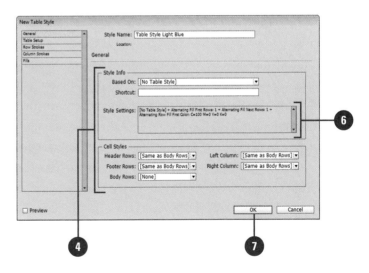

Using Quick Apply

The Quick Apply button that is available on the right side of the Control panel and any of the style panels provides an easy way to apply any style in your InDesign document. You can use all available keyboard shortcuts to speed up the process. If you want to edit a style, you can access the style dialog box to make changes. If the list of styles is so long it is hard to find the one you want, you can use the Search box to help you find a style by name or style prefix. The prefixes are internally set by InDesign. The prefixes include *p:* for paragraph styles, *c:* for character styles, and *o:* for object styles, to name a few. In addition to styles, you can also use Quick Apply to apply menu commands, text variables, and scripts.

Use Quick Apply

1. Select the text, table, or object to which you want to apply the style.

2. Click the **Quick Apply** button on the Control panel or any of the style panels.

   TIMESAVER *Press Ctrl (Win) or* ⌘ *(Mac), and then press Enter (Win) or Return (Mac).*

   ◆ Quick Apply remembers your last selected style, so you can simply press Enter (Win) or Return (Mac) to apply it.

3. To narrow down the list of styles, type the first letters in the style name.

4. Use the Up and Down arrow keys to move up and down the list of styles to find the one you want.

5. Click the style you want to apply or press Enter (Win) or Return (Mac) to apply the selected style.

   The Quick Apply dialog box closes.

6. To apply a style without closing the Quick Apply dialog box, press Shift+Enter (Win) or Shift+Return (Mac).

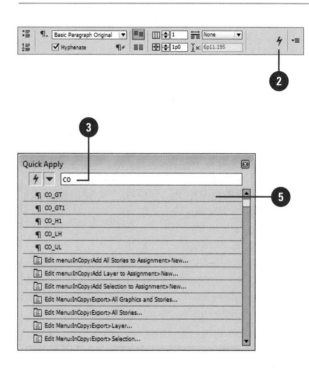

Edit Styles with Quick Apply

1. Click the **Quick Apply** button on the Control panel or any of the style panels.

2. To narrow down the list of styles, type the first letters in the style name.

3. Use the Up and Down arrow keys to move up and down the list of styles to find the one you want.

4. Press Ctrl+Enter (Win) or ⌘+Return (Mac) to open the dialog box for the selected style.

5. Make the changes you want, and then click **OK**.

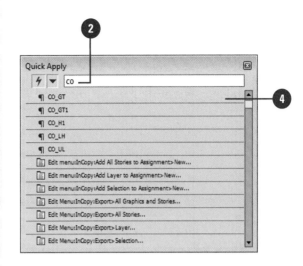

Use Letter Commands with Quick Apply

1. Click the **Quick Apply** button on the Control panel or any of the style panels.

2. To narrow down the list of styles, click the **Down** Arrow, and then select (check) or deselect (uncheck) the styles you want to view in the list.

3. Type the prefix for the style type (see illustration for prefixes) and then continue to type the first letters in the style name.

4. Use the Up and Down arrow keys to move up and down the list of styles to find the one you want.

5. Press Enter (Win) or Return (Mac) to apply the selected style.

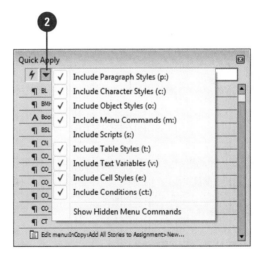

Mapping Styles to Export Tags

In order to prepare your document styles for export in EPUB, HTML, or PDF output, you need to map styles to export tags. Mapping styles to export tags specifies how you want to translate your paragraph, character and object (**New!**) styles into HTML or PDF tags. By mapping styles to tags, you'll ensure the best export results. For EPUB and HTML, you can specify CSS (Cascading Style Sheets) class names (optional) to differentiate between variations in styling. For example, you can map an InDesign body text style to an HTML <p> tag, and then add a class named paragraph1 to differentiate between a typical paragraph and the first paragraph. You can define individual mapping styles using the paragraph, character or object Style Options dialog box or all mapping styles (not object) in one place using the Edit All Export Tags dialog box.

Map Styles to Export Tags

1 Select the **Object Styles (New!)**, **Paragraph Styles**, or **Character Styles** panel.

◆ Click the **Type** menu, and then click **Object Styles**, **Paragraph Styles**, or **Character Styles**.

2 Select the style you want to map.

3 Click the **Options** button, and then click **Style Options**.

4 Select the **Export Tagging** category, and then specify the following:

◆ **Tag (EPUB and HTML)**. Select a tag for EPUB and HTML output.

◆ **Class (EPUB and HTML)**. Specify a class to generate style definitions for tags (optional).

◆ **Emit CSS (EPUB and HTML)**. Select to use the set class name if a conflict occurs (**New!**).

◆ **Split Document (EPUB)**. Adds a break after the style.

◆ **Tag (PDF)** Select a tag for PDF output; paragraph styles only.

5 Click **OK**.

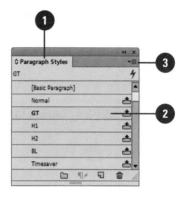

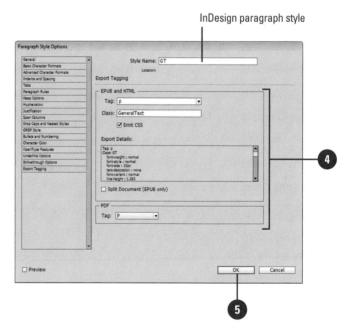

InDesign paragraph style

See Also

See "Exporting Tags for EPUB and HTML" on page 451 for details on using the Edit All Export Tags dialog box.

Finalizing a Document

Introduction

Finalizing your document is an important thing to do prior to printing. Of course, no document should be printed without first going through the spell checker to check your spelling. You can add personalized names, terms, and company information to a user dictionary, so that when you are using the spell checker, there won't be unnecessary stops on words that are spelled and used correctly. If you need to make text fit in text frames and on pages, you can adjust the hyphenation, choose to keep lines together, and change justification options to help you finalize your document.

Sometimes you use a certain font in a document, but later you decide to change it. Instead of manually changing each use of the font, you can use the Find Font command to quickly find and change every instance of the font in your document. You can also use the Find/Change dialog box to find and replace elements—including text, GREP expressions, glyphs, and objects—in your document. The dialog box provides powerful features to find and change special characters, including tabs, line breaks, end of paragraph returns, symbols, markers, hyphens and dashes, white space, variables, and wildcards to name a few.

If you want to focus solely on the text in your document, the Story Editor is the tool for you. The Story Editor displays text and tables in a separate window with unformatted sequential columns and rows for easy editing. Any graphics, shapes, text formatting, and other design elements in your document do not appear in the Story Editor.

What You'll Do

Use Spell Check

Use Custom Dictionaries

Find and Change Fonts

Use Find and Change

Search for Text

Search Using GREP

Search for Glyphs

Search for Objects

Work with Hyphenation

Keep Lines Together

Change Justification Options

Use the Story Editor

Add Footnotes

Change Case

Using Spell Check

There's nothing more embarrassing than creating a document that contains misspelled words. InDesign includes a fully functional spell checking system, which lets you make sure all of your words are spelled correctly. Instead of using Spell Check, you can also use dynamic spelling, which displays misspelled or unrecognized words in your document with a red underline as you type. You can right-click (Win) or Control-click (Mac) the word to select a correction on the context menu.

Use Spell Check on a Document

1 Click the **Edit** menu, point to **Spelling**, and then click **Check Spelling**.

   TIMESAVER *Ctrl+I (Win) or* ⌘+I *(Mac).*

2 Click **Start**, if necessary.

3 When InDesign encounters a word not in the dictionary, it displays that word, and allows you to choose one of the following options:

   ◆ **Skip.** Leaves the word alone and moves on.

   ◆ **Change.** Changes the word, based on the selected suggestion.

   ◆ **Ignore All.** Ignores all instances of this word in the document.

   ◆ **Change All.** Changes all occurrences of the word, based on the selected suggestion.

   ◆ **Dictionary.** Opens the Dictionary dialog box.

   ◆ **Add.** Adds the word to the selected dictionary. Click the Add To list arrow to select a dictionary.

   InDesign continues to highlight misspelled and other incorrectly used words until the document is completely scanned.

4 When you're finished, click **Done**.

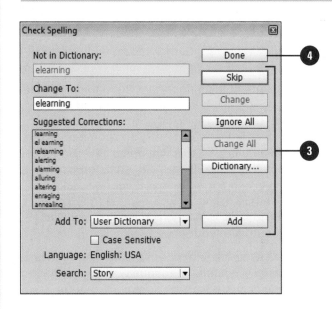

Use Spell Check Options

1. To spell check a text frame, click to place the insertion point.

2. Click the **Edit** menu, point to **Spelling**, and then click **Check Spelling**.

3. Click the **Search** list arrow, and then select a search option:

   ◆ **All Documents.** Checks all open documents.

   ◆ **Document.** Checks the active document.

   ◆ **Story.** Checks all the linked frames of the selected text.

   ◆ **To End of Story.** Checks from the insertion point to the end of the story.

   ◆ **Selection.** Checks only the selected text.

4. Select the **Case Sensitive** check box to require a match of lower and uppercase characters.

5. When you're finished, click **Done**.

Use Dynamic Spelling

1. To enable dynamic spelling, click the **Edit** menu, point to **Spelling**, and then click **Dynamic Spelling**.

2. Right-click (Win) or Control-click (Mac) a word with a red underline, and then select a word correction or an option to **Ignore All** or **Add** "*Word*" **To User Dictionary**.

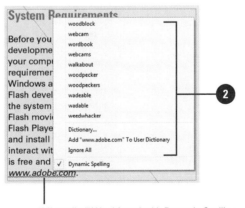

"Misspelled" Word found with Dynamic Spelling

Using Custom Dictionaries

InDesign comes with a custom dictionary for the spell checker. If you need to manage dictionary content, you can use the Edit Custom Dictionary dialog box to add, delete, or edit words. The ability to edit the dictionary becomes useful when you accidentally enter a word that you don't want in the dictionary, or you have some specialty words that you want to enter in all at once. When you add a custom word, name, or phrase to a custom dictionary, all languages treat the item as correctly spelled. InDesign supports the user dictionary to verify spelling and to hyphenate words. In addition, you can find Hunspell dictionaries at Adobe.com from InDesign.

Use a Custom Dictionary

1. Click the **Edit** menu, point to **Spelling,** and then click **Dictionary**.

   ◆ You can also click **Dictionary** in the Check Spelling dialog box.

2. Click the **Target** list arrow, and then select the dictionary you want to use.

3. Click the **Language** list arrow, and then select the language you want to use.

4. Click the **Dictionary List** list arrow, and then click **Added Words, Removed Words,** or **Ignored Words**.

5. Select the **Case Sensitive** check box to specify a match of lower and uppercase characters.

6. Type the word you want to add or select the word you want to remove or be ignored by the spell checker.

7. Click **Add** or **Remove**.

8. If you want to export or import dictionary entries, click **Export** to name and save the file or click **Import** to locate and open (import) the file.

9. When you're finished, click **Done**.

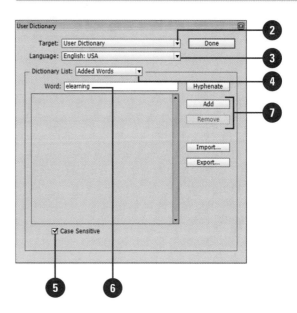

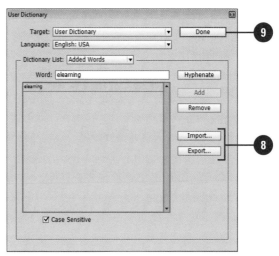

Finding and Changing Fonts

Say you create some text using a certain font. After customer or client reviews, you're asked to change it. Instead of manually changing each use of the font, you can use the Find Font command to quickly find and change every instance of the font in your document. If you're not sure what fonts are used in your document, the Find Font dialog box gives you a list.

Find or Change a Font

1. Click the **Type** menu, and then click **Find Font**.

   The fonts in the top list are the ones currently used in your document. The list at the bottom displays fonts in your document or on your computer, depending on your setting.

2. To find a specific font, select it in the top list.

3. To replace the font in the top list, click the **Font Family** and **Font Style** list arrows, and then select a replacement font and style.

4. Select the **Redefine Style When Changing All** check box to redefine the replaced style for Change All.

5. Click **Find Next** to display the first instance of the font, and then click **Change** to replace it, or click **Change All** to replace all uses of the font in your document.

6. When you're done, click **Done**.

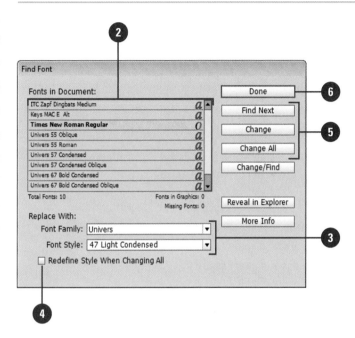

Did You Know?

You can make fonts available for a document. If you store any fonts in a Document Fonts folder in the same location as an InDesign document, the fonts in the folder are available in the opened InDesign document.

Using Find and Change

The Find/Change command on the Edit menu allows you to find and change text, font characters, or object attributes in a document. You can use tabs to search for specific elements in a document, including text, GREP patterns, glyphs, and objects. I'll focus on the basics of using the Find/Change dialog box in this topic. Other topics in this chapter go into specifics for each search type. After you create a search, you can save it as a query for later use. InDesign also comes with some built-in queries that you can use.

Use Find and Change

1. Click the **Edit** menu, and then click **Find/Change**.

   TIMESAVER *Ctrl+F (Win) or ⌘+F (Mac).*

2. To use a search query, click the **Query** list arrow, and then select a built-in or custom query.

3. Click one of the following tabs to specify the type of search you want to perform:

   ◆ **Text.** Finds and changes text and text formatting.

   ◆ **GREP.** Finds and changes search expressions for patterns within text.

   ◆ **Glyph.** Finds and changes glyphs using unicode or GID/CID values.

   ◆ **Object.** Finds and changes objects with specific formatting.

4. Specify what you want to find. The method varies depending on the search type.

5. Specify what you want to change the find item to. The method varies depending on the search type.

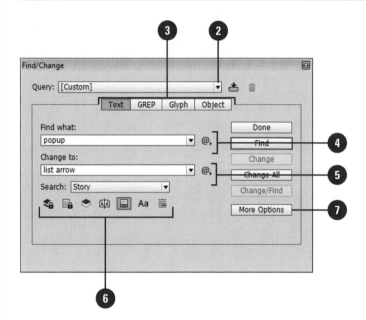

6 Click the following buttons, which toggle on and off, to allow or not allow a search in the specified area:

- **Locked Layer.** Searches on locked layers. You can't make changes on a locked layer.

- **Locked Stories.** Searches in locked stories. You can't make changes in locked stories.

- **Hidden Layers.** Finds and changes in hidden layers.

- **Master Pages.** Finds and changes in master pages.

- **Footnotes.** Finds and changes in footnotes.

7 To display more options, if available, click **More Options**.

The button toggles to Fewer Options.

8 Use the following buttons to find or change the search items:

- **Find.** Starts the search for the specified find items.

- **Change.** Changes the selected find item to the specified change.

- **Change All.** Changes all find items to the specified change.

- **Change/Find.** Changes the selected find item to the specified change, and then continues the search for the next find item.

9 To save a search as a query for use in the future, click the **Save Query** button, enter a name, and then click **OK**.

10 To delete a custom query, select it, and then click the **Delete Query** button.

11 When you're finished, click **Done**.

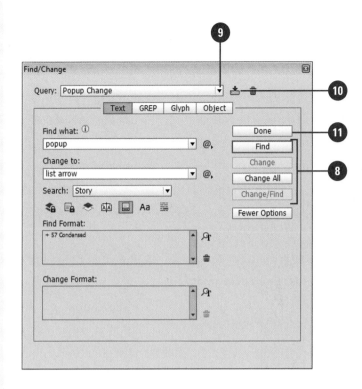

Searching for Text

The Find/Change command on the Edit menu allows you to find and change text, text formatting, and special characters in a document. The special characters, known as **metacharacters**, include tabs, line breaks, end of paragraph returns, symbols, markers, hyphens and dashes, white space, variables, and wildcards to name a few. Wildcards allow you to create more general searches. You can select special characters from a menu in the Find/Change dialog box. The special characters appear in the Find/Change dialog box as a character code. In addition to text, you can also find and change text formatting. You can specify the same formatting find and change options as the ones for creating styles.

Search for Text

1. To find and change text in a specific text frame, click to place the insertion point in the text.

2. Click the **Edit** menu, and then click **Find/Change**.

   TIMESAVER *Ctrl+F (Win) or* ⌘+F *(Mac).*

3. Click the **Text** tab.

4. Specify what you want to find in the **Find What** box, and then specify what you want to change the find item to in the **Change To** box.

   - ◆ **Include Special Characters.** Click the @ menu, and then use the menus to select the special characters you want to add to the find. A character code appears for the special character in the Find What and Change To boxes.

   - ◆ **Include Wildcards.** Click the @ menu, point to **Wildcards**, and then click **Any Digit**, **Any Letter**, **Any Character**, or **Any White Space**.

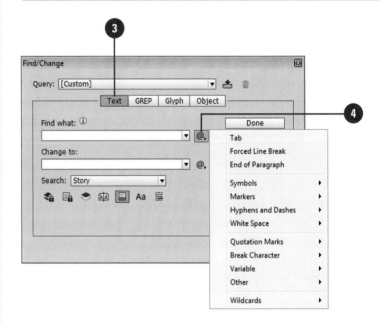

5 Click the **Search** list arrow, and then select a search option:

- ◆ **All Documents.** Searches all open documents.
- ◆ **Document.** Searches the active document.
- ◆ **Story.** Searches all the linked frames of the selected text.
- ◆ **To End of Story.** Searches from the insertion point to the end of the story.
- ◆ **Selection.** Searches only the selected text.

6 Click the **Case Sensitive** button to require a match of lower and uppercase characters.

7 Click the **Whole Word** button to ignore text contained within other words.

8 To display more options, if available, click **More Options**.

The button toggles to Fewer Options.

9 To find and change formatting, click the **Format** button for Find or Change, select the formatting options that you want, and then click **OK**.

- ◆ To delete a formatting search, click the **Delete** button.

10 Use the Find and Change buttons to perform the search and make changes.

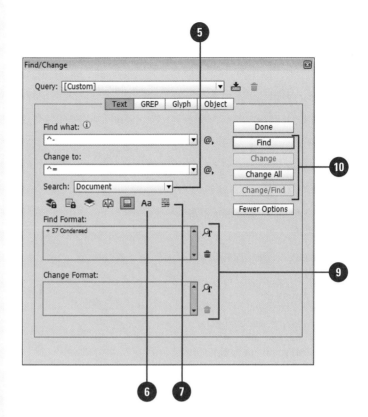

See Also

See "Using Find and Change" on pages 328 for information on common Find/Change dialog box options.

Searching Using GREP

GREP stands for Global Regular Expression and Print. The Find/Change command on the Edit menu allows you to to find and replace text and special characters, such as tabs, end of paragraph, white space, variables, and wildcards. In the Find What and Change To boxes, you can build GREP search expressions for patterns within text. For example, you could build a search to find any text variable, and then change the formatting to bold. You can select a character or paragraph style in the Find/Change and GREP Styles dialog boxes and create a style without having to exit the dialog box.

Search Using GREP

1. Click the **Edit** menu, and then click **Find/Change**.

   TIMESAVER *Ctrl+F (Win) or* ⌘+F (Mac).

2. Click the **GREP** tab.

3. Specify what you want to find in the **Find What** box, and then specify what you want to change the find item to in the **Change To** box.

4. Click the @ menu for **Find What** and **Change To**, and then use the menus to select the special characters you want to add to the find. A character code appears for the special character in the Find What and Change To boxes.

5. Specify the other text search options. *See "Searching for Text" on pages 330-331 for details on text search options.*

6. Use the Find and Change buttons to perform the search.

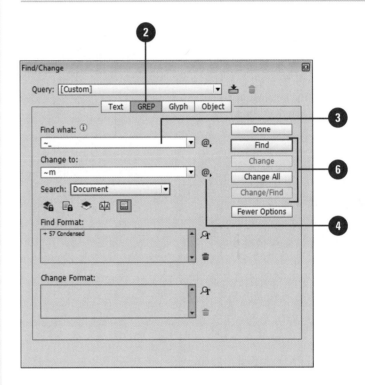

See Also

See "Using Find and Change" on pages 328 for information on common Find/ Change dialog box options.

Searching for Glyphs

A glyph is a style variation—such as ligatures, ordinals, swashes, and fractions—for a given character in an OpenType font. For example, you can change fractions with numerals and slashes to properly formatted fractions. You can automatically insert alternate glyphs with the OpenType panel or insert them manually with the Glyphs panel to extend the font format. In the Find/Change dialog box, you can search for alternate glyphs using special ID codes or symbols.

Search for Glyphs

1. Click the **Edit** menu, and then click **Find/Change**.

   TIMESAVER *Ctrl+F (Win) or* ⌘+F (Mac).

2. Click the **Glyph** tab.

3. Specify the following options for Find Glyph and Change Glyph:

   ◆ **Font Family.** Select a font typeface.

   ◆ **Font Style.** Select a font style.

   ◆ **ID.** Select the Unicode or GID/CID numbering system, and then enter a code for the glyph you want to find or change.

   ◆ **Glyph.** Select a glyph symbol from the display panel.

4. Specify the other search options.

5. To clear all the information from the glyph field, click **Clear Glyphs**.

6. Use the Find and Change buttons to perform the search.

See Also

See "Using Find and Change" on pages 328-329 for information on common Find/Change dialog box options.

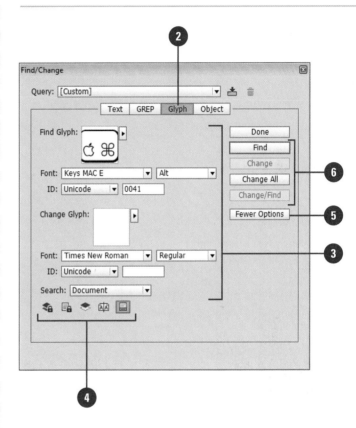

Searching for Objects

In addition to text-related searches, you can also use the Find/Change dialog box to search for objects with certain formatting and then apply other attributes. You can specify the formatting that you want to find for all or specific types of objects, such as text frames, graphic frames, or unassigned frames.

Search for Objects

1. Click the **Edit** menu, and then click **Find/Change**.

    TIMESAVER *Ctrl+F (Win) or ⌘+F (Mac).*

2. Click the **Object** tab.

3. To find and change formatting, click the **Format** button for Find or Change, select the formatting options that you want, and then click **OK**.

    ◆ To delete a formatting search, click the **Delete** button.

4. Click the **Search** list arrow, and then select a search option.

5. Click the **Type** list arrow, and then select a frame option: **All Frames**, **Text Frames**, **Graphic Frames**, or **Unassigned Frames**.

6. Use the Find and Change buttons to perform the search.

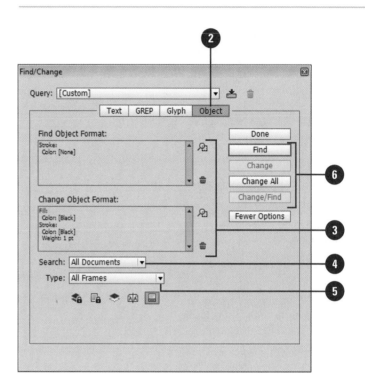

See Also

See "Using Find and Change" on pages 328-329 for information on common Find/Change dialog box options.

Working with Hyphenation

When you select the Hyphenate check box in the Paragraph panel, InDesign automatically adds hyphenation as you need it based on the options set in the Hyphenation dialog box. If you want to manually set hyphenation, deselect the check box. The Hyphenation options allow you to specify how long a word needs to be before hyphenation takes place, the maximum number of hyphens you can use, and what balance you want between better spacing and fewer hyphens.

Change Hyphenation Options

1. Click in the text frame where you want to enable hyphenation.

2. Select the **Paragraph** panel.

3. To enable hyphenation, select the **Hyphenate** check box.

4. Click the **Options** button, and then click **Hyphenation**.

5. Specify the following options:

   ◆ **Words With At Least.** Enter the minimum number of characters in a word before hyphens are added.

   ◆ **After First.** Enter the minimum number of characters that can occur before a hyphen.

   ◆ **Before Last.** Enter the minimum number of characters that can occur after a hyphen on the next line.

   ◆ **Hyphen Limit.** Enter the maximum number of hyphens in a row (0-25).

   ◆ **Hyphenation Zone.** Drag the slider to adjust the balance of hyphenation between better spacing and fewer hyphens.

   ◆ **Hyphenate Capitalized Words.** Select to hyphenate capitalized words.

   ◆ **Hyphenate Across Column.** Select to hyphenate across columns.

   ◆ **Hyphenate Last Word.** Select to hyphenate the last word.

6. Click **OK**.

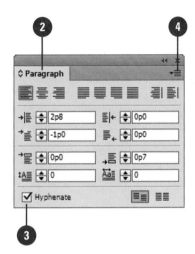

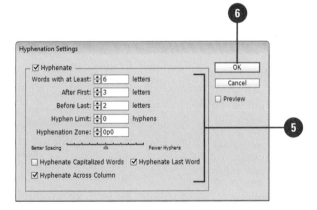

Keeping Lines Together

With Keep Options from the Paragraph panel, you can have InDesign automatically keeps paragraphs together based on the number of lines that you want, instead of allowing them to break naturally into other columns or on to other pages. The Keep Lines Together options allow you to specify the number of lines in a paragraph that you want to stay in the same column or page, and where you want paragraph lines to move, such as Anywhere, In Next Column, In Next Frame, or On Next Page. Keep options are applied to paragraphs that span or split columns.

Change Keep Options

1. Click in the text frame for which you want to set keep options.

2. Select the **Paragraph** panel.

3. Click the **Options** button, and then click **Keep Options**.

4. Select the **Keep with Previous** check box to keep the first line of the current paragraph with the last line of the previous paragraph.

5. Enter a **Keep with Next** value to force the last line in a paragraph to stay in the same column or page with a specified number of lines.

6. Select the **Keep Lines Together** check box.

7. Click the **All Lines in Paragraph** option to keep all paragraph lines together or click the **At Start/End of Paragraph** option to specify the number of lines that you want to remain with the paragraph.

8. Click the **Start Paragraph** list arrow, and then select an option to indicate where the lines appear.

9. Click **OK**.

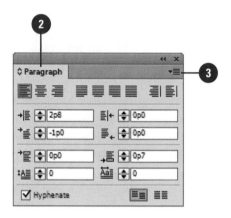

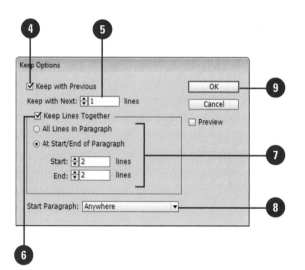

Did You Know?

You can balance uneven line breaks. Select the text, select the Paragraph panel, click the Options button, and then select Balance Ragged Lines.

Changing Justification Options

When you use Justify buttons on the Control panel or Paragraph panel, you can further adjust settings in the Justification dialog box. The justification settings allow you to specify how lines fit between margins in a document. In InDesign, there are three justification controls: word spacing, letter spacing, and glyph spacing. For each control, you can set a minimum, desired, and maximum percentage to specify the justification levels you want. The default percentages are recommended for most uses. However, if you need to make information fit on a page, you can change the percentage values. The best way to adjust justification settings is to use the Preview option to view your changes in the document window.

Change Justification Options

1. Click in the text frame for which you want to set justification options.

2. Select the **Paragraph** panel.

3. Click the **Options** button, and then click **Justification**.

4. Select the **Preview** check box to view your results in the document window.

5. Specify the following options:

   ◆ **Word Spacing.** Specifies the spacing between words.

   ◆ **Letter Spacing.** Specifies the spacing between characters.

   ◆ **Glyph Scaling.** Specifies the horizontal scaling for glyphs.

   ◆ **Auto Leading.** Specifies how much space to use between lines for the Auto Leading option.

   ◆ **Single Word Justification.** Select an option to specify how you want to justify a single word on a line.

   ◆ **Composer.** Select an option to specify the best way to justify text, either as a line or an entire paragraph.

6. Click **OK**.

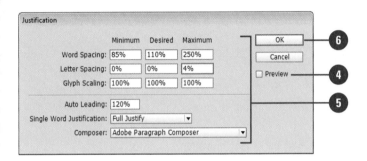

For Your Information

Setting Optical Margin Alignment

If you have punctuation along a margin with justified text, you can set optical margin adjustment to create a more uniform appearance for the edge of the text. This moves the punctuation slightly outside of the text margin so the type appears aligned. To set the option, select the text, click the Type menu, click Story, select the Optical Margin Alignment check box in the Story panel, and then enter a size value for adjustment.

Using the Story Editor

If you want to focus solely on text in your document, the Story Editor is the tool for you. The Story Editor displays text and tables in a separate window with unformatted sequential columns and rows for easy editing. Any graphics, shapes, text formatting, or other design elements in your document do not appear in the Story Editor. The left side of the Story Editor displays the paragraph style, while the right side displays the editable text. You don't have to close the Story Editor to work in layout view. You can switch back and forth by clicking in the layout window. When you close and reopen a Story Editor window, the window opens to its previous width, height, and location on the screen. You can change the display of the Story Editor window by showing or hiding elements—such as track changes, Style Name column, depth ruler, paragraph break markers, and footnotes—using the Story Editor submenu on the View menu or changing Story Editor Display preferences.

Edit Text and Tables in the Story Editor

1. Click in the text frame that you want to edit using Story Editor.

2. Click the **Edit** menu, and then click **Edit in Story Editor**.

3. Drag the pointer to highlight the text, or click in the document to place the insertion point where you want to make a change.

4. Perform one of the following editing commands:

   ◆ To replace text, type your text.

   ◆ To delete text, press the Backspace key or the Delete key.

   ◆ Drag the selection to a new location.

5. Click the **Close** button.

Style for text frame

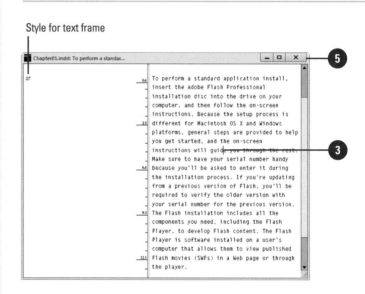

Show or Hide Elements in the Story Editor

1. Click in the text frame that you want to edit using Story Editor.

2. Click the **Edit** menu, and then click **Edit in Story Editor**.

3. Click the **View** menu, point to **Story Editor**.

4. Click any of the following commands:

   ◆ **Hide/Show Changes.** Hides or shows track changes.

   ◆ **Hide/Show Style Name Column.** Hides or shows the column on the left that displays style names and depth ruler.

   ◆ **Hide/Show Depth Ruler.** Hides or shows the depth ruler in the Style Name column.

   ◆ **Hide/Show Paragraph Break Marks.** Hides or shows paragraph break marks.

   ◆ **Expand All Footnotes.** Expands all footnotes to display them.

5. Click the **Close** button.

See Also

See "Setting Story Editor Display Preferences" on page 498 for more information on setting Story Editor preferences.

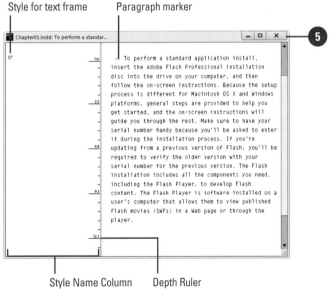

Style for text frame   Paragraph marker

Style Name Column   Depth Ruler

Adding Footnotes

A footnote is a note placed at the bottom of a text frame to cite a reference in the text. Footnote reference marks appear as numeric characters (1, 2, 3, etc.). InDesign provides you with various options in order to customize the reference marks. If you'd like to change your footnotes to alpha characters (a, b, c, etc.) or Roman numerals (i, ii, iii, etc.), you can do that through the Footnote Options dialog box. You can also have InDesign renumber your footnotes after each page, section, or spread in your document, and change the style and other formatting for reference marks.

Add Footnotes

1. Click to place the insertion point where you want the footnote reference to appear.

2. Click the **Type** menu, and then click **Insert Footnote**.

3. Type or paste the text for the footnote.

Did You Know?

You can import footnotes and endnotes from Microsoft Word. When you place a Word document with footnotes and endnotes into an InDesign document, you can include them when importing the text by using the Import Options dialog box. Footnotes from Word are converted to InDesign footnotes, while endnotes are converted to normal text.

and Windows. Flash is the world's most pervasive software platform, used by over one million professionals and reaching more than 97% of Web-enabled desktops worldwide, as well as a wide range of consumer electronic devices, such as PDAs and mobile phones. ————————— 1

and Windows. Flash is the world's most pervasive software platform, used by over one million professionals and reaching more than 97% of Web-enabled desktops worldwide, as well as a wide range of consumer electronic devices, such as PDAs and mobile phones[1].

Flash operates virtually the same on both Macintosh and Windows versions, except for a few keyboard commands that have equivalent functions. You use the [Ctrl] and [Alt] keys in Windows, and the ⌘ and [Option] keys on a Macintosh computer. Also, the term *popup* on the Macintosh and *list arrow* in Windows refer to the same type of option.

1   World Marketing Research data: 2012 ————————— 3

Change Footnote Options

① Click the **Type** menu, and then click **Document Footnote Options**.

② Click the **Numbering and Formatting** tab.

③ Select the various options you want to use:

- ◆ Numbering. Specify a style, start number, and select options to restart numbering and show and specify prefix or suffix characters.

- ◆ Footnote Reference Number in Text. Specify a position and character style.

- ◆ Footnote Formatting. Specify a paragraph style and special character separator.

④ Click the **Layout** tab.

⑤ Select the various options you want to use:

- ◆ Spacing Options. Specify options for spacing before the first footnote and between footnotes.

- ◆ First Baseline. Specify an offset for the baseline shift.

- ◆ Placement Options. Specify options to place end of story footnotes at bottom of text and allow split footnotes in different columns.

- ◆ Rule Above. Specify options to create a rule line above the footnote.

⑥ Click **OK**.

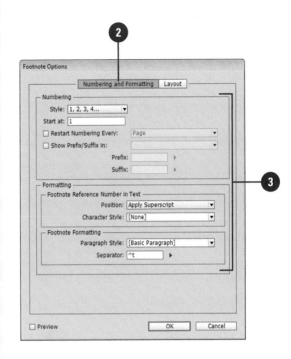

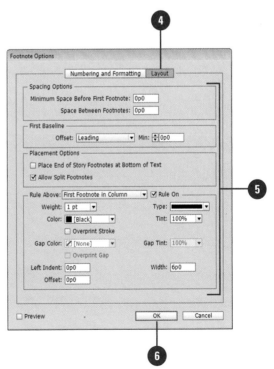

Changing Case

If there are paragraphs with inconsistent use of capitalization in your document, you can use change case options to fix them. You can set options to create text as UPPERCASE, lowercase, Title Case, or Sentence case. Title Case capitalizes each word in a title, while Sentence case capitalizes the first word in the sentence.

Change Case

1. Select the type for which you want to change case.

2. Click the **Type** menu, and then point to **Change Case**.

3. Select one of the following:

   ◆ **UPPERCASE.**

   ◆ **lowercase.**

   ◆ **Title Case.**

   ◆ **Sentence case.**

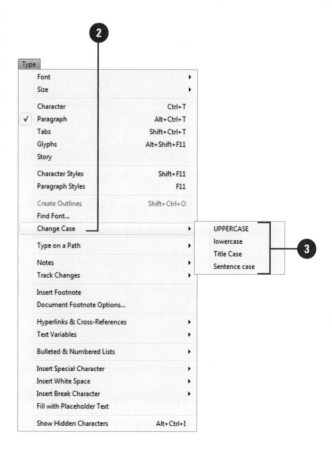

Creating an Interactive Document

Introduction

In the past, desktop publishing was exclusively considered a print-based medium. However, with the introduction and popularity of the PDF (Portable Document Format) file format and the Adobe Reader as well as the SWF (ShockWave Flash) file format and the Adobe Flash Player, interactive documents are more popular than ever. Instead of creating a document just for printing, you can now create an interactive document with hyperlinks, bookmarks, and buttons for presentations. You can even add animation using motion presets, page transitions, such as a wipe or dissolve, when you turn a page and insert sounds and videos into an InDesign document in addition to graphics.

With the Hyperlinks panel, you can create hyperlinks that navigate to external URLs, link to files with supplemental information, launch an e-mail client, or jump to a page or section of a page within the same or even a different document. You can also verify your hyperlinks directly in InDesign with no need to export the document to a PDF or Flash (SWF) file for testing.

The Buttons and Forms panel is a centralized place to work with interactive buttons and forms in InDesign. The Buttons and Forms panel makes it easy to create interactive buttons that perform actions when the document is exported to Flash (SWF file) or Acrobat (PDF). You can create a custom button from a selected object in an InDesign document or select a button from the built-in Samples button library. When you create an interactive button, you can add events and actions to enable navigation within a document, launch a movie, play a sound, or open a web page.

When you're finished with your interactive document, you can use the SWF Preview panel to view animation and interactivity for the current selection, current spread, or the entire document.

What You'll Do

Define Hyperlink Destinations

Create Hyperlinks

Convert and Stylize Hyperlinks

Use the Hyperlinks Panel

Create Cross-References

Create Bookmarks

Add Media

Set Media Options

Add Animation with Motion Presets

Work with Animations

Change Animation Order

Add Page Transitions

Use the Buttons and Forms Panel

Create Buttons and Forms

Work with Events and Actions

Work with Button States

Set Tab Order

Create Multi-State Objects

Insert HTML Content

Create QR Code

Use the SWF Preview Panel

Defining Hyperlink Destinations

A **hyperlink** is a text or graphic object that is linked to other parts of the document, other documents, or web pages. A hyperlink consists of a source and a destination. The **source** is the text or graphic object that you click to jump to the hyperlink location while the **destination** is the place that InDesign sends you to. The destination can be in the same document, another document, an e-mail message, or a web page on the Internet. You need to define a destination before you can define the source.

Create a Hyperlink Destination

1. Select the **Hyperlinks** panel.

   ◆ Click the **Window** menu, point to **Interactive**, and then click **Hyperlinks**.

2. Click the **Options** button, and then click **New Hyperlink Destination**.

3. Click the **Type** list arrow, and then select a hyperlink type:

   ◆ **Page.** Creates a link to a page in the same document.

   ◆ **Text Anchor.** Creates a link to a selected area of text.

   ◆ **URL.** Creates a link to a web page on the Internet.

4. Specify the options related to the hyperlink type; options vary depending on the type.

   ◆ **For a Page.** Specify a page name, page number, and zoom setting.

   ◆ **For a Text Anchor.** Specify a name for the anchor.

   ◆ **For an URL.** Specify a name and address for the URL (Uniform Resource Locator).

5. Click **OK**.

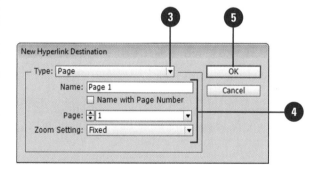

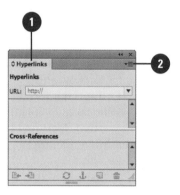

Text Anchor

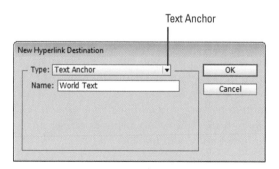

Edit or Delete a Hyperlink Destination

1. Select the **Hyperlinks** panel.

   ◆ Click the **Window** menu, point to **Interactive**, and then click **Hyperlinks**.

2. Click the **Options** button, and then click **Hyperlink Destination Options**.

3. Click the **Destination** list arrow, and then select a destination.

4. Click **Edit** or **Delete**.

5. If editing, make the changes you want for the destination.

6. Click **OK**.

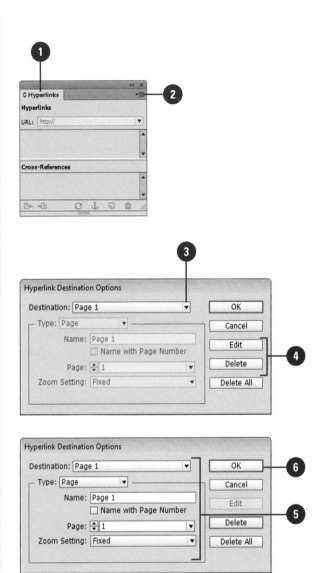

Creating Hyperlinks

Before you can create a hyperlink, you need to define a hyperlink destination. After you create one or more hyperlink destinations, you can create a hyperlink source, which is a text or graphic object that you click to jump to a hyperlink destination. You can link a hyperlink to several different destination types, including URL, File, Email, Page, Text Anchor, and Shared Destination. If you need a quick hyperlink to an URL, you can create one with the New Hyperlink From URL command.

Create a Hyperlink

1. Select the text or graphic you want to use as the hyperlink.

2. Select the **Hyperlinks** panel.

   ◆ Click the **Window** menu, point to **Interactive**, and then click **Hyperlinks**.

3. Click the **Options** button, and then click **New Hyperlink**.

4. Click the **Link To** list arrow, and then select an option:

   ◆ **URL.** Creates a link to a web page on the Internet.

   ◆ **File.** Creates a link to a document.

   ◆ **Email.** Creates an e-mail message link, which opens your default e-mail program.

   ◆ **Page.** Creates a link to a page in the same document.

   ◆ **Text Anchor.** Creates a link to a selected area of text.

   ◆ **Shared Destination.** Creates a link to the same destination from multiple sources.

5. Specify the options related to the hyperlink type; options vary depending on the type.

   ◆ **For an URL.** Specify a name and address for the URL (Uniform Resource Locator).

   ◆ **For a File.** Use the Browse button to select a file to link.

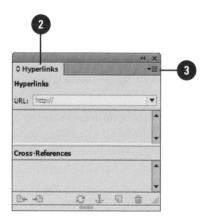

- ◆ **For an Email.** Specify an e-mail address and message subject line.

- ◆ **For a Page.** Specify a page name, page number, and zoom setting.

- ◆ **For a Text Anchor.** Specify a name for the anchor.

- ◆ **For a Shared Destination.** Specify a document name, and hyperlink destination.

6 Specify a character style for the text and appearance options for the hyperlink.

7 Click **OK**.

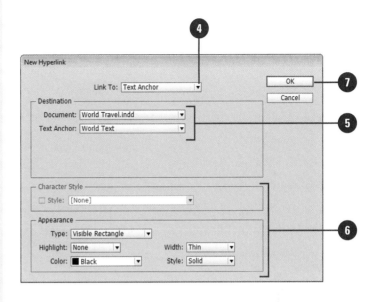

Create a Hyperlink From an URL

1 Select the text that you want to use to create a URL.

2 Select the **Hyperlinks** panel.

- ◆ Click the **Window** menu, point to **Interactive**, and then click **Hyperlinks**.

3 Click the **Options** button, and then click **New Hyperlink From URL**.

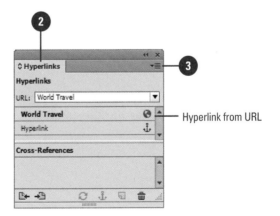

Hyperlink from URL

Converting and Stylizing Hyperlinks

If you have one or more URLs in your document, you can use the Convert URLs to Hyperlink command to search the current selection, story, or document for URL strings and convert them to hyperlinks. The Convert URLs to Hyperlinks dialog box works like the Find/Change dialog box. You can find URLs and convert one URL at a time or convert them all at once. In addition to converting URLs to hyperlinks, you can also apply a character style to create a consistent look. However, if you don't want them all the same, you can change the style and appearance of individual hyperlinks.

Convert and Stylize URLs to Hyperlinks

1. Select the **Hyperlinks** panel.
   - Click the **Window** menu, point to **Interactive**, and then click **Hyperlinks**.

2. Click the **Options** button, and then click **Convert URLs to Hyperlinks**.

3. Click the **Search** list arrow, and then select the scope option you want: **Document**, **Story**, or **Selection**.

4. To apply a character style to the converted hyperlinks, select the **Apply to Hyperlink** check box, click the **Character Style** list arrow, and then select a character style.

5. Use the following buttons to find or convert the URL strings:
   - **Find.** Starts the search for the next URL string.
   - **Convert.** Converts the selected URL string to a hyperlink.
   - **Convert All.** Changes all find URL strings to hyperlinks.

6. If the Finished Finding URLs alert dialog box appears, click **OK**.

7. When you're finished, click **Done**.

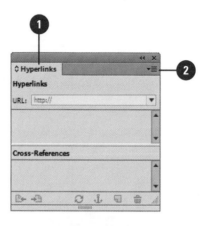

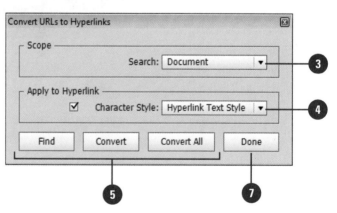

Change the Appearance of a Hyperlink

1. Select the **Hyperlinks** panel.
   - ◆ Click the **Window** menu, point to **Interactive**, and then click **Hyperlinks**.

2. Select the hyperlink you want to edit.

3. Click the **Options** button, and then click **Hyperlink Options**.
   - ◆ You can also double-click a hyperlink in the Hyperlinks panel.

4. Double-click the hyperlink in the Hyperlinks panel.

5. For text, select the **Style** check box, and then select a character style.

6. Make the changes you want for the hyperlink appearance.
   - ◆ **Type.** Specify a visibility setting for the hyperlink.
   - ◆ **Highlight.** Specify a highlight setting for the hotspot.
   - ◆ **Color.** Specify a color for the hyperlink.
   - ◆ **Width.** Specify a thickness for the visible rectangle type.
   - ◆ **Style.** Specify a line style for the visible rectangle type.

7. Click **OK**.

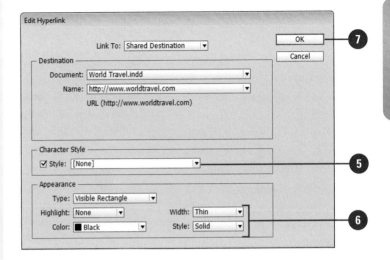

Using the Hyperlinks Panel

The Hyperlinks panel is a centralized place to work with hyperlinks and cross references in InDesign. The redesigned Hyperlinks panel makes it easy to create hyperlinks that navigate to external URLs, link to files with supplemental information, launch an e-mail client, or jump to a page or section of a page within the same or even a different document. You can also verify your hyperlinks directly in InDesign with no need to export the document to a PDF or Flash (SWF file) for testing. You can use buttons on the bottom of the panel to go to the hyperlink source or destination, create a new hyperlink, or delete hyperlinks.

Use the Hyperlinks Panel

1. Select the **Hyperlinks** panel.

   ◆ Click the **Window** menu, point to **Interactive**, and then click **Hyperlinks**.

2. Use any of the following buttons or commands to perform an operation:

   ◆ Go to the Hyperlink Source. Select the hyperlink, and then click the **Go to Source** button.

   ◆ Go to the Hyperlink Destination. Select the hyperlink, and then click the **Go to Destination** button.

   ◆ Create a New Hyperlink. Create a destination, and then click the **Create New Hyperlink** button.

   ◆ Delete a Hyperlink. Select the hyperlink, click the **Delete Selected Hyperlinks** button, and then click **Yes**.

   ◆ Reset a Hyperlink. Select the hyperlink, click the **Options** button, and then click **Reset Hyperlink**.

   ◆ Update a Hyperlink. Select the hyperlink, click the **Options** button, and then click **Update Hyperlink**.

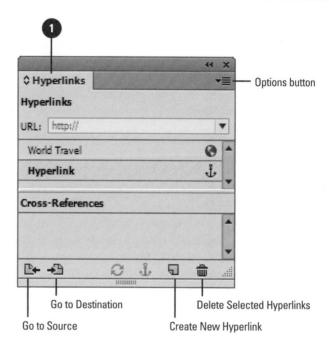

Edit a Hyperlink

1 Select the **Hyperlinks** panel.

◆ Click the **Window** menu, point to **Interactive**, and then click **Hyperlinks**.

2 Select the hyperlink you want to edit.

3 Click the **Options** button, and then click **Hyperlink Options**.

◆ You can also double-click a hyperlink in the Hyperlinks panel.

4 Click the **Link To** list arrow, and then select an option:

◆ **URL.** Creates a link to a web page on the Internet.

◆ **File.** Creates a link to a document.

◆ **Email.** Creates an e-mail message link, which opens your default e-mail program.

◆ **Page.** Creates a link to a page in the same document.

◆ **Text Anchor.** Creates a link to a selected area of text.

◆ **Shared Destination.** Creates a link to the same destination from multiple sources.

5 Specify the options related to the hyperlink type; options vary depending on the Link To type.

6 Click **OK**.

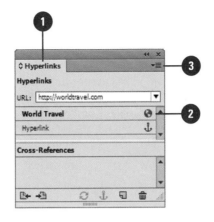

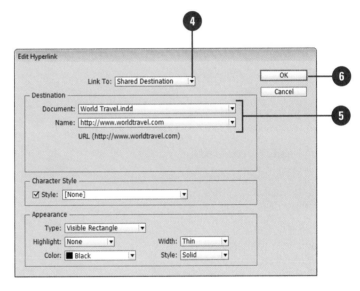

See Also

See "Creating Hyperlinks" on page 346 for more information on setting options for editing a hyperlink.

Creating Cross-References

A cross-reference refers a reader from one section of a document to another. For example, *For more information, see "Using the Hyperlinks Panel" on page 350.* The text being referred to is the destination text, while the text generated from the destination is the source cross-reference, which is editable. The Hyperlinks panel is a centralized place to create and work with hyperlinks and cross references in InDesign. You can use buttons on the bottom of the panel to go to the cross-reference source or destination, create a new cross-reference, or delete cross-references. When you create or edit a cross-reference, you can select format and appearance settings for the reference.

Create a Cross-Reference

1. Click to place the insertion point where you want the cross-reference.

2. Select the **Hyperlinks** panel.
   - Click the **Window** menu, point to **Type & Tables**, and then click **Cross-References**.

3. Click the **New Cross-Reference** button on the panel.

4. Click the **Link To** list arrow, and then select a link type.

5. Click the **Document** list arrow, and then select a document location.

6. Select a paragraph in the document or a hyperlink destination for the text anchor.

7. Click the **Format** list arrow, and then select a cross-reference format.

8. Make the changes you want for the cross-reference appearance.
   - **Type.** Specify a visibility setting.
   - **Highlight.** Specify a highlight setting for the hotspot.
   - **Color.** Specify a color.
   - **Width.** Specify a thickness for the visible rectangle type.
   - **Style.** Specify a line style for the visible rectangle type.

9. Click **OK**.

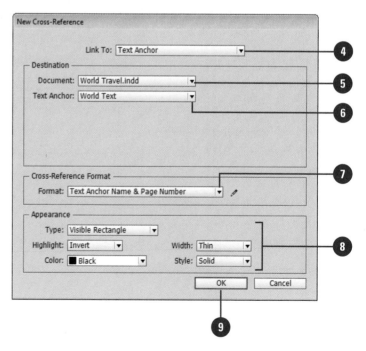

Work with Cross-References

1 Select the **Hyperlinks** panel.

- ◆ Click the **Window** menu, point to **Interactive**, and then click **Hyperlinks**.

2 Use any of the following buttons or commands to perform an operation:

- ◆ Go to the Cross-Reference Source. Select the reference, and then click the **Go to Source** button.

- ◆ Go to the Cross-Reference Destination. Select the reference, and then click the **Go to Destination** button.

- ◆ Create a New Cross-Reference. Select the cross-reference text, and then click the **Create New Cross-Reference** button.

- ◆ Edit a Cross-Reference. Double-click the cross-reference in the panel.

- ◆ Delete a New Cross-Reference. Select the reference, click the **Delete Selected Cross-Reference** button, and then click **Yes**.

- ◆ Reset a New Cross-Reference. Select the reference, click the **Options** button, and then click **Reset Cross-Reference**.

- ◆ Update a Cross-Reference. Select the reference, click the **Options** button, and then click **Update Cross-Reference**.

- ◆ Relink a Cross-Reference. Select the reference, click the **Options** button, click **Relink Cross-Reference**, select the reference, and then click **OK**.

Options button

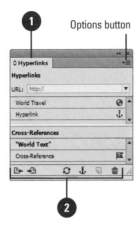

Out of date

Missing link

Cross-reference

Creating Bookmarks

Bookmarks provide another way to navigate through a document. You can create bookmarks that will point to a place in a text frame, any selected text, a frame, or a page. You can create and work with bookmarks in the Bookmarks panel. When you create a PDF of your document, readers can use the bookmarks to navigate from one location to another by using the Bookmarks panel.

Create and Rename a Bookmark

1 Do one of the following to select a bookmark location:

◆ **Insertion Point.** Click to place the insertion point where you want the bookmark.

◆ **Text.** Select any text to specify a location.

◆ **Frame.** Select a text or graphic frame to specify a location.

◆ **Page.** Double-click a page in the Pages panel to specify a page location.

2 Select the **Bookmarks** panel.

◆ Click the **Window** menu, point to **Interactive**, and then click **Bookmarks**.

3 Click the **New Bookmark** button on the panel.

4 Click the bookmark to select it.

5 Click the bookmark again to make the name editable.

◆ You can also click the **Options** button, click **Rename Bookmark**, enter a name, and then click **OK**.

6 Type a name for the bookmark, and then press Enter (Win) or Return (Mac).

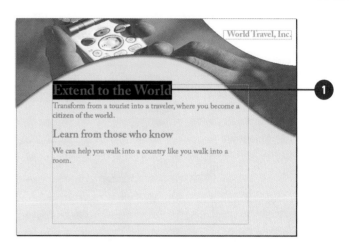

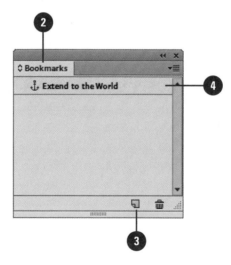

Use the Bookmarks Panel

1. Select the **Bookmarks** panel.

   ◆ Click the **Window** menu, point to **Interactive**, and then click **Bookmarks**.

2. Use any of the following buttons or commands to perform an operation:

   ◆ **Create a New Bookmark.** Select a location, and then click the **Create New Bookmark** button.

   ◆ **Delete a Bookmark.** Select the bookmark, click the **Delete Selected Bookmarks** button, and then click **OK**.

   ◆ **Rename a Bookmark.** Select the bookmark, click the **Options** button, click **Rename Bookmark**, type a name, and then click **OK**.

   ◆ **Go to a Selected Bookmark.** Select the bookmark, click the **Options** button, and then click **Go to Selected Bookmark**.

   ◆ **Sort Bookmarks.** Click the **Options** button, and then click **Sort Bookmarks**.

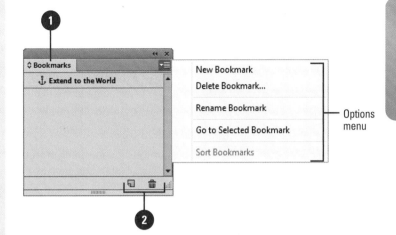

Adding Media

With the Place command or Media panel, you can import the sound or video clips that you want to play in your interactive document. You can import video files in Flash Video format (FLV and F4Vm), H.264-encoded files (such as MP4), and SWF (ShockWave Flash) files. You can import audio files in MP3 format. Legacy media files, such as QuickTime (MOV), AVI, WMV, and MPEG, are still supported. However, if you want to take advantage of the rich media support in Acrobat 9 or later, Adobe Reader 9 or later, and Adobe Flash Player 10 or later, you need to convert and relink your legacy media to FLV, F4V, SWF, MP4, or MP3 using Adobe Media Encoder CC or later. With the Preset Browser, you can select user conversion presets for systems, such as desktops and the web, and devices, such as Apple iOS and Android. After you import sound and video files, you can preview them in the SWF Preview panel in InDesign or export them to Adobe PDF or SWF, or XML. You can export legacy media files to PDF files, but not to SWF or FLA files. If you have video on a web server, you can place the video from a URL. If you're not sure what to play, you can create an empty frame (with diagonal lines) and then import the clip later. When you import a media file, a poster image appears, which you can change or remove later.

Insert a Media File

1. Click the **File** menu, and then click **Place**, or select the **Media** panel, and then click the **Place Video or Audio File** button on the panel.

   ◆ **Place a Video from a URL.** Select the **Media** panel, click the **Place Video From URL** button on the panel, type the URL, and then click **OK**.

2. Navigate to the location with the file you want to import.

3. Select the sound or video file you want to place.

4. Click **Open**.

   The imported sound or movie is placed in a loaded preview cursor.

5. Click or drag a rectangle frame with the loaded cursor to place the clip in a new sound or movie frame, or click in an empty sound or movie frame (designated by diagonal lines) to place it in an empty frame.

Place Video From URL button ❶

URL to a video on a web server

Convert and Relink Media Files Using Adobe Media Encoder

① Start Adobe Media Encoder from the Start menu or screen (Win) or the Applications folder (Mac).

② Click the **Add Source** button (+), select the media files you want to convert, and then click **Open**.

③ Select each media file, click the **Format** list arrow, and then select a conversion file format. Click the **Preset** list arrow and then select a predefined setting.

◆ **Preset Browser.** Select a file, select a preset, and then click **Apply Preset**.

◆ **Presets.** Use toolbar buttons to create, delete, group, view settings, import, and export presets.

④ Click the **Start Queue** button.

The media files are converted to the new media format and placed in the same folder as the original.

⑤ When you're done, click the **Close** button to exit the program.

⑥ To relink the media files in InDesign, select the Links panel, Alt (Win) or Option (Mac) click the **Relink** button on the panel, select the replacement media file for each one (or click Skip if not available), and then click **Open**.

Did You Know?

You can preserve transformation when you update or reestablish a link. Click the Edit (Win) or InDesign (Mac) menu, point to Preferences, click File Handling, select the Preserve Image Dimensions When Relinking check box, and then click OK.

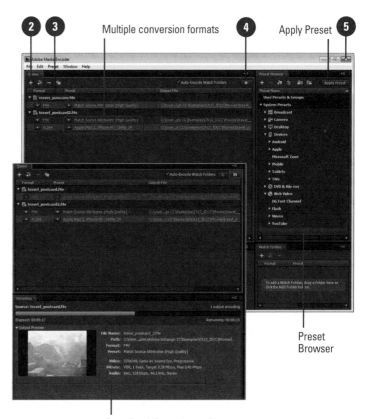

Multiple conversion formats — Apply Preset

Preset Browser

Encoding information and progress

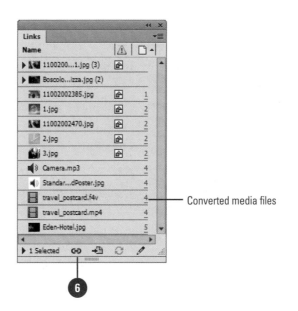

Converted media files

Setting Media Options

After you import media files into a document, you can use the Media panel to preview media, set playback and other properties. You can preview FLV, F4V, SWF, MP4, and MP3 files directly in InDesign; all other legacy media cannot be viewed in the Media panel. You can select the playback controls you want, and select the placeholder poster image for FLV, F4V, and MP4 files. A placeholder poster image is the still image that appears for the media in the frame, which you can change or remove later. In addition, you can create navigation points, which are time-code markers, that you can use with button actions to play a video starting from any of the navigation points. You can work with media frames like any other frame in InDesign.

Set Sound Options

1. Select the sound clip.

2. Select the **Media** panel.

   ◆ Click the **Window** menu, point to **Interactive**, and then click **Media**.

3. Select any of the following check boxes to enable the option:

   ◆ **Play on Page Load.** Select to play the sound when the page is loaded. If other objects are set to play, the Timing panel determines the order.

   ◆ **Stop on Page Turn.** Select to stop playing an MP3 sound when turned to a different page.

   ◆ **Loop.** Select to play the MP3 sound repeatedly.

4. Click the **Poster** list arrow, and then select a poster option:

   ◆ **None.** Removes poster image.

   ◆ **Standard.** Uses the file: *StandardSoundPoster.jpg*.

   ◆ **Choose Image.** Use the Browse button to select a bitmap graphic (BMP).

5. To preview in the SWF Preview panel, click the **Preview Spread** button.

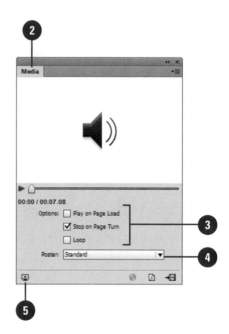

Poster image

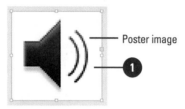

Set Video Options

1 Select the video clip.

2 Select the **Media** panel.

◆ Click the **Window** menu, point to **Interactive**, and then click **Media**.

3 Select any of the following check boxes to enable the option:

◆ **Play on Page Load.** Select to play the video when the page is loaded. If other objects are set to play, the Timing panel determines the order.

◆ **Loop (Except PDF).** Select to play the video repeatedly; not included for PDFs.

4 Click the **Poster** list arrow, and then select a poster option:

◆ **None.** Removes poster image.

◆ **Standard.** Uses the file: *StandardMoviePoster.jpg*.

◆ **From Current Frame.** Uses the current frame displayed in the Media panel. Use the slider to change it, and then click the **Use Current Frame** button.

◆ **Choose Image.** Use the Browse button to select a bitmap graphic (BMP).

5 Click the **Controller** list arrow, select a playback control skin.

◆ **Show Controller on Rollover.** Select to show the controller when you point to the media.

6 To create a navigation point, drag the slider to a frame, and then click the **Add Nav Point** button, type a name, and then press Enter (Win) or Return (Mac). To remove a navigation point, select the point name in the list, and then click the **Delete Nav Point** button.

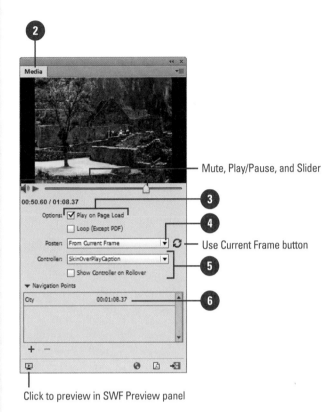

Mute, Play/Pause, and Slider

Use Current Frame button

Click to preview in SWF Preview panel

Added video

Adding Animation with Motion Presets

In an InDesign document, you can add animation to objects for use in exported SWF files, not in an Interactive PDF. To add animation to a PDF, export a selection as a SWF and place it in an InDesign document, and then export it as a PDF. With the Animation panel, you can animate an object quickly using motion presets, which are pre-defined animations that come along with InDesign. The motion presets are the same ones used in Adobe Flash Professional CS6 or later. You can import any custom presets from XML created in Flash or save your own in InDesign. After you apply a motion preset, you can modify animation settings, such as speed, duration, and when the animation plays. If you no longer want to use an animation, you can remove it.

Apply an Animation Motion Preset and Set Options

1. Select the object you want to animate.

2. Select the **Animation** panel.

   ◆ Click the **Window** menu, point to **Interactive**, and then click **Animation**.

3. Type a descriptive name for the animation. The name is also used when you set up an action to play the animation.

4. Click the **Preset** list arrow, and then select a motion preset.

5. Click the **Event(s)** list arrow, and then select an event to play the animated object in the SWF file.

   ◆ **On Page Load.** Plays when the page is loaded (selected by default).

   ◆ **On Page Click.** Plays when the page is clicked.

   ◆ **On Click (Self).** Plays when the object is clicked.

   ◆ **On Roll Over (Self).** Plays when the object is pointed to. To reverse the action when you point off the object, select the **Reverse On Roll Off** check box.

   ◆ **On Button Event.** Plays when a button action takes place.

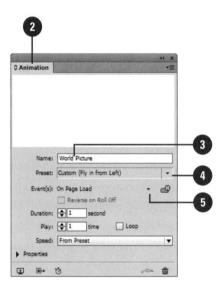

6 To create a button trigger, click the **Create Button Trigger** button, click an object to convert it to a button, and then set options in the Buttons and Forms panel.

7 Specify a duration for the animation and the number of time the animation plays, or select the **Loop** check box to repeatedly play the animation.

8 Click the **Speed** list arrow, and then select an option: **From Preset** for the default, **None** for a steady rate, **Ease In** to start slow and speeds up, or **Ease Out** to start fast and slows down.

9 To use advanced options, click the **Properties** arrow, and then do any of the following:

◆ Animate. Select **From Current Appearance** or **To Current Appearance** to use the object's current properties as the starting or ending point. Select **To Current Location** to use the object's properties as the starting and ending point.

◆ Rotate. Specify a rotation angle the object completes.

◆ Origin. Uses the proxy to specify the origin point of the motion path.

◆ Scale. Specify a percentage to increase or decrease the size.

◆ Opacity. Select **None** (remains solid), **Fade In** (goes to visible), or **Fade Out** (goes to invisible).

◆ Visibility. Select the **Hide Until Animated** or **Hide After Animating** check boxes to make an object invisible before or after playback.

10 To remove an animation from an object, select the object, and then click the **Delete** button on the Animation panel.

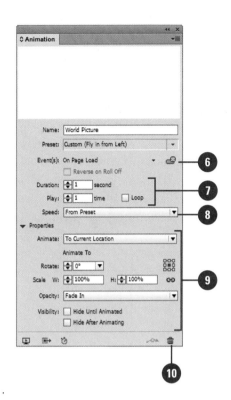

Working with Animations

With the Animation panel, you can import any custom motion presets from XML created in Flash or InDesign, or save your own in InDesign. If you want to share your motion presets with other InDesign users, you can save them as an XML file, which they can in turn import. After you import, save, or duplicate motion presets, you can delete the ones you don't want. After you apply a motion preset to an object, you can change the motion path with the Direct Selection tool or Pen tool just like any other path in InDesign.

Manage Animation Motion Presets

1 Select the **Animation** panel.

- ◆ Click the **Window** menu, point to **Interactive**, and then click **Animation**.

2 Perform any of the following management options:

- ◆ **Save Motion Presets.** Specify the settings you want to save, click the **Options** button, click **Save**, type a name, and then click **OK**.

- ◆ **Delete Motion Presets.** Click the **Options** button, click **Manage Presets**, select a preset, and then click **Delete**.

- ◆ **Duplicate Motion Presets.** Click the **Options** button, click **Manage Presets**, select a preset, and then click **Duplicate**.

- ◆ **Save Motion Presets as XML.** Click the **Options** button, click **Manage Presets**, select a preset, click **Save As**, type a name, specify a location, and then click **Save**.

- ◆ **Import Motion Presets as XML.** Click the **Options** button, click **Manage Presets**, click **Load**, and then double-click the XML file you want.

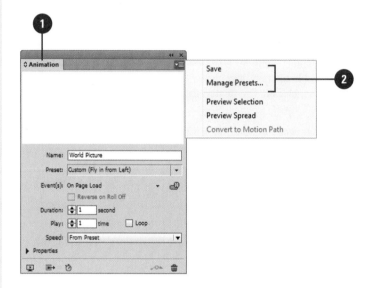

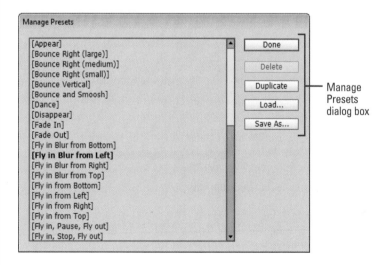

Manage Presets dialog box

Edit a Motion Path

1. Select the **Direct Selection** tool on the Tools panel.

2. Click a blank area to deselect all points.

3. To select and move multiple anchor points and segments, hold the Shift key, and then click the anchor points or segments you want, or drag a rectangle marquee around the ones you want.

4. Drag an anchor point or drag the middle of a segment.

   ◆ For a smaller move, click the anchor point or segment, and then press an arrow key.

   ◆ To constrain the movement of anchor points or segments to 45 degrees, hold down Shift while dragging.

5. To reshape a curve segment, click an anchor point or a curve segment, and then drag a direction point at the end of the direction handle.

Did You Know?

You can convert selected objects to a motion path. Select the object you want to animate and the path you want to use as the motion path (cannot select more than two objects), select the Animation panel, click the Convert To Motion Path button on the panel, and then change settings in the panel.

You can change the direction of the motion path. Select the motion path, click the Object menu, point to Paths, and then click Reverse Path.

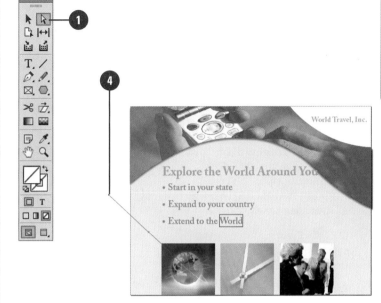

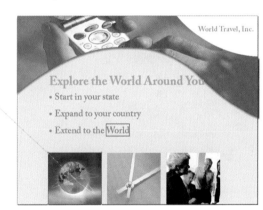

Edited motion path

Changing Animation Order

With the Timing panel, you can change the order of when objects play an animation. Animated objects on the current spread appear in the Timing panel based on the page event assigned to each object animation, either On Page Load, On Page Click, or Unassigned. You can change the animation order, delay time, event assignment, and play animations together, separately, or linked.

Use the Timing Panel

1 Select the **Timing** panel.

◆ Click the **Window** menu, point to **Interactive**, and then click **Timing**, or click the **Show Timing Panel** button on the Animation panel.

2 Click the **Event** list arrow, and then select an event type: **On Page Load**, **On Page Click**, or **Unassigned**.

3 Perform any of the following:

◆ Animation Order. Drag elements up or down the list. Items at the top play first.

◆ Delay Animation. Select a element, and then specify the delay in seconds.

◆ Play Multiple Animations Together. Select the elements, click the **Play Together** button on the panel to link them. To unlink Play Together elements, select them, and then click the **Play Separately** button on the panel.

◆ Play Linked Animations. Select the linked elements, and then specify the number of play times or select the **Loop** check box.

◆ Remove Animation. Select a element, click the **Options** button, and then click **Remove Item**.

◆ Reassign Animation. Select a element, click the **Options** button, and then click **Reassign to On Page Load** or **Reassign to On Page Click**.

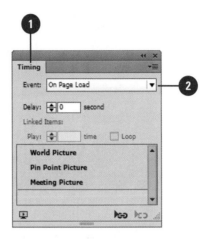

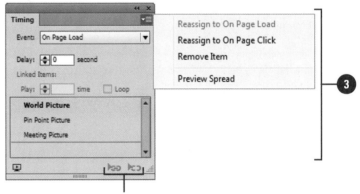

Play Together and Play Separately buttons

Adding Page Transitions

A page transition displays a visual effect, such as a wipe or dissolve, when you turn the page in an interactive document. You can apply page transitions directly in InDesign to individual pages or to all spreads at once with a single click. See previews of available transition types in the Page Transitions dialog box, and control the direction and speed of your transitions for export to Flash (SWF file) or PDF. When you export your document to a PDF, select the Interactive Elements option in the Export PDF dialog box to include page transitions. You can view the page transitions in Full Screen Mode in the PDF by pressing Ctrl+L (Win) or ⌘L (Mac) in Adobe Acrobat or Reader; press Esc to exit from Full Screen Mode.

Apply a Page Transition

1. Select the **Pages** panel, and then select the spread to which you want to apply a page transition.

2. Select the **Page Transitions** panel.

   ◆ Click the **Window** menu, point to **Interactive**, and then click **Page Transitions**.

3. Click the **Transition** list arrow, and then select a transition.

   ◆ To select a page transition from the Page Transitions dialog box, click the **Options** button, click **Choose**, select a transition, select the **Apply to All Spreads** check box as desired, and then click **OK**.

4. Click the **Direction** list arrow, and then select a transition direction.

5. Click the **Speed** list arrow, and then select a transition speed.

6. To apply the current transition to all spreads, click the **Apply To All Spreads** button on the panel.

7. To clear all page transitions, do either of the following:

   ◆ Click the **Transition** list arrow, and then click **None**.

   ◆ Click the **Options** button, and then click **Clear All**.

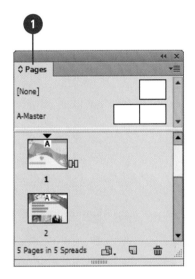

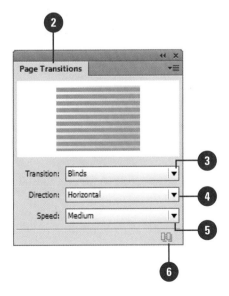

Using the Buttons and Forms Panel

The Buttons and Forms panel is a centralized place to work with interactive buttons and form controls in InDesign. The Buttons and Forms panel makes it easy to create interactive buttons that perform actions when the document is exported to Flash (SWF file) or PDF. You can use buttons on the bottom of the panel to convert an object to a button and to delete buttons. You can also use the Options menu to view and use sample buttons and forms, reset all buttons to the normal state, as well as set panel options. At the bottom of the panel, you can set PDF options based on the selected element, such as button, check box, combo box, list box, radio button, signature field, or text field. The PDF option vary depending on the selected element.

Use the Buttons and Forms Panel

1. Select the **Selection** tool on the tools panel, and then select a button to view or change.

2. Select the **Buttons and Forms** panel.

   ◆ Click the **Window** menu, point to **Interactive**, and then click **Buttons and Forms**.

3. Click the **Options** button, and then select one of the following options:

   ◆ **Sample Buttons and Forms.** Opens the Sample Buttons and Forms panel to use pre-built button and form control elements.

   ◆ **Reset All Buttons to Normal State.** Resets all buttons back to the normal state.

   ◆ **Panel Options.** Changes the thumbnail size in the panel.

4. Select the **Hidden Until Triggered** check box to hide the element until triggered.

5. Click the **PDF Options** arrow to expand the panel.

   ◆ Type a description to provide alternative text for visually impaired users.

   ◆ Common options include **Printable**, **Required**, and **Read Only** check boxes.

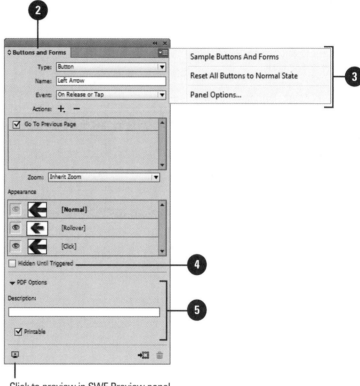

Click to preview in SWF Preview panel

Change the Buttons and Forms Panel Display

1. Select the **Selection** tool on the tools panel, and then select a button to view or change.

2. Select the **Buttons and Forms** panel.

   ◆ Click the **Window** menu, point to **Interactive**, and then click **Buttons and Forms**.

3. Click the **Options** button, and then click **Panel Options**.

4. Select a thumbnail size.

5. Click **OK**.

Did You Know?

You can delete a button. Select the Buttons and Forms panel, select the button, click the Delete button on the panel, and then click OK.

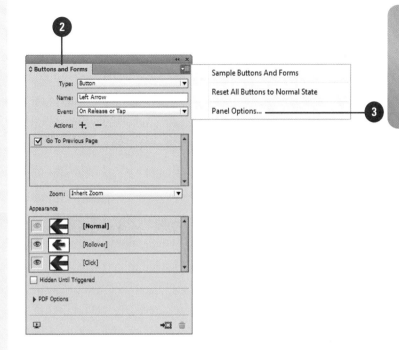

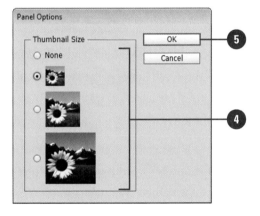

Creating Buttons

You can build interactive buttons to perform an action using the Buttons and Forms panel. For example, you can create a button to navigate within a dynamic document, launch a movie, play a sound, or open a web page or add controls to create a PDF form. You can create a custom button from a selected object in an InDesign document or select a button from the built-in Sample Buttons and Forms panel. The sample buttons include effects, such as adding gradient feathers and drop shadows. There are also assigned actions. For example, the arrow buttons are assigned the Go To Next Page or Go To Previous Page action.

Create a Button from a Sample

1. Select the **Buttons and Forms** panel.

   ◆ Click the **Window** menu, point to **Interactive**, and then click **Buttons and Forms**.

2. Click the **Options** button, and then click **Sample Buttons and Forms**.

3. Drag a button from the Sample Buttons and Forms panel to the document.

4. Click the **Close** button on the Sample Buttons and Forms panel.

5. Select the button using the **Selection** tool on the Tools panel.

   ◆ You can drag a resize handle to change the size of the button, and then drag to move.

6. Enter a name and make changes to the button settings.

   ◆ The default type is set to Button and the Event is set to On Release or Tap.

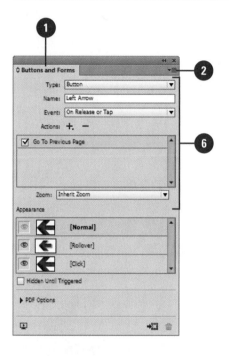

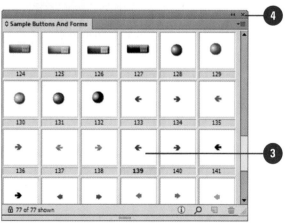

Did You Know?

You can convert a button to an object. Select the button, select the Buttons and Forms panel, click the Convert To Object button, and then click OK.

Convert an Object to a Button

1. Create and select an object that you want to convert to a button.

   IMPORTANT *You can convert any object to a button except a sound, movie, or poster.*

2. Select the **Buttons and Forms** panel.

   ◆ Click the **Window** menu, point to **Interactive**, and then click **Buttons and Forms**.

3. Click the **Convert Object to Button** button on the panel.

   The default type is set to Button.

4. Type a name for the button.

5. Click the **Event** list arrow, and then select an event type.

   ◆ The options include On Release or Tap, On Click, On Roll Over, On Roll Off, On Focus (PDF), and On Blur (PDF).

6. Click the **Add New Action** button, and then select an action to perform for the button.

   ◆ The options include Close, Exit, Go To First Page, Go To URL, Movie, Sound, and Open File, among others.

7. Specify options for the selected action type (options vary).

Did You Know?

You can convert an object to a button.
Select the object, click the Object menu, point to Interactive, and then click Convert to Button. Make changes in the Buttons and Forms panel.

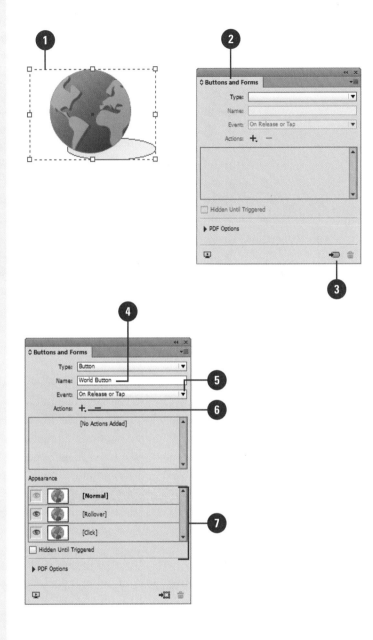

Creating Forms

You can build interactive forms to perform an action using the Buttons and Forms panel. For example, you can add controls—such as a check box, combo box, list box, radio button, signature field, or text field—to create a PDF form. You can create a custom form control from a selected object in an InDesign document or select a form control—either a check box, combo box, or radio button—from the built-in Sample Buttons and Forms panel. The sample form controls include effects, such as adding gradient feathers and drop shadows. After you create a form control, you can enter a description to provide alternative text for visually impaired users, and specify control specific options, which include Printable, Required, and Read Only.

Create a Form from a Sample

1. Select the **Buttons and Forms** panel.

   ◆ Click the **Window** menu, point to **Interactive**, and then click **Buttons and Forms**.

2. Click the **Options** button, and then click **Sample Buttons and Forms**.

3. Drag a form control—either a check box, combo box, or radio button—from the Sample Buttons and Forms panel to the document.

4. Click the **Close** button on the Sample Buttons and Forms panel.

5. Select the form control using the **Selection** tool on the Tools panel.

   ◆ You can drag a resize handle to change the size of the control, and then drag to move it.

6. Enter a name and make changes to the form control settings in the Buttons and Forms panel.

   ◆ The default Event is set to On Release or Tap.

7. Click the **PDF Options** arrow to expand the panel, if necessary, and set control specific options based on the type.

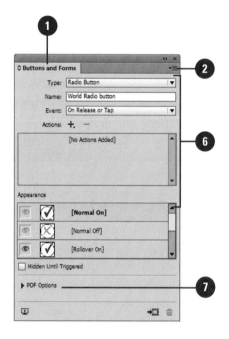

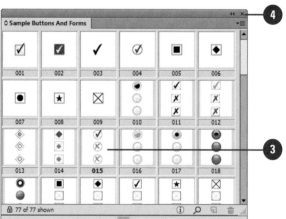

Create a Form Control

1. Create and select an object that you want to use as a form control.

2. Select the **Buttons and Forms** panel.

   - Click the **Window** menu, point to **Interactive**, and then click **Buttons and Forms**.

3. Click the **Type** list arrow on the panel, and then select a form type: **Check Box**, **Combo Box**, **List Box**, **Radio Button**, **Signature Field**, or **Text Field**.

4. Type a name for the form control.

5. Click the **Event** list arrow, and then select an event type.

6. Click the **Add New Action** button, and then select an action to perform for the form control.

7. Click the **PDF Options** arrow to expand the panel, if necessary.

   - Type a description to provide alternative text for visually impaired users.

   - Common options include **Printable**, **Required**, and **Read Only** check boxes.

   - For a Combo Box or List Box, add or delete list items and specify a font size.

Did You Know?

You can convert an object to a form control. Select the object, click the Object menu, point to Interactive, and then select a convert to form command: Check Box, Combo Box, List Box, Radio Button, Signature Field, or Text Field. Make changes in the Buttons and Forms panel.

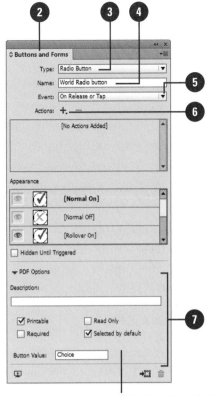

PDF options for Radio Button

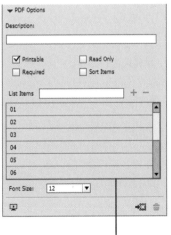

PDF options for a Combo Box

Working with Events and Actions

An event determines when to trigger an action that will execute a button or form control operation. For example, the On Release or Tap event triggers an action when the mouse button is released after a button click or when a tap is pressed from a gesture. An action is associated with an event. You can assign an action type to a button to perform an action. For example, the Go To URL action type opens a web page in your default browser from the PDF document with the interactive button. You can create actions to navigate to anchor text or bookmarks, document pages and views, to launch a movie, play a sound, or open a web page. You can work with events and actions for a selected button or form control in the Buttons and Forms panel.

Select Events for a Button or Form Control

1. Select the **Selection** tool on the tools panel, and then select a button or form control to change.

2. Select the **Buttons and Forms** panel.

   ◆ Click the **Window** menu, point to **Interactive**, and then click **Buttons and Forms**.

3. Click the **Event** list arrow, and then select an event type.

   ◆ **On Release or Tap.** Event occurs when the mouse button is released after a click or a pressed tap.

   ◆ **On Click.** Event occurs when the mouse button is clicked.

   ◆ **On Roll Over.** Event occurs when the mouse pointer enters the button or form control.

   ◆ **On Roll Off.** Event occurs when the mouse pointer moves off the button or form control.

   ◆ **On Focus (PDF).** Event occurs when the button or form control gets the focus using the Tab key.

   ◆ **On Blur (PDF).** Event occurs when the focus moves to another button or form control using the Tab key or mouse click.

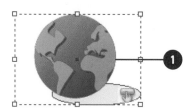

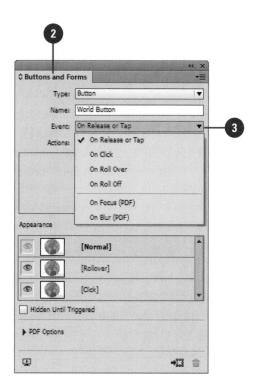

Add or Edit Actions for a Button or Form Control

1. Select the **Selection** tool on the tools panel, and then select a button or form control to change.

2. Select the **Buttons and Forms** panel.

   ◆ Click the **Window** menu, point to **Interactive**, and then click **Buttons and Forms**.

3. Click the **Event** list arrow, and then select an event type.

4. Click the **Add New Action** button, and then select an action to perform for the button or form control.

   ◆ **General.** Options include Go To First Page, Go To URL, Video, and Sound, among others.

   ◆ **HTML5 and SWF.** Options include Animation, Go To Page, Go To State, Go To Next State, and Go To Previous State.

   ◆ **PDF.** Options include Open File, Clear Form , Print Form, and Submit Form, among others.

5. Specify the various options for the selected action type (options vary).

6. To enable or disable an action, select or deselect the check box next to the action name.

7. To delete an action, select the action, click the **Delete Selected Action** button, and then click **OK**.

8. To change an action order, drag an action to a new position.

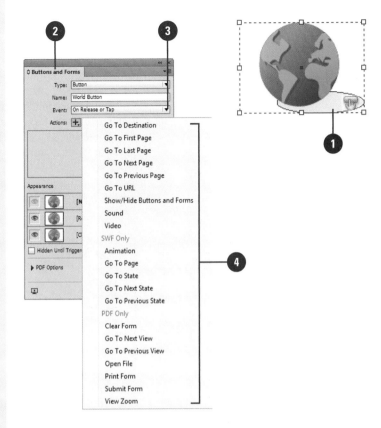

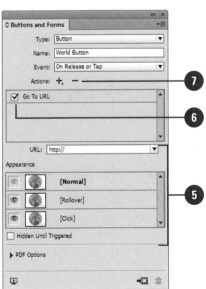

Working with Button States

A button consists of a group of individual objects. When you view a button, an object appears. When you point to or click on a button, another object appears. Each object represents a button state. Each button can have up to three states: Normal, Rollover, and Click. The button is in Normal state when you don't point to or click on the button, Rollover occurs when you point to the button, and Click occurs when you click the button. When you're working with form controls for a PDF, the Radio Button and Check Box controls include button states, which you can change the same way. You can work with button states for a selected button or form control in the Buttons and Forms panel. When you activate a state in the Buttons and Forms panel, the Normal state (default) is copied to it. After it's copied, you can change the appearance of the element using InDesign color, text, and image tools.

Work with Button States

1. Use the **Selection** tool to select a button or use the **Direct Selection** tool to select a button as an individual object (state).

2. Select the **Buttons and Forms** panel.

    ◆ Click the **Window** menu, point to **Interactive**, and then click **Buttons and Forms**.

3. Click the state to activate it.

4. Use any of the following to change the appearance in the layout view.

    ◆ Change Color. Use the **Color** and **Swatches** panel to select a color.

    ◆ Add Text. Select the **Type** tool, click a button, and then type.

    ◆ Insert Graphic. Click the **File** menu, click **Place**, and then double-click a graphic file.

5. To disable/enable a state, click the **Eye** icon next to the state. Disabled states (no Eye icon) are not exported to the SWF or PDF.

6. To delete a state, select it, click the **Delete** button on the panel (you can't delete Normal), and then click **OK**.

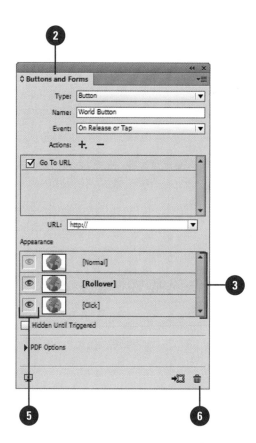

Setting Tab Order

The tab order determines when a button receives focus as you press the Tab key in a SWF or PDF document. When a button or form control receives focus, you can press Enter (Win) or Return (Mac) to execute it. You can also use the On Focus event to trigger an action when a button or form control gets the focus. In the Tab Order dialog box, you can change the tab order for optimal use. The tab order includes buttons or form controls on hidden layers, but not ones on master pages.

Set the Tab Order

1. Select the **Pages** panel, and then double-click the page containing the buttons and form controls you want to set the tab order for.

2. Click the **Object** menu, point to **Interactive**, and then click **Set Tab Order**.

   ◆ The tab order includes buttons or form controls on hidden layers, but not ones on master pages.

3. Select the button or form control you want to move.

4. Click the **Move Up** or **Move Down** buttons to adjust the order.

5. Click **OK**.

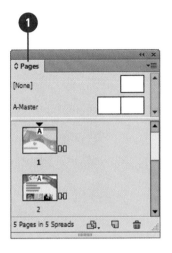

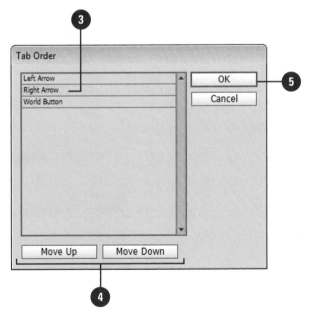

Creating Multi-State Objects

With the Object States panel, you can create multiple versions of an object, known as a state, on a page. An object with multiple states is called a multi-state object. Each time you create a new state, you create a new version of the selected object to the page. Only one state is visible on the page at a time. For example, you can create a slide show for use in a PDF or SWF, where each image is stacked and aligned on top of each other as a multi-state object. When you print the document or export it as a PDF, only the active state appears. After you create a multi-state object, you can edit it in a variety of ways. You can edit an object in a state, add to or duplicate objects in a state, or delete a state and its contents. If you want to break apart a multi-state object, you can convert it to independent objects.

Create a Multi-State Object

1 Select the objects you want to convert into a multi-state object.

2 To stack the objects on top of each other, click the **Align Horizontal Centers** and **Align Vertical Centers** buttons on the Control or Align panel.

3 Select the **Object States** panel.

◆ Click the **Window** menu, point to **Interactive**, and then click **Object States**.

4 Click the **Convert Selection To Multi-State Object** button on the panel.

The objects appears as states in the panel and a dashed frame border appears around them in the document.

5 Type a name for the multi-state object.

6 Click the default state name, type name, and then press Enter (Win) or Return (Mac).

7 To select the multi-state object, click the **Multi-State** button.

◆ To select a state, click the state in the list.

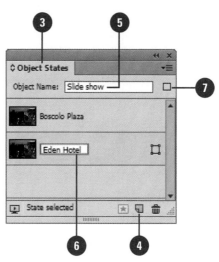

Edit a Multi-State Object

1. Select a multi-state object.

2. Select the **Object States** panel.

   ◆ Click the **Window** menu, point to **Interactive**, and then click **Object States**.

3. Perform any of the following:

   ◆ **Edit a State.** Select the state in the panel, and then edit it in the document.

   ◆ **Add an Object to an Existing State.** Select the object and multi-state object, and then click the **Add Objects To Visible State** button on the panel.

   ◆ **Paste an Object to an Existing State.** Cut or copy the object to the Clipboard, select the multi-state object, select the state in the panel, click the **Options** button, and then click **Paste Into State**.

   ◆ **Duplicate a State.** Select the state in the panel, click the **Options** button, and then click **New State**.

   ◆ **Delete a State and Remove Contents.** Select the state in the panel, click the **Options** button, and then click **Delete State**.

   ◆ **Convert a Multi-State Object to Independent Objects.** Select the state in the panel, click the **Options** button, and then click **Release State To Objects**.

   ◆ **Hide a Multi-State Object in an Export Until Triggered.** Click the **Options** button, and then click **Hidden Until Triggered**.

   ◆ **Reset All Multi-State Objects to the First State.** Click the **Options** button, and then click **Reset All Multi-State Objects To First State**.

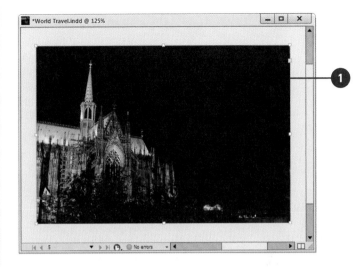

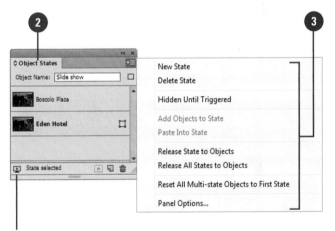

Click to preview in SWF Preview panel

Inserting HTML Content

If you're familiar with HTML code snippets, you can place them in an HTML object on a page in InDesign. You can write your own code or paste in existing code, such as the ones found on web sites like YouTube or Google Maps, or interactivity and animation created in programs like Adobe Edge Animate. InDesign renders a poster image of the code on the page in Document view. If you want to preview the HTML code, you can use the SWF Preview panel, or preview the document in an HTML browser. When you export as HTML, the code is passed through, where a web browser can interpret and display it.

Insert HTML Content

1. Select the **Selection** tool on the Tools panel.

2. Click the **Object** menu, and then click **Insert HTML**.

3. Enter the HTML code.

   ◆ The best way to enter code is to copy the source code and paste it into the dialog box.

4. Click **OK**.

   InDesign creates a text frame with the snippet content.

5. To preview the HTML code, select from the following:

   ◆ **SWF Preview panel.** Click the **Window** menu, point to **Interactive**, and then click **SWF Preview**.

   ◆ **Browser.** Select the **SWF Preview** panel, click the **Options** button, and then click **Test in Browser**.

   ◆ **Export.** Click the **File** menu, click **Export**, select **HTML** as the file type, click **Save**, specify options, and then click **OK**.

6. To edit HTML in a text frame, right-click the text frame, click **Edit HTML**, make any changes, and then click **OK**.

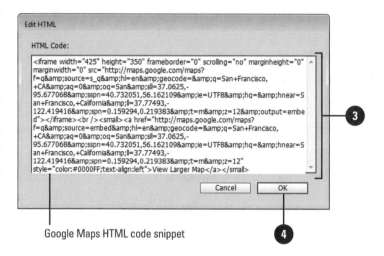

Google Maps HTML code snippet

Google Maps in InDesign

Creating QR Codes

A QR code, short for Quick Response Code, is a type of matrix barcode, which can be read by an imaging device, such as a camera, and contains information related to a specific item. A QR code consists of black modules (square dots) arranged in a square grid on a transparent background. Data is interpreted from patterns present in both horizontal and vertical components for the QR code image. Within InDesign, you can create or edit high quality QR code image (**New!**) as a vector EPS image with your specified content and color. After you create it, you can transform and scale the object, fill it with colors, and apply effects, transparency, and printing attributes, such as over printing, spot inks, and trappings, just like any other object. In addition, you can copy and paste it into Adobe Illustrator, a vector graphics program.

Create a QR Code

1. Click the **Object** menu, and then click **Generate QR Code (New!)**.

   ◆ To edit an existing QR code image, select the object, click the **Object** menu, and then click **Edit QR Code (New!)**.

2. Click the **Content** tab.

3. Click the **Type** list arrow, and then select an information type option: **Web Hyperlink**, **Plain Text**, **Text Message**, **Email**, or **Business Card**.

4. Enter the content associated with the selected type.

5. Click the **Color** tab.

6. Select the color swatch you want to apply to the QR code image.

7. Click **OK**.

   The QR code image is placed in a loaded preview cursor.

8. Click (to create 30x30 cm) or drag a rectangle frame with the loaded cursor to place the graphic in a new frame, or click in an empty frame or Alt-click a frame to place or replace it in the frame.

9. To preview information associated with a QR code image, point to the object to display a ScreenTip.

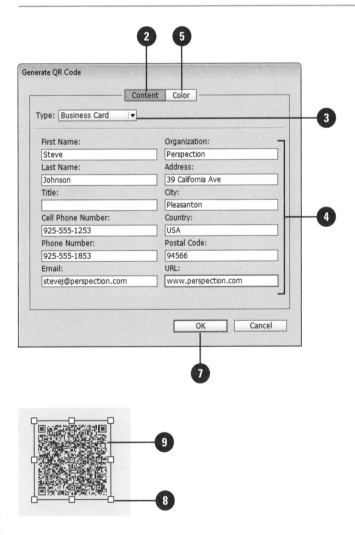

Using the SWF Preview Panel

If you're working on an interactive document, you can use the SWF Preview panel to view animation and interactivity for the current selection, current spread, or the entire document. If you want to test your interactive document in your browser, you can open it from the SWF Preview panel. If the preview display is not exactly what you want, you can set general and advanced options in the Preview Settings dialog box to change it. Some of the options include size, background, interactivity and media, page transitions, frame rate, and image handling resolution, compression and quality.

Use the SWF Preview Panel

1. Select the object or display the spread or document (interactive) you want to preview.

2. Select the **SWF Preview** panel.

   ◆ Click the **Window** menu, point to **Interactive**, and then click **SWF Preview**.

   TIMESAVER *Press Shift+Ctrl+Enter (Win) or Shift+⌘+Return (Mac) to open the SWF Preview panel.*

3. Click a preview mode button on the panel: **Set Preview Selection Mode**, **Set Preview Spread Mode**, or **Set Preview Document Mode**.

4. To play the preview, click the **Play Preview** button on the panel.

   ◆ To erase the preview, click the **Clear Preview** button on the panel.

5. To set preview settings, click the **Options** button, click **Edit Preview Settings**, select the options you want on the General and Advanced tabs, and then click **Save Settings**.

6. To test in your browser, click the **Options** button, and then click **Test in Browser**.

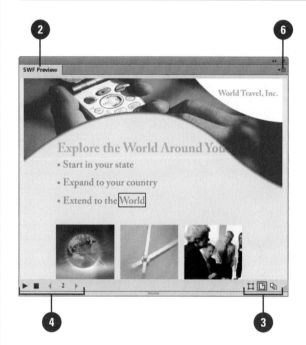

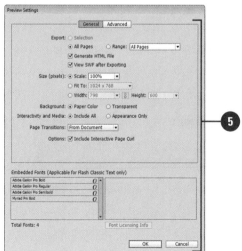

Creating a Digital Publication

Introduction

In addition to creating print and interactive documents, you can also create a digital publication for use on mobile devices, such as an iPad or iPhone, as well as your desktop.

If you create a document with a primary layout, yet need another unique layout for another orientation or different device class, such as a tablet, you can create an alternate layout to create new linked pages based on an existing layout. This allows you to leverage content on the primary layout to create an alternate one. After you create a document with a primary layout, you can apply Liquid Layout options to allow page content to adapt to different aspect ratios within a device class.

Adobe Digital Publishing Suite (DPS) is a set of tools used by publishers to create, distribute, and sell interactive publications for tablet devices. The DPS fee-based solution is available at *www.adobe.com* under Products; the Single Edition allows for publishing to iPad. DPS tools are integrated into InDesign by adding the Folio Overlays and Folio Builder panels and Preview commands on the File menu. The Folio Overlays panel allows you to create the interactive content, while the Folio Builder panel assembles (in a container) all of the necessary files into a format compatible with tablets. After you finish a folio publication, you can preview it on a device with the Adobe Content Viewer application (available free from Adobe).

What You'll Do

Create Liquid Layouts

Create Alternate Layouts

Work with Alternate Layouts

Adjust Layouts

Get Started with Digital Publishing Suite

Create a Folio Overlay

Create a Folio Publication

Import Articles into a Folio Publication

Set Folio and Article Properties

Preview a Folio Publication

Creating Liquid Layouts

Instead of creating multiple fixed positioned layouts for every possible size and orientation, Liquid Layout allows page layout content to adapt to different page dimensions within the same category of devices, known as a device class, such as smartphones, tablets, laptops, desktops, or televisions. After you create a document with a primary layout (using a specified intent—either print, web, or digital publishing—and page size), you can apply Liquid Layout options to allow page content to adapt to different aspect ratios within a device class. Liquid Layout applies Liquid Page Rules: Off, Scale, Re-center, Object-based, Guide-based and Controlled by Master. Except for the Object-based option, all rules are applied to all elements on a page. If you need a layout for a new device class or another orientation, you need to create an alternate layout to create new pages.

Create a Liquid Layout

1. Click the **Layout** menu, and then click **Liquid Layout**.

   ◆ You can also click the **Window** menu, point to **Interactive**, and then click **Liquid Layout**.

2. Display the page you want to specify liquid layout options.

3. Click the **Liquid Page Rule** list arrow, and then select from the following options:

   ◆ **Off.** Turn off adjustment.

   ◆ **Scale.** All objects work as a group and scale proportional. For different aspect ratios, a black band may appear on top and bottom or left and right.

   ◆ **Re-center.** Objects are centered no matter the width; not resized.

   ◆ **Object-based.** Object edges are defined as fixed or fluid relative to the corresponding page edge. A filled circle pins elements as fixed while an unfilled circle pins as fluid.

   ◆ **Guide-based.** Similar to the concept of 3 & 9 slice scaling. Slice guides define a straight line across the page where elements can resize. Anything a

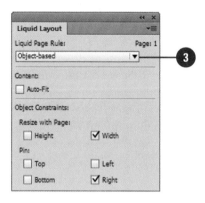

For Your Information

Using the Page Tool to Set Liquid Page Rules

In addition to the Liquid Layout panel, you can also use the Page tool on the Tools panel along with the Control panel to set Liquid Page Rules for a specific page. Select the Page tool on the Tools panel, select the page you want to resize in the layout, click the Liquid Page Rule list arrow on the Control panel, and then select a rule. You can apply a rule to any page. when you create an alternate layout, you can select the Preserve Existing option to use the options set on each page. See "Changing the Page Size," on pages 62-63 for more information on using the Page tool to set Liquid Page Rules.

guide touches will resize, while anything not touching will not. You add slide guides by dragging from the ruler (dashed lines), like ruler guides.

◆ **Controlled by Master.** Let the master determine it.

④ Select the **Auto-Fit** check box to resize an image when a graphic frame size changes. Deselect to keep the image size the same regardless of the frame change.

⑤ With the Liquid Page Rule set to Object-based, select an object (highlighted with blue edge), and then select from the following Object Constraints options:

◆ Resize with Page. **Height and Width.** Select to resize object's height or width as the page's height or width changes.

Inside the object, a spring icon appears in the middle of a dashed line with unfilled circles at each end. Deselect to lock the height or width. The circles appear filled.

TIMESAVER *You can click pins to toggle height and width between fixed and fluid.*

◆ Pin. **Top, Bottom, Left and Right.** Select to pin an object edge relative to the page edge.

Outside the object, a filled circle appears at the page edge to pin it as fixed. Deselect to unpin an object as fluid. An unfilled circle appears next to the object.

TIMESAVER *You can click pins to toggle top, bottom, left, and right between fixed and fluid.*

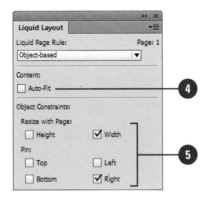

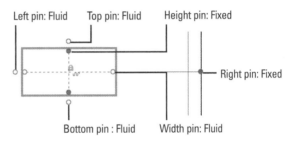

Left pin: Fluid   Top pin: Fluid   Height pin: Fixed

Right pin: Fixed

Bottom pin : Fluid   Width pin: Fluid

Object-based Liquid Page Rule

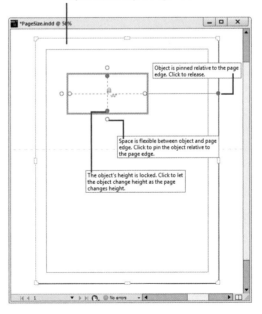

Creating Alternate Layouts

If you create a document with a primary layout (using a specified intent—either print, web, or digital publishing—and page size), yet need another unique layout for another orientation or different device class, you can create an alternate layout to create new linked pages based on an existing layout all in the same document. This allows you to leverage content on the primary layout to create an alternate one. When you update the primary layout, you can update the link for the alternate one to keep the content consistent. If you want to adapt the content in the layout for use in the same device class, you can use Liquid Layout options. As you create alternate layouts, it's important to name them by target device and orientation for easy identification later. For example, iPad-H and iPad-V. InDesign creates new masters for an alternate layout and preserves the use of a primary text frame.

Create an Alternate Layout

1. Click the **Layout** menu, and then click **Create Alternate Layout**.

2. Enter a name.

    The name ends with an H or V to indicate the orientation type of the page, either Horizontal or Vertical.

3. Click the **From Source Pages** list arrow, and then select the source page to base the alternate layout.

4. Specify the following settings:

    ◆ **W and H Values, Preset, or Custom.** Specify the **Width** and **Height** for the selected page or select a preset from the **Page Size** list; click **Custom** to create or delete a custom size.

        ◆ The available preset page sizes are based on the document intent.

    ◆ **Orientation.** Click the **Portrait** or **Landscape** button.

5. Click the **Liquid Page Rule** list arrow, and then select from the following options:

    ◆ **Off.** Turn off adjustment.

    ◆ **Scale.** All objects work as a group and scale proportional. For different aspect ratios, a black band may appear on top and bottom or left and right.

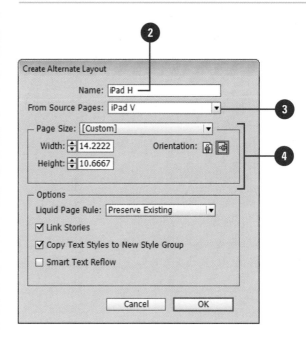

- ◆ **Re-center.** Objects are centered no matter the width; not resized.

- ◆ **Guide-based.** Similar to the concept of 3 & 9 slice scaling. Slice guides define a straight line across the page where elements can resize. You add slide guides by dragging from the ruler (dashed lines), like ruler guides.

- ◆ **Object-based.** Object edges are defined as fixed or fluid relative to the corresponding page edge. A filled circle pins elements as fixed while an unfilled circle pins as fluid.

- ◆ **Preserve Existing.** Let the liquid layout rules for the existing pages determine it.

⑥ Select from the following options:

- ◆ **Link Stories.** Select to link each story in the source layout to the copied stories in new layout.

- ◆ **Copy Text Styles to New Style Group.** Select to copy text styles in the source layout to a new style folder with custom mapping to new style group. This allows you to modify styles for the needs of the new layout.

- ◆ **Smart Text Reflow.** Select to turn on Smart Reflow in Type preferences.

⑦ Click **OK**.

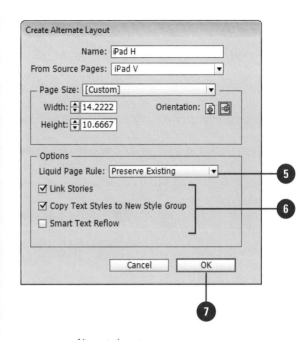

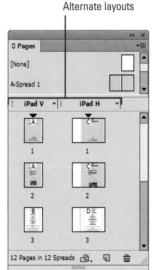

Alternate layouts

Did You Know?

You can rename alternative layouts. In the Pages panel, double-click the layout name, edit the name, and then press Enter (Win) or Return (Mac).

You can shuffle alternative layout columns. In the Pages panel, drag the layout names.

Working with Alternate Layouts

After you create an alternate layout, you can view pages using the Pages panel. On the Options menu, you can use View Pages to switch between layout views: Horizontally, Vertically, and By Alternate Layout. When you view pages By Alternate Layout, columns appear for each layout with the pages shown vertically. You can use the rename layouts and shuffle columns directly in the Pages panel. Each layout has a Layout Options menu where you can access commands, including Create Alternate Layout, Delete Alternate Layout, Delete Pages, and Split Window to Compare Layouts, which makes it easy to view and compare multiple layouts at the same time in side-by-side windows.

Work with Alternate Layouts

1. Select the **Pages** panel.

   ◆ Click the **Window** menu, and then click **Pages**.

2. Click the **Options** button, point to **View Pages**, and then click **By Alternate Layout**.

3. Click the **Layout Options** menu, and then select from the following options:

   ◆ **Create Alternate Layout.** Select to creates a new alternate layout.

   ◆ **Delete Alternate Layout.** Select to delete the selected alternate layout.

   ◆ **Delete Pages.** Select to delete the selected pages in the alternate layout.

   ◆ **Split Window to Compare Layouts** or **Unsplit Window.** Select to display alternate layouts in side-by-side windows.

      ◆ You can also click the **Split Layout View** button on the bottom right-corner of the document window to split and unsplit windows.

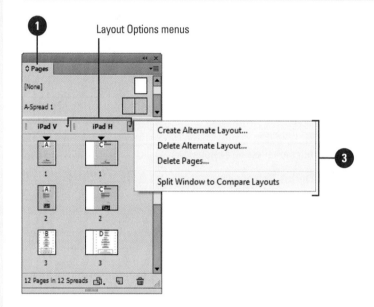

Layout Options menus

Adjusting Layouts

If you ever need to change the page size or margins after you have already added a document page or created a master page, you can enable the Layout Adjustment option to have InDesign adjust the layout and position of elements on document and master pages. The Layout Adjustment dialog box allows you to enable the option and set other related adjustment options, such as Allow Graphics and Groups to Resize and Ignore Object and Layer Locks. The Layout Adjustment options are available for backwards compatibility and not compatible with Liquid Layout options. You need to turn off Liquid Layout to use the Layout Adjustment options.

Enable Layout Adjustment and Change Options

1. Click the **Layout** menu, and then click **Liquid Layout**.

2. Click the **Options** button, and then click **Layout Adjustment**.

3. Select the **Enable Layout Adjustment** check box.

4. Select from the following options:

   ◆ **Snap Zone.** Enter a distance value for snapping an object to a margin, column guide, or page boundary.

   ◆ **Allow Graphics and Groups to Resize.** Select to allow graphics and groups to resize during the adjustment.

   ◆ **Allow Ruler Guides to Move.** Select to allow ruler guides to move during the adjustment.

   ◆ **Ignore Ruler Guide Alignments.** Select to keep objects from moving along ruler guides during the adjustment.

   ◆ **Ignore Object and Layer Locks.** Select to move locked objects and layers during the adjustment.

5. Click **OK**.

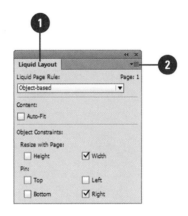

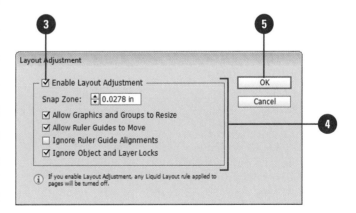

Getting Started with Digital Publishing Suite

Adobe Digital Publishing Suite (DPS) is a set of tools used by larger publishers to create, distribute, and sell interactive publications for tablet devices. The DPS fee-based solution is available at *www.adobe.com* under Products; the Single Edition allows for publishing to iPad. DPS tools are integrated into InDesign by adding the Folio Overlays and Folio Builder panels. The Folio Overlays panel allows you to create the interactive content, while the Folio Builder panel assembles (in a container) all of the necessary files into a format compatible with tablets. You can create local or online publications. For online publications, you need an Adobe ID (available free) to access Adobe DPS and the Adobe Cloud, where documents are stored and distributed to tablets. As an InDesign user, you can use DPS to create one free online publication to try it out and share it with as many people as you want. Before you can get started, you need to download Folio Producer tools (Folio Overlays panel, Digital Publishing plug-in, and Content Viewer for Desktop) and the Folio Builder panel update for InDesign CS6 or later, and install them on your computer. When you sign in to DPS with your Adobe ID on a tablet, it allows you to download and view it.

Get Started with DPS

1. Select the **Folio Builder** panel.
   - Click the **Window** menu, and then click **Folio Builder**.
2. On first use, click **Download Update**.
   - If prompted to update InDesign, click the **Help** menu, and then click **Updates**.

   Your browser opens, displaying an Adobe.com page to download the needed software.
3. Follow the on-screen instructions to download Folio Producer tools and Folio Builder panel update for InDesign CS6 or later.
4. Quit InDesign.
5. Start the Setup program for Folio Producer tools and Folio Builder panel, and then follow the on-screen instructions.
6. Start InDesign.
7. Select the **Folio Builder** and **Folio Overlays** panels to view them.

Sign In and Sign Out from DPS

1. Select the **Folio Builder** panel.

   ◆ Click the **Window** menu, and then click **Folio Builder**.

2. To sign in, click the **Sign in** link to connect to DPS (enter email address and password) or click the **Sign up** link to create an Adobe ID and DPS account.

   A bulls eye appears in a circle in the upper-right corner of the Folio Builder panel.

3. To sign out, click the **Options** button, and then click **Sign Out**.

   The bulls eye in a circle is removed in the upper-right corner of the Folio Builder panel.

4. To access DPS on the web, click the **Options** button, and then click **Folio Producer**.

   Your browser opens, displaying the Adobe Digital Publishing Suite at Acrobat.com.

   ◆ To sign in to DPS online, click the **Sign in** link, enter email address and password, and then click **Sign in**.

Did You Know?

DPS adds commands to InDesign. Two DPS related menu commands—Folio Preview and Folio Preview Settings—appear on the File menu, which display a folio preview, and two—Folio Builder and Folio Overlays—appear on the Window menu, which open folio related panels.

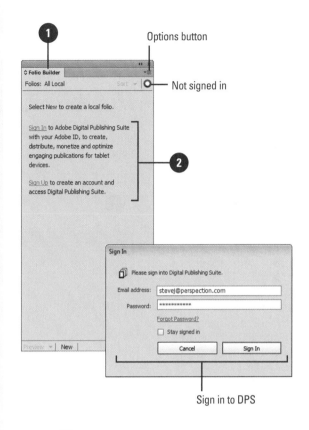

Options button

Not signed in

Sign in to DPS

Creating a Folio Overlay

The Folio Overlays panel allows you to create the interactive content with hyperlinks (links or buttons), slide shows, image sequences (rotating 360 effect with images), audio & video, panoramas (360 views), web content (access URLs or embed HTML), and pan & zoom for display on tablet devices. The interactive content is an overlay on top of all noninteractive elements, which are compressed into a single image in the background. When you create a publication for a tablet, known as a folio, you need to create horizontal and vertical layouts in separate InDesign documents. In a folio, you cannot mix and match orientations; it must be portrait, landscape, or dual (both for when a device rotates).

Use the Folio Overlays Panel

1. Select the **Folio Overlays** panel.

   ◆ Click the **Window** menu, and then click **Folio Overlays**.

2. Add interactivity to your document using the following:

   ◆ **Hyperlink.** Create a hyperlink using the Hyperlinks panel (as text) or the Buttons and Forms panel (as a button). In the Buttons and Forms panel, create a Go To URL.

   ◆ **Slideshow.** Create a multi-state object using the Object States panel.

   ◆ **Image Sequence.** Create a folder that contains the images for the sequence. Name the images using ascending numbers, such as image001.jpg, image002.jpg, and so on. Create a placeholder image frame.

   ◆ **Audio & Video.** Place an audio (mp3) or video (mp4 with h.264) file and set options in the Media panel. To display an audio controller, create a folder that contains a set of image buttons for play and pause, named audio_play.png and audio_pause.png.

   ◆ **Panorama.** Create a folder containing the six images that represent a cube (four outside images, top and bottom). Create a placeholder image frame.

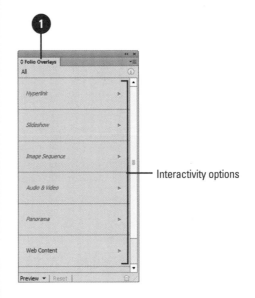

Interactivity options

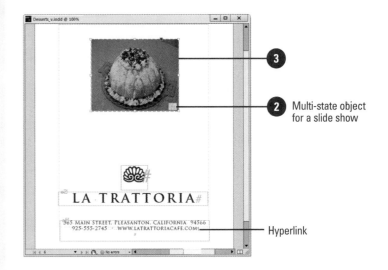

Multi-state object for a slide show

Hyperlink

- ◆ **Web Content.** Go to a URL (need Internet access) or embed HTML content (don't need Internet access); use the home page, such as *index.html*.

  See *"Inserting HTML Content,"* on page 378 for details.

- ◆ **Pan & Zoom.** Place an image and resize the frame to crop the image to the view area in which the content scrolls.

  To create a scrolling text frame, create a text frame and a container frame. Cut the text frame and use the Paste Into command on the Edit menu to paste it into the container frame.

③ Select a media object frame in your document.

④ If necessary, click the interactivity overlay you want to create for the media object.

⑤ Specify the options in the Folio Overlays panel for the selected media object.

Options vary depending on the media object type selected.

⑥ To display all the overlays, click the **Back** arrow.

⑦ To display your interactive document on a tablet, select the Folio Builder panel, create a folio publication, and then add articles to it for use with DPS.

- ◆ See *"Creating a Folio Publication,"* on pages 392-393 for details.

⑧ To preview the publication on your desktop with Adobe Content Viewer, click the **Preview** button on the Folio Builder panel.

- ◆ You can also click the **File** menu, and then click **Folio Preview**.

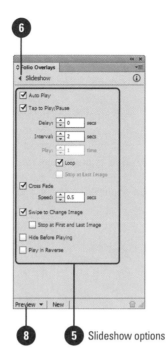

Slideshow options

Pan & Zoom options

Creating a Folio Publication

After you add interactivity to an InDesign document using the Folio Overlays panel and InDesign media tools, you can use the Folio Builder panel to assemble all of the individual InDesign files, called articles, into a format for tablet devices. The Folio Builder panel works in conjunction with Adobe Digital Publishing Suite (DPS) at *acrobat.com* to create, distribute, and sell interactive publications for tablet devices. You can create local or online publications. For online publications, you need an Adobe ID (available free) to access Adobe DPS and the Adobe Cloud, where documents are stored and distributed to tablets. You can use DPS to create one free online publication to try it out and share it with others. The process is easy: (1) create a new folio publication, (2) add and order articles, and (3) change folio and article properties.

Create a Folio Publication

1. Select the **Folio Builder** panel, and then sign in to use online DPS.
   - ◆ Click the **Window** menu, and then click **Folio Builder**.

2. Click **New** on the Folio Builder panel.

3. Enter a name for the folio.

4. Click the **Size** list arrow, and then select a size, or enter a custom Width and Height.

5. Click an orientation option: **Portrait Only Folio**, **Landscape Only Folio**, or **Portrait and Landscape Folio**.

6. Click the **Default Format** list arrow, and then select a format for any default article, either Liquid or Static. Liquid creates HTML code that reflows in multiple platforms, while Static creates raster (bitmap) images that scale.

7. Click the **Default JPEG Quality** list arrow, and then select a quality. Higher the quality, bigger the file.

8. If you select Liquid, specify a default raster (bitmap) format, default resolution (ppi), and whether to ignore Object Export Settings.

9. Click **OK**.

   This creates a .folio file with DPS.

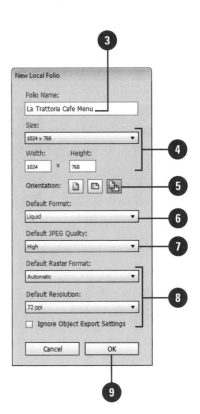

Add Articles to a Folio Publication

1. Select the **Folio Builder** panel.
   - Click the **Window** menu, and then click **Folio Builder**.
2. Select the folio publication you want to use, and then click an **Expand** arrow to open a view.
3. Open the InDesign file with the article or layout you want to add.
4. Click **Add** on the Folio Builder panel to add article or layout.
5. Enter an article name.
6. Click the **Format** list arrow, and then select a format for any default article, either Liquid or Static. Liquid creates HTML code that reflows in multiple platforms, while Static creates raster (bitmap) images that scale.
7. Click the **JPEG Quality** list arrow, and then select a quality. Higher the quality, bigger the file.
8. Specify options:
   - **Liquid.** Specify a default raster (bitmap) format, default resolution (ppi), and whether to ignore Object Export Settings.
   - **Static.** Use for a long, single-page document (width matches device width) to scroll vertically.
9. Click **OK**, and then click **Continue** (don't save document) or **Save**.

   This updates/uploads the article to the folio.
10. To reorder articles, drag an article to another position; the panel list order determines the folio order.
11. To display all folio publications, click the **Back** arrow.

Delete folio

Articles view

Delete article

Layout view

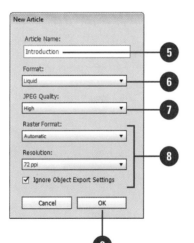

Importing Articles into a Folio Publication

Instead of adding one article at a time in the Folio Builder panel, you can import multiple articles all at one time. Before you can import articles, you need to set up the InDesign files (articles) according to a set of folder structure and file naming conventions. In Windows Explorer (Win) or Finder (Mac), create a folder for the folio that consists of individual article folders. Each article folder contains one (single orientation) or two (dual orientation) article documents named with a suffix of "_v" (vertical layout) or "_h" (horizontal layout), such as article_v.indd. You cannot mix and match orientations; it can only be one orientation. Each article folder can also contain a PNG file for table-of-contents thumbnails. If this file is missing, the TOC image is generated automatically. Any files you link to in InDesign do not have to be in the article folder; the links simply need to corrected linked.

Import Articles into a Folio Publication

1. Create a folio folder that consists of multiple article folders. Name article documents with a "_v" or "_h" suffix, where v is vertical layout and h is horizontal layout, such as article_v.indd.

2. In InDesign, select the **Folio Builder** panel.

   ◆ Click the **Window** menu, and then click **Folio Builder**.

3. Click the **Expand** arrow for the folio to open Articles view.

4. Click the **Options** button, and then click **Import**.

5. Click the **Import a Single Article** or **Import Multiple Articles** option.

6. For a single article, enter a name, and then select a Format, JPEG Quality, Raster Format, Resolution, and whether to ignore Object Export Settings.

7. Click the **Folder** icon, select the root folder for the folio, and then click **OK**.

8. Click **OK**.

9. To reorder articles, drag an article to another position; the panel list order determines the folio order.

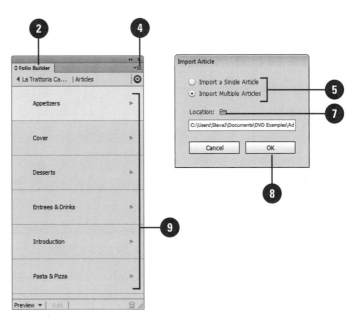

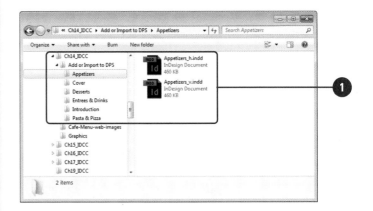

Setting Folio and Article Properties

After you create a folio publication and add/order articles, you can change folio and article properties. You can set properties in the Folio Builder panel. Properties you can set for a folio include the publication name that appears on the tablet device and a cover image. For an article, you can set properties for the table of contents (TOC).

Set Folio and Article Properties

1. Select the **Folio Builder** panel.
   - ◆ Click the **Window** menu, and then click **Folio Builder**.
2. Select the folio publication.
3. Click the **Options** button, and then click **Properties**.
4. Specify options:
   - ◆ **Name.** Enter a publication name (appears on the tablet device).
   - ◆ **Size.** Specify a publication size.
   - ◆ **Cover.** Click the **Browse** button to select a Vertical and/or Horizontal image cover file.
5. Click **OK**.
6. Click the folio **Expand** arrow.
7. Select a folio article.
8. Click the **Options** button, and then click **Properties**.
9. Specify options:
   - ◆ **Title and Description.** Enter or edit an article name for the TOC, and a brief description.
   - ◆ **Table of Contents Preview.** Select a preview image.
   - ◆ **Smooth Scrolling.** Use for a long, single-page document (width matches device width) to scroll vertically.
   - ◆ **Horizontal Swipe.** Select to enable horizontal swipe.
   - ◆ **Byline and Kicker.** Enter an author name and description.
   - ◆ **Advertisement.** Select to not have the article in the TOC.
10. Click **OK**.

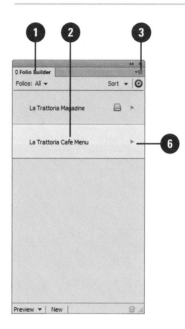

Go back to folios

Previewing a Folio Publication

Before you publish a folio publication, it's important to preview it to make sure your content looks the way you want. To view a folio publication on a desktop, tablet, or other device, you need to have the Adobe Content Viewer application installed (available free from Adobe). When you install Folio Producer tools for InDesign, the Adobe Content Viewer is automatically installed. Two menu commands are also installed for InDesign: Folio Preview and Folio Preview Settings, which you can use to set preview options.

Preview a Folio Publication

1. Select the **Folio Builder** panel.
   - Click the **Window** menu, and then click **Folio Builder**.

2. Click **Preview** on the Folio Builder panel, and then click **Preview on Desktop**, if necessary.

   TIMESAVER *Click the File menu, and then click Folio Preview.*

   Adobe Content Viewer opens, displaying the current folio publication.

   To set folio preview settings, continue.

3. Click the **File** menu, and then click **Folio Preview Settings**.

4. Specify options:
   - **Format.** Select Auto to use document setting, Liquid, or Static.
   - **Raster Format.** Select Auto to use document setting, or a graphic format.
   - **JPEG Quality.** Select a quality; higher the quality, better the display, bigger the file size.
   - **Ignore Object Export Options.** Select to ignore option.
   - **Resolution.** Select a resolution best for the device: OS & web is 72 or 96, tablets are 150, and iPhone is 300.
   - **Preview Current Layout.** Select to preview the current layout.

5. Click **OK**.

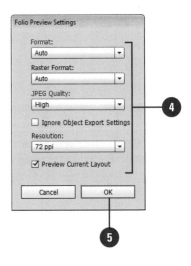

For Your Information

Sharing a Folio Publication

Instead of publishing a folio publication to a wide audience, you can share it with individuals. This is a great way to have co-workers and friends review your publication. In the Folio Builder panel, select the folio, click the Options button, click Share, enter email addresses, a subject, and a personal message, and then click Share. The email provides a connection link to the DPS folio publication. To view the publication on a tablet, the user needs to have Adobe Content Viewer installed on the device (available for free from Adobe).

Automating the Way You Work

Introduction

A library stores InDesign items, such as text frames, graphics frames, shapes, buttons, sounds, and movies so you can use them in other documents. A library is not an InDesign document; it's a separate file (INDL). After you add items to a library, you can use them in any InDesign document. A snippet is an item from an InDesign document that you can save as an external InDesign Snippet file (IDMS) for use later. Snippets and libraries are similar. However, there are a few differences. Libraries are composed of a group of items, while snippets as individual items. You can store hundreds of items in a library. You may not want to do that, but you can if you want. When a library contains a lot of items, it can be hard to find the one you want. You can use the Show Subset dialog box to search for any item in a library. The powerful search features allow you to specify one or more levels of search criteria to find exactly what you want.

Conditional text allows you to create different versions of the same document. If you want to create two versions of the same document without having to create two separate files, you can create conditions for different text, and then show and hide conditions to create multiple versions. You can also merge data between documents. With the Data Merge panel, you can create a form letter, envelopes, or mailing labels by merging data from a source file with an InDesign target document.

A script is external code that allows you to extend the functionality of InDesign. InDesign comes with a set of sample scripts that you can run at any time. If you know how to write code for a script, you can create your own. XML (Extensible Markup Language) provides a way to reuse data from one file in another file. If you have some experience with XML, it's a good way to reuse information and automate the way you work with content.

What You'll Do

Create a Library

Use and Update a Library

Change Library Item Information

Search and Sort Libraries

Create and Use Snippets

Create Conditional Text

Collect and Place Content

Create Linked Content

Link Content Across Documents

Manage Linked Content

Use and Run Scripts

Use Data Merge

Work with XML

Export XML or IDML

Creating a Library

A library stores InDesign items, such as text frames, graphics frames, shapes, buttons, sounds, and movies so you can use them in other documents. A library is not an InDesign document; it's a separate file (INDL). When you create a new library or open an existing library, the Library panel appears, displaying the library name in the title tab. In the Library panel, you can add, remove, or update items. You can add items to the library one at a time, all items from a page, or as a whole page.

Create a New Library

1. Click the **File** menu, point to **New**, and then click **Library**.

2. Enter a name for the library file.

3. Navigate to the location where you want to save the library.

4. Click **Save**.

   The tab for the Library panel displays the name of the library.

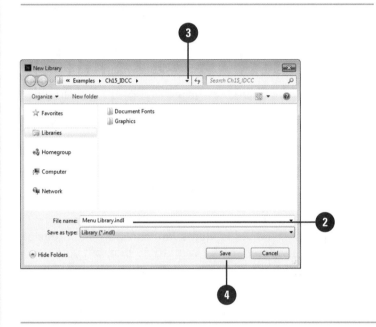

Open an Existing Library

1. Click the **File** menu, and then click **Open**.

2. Navigate to the location where the library you want to open is stored.

3. Select the library file you want to open.

4. Click **Open**.

   The Library panel opens.

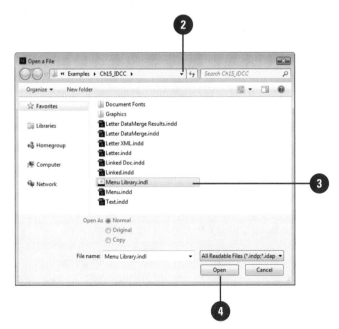

Add or Delete Items in a Library

1. Open the library you want to edit.

2. Do any of the following:

   ◆ **Add an Item.** Select the item in layout view, and then click the **New Library Item** button on the panel.

   ◆ **Add a Page.** Display the page in layout view, click the **Options** button, and then click **Add Items on "Page."**

   ◆ **Add All Items on a Page as Separate Objects.** Display the page in layout view, click the **Options** button, and then click **Add Items on "Page" as Separate Objects**.

   ◆ **Delete Items.** Select the items in the Library panel, click the **Delete Library Item** button on the panel, and then click **Yes**.

      ◆ Press Ctrl (Win) or ⌘ (Mac) to select multiple non-contiguous items or press Shift to select multiple contiguous items.

      ◆ Press Alt (Win) or Option (Mac) to bypass the confirmation dialog box.

3. Click the **Close** button to exit the library.

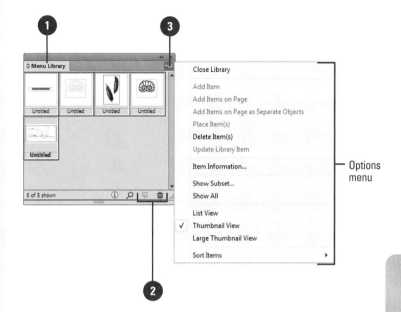

Options menu

Did You Know?

You can use libraries from Adobe Bridge. A library file (INDL) appears in Adobe Bridge like any other file. However, the files appears as icons, not as preview documents. You can open a library from Bridge as you would any InDesign file.

Using and Updating a Library

After you add items to a library, you can use them in any InDesign document. You can add library items to a page by dragging them individually, dragging a selection, or by using the Place Item(s) command on the Options menu. If you change a library item in your document, you can use the Update Library Item on the Options menu to replace the existing item in the library with the updated one.

Place Library Items on a Page

1. Open the library you want to use.

2. Select the items that you want to place on a page.

   ◆ Press Ctrl (Win) or ⌘ (Mac) to select multiple non-contiguous items or press Shift to select multiple contiguous items.

3. Drag the selection from the Library panel onto the page.

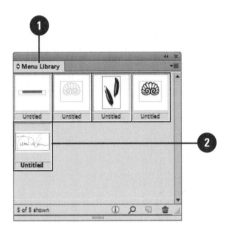

Update a Library Item in the Library

1. Select and modify the library item that you want to update in the Library panel.

2. Open the library you want to use.

3. Click the **Options** button, and then click **Update Library Item**.

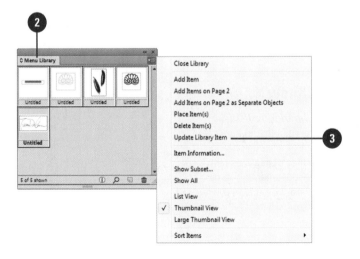

Changing Library Item Information

When you add items to a library, the item appears as an untitled element. You'll want to name the items for searching and sorting purposes. InDesign tries to assign an object type to the item, but it may not always be what you want. If an item contains multiple objects, such as a shape with text or a button with text, you may want to change the object type. You can change the item name and object type, as well as add a short description in the Item Information dialog box.

Change Library Item Information

1. Open the library you want to use.

2. Select the item that you want to change.

3. Click the **Library Item Information** button on the panel.

   ◆ You can also double-click a library item.

4. Enter a name for the item.

5. Click the **Object Type** list arrow, and then select an object type:

   ◆ **Image.** Specifies a raster graphic.

   ◆ **EPS.** Specifies an EPS file.

   ◆ **PDF.** Specifies a PDF file.

   ◆ **Geometry.** Specifies frames and rules that don't contain graphics or text.

   ◆ **Page.** Specifies an entire page.

   ◆ **Text.** Specifies a text frame.

   ◆ **Structure.** Specifies an XML element.

   ◆ **InDesign File.** Specifies an InDesign file.

6. Enter a short description for the item.

7. Click **OK**.

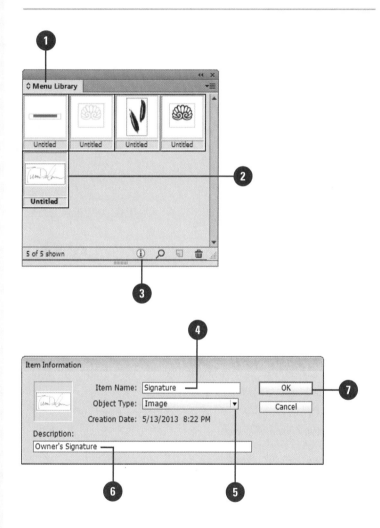

Searching and Sorting Libraries

You can store hundreds of items in a library. You may not want to do that, but you can if you want. When a library contains a lot of items, it can be hard to find the one you want. You can use the Show Subset dialog box to search for any item in a library. The powerful search features allow you to specify one or more levels of search criteria to find what you want. In addition to searching for items, you can also sort items in a library by name, newest, oldest, and type. A library panel displays items as thumbnails by default. If your prefer using a list to help you find what you want, you can change the library display.

Search in a Library

1. Open the library you want to use.

2. Click the **Show Library Subset** button on the panel.

3. Click the **Search Entire Library** option to search all items in the library or click the **Search Currently Shown Items** option to search only those items currently displayed in the library.

4. Use the list arrows under Parameters to specify the search criteria you want.

5. If you want to add multiple levels of search criteria, click **More Choices**.

6. With More Choices, use the list arrows to specify the next level of search criteria you want, and then click the **Match All** or **Match Any One** option.

7. To remove a level of search criteria, click **Fewer Choices**. To add more levels of criteria, click More Choices again.

8. Click **OK**.

   All the items that match the search criteria appear in the library.

9. To show all library items, click the **Options** button, and then click **Show All**.

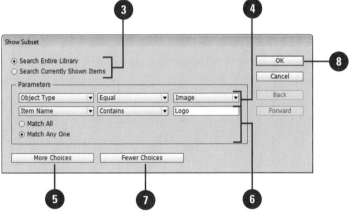

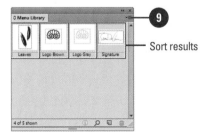

Sort results

Sort Library Items

1. Open the library you want to use.

2. Click the **Options** button, point to **Sort Items**, and then select a sort command:

   ◆ **by Name.** Sorts library items by name.

   ◆ **by Newest.** Sorts library items from newest to oldest.

   ◆ **by Oldest.** Sorts library items from oldest to newest.

   ◆ **by Type.** Sorts library items into groups by object type.

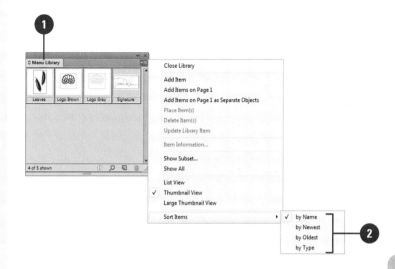

Change the Library Display

1. Open the library you want to use.

2. Click the **Options** button, and then select a display command:

   ◆ **List View.** Displays library items with a name and an icon that indicates the item type.

   ◆ **Thumbnail View.** Displays library items with a name and image preview.

   ◆ **Large Thumbnail View.** Displays library items with a name and large image preview.

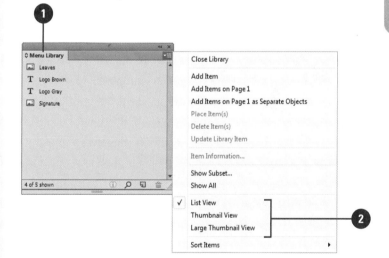

Creating and Using Snippets

A snippet is an item from an InDesign document, such as a text frame, graphics frame, shape, button, sound, or movie, that you can save as an external InDesign Snippet file (IDMS) for use later. You can't use a text selection as a snippet, but you can use a text frame. Snippets and libraries are similar. However, there are a few differences. Libraries are composed of a group of items, while snippets individual items. You can drag individual snippets from a folder, desktop, or the Adobe Bridge into an InDesign document, which you can't do with library items. Since snippets are individual items, you can preview them (unlike library items). Snippets also typically have a smaller file size than a library file.

Create a Snippet

1. Select the items on the page that you want to use to create a snippet.

2. Click the **File** menu, and then click **Export**.

3. Enter a name for the file.

4. Click the **Save as Type** list arrow (Win) or **Format** popup (Mac), and then click **InDesign Snippet**.

5. Navigate to the location where you want to save the snippet.

6. Click **Save**.

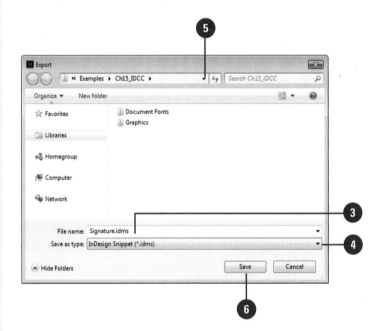

Create a Snippet by Dragging

1 Select the items on the page that you want to use to create a snippet.

2 Drag the items into a folder or onto the desktop.

The snippet appears with a file name assigned by InDesign, and a file extension of .idms.

3 Click the icon name, type a new name, and then press Enter (Win) or Return (Mac).

Use a Snippet

1 Select the snippet in a folder, on the desktop, or from Adobe Bridge.

2 Drag the snippet icon onto the InDesign document page.

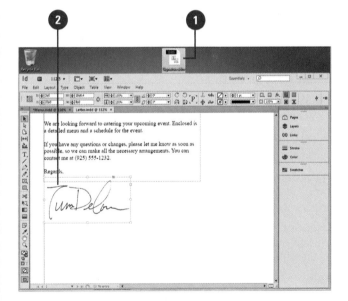

Creating Conditional Text

Conditional text allows you to create different versions of the same document. If you want to create two versions of the same document without having to create two separate files, you can create conditions for different text, and then show and hide different conditions to create multiple versions. For example, if you're creating a computer book for the Macintosh and Windows operating systems, like the one you're reading, you can create text conditions for each Macintosh and Windows step instead of creating two separate files. You can apply conditions to text in a frame or table. A condition includes formatting indicators to make each condition easy to see in a document. To display different versions quickly, you can create condition sets. A condition set saves the visibility settings (the Eye icon) for all conditions.

Create and Apply a Condition

1. To create a condition for all new documents, close all documents. Otherwise any new conditions are saved only with the current document.

2. Select the **Conditional Text** panel.

   ◆ Click the **Window** menu, point to **Type & Tables**, and then click **Conditional Text**.

3. Click the **New Condition** button on the panel.

4. Enter a name for the condition.

5. Specify the following condition indicator options:

   ◆ **Method.** Highlights or underlines the conditional text.

   ◆ **Appearance.** Displays an underline style for the conditional text.

   ◆ **Color.** Displays a color for highlighted conditional text or for the underline indicator.

6. Click **OK**.

7. To apply a condition, select the text you want, and then click the condition name on the panel.

   ◆ To remove a condition, deselect the check box next to the condition name on the panel.

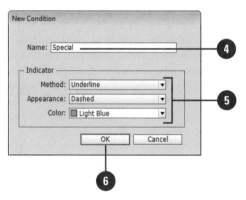

Specials — Selected text

Specials — Applied XML tag

Use the Conditional Text Panel

1 Select the **Conditional Text** panel.

- Click the **Window** menu, point to **Type & Tables**, and then click **Conditional Text**.

2 Use any of the following buttons or commands:

- **Apply a Condition.** Select text, and then click a condition.

- **Show or Hide Conditions.** Click the **Eye** icon to toggle on/off.

- **Delete a Condition.** Select a condition, and then click the **Delete Condition** button.

- **Edit a Condition.** Double-click a condition and make changes.

- **Condition Indicators.** Specify an option: **Show**, **Show and Print**, or **Hide**.

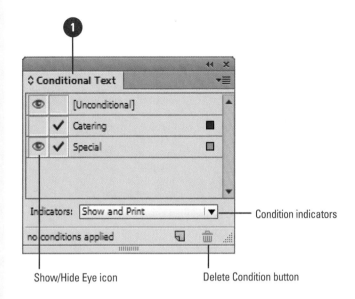

Condition indicators

Show/Hide Eye icon   Delete Condition button

Create a Condition Set

1 Apply conditions to text.

2 Select the **Conditional Text** panel.

3 Click the **Set** list arrow, and then click **Create New Set**.

- If the Set menu doesn't appear, click the **Options** button, and then click **Show Options**.

4 Enter a name for the condition set.

5 Click **OK**.

6 To use a condition set, click the **Set** list arrow, and then select a sort command:

- **Set Name.** Applies the condition set to the document.

- **Delete Set.** Deletes the condition set.

- **Rename/Redefine.** Renames or redefines the condition set.

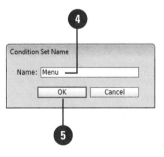

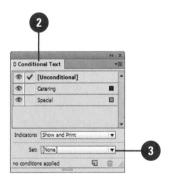

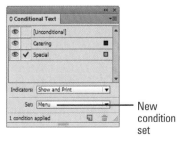

New condition set

Collecting and Placing Content

With the Content Collector and Content Placer tools on the Tools panel, you can quickly collect page elements in the Conveyor and then place them in other parts of your document or in different documents. When you collect an element, the Conveyor appears at the bottom of the screen, where you can view the collected elements, switch between the Content Collector and Content Placer tools, select placement options and specify whether to create a link or map text styles. You can load as many elements as you want. The Content Collector loads elements into the Conveyor, and the Content Placer puts the elements in a loaded cursor where you can place them one at a time.

Collect Content to the Conveyor

1. Select the **Content Collector** tool on the Tools panel.

   By default, the Conveyor appears at the bottom of the screen.

   ◆ To show or hide the Conveyor when you select the Content Collector or Content Placer tool, click the **View** menu, point to **Extras**, and then click **Show** or **Hide Conveyor**.

2. Point to an element on the page you want to add to the Conveyor.

   The element is highlighted with a light blue selection.

3. Click the element to add it to the Conveyor, and then continue to add the elements you want.

   The cursor indicates the number of items collected.

4. Select the **Collect All Threaded Frames** check box to include all threads in a text frame.

5. To change the way the Content Collector loads elements, click the **Load Conveyor** button, select the options you want, and then click **OK**.

6. To close the Conveyor, click the **Close** button or another button on the Tools panel.

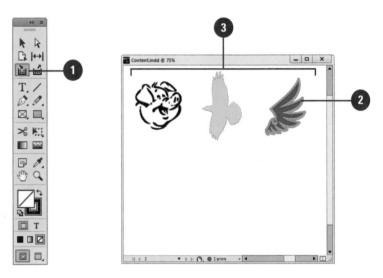

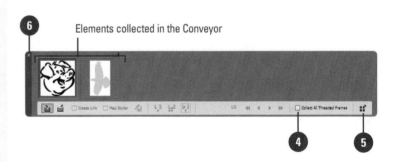

Elements collected in the Conveyor

Load Conveyor options

Place Content from Conveyor

1. Select the **Content Placer** tool on the Tools panel.

   By default, the Conveyor appears at the bottom of the screen.

   ◆ To show or hide the Conveyor when you select the Content Collector or Content Placer tool, click the **View** menu, point to **Extras**, and then click **Show** or **Hide Conveyor**.

2. Select a placement button.

   ◆ **Place (item), remove from Conveyor and load next (one).**

   ◆ **Place (item) multiple (times) and keep in Conveyor.**

   ◆ **Place (item), keep in Conveyor and load next (one).**

3. To switch element positions in the Conveyor, click the **Next Cluster**, **Next**, **Previous**, or **Previous Cluster** buttons.

4. Select linking options as desired.

   ◆ **Create Link.** Select to create a link with the selected item in the Conveyor.

   ◆ **Map Styles.** Select to use text style mapping.

   ◆ **Edit Custom Style Mapping.** Click to specify custom text style mapping.

5. Click the loaded cursor to place an element one at a time on a page based on the placement option.

   The cursor indicates the number of items to place.

   ◆ You can press Esc to delete the current element in the loaded cursor.

6. To close the Conveyor, click the **Close** button or another button on the Tools panel.

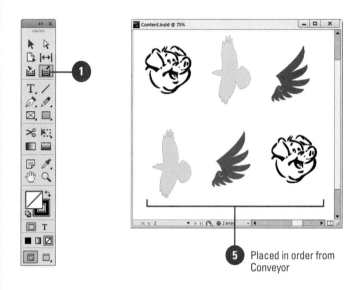

5 Placed in order from Conveyor

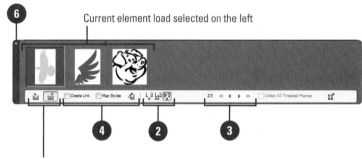

Current element load selected on the left

Content Collector and Content Placer tools

Creating Linked Content

With the Place and Link command, you can reuse content—including text, shapes, graphics, groups and interactivity elements (such as a button)—in the same InDesign document or in other documents. By creating a link (to a parent), you create an identical object (child) in a layout, which you can update as desired as content changes. This is useful when you want to create stationery and want to use boilerplate text and logo on different size letterhead or envelopes or when you want to create an InDesign document as a centralized repository to storage and manage reusable content. When content is placed, one or more links appear in the Links panel, where you can update all or individual linked content. InDesign views content and frames as unique elements to differentiate between the content and container. Any unique changes to child content are overwritten by parent content, except for specified style mapping exceptions and local edits.

Reuse Linked Text

① Select the **Selection** tool on the Tools panel.

② Click to place the insertion point in the text frame (parent story) you want to reuse as linked text.

③ Click the **Edit** menu, and then click **Place and Link**.

◆ If the Conveyor opens, click the **Close** button on the Conveyor.

④ Click or drag a text frame or click an existing empty text frame with the loaded text cursor to place the text where you want it (child story).

⑤ To show or hide the linked Badge icon, click the **View** menu, point to **Extras**, and then click **Show** or **Hide Linked Badge**.

⑥ Select the **Type** tool on the Tools panel, and then make changes to the parent story content or format.

⑦ Click the **Window** menu, and then click **Links** to open the Links panel.

⑧ Select the child linked text item in the Links panel to display link info.

⑨ To update child linked stories, double-click the Badge icon next to the text item.

Adobe Flash Professional On Demand

Copyright © by Perspection, Inc. ——————— ②
All rights reserved. No part of this book shall be reproduced, stored in a retrieval system, or transmitted by any means, electronic, mechanical, photocopying, recording, or otherwise, without written permission from the publisher. No patent liability is assumed with respect to the use of the information contained herein. Although every precaution has been taken in the preparation of this book, the publisher and author assume no responsibility for errors or omissions. Nor is any liability assumed for damages resulting from the use of the information contained herein.

Status icon indicates a linked (child) story

Adobe Flash Professional On Demand

Copyright © by Perspection, Inc.
All rights reserved. No part of this book shall be reproduced, stored in a retrieval system, or transmitted by any means, electronic, mechanical, photocopying, recording, or otherwise, without written permission from the publisher. No patent liability is assumed with respect to the use of the information contained herein. Although every precaution has been taken in the preparation of this book, the publisher and author assume no responsibility for errors or omissions. Nor is any liability assumed for damages resulting from the use of the information contained herein.

④

⑦ ⑧ ⑨

Links
Name
▶ que_b_cmyk.tif (2)
  <Adobe®... Dem...>   1
  <que_b_cmyk.tif>   1

▶ 1 Selected

Go to Link, Update Link, and Edit Original buttons

Reuse Linked Objects

1. Select the **Selection** tool on the Tools panel.

2. Select the object frame—shape, graphic, text, group, or interactivity element (such as a button)—you want to reuse.

3. Click the **Edit** menu, and then click **Place and Link**.

   ◆ If the Conveyor opens, click the **Close** button on the Conveyor.

4. Click or drag a frame with the loaded cursor to place the content where you want it (child).

   A link appears for the frame and another one appears for the object itself. Related items are grouped together. You can click the **Expand/Collapse** arrow to view or hide its contents.

5. To show or hide the linked Badge icon, click the **View** menu, point to **Extras**, and then click **Show** or **Hide Linked Badge**.

6. Make changes to the parent frame or object content.

7. Click the **Window** menu, and then click **Links** to open the Links panel.

8. Select the child linked item in the Links panel to display link info.

9. To update child linked items, double-click the Badge icon.

See Also

See "Collecting and Placing Content," on page 408 for more information on using the Conveyor.

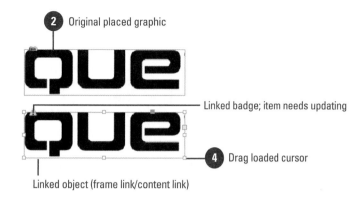

2 Original placed graphic

Linked badge; item needs updating

4 Drag loaded cursor

Linked object (frame link/content link)

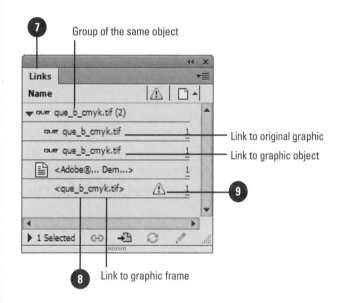

7 Group of the same object

Link to original graphic

Link to graphic object

9

8 Link to graphic frame

Linking Content Across Documents

With the Place and Link command, you can reuse content in the same document, however, you can also reuse content in another InDesign document. This allows you to use an InDesign document as a centralized repository to storage and manage reusable content. When the linked content is placed in another document, one or more links appear in the destination's Links panel, where you can update all or individual linked content. InDesign views content and frames as unique elements to differentiate between the content and container. Any unique changes to child content are overwritten by parent content, except for specified style mapping exceptions and local edits.

Link Content Across Documents

1. Select the **Selection** tool on the Tools panel.

2. Select the object frame or place the insertion point in a text frame you want to reuse.

3. Click the **Edit** menu, and then click **Place and Link**.

    ◆ If the Conveyor opens, click the **Close** button on the Conveyor.

4. Switch to another document for the destination content.

5. Click or drag a frame with the loaded cursor to place the content where you want it (child).

6. To show or hide the linked Badge icon, click the **View** menu, point to **Extras**, and then click **Show** or **Hide Linked Badge**.

7. Make changes to the parent frame or object content.

8. Click the **Window** menu, and then click **Links** to open the Links panel.

9. Select the child linked object in the Links panel to display link info.

10. To update linked child items, double-click the Badge icon.

11. To view the source object, select the child linked object, click the **Options** button, and then click **Go To Source**.

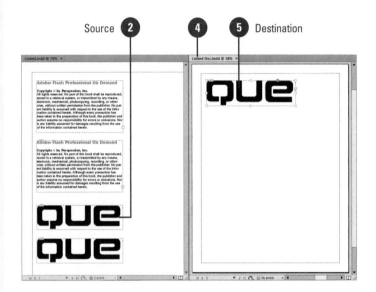

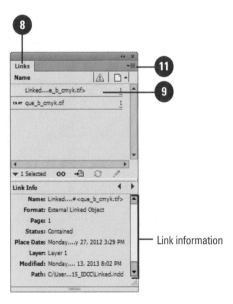

Link information

Managing Linked Content

When you link content in the same document or in a different document, the child element is set by default to update to exactly the same as the parent. However, there are situations where you want the child to be a little different than the parent. For example, between the print and digital version of the same document publication, you want the headline and body text to be larger in the digital version than the print version. With the Link Options dialog box, you can set options to preserve local edits while updating object links and specify style mapping exceptions. In addition, there are options to update links when saving a document or display a warning if an update will overwrite local edits.

Manage Linked Content

1. Select the **Selection** tool on the Tools panel.

2. Select the child linked object you want to manage and set linked options.

3. Click the **Options** button, and then click **Link Options**.

4. Specify the following options:

   ◆ **Update Link When Saving Document.** Select to update links when you save a document.

   ◆ **Warn if Update Edits Will Overwrite Local Edits.** Select to display a warning dialog box if an update tries to overwrite local edits.

5. Select the check boxes with the items you want to preserve local edits while updating object links.

6. Specify the following options for text links:

   ◆ **Remove Forced Line Breaks from Story.** Select to delete forced line breaks.

   ◆ **Define Custom Style Mapping.** Click **Settings** to set or create style mappings for the text or page between parent and child.

7. Click **OK**.

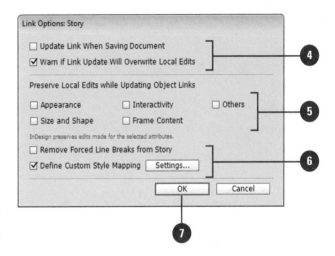

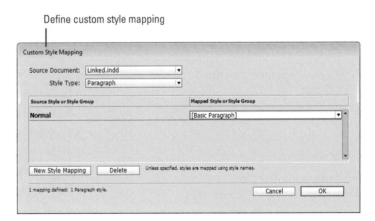

Define custom style mapping

Using and Running Scripts

A script is external code that allows you to extend the functionality of InDesign. InDesign comes with a set of sample scripts that you can run at any time. If you know how to write code for a script, you can create your own. InDesign works with AppleScripts on the Macintosh and Visual Basic scripts in Windows. If you want to use the same scripts on both platforms, you can use JavaScript. The Scripts panel displays all the available scripts in InDesign. The sample scripts are located in the Samples folder within the InDesign application folder. You can double-click a script in the Scripts panel to run it, or you can run scripts using Quick Apply on the Control panel. You can also attach text to an object on a page using the Script Label panel. The text you attach can be any text, which you can search for or manipulate using a script.

Run a Script

1. If a specific script requires it, select an object or text.

2. Select the **Scripts** panel.

   ◆ Click the **Window** menu, point to **Utilities**, and then click **Scripts**.

   TIMESAVER *Press Alt+Ctrl+ F11 (Win) or Option +⌃⌘+F11 (Mac) to open the Scripts panel.*

3. Click the triangle to expand folders in the Scripts panel to locate a script.

4. Double-click the script name.

   ◆ You can also click the **Options** button, and then click **Run Script**.

   The script runs.

See Also

See "Defining Shortcut Keys" on page 503 for more information on assigning keyboard shortcuts to scripts.

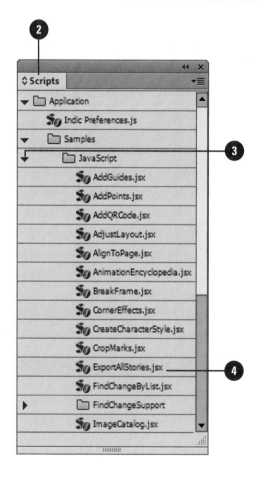

Use the Scripts Panel

① To display your own scripts in the Scripts panel, put the script file in the Scripts Panel folder.

- ◆ **Scripts Panel Folder Location.** Select the **Scripts** panel, click the **Options** button, and then click **Select in Explorer** (Win) or **Select in Finder** (Mac).

② Select the **Scripts** panel.

- ◆ Click the **Window** menu, point to **Utilities**, and then click **Scripts**.

③ Click the triangle to expand folders in the Scripts panel to locate a script.

④ Select a script.

⑤ Click the **Options** button, and then select any of the following commands:

- ◆ **Run Script.** Runs the selected script file.

- ◆ **Edit Script.** Opens the selected script file in a code editor.

- ◆ **Reveal in Explorer (Win)** or **Finder (Mac).** Displays the script file in Windows Explorer or Macintosh Finder.

- ◆ **Delete Script File.** Deletes the selected script file.

- ◆ **Enable Redraw.** Enables or disables script redraw.

- ◆ **Display Unsupported Files.** Displays all available script files in the Scripts Panel folder.

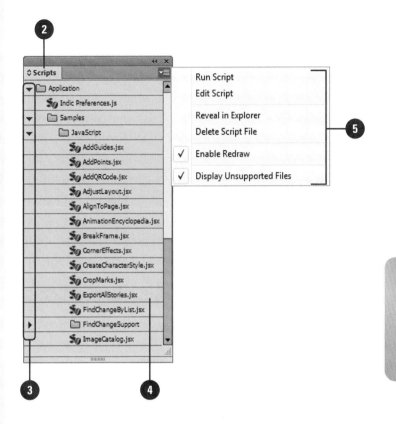

For Your Information

Creating a Script Label

Select an object, select the Script Label panel (click the Window menu, point to Utilities, and then click Script Label), type the label text, and then click in a blank area to deselect.

You can use a script statement to select the text in the script label:

```
app.selection[ 0] .label = "Label_Text";
```

Using Data Merge

With the Data Merge panel, you can create a form letter, envelopes, or mailing labels by merging data from a source file with an InDesign target document. The source file, such as a Microsoft Excel spreadsheet, in CSV (comma-delimited) or TXT (tab-delimited) contains data **fields** (columns) and **records** (rows). Each column of data is a field, such as Name, Address, and so on, while each row of data is a record. If you want to add images to the source file, type an @ before the field name, such as @Photo, and enter the path to the image for each record. The merged document is the result of the data merge between the source and target, which is then exported to a PDF document.

Create a Data Merge

1. Select the **Data Merge** panel.

   ◆ Click the **Window** menu, point to **Utilities**, and then click **Data Merge**.

2. Click the **Options** button, and then click **Select Data Source**.

3. Navigate to the folder location, select the source file (CSV or TXT), and then click **Open**.

   ◆ Select the **Show Import Options** check box to change options. Specify import options, and then click **OK**.

4. Click to place the insertion point in the text frame (document or master page) where you want data field.

5. Click a field in the Data Merge panel list.

   ◆ For image data, drag the image field onto an empty frame or existing graphics frame.

   Text fields appear with double angled brackets, like <<Name>>.

6. Select the **Preview** check box on the panel to preview data in the target document.

7. Click the **Preview First Record**, **Preview Previous Record**, **Preview Next Record**, or **Preview Last Record** button on the panel to view the record data in the target document.

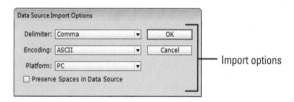

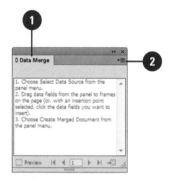

Import options

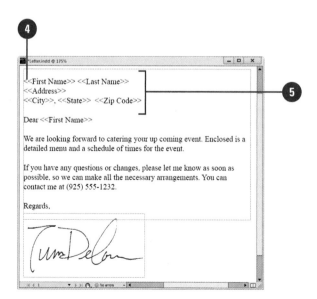

8 To work with the data source, do any of the following:

◆ Update. Edit the data source file in the source program, click the **Options** button, and then click **Update Data Source**.

◆ Remove Connection. Click the **Options** button, and then click **Remove Data Source**.

◆ Replace. Click the **Options** button, click **Select Data Source**, select a new file, and then click **Open**.

◆ Image Placement. Click the **Options** button, click **Content Placement Options**, select options, and then click **OK**.

9 Click the **Create Merged Document** button on the panel.

10 Specify the following options on the Records tab:

◆ Records To Merge. Specify the records you want to merge.

◆ Records Per Document Page. Select **Single Record** to start each record at the top of the next page, or select **Multiple Records** to create more than one record per page.

11 If you select Multiple Records, click the **Multiple Record Layout** tab, and then specify settings for margins, and the column and row record layout.

◆ Select the **Preview Multiple Record Layout** check box to preview the data.

12 Click **OK**.

13 Specify options to export the merged document to a PDF (see Chapter 16 for details), and then click **Export**.

14 Enter a name, specify a location, and then click **Save**.

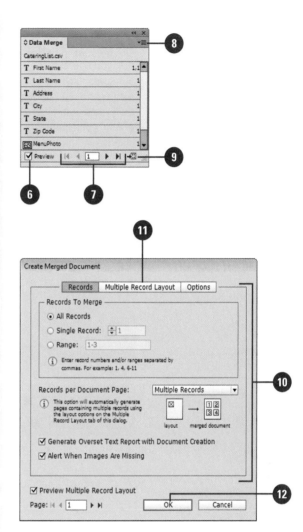

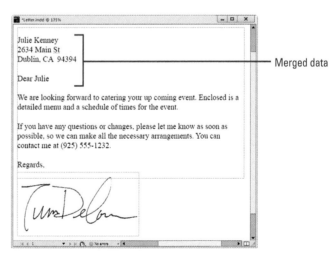

Merged data

Working with XML

XML (Extensible Markup Language) provides a way to reuse data from one file in another file. XML uses tags to describe data in the XML file that you can export into a different file. Tagged data are called **elements**. InDesign can create and use XML data. You can tag data as elements in an InDesign document, save and export data as XML, and then reuse it in other documents. InDesign provides the Structure pane and the Tags panel for working with XML data. The Structure pane shows you the hierarchy and structure of XML data and text snippets for viewing purposes, while the Tags panel lists tags for elements and provides tools to import, export, add, delete, and rename tags.

Create an XML Tag

1. Select the **Tags** panel.

   ◆ Click the **Window** menu, point to **Utilities**, and then click **Tags**.

2. Click the **New Tag** button on the panel.

3. Type a name for the tag (no spaces or non-standard characters), and then press Enter (Win) or Return (Mac).

4. Double-click the tag, select a color, and then click **OK**.

   The color appears when you apply the tag to a frame or text.

Did You Know?

You can delete a tag. Select the Tags panel, select the tag, and then click the Delete Tag button on the panel.

Place XML Tags in a Document

1. Click the **View** menu, point to **Structure**, and then click **Show Structure**.

2. Select the **Tags** panel.

   ◆ Click the **Window** menu, point to **Utilities**, and then click **Tags**.

3. Select the text frame or individual text.

4. Click a tag in the Tags panel.

   ◆ To untag an item, select the element in the Structure pane, and then click **Untag** in the Tags panel.

5. To show tagged frames or text or frames, click the **View** menu, point to **Structure**, and then click **Show Tag Markers** or **Show Tagged Frames**.

6. To map XML tags to styles in your document for formatting, click the **Options** button, click **Map Tags To Styles**, select a style for each tag, and then click **OK**.

Did You Know?

You can import XML data. Create a placeholder frame, click the File menu, click Import XML, select the Show XML Import Options check box, click the Merge Content or Append Content option, select the XML file, click Open, select the options you want, and then click OK.

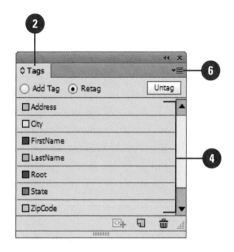

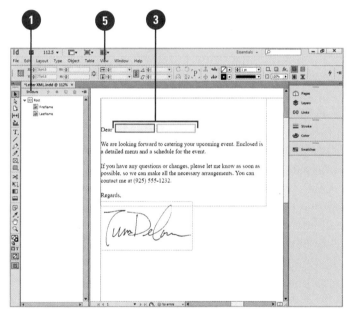

Exporting XML or IDML

After you finish creating or loading element tags, applying them to items on the page in your document, and making any final adjustments in the hierarchy of the tagged elements in the Structure pane, you're ready to export your document to XML for use in other documents. In addition to XML files, you can also export to the InDesign Markup Language (IDML) format, which is an XML-based format. This allows you to create (export) and open XML InDesign documents using standard XML tools. If you're exporting large documents to PDF or IDML, you can continue to work on your document as InDesign works in the background.

Export XML or IDML

1. Click the **File** menu, and then click **Export**.

2. Enter a name for the file.

3. Click the **Save as Type** list arrow (Win) or **Format** popup (Mac), and then click **XML** or **InDesign Markup (IDML)**.

4. Navigate to the location where you want to save the XML document.

5. Click **Save**.

6. For XML, specify any of the following options on the General tab:

   ◆ **Include DTD Declaration**. Uses the DTD along with the XML.

   ◆ **View XML Using**. Opens the exported file in a browser.

   ◆ **Export From Selected Element**. Starts the export from the selected element in the Structure pane.

   ◆ **Export Untagged Tables as CALS XML**. Exports untagged tables in the CALS XML format.

   ◆ **Remap Break, Whitespace, and Special Characters**. Exports items as decimal characters.

   ◆ **Apply XSLT**. Applies a stylesheet (XSLT) to define the transformed, exported XML.

   ◆ **Encoding**. Specifies an encoding method.

7. Click **Export**.

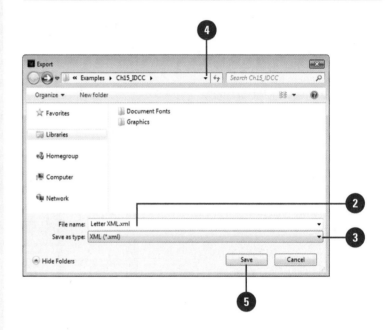

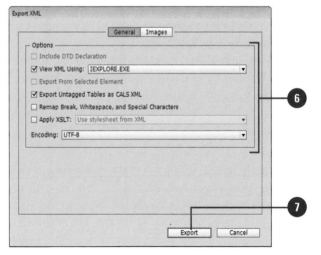

Exporting a Document

Introduction

After you finish creating your document in InDesign, you can export your work in another file format for use in other programs. There are eight main file formats to which you can export your document, which include Adobe Flash Professional (FLA), Adobe PDF (Portable Document Format) for print or interactive, EPS (Encapsulated PostScript), JPEG, Flash SWF (ShockWave Flash), and XML (Extensible Markup Language). In addition to these file formats, you can also export text in the Adobe InDesign Tagged Text, Rich Text Format, and Text Only file formats. When you export from InDesign, your content can be altered using the Options dialog box for the specific file format.

If a co-worker or client doesn't have InDesign, you can create an Adobe PDF of a print or interactive document for them to review your work. Adobe PDF is a useful file format for document sharing, viewing, and proofing with Adobe Acrobat Reader or Adobe Acrobat Professional, which can be used to add comments and annotations. If you frequently use custom settings to export an InDesign document to an Adobe PDF file, you can save time by creating a preset.

If you use Adobe Flash Professional CS6 or later to create vector-based animation and interactivity, you can export content from InDesign to the FLA format for use in Flash. You can open FLA files in Flash and then use the authoring environment to add video, audio, animation, and complex interactivity. If you want to use InDesign content on the web, you can export your document as a Digital Editions eBook file or a HTML file, which you can open in Adobe Dreamweaver. A digital edition is a XHTML-based EPUB ebook that is compatible with the Adobe Digital Editions reader software. Dreamweaver is a HTML editor that allows you to create and manage web sites and pages.

What You'll Do

Export a Document

Understand Export File Formats

Export as a Print PDF

Set PDF General Options

Set PDF Compression Options

Set PDF Marks and Bleeds Options

Set PDF Output Options

Set PDF Advanced Options

Set PDF Security Options

Export with PDF Presets

Export PDF Files in the Background

Set PDF Media Options

Export as an Interactive PDF

Export as an EPS, JPEG, or PNG

Export as a Flash Movie or File

Order Content in the Article Panel

Export as an Accessible PDF

Apply Tags for a PDF

Export Tags for EPUB and HTML

Export as an EPUB eBook

Export as an HTML

Set EPUB and HTML Options

Exporting a Document

After you finish creating your document in InDesign, you can export it for use in other programs. If you want to share a document with someone who doesn't have InDesign, you can export the file as a PDF (Portable Document Format) in print or interactive form. If you have a document that is composed primarily of text, you can export the file as a text document, which you can open in a word processing program. If you have a document composed mostly of artwork, you can export it as a JPEG or PNG file (for use on the web). If you want to use content from an InDesign document in Adobe Flash CS6 Professional or later, you can export it as a FLA file. If you want to use content from your InDesign document on the web, you can export your document as an eBook EPUB file or HTML file. In addition, you can export a document as a SWF movie for use in the Flash Player. If you want to open an InDesign document in InDesign CS4 or later (make sure software is updated), you can export it to IDML (InDesign Markup).

Export a Document

1. Click the **File** menu, and then click **Export**.

2. Enter a name for the file in the File Name (Win) or Save As (Mac) box.

3. Click the **Save as Type** list arrow (Win) or **Format** popup (Mac), and then select a file format.

   ◆ All the formats don't display unless you place the insertion point in a text frame.

   ◆ InDesign also remembers your last export format for next time.

   See the list on the next page for more information about all the file formats.

4. Navigate to a save location.

5. Click **Save**.

   For some formats, an Options dialog box appears, prompting you for additional settings.

6. If prompted, specify the options that you want, and then click **Export**.

   ◆ For help, point to an option to display a description at the bottom of the dialog box.

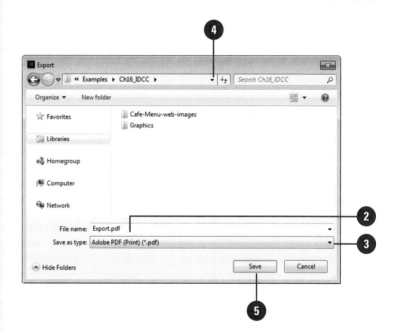

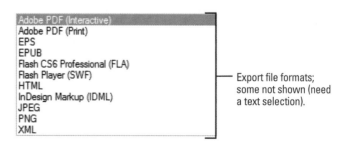

Export file formats; some not shown (need a text selection).

Understanding Export File Formats

Export File Formats

Format	Usage
Adobe InDesign Tagged Text	Creates a text file formatted with text codes.
Adobe PDF (Interactive)	Creates a file in the PDF (Portable Document Format) optimized for rich media content display in Adobe Reader.
Adobe PDF (Print)	Creates a file in the PDF (Portable Document Format) optimized for print content display and print in Adobe Reader.
EPS	Creates a file in the EPS (Encapsulated PostScript) format for use as a graphic document.
EPUB	Creates a file in an XHTML-based ebook (EPUB) document that is compatible with the Adobe Digital Editions reader software.
Flash CS6 Professional (FLA)	Creates a file in the FLA format for use in Adobe Flash CS6 Professional or later.
Flash Player (SWF)	Creates a file in the SWF (ShockWave Flash) movie format for use on the web using the Flash player.
HTML	Creates a file in the HTML format for use in Adobe Dreamweaver or other web page editor and display is web browsers.
InCopy Document	Creates a file for use in InCopy.
InDesign Markup (IDML)	Creates a file in the IDML (InDesign Markup Language) format, an XML-based format for use with documents that will be created and modified outside of InDesign or previous versions of InDesign. This format is especially useful for back saving documents you want to open in InDesign CS4 or later (make sure InDesign is the latest version; click the Help menu, and then click Updates). This format is also useful for saving QuarkXPress or PageMaker files opened in InDesign with compatibility problems.
JPEG	Creates a file in the JPG or JPEG (Joint Photographic Experts Group) format for use as a compression method to reduce the size of image files primarily for the web.
Rich Text Format	Creates a file in the RTF (Rich Text Format) format for use as formatted text.
Text Only	Creates a file in the TXT format for use as a plain text document.
PNG	Creates a file in the PNG (Portable Network Graphic) format for use as a graphic document.
XML	Creates a file in the XML (Extensible Markup Language) format for use as a reusable document with customized definitions and tags.

Exporting as a Print PDF

If a co-worker or client doesn't have InDesign, you can create an Adobe PDF of a document for them to review your work in a print or interactive form. Adobe PDF (Portable Document Format) is a useful file format for document sharing, viewing, and proofing with Adobe Acrobat Reader, which is free for download on the web at *www.adobe.com*. InDesign, you have two PDF export options. You can export and optimize your PDF document for print using the Adobe PDF (Print) format or for interactivity using the Adobe PDF (Interactive) format.

Export to a Document as a PDF Print File

1. Click the **File** menu, and then click **Export**.

2. Enter a name for the file in the File Name (Win) or Save As (Mac) box.

3. Click the **Save as Type** list arrow (Win) or **Format** popup (Mac), and then click **Adobe PDF (Print)**.

4. Navigate to the location where you want to save the document.

5. Click **Save**.

6. Click the **Adobe PDF Preset** list arrow, and then select a preset option, or specify your own options to create a custom preset.

   ◆ To create a preset that you can use later, set your options, click **Save Preset**, enter a name, and then click **OK**.

7. Select each category on the left and then select the options you want.

   See topics on the following pages that describe the available options in detail.

   ◆ To reset options to the defaults, hold down Alt (Win) or Option (Mac), and then click **Reset**.

8. Click **Export**.

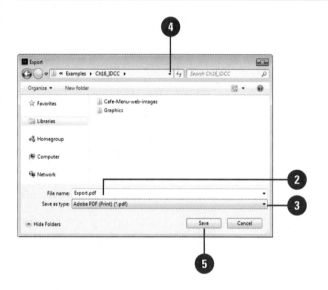

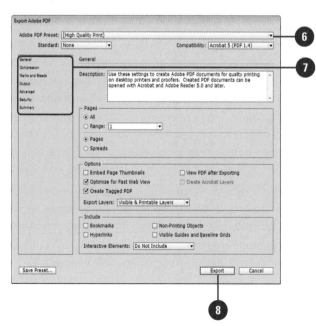

Use Adobe PDF Preset Options

1. Follow steps 1 through 5 on the previous page.

2. Click the **Adobe PDF Preset** list arrow, and then select one of the following presets:

   ◆ **High Quality Print.** Creates PDFs for quality printing on desktop printers and proofing devices.

   ◆ **PDF/X-1a:2001.** Creates PDFs that meet printing standards for PDF/X-1a:2001 or 2003 and Acrobat Reader 4.0 or later (PDF 1.3). Useful for a CMYK or spot color job.

   ◆ **PDF/X-3:2002.** Creates PDFs that meet printing standards for PDF/X-3:2002 or 2003 and Acrobat Reader 4.0 or later (PDF 1.6). Useful for a color-managed workflow. May contain RGB/ LAB/... colors, which are converted to CMYK.

   ◆ **PDF/X-4:2008.** Creates PDFs that meet printing standards for PDF/X-4:2010 and Acrobat Reader 7.0 or later (PDF 1.6). Useful for a color-managed workflow with added support for preserving transparency, layers, and JPEG2000 compression.

   ◆ **Press Quality.** Creates PDFs for high quality print production (digital printing or separations).

   ◆ **Smallest File Size.** Creates compressed PDFs for use on the web or e-mail distribution.

3. Click **Export**.

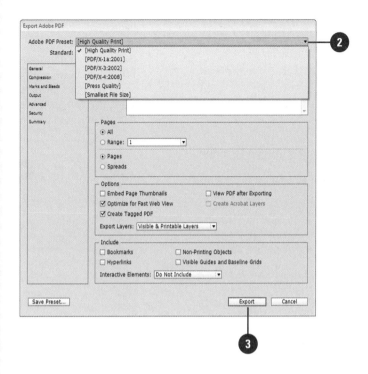

Understanding PDF/X Formats

PDF/X is a standard—a defined set of rules—that ensures page layout or graphic files are consistent, predictable, and compliant for print-ready purposes. PDF/X rules require certain content, prohibit others, and leaves some alone. Using PDF/X compliant files eliminates many common errors in file preparation, such as fonts not embedded, incorrect color spaces, missing images, and overprinting and trapping issues. There are three PDF/X formats: PDF/X-1a, PDF/X-3 and PDF/X-4. Each format has different versions. InDesign supports PDF/X-4:2010, which is the same as PDF/X-4:2008, except that it relaxes certain restrictions on how layers can be specified in the PDF. This provides the functionality to create layers in an exported PDF and PDF 1.6 compatibility. In addition, PDF 1.6 allows JPEG2000 compression as an option for the color and grayscale images.

Setting PDF General Options

The General PDF Print options allow you to specify PDF compatibility, a page range, conversion options, and to choose what elements to include in the PDF file. The important options to consider here are the page range, Export Layers, and the elements you want to include in the PDF file. Some of the important options include Bookmarks, Hyperlinks, and Interactive Elements. If you have sounds and movies in your document, you can specify options to use current media settings or override them to link or embed all of them in the PDF document.

Set PDF Print General Options

1. Click the **File** menu, and then click **Export**.

2. Enter a name, specify a location, select the **Adobe PDF (Print)** format, and then click **Save**.

3. Click the **Compatibility** list arrow, and then select which version of Acrobat you want your file to be compatible.

4. Click the **Standard** list arrow, and then select a PDF/x option.

   The PDF/X options use ISO international standards for compatibility with printing. See the previous page and the table on the next page for help selecting an option.

5. Click the **General** category.

6. Specify any of the following General options:

   ◆ **Pages.** Select the All or Range option, and specify a range, and then select the Pages or Spreads (keep pages within spreads together) option.

   ◆ **Embed Page Thumbnails.** Select to add a thumbnail image for each page; only necessary for Acrobat 5 or earlier.

   ◆ **Optimize for Fast Web View.** Select to optimize the document for downloading from web servers.

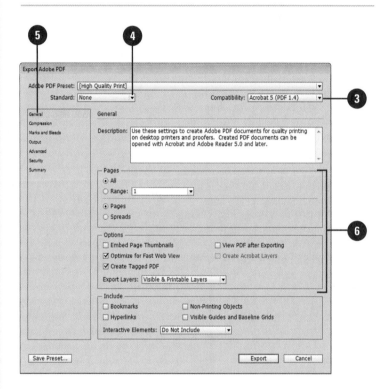

- ◆ **Create Tagged PDF.** Select to add tags for use with screen readers to create an accessible PDF.

- ◆ **View PDF after Exporting.** Select to open the PDF file in Adobe Reader or Acrobat Pro.

- ◆ **Create Acrobat Layers.** Select to convert InDesign layers into Acrobat layers.

- ◆ **Export Layers.** Select the option to export layers.

7️⃣ Specify any of the following Include options:

- ◆ **Bookmarks.** Select to create bookmarks for entries in a table of contents.

- ◆ **Hyperlinks.** Select to convert InDesign hyperlinks, table of contents, and index entries into Acrobat hyperlinks.

- ◆ **Non-Printing Objects.** Select to export objects with the non-printing option.

- ◆ **Visible Guides and Baseline Grids.** Select to use current guides and grids in the PDF document.

- ◆ **Interactive Elements.** Select the option to Include Appearance or Do Not Include.

8️⃣ Click **Export**.

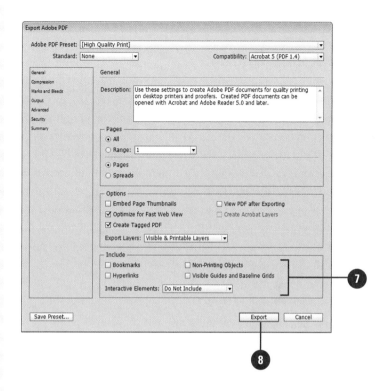

Did You Know?

What is the PDF/X file format? The PDF/X file format is a set of rules that provide predictable and consistent PDF files for a prepress environment. The rules enforce PDF functions for printing purposes and forbid the use of irrelevant ones.

PDF/X Standards

Standard	Description
PDF/X-1a:2001 or 2003	Creates PDFs that meet printing standards and Acrobat Reader 4.0 or later (PDF 1.3). Useful for a CMYK or spot color job.
PDF/X-3:2002 or 2003	Creates PDFs that meet printing standards and Acrobat Reader 4.0 or later (PDF 1.3). Useful for a color- managed workflow. May contain RGB/LAB/... colors, which are converted to CMYK.
PDF/X-4:2010	Creates PDFs that meet printing standards and Acrobat Reader 7.0 or later (PDF 1.6). Useful for a color-managed workflow with added support for preserving transparency, layers, and JPEG2000 compression for color and grayscale images. Identical to PDF/X-4:2008 except for layers and JPEG2000 compression.

Setting PDF Compression Options

The Compression PDF Print options allow you to specify compression settings for color, grayscale, and monochrome (black and white) images. The important settings to consider are sampling, compression method, and image quality. The sampling option allows you to select how much downsampling of pixels takes place. The greater the downsampling, the greater compression and lower the quality. The compression option lets you select a compression method. Automatic (JPEG) is recommended. The higher the image quality level, the lower the compression and vice versa. So, choose an image quality level that best suits your needs.

Set PDF Print Compression Options

1. Click the **File** menu, and then click **Export**.

2. Enter a name, specify a location, select the **Adobe PDF (Print)** format, and then click **Save**.

3. Click the **Compression** category.

4. Specify the following options for Color, Grayscale, and Monochrome Images:

   ◆ **Sampling.** Select from the following options:

      ◆ **Do Not Downsample.** Retains all pixels.

      ◆ **Average Downsampling to.** Averages pixels in an area.

      ◆ **Subsampling to.** Fastest results with low quality.

      ◆ **Bicubic downsampling to.** Slowest results with high quality.

   ◆ **Compression.** Select a compression method.

   ◆ **Image Quality.** Select an image quality level.

   ◆ **Resolution.** Enter resolution settings for all the options.

   ◆ **Compress Text and Line Art.** Select to compress text or art.

   ◆ **Crop Image Data to Frames.** Select to crop and reduce size.

5. Click **Export**.

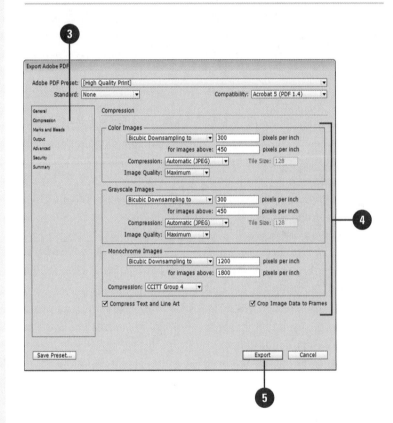

Setting PDF Marks and Bleeds Options

The Marks and Bleeds PDF Print options allow you to specify what printer's marks—crop marks, bleed marks, registration marks, color bars, and page numbers—you want to include in the PDF file. Printer's marks appear outside of the page boundary for commercial printing purposes. They don't affect the visual display of the page. You can also set options for the bleed and slug. The bleed is an area outside the trim of the page where objects still print, while the slug is an area outside the page trim that may or may not print. The slug is typically used to add non-printing information to a document.

Set PDF Print Marks and Bleeds Options

1. Click the **File** menu, and then click **Export**.

2. Enter a name, specify a location, select the **Adobe PDF (Print)** format, and then click **Save**.

3. Click the **Marks and Bleeds** category.

4. Select the **All Printer's Marks** check box to display the available printer's marks options.

5. Select the check boxes for the printer's marks you want to include in the PDF document.

6. Select the bleed and slug options you want:

   ◆ **Use Document Bleed Settings.** Select to use document settings for the bleed.

   ◆ **Bleed.** Specify the bleed values for top, bottom, inside and outside.

   ◆ **Make All Settings the Same.** Click the chain icon to make all settings the same.

   ◆ **Include Slug Area.** Select to include the slug area in the export.

7. Click **Export**.

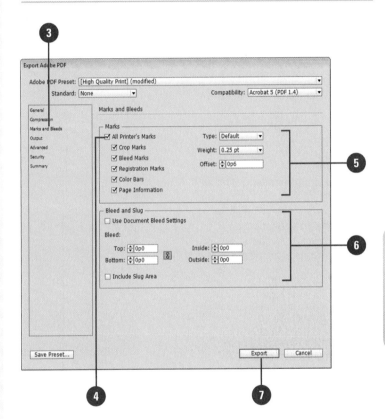

Setting PDF Output Options

The Output PDF Print options allow you to specify color options and PDF/X compatibility settings. The important options to consider here are color conversion, destination, and profile inclusion policy. The color conversion option allows you to select whether to use the current color profile in the destination PDF document. The destination option lets you choose a color or grayscale profile for the destination PDF document, while the profile include policy lets you choose how it's used. You can also set PDF/X options, if you need to.

Set PDF Print Output Options

① Click the **File** menu, and then click **Export**.

② Enter a name, specify a location, select the **Adobe PDF (Print)** format, and then click **Save**.

③ Click the **Output** category.

④ Specify the following Color options:

- ◆ **Color Conversion**. Select an option: No Color Conversion, Convert to Destination, or Convert to Destination (Preserve Numbers), which converts to the destination only if the embedded profile is different.

- ◆ **Destination**. Select a color or grayscale profile.

- ◆ **Profile Inclusion Policy**. Select an option: Don't Include Profiles, Include All Profiles, Include Tagged Source Profiles (for output calibrated output devices), or Include All RGB and Tagged Source CMYK Profiles (for output calibrated RGB and CMYK files).

⑤ Select the **Simulate Overprint** check box to simulate overprinting on the screen.

⑥ To control ink type, density, and sequence for process and spot colors, click **Ink Manager**.

⑦ Click **Export**.

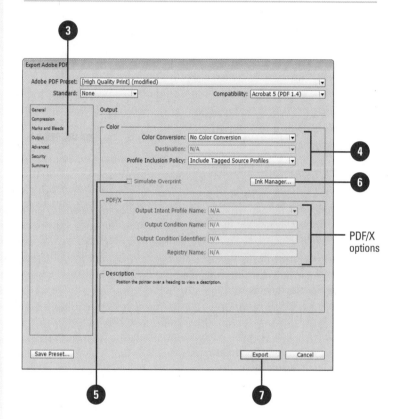

Setting PDF Advanced Options

The Advanced PDF Print options allow you to specify when all characters of the font are embedded, whether to use OPI (Open Prepress Interface) with document graphics, and what resolution to use for transparency flattening. OPI options are used when you send files to Scitex and Kodak prepress systems. OPI uses low-resolution images for layout and high-resolution images for printing. When you use transparency in a document, you need to specify a resolution setting to flatten, or convert, the effect into vector and raster images.

Set PDF Print Advanced Options

① Click the **File** menu, and then click **Export**.

② Enter a name, specify a location, select the **Adobe PDF (Print)** format, and then click **Save**.

③ Click the **Advanced** category.

④ Specify the following Advanced options:

◆ **Fonts.** Enter a percentage amount for the threshold when all characters of the font are embedded.

◆ **OPI.** OPI uses low-resolution images for layout and uses high-resolution images for printing. Select the check boxes for the image types to which you want to apply the OPI setting.

◆ **Transparency Flattener Preset.** Select a resolution to convert transparency into rasterized images.

◆ **Ignore Spread Overrides.** Select if you flatten individual spreads using the Pages panel.

⑤ Select the **Create JDF File Using Acrobat** check box to add job definition format information to the PDF document.

◆ You need Acrobat 7 Pro or later installed for this option.

⑥ Click **Export**.

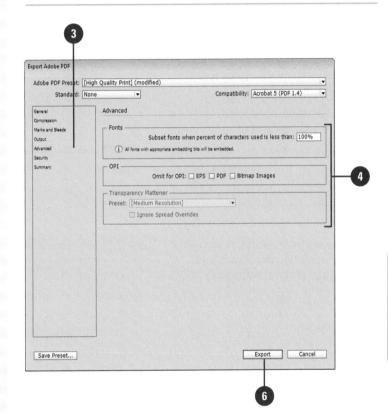

Setting PDF Security Options

If you only want certain users to open the exported PDF file, you can use Security PDF Print options to require a password. If you don't want to restrict complete access to the PDF file, yet you still want to have some restrictions in place, you can require a password for printing, editing, and other tasks. You can specify what a user can print and change. The password to open the document needs to be different than the one required to print, edit, or perform other tasks. Passwords are case-sensitive, so you can use upper and lowercase letter as well as numbers to create a secure password.

Set PDF Print Security Options

1. Click the **File** menu, and then click **Export**.

2. Enter a name, specify a location, select the **Adobe PDF (Print)** format, and then click **Save**.

3. Click the **Security** category.

4. To require a password, select the **Require a password to open the document** check box, and then enter a password in the box.

5. To require a password for certain tasks, select the **Use a password to restrict printing, editing and other tasks** check box, and then enter a password in the box.

   ◆ **Printing Allowed.** Select an option: None, Low Resolution (150 dpi), or High Resolution.

   ◆ **Changes Allowed.** Select an option: None; Inserting, deleting and rotating pages; Filling in form fields and signing; Commenting, filling in form fields, and signing; and Any except extracting pages.

   ◆ **Enable copying of text, images and other content.** Select to allow content copying.

   ◆ **Enable text access of screen reader devices for the visually impaired.**

6. Click **Export**.

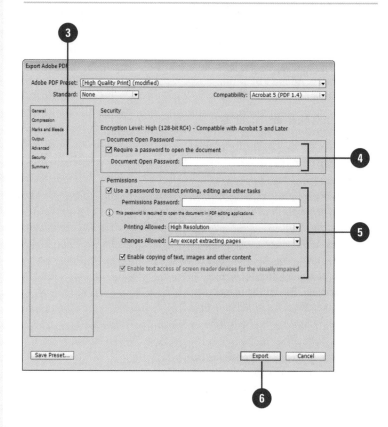

Exporting with PDF Presets

If you frequently use custom settings to export an InDesign document to an Adobe PDF file, you can save time by creating a preset. Adobe programs, including InDesign, Illustrator, Photoshop, and Acrobat, provide built-in presets that you can use in any of the programs. When you create your own preset, you can also use it in other Adobe programs. The process for creating a preset for an Adobe PDF is similar to creating a preset in other Adobe programs.

Create a Preset for an Adobe PDF

1. Click the **File** menu, point to **Adobe PDF Presets**, and then click **Define**.

2. Perform any of the following:

   ◆ New. Click **New**, specify the options that you want, and then click **OK**.

   ◆ Edit. Select a custom preset (not a predefined one), click **Edit**, change the options, and then click **OK**.

   ◆ Delete. Select a custom preset (not a predefined one), and then click **Delete**.

   ◆ Import. Click **Load**, navigate to the preset file, select it, and then click **Open**.

   ◆ Export. Select a preset, click **Save As**, specify a location and name, and then click **Save**.

   For PDF files, the preset is saved with the *.joboptions* extension.

3. Click **Done**.

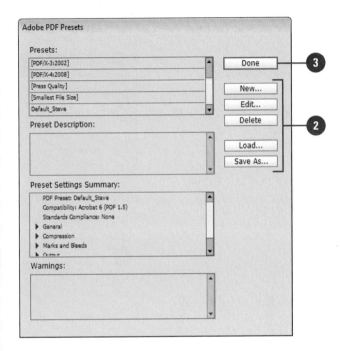

Exporting PDF Files in the Background

When you export one or more documents to a PDF or IDML (InDesign Markup), the process can sometimes take a little while. Instead of waiting for the process to complete, you can continue working on your documents while the process continues in the background. You can use the Background Tasks panel to view the progress of the export processes. When you queue up several PDF exports, you can view the multiple jobs in the Background Tasks panel.

View Exported PDF or IDML Files in the Background Tasks Panel

1. Select the **Background Tasks** panel.

   ◆ Click the **Window** menu, point to **Utilities**, and then click **Background Tasks**.

2. Follow steps on page 420, "*Exporting XML or IDML*," and on page 424, "*Exporting as a Print PDF*," to export one or more documents to an IDML or PDF format.

3. View the progress of the PDF exports.

4. To stop a process, click the **Cancel** button.

5. Click the **Alerts** triangle to expand the panel.

6. To clear alerts, click the **Clear Alerts** button on the panel.

Setting PDF Media Options

Before you export a document with media files, you should set options for playback in the interactive PDF document. The PDF media options allow you to play video in a separate window, and provide a message if the media cannot be played in Acrobat or as alternative text for visually impaired users. You can set these options in the PDF Options dialog box, which you can open from the Media panel. When you import a video, the video object and the poster appear in a frame. When you export to PDF, the video object's frame determines the size of the video in the PDF document, not the frame or poster size. If you keep the video frame size and the poster and frame size the same, you shouldn't have any problems on export to PDF. Also, be aware that videos always appear and play on the topmost layer of a PDF document, even if you overlay an object on the movie in InDesign.

Set PDF Media Options

1. Select the media clip.

2. Select the **Media** panel.

   ◆ Click the **Window** menu, point to **Interactive**, and then click **Media**.

3. Click the **Set Options For Exporting Interactive PDF** button on the panel.

4. Type a description to be displayed if the media cannot be played in Acrobat. The description also provides alternative text for visually impaired users.

5. Select the **Play Video In Floating Window** check box to play the video in a separate window (not available for SWF or audio files). If you select the option, specify the following:

   ◆ Size. Select a size ratio based on the size of the original video (not a scaled version). As you increase the ratio, the image quality of the video may reduce.

   ◆ Position. Select a position on the screen for the window.

6. Click **OK**.

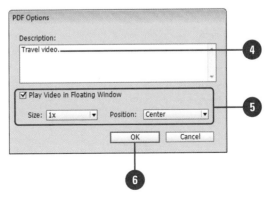

Exporting as an Interactive PDF

When you create an interactive document with buttons, page transitions, and animations in InDesign that you want to share with others, you can export the file as an interactive PDF (Portable Document Format) for display in Adobe Acrobat Reader. In InDesign, you have two PDF export options. You can export and optimize your PDF document for print using the Adobe PDF (Print) format or for interactivity as pages or spreads using the Adobe PDF (Interactive) format.

Export a Document as an Interactive PDF File

1. Click the **File** menu, and then click **Export**.

2. Enter a name for the file in the File Name (Win) or Save As (Mac) box.

3. Click the **Save as Type** list arrow (Win) or **Format** popup (Mac), and then click **Adobe PDF (Interactive)**.

4. Navigate to the location where you want to save the document.

5. Click **Save**.

6. Specify any of the following options:

   ◆ **Pages.** Select the All or Range option, and specify a range, and then select the Pages or Spreads (keep pages within spreads together) option.

   ◆ **View After Exporting.** Select to open the PDF file in Adobe Reader or Acrobat Pro.

   ◆ **Embed Page Thumbnails.** Select to add a thumbnail image for each page; only necessary for Acrobat 5 or earlier.

   ◆ **Create Acrobat Layers.** Select to convert InDesign layers into Acrobat layers.

   ◆ **View.** Select a view option to display the PDF file, such as Actual Size, Fit Page, Fit Visible, 25%, or 100%.

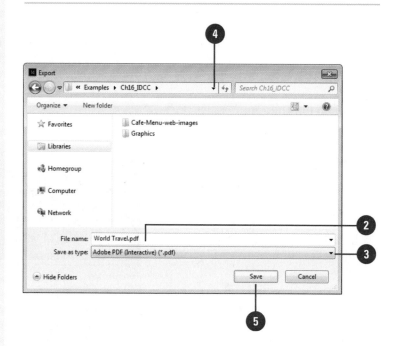

- **Layout.** Select a page spread option to display pages, such as Single Page, Two-Up (Facing), or Two-Up Continuous (Facing).

- **Open in Full Screen Mode.** Select to open the PDF file in full screen mode.

  If you select this option, select the **Flip Pages Every X seconds** check box to automatically flip through pages based on the duration.

- **Page Transitions.** Select a page transition to include.

- **Forms and Media.** Select the Include All or Appearance Only option. Select Include All to use bookmarks, hyperlinks, and cross-references.

- **Create Tagged PDF.** Select to add tags for use with screen readers. If so, you can select the Use Structure for Tab Order check box to use it.

7. Specify any of the following Image Handling options:

- **Compression.** Select Automatic to let InDesign handle it, JPEG (Lossy) for use with grayscale and color images, or PNG (Lossless) to not compress.

- **JPEG Quality.** Select a quality level. The higher the quality, the higher the file size and slower the display.

- **Resolution (ppi).** Select a resolution for bitmaps.

8. To set security options, click **Security**, select the options you want, and then click **OK**.

- See "*Setting PDF Security Options*," on page 432 for information about the options.

9. Click **OK**.

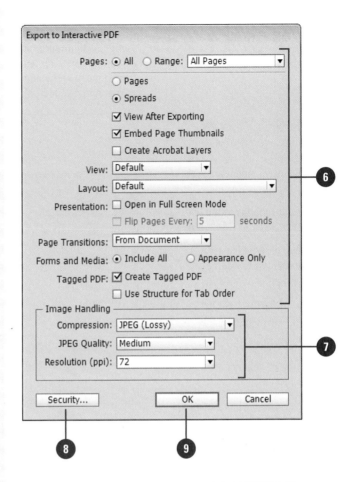

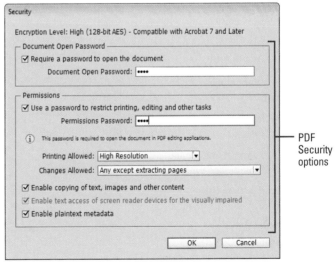

PDF Security options

Exporting as an EPS

EPS (Encapsulated PostScript) is a commonly used file format that you can import into graphics, word processing, and page layout programs. An EPS file can contain vector and bitmap graphics, so it makes the format more versatile for use in other programs. EPS does a good job of preserving graphic objects in an InDesign document.

Export a Document as an EPS File

1. Click the **File** menu, and then click **Export**.

2. Enter a name for the file in the File Name (Win) or Save As (Mac) box.

3. Click the **Save as Type** list arrow (Win) or **Format** popup (Mac), and then click **EPS**.

4. Navigate to the location where you want to save the document.

5. Click **Save**.

6. Specify any of the following General options:

   ◆ **Pages.** Select the All or Range option, and specify a range, and then select the Pages or Spreads (keep pages within spreads together) option.

   ◆ **PostScript.** Select Level 2 for older printers or Level 3 for newer printers. Check your specific printer for capabilities.

   ◆ **Color.** Select from the following options or select **Leave Unchanged**:

      ◆ **CMYK.** Uses CMYK. Useful for separations.

      ◆ **Gray.** Converts to grayscale. Useful for black and white.

      ◆ **RGB.** Converts to RGB. Useful for onscreen images.

      ◆ **PostScript Color Management.** Uses the PostScript printer to control the color separations.

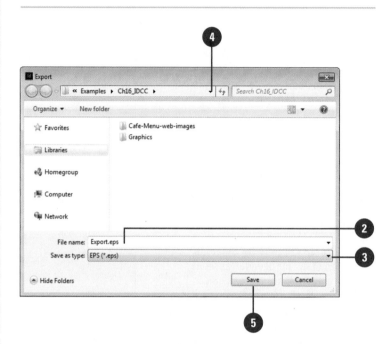

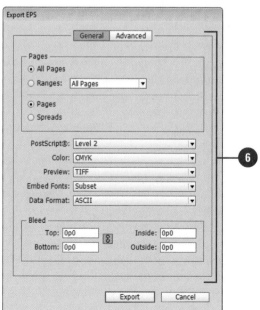

- **Preview.** Select None for no preview, TIFF for an image preview (Mac and Win), or PICT for an image preview (Mac only).

- **Embed Fonts.** Select None to not embed, Complete to embed all characters in fonts, or Subset to embed only the characters used in the file.

- **Data Format.** Select Binary for universal use or ASCII for use on PC computers.

- **Bleed.** Specify the bleed values for top, bottom, inside and outside.

7 Click the **Advanced** tab.

8 Specify the following Advanced options:

- **Send Data.** Sends All image data in high resolution or Proxy in low resolution.

- **OPI.** OPI uses low-resolution images for layout and high-resolution images for printing. Select the check boxes for the image types you want to apply the OPI setting.

- **Transparency Flattener Preset.** Select a resolution to convert transparency into rasterized images.

- **Ignore Spread Overrides.** Select if you flatten individual spreads using the Pages panel.

9 To control ink type, density, and sequence for process and spot colors, click **Ink Manager**.

10 Click **Export**.

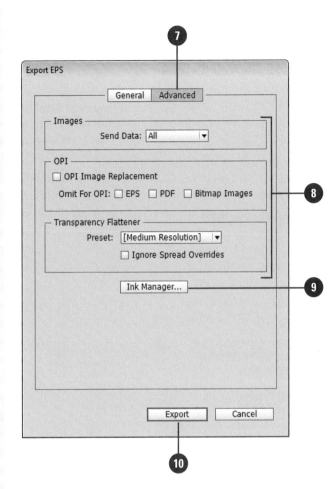

Exporting as a JPEG or PNG

If you have a document that you want to post on the web, you can export it as a JPEG (Joint Photographic Experts Group) or PNG (Portable Network Graphic) file. The Export command for JPEG or PNG gives you options to specify image quality and resolution, select the color space, use anti-alias to smooth jagged edges for text and images, use document bleed settings, and simulate overprinting. For JPEG, you can also set options to embed the color profile and specify how you want to display the image on the screen (format method). For PNG, you can also set an option to use a transparent background. JPEG and PNG are a compressed format with relatively high quality, so it's a common file format for the web.

Export a Document as a JPEG or PNG File

1. Click the **File** menu, and then click **Export**.

2. Enter a name for the file in the File Name (Win) or Save As (Mac) box.

3. Click the **Save as Type** list arrow (Win) or **Format** popup (Mac), and then click **JPEG** or **PNG**.

4. Navigate to the location where you want to save the document.

5. Click **Save**.

6. Specify any of the following options:

    ◆ **Pages.** Select the All or Range option, and specify a range, and then select the Pages or Spreads (keep pages within spreads together) option.

    ◆ **Quality.** Select a quality level. The higher the quality, the higher the file size and slower the display.

    ◆ **Format Method (JPEG).** Select Progressive to create an image that appears gradually on the page, or select Baseline to create an image that appears all at once, which is slower.

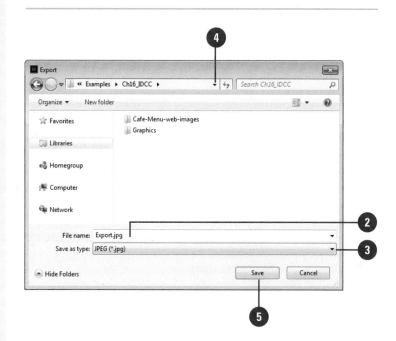

- **Resolution (ppi).** Specify a resolution. 72 ppi is common for the web.

- **Color Space.** Specify a color palette: RGB, CMYK, or Gray.

- **Embed Color Profile (JPEG).** Select to embed the document's color profile in the exported JPEG file. The name of the color profile appears to the right of the option.

- **Transparent Background (PNG).** Select to use a transparent background.

- **Anti-alias.** Select to smooth out jagged edges in text and bitmap images.

- **Use Document Bleed Settings.** Select to use the bleed settings in Document Setup in the exported JPEG or PNG.

- **Simulate Overprint.** Select to apply the Overprint Preview option for any of the selected color spaces. The exported JPEG or PNG simulates the effects of overprinting spot inks by converting spot colors to process colors for printing.

7 Click **Export**.

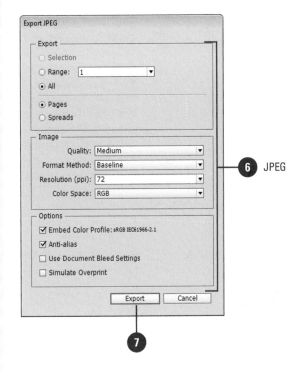

6 JPEG

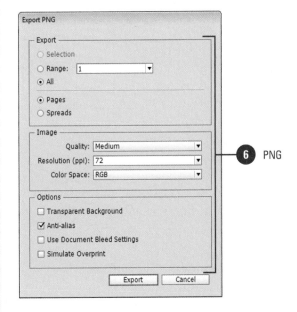

6 PNG

Exporting as a Flash Movie

The SWF file format delivers vector graphics, text, video, and sound to the web using Adobe Flash player or Adobe AIR software. Adobe Flash Pro produces SWF (ShockWave Flash) movie files as a native format. However, you can also create SWF files directly from InDesign by using the Export command. The Export command for SWF gives you general and advanced options to specify how you want to create a SWF movie. You can export a selection, all pages, or a range of pages. When you export SWF files from within InDesign, you can include interactivity and media or just their appearance. When InDesign finishes the export, you can have your browser automatically open and display the SWF file using the Adobe Flash Player.

Export a Document as a Flash SWF Movie

1 Click the **File** menu, and then click **Export**.

2 Enter a name for the file in the File Name (Win) or Save As (Mac) box.

3 Click the **Save as Type** list arrow (Win) or **Format** popup (Mac), and then click **Flash Player (SWF)**.

4 Navigate to the location where you want to save the document.

5 Click **Save**.

6 Click the **General** tab.

7 Specify any of the Export options:

- **Selection.** Select to export the selected element.

- **Pages.** Select the All Pages or Range option, and then select a range option.

- **Generate HTML File.** Select to create a HTML file that plays back the SWF.

- **View SWF After Exporting.** Select to open the SWF file in your browser after exporting.

8 Select a Size (pixels) option:

- **Scale.** Increases or decreases the original size by a percentage.

- **Fit To.** Changes the size to fit a certain screen size.

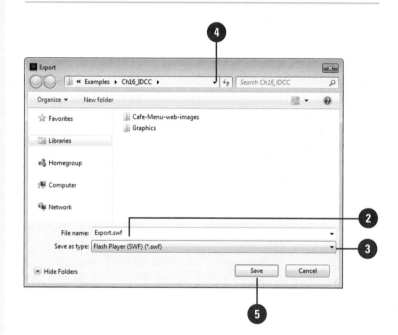

- **Width and Height.** Changes the size to exact width and height settings.

9. Specify any of the options:

- **Background.** Select the Paper Color or Transparent option for the background.

- **Interactivity and Media.** Select the Include All or Appearance Only option.

- **Include Page Transitions.** Select a page transition to include.

- **Include Interactive Page Curl.** Select to enable users to drag a corner of the page to turn it.

10. Click the **Advanced** tab, and then specify any of the options:

- **Frame Rate.** Specify a rate for frames per second. The higher rate, the smoother animations.

- **Text.** Select an option to convert text to Flash Classic Text, Outlines (vector paths), or Pixels (raster image).

- **Rasterize Pages.** Select to create pages as bitmap images.

- **Flatten Transparency.** Select to remove live transparency; this also removes interactivity.

- **Compression.** Select Automatic to let InDesign handle it, JPEG (Lossy) for use with grayscale and color images, or PNG (Lossless) to not compress.

- **JPEG Quality.** Select a quality level. The higher the quality, the higher the file size and slower the display.

- **Resolution (ppi).** Select a resolution for bitmaps.

11. Click **OK**.

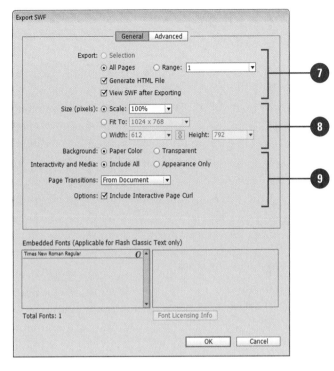

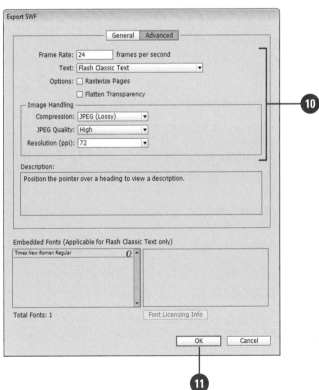

Exporting as a Flash File

If you use Adobe Flash CS6 Professional or later to create vector-based animation and interactivity, you can export content from InDesign to the FLA format for use in Flash; this replaces XFL export in InDesign CS4. You can open FLA files (default file format) in Flash and then use the authoring environment to add video, audio, animation, and complex interactivity. You can export a selection, all pages, or a range of pages. InDesign text exported as FLA remains fully editable when the FLA file is opened in Flash. InDesign automatically converts high-resolution print assets (CMYK) to low-resolution web assets (RGB) upon export as an FLA file. An image placed multiple times in your InDesign document is saved as a single image asset with shared locations when exported as an FLA file.

Export a Document as a Flash FLA File

1. Click the **File** menu, and then click **Export**.

2. Enter a name for the file in the File Name (Win) or Save As (Mac) box.

3. Click the **Save as Type** list arrow (Win) or **Format** popup (Mac), and then click **Flash CS6 Professional (FLA)**.

4. Navigate to the location where you want to save the document.

5. Click **Save**.

6. Specify any of the Export options:

   ◆ **Selection.** Select to export the selected element.

   ◆ **Pages.** Select the All Pages or Range option, and then select a range option.

   ◆ **Rasterize Pages.** Select to create pages as bitmap images.

   ◆ **Flatten Transparency.** Select to flatten all objects with transparency.

7. Select a Size option:

   ◆ **Scale.** Increases or decreases the size of the original by a percentage.

   ◆ **Fit To.** Changes the size to fit a certain screen size.

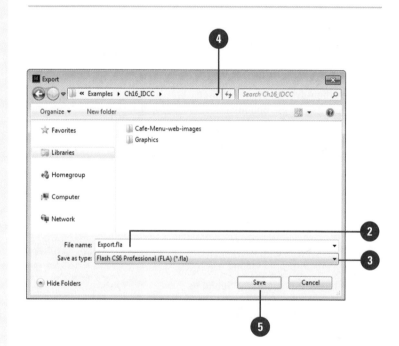

◆ **Width and Height.** Changes the size to exact width and height settings.

⑧ Specify any of the options:

◆ **Interactivity and Media.** Select the Include All or Appearance Only option.

◆ **Text.** Select an option to convert text to Flash Classic Text, Flash TLF Text, Convert to Outlines (vector paths), or Convert to Pixels (raster image).

◆ **Insert Discretionary Hyphenation Points.** If you select Flash TLF Text option for Text, select to allow hyphenation.

⑨ Specify any of the following Image Handling options:

◆ **Compression.** Select Automatic to let InDesign handle it, JPEG (Lossy) for use with grayscale and color images, or PNG (Lossless) to not compress.

◆ **JPEG Quality.** Select a quality level. The higher the quality, the higher the file size and slower the display.

◆ **Resolution (ppi).** Select a resolution for bitmaps.

⑩ Click **OK**.

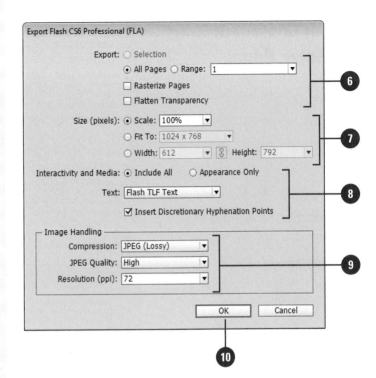

Ordering Content in the Articles Panel

The Articles panel allows you to specify the content reading order of your document for EPUB, HTML, or Accessible PDFs without using the Structure panel. It's a simple drag and drop objects from a page (including Master Page objects) to the Articles panel. InDesign uses the Layers panel to help order the initial placement of the content in the Articles panel. Once the content is in the Articles panel, you can manually reorder it to meet your needs. For EPUB and HTML, you are good to go. For Accessible PDFs, you need to enable an option to use the structure in the Articles panel in Acrobat. The Articles panel allows you to create multiple articles and order them in the sequence you want and then export the ones you want to create custom content.

Order Content in the Articles Panel

1. Select the **Articles** panel.
   - Click the **Window** menu, and then click **Articles**.

2. Display the page you want to use, and then select one or more objects you want order.
   - If you select a threaded story that spans multiple pages, the entire story gets added to the Articles panel.

   TIMESAVER *When you Shift-click to select objects, InDesign places the objects in the Articles panel in the selected order.*

3. Drag the objects to the Articles panel where you want them to appear. A thick black line appears, indicating the position when you release the mouse.
   - **Create New Article**. You can click the **Create New Article** button on the Articles panel to add the selected element to a new article.
   - **Add to Existing Article**. You can click the **Add Selection to Articles** button on the Articles panel to add the selected element to the selected article in the Articles panel.

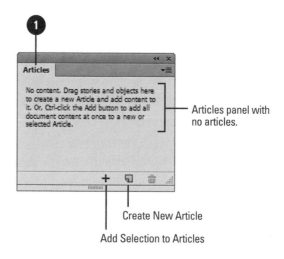

Articles panel with no articles.

Create New Article

Add Selection to Articles

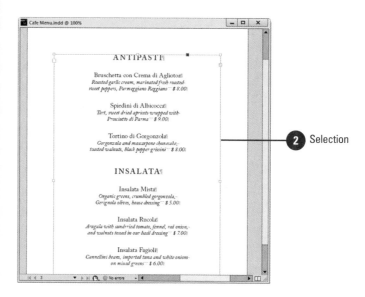

Selection

TIMESAVER *Ctrl-click (Win) or ⌘+click (Mac) the Add Selection to Articles button on the Articles panel to add all page items to an article in the Articles panel.*

④ Enter a name for the article.

⑤ Select the **Include When Exporting** check box, if necessary, to include the article for export.

⑥ Click **OK**.

⑦ To view an item in the Articles panel on the page, click the arrow to expand/collapse content (if necessary), and then double-click the item in the panel.

◆ When you select an item in the page layout, a blue box appears in the Articles panel, so you can quickly locate it.

⑧ To reorder an item in the Articles panel, drag it to another position.

A thick black line appears indicating the location.

⑨ Specify the following options:

◆ **Remove an item or article.** Select the item or article in the Articles panel, and then click the **Delete** button on the panel.

◆ **Rename an article.** Double-click the article in the Articles panel, change the name, and then click **OK**

⑩ To enable or disable an article for export, select or deselect the check box next to it in the Articles panel.

⑪ For an accessible PDF, click the **Options** button, and then click **Use for Reading Order in Tagged PDF** to select it.

⑫ Close the Articles panel.

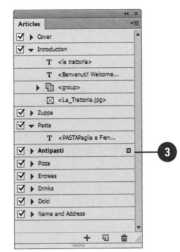

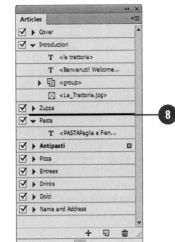

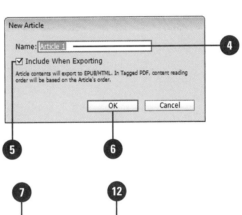

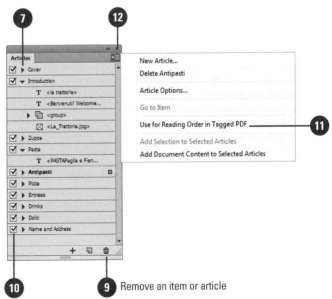

Remove an item or article

Exporting as an Accessible PDF

With InDesign, you can more efficiently create an accessible PDF that people with disabilities can access using a screen reader or assistive device. You can establish content reading order in the Article panel, add alt text to graphics, add tags to paragraph styles, and anchor objects. InDesign automatically creates tags for tables, nested tables, lists, nested lists, footnotes, bookmarks, hyperlinks, and cross-references and translates them directly from InDesign to Acrobat. In order to finalize an accessible PDF, you need to make some changes in Acrobat that you can't do in InDesign. You need to set the document language, remove unnecessary information in a Properties field, and set the tab order to use the order from the Articles panel in InDesign.

Export a Document as an Accessible PDF File

1. Prepare the document for accessibility using the following:

   ◆ **Content Order.** Open the Articles panel, select page items, and then drag them to the panel in the order you want.

   ◆ **Add Alt Text to Graphics.** Select a graphic, click the **Object** menu, click **Object Export Options**, click **Alt Text** tab, and then specify options.

   ◆ **Add Tags to Paragraph Styles.** In Paragraph Styles panel, click the **Options** button, click **Edit All Export Tags**, click **PDF**, and then set tags.

   ◆ **Anchor Objects.** On a graphic frame, drag the blue square to the anchor text point.

   ◆ **Bookmarks, Hyperlinks, and Cross References.** Add items to the document as desired.

2. Click the **File** menu, and then click **Export**.

3. Enter a name, specify a location, select the **Adobe PDF (Interactive)** format, and then click **Save**.

4. Select the **Create Tagged PDF** and **View After Exporting** check boxes. If desired, select the **Use Structure for Tab Order** check box.

5. Click **OK**.

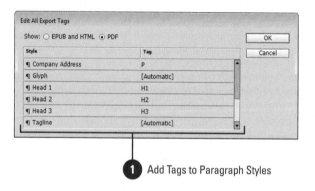

1 Add Tags to Paragraph Styles

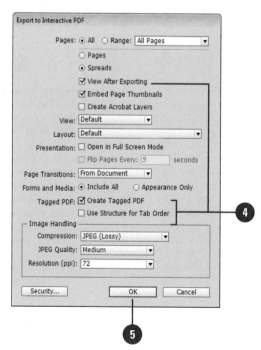

Finish an Accessible PDF in Acrobat X Pro

1. Open the exported Accessible PDF from InDesign in Acrobat.

2. Click the **File** menu, click **Properties**, click the **Advanced** tab, click the **Language** list arrow, and then select a language.

3. Click the **General** tag, and then delete the extra semi-colon and space at the beginning of the Keywords field.

4. Click **OK**.

5. Open the **Page Thumbnails** panel, select all the pages (Ctrl+A or ⌘+A), click the Thumbnails **Options** button, click **Page Properties**, click the **Use Document Structure** option, and then click **OK**.

6. To view and check tags, open the Tags panel, Alt-click (Win) or Option-click (Mac) the expand arrow next to the Tags icon.

   ◆ **Display Selected Tags in Blue.** Click the Tags **Options** button, and then click **Highlight Content**. Click a tag to select it.

   ◆ **Find Tag From Selection.** Select an item on the page, click the Tags **Options** button, and then click **Find Tag From Selection**.

7. Quit Acrobat.

Did You Know?

You can view and use accessible PDFs in different software. When you create an accessible PDF, you can use it in Adobe Acrobat (view and change), Adobe Acrobat Reader (view), or other software, such as screen readers.

For Your Information

Automating Accessible PDF in Acrobat

Instead of manually finalizing the Accessible PDF in Acrobat, you can automate the process with an action. The action is available for free online from the Accessibility page at Adobe.com. Simply search for the file InDesign Accessibility Touchup.sequ, and then download it. Once you have it, click Tools, click Action Wizard, click Edit Actions, click Import, select the file, and then click Open. Click Run and follow the on-screen instructions. The action is now available for use in the Action Wizard panel.

Applying Tags to a PDF

In addition to normal content, such as text, graphics, and links, PDFs also include a structure. The structure is a set of tags that define the content layout, such as the correct reading order, and the meaning of elements, such as figures, lists, and tables. A PDF with well-formed tags may be reflowed to fit different pages or screen widths. The more you tag a PDF, the more control you have over the output. Tagged PDFs work well with screen-readers as well as make the file compliant with Section 508 of the Rehabilitation Act of 1973, which makes web content accessible to people with disabilities. You can use the Object Export Options dialog box to apply tags and actual text, which is a way to apply text (as an image) to graphics elements within tagged PDFs.

Apply Tags to a PDF

1. Select the **Selection** tool on the Tools panel.

2. Select the frame or group that you want to add a tag.

3. Click the **Object** menu, and then click **Object Export Options**.

4. Click the **Tagged PDF** tab.

5. Click the **Apply Tag** list arrow, and then select an option:

   ◆ **From Structure.** Use text as specified in the Structure pane; items marked with XML tags.

   ◆ **Artifact.** Use to tag a Artifact, an element with no meaning.

   ◆ **Based On Object.** Lets InDesign determine the tag; it sets text or graphics to story or figure tag.

6. Click the **Actual Text Source** list arrow, and then select an option:

   ◆ **Custom.** Enter text manually.

   ◆ **From Structure.** Same as above.

   ◆ **From XMP: Title, Description, or Headline.** Use data stored in specified XMP fields.

   ◆ **From Other XMP.** Use data stored in another XMP field.

7. Select another object to apply settings; the dialog box stays open.

8. Click **Done**.

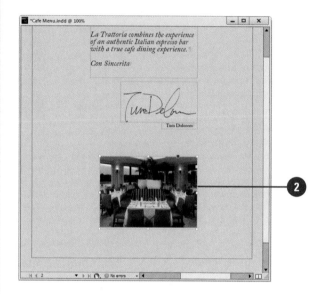

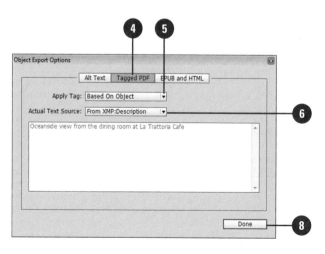

Exporting Tags for EPUB and HTML

In InDesign, the layout of text and objects are based on styles. When you export a document or book to EPUB or HTML, the layout of text and objects are based on HTML and CSS, where you use tags and classes. For exporting control to EPUB or HTML, you can specify and map text and object (**New!**) styles in the InDesign document to tags, such as <p> or <h1> to <h6>, and classes in the EPUB or HTML document. Class names are used to generate style definitions. In addition, you can also set options to Split EPUB or Emit CSS. The Split EPUB option applies a document break after the specified style. This creates a larger number of HTML files in the EPUB package, which can be useful for breaking up long files to increase performance. The Emit CSS option (**New!**) ensures the specified class name is used for the style even if a conflict occurs. It also defines the class name based on the style (**New!**).

Map Styles to Export Tags

1. Select the **Object Styles (New!)**, **Paragraph Styles** or **Character Styles** panel.

   ◆ Click the **Type** menu, and then click **Object Styles**, **Paragraph Styles**, or **Character Styles**.

2. Click the **Options** button, click **Edit All Export Tags**.

3. Click the **EPUB and HTML** option.

4. Select the style you want to map.

5. Select or specify any of the following available options:

   ◆ **Tag.** Click the current setting, click the list arrow, and then select a tag. Default set to [Automatic].

   ◆ **Class.** Specify a class to generate style definitions for tags. You can specify multiple class names (**New!**) separated by one or more spaces.

   ◆ **Split EPUB.** Select to add a document break after the style.

   ◆ **Emit CSS.** Select to use the set class name if a conflict or multiple classes (use first one) occurs (**New!**). The CSS class is defined based on the style.

6. Click **OK**.

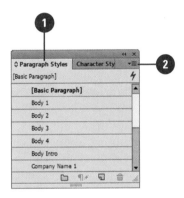

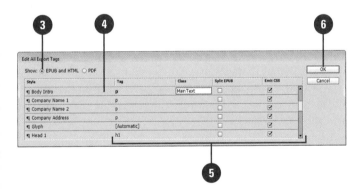

Exporting as an EPUB eBook

An ebook is an electronic book file that displays content in a linear, reflowing format with different sizes of viewing. The EPUB or OEBPS format is one of the most widely supported file formats for ebooks. EPUB is compatible with the Adobe Digital Editions reader software and devices, such as Barnes & Noble Nook, Sony Reader, iRiver, Kobo, and Apple iOS (iPhone, iPod Touch, and iPad). The exception is Amazon Kindle (MOBI), however there is a plug-in available. EPUB is an XHTML-based format that can display text, graphics, and audio/video (Apple iOS only). You can export a document or book as an EPUB with version 2.0.1 (2007 standard) or 3.0 (2011 standard). You can specify book metadata for search engines, a book cover, content ordering and formatting options, image display and conversion settings, and the use (**New!**) of style classes and CSS (Cascading Style Sheets: formatting rules that control page look). See "New Features" on page 543 for conversion details.

Export a Document as an EPUB

1. Click the **File** menu, and then click **Export**.

2. Enter a name, specify a location, select the **EPUB** format, and then click **Save**.

3. Specify **General** options:

    ◆ **Version.** Select an EPUB version: 2.0.1 or 3.0

    ◆ **Cover.** Select a cover option: none, rasterize (bitmap) of first page, or use an existing image.

    ◆ **Navigation.** Select File Name (**New!**) or TOC Style. Select an option: [None], [Default], or a style to create a TOC.

    ◆ **Margins.** Specify a value for each side in pixels.

    ◆ **Content Order.** Select an option to base reading order on the page layout, XML tag structure, or Articles panel.

    ◆ **Place Footnote After Paragraph.** Select to place or deselect to convert to end-notes.

    ◆ **Remove Forced Line Breaks.** Select to remove all soft-returns, Shift+Enter.

    ◆ **Bullets and Numbers.** Select conversion options (**New!**); see details on page 454 in Step 4.

General category

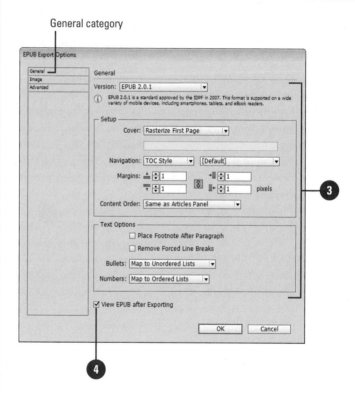

④ To open the file in Adobe Digital Edition Reader, select the **View EPUB after Exporting** check box.

⑤ Click the **Images** category.

⑥ Click the **Copy Images** list arrow, click **Original**, **Optimized**, or **Link to Server Path**, and then select image export options; see details on page 455 in Step 7.

⑦ Click the **Advanced** category.

⑧ Specify the following options:

◆ **Split Document.** Select a split option: **Do Not Split**, **Based on Paragraph Style Export Tags**, or based on a style.

◆ **EPUB Metadata.** Specify options to include metadata, add publisher information (such as a URL), and supply a unique identifier (required for EPUB).

◆ **CSS Options.** Select or deselect **Generate CSS (New!)**; select or deselect **Preserve Local Overrides** to preserve manual formatting or match style definitions to CSS, or **Include Embeddable Fonts**; click **Add Style Sheet** (use external file) or **Add Script** (add JavaScript).

⑨ Click **OK**. If an export warning (**New!**) appears with one or more errors, read it, and then click **OK**.

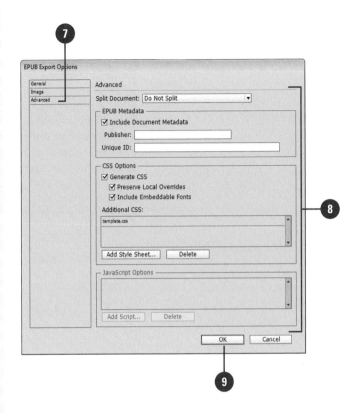

Did You Know?

You can export to Kindle with a plug-in. Amazon has created a plug-in for InDesign CS4 or later that allows you to export to the Kindle format (.mobi & .azw). Go to *www.amazon.com* and search for Kindle Publishing Programs under Kindle Store. Download and install the program. In InDesign, click the File menu, click Export for Kindle, and then follow the instructions.

For Your Information

Looking Inside the ePUB Structure

An ePUB file is a collection of files in a zip file. If you change its extension from .epub to .zip, the file becomes a ZIP file that you can unzip. The most important folder is the OEBPS folder, which contains the ePub content. The OEBPS folder includes the following: content.opf, template.css, .xhtml or .html files, toc.ncx, images folder, and fonts folder. If you want to get into it, you can unzip it on Windows, or use Springy (third-party app) on the Mac. At this point, you can open the OEBPS folder as a site in Adobe Dreamweaver, view the content in Live view, and edit the HTML code to tweak or customize it. When you're done, rezip it or bring it back into Springy.

Exporting as an HTML

If you want to use your document on the web, you can export it as a HTML file. During the export, you can control the output; InDesign uses the names of paragraph, character, object, table, and cell styles to create CSS (Cascading Style Sheets) style classes (**New!**) in HTML. InDesign exports the following: stories, linked and embedded graphics, SWF files, footnotes, text variables (as text), bulleted and numbered lists (**New!**), cross-references, hyperlinks (to text and web pages), and tables along with some formatting. For exported audio and h.264 video, files are enclosed in HTML5 <audio> and <video> tags. There are some elements that don't get exported, such as drawn objects, pasted objects, text converted to outlines, XML tags, books, bookmarks, SING glyphlets, page transitions, index markers, objects on the pasteboard (not selected), and master page items (unless overridden or selected).

Export a Document as an HTML

1. Deselect everything to export the entire document or select the elements you want to export.

2. Click the **File** menu, and then click **Export**.

3. Enter a name, specify a location, select the **HTML** format, and then click **Save**.

4. Specify **General** options:

   ◆ **Export.** Specify an option to export the current selection or entire document.

   ◆ **Content Order.** Select an option to base reading order on the page layout, XML tag structure, or Articles panel.

   ◆ **Bullets.** Select options (**New!**): Map To Unordered List exports to <ul> tag, while Convert To Text exports to <p> tag with bullets.

   ◆ **Numbers.** Select options (**New!**): Map To Ordered List exports to <ol> tag, and Convert To Text exports to <p> tag with paragraph's number.

5. To view HTML file, select the **View HTML after Exporting** check box.

General category

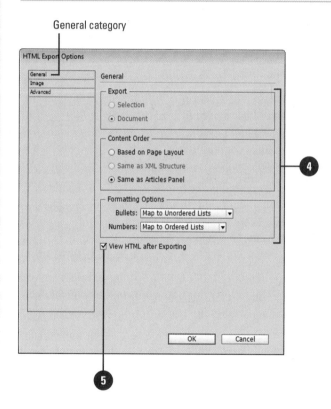

6 Click the **Image** category.

7 Click the **Copy Images** list arrow, and then click **Original**, **Optimized**, or **Link to Server Path**.

◆ **Optimized.** Specify options:

  ◆ **Preserve Appearance from Layout.** Use image attributes from the layout.

  ◆ **Resolution (ppi).** OS is 72 or 96. Mobile is 132 (iPad), 172 (Sony Reader), 150 (ebook) to over 300 (iPhone).

  ◆ **Image Size.** Stay fixed or rescale by percentage relative to the page.

  ◆ **Alignment and Spacing.** Set aligning and padding.

  ◆ **Settings Apply to Anchored Objects.** Apply settings to anchored objects.

  ◆ **Image Conversion.** Select Automatic, GIF, JPEG, or PNG (supports transparency).

  ◆ **GIF and JPEG Options.** See option details on page 456.

  ◆ **Ignore Object Export Settings.** Ignore settings on individual images.

◆ **Link to Server Path.** Enter a path to a local URL and file extension.

8 Click the **Advanced** category.

9 Specify the following options:

◆ **CSS Options.** Select or deselect **Generate CSS** (**New!**); select or deselect **Preserve Local Overrides** to preserve manual formatting or match style definitions to CSS; click **Add Style Sheet** to select a CSS file.

◆ **Add JavaScript.** Click to select a file to run a JavaScript when the HTML page opens.

10 Click **OK**. If an export warning (**New!**) appears with one or more errors, read it, and then click **OK**.

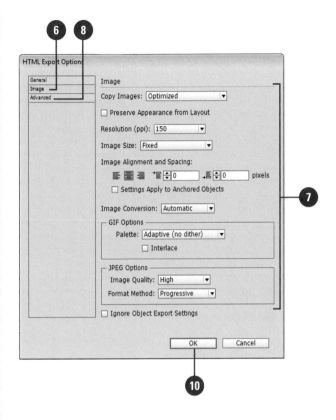

For Your Information

More About EPUB and HTML Export Options

InDesign provides an improved workflow and options for exporting documents to EPUB eBook and HTML files. You can define margins, use article ordering, define image resolution and size, use the PNG file type (supports transparency), specify alignment and spacing settings, insert page breaks, use paragraph styles, export table headers and footers, export sublists as nested lists, support j-language for vertical text and Ruby characters, automatically insert publish date as metadata, include a table of contents in EPUB, and use audio and video tags in HTML.

Setting EPUB and HTML Options

EPUB and HTML options in the Object Export Options dialog box allow you to specify custom image conversion and image alignment and spacing settings for selected objects. The conversion options include size, resolution (ppi), file format, compression quality, and display method. The custom layout options include float left or right (**New!**), alignment and spacing, and whether to insert page breaks. You can also set these options in Object Styles (**New!**); for details, see the topic on page 316. If these options are not set, the EPUB or HTML export settings are used.

Set EPUB and HTML Options

① Select the **Selection** tool on the Tools panel.

② Select the frame or group that you want to set options.

③ Click the **Object** menu, and then click **Object Export Options**.

④ Click the **EPUB and HTML** tab.

⑤ Click the **Custom Rasterization** check box, and then select options:

◆ **Size.** Stay fixed or rescale by percentage relative to the page.

◆ **Format.** GIF, JPEG, or PNG.

◆ **Palette.** Controls colors when optimizing GIF files.

◆ **Resolution.** Specify in pixels per inch (ppi).

◆ **Quality.** High is low compression; Low is high compression.

◆ **Method.** Web display method on the web. Progressive is gradual while download. Baseline is after download is complete.

⑥ Select the **Custom Layout** check box, select **Float Left (New!)**, **Float Right (New!)**, or **Alignment and Spacing**, and then select options:

◆ **Align.** Left, Center, or Right.

◆ **Space Before and After.** Specify top and bottom padding space.

◆ **Insert Page Break.** Select to insert page breaks with images.

⑦ Select another object to apply settings; the dialog box stays open.

⑧ Click **Done**.

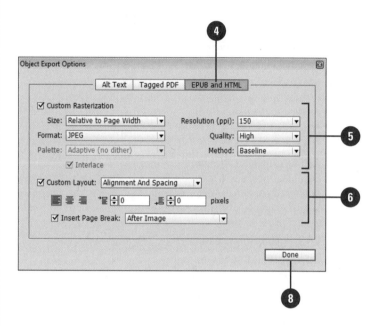

Resolution	
Device	**Resolution (ppi)**
Operating System (OS)	72 or 96
iPad	132
Sony Reader	172
ebooks (general)	150
iPhone	300

Printing and Outputting a Document

Introduction

The Print command is probably the most used of all InDesign's print options. The Print command is a portal to other menus that let you control specific printing functions, such as crop marks and bleeds, output ink, graphics, and color management. Color separations divide artwork into four plates by color, known as process colors. Each plate represents a CMYK (Cyan, Magenta, Yellow, and Black) color. The Separations Preview panel allows you to preview color separations on your screen. If you frequently use custom settings to send an InDesign document to a local printer or commercial printer for printing, you can save time by creating a preset. Before you print your document, it's important to check the Summary category in the Print dialog box. The summary information is good to check if you're having problems printing your job at a commercial printer.

When you print a document with spreads (for example, as a booklet), the pages need to be arranged as imposing pages, also known as printer's spreads. For example, page one of a 4 page project is paired with page four while page two and page three are paired together. You can arrange your document into imposing pages by using the Print Booklet command on the File menu.

Before you print or send your document to a commercial printer or service provider, you can should check your document for errors. Catching errors before you send out a print job can save you time and lower production costs. You can use live preflighting in the Preflight panel to catch errors, such as missing files or fonts, low-resolution images, and overset text. When you're ready to send a document, you can create a package file, which gathers together all the files related to your document, including linked graphics and fonts, to make it easy to deliver.

What You'll Do

Print a Document

Print with Presets

Set General and Setup Print Options

Set Marks and Bleed Options

Set Graphics Options

Preview Color Separations

Set Output Options

Set Trapping Options

Set Advanced Options

Set Color Management Options

Create a Print Summary

Print Spreads in a Booklet

Use Live Preflight

Insert File Information

Create a Package

Use Document Fonts

Printing a Document

The Print command is probably the most used of all InDesign's print options. The Print command is a portal to other menus that let you control specific printing functions, such as crop marks and bleeds, output ink, graphics, and color management. Understand that the options available for the Print command will be partially determined by your default printer. For example, if your default printer uses more than one paper tray, you will see options for selecting a specific tray for the current print job. In spite of the differences, there are some universal options for all print jobs, and these are covered here.

Print a Document

1 Click the **File** menu, and then click **Print**.

TIMESAVER *Ctrl+P (Win) or* ⌘*+P (Mac).*

2 Click the **Print Preset** list arrow, and then select a preset.

3 Click the **Printer** list arrow, and then select an available printer.

4 Click the **PPD** list arrow, and then select a PPD (if available).

- ◆ A PPD (PostScript Printer Description) is a printer driver, a specific file used by commercial and specialty printers to define an output device.

5 Select a print category (**General**, **Setup**, **Marks and Bleed**, **Output**, **Graphics**, **Color Management**, **Advanced**) with your desired settings.

6 Select the options that you want; see other pages in this chapter for option specifics.

7 Click the Preview to display information about the document.

8 When you're finished, click **Print**.

- ◆ If you select a PostScript printer, click **Save**, specify a name and location, and then click **Save**.

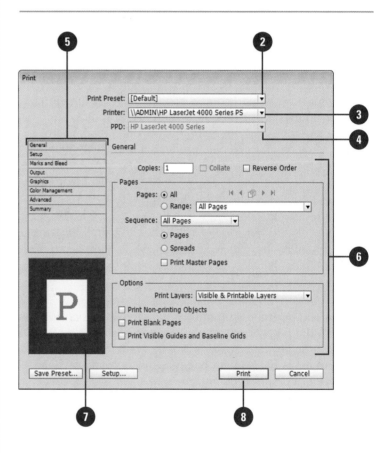

Printing with Presets

If you frequently use custom settings to send an InDesign document to a local printer or commercial printer for printing, you can save time by creating a preset. Adobe programs, including InDesign, Illustrator, Photoshop, and Acrobat, provide built-in presets that you can use in any of the other programs. When you create your own preset, you can also use it in other Adobe programs.

Create a Preset for Printing

1. Click the **File** menu, point to **Print Presets**, and then click **Define**.

2. Perform any of the following:

   ◆ New. Click **New**, specify the options that you want, and then click **OK**.

   ◆ Edit. Select a custom preset (not a predefined one), click **Edit**, change the options, and then click **OK**.

   ◆ Delete. Select a custom preset (not a predefined one), and then click **Delete**.

   ◆ Import. Click **Load**, navigate to the preset file, select it, and then click **Open**.

   ◆ Export. Select a preset, click **Save**, specify a location and name, and then click **Save**.

3. Click **OK**.

Print preset

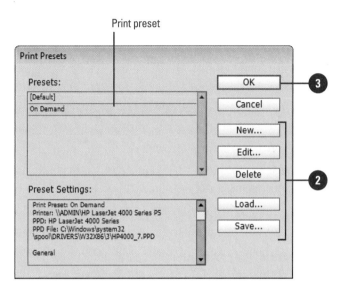

Setting General and Setup Print Options

The General and Setup categories in the Print dialog box allow you to set the page size and orientation (Portrait Up, Portrait Down, Landscape Left, Landscape Right), number of pages to print, and page scaling and tiling options. If you have different pages sizes in your document, you can select same size pages for easy printing. You can also ignore blank pages for printing. In addition, you can specify which layers you want to print: Visible & Printable Layers, Visible Layers, or All Layers.

Set General and Setup Print Options

1. Click the **File** menu, and then click **Print**.

2. Click the **General** category.

3. Select from the various General options:

   ◆ **Copies.** Enter the number of copies you want to print.

   ◆ **Collate.** Select to print pages in collated order.

   ◆ **Reverse Order.** Select to print pages in the reverse order.

   ◆ **All or Range.** Select an option to print all pages or only even or odd pages.

   ◆ **Select Same Size Pages.** Click the buttons to select the first, previous, next, or last range of same-size pages.

   ◆ **Select Matching Size Pages.** Click the Select All Pages Matching Current Page button.

   ◆ **Sequence.** Select an option to print all or a range of pages.

   ◆ **Spreads.** Select to keep spreads together.

   ◆ **Print Master Pages.** Select to print master pages.

   ◆ **Print Layers.** Select an option to print layers: Visible & Printable Layers, Visible Layers, or All Layers.

Buttons to select same size pages

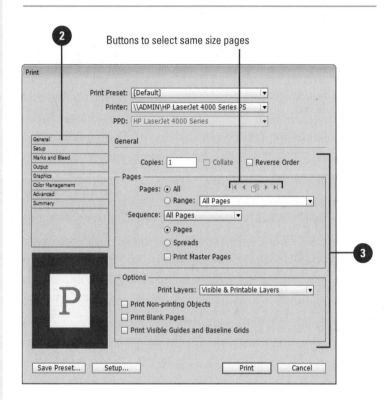

- ◆ **Print Non-printing Objects.** Select to print nonprinting objects.

- ◆ **Print Blank Pages.** Select to print blank pages.

- ◆ **Print Visible Guides and Baseline Grids.** Select to print guides and baseline grids.

4 Click the **Setup** category.

5 Select from the various Setup options:

- ◆ **Page Size.** Select a page size, such as Letter, Legal, 11x17, A3, A4, and Envelope #10.

  For Custom, specify **Width** and **Height** values.

- ◆ **Orientation.** Click an icon to select a page orientation.

- ◆ **Transverse.** Select to rotate the printed document 90 degrees.

- ◆ **Scale.** Select an option: Width to enter width and height percentages or Scale To Fit to scale to fit the page.

- ◆ **Page Position.** Select to position the page during printing (Upper Left, Centered, etc.).

- ◆ **Thumbnails.** Select to print small versions of the pages on a page, and then specify a number per page.

- ◆ **Tile.** Select to print pages that are larger than the page on multiple pages, and then specify a tiling option, and overlap settings.

  Select **Auto** to tile automatically on the page, **Auto Justified** to tile automatically to the right edge of the page, or **Manual** to set the tile position in the document yourself. View the preview to see results.

6 When you're finished, click **Print**.

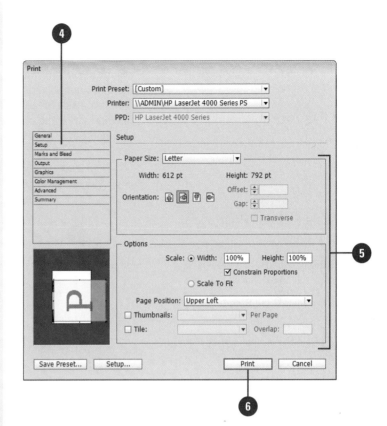

Setting Marks and Bleed Options

The Marks and Bleed category in the Print dialog box allows you to select printer's marks and create a bleed. Printer's marks appear at the edge of the printable page. Commercial printers use printer's marks to trim the paper, registration marks to align printing plates, and color bars to print colors properly. Bleed is the amount of the document that appears outside of the printing area, which includes the bounding box and trim marks. The bleed is useful to give you a margin of error. Having a bleed ensures that ink is printed all the way to the edge of the page so there are no gaps between the page and the edge of the trimmed document page. Your commercial printer can advise you on the best bleed settings based on your print job.

Set Marks and Bleed Print Options

1. Click the **File** menu, and then click **Print**.

2. Click the **Marks and Bleed** category.

3. Select from the various Marks options:

   ◆ **All Printer's Marks.** Select to enable the following check boxes: Crop Marks, Bleed Marks, Registration Marks, Color Bars, and Page Information.

   ◆ **Crop Marks.** Select to add crop marks where the page is trimmed. When you print spreads, fold marks are printed as solid lines.

   ◆ **Bleed Marks.** Select to show bleed marks outside the crop marks for the printer.

   ◆ **Registration Marks.** Select to add small targets for aligning color separations.

   ◆ **Color Bars.** Select to add small color squares with color information for the printer.

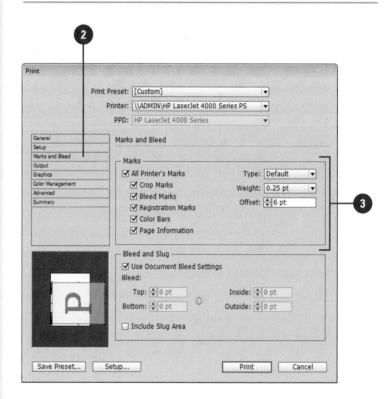

- ◆ **Page Information.** Select to add labels with document information such as: name, page number, time and date, plate color, and screen angle.

- ◆ **Type.** Specify a set of marks for custom use, such as for Japanese printing.

- ◆ **Weight.** Enter an amount for the thickness of the crop marks.

- ◆ **Offset.** Specify an offset value (0-72 points) for the distance between trim marks and the bounding box.

  Enter an offset value to make sure that any printer's marks will not be overlapped by the bleed.

4 Select from the various Bleed and Slug options:

- ◆ **Use Document Bleed Settings.** Select to use bleed settings defined in the New Document dialog box.

- ◆ **Top, Bottom, Inside and Outside.** Enter values to define the bleed area.

  Your commercial printer can advise you on the best bleed settings based on your print job.

- ◆ **Include Slug Area.** Select to include the slug area in the printed file.

5 When you're finished, click **Print**.

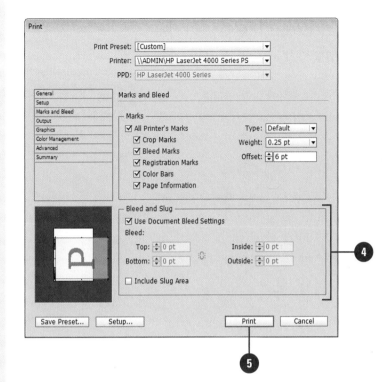

Setting Graphics Options

The Graphics category in the Print dialog box allows you to set printing options for image data, fonts, and PostScript files. When you send graphics to a printer, you can control how much information gets sent to the output device. You can include all image information or an optimized subset. When you include typeface fonts in your document, the fonts that you have used need to be downloaded to your printer. You can choose to download all or a subset of the characters used in your document.

Set Graphics Print Options

1. Click the **File** menu, and then click **Print**.

2. Click the **Graphics** category.

3. Select from the various Graphics options:

   ♦ **Send Data (Images).** Select from the following options:

     ♦ **All.** Sends all image data (slowest option).

     ♦ **Optimized Subsampling.** Sends only the image data needed by the output device.

     ♦ **Proxy.** Sends only a 72-ppi version of the image.

     ♦ **None.** Replaces the image with crosshairs. Useful for proofing text.

   ♦ **Download (Fonts).** Select a download option: None, Subset (only characters, or glyphs, used), or Complete (all fonts used). Select the **Download PPD Fonts** check box to send all fonts to the printer.

   ♦ **PostScript.** Choose from Language Level 2 or Language Level 3. Level 3 delivers the best speed and quality if you are printing to a PostScript 3 device (for PostScript printer).

   ♦ **Data Format.** Choose ASCII or Binary to determine how the data is sent to the printer.

4. When you're finished, click **Print**.

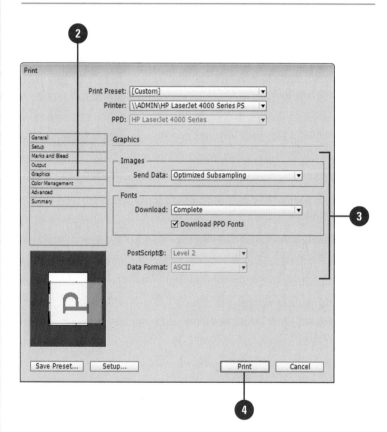

Previewing Color Separations

Color separations divide content into four plates by color, known as process colors. Each plate represents a CMYK (Cyan, Magenta, Yellow, and Black) color. The Separations Preview panel allows you to preview color separations on your screen. As you move your cursor around the page, the panel displays an ink percentage usage for the item next to each plate. In the panel, you can use the Visibility column to show and hide different separation color inks to preview your content on the page. Printers have ink limits, typically 300%. You can use the panel to check ink limits to make sure you have not exceeded them.

Preview Color Separations with the Separations Preview Panel

1 Select the **Separations Preview** panel.

◆ Click the **Window** menu, point to **Output**, and then click **Separations Preview**.

2 Click the **View** list arrow, and then click **Separations**.

3 Do any of the following:

◆ **View Ink Amounts.** Move the cursor around the page to display ink percentages on the panel.

◆ **Hide/Show Separation Ink.** Click the eye icon for each ink you want to hide. Click the eye icon again to make the effects of the ink visible.

◆ **View All Inks.** Click the CMYK eye icon.

4 To make sure inks don't exceed printer limits, click the **View** list arrow, and then click **Ink Limit**.

In Ink Limit view, the document preview changes to a grayscale image. Any areas over the limit appear in red.

5 To turn separations view off, click the **View** list arrow, and then click **Off**.

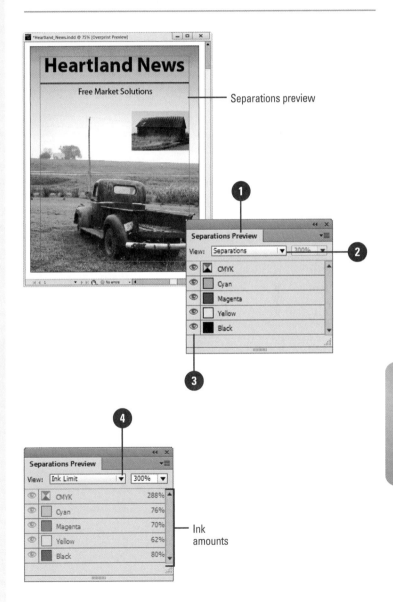

Separations preview

Ink amounts

Setting Output Options

The Output category in the Print dialog box allows you to create and print color composites and separations. A composite prints all colors together on a page, while separations prints each color on a separate page. When you choose to create color separations, you also have the option of selecting which color plates that you want to print. The Inks area allows you to control how inks are separated and printed. If you have spot colors, you can use the Ink Manager to convert them to process inks or map one color to another. Since options vary from job to job, check with your commercial printer for help with specific values for your print job.

Set Output Print Options

① Click the **File** menu, and then click **Print**.

② Click the **Output** category.

Check with your commercial printer for help with specific values for your print job.

③ Click the **Color** list arrow, and then select an option:

- ◆ **Composite Leave Unchanged.** Use current composite settings.

- ◆ **Composite Gray, RGB, or CMYK.** Use to print with no separations using Gray, RGB, or CMYK.

- ◆ **Separations.** Use to create separations.

- ◆ **In-RIP Separations.** Use to have InDesign create a PostScript file that creates the separations in RIP (Raster Image Processing).

④ Select from the various options:

- ◆ **Text as Black.** Select to print colored text as black.

- ◆ **Trapping.** For separations, select an option to compensate for the misregistration of printing plates.

- ◆ **Negative.** Select to create a negative. Useful for creating film separations.

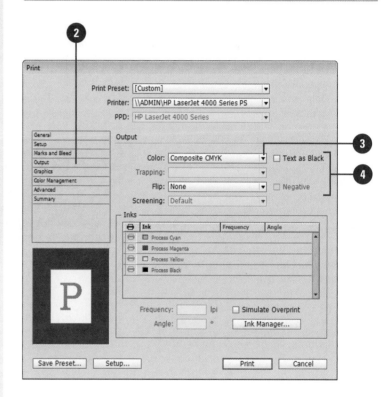

◆ **Flip.** Select an option to flip the orientation of the page.

5 For separations, click the **Screening** list arrow, and then select a frequency and angle.

◆ In the Inks area, select a color, and then enter values for **Frequency** and **Angle**.

Check with your commercial printer for these settings.

6 Select the **Simulate Overprint** check box to simulate overprinting on the screen.

7 To control ink type, density, and sequence for process and spot colors, click **Ink Manager**.

8 When you're finished, click **Print**.

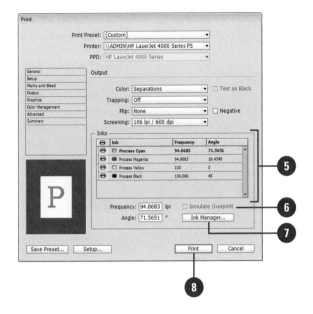

Use the Ink Manager

1 Click the **File** menu, and then click **Print**.

2 Click the **Output** category.

3 Click **Ink Manager**.

4 To convert spot color to process inks, do any of the following:

◆ **Individual.** Click the color icon next to the name to toggle between CMYK or spot color.

◆ **All.** Select the **All Spots to Process** check box.

◆ **Use Standard Lab Values for Spots.** Select to use built-in values.

5 To change ink density, select a color, and then enter an ink value.

6 To map a color to another color, select a color you want to map, click the **Ink Alias** list arrow, and then click a color.

7 Click **OK**.

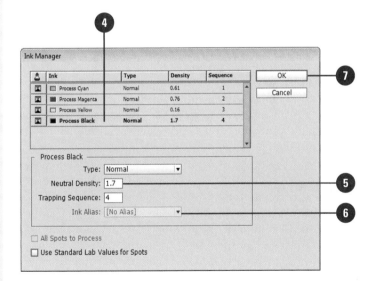

Setting Trapping Options

In the Output section of the Print dialog box, you can set a trapping option to correct for misregistration of printing plates. Trapping slightly expands one object so it overlaps with another to prevent color gaps. Trapping requires inks to overprint each other to prevent knockouts. You can use Adobe InDesign built-in trapping or Adobe In-RIP Trapping to trap text and graphics in your document. Both work well. You can also apply trapping settings to a page or page range by using trap presets in the Trap Presets panel. Since options vary from job to job, check with your commercial printer for help with specific values for your print job.

Create a Trap Preset

1. Select the **Trap Presets** panel.

   ◆ Click the **Window** menu, point to **Output**, and then click **Trap Presets**.

2. Click the **Create New Trap Preset** button on the panel.

3. Double-click the new trap preset.

4. Enter a name for the preset.

5. Specify the trap settings you want for your document.

   Since options vary from job to job, check with your commercial printer for help with specific values for your print job.

6. Click **OK**.

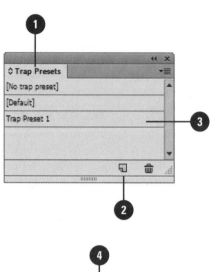

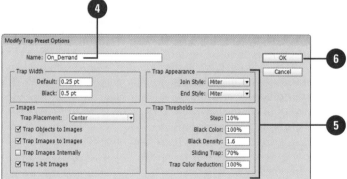

Did You Know?

You can delete a trap preset. Select the Trap Presets panel, select the trap preset, click the Delete Selected Preset button on the panel, and then click Yes.

Assign a Trap Preset to Pages

1. Select the **Trap Presets** panel.

   ◆ Click the **Window** menu, point to **Output**, and then click **Trap Presets**.

2. Click the **Options** menu, and then click **Assign Trap Presets**.

3. Click the **Trap Preset** list arrow, and then select a preset.

4. Click the **All** or **Range** option, and then specify a range as needed.

5. Click **Assign**.

6. Click **Done**.

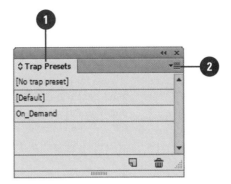

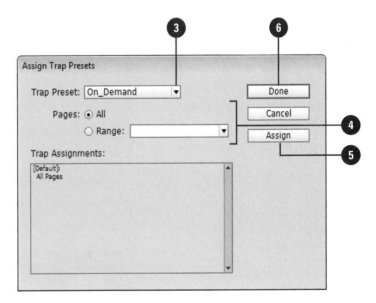

Setting Advanced Options

The Advanced category in the Print dialog box allows you to specify when all characters of the font are embedded, whether to use OPI (Open Prepress Interface) with document graphics, and what resolution to use for transparency flattening. OPI options are used when you send files to Scitex and Kodak prepress systems. OPI uses low-resolution images for layout and high-resolution images for printing. When you use transparency in a document, you need to specify a resolution setting to flatten, or convert, the effects into vector and raster images. You can use the Flattener Preview panel to highlight the areas affected by flattening images. If you have problems printing vector objects to a non-PostScript printer, select the Print as Bitmap option to convert vector objects to bitmap raster images for print purposes.

Set Advanced Print Options

1. Click the **File** menu, and then click **Print**.

2. Click the **Advanced** category.

3. Select from the various Advanced options:

   ◆ **Print as Bitmap.** Select if you have problems printing vector objects to a non-PostScript printer.

   ◆ **OPI.** OPI uses low-resolution images for layout and high-resolution images for printing. Select the check boxes for the image types to which you want to apply OPI.

   ◆ **Transparency Flatter Preset.** Select a resolution to convert transparency into rasterized images.

   ◆ **Ignore Spread Overrides.** Select if you flatten individual spreads using the Pages panel.

4. When you're finished, click **Print**.

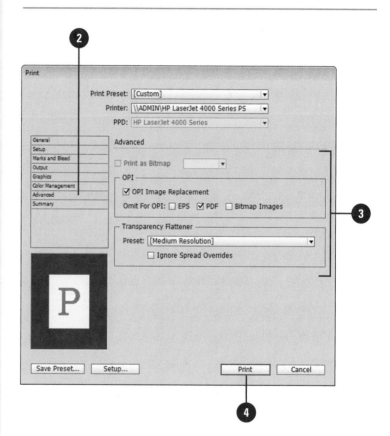

Preview Flattened Artwork

1. Click the **Window** menu, point to **Output**, and then click **Flattener Preview**.

2. Click the **Highlight** list arrow, and then select a highlight option.

3. Click the **Preset** list arrow, and then select a flattener preset.

4. Select the **Auto Refresh Highlight** check box or click **Refresh** to display a fresh preview.

5. Select the **Ignore Spread Overrides** check box to use for the setting in the Preset menu.

6. Click **Apply Settings to Print** to apply settings to Advanced options in the Print dialog box.

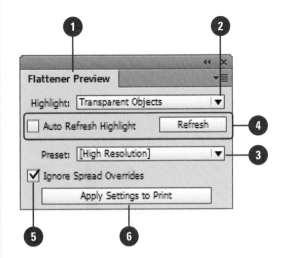

Create a Preset for Transparency Flattener

1. Click the **Edit** menu, and then click **Transparency Flattener Presets**.

2. Perform any of the following:

   ◆ New. Click **New**, specify the options that you want, and then click **OK**.

   ◆ Edit. Select a custom preset (not a predefined one), click **Edit**, change the options, and then click **OK**.

   ◆ Delete. Select a custom preset (not a predefined one), and then click **Delete**.

   ◆ Load. Click **Load**, navigate to the preset file, select it, and then click **Open**.

   ◆ Save. Select a preset, click **Save**, specify a location and name, and then click **Save**.

3. Click **OK**.

Transparency Flattener preset

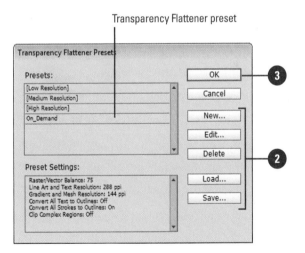

Transparency Flattener preset options

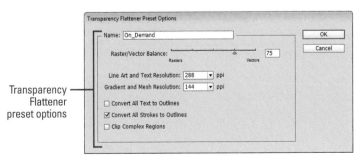

Setting Color Management Options

The Color Management category in the Print dialog box allows you to select a document profile for printing and a printer profile. A document profile and an output profile for a device can be different, so you can select color management options for the best results. In most cases, it's best to use the default options for Color Management unless you've been give specific instructions from a printer to change them.

Set Color Management Print Options

1. Click the **File** menu, and then click **Print**.

2. Click the **Color Management** category.

3. Select from the various Color Management options:

   ◆ **Print Profile.** Select an option: **Document** to use the current Document profile or **Proof** to emulate the profile for the device.

   ◆ **Color Handling.** Select a color option: **Let InDesign Determine Colors** or **Let PostScript Printer Determine Colors**.

   ◆ **Printer Profile.** Select the profile for your output device.

   ◆ **Preserve Color Numbers.** Select to preserve the color mode when a color profile is not available. Deselect to have InDesign convert colors for use on the output device.

   ◆ **Simulate Paper Color.** Select to simulate how colors look on paper for the output device.

4. When you're finished, click **Print**.

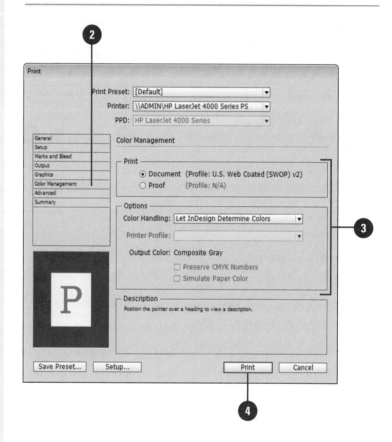

Creating a Print Summary

Before you print your document, it's important to check the Summary category in the Print dialog box. The summary information is good to check if you're having problems printing your job at a commercial printer. You can save the information and send it to the printer to help diagnose the problem.

View and Save Summary Print Options

1. Click the **File** menu, and then click **Print**.

2. Click the **Summary** category.

3. Scroll through the print summary to review your print settings.

4. To print the summary information to a file, click **Save Summary**, enter a name, specify a location, and then click **Save**.

5. When you're finished, click **Print**.

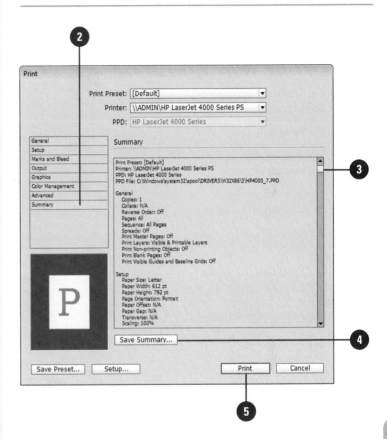

Printing Spreads in a Booklet

When you work on page spreads in a document, two pages appear side by side. However, when you print a document with spreads, the pages need to be arranged as imposing pages, also known as printer's spreads. For example, page one of a four-page project is paired with page four while page two and page three are paired together. You can arrange your document into imposing pages by using the Print Booklet command on the File menu. To use Print Booklet, your document pages need to be the same size.

Print Spreads in a Booklet

1. Click the **File** menu, and then click **Print Booklet**.

2. Click the **Setup** category.

3. Click the **Print Preset** list arrow, and then select a preset.

4. Click the **All** or **Range** option, and then specify a range as needed.

5. Click the **Booklet Type** list arrow, and then select an option:

   ◆ **2-up Saddle Stitch.** Creates two-page, side-by-side printer spreads. You can print on both sides, collate, fold, and staple.

   ◆ **2-up Perfect Bound.** Creates two-page, side-by-side printer spreads and adds blank pages to fit the signature. You can print on both sides, cut, and bind to a cover.

   ◆ **Consecutive.** Creates two-, three-, or four-page panels for a foldout booklet or brochure.

6. Specify the following values (options vary depending on the Booklet type):

   ◆ **Space Between Pages.** Specify the amount of space between pages.

   ◆ **Bleed Between Pages.** Specify the amount of space added around pages.

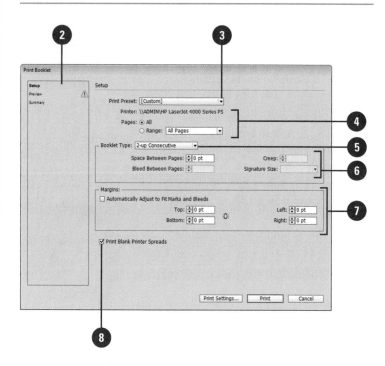

- ◆ **Creep.** Specify the amount of space for the thickness of folded pages.

- ◆ **Signature Size.** Specify the number of pages bound together.

7 Select the **Automatically Adjust to Fit Marks and Bleeds** check box to automatically fit printer's marks and bleeds. Deselect to enter your own values.

8 Select the **Print Blank Printer Spreads** check box to print empty page spreads.

9 Click the **Preview** category.

10 Scroll through the pages to preview the imposed pages.

11 Check the Messages and Warning boxes for information or problems that you should know about or fix before you print.

12 Click the **Summary** category.

13 Scroll through the print summary to review your print settings.

14 To print the summary information to a file, click **Save Summary**, enter a name, specify a location, and then click **Save**.

15 When you're finished, click **Print**.

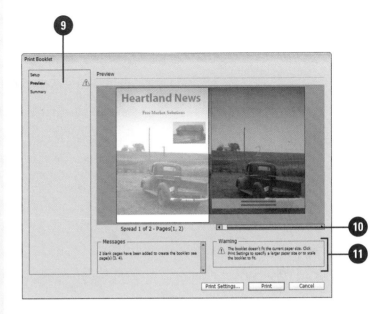

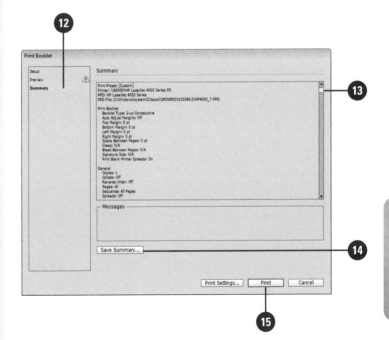

Using Live Preflight

Before you print or send your document to a service provider or for digital publishing, you should check your document for errors. Catching errors before you send out a print or digital job can save you time and lower production costs. Instead of using an external program, you can use live preflighting in the Preflight panel to catch errors, such as missing files or fonts, low-resolution images, and overset text. You can use the built-in Basic or Digital Publishing profile or create one of your own to catch the type of errors you want. If you create your own, you can embed the profile into your document for use on other computers. The Preflight panel lets you navigate to and select the objects that are triggering preflight errors. View contextual tips to help you correct errors directly in layout.

Create a Preflight Profile

1. Select the **Preflight** panel.

   ◆ Click the **Window** menu, point to **Output**, and then click **Preflight**.

   TIMESAVER *Double-click the Preflight icon on the bottom of the document window.*

2. Click the **Options** menu, and then click **Define Profiles**.

3. Click the **New Preflight Profile** button.

4. Enter a name for the profile.

5. Click the triangles to expand settings for each of the categories (**Links**, **Color**, **Images and Objects**, **Text**, and **Document**), and then select the options you want and deselect the ones you don't.

   A shaded check box indicates some items are selected.

6. Click **OK**.

7. Click the **Profile** list arrow, and then select a custom profile.

   ◆ You can also select the **[Basic]** or **Digital Publishing** profile.

8. Click the **Embed** button on the panel.

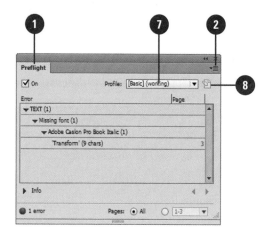

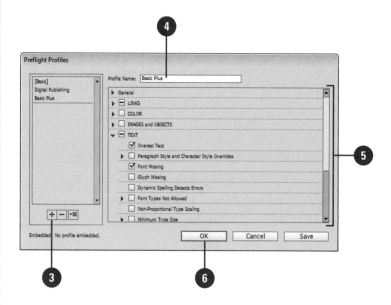

Use the Preflight Panel

1. Select the **Preflight** panel.
   - ◆ Click the **Window** menu, point to **Output**, and then click **Preflight**.

2. Use any of the following to perform a preflight operation:
   - ◆ **Enable/Disable Live Preflight.** Select or deselect the **On** check box on the panel.
   - ◆ **Select a Profile.** Click the **Profile** list arrow, and then select a profile.
   - ◆ **Resolve Errors.** Double-click a row or page number, click the Info arrow to view information about the problem and suggestions for resolving it.
   - ◆ **Limit Number of Rows Per Error.** Click the **Options** menu, point to **Limit Number of Rows Per Error**, and then select a number or **No Limit**.
   - ◆ **Specify Pages.** Specify a page range or use **All** on the panel.
   - ◆ **Set Preflight Options.** Click the **Options** menu, click **Preflight Options**, select a profile, specify options for profile use, including layers, and other objects, and then click **OK**.
   - ◆ **Create a PDF Report.** Click the **Options** menu, click **Save Report**, specify a name and location, and then click **Save**.
   - ◆ **Delete a Profile.** Click the **Options** menu, click **Define Profiles**, select a profile, click the **Delete Preflight Profile** button, and then click **OK**.
   - ◆ **Unembed a Profile.** Click the **Options** menu, click **Define Profiles**, select a profile, click the **Preflight Profile** menu, and then click **Unembed Profile**.

Turn on/off   Preflight profiles

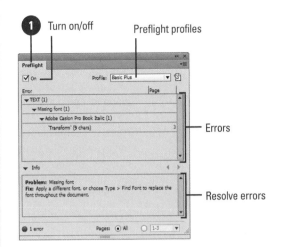

Errors

Resolve errors

Preflight options

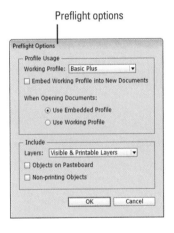

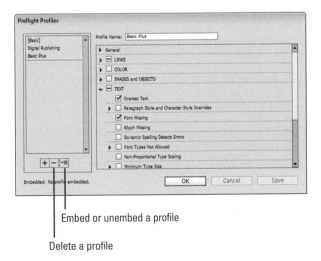

Embed or unembed a profile

Delete a profile

Inserting File Information

When you save a document, you have the ability to save more than just InDesign information. You can save title, author, keywords, copyright, contact, and even image category information. This data is saved with the file as metadata in the XMP format (Extensible Metadata Platform) in InDesign files, and can be recognized and accessed by any application, such as Adobe Bridge, that reads XMP metadata. In addition, if an image is a photograph, you can save data specifying the type of image, where it was shot, the camera used, GPS data, and IPTC (International Press Telecommunications Council) core and extension metadata. You can even get information on shutter speed and f-stop. You can do the same with video and audio data. That information will not only protect your intellectual property, but will supply you with vital statistics on exactly how you created that one-of-a-kind document.

Insert File Information into a Document

1. Open a document.

2. Click the **File** menu, and then click **File Info**.

3. Click the **Description** tab, and then enter information concerning the document title, description of file, author and any copyright information.

4. Click the **IPTC** and **IPTC Extension** tabs to enter information about the image's creator, description and keywords, location taken, date created, copyright, and usage terms.

5. Click the **Camera Data** tab, which reveals information about the camera that took the image.

6. Click the **GPS Data** tab to reveal information about the camera location and subject location.

7. Click the **Video Data** tab or **Audio Data** tab to reveal information about video and audio data, and then enter any custom video and audio data.

8. Click the **Mobile SWF** tab, and then enter the file information for a mobile SWF document.

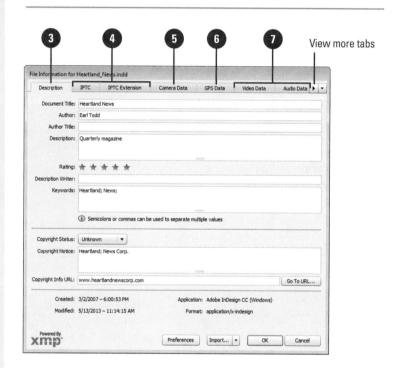

9 Click the **Categories** tab, and then enter category keywords for search purposes.

10 Click the **Origin** tab, and then enter data pertaining to the origin of the image.

11 Click the **DICOM** tab, and then enter data pertaining to the Digital Imaging and Communications in Medicine options (patient name, ID, etc.).

12 Click the **History** tab to view historical information about the active document, such as dates last opened and saved, and a list of image adjustments.

13 Click the **Advanced** tab to view additional information on the active document, such as EXIF, and PDF document properties.

14 Click the **Raw Data** tab to view raw RDF/XML information.

15 Click **OK**.

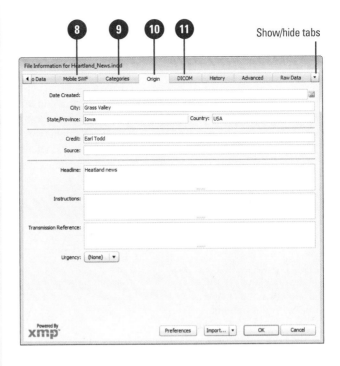

Show/hide tabs

Did You Know?

You can add metadata to files saved in the PSD, PDF, EPS, PNG, GIF, JPEG, and TIFF formats. The information is embedded in the file using XMP (Extensible Metadata Platform). This allows metadata to be exchanged between Adobe applications and across operating systems.

You can use the XMP Software Development Kit to customize the creation, processing, and interchange of metadata. You can also use the XMP kit to add fields to the File Info dialog box. For information on XMP and the XMP SDK, check the Adobe Solutions Network.

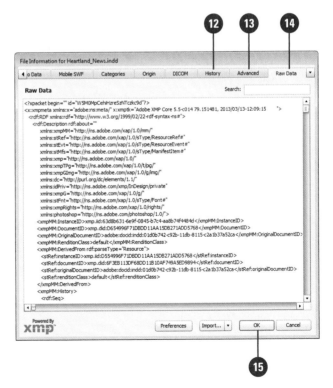

Creating a Package

A package file gathers all the files related to your document or book, including linked graphics and fonts, to make it easy to deliver to a printer or service provider. During the packaging process, you can display any problems, so you can fix them before you continue. When you create a package, you create a folder that contains your document, linked graphics and InDesign content, text files, any fonts (in a Document Fonts subfolder), and a customized report. Externally linked InDesign content will not show missing links, but it may or may not be updated. The report includes information about all the files in the package and any printer instructions required to print your document.

Create a Package

1. Click the **File** menu, and then click **Package**.

    ◆ To package a book or a document in a book, open the book, select a document as desired, click the **Options** menu, and then click **Package Book For Print** or **Package Selected Documents For Print**.

2. Review the summary information for your document.

3. Select the **Show Data For Hidden and Non-Printing Layers** check box to show the data and layers in the Package.

4. Select the **Fonts** category.

5. Select the **Show Problems Only** check box to view any problems with fonts.

    ◆ If there are any problems, select the font, and then click **Find Font** to locate and fix the problem.

6. Select the **Links and Images** category.

7. Select the **Show Problems Only** check box to view any problems with links and images.

    ◆ If there are any problems, select it, and then click **Update** to locate and fix the problem or click **Repair All**.

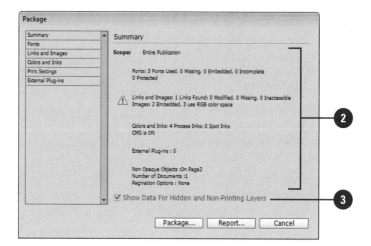

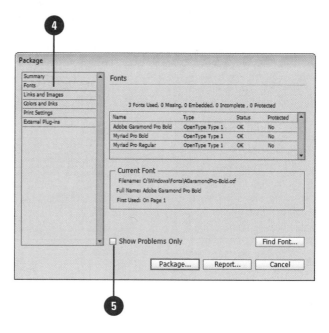

8 Select the **Colors and Inks**, **Print Settings**, and **External Plug-ins** categories, and then view the current settings.

9 To create a report, click **Report**, enter a name, specify a location, and then click **Save**.

10 Click **Package**.

♦ If prompted, click **Save** to save your document.

11 Enter contact information in the Printing Instructions dialog box, and then click **Continue**.

12 Enter a name for the package, and then specify a location.

13 Select/Deselect any of the following check boxes:

♦ **Copy Fonts (Except CJK).** Copies all fonts used in your document, except double-byte fonts, such as Japanese.

♦ **Copy Linked Graphics.** Copies linked images. Embedded images stay with the document.

♦ **Update Graphic Links In Package.** Updates any modified linked graphics.

♦ **Use Document Hyphenation Exceptions Only.** Uses only the hyphenation exceptions from the document.

♦ **Include Fonts and Links From Hidden and Non-Printing Content.** Includes fonts and graphic links from hidden and non-printing items.

♦ **View Report.** Opens a text editor and the package report.

14 Click **Package**.

♦ If a warning alert appears, click **OK**.

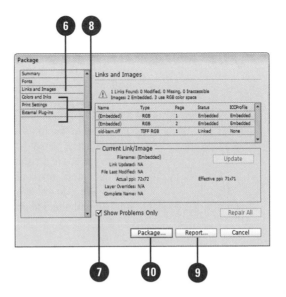

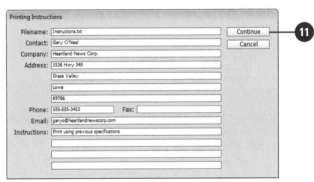

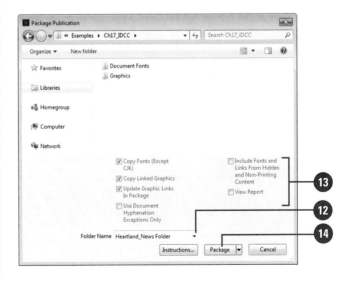

Using Document Fonts

A document font is a font that is only available in an open InDesign document. Document fonts are any fonts in a Document Fonts folder located in the same location as an InDesign document. When the InDesign document is open, the fonts are used and available; they appear in the Font submenu. When you close the document, the fonts are not available. Fonts used by one document are not available to other documents unless the documents are in the same folder. Document fonts are not the same as the fonts available from your operating system. They are separate, yet displayed together in InDesign when the document is open. If there is a system font with the same name as a document font, the document font is used in its place. When you package an InDesign document, you create a Document Fonts folder with any necessary fonts for use with the document on another computer.

Use Document Fonts

1. Create a folder named *Document Fonts* in the same folder as your InDesign document, and then copy the font files into the Document Fonts folder.

2. Open the InDesign document.

   The fonts are now available in the InDesign document.

3. Click the **Type** menu, and then point to **Fonts**. If needed, point to a font family name to display a submenu with individual fonts.

   The fonts in the Document Fonts are available in the document.

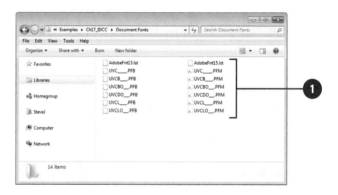

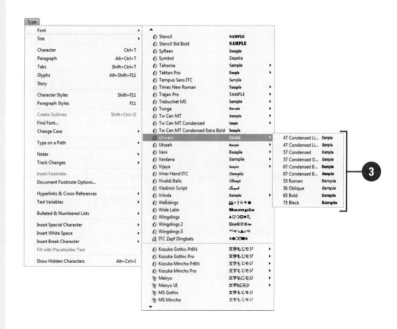

Customizing the Way You Work

Introduction

No description of Adobe InDesign would be complete without that well-known, but little utilized area called Preferences. InDesign preferences serve several purposes. They help customize the program to your particular designing style, and they help you utilize available computer resources to increase the overall performance of the program.

As you use InDesign, you'll come to realize the importance of working with units and rulers. Precision is the name of the game when you are working with graphic designs and text. What about the color of your guides and grids? No big deal, you say. Well, if you've ever tried viewing a blue guide against predominantly blue artwork, you know exactly why guide color is important. By setting your own preferences, such as Display Performance, you can increase speed by up to 20%.

In addition, customizing the program helps make you more comfortable, and studies show that the more comfortable you are as a designer, the better your designs. Plus, being comfortable allows you to work faster, and that means you'll accomplish more in the same amount of time. What does setting up preferences do for you? They make InDesign run faster, you work more efficiently, and your designs are better. That's a pretty good combination. InDesign doesn't give you Preferences to confuse you, but to give you choices, and those choices give you control.

What You'll Do

Set General Preferences

Set Interface Preferences

Set Type Preferences

Set Advanced Type Preferences

Set Composition Preferences

Set Units & Increments Preferences

Set Dictionary Preferences

Set Spelling Preferences

Set Notes Preferences

Work with Appearance of Black Preferences

Set Story Editor Display Preferences

Set File Handling Preferences

Set Clipboard Handling Preferences

Define Shortcut Keys

Customize Menus

Configure Plug-Ins and Extensions

Customize the Control Panel

Setting General Preferences

InDesign's General preferences help you configure some of the more general features of the program. Some of the options include how to implement page numbering, font downloading and embedding, and text scaling. You can also enable or disable the use of JavaScript in your document. Disabling JavaScript can protect your computer from harmful security threats. Enable it only when you know the script is safe. You can also click the Reset All Warning Dialogs to allow warnings for which you previously selected the Don't Show Again check box.

Set General Preferences

1. Click the **Edit** (Win) or **InDesign** (Mac) menu, and then point to **Preferences**.

2. Click **General**.

   TIMESAVER *Ctrl+K (Win) or* ⌃⌘*+K (Mac).*

3. Select the various options you want to use:

   ◆ **Page Numbering View.** Select **Absolute Number** to use the physical placement number of the page or **Section Numbering** to use section numbers.

   ◆ **Font Downloading and Embedding.** Enter a minimum number of glyphs to activate the use subset of fonts.

   ◆ **Prevent Selection of Locked Objects.** Select to prevent the selection of locked objects.

   ◆ **When Scaling.** Select **Apply to Content** to scale text with point size changes or **Adjust Scaling Percentage** to scale text with point size changes, but still display new and old scale.

   ◆ **Reset All Warning Dialogs.** Click to allow warnings for which you previously selected the Don't Show Again check box.

4. Click **OK**.

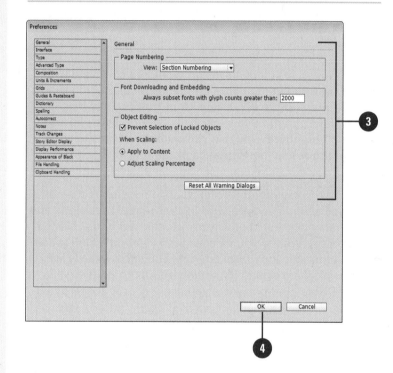

Setting Interface Preferences

Interface preferences give you control over some user interface features. You can change the user interface color from dark to light gray (**New!**). When you place text or graphics or transform objects, you can show the Smart Cursor changes to display information. In addition, you can also set options to automatically collapse icon panels or show hidden panels when you click away, and change how documents open.

Set Interface Preferences

1. Click the **Edit** (Win) or **InDesign** (Mac) menu, and then point to **Preferences**.

2. Click **Interface**.

3. Select the options you want to use:

   ◆ **Color Theme.** Specify a UI color (**New!**) and an option to Match Pasteboard to Theme Color.

   ◆ **Tool Tips.** Select option showing tips when pointing to an element.

   ◆ **Show Thumbnails on Place.** Select to show preview with the loaded cursor when you place.

   ◆ **Show Transformation Values.** Select to show Smart Cursor X/Y values in a gray tag as you work.

   ◆ **Enable Multi-Touch Gestures.** Select to use touch gestures.

   ◆ **Highlight Object Under Selection Tool.** Select to highlight object on mouse over.

   ◆ **Floating Tools Panel.** Specify an option for the Tools panel.

   ◆ **Auto-Collapse Icon Panels.** Select to have an expanded panel icon automatically collapse when you click away.

   ◆ **Auto-Show Hidden Panels.** Select to have a hidden panel icon automatically revealed when you click away.

   ◆ **Open Documents as Tabs.** Select to open in tabbed windows; deselect for floating windows.

   ◆ **Enable Floating Document Window Docking.** Select to allow window docking.

4. Click **OK**.

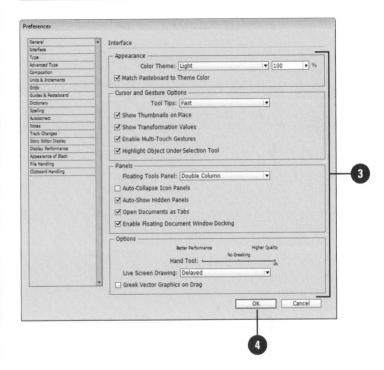

Setting Type Preferences

InDesign is by definition a typesetting application, so it contains some powerful type features. Instead of manually threading text from text frame to text frame, you can let InDesign add or remove pages automatically when you type text or change your text flow. InDesign allows you to set options to customize the way you display, select, and drag-and-drop text. The Type menu lets you quickly access recently used fonts at the top of the font list and see fonts exactly as they will print or display. For designers who use a lot of fonts, this WYSIWYG (What You See Is What You Get) font menu is a big timesaver. You can use Type preferences to help you select the type and font options you want to use.

Set Type Preferences

1. Click the **Edit** (Win) or **InDesign** (Mac) menu, and then point to **Preferences**.

2. Click **Type**.

3. Select the Type options you want to use:

   ◆ **Use Typographer's Quotes.** Select to automatically change straight quotes to curly quotes as you type.

   ◆ **Type Tool Converts Frames to Text Frames.** Select to be able to double-click a frame to change from one of the Selection tools to the Type tool.

   ◆ **Automatically Use Correct Optical Size.** Select to automatically set the correct value for the optical size of multiple master fonts.

   ◆ **Triple Click to Select a Line.** Select to use triple-click to select a line. Deselect to use triple-click to select a paragraph.

   ◆ **Apply Leading to Entire Paragraphs.** Select to apply leading to an entire paragraph.

   ◆ **Adjust Spacing Automatically When Cutting and Pasting Words.** Select to prevent from adding two spaces when pasting text from one location to another.

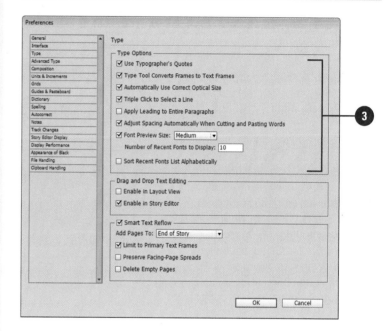

- **Font Preview Size.** Select to enable font preview on the Type menu, and then specify the size of the preview fonts (Medium is default). The Large option takes longer to display.

- **Number of Recent Fonts to Display.** Enter the number of recently used fonts to display in the fonts list.

- **Sort Recent Fonts List Alphabetically.** Select to sort and display recently used fonts in alphabetical order. Deselect to display in order used.

4. Select the Drag and Drop Text Editing options you want to use:

- **Enable in Layout View.** Select to enable drag-and-drop text within frames.

- **Enable in Story Editor.** Select to enable drag-and-drop text within the Story Editor.

5. Select the Smart Text Reflow options you want to use:

- **Smart Text Reflow.** Select to enable Smart Text Reflow.

- **Limit to Primary Text Frames.** Select to limit the use of reflowed text to primary text frames.

- **Preserve Facing-Page Spreads.** Select to preserve facing-page spreads during a reflow of text to new pages.

- **Delete Empty Pages.** Select to delete empty pages when text is removed during a reflow.

6. Click **OK**.

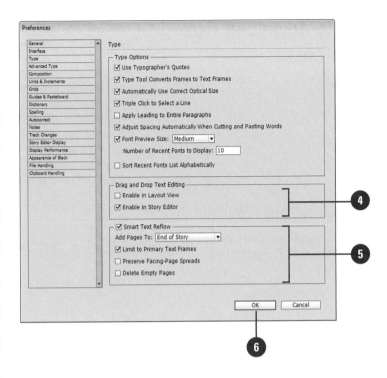

For Your Information

Setting Text to Be Greeked

Greeked text describes text that appears as a gray band when it's too small to display individual characters. Click the Edit (Win) or InDesign (Mac) menu, point to Preferences, click Display Performance, enter a minimum greek level, and then click OK.

Setting Advanced Type Preferences

Advanced Type preferences allow you to control text character setting options for superscript, subscript and small caps, and specify the language you want to use. For superscript, subscript and small caps, you can set size and position values to control the size and position above or below the baseline of characters. Latin typefaces, such as English, French, and Spanish, use a different character structure and paragraph layout than other non-latin languages, such as Japanese, Korean, and Chinese. If you want to use a non-latin language, you need to enable options (**New!**) to use the Windows or Macintosh controls for language input, layout composition (Adobe composer for single-line or paragraph justification), and missing characters (glyphs).

Set Advanced Type Preferences

1. Click the **Edit** (Win) or **InDesign** (Mac) menu, and then point to **Preferences**.

2. Click **Advanced Type**.

3. Select character settings for size and position for **Superscript**, **Subscript**, and **Small Cap** text:

   ◆ **Size.** Enter Size values to control the size of characters.

   ◆ **Position.** Enter Position values to control text position above or below the baseline.

4. Select input method options:

   ◆ **Use Inline Input for Non-Latin Text.** Select to use non-latin text, such as Japanese, Korean, and Chinese.

   ◆ **Use Native Digits When Typing in Arabic Scripts.** Select to use native numbers (**New!**).

5. Select the **Protect While Typing** and/or **Protect When Apply Fonts** check box (**New!**) to protect against missing character glyphs for non-latin text.

6. Select a composer (**New!**): Adobe World-Ready for middle-eastern or mixed languages; Adobe Japanese for asian languages or Adobe general for latin languages.

7. Click **OK**.

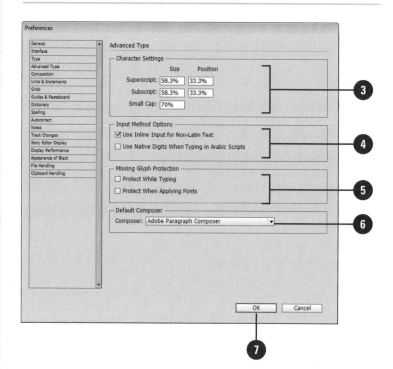

Setting Composition Preferences

Composition preferences enable the program to highlight text when composition or typographic violations and substitutions are made by InDesign based on other settings, and control how text wraps around an object. For example, you can highlight text with tracking or kerning applied or substituted fonts or Open Type characters with glyphs. When you wrap text around an object, you can set options to justify text, and adjust leading, change text position.

Set Composition Preferences

1. Click the **Edit** (Win) or **InDesign** (Mac) menu, and then point to **Preferences**.

2. Click **Composition**.

3. Select the various options you want to use:

   ◆ **Keep Violations.** Select to display lines that violate Keep With settings.

   ◆ **H&J Violations.** Select to highlight text that violate hyphenation or justification settings.

   ◆ **Custom Tracking/Kerning.** Select to highlight text with tracking or kerning applied.

   ◆ **Substituted Fonts.** Select to highlight substituted fonts.

   ◆ **Substituted Glyphs.** Select to highlight substituted Open Type characters with glyphs.

   ◆ **Justify Text Next to an Object.** Select to justify text that is wrapped around an object.

   ◆ **Skip by Leading.** Select to adjust text to the next leading increment that is wrapped around an object.

   ◆ **Text Wrap Only Affects Text Beneath.** Select to wrap text around an object only below the object.

4. Click **OK**.

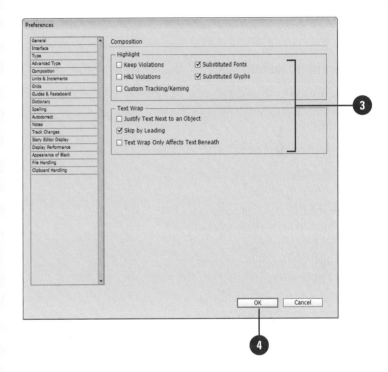

Setting Units & Increments Preferences

Units & Increments preferences allow you to set ruler measurement units, text size and stroke measurement units, the number of points per inch, and the amount that keyboard shortcuts change text. When you use a ruler in a document, InDesign uses the settings in the Ruler Units section to display the ruler with the measurement system and origin you want. You can also set the number of points per inch. Typically this is set to PostScript (72 pts/inch). This is the recommended setting unless a commercial printer asks you to change it. When you change text, such as size/leading, baseline shift, or kerning/tracking using keyboard shortcuts, you can specify the amounts you want to apply for each keystroke.

Set Ruler Units Preferences

1 Click the **Edit** (Win) or **InDesign** (Mac) menu, and then point to **Preferences**.

2 Click **Units & Increments**.

3 Click the **Origin** list arrow, and then select an option:

◆ **Spread.** Displays rulers for two pages at a time, as in a book or magazine.

◆ **Page.** Displays rulers for one page at a time.

◆ **Spine.** Displays rulers for the area where two page spreads are bound together.

4 Click the **Horizontal** and **Vertical** list arrows, and then select a measurement option.

◆ If you selected **Custom**, enter the number of points for each unit on the ruler.

5 Click the **Stroke** list arrow, and then select a measurement option.

6 To set an exact number for points per inch, click the **Points/Inch** list arrow, and then select an option.

7 Click **OK**.

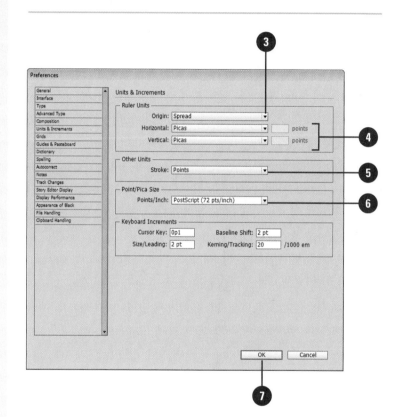

Set Keyboard Increments Preferences

1. Click the **Edit** (Win) or **InDesign** (Mac) menu, and then point to **Preferences**.

2. Click **Units & Increments**.

3. Enter the Keyboard Increments values you want to use:

   ◆ **Cursor Key.** Enter a value to move objects with the arrows keys.

   ◆ **Size/Leading.** Enter a default value to control type size and leading.

   ◆ **Baseline Shift.** Enter a default value to control text baseline shift.

   ◆ **Kerning/Tracking.** Enter a default value to control text kerning and tracking.

4. Click **OK**.

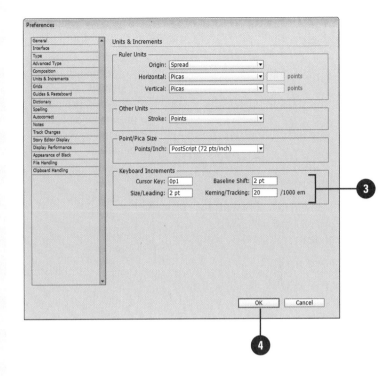

Setting Dictionary Preferences

InDesign uses open-source dictionaries, including Proximity, HunSpell, or Winsoft, or the user dictionary, for most languages to verify spelling and to hyphenate words. You can find HunSpell dictionaries at Adobe.com. Dictionary preferences allow you to specify and use different languages and dictionaries for text in your documents and set options to avoid flagging correctly spelled words as unrecognized words. Many words are flagged as misspelled because of hyphenation. You can set options for hyphenation exceptions to reduce the annoyance. If you work with a unique set of words for your profession, you can create a new dictionary, which you can share with others.

Set Dictionary Preferences

1. Click the **Edit** (Win) or **InDesign** (Mac) menu, and then point to **Preferences**.

2. Click **Dictionary**.

3. Click the **Language** list arrow, and then select a language for the dictionary.

4. Use any of the following to work with User Dictionaries:

   - **Relink User Dictionary.** Relinks an existing dictionary that has been moved to another folder.

   - **New User Dictionary.** Creates a new user dictionary.

   - **Add User Dictionary.** Adds an existing user dictionary for use in your documents.

   - **Remove User Dictionary.** Removes a user dictionary from the list. The default dictionary cannot be deleted.

5. Select the various options you want to use:

   - **Hyphenation.** Select an installed open-source dictionary option for hyphenation: HunSpell, Proximity, or WinSoft, or User Dictionary Only.

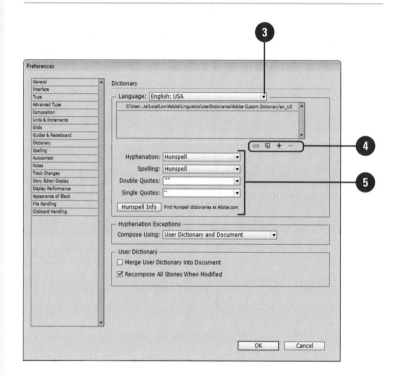

- **Spelling.** Select an installed open-source dictionary option for spelling: HunSpell, Proximity, or WinSoft, or User Dictionary Only.

- **Double Quotes.** Specify a default style for double quotation marks.

- **Single Quotes.** Specify a default style for single quotation marks.

- **Hunspell Info.** Click to find Hunspell dictionaries at Adobe.com; Internet connection required.

6 Click the **Compose Using** list arrow, and then select an option to apply hyphenation exceptions:

- **User Dictionary.** Uses only the hyphenation exceptions set by editing the dictionary.

- **Document.** Uses the hyphenation exceptions list in the document.

- **User Dictionary and Document.** Merges the hyphenation exceptions in the user dictionary and document.

7 Select the User Dictionary options you want to use:

- **Merge User Dictionary into Document.** Select to merge the hyphenation exceptions in the document with the user dictionary.

- **Recompose All Stories When Modified.** Select to apply the new hyphenation exceptions in the user dictionary or any added or deleted dictionary words to all stories in the document.

8 Click **OK**.

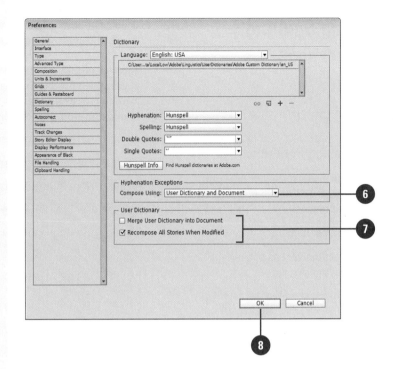

Setting Spelling Preferences

Spelling preferences allow you to set options to control what types of words and sentences get flagged as unrecognized, misspelled, repeated, or incorrectly capitalized in the spelling checker, and enable and set options for dynamic spelling. Dynamic spelling highlights errors in your document as they happen. You can specify underline colors for the different types of errors that appear, such as misspelled words, repeated words, and uncapitalized word or sentences.

Set Spelling Preferences

1. Click the **Edit** (Win) or **InDesign** (Mac) menu, and then point to **Preferences**.

2. Click **Spelling**.

3. Select the various options you want to use:

   ◆ **Misspelled Words.** Select to find and flag unrecognized words in the spelling dictionary.

   ◆ **Repeated Words.** Select to find and flag repeated words next to each other in a document. For example, "The the Spelling preferences dialog box ..."

   ◆ **Uncapitalized Words.** Select to find and flag uncapitalized proper nouns in the spelling dictionary (for example, proper name, such as "Steve").

   ◆ **Uncapitalized Sentences.** Select to find and flag uncapitalized words in the spelling dictionary that begin sentences.

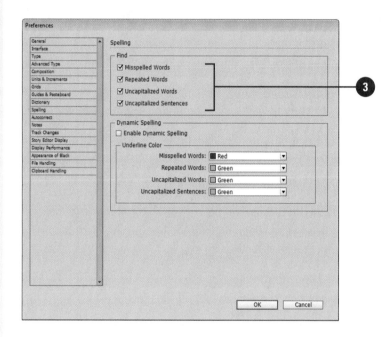

④ Select the Dynamic Spelling options you want to use:

◆ **Enable Dynamic Spelling.** Select to enable dynamic spelling, which highlights errors in your document as they occur.

◆ **Misspelled Words.** Select a color to highlight unrecognized words in the spelling dictionary.

◆ **Repeated Words.** Select a color to highlight repeated words next to each other in a document. For example, "The the Spelling preferences dialog box ..."

◆ **Uncapitalized Words.** Select a color to highlight uncapitalized proper words in the spelling dictionary (for example, proper name, such as "Steve").

◆ **Uncapitalized Sentences.** Select a color to highlight uncapitalized words in the spelling dictionary that begin sentences.

⑤ Click **OK**.

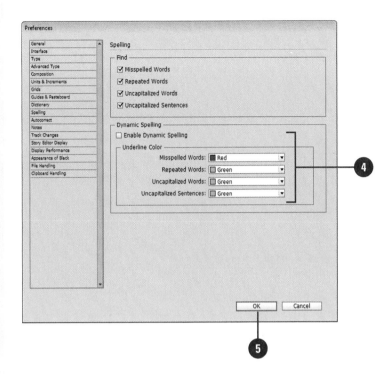

Setting Notes Preferences

When you work with more than one person on the same document, it's important to communicate changes and other information with each other. Notes are a great way to communicate with others and keep a record of it along with the document. Notes preferences allow you to select a user note color to make it easier to identify who wrote notes, show or hide note tooltips, and specify whether to include Notes text when you check spelling or use the Find/Change command.

Set Notes Preferences

1. Click the **Edit** (Win) or **InDesign** (Mac) menu, and then point to **Preferences**.

2. Click **Notes**.

3. Select the various options you want to use:

   ◆ **Note Color.** Specify a color for user notes.

   ◆ **Show Note Tooltips.** Select to display the text for a note when you point to it.

   ◆ **Include Note Content When Checking Spelling.** Select to check spelling for text in notes.

   ◆ **Include Note Content in Find/Change Operations.** Select to include text from notes in the Find/Change command on the Edit menu.

   ◆ **Inline Background Color.** Specify a background color for notes in the Story Editor.

4. Click **OK**.

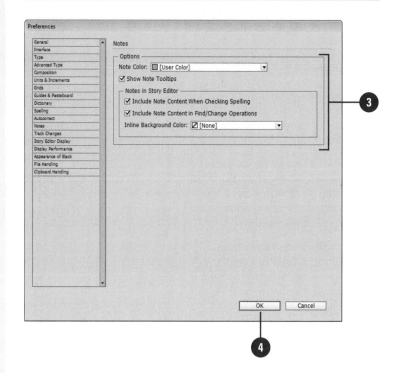

Working with Appearance of Black Preferences

If a printer uses a combination of CMYK inks instead of the actual 100K black tone to create a rich black look, you can set options in the Appearance of Black preferences to specify how you want to create the appearance of black in your documents. There are two available options to determine the appearance of black in your document: one for On Screen and another one for Printing/Exporting. Each of the options allows you to specify how you want to work with the appearance of black (true black or rich black) in your documents.

Work with Appearance of Black Preferences

1. Click the **Edit** (Win) or **InDesign** (Mac) menu, and then point to **Preferences**.

2. Click **Appearance of Black**.

3. Select from the following Appearance of Black options:

   ◆ On Screen. Select **Display All Blacks Accurately** to display blacks based on actual CMYK color values or select **Display All Blacks as Rich Black** to display all blacks as rich blacks (a mix of CMYK values).

   ◆ Printing / Exporting. Select **Output All Blacks Accurately** to print blacks using actual CMYK color values on RGB and grayscale devices, or select **Output All Blacks as Rich Black** to print blacks as rich blacks (a mix of CMYK values) on RGB devices.

4. Select the **Overprint [Black] Swatch at 100%** check box to improve printing or saving separations for objects that use the [Black] (100K) swatch. This applies to PostScript and PDF output. Deselect to knock out objects below.

5. Click **OK**.

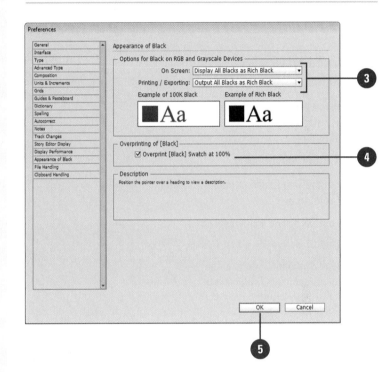

Setting Story Editor Display Preferences

The Story Editor is a separate window that only displays the text in your document. This is helpful when you want to focus just on the text and not on any of the other elements in your document. Story Editor Display preferences allow you to set text and background display options for the Story Editor window. You can specify the display font, font size, line spacing, text color, background or theme, and cursor or insertion point, style. A theme is a preset background and text color. If you want to display smoother text, you can enable the anti-aliasing option and select the type of anti-aliasing that best works for you. If the insertion point cursor is hard to see in the Story Editor, you can select cursor options to make it easier to see.

Set Story Editor Display Preferences

1 Click the **Edit** (Win) or **InDesign** (Mac) menu, and then point to **Preferences**.

2 Click **Story Editor Display**.

3 Select the Text Display Options you want to use:

- ◆ **Font.** Specify a font typeface.

- ◆ **Font Size.** Specify a font size.

- ◆ **Line Spacing.** Specify a line spacing option: Singlespace, 150% space, Doublespace, or Triplespace.

- ◆ **Text Color.** Specify a text color.

- ◆ **Background.** Specify a background color.

- ◆ **Theme.** Specify a preset font color and background: Ink on Paper, Amber Monochrome, Classic System, or Terminal.

4 Select the **Enable Anti-aliasing** check box to soften the edges of text.

5 If you selected the Enable Anti-aliasing check box, click the **Type** list arrow, and then select one of the following options:

- ◆ **Default.** Uses normal anti-aliasing.

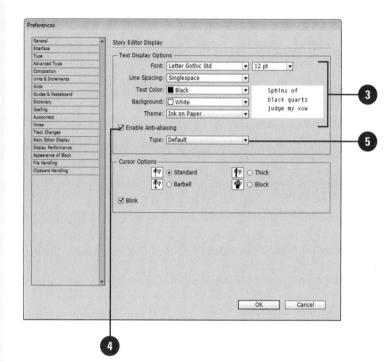

- ◆ **LCD Optimized.** Optimizes the display for light colored backgrounds with black text.

- ◆ **Soft.** Creates a softer look than the default setting.

⑥ Select the Cursor Options you want to use:

- ◆ **Cursor.** Select a cursor display type: Standard (default), Barbell, Thick, or Block.

- ◆ **Blink.** Select to have the cursor blink on and off within the text.

⑦ Click **OK**.

Did You Know?

You can select or deselect anti-aliasing for display performance. Click the Edit (Win) or InDesign (Mac) menu, point to Preferences, click Display Performance, select the Enable Anti-aliasing check box, and then click OK.

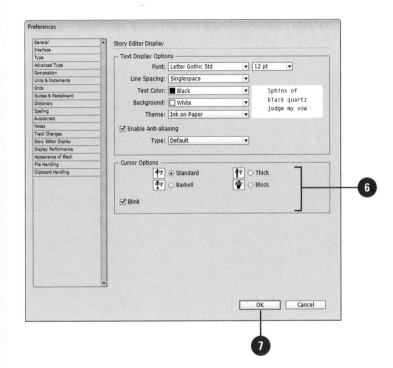

Setting File Handling Preferences

File Handling preferences allow you to specify a document recovery data folder, create one or more preview thumbnails with saved documents, control the location of imported snippets when you drag them into a document, and control how graphic links are maintained and updated. You can also specify the number of files you want to display in the Recent Items list on the Welcome Screen or the Open Recent submenu on the File menu.

Set File Handling Preferences

1. Click the **Edit** (Win) or **InDesign** (Mac) menu, and then point to **Preferences**.

2. Click **File Handling**.

3. To specify a document recovery data folder, click **Browse** (Win) or **Choose** (Mac), navigate to the folder, and then click **Select**.

4. Select the Saving InDesign Files options you want to use:

   ◆ **Number of Recent Items to Display.** Specify the number of files you want to display in the Recent Items list on the Welcome Screen or on the Open Recent submenu on the File menu.

   ◆ **Always Save Preview Images with Documents.** Select to save a preview image of the InDesign document along with the document for preview purposes in Open dialog boxes and other thumbnails.

     ◆ Click the **Pages** list arrow, and then select the number of pages you want to save: First Page, First 2 Pages, First 5 Pages, First 10 Pages, or All Pages.

     ◆ Click the **Preview Size** list arrow, and then select a thumbnail size.

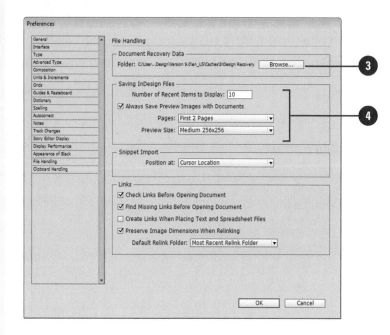

5 Click the **Snippet Import** list arrow, and then select the option you want to use when you drag a snippet onto a page:

◆ **Original Location.** Places the snippet at its original location.

◆ **Cursor Location.** Places the snippet at the current cursor location instead of the original location.

6 Select the Links options you want to use:

◆ **Check Links Before Opening Document.** Select to check graphic links before opening a document.

◆ **Find Missing Links Before Opening Document.** Select to prompt you to locate missing linked graphics before opening a document.

◆ **Create Links When Placing Text and Spreadsheet Files.** Select to create links to styles from original text and spreadsheet files to your new document.

◆ **Preserve Image Dimensions When Relinking.** Select to maintain graphic size when relinking the file.

7 Click **OK**.

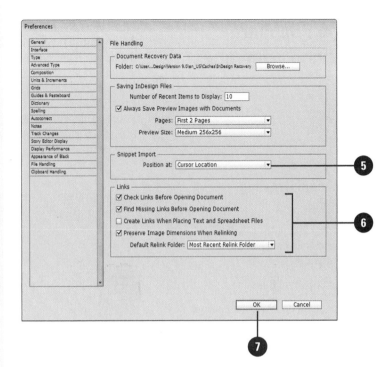

Setting Clipboard Handling Preferences

When you copy and paste information into an InDesign document, the information is temporarily stored on the Clipboard until something else replaces it. Copying and pasting information from other programs is an important part of creating an InDesign document, so InDesign allows you to set Clipboard preferences. Clipboard preferences allow you to specify how you want information to be pasted into a document. For example, you can have graphics or data pasted into a document as a PDF file, or paste text and tables from other programs with or without formatting.

Set Clipboard Handling Preferences

1. Click the **Edit** (Win) or **InDesign** (Mac) menu, and then point to **Preferences**.

2. Click **Clipboard Handling**.

3. Select the Clipboard options you want to use:

   ◆ **Prefer PDF When Pasting.** Select to paste graphics as independent PDF files.

   ◆ **Copy PDF to Clipboard.** Select to copy data as PDF files.

   ◆ **Preserve PDF Data at Quit.** Select to maintain copied PDF information on the Clipboard when you exit InDesign.

4. Click the **All Information or Text Only** option to either maintain formatting for all imported information or remove formatting for imported plain text.

5. Click **OK**.

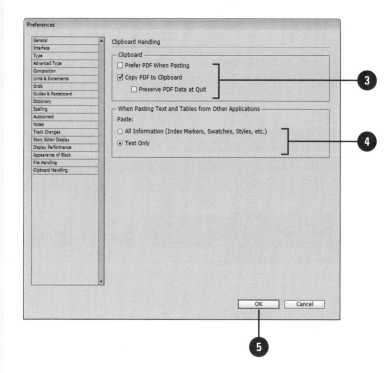

Defining Shortcut Keys

A wise man once wrote "time is money," and InDesign is a program that can consume a lot of time. That's why the InDesign application uses keyboard shortcuts. **Keyboard Shortcuts**, as their name implies, let you perform tasks in a shorter period of time. For example, if you want to open a new document in InDesign, you can click the File menu, and then click New, or you can abandon the mouse and press Ctrl+N (Win) or ⌘+N (Mac) to use shortcut keys. Using shortcut keys reduces the use of the mouse and speeds up operations. InDesign raises the bar by not only giving you hundreds of possible shortcut keys, but also actually allowing you to define your own shortcuts. In fact, you can select options to create shortcuts for menus, panels, tools, and object editing, such as scaling and sizing objects. In addition to adding shortcuts, you can delete any of them you don't want and even print out a summary of shortcuts defined in InDesign.

Create or Edit a Keyboard Shortcut

1. Click the **Edit** menu, and then click **Keyboard Shortcuts**.

2. Click the **Set** list arrow, and then select a set.

3. Click the **Product Area** list arrow, and then select the area that contains the command for which you want to create or edit a shortcut.

4. Select an item from the Commands list.

5. Use the keyboard to create or change the shortcut. For example, press Ctrl+N (Win) or ⌘+N (Mac), and then click **Assign**.

6. Click **OK**.

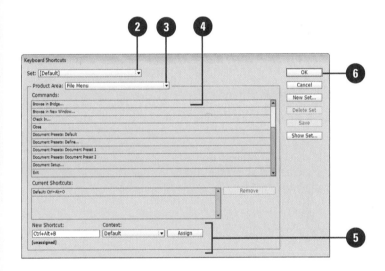

Did You Know?

You can print out a list of keyboard shortcuts. Click the Edit menu, click Keyboard Shortcuts, select a set, click Show Set to display the shortcuts in Notepad (Win) or TextEdit (Mac), and then print the text file.

For Your Information

Working with Keyboard Shortcuts Sets

A set is a collection of keyboard shortcuts, such as Shortcuts for PageMaker 7.0 and Shortcuts for QuarkXPress 4.0. You can create your own set or modify an existing one. Click the Edit menu, click Keyboard Shortcuts, and then use the appropriate buttons, such as Save (Shortcut Set), Delete Set (Shortcut Set), Remove (remove shortcut), or New Set (create Shortcut Set) to perform the tasks you want.

Customizing Menus

InDesign's pull-down menus actually contain hundreds of options (yes, I did say hundreds). If you find navigating through menus a hassle, then Adobe has the answer to your problem with a customizable user interface. In InDesign, you have the ability to choose what menu items appear on the pull-down menus and you can even colorize certain menu items for easier visibility.

Customize Menus

1. Click the **Edit** menu, and then click **Menus**.

2. Click the **Set** list arrow, and then select a listing of modified User Interfaces (if available) or customize the InDesign Defaults set to make your own.

3. To create a new set based on the current active set, click **Save As**, enter a name, and then click **Save**.

4. Click the **Category** list arrow, and then click **Application Menus** or **Context & Panel Menus** with the items you want to modify.

5. Click an arrow (left column) to expand the menu that contains the command you want to modify.

6. Click the **Visibility** icon associated with a command to show or hide the command.

7. Click the **Color** list arrow, and select a color for the selected command.

8. Click **Save** to save the new customized User Interface.

9. Click **OK**.

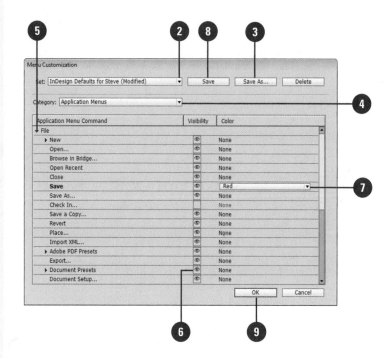

Configuring Plug-In and Extensions

Plug-ins are external programs, also known as extensions, that provide additional functionality for the program. InDesign uses plug-ins to perform standard operations in the program. If you want to add more functionality, you can download and install a plug-in. InDesign uses Adobe Extension Manager CC to help you work with plug-ins and extensions for InDesign and other Adobe programs. Extension Manager is available from the Help menu in InDesign. You can use Extension Manager or the Adobe Exchange panel (**New!**)—available on the Extensions submenu on the Window menu—to access the Adobe Exchange site, where you can locate, research, and download many different types of extensions. Some are free and some are not. With Extension Manager, you can search and filter, enable, disable, remove, and install—for all users or only the current user—extensions using the ZXP file format (still compatible with MXP). ZXP is an Adobe Zip Format Extension Package file. Extension Manager can recognize dependency between different extensions and employs the information when using them.

Work with Extension Manager

① Click the **Help** (Win) or **InDesign** (Mac) menu, and then click **Manage Extensions**.

② To locate a plug-in or extension, click **Exchange** to access the Exchange web site, download an extension, and then save it.

③ To install an extension, click **Install**, locate and select the extension (.zxp or .mxp), and then click **Open**.

④ Perform any of the following:

   ◆ Search. Select a filter from the down arrow, and then enter search name.

   ◆ Extension Set. Click the down arrow to select a set.

   ◆ Sort. Click a column heading.

   ◆ Enable or Disable. Select or deselect the **Enabled** check box next to the extension.

   ◆ Remove. Select the extension, and then click **Remove.**

⑤ When you're done, click the **Close** button.

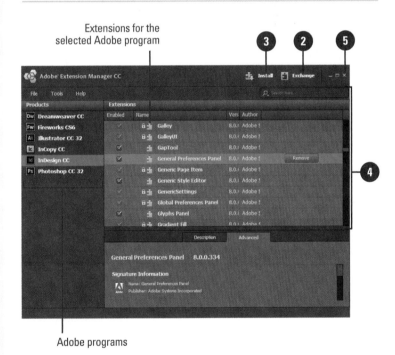

Extensions for the selected Adobe program

Adobe programs

Customizing the Control Panel

The Control panel appears at the top of the document window. The Control panel displays the options for the currently selected tool. However, if you want to display additional tools, you can use the Customize Control Panel dialog box to select the tools you want or remove the ones you don't. If you prefer the Control panel in a different location, you can select options on the Control Panel menu (located on the far right-side of the panel).

Customize the Control Panel

1. Click the **Control Panel** menu, and then click **Customize**.

2. Click the triangle to expand the settings category.

3. Select or deselect the check boxes with the options you want and don't want on the Control panel.

4. Click **OK**.

5. To change the position of the Control panel, click the **Control Panel** menu, and then select one of the following:

    ◆ **Dock at Top.** Docks the Control panel at the top of the document window.

    ◆ **Dock at Bottom.** Docks the Control panel at the bottom of the document window.

    ◆ **Float.** Undocks the Control panel into a floating window.

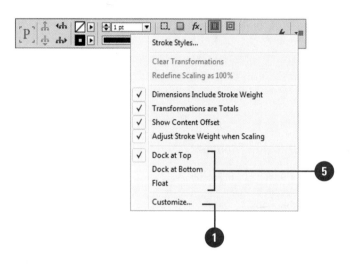

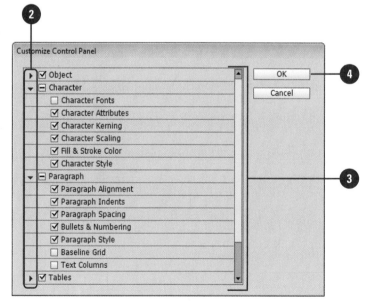

Collaborating with Others

Introduction

InDesign allows you to collaborate with others using several different program features. You can add notes to a document to make comments, track changes to review document content or text, or use Adobe InCopy to manage content development.

When you work with more than one person on a document, it's important to communicate changes and other information with each other. Notes are a great way to communicate and record the notes along with the document. With the Notes panel, you can create and manage notes in a document for others to read and respond.

With Track Changes, you can manage and view the changes made to text in your document. With the Track Changes panel (InDesign) or the Track Changes toolbar (InCopy), you can turn Track Changes on and off in the current story or all stories, and show, hide, accept and reject changes in your document.

Adobe InCopy is a stand-alone writing and editing program that allows you to work seamlessly with Adobe InDesign. The integration with InCopy allows InDesign users to select text and graphics in a document, and then assign the content to InCopy users for writing and editing. Exporting content from InDesign allows you to make content available to InCopy users to check out and change while still maintaining a link back to the original document. The Assignments panel is a centralized place to work with content assignment in InDesign. You can quickly identify the assigned user, update content, check out content, create new assignments, and delete assignments.

What You'll Do

Create and Work with Notes

Track Text Changes

Share Content with Adobe InCopy

Set Up User Identification

Export Content from InDesign

Use the Assignments Panel

Create an Assignment

Check Content Out and In

Update Content

Work with InCopy

Creating and Working with Notes

When you work with more than one person on a document, it's important to communicate changes and other information with each other. Notes are a great way to communicate with others and record the notes along with the document. You can add inline notes in text and tables to collaborate more effectively. Notes are linked to specific locations in text and tables. When you create a note with the Notes tool on the Tools panel, you type text directly in the Notes panel. In the Notes panel, you can show and hide notes, go to the note anchor in the document, browse notes, create notes, and delete notes. The top of the Notes panel displays information about the active note, including author name, created date, modified date, story location, page number, and the number of characters and words in the note.

Create Notes

1. Select the **Notes** tool on the Tools panel.

   The cursor changes to a notepad icon.

2. Click in the text or table where you want to insert an note.

   The Notes panel appears.

3. Type the notes you want in the Notes panel window.

4. To create additional notes, click in the text or table where you want to insert a note, and then type the notes you want.

Did You Know?

You can convert text to a note. Select the text you want to convert, select the Notes panel, click the Options menu, and then click Convert To Note.

See Also

See "Setting Notes Preferences" on page 496 for more information on setting Notes preferences.

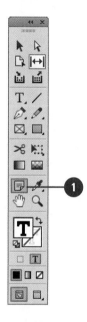

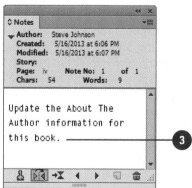

Work with Notes in the Notes Panel

① Select the **Notes** panel.

- Click the **Window** menu, point to **Editorial**, and then click **Notes**.

② Use any of the following buttons or commands to perform an operation:

- **Identify Note Color.** The icon on the bottom of the panel to the left shows you the color of the note.

- **Show or Hide Notes.** Click the **Show/Hide** button on the panel.

- **Go to Note Location.** Click the **Go to Note Anchor** button on the panel.

- **Display Previous or Next Notes.** Click the **Go to Previous Note** or **Go to Next Note** button on the panel.

- **Create a Note.** Click to place the insertion point where you want the note, and then click the **New Note** button on the panel.

- **Delete a Note.** Display the note you want to delete, and then click the **Delete Note** button on the panel.

  - To remove all notes, click the **Options** menu, and then click **Remove All Notes**.

- **Convert a Note to Text.** Display the note you want to convert, click the **Options** menu, and then click **Convert to Text**.

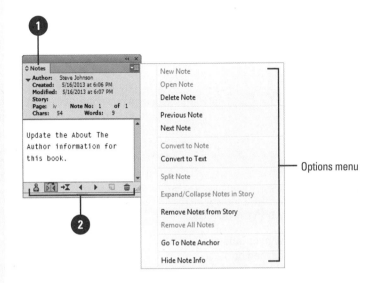

Options menu

Note indicator

About The Author

Steve Johnson has written more than 80 books on a variety of computer software, including Microsoft Office 2013 and 2010, Microsoft Windows 8 and 7, Apple Mac OS X Mountain Lion, Adobe Dreamweaver CS6, Adobe Illustrator CS6, Adobe InDesign CS6, Adobe Photoshop CS6, and Adobe Edge Animate. In 1991, after working for Apple Computer and Microsoft, Steve founded Perspection, Inc., which writes and produces software training. When he is not staying up late writing, he enjoys playing golf, gardening, and spending time with his wife, Holly, and three children, JP, Brett, and Hannah. When time permits, he likes to travel to such places as New Hampshire in October, and Hawaii. Steve and his family live in Pleasanton, California, but can also be found visiting family all over the western United States.

Tracking Text Changes

With Track Changes, you can manage the changes made to text in your document. You can view the changes on a per user basis in the Story Editor in InDesign or the Gallery and Story view in InCopy. With the Track Changes panel (InDesign) or the Track Changes toolbar (InCopy), you can turn Track Changes on and off in the current story or all stories, and show, hide, accept and reject changes—such as deleting text, moving text, and inserting text—in your document. Before you start track changes, it's important to specify what you want to track and how and where you want to track it in Track Changes preferences. You can use the User command on the File menu or the Options menu on the Assignments panel to specify a user name and color for track changes as well as file check in and out with InCopy.

Set Track Changes Preferences

1. Click the **Edit** (Win) or **InDesign** (Mac) menu, and then point to **Preferences**.

2. Click **Track Changes**.

3. Select the check box for the type of changes to track: **Added Text**, **Deleted Text**, or **Moved Text**.

4. For each type of tracked change, select a **Text** and **Background** color, and a **Marking** option, such as Strikethrough, Underline, Outline, or None.

5. Select the **Prevent Duplicate User Colors** check box to make sure all users are assigned different colors.

6. To show change bars, select the **Change Bars** check box, and then select a **Change Bar Color** and **Location** for the change bar.

7. Select the **Included Deleted Text When Spellchecking** check box to mark spell-checked text to be deleted (in Story view only).

8. Click **OK**.

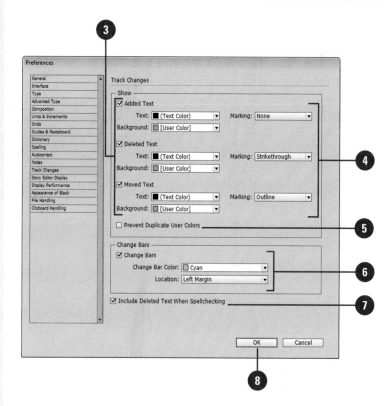

Track Text Changes

1. Click the **Edit** menu, and then click **Edit in Story Editor**.

2. Select the **Track Changes** panel.

   ◆ Click the **Window** menu, point to **Editorial**, and then click **Track Changes**.

3. To enable/disable track changes, click the **Enable/Disable Track Changes in Current Story** button on the panel.

   ◆ **All Stories.** Click the **Options** menu, and then click the **Enable /Disable Tracking In All Stories**.

4. Add, delete, or move text as desired in the Story Editor or Layout view. Each change is marked based on the settings in Track Changes preferences along with the changer's user name, date and time, and change type, which appear in the Track Changes panel.

5. To show or hide changes, click the **Show/Hide Changes** button on the panel.

6. To accept or reject changes, use the buttons on the panel or commands on the Options menu:

   ◆ **Previous Change** or **Next Change.** Select to highlight the previous or next change.

   ◆ **Accept Change** or **Accept All Changes.** Select to accept the highlighted change or all changes without review.

   ◆ **Reject Change** or **Reject All Changes.** Select to reject the highlighted change or all changes without review.

   TIMESAVER *To accept or reject a change and select the next change, Alt-click (Win) or Option-click (Mac) the Accept Change or Reject Change button.*

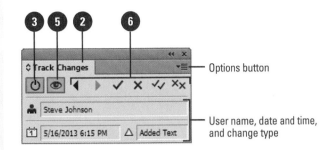

Options button

User name, date and time, and change type

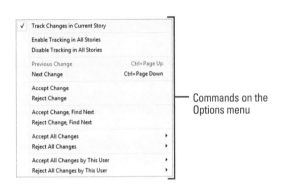

Commands on the Options menu

Highlighted change

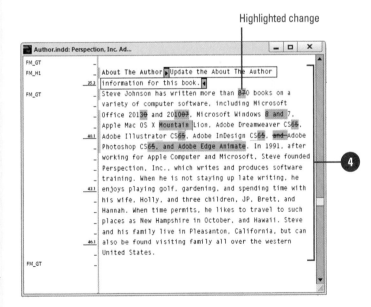

Sharing Content with Adobe InCopy

Adobe InCopy is a stand-alone writing and editing program that allows you to work seamlessly with Adobe InDesign. The integration with InCopy allows InDesign users to select text and graphics in a document, and then assign the content to InCopy users for writing and editing. Content designates either a body of text that flows through one or more frames or an imported graphic.

InCopy users can open an assignment file with only the material assigned to them and then make changes to it. An assignment file is a container that stores a piece of content from an InDesign document and other related file-locking and notification tools. You can share assignment files on a server for easy access or through assignment packages.

InCopy uses live layout view to display how the content changes affect the InDesign document. Multiple InCopy or InDesign users can open the same content file at the same time as a read-only file. However, only one user can check out the content file to make changes. You can open a content file by opening an assignment file, assignment package, linked InCopy file, or InDesign file with linked content. An assignment package is a compressed version of an assignment file. If users don't have access to a common network server, you can can create assignment packages and then send them to the assigned user as an e-mail attachment. The assigned user can open the assignment package, make changes, and then return it. If an assigned user is done with the update or you no longer want the user to make changes, you can unlink or cancel the assignment.

Working Together on a Local Server

1. In InDesign, create assignments and add content to them.

2. Save the assignment files for InCopy users on a local server.

3. In InCopy, open the assignment file, and check out and edit the content. When you finish, check in the content.

4. In InDesign, while the content is checked out, you can still make changes to the rest of the InDesign document. When the content file is checked back in, you can make changes to the content.

5. In InCopy, open the assignment file, check out, and edit a story or graphic.

Exporting content from InDesign allows you to make content available to InCopy users to check out and change while still maintaining a link back to the original document. You can export content from an InDesign document to InCopy by creating an assignment file, or by exporting text and graphics frames separately as files. After you export content to InCopy, the file is called a **managed file**. Icons appear at the top left of the exported frames in InDesign and InCopy, and in the Assignments panel to indicate the content is currently assigned to another person. A link to the exported file also appears in the Links panel.

Setting Up User Identification

When you work with InCopy, all users who want to check files in and out or make and track text changes in a document need to have a unique identification name. You can specify or change a unique user Identification name and select a linked color by using the User command on the File menu or the Options menu on the Assignments panel. If you want to change a user identification name, make sure you don't have any files checked out.

Set Up User Identification

1. Click the **File** menu, and then click **User**.

2. Type a unique name.

3. Click the **Color** list arrow, and then select a color.

4. Click **OK**.

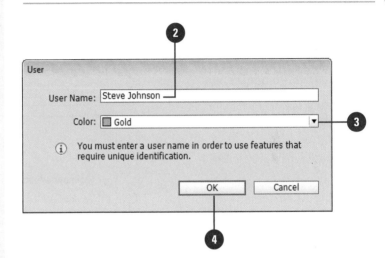

Did You Know?

You can add notes and track changes. When you add notes to managed files, the information in the notes is pasted along with content for viewing and changing in InCopy. Use commands on the Notes submenu on the Type menu to create and manage notes.

Exporting Content from InDesign

Exporting content from InDesign allows you to make content available to InCopy users to check out and change while still maintaining a link back to the original document. You can export content from an InDesign document to InCopy by creating an assignment file (ICMA for CC), or by exporting text and graphics frames separately as files (ICML for CC) using one of the Export commands for InCopy. When you use one of the Export commands, the managed file is unassigned, which you can change later. Icons appear at the top left of the exported frame in InDesign and InCopy, and in the Assignments panel to indicate the content is currently assigned to another person for changes. A link to the exported file also appears in the Links panel.

Export Content from InDesign

1. Select the text or graphics frames that you want to export.

2. Click the **Edit** menu, point to **InCopy**, and then point to **Export**.

3. Click one of the following commands:

   - **Selection.** Use to export all selected text or graphics frames.

   - **Layer.** Use to export all content on the selected layer.

   - **All Stories.** Use to export all text in stories that have not been exported already.

   - **All Graphics.** Use to export all graphics that has not been exported already.

   - **All Graphics and Stories.** Use to export all graphics and text in stories that have not been exported already.

4. Enter a name for the file.

5. Navigate to the location where you want to save the content file.

6. Click **Save**.

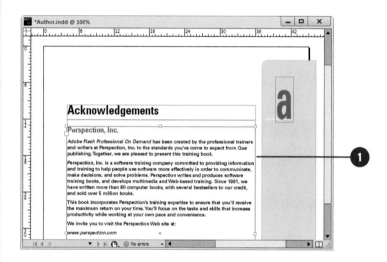

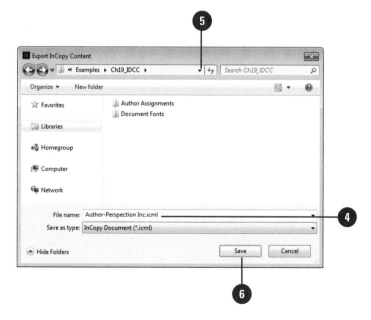

Using the Assignments Panel

The Assignments panel is a centralized place to work with content assignment in InDesign. The panel displays the content files exported from the current document and an icon indicating the status of the content. You can use buttons on the bottom of the panel to quickly identify the assigned user, update content, check out content, create new assignments, and delete assignments. You can also use the Options menu to select these and other commands. For example, you can select commands to update assignments for selected, out-of-date, or all content. Before you can make an assignment, you need to save your InDesign document. If you have not yet saved the file, InDesign will prompt you to save it.

Use the Assignments Panel

1. Select the **Assignments** panel.

   ◆ Click the **Window** menu, point to **Editorial**, and then click **Assignments**.

2. Use any of the following buttons to perform an operation:

   ◆ Update Content. Select the assignment, and then click the **Update Content** button.

   ◆ Check Out/Check In Content. Select the assignment, and then click the **Check Out/Check In Selection** button.

   ◆ Create New Assignment. Click the **New Assignment** button, enter information, select options, and then click **OK**.

   ◆ Delete Assignment. Select the assignment, and then click the **Delete** button.

3. To locate and select the text and graphics associated with an assignment, double-click the assignment name in the panel.

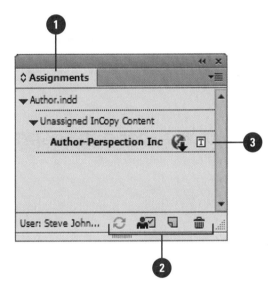

Creating an Assignment

You can create an assignment file several ways. One is to create an empty assignment file and add content to it later. Another is to create an assignment and add content at the same time. The last way is to add content to an existing assignment. When you create an assignment, a folder is created in the same location as the InDesign document file in order to store the assignment files (ICMA) and any exported InCopy story files (ICML). After you create an assignment, you can move the folder into a location where all users have access to it or create and distribute an assignment package.

Create an Assignment and Add Content

① Select the **Assignments** panel.

   ◆ Click the **Window** menu, point to **Editorial**, and then click **Assignments**.

② Click the **New Assignment** button on the panel.

③ Specify the following New Assignment options:

   ◆ **Assignment Name.** Enter a unique name for the assignment.

   ◆ **Assigned To.** Enter a name to associate with the assignment.

   ◆ **Color.** Select a color to associate with the assignment.

   ◆ **Change.** Click to specify a new location for the assignment file.

   ◆ **Include.** Select an option to include placeholder frames, assigned spreads, or all spreads.

   ◆ **Linked Image Files when Packaging.** Select to include linked image files when packaging. This keeps all the content together, so you can send everything in one file.

④ Click **OK**.

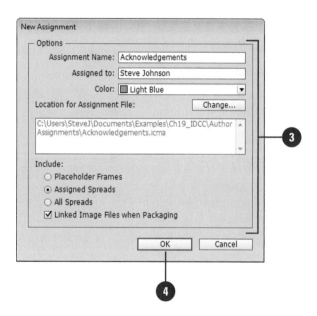

For Your Information

Creating and Opening an Assignment Package

If users don't have access to a common network server, you can create assignment packages and then send them to the assigned user. To create a package, select the assignment, click the Options menu, click Package for InCopy, specify a name and location, and then click Save. To create a package and send it in an e-mail message in your default e-mail program, use the Package for InCopy and Email command on the Options menu. To open a package, use the Open Package command on the Options menu in InDesign or the Open button on the Command Bar in InCopy.

Create an Assignment and Add Content at the Same Time

1. Select the text and graphics frames you want to include in a new assignment file.

2. Click the **Edit** menu, point to **InCopy**, and then point to one of the following commands:

   ◆ **Add Selection to Assignment.**

   ◆ **Add Layer to Assignment.**

   ◆ **Add All Stories to Assignment.**

   ◆ **Add All Graphics to Assignment.**

3. Click **New** on the submenu.

4. Specify the new assignment options; see the previous page for details.

5. Click **OK**.

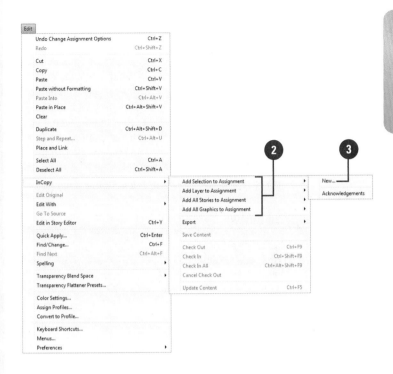

Add to an Existing Assignment

1. Select the text and graphics frames you want to include in an existing assignment file.

2. Click the **Edit** menu, point to **InCopy**, and then point to one of the following commands:

   ◆ **Add Selection to Assignment.**

   ◆ **Add Layer to Assignment.**

   ◆ **Add All Stories to Assignment.**

   ◆ **Add All Graphics to Assignment.**

3. Select an assignment name on the submenu.

4. Click the **Options** menu, and then click **Update All Assignments** or **Update Selected Assignments**.

Checking Content Out and In

Anyone can open an assignment file for review. However, only one user at a time can open and edit the file. Before you can open and edit an assignment file, the content needs to be checked out. This prevents two users from accidentally editing the same file at the same time. When you check out a file, a hidden lock file (IDLK) is attached to the file on your computer. Once the file is locked, no one else can access it. The user who checked out the file has exclusive use of it until the file is checked in, even if you exit the program and come back later. You can make changes to an assignment file (INCA) in InCopy or in the InDesign document (INDD) that contains the assigned content. In this case, I'm focusing on InCopy. The same commands are available in InDesign on the InCopy submenu on the Edit menu.

Check Content Out and In

1. In InDesign, select the text or graphic frames that you want to check out.

2. Click the **Check Out** button on the Assignments panel.

   - You can also click the **Edit** menu, point to **InCopy**, and then click **Check Out**.

   A pencil icon appears on the InDesign frame indicating the content is checked out.

3. In InCopy, click the **File** menu, and then click **Open**.

4. Navigate to the location where the file is stored, and then select it.

5. Click **Open**.

6. Make the changes you want to the content. Story view provides a quick and easy way to write and edit text.

   A pencil with line icon appears on the frame indicating the content is in use.

7. Click the **File** menu, and then click **Save Content**.

8. When you're done, click the **File** menu, and then click **Check In** or **Check In All**.

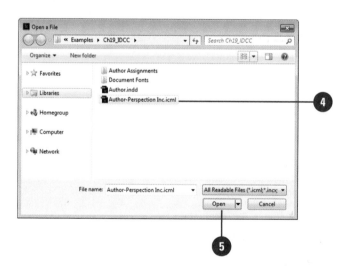

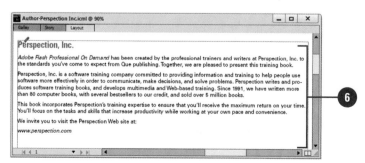

Updating Content

When content is updated in InCopy or InDesign by the assigned user, an out-of-date icon appears in the Assignments and Links panel. In the Assignments panel, you can update the content in the original document by choosing update commands on the Options menu for selected, out-of-date, or all content. If an assignment file was moved during the editing process, the original document is not going to know where the file is located. You can also use the same update commands to help you locate and relink the file.

Update or Relink Content

1. In InDesign, open the document with the content you want to update.

2. Select the **Assignments** panel.

   ◆ Click the **Window** menu, point to **Editorial**, and then click **Assignments**.

3. Select the assignment you want to update.

4. Click the **Options** menu, and then select any of the following:

   ◆ **Update Selected Assignments.**

   ◆ **Update Out-of-Date Assignments.**

   ◆ **Update All Assignments.**

5. To update content from the document window, select the text or graphics frames, click the **Edit** menu, point to **InCopy**, and then click **Update Content**.

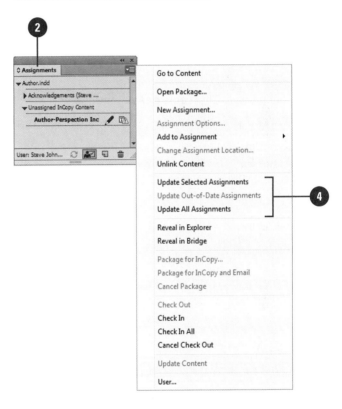

Did You Know?

You can override locked files. If you need access to a locked file, you can take back ownership. In InDesign, select the Assignments panel, select the assignment file you want back, click the Options menu, and then click Unlink Content.

Working with InCopy

When you start InCopy, the program window displays several windows of varying types you can use to work with documents.

A **menu** is a list of commands that you use to accomplish specific tasks. A **command** is a directive that accesses a feature of a program. InCopy has its own set of menus. The **Application bar** provides easy access to commonly used features, such as choosing zoom levels, view options, screen mode, document arrangement, workspaces, and searching InCopy's online Help. The **Tools panel** contains a set of tools you can use to work with text, create notes, and change the display view. Additional options and tools are available on the **Command Bar**. The **Document window** displays open InCopy documents. InCopy includes tabs to make it easier to switch back and forth between documents and a close button to quickly close a document. Each document tab includes View tabs to switch between display views. In InCopy, a collection of panels are available to help you work with documents. A **panel** is a window you can collapse, expand, and group with other panels, known as a **panel group**, to improve accessibility and workflow. A panel group consists of either individual panels stacked one on top of the other or related panels organized together with tabs to navigate from one panel to another. InCopy displays the following panels for the Essentials workspace by default: Command Bar, Tools, Copyfit Info, and Gallery & Story Appearance.

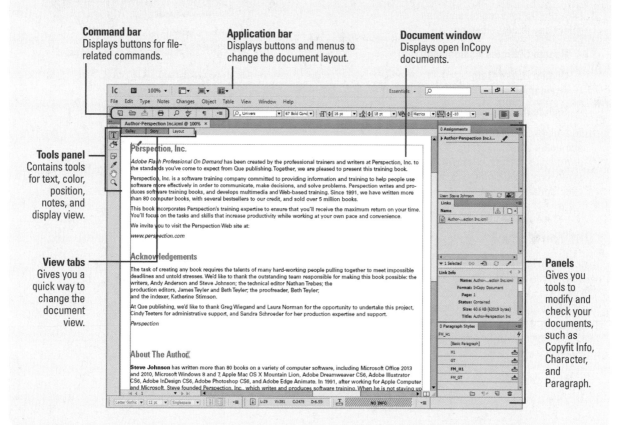

Command bar
Displays buttons for file-related commands.

Application bar
Displays buttons and menus to change the document layout.

Document window
Displays open InCopy documents.

Tools panel
Contains tools for text, color, position, notes, and display view.

View tabs
Gives you a quick way to change the document view.

Panels
Gives you tools to modify and check your documents, such as Copyfit Info, Character, and Paragraph.

Working Together with Adobe Programs

Introduction

Adobe Creative Cloud (CC) provides access to an integrated collection of professional programs—including Illustrator, InDesign, Photoshop, and Dreamweaver to name a few—that work together to help you create designs in print, on the web, or on mobile devices. Adobe CC programs are designed to work together so you can focus on what you need to do, rather than on how to do it. In fact, the Adobe CC programs share tools and features for common tasks so you can work uninterrupted and move seamlessly from one program to another. With your Adobe CC program, you can sign in to Creative Cloud and Adobe.com with your Adobe ID to access online cloud services. Creative Cloud is a membership-based cloud solution that allows you to access and download Adobe software, tools, services, personal files, tutorial videos, and sync Adobe CC program settings online from any computer or device. You can go to *www.creativecloud.com* or *www.adobe.com* for more details.

Along with the professional programs, Creative Cloud also includes additional Adobe services and tools (available for download)—such as Bridge, Camera Raw plug-in, Media Encoder, Extension Manager, and ExtendScript Toolkit—to help you perform specific jobs, such as locating, downloading, and modifying images for projects, managing files and program plug-ins and extensions, testing files for different mobile devices, and creating scripts.

For example, Adobe Bridge is a program that lets you view, open, modify, and manage images located on your computer from any Adobe CC program. Bridge allows you to search, sort, filter, manage, and process image files one at a time or in batches. You can also import files from your digital camera and view file information and metadata.

What You'll Do

Explore Adobe Programs

Explore Adobe Bridge

Get Started with Adobe Bridge

Get Photos from a Digital Camera

Work with Raw Images from a Digital Camera

Modify Images in Camera Raw

Work with Images Using Adobe Bridge

Set Preferences in Adobe Bridge

Apply Image Adjustments

Automate Tasks in Adobe Bridge

Use Mini Bridge

Script with Adobe ExtendScript Toolkit

Work with Adobe Media Encoder

Work with Adobe Extension Manager

Use the Adobe Exchange Panel

Access Adobe Creative Cloud

Exploring Adobe Programs

Adobe Creative Cloud

Adobe Creative Cloud is a membership-based cloud solution that allows you to access and download Adobe software, tools, services, personal files, tutorial videos, and sync program settings online from any computer or device. Creative Cloud includes an integrated collection of professional programs that work together to help you create designs in print, on the web, or on mobile devices. The Adobe programs for print design include InDesign and Acrobat Pro; for graphic design the programs include Photoshop, Illustrator, and Fireworks; for video and sound design the programs include Premiere Pro, After Effects, Encore, and Soundbooth; and for web design the programs include Flash Professional, Dreamweaver, Edge Animate, and Fireworks.

Working with Adobe Tools

With an Adobe program, you can also use additional Adobe tools—including Bridge, Camera Raw plug-in, Media Encoder, Extension Manager, and ExtendScript Toolkit—to help you perform related tasks, such as managing files and extensions and automating tasks with scripts.

Adobe Bridge

Adobe Bridge is a file management/batching program that manages and processes images while you work. To use Bridge, click Browse in Bridge on the File menu or the Go to Bridge button on the Applications bar within an Adobe program or from the Start menu or screen (Win) or the App folder (Mac).

Camera Raw Plug-In

The Camera Raw plug-in—available in Adobe Bridge, Adobe Photoshop, and other Adobe programs—allows you to open and process with fine control RAW image formats (not processed, also known as digital negatives) produced by digital cameras. Raw image formats are intended to capture as closely as possible the characteristics of the picture. DNG (Digital NeGative) is a raw format developed by Adobe.

Adobe Media Encoder

Adobe Media Encoder allows you to encode and compress video and audio files and convert them to distribution formats: F4V, FLV, H.264, and MP3. You can select a format and preset for systems—such as high-definition (HD), desktops, and the web (Flash, Vimeo, and YouTube)—and devices—such as Apple TV, iPad, iPhone, and Android. The presets include: size, bitrate (data rate), and frames per second (fps) rate.

Adobe Extension Manager

Adobe Extension Manager allows you to install and delete added program functionality, known as extensions, to many Adobe programs. You can use the Extension Manager to access the **Adobe Exchange** site (which is also available within an Adobe CC program using the Adobe Exchange panel (**New!**)), where you can locate, research, and download many different types of extensions, plug-ins, and other resources for use in Adobe programs.

Adobe ExtendScript Toolkit

Adobe ExtendScript Toolkit allows you to create, edit, and debug an extended version of JavaScript, called ExtendScript, to be used for scripting Adobe programs. If you perform the same set of tasks on a regular basis, you can use scripting as a powerful tool to make a lengthy set of tasks simple.

Exploring Adobe Bridge

Favorites panel
Displays links to common features and favorite places.

Folders panel
Displays the folders on your computer in a tree structure.

Workspaces
Choose from common workspaces.

Quick Search
Search for file names, keywords, folder names.

Preview panel
Displays a preview of the selected image.

File path
To trace file back to its folder.

Filter panel
Displays files based on filter criteria.

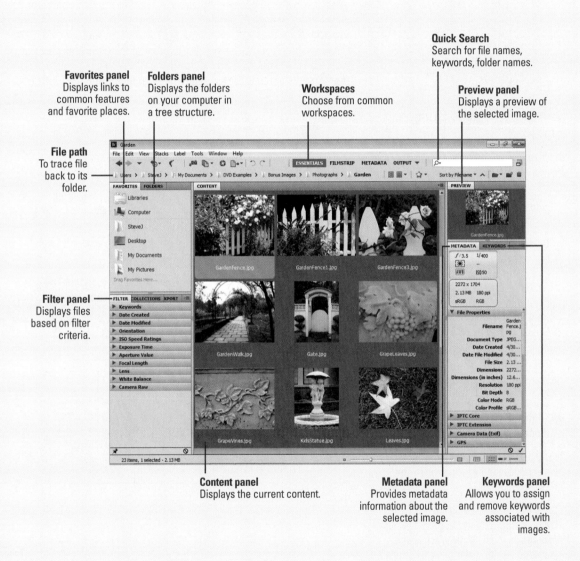

Content panel
Displays the current content.

Metadata panel
Provides metadata information about the selected image.

Keywords panel
Allows you to assign and remove keywords associated with images.

Getting Started with Adobe Bridge

Adobe Bridge CC is a stand-alone program—available for download from Creative Cloud—that lets you view, open, and manage images located on your computer from any Adobe CC program. Adobe Bridge is literally the glue that binds Adobe CC programs and shared tools into one cohesive unit. The Bridge program provides a set of panels that make it easy to find, view, and manage the files on your computer or network. As you work with Bridge, you'll open, close, and move (dock and undock) the panels to meet your individual needs. After you customize the workspace, you can save the location of the panels as a custom workspace, which you can display using the Workspace command on the Window menu. Bridge also provides some predefined workspaces.

Get Started with Adobe Bridge

1. Start your Adobe CC program, click the **File** menu, and then click **Browse in Bridge**.

   ◆ If prompted, install/update from Adobe Application Manager.

   ◆ You can also click the **Go to Bridge** button on the Application bar (if available). Ctrl (Win) or ⌘ (Mac)+ click for a maximized view, Alt (Win) or Option (Mac)+click to open a new Bridge window, or Shift+click to open Mini Bridge.

   ◆ You can also start Bridge from the Start menu/screen (Win) or the Applications folder (Mac).

2. To open and close a panel, click the **Window** menu, and then click the panel name you want.

3. To move a panel, drag the panel tab you want to another location in the Bridge window.

4. To save a workspace, click the **Window** menu, point to **Workspace**, click **New Workspace**, type a name, and then click **OK**.

5. To display a workspace, click the **Window** menu, point to **Workspace**, and then click the workspace you want.

6. When you're done, click the **Close** button in the Bridge window.

1. The Go to Bridge button on the Application bar in InDesign

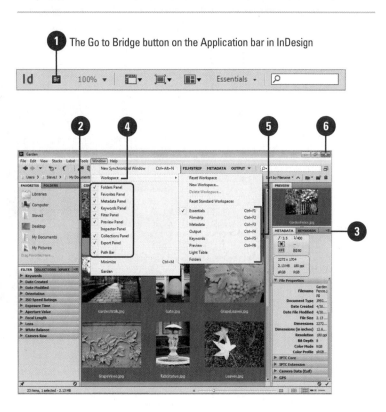

Getting Photos from a Digital Camera

If you have raw or other images from your digital camera, you can use the Get Photos from Camera command in Adobe Bridge to retrieve and copy them to your computer. This allows you to specify where you want to store the files, rename them if you want, preserve metadata, or convert them to the DNG format. When you convert raw files to the DNG format, you specify preview size, compression, and whether to preserve the raw image data or embed the original raw file.

Import Raw and Other Files from a Camera

1. In Adobe Bridge, click the **File** menu, and then click **Get Photos from Camera** or click the camera icon on the Application bar.

2. Click the **Get Photos From** list arrow, and then select the source camera or memory card.

3. Click the **Browse** button to select a folder location, and then create a new subfolder to store the images (optional).

4. To rename the files, select a method, and then enter file name text.

5. Select the options you want:

   ◆ **Preserve Current Filename in XMP.** Select to save the current filename as image metadata.

   ◆ **Open Adobe Bridge.** Select to open and display the files in Adobe Bridge.

   ◆ **Convert To DNG.** Select to convert Camera Raw files to DNG. Click Settings to set DNG conversion options.

   ◆ **Delete Original Files.** Select to delete original files from camera or memory card.

   ◆ **Save Copies To.** Select to save copies to another folder for backup.

6. To apply metadata to the files, click **Advanced Dialog**.

7. Click **Get Photos**.

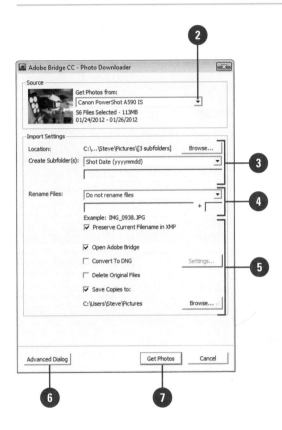

Working with Raw Images from a Digital Camera

Raw image file formats are created by most mid- to high-end digital cameras and contain information about how the image was taken. The raw format turns off all camera adjustments, and simply saves the image information. Using the raw format is as close to using traditional film as a digital camera can get. Raw images are larger; however, the increase in file size gives you more information that can be used by Camera Raw to adjust the image. Camera Raw version 8 (**New!**) is installed along with an Adobe CC program, such as Bridge and Photoshop, as a plug-in. It supports more than 400 cameras. Before you get started with Camera Raw, you can set preferences to apply default image options and specify how you want to open and work with work with DNG (Digital Negative), JPEG, and TIFF images. After you make Camera Raw adjustments, you can save the settings as a preset so you can use them later.

Set Camera Raw Preferences

1. In Adobe Bridge, click the **Edit** (Win) or **Adobe Bridge** (Mac) menu, and then click **Camera Raw Preferences**.

   ◆ In the Camera Raw dialog box, you can also click the **Open Preferences Dialog** button on the toolbar to access camera raw preferences.

2. Select the preferences you want:

   ◆ **General.** Specify where Camera Raw file settings are stored. Use Sidecar XMP files to store settings separately, or Camera Raw Database to store settings in a searchable database.

   ◆ **Default Image Settings.** Select options to automatically apply settings or set defaults.

   ◆ **Camera Raw Cache.** Set a cache size to shorten loading time for thumbnails and previews.

   ◆ **DNG File Handling.** Select options to ignore XMP files or update embedded content.

   ◆ **JPEG and TIFF Handling.** Automatically open JPEGs and/or TIFFs in Camera Raw.

3. Click **OK**.

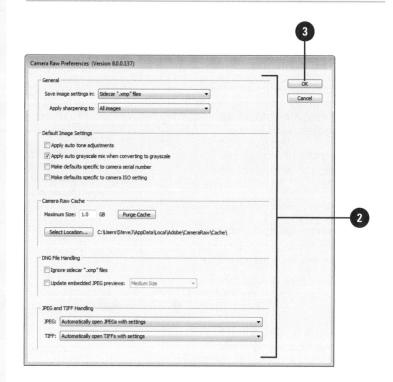

Work with Images in Camera Raw

1. In Adobe Bridge, select the images (camera raw, TIFF or JPEG), right-click the selection, and then click **Open in Camera Raw**.

   ◆ In Photoshop, you can use the Open dialog box to open a file in Camera Raw.

   The Camera Raw dialog box opens.

2. Click any of the tools to modify or enhance the image, and select the **Preview** check box to see all changes that have been made.

3. Click any of the tabs to modify or enhance the image.

   The Basics tab is easier to use with all sliders having a starting point in the middle.

4. Click the **Camera Raw Menu** button to **Load**, **Save**, or **Apply** a specific set of Raw settings.

   ◆ You can use the **Presets** tab to apply, create, or delete presets.

5. Click **Save Image(s)** to specify a folder destination, file name, and format for the processed images.

6. When you're done, click **Done** to process the file, but not open it, or click **Open Image(s)** to process and open it in Photoshop. Hold Alt (Win) or Option (Mac) to use **Open Copy** or **Reset**.

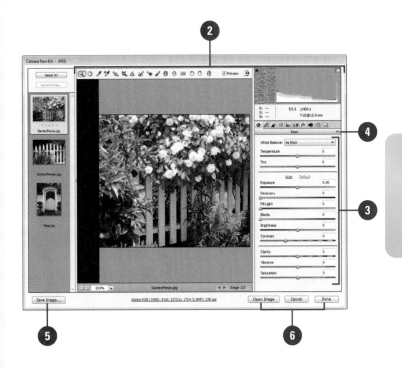

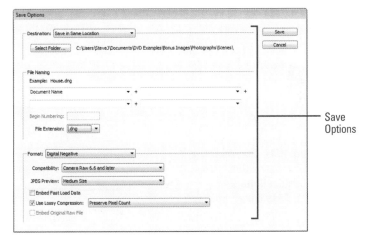

Save Options

Modifying Images in Camera Raw

From Adobe Bridge or Photoshop, you can use Camera Raw version 8 (**New!**) to open raw files (extensions vary with digital cameras), JPEG, and TIFF files to make image touch-ups and enhancements. If you're not sure what to do, you can click Auto to have Camera Raw do it or drag sliders to adjust options manually. You can set white balance with presets (**New!**) (remove color casts), color temperature (warm or cool light source), image exposure, contrast, highlights, shadows, clarity, and vibrance (color vividness). In addition, you can adjust color tones (Hue, Saturation, and Luminance or grayscale), reduce luminance and color noise, add grain, add sharpening, correct for lens defects (including the Upright tool (**New!**) to straighten horizons and apply perspective corrections), add post-crop vignetting and effects, apply graduated (exposure) or radial (**New!**) (inside/outside circular area) filters and retouch images with the Spot Removal—Heal (**New!**) and Clone—and Red Eye tools. In addition, raw images can be converted into 16-bit mode, which provides control over adjustments such as tonal and color correction. Once processed, raw images can be saved in the DNG (Digital Negative), TIFF, PSD, or JPEG formats. All changes made to raw images are non-destructive, meaning only the metadata is changed to make different versions, leaving the original data unchanged.

Modify Images in Camera Raw

1. In Adobe Bridge, select the images, right-click the selection, and then click **Open in Camera Raw**.

   ◆ In Photoshop, you can use the Open dialog box to open a file in Camera Raw.

   The Camera Raw dialog box opens.

2. Click a tab: **Basic**, **Tone Curve**, **Detail** (Sharpen & Noise Reduction), **HSL / Grayscale**, **Split Toning**, **Lens Corrections** (**New!**), **Effects**, **Camera Calibration**, **Presets**, or **Snapshots**.

3. To automatically make tonal adjustments, click **Auto** on the Basic tab.

4. Use sliders or enter values to make any other manual adjustments.

   ◆ **Basic.** Select a White Balance preset (**New!**); use sliders for Temperature, Tint, Exposure, Contrast, Highlights, Shadows, Whites, Blacks, Clarity, Vibrance, and Saturation.

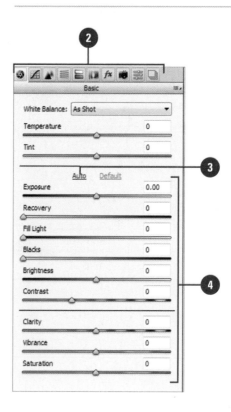

5 Use tools to modify the image:

◆ Use the **Zoom**, **Hand**, **Rotate**, **Crop**, and **Straighten** tools to change the size, orientation, and position of the image.

◆ Use the **White Balance** tool to adjust color cast or the **Color Sampler** tool to sample a color from the image.

◆ Use the **Spot Removal** (**New!**) (Heal or Clone) or **Red Eye Removal** tool to fix the image.

◆ Use the **Adjustment Brush**, **Graduated Filter**, **Radial Filter** (**New!**), or **Targeted Adjustment** tool to make adjustments to exposure, brightness, contrast, saturation, clarity, sharpness, and color.

6 Use options to view the image:

◆ **Preview.** Select to display the image with all changes that have been made.

◆ **Zoom Level.** Changes to the level of image magnification can be made here.

7 Click the file name to change the (color) Space, (bit) Depth, Size, and Resolution of the image.

8 Click **Save Image(s)** to specify a folder destination, file name, and format for the processed images.

9 Select the images you want to synchronize (apply settings) in the Filmstrip (if desired, click **Select All**), and then click **Synchronize**.

10 When you're done, click **Done** to process the file, but not open it, or click **Open Image(s)** to process and open it in Photoshop. Hold Alt (Win) or Option (Mac) to use **Open Copy** or **Reset**.

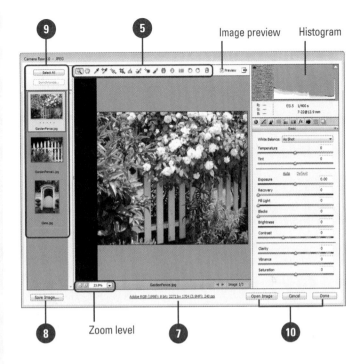

Image preview   Histogram

Zoom level

For Your Information

What is the DNG File Format?

The DNG, or Digital Negative, format is an openly published raw file format from Adobe that stores "raw" pixel data captured by digital cameras before it has been converted to another format, such as TIFF or JPEG. In addition, it captures standard 'EXIF' metadata, such as date, time, camera used, and camera settings. Saving raw files in the DNG format provides several advantages. DNG files are smaller than uncompressed TIFFs, and they do not have the artifacts of compressed JPEGs. Many key camera parameters, such as white balance, can be modified even after the image is captured. You have access to 16-bit data for greater detail and fidelity, and the added flexibility of converting a single file using multiple conversion settings. When you convert raw images into the DNG format, you are using a format that is openly published by Adobe and usable by other software and hardware vendors, which makes it a safe format for the long-term storage and archiving of digital images. The raw format used by digital cameras is proprietary to the specific camera (e.g., NEF for Nikon, CR2 for Canon, RAF for Fuji), so the format might not be supported once that camera and its proprietary software is obsolete, which means at some point in the future, you might not be able to open any of your archived raw images. The DNG format solves that problem. To get a free copy of the DNG converter, go to *www.adobe.com* and then search for DNG converter.

Working with Images Using Adobe Bridge

With Adobe Bridge, you can drag assets into your layouts as needed, preview them, and add metadata to them. Bridge allows you to search, sort, filter, manage, and process image files one at a time or in batches. You can also use Bridge to create new folders; rename, move, delete and group files (known as stacking); edit metadata; rotate images; and run batch commands. You can also view information about files and data imported from your digital camera.

Work with Images Using Bridge

1. Start your Adobe CC program, click the **File** menu, and then click **Browse in Bridge**, or click the **Launch Bridge** button (if available).

2. Click the **Folder** path, and then select a folder.

3. Click the **Folders** tab and choose a folder from the scrolling list.

4. Click the **Favorites** tab to choose from a listing of user-defined items, such as Pictures.

5. Click an image within the preview window to select it.

6. Click the **Metadata** tab to view image information, including date and time the image was shot, and aperture, shutter speed, and f-stop.

7. Click the **IPTC Core** or **IPTC Extension** arrow to add user-defined metadata, such as creator and copyright information, or captions.

8. Click the **Preview** tab to view a larger thumbnail of the selected image. Multiple images appear when you select them.

   ◆ Click the image in the Preview tab to display a Loupe tool for zooming. Drag magnified box to change positions. Click it to deactivate the tool.

9. Drag the **Zoom** slider to increase or decrease the thumbnail views.

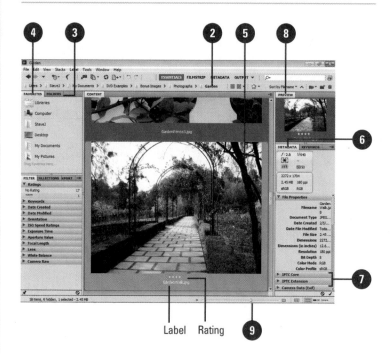

Label   Rating

For Your Information

What is Metadata?

Metadata is information about an image file, such as its author, copyright, creation date, size, version, color space, resolution, and searchable keywords. This data is stored in the file or in a separate file known as a **sidecar file**, using a standard format called **Extensible Metadata Platform (XMP)**. Bridge uses XMP files to help you organize and search for files on your computer. Metadata is also stored in other formats, such as EXIF (digital camera data), IPTC (photographer and image data), GPS (global positioning system data), and TIFF, which are all synchronized with XMP.

10 Click the preview buttons to select a different view of the workspace you have chosen. If you want to view your images in filmstrip or metadata focus mode, choose that workspace from the Window menu.

◆ **View Content as Thumbnails.** Default view. Displays the images as thumbnails with the file name underneath.

◆ **View Content as Details.** Displays a thumbnail of each image with selected details about the image such as date created, document type, resolution.

◆ **View Content as List.** Displays a small thumbnail of each image with metadata information details, such as date created and file size.

11 Use the file management buttons to sort, open or delete images, or create a new folder.

12 To narrow down the list of images using a filter, click the criteria you want to use in the Filter panel.

13 To add a label or rating to images, select the ones you want, click the **Label** menu, and then select the label or rating you want.

14 To group related images as a stacked group, select the images, click the **Stacks** menu, and then click **Group as Stack**.

◆ Use the Stacks menu to ungroup, open, expand, or collapse stacks.

15 Double-click on a thumbnail to open it in the default program, or drag the thumbnail from Bridge into an open Adobe application.

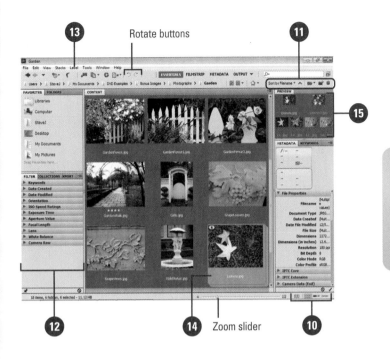

Rotate buttons

Zoom slider

For Your Information

Creating a Web Photo Gallery

Adobe Bridge takes the drudgery out of creating a Web Photo Gallery (thumbnail images on web pages) with the use of Adobe Output Module (AOM)—available from Creative Cloud. The pages generated with this command display small thumbnails of a group of images—when you click on an image, a larger version is displayed within another window or section of the page. If your goal is to show the world your photographs, but you don't want to write all the HTML code involved in making that happen, then the Web Photo Gallery is just what you need. In Bridge, select the images that you want to use for the photo gallery, click the Workspace menu, click Output, and then click the Web Gallery button. Select a template, and then use the Site Info, Color Palette, and Appearance panels to customize the Web gallery. When you're done, enter a gallery name, and then select a creation option, either Save to Disk or Upload.

Setting Preferences in Adobe Bridge

Adobe Bridge allows you to set preferences to customize the way you work. The Preferences dialog box is organized into categories—including General, Thumbnails, Playback, Metadata, Keywords, Labels, File Type Associations, Cache, Startup Scripts, Advanced, and Output. You can set specific options within these categories to suit your particular needs. For example, you can choose to display more metadata information with thumbnails, such as dimensions, size, keywords, color mode, label, etc. In addition, you can change the user interface with a color theme, brightness, backdrop, and accent color.

Set Bridge Preferences

1. In Adobe Bridge, click the **Edit** (Win) or **Bridge** (Mac) menu, and then click **Preferences**.

2. Click the **General** category.

3. Select the appearance, behavior, and Favorite Items you want.

   ◆ **Appearance.** Select options for color theme, user interface brightness, image backdrop, and accent color.

   ◆ **Favorite Items.** Select the items you want to access and use.

4. Click the **Thumbnails** category.

5. Specify the performance and details options you want:

   ◆ **Performance and File Handling.** Choose the maximum size of file to be processed (default: 1000 MB).

   ◆ **Details.** Select the metadata details you want to show with the thumbnail.

6. Click the **Metadata** category.

7. Select the check boxes with the metadata you want and clear the ones you don't want.

8. Click the **Labels** category.

9. Enter names for labels you want to be associated with a specific color.

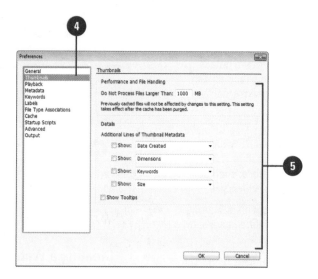

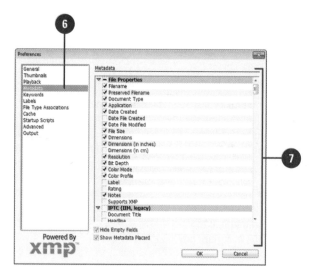

10 Click the **File Type Associations** category.

The left column displays the file type and the right column displays the current program that will open the file by default.

11 To change the default program, click the list arrow next to the file type, and then select a program or choose Browse to locate another application you would like to use.

12 Click the **Cache** category.

13 Choose where to store the cache, choose a cache size, and optimize or purge the cache from here.

14 Click the **Startup Scripts** category.

15 Select the check boxes with the programs you want to enable and clear the ones you want to disable.

16 Click the **Advanced** category, and specify whether to use software rendering and monitor-size previews, and then choose the language and keyboard options you want. You can also choose to have Bridge start automatically at login.

17 Click **OK**.

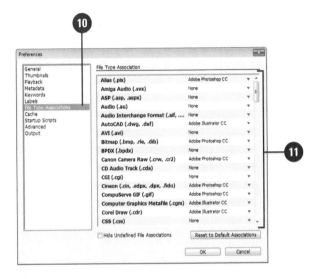

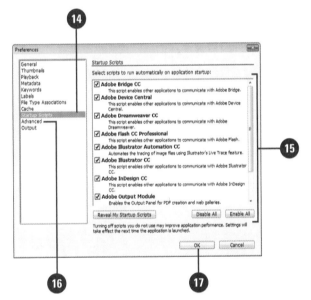

Applying Image Adjustments

Adobe Bridge makes it easy to make adjustments to one image in Camera Raw and then apply those adjustments to other images directly from Bridge without going back into Camera Raw. For instance, you may be correcting the white balance for an image and have many other images that were shot at the same time, under the same lighting conditions. You can use the initial settings to correct the rest of your images right from Bridge. You can also make a preset from your favorite adjustments, which will then be available as a develop setting within Bridge.

Modify Images in Adobe Bridge

① In Adobe Bridge, display and select the images that you want to adjust.

② Use any of the following methods to modify an image:

◆ **Apply a Preset Adjustment.** Click the **Edit** menu, point to **Develop Settings**, and then select a preset adjustment.

◆ **Copy and Paste Settings.** Click the **Edit** menu, point to **Develop Settings**, and then click **Copy Settings**. Select the image(s) to which you want to apply the settings. Click the **Edit** menu, point to **Develop Settings**, and then click **Paste Settings**. Select the options to apply, and then click **OK**.

◆ **Apply the Most Recent Adjustment.** Click the **Edit** menu, point to **Develop Settings**, and then click **Previous Conversion**.

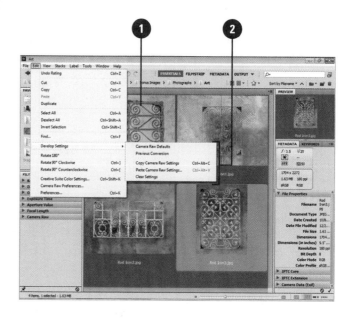

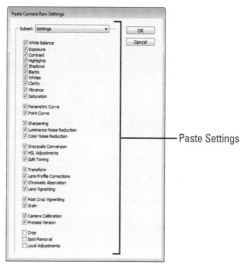

Paste Settings

Automating Tasks in Adobe Bridge

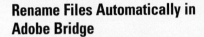

The Tools menu provides commands you can use to automate tasks in Bridge. For example, you can automate the process of renaming a group of files using the Batch Rename command. If you use Photoshop, or InDesign, you can use commands on submenus to run automated tasks, such as processing raw images with Photoshop, or you can create a contact sheet of images in InDesign. You can also use the Tools menu to start other Adobe programs as well as create and edit Metadata templates, which you can use to append or replace metadata in InDesign or other XMP-enabled programs.

Rename Files Automatically in Adobe Bridge

1. In Adobe Bridge, select the files or folders you want to use.

2. Click the **Tools** menu, and then click **Batch Rename**.

3. Select the Destination Folder option you want: **Rename in same folder**, **Move to other folder**, or **Copy to other folder**, and then click **Browse** to specify a new folder location.

4. Click the **Element** drop-down, and then select options to specify how you want to name the files:

   ◆ Text, New Extension, Current Filename, Preserved Filename, Sequence Number, Sequence Letter, Date/Time, Metadata, or Folder Name.

5. Enter the text you want to use in conjunction with the Element selection to name the files.

6. Select the **Preserve Current File Name In XMP Metadata** check box to retain the original filename in the metadata.

7. Select the check boxes for the operating systems with which you want the renamed files to be compatible.

8. Click **Rename**.

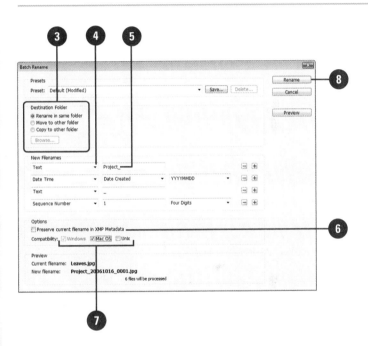

Using Mini Bridge

Adobe Mini Bridge is a condensed version of Adobe Bridge available in a panel within an Adobe CC program (Photoshop, InDesign, and InCopy). Mini Bridge—available when Adobe Bridge is installed—allows you to directly access graphics within a CC program, where you can drag and drop them in a document. Within Mini Bridge, you can navigate to different locations on your computer, search, sort, filter, and preview content as well as access Adobe Bridge. In Photoshop, the Mini Bridge panel appears in film strip mode, like in Lightroom.

Use Mini Bridge

1. Start your Adobe CC program, and then start Mini Bridge:

   ◆ **Photoshop.** Click the **File** menu, and then click **Browse in Mini Bridge** or click the **Window** menu, point to **Extensions**, and then click **Mini Bridge**.

   ◆ **InDesign/InCopy.** Shift+click the **Go to Bridge** button on the Application bar.

   If prompted, click **Launch Bridge**.

   Mini Bridge opens in the panel.

2. Use the Path or **Path** button and the Navigation pod to locate the graphics you want to view.

3. Use the buttons (**View**, **Sort**, and **Filter**) on the Tool bar to show, select, sort, and filter files.

4. To preview files, click the **View** button, and then click an option:

   ◆ **Slideshow.** Displays a slide show of the viewed files.

   ◆ **Review Mode.** Displays a full screen preview of the viewed files.

   ◆ **Full Screen Preview.** Displays a full screen preview. You can also press the Spacebar.

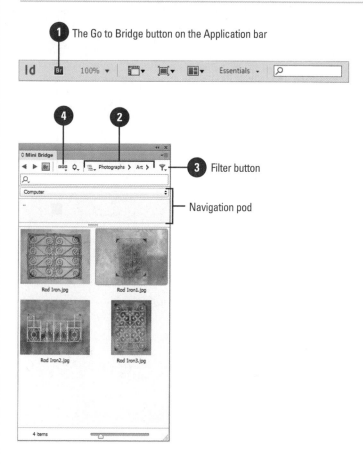

1 The Go to Bridge button on the Application bar

3 Filter button

Navigation pod

Scripting with Adobe ExtendScript Toolkit

Adobe ExtendScript Toolkit is a program—available for download from Creative Cloud—you can use to create and test scripts to control and automate features in many Adobe programs. If you perform the same set of tasks on a regular basis, you can use scripting as a powerful tool to make a lengthy set of tasks simple. A script is a series of statements in a language—an extended version of JavaScript, called ExtendScript—that tells a program what to do. For example, you can write a script to open an image in Photoshop, make some enhancements, and then insert the image into an InDesign document. If you're new to scripting, take a look at the Adobe Intro To Scripting document, which you can open from the Help menu. You can also use the Scripts panel to access favorite and sample scripts by target program. You can open the script, modify it, save it, and run it within the target program. Another option is the search the web for Extend-Script sample scripts. ExtendScript programs and scripts end with the extension JSX. A normal JavaScript file ends with the extension JS.

Use ExtendScript Toolkit to Work with Scripts

1. Start Adobe ExtendScript Toolkit from the Start menu or screen (Win) or the Applications folder (Mac).

2. To use a built-in script, select the **Scripts** panel, select a target program, and then navigate to a script, and then double-click it to open it.

3. To start a new script, click the **File** menu, and then click **New JavaScript**.

4. Enter or edit the script in the Document window.

5. To start, stop, pause, or step through the script, click the buttons on the Document window toolbar.

   ◆ You can also use commands on the Debug menu.

6. Click the **File** menu, and then click **Save**. If a new script, enter a name, specify a location, and then click **Save**.

7. When you're done, click the **Close** button to exit the program.

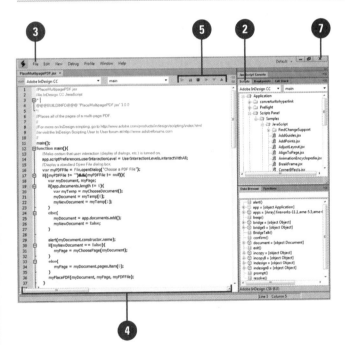

Working with Adobe Media Encoder

Adobe Media Encoder is a program—available for download from Creative Cloud—you can use to encode and compress video and audio files and convert them to a variety of distribution formats: F4V, FLV, H.264, and MP3. With the Preset Browser, you can select a format and preset for systems—such as high-definition (HD), desktops and the web (Flash, Vimeo, and YouTube)—and devices—such as Apple TV, iPad, iPhone, and Android. The presets include: size, bitrate (data rate), and frames per second (fps) rate. When you export a movie for playback on a specific type of device at a certain bandwidth, you select an encoder (codec). Each encoder has a corresponding decoder that decompresses and interprets the data for playback. You can batch process multiple media files to expedite the workflow process. For example, you can add, reorder, and change the encoding settings of files in the batch processing queue while Media Encoder encodes other files. You can also use the Watch folder to help you automate the process. It's a folder you add to the Watch folder list that automatically encodes any files in it.

Convert Media Files Using Presets

1. Start Adobe Media Encoder from the Start menu or screen (Win) or the Applications folder (Mac).

2. Click the **Add Source** button (+), select the media files you want to convert, and then click **Open**.

3. Select each media file, click the **Format** list arrow, and then select a conversion file format. Click the **Preset** list arrow, and then select a predefined setting.

4. To use the Preset Browser, select the media file, select a preset, and then click **Apply Preset**.

   This adds a copy of the selected file with the preset applied.

   ◆ Presets. Use toolbar buttons to create, delete, group, view settings, import, and export presets.

5. Click the **Start Queue** button.

   The media files are converted to the new media format and placed in the same folder as the original.

6. When you're done, click the **Close** button to exit the program.

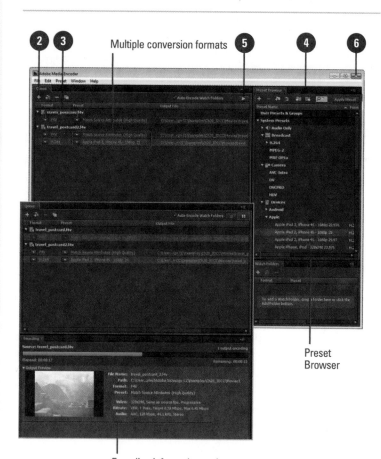

Multiple conversion formats

Preset Browser

Encoding information and progress

Convert Media Files Using Custom Settings

1. Start Adobe Media Encoder from the Start menu or screen (Win) or the Applications folder (Mac).

2. Click the **Add Source** button (+), select the media files you want to convert, and then click **Open**.

   TIMESAVER *You can drag one or more files from the desktop or file window directly into the queue.*

3. To create a duplicate copy of a media file to set different settings, select the media file, and then click the **Duplicate** button.

4. To apply custom export settings, select the media file, click the **Edit** menu, click **Export Settings**, specify the settings you want, and then click **OK**.

5. To use a watch folder, click the **Add Folder** button (+), select the folder you want to use, and then click **OK**.

   ◆ Select each folder, click the **Format** list arrow, and then select a conversion file format. Click the **Preset** list arrow, and then select a predefined setting.

   TIMESAVER *You can drag one or more folders from the desktop or file window directly into the queue.*

6. Click the **Start Queue** button.

   The media files are converted to the new media format and placed in the same folder as the original.

7. When you're done, click the **Close** button to exit the program.

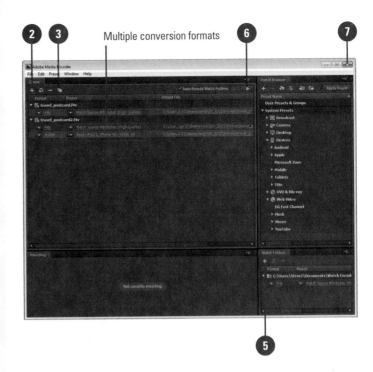

Multiple conversion formats

Working with Adobe Extension Manager

Adobe Extension Manager CC is a program—available for download from Creative Cloud—you can use to install and delete added program functionality, known as extensions, to many Adobe programs. The Extension Manager is available from the Help menu in Dreamweaver, Flash, InDesign, or Fireworks. You can use the Extension Manager or the Adobe Exchange panel (**New!**)—available on the Extensions sub-menu on the Window menu—to access the Adobe Exchange site, where you can locate, research, and download many different types of extensions with the ZXP or MXP (for compatibility) file format. ZXP is an Adobe Zip Format Extension Package file. Some are free and some are not. After you download an extension, you can use Extension Manager to install it for all users or only the current user. In Extension Manager, you can search and filter, enable, disable, and remove extensions.

Install and Use an Extension

1. Start Adobe Extension Manager from the Start menu or screen (Win) or the Applications folder (Mac).

   TIMESAVER *In Flash, InDesign, Dreamweaver, or Fireworks, click the Help menu, and then click Manage Extensions.*

2. To locate an extension, click **Exchange** to access the Exchange web site, download an extension, and then save it.

3. To install an extension, click **Install**, locate and select the extension (.zxp or .mxp), and then click **Open**.

4. Perform any of the following:

   ◆ **Search.** Select a filter from the down arrow, and then enter search name.

   ◆ **Sort.** Click a column heading.

   ◆ **Enable or Disable.** Select or deselect the **Enabled** check box.

   ◆ **Remove.** Select the extension, and then click **Remove.**

5. When you're done, click the **Close** button.

Installed Extensions

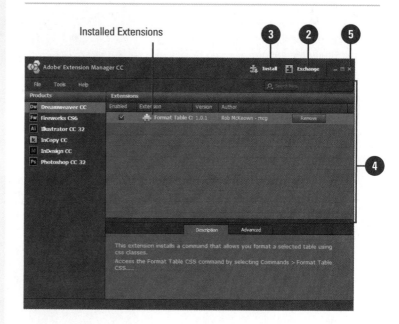

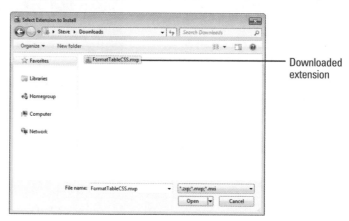

Downloaded extension

Using the Adobe Exchange Panel

Adobe Exchange is a web site to get resources for Adobe programs. You can find brushes and textures to use in your documents and plug-ins and extensions to add functionality to your Adobe program. You can access the Adobe Exchange directly from Adobe CC programs with the Adobe Exchange panel (**New!**). With the Adobe Exchange panel, you can find, purchase (if needed), download, and install resources, extensions, and plug-ins for Adobe programs. In order to use Adobe Exchange, you'll need your Adobe ID to access, store, and manage your resources online in My Stuff. From the Options menu in the Adobe Exchange panel, you can also install or launch Adobe Extension Manager CC (**New!**) to work with extensions for all Adobe programs.

Add Resources with the Adobe Exchange Panel

1. In your Adobe CC program, select the **Adobe Exchange** panel.

   ◆ Click the **Window** menu, point to **Extensions**, and then click **Adobe Exchange** (**New!**).

2. To display the home screen with features and new resources, click the **Home** button.

3. To search for a resource, click in the Search box, enter a keyword, and then press Enter (Win) or Return (Mac).

4. Click any of the following tabs on the panel:

   ◆ **All.** Displays all resources.

   ◆ **Paid.** Display resources that cost a price.

   ◆ **Free.** Display resources that are free.

   ◆ **My Stuff.** Display all resources you downloaded.

5. To download and install a resource (add to My Stuff), click the item, click the tabs, click the **Free** or **Price** button, and then follow the on-screen instructions

6. To use Adobe Extension Manager, click the **Options** button, and then click **Launch Extension Manager** or Install Extension Manager.

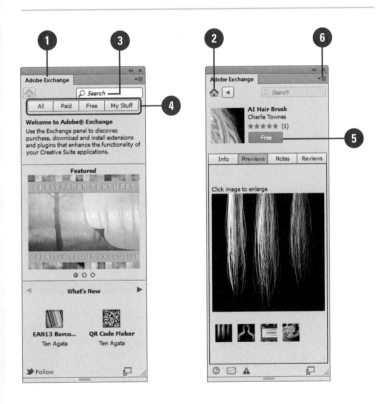

Accessing Adobe Creative Cloud

Creative Cloud is a membership-based cloud solution that allows you to access and download Adobe software, tools, services, tutorial videos, personal files, and sync Adobe CC program settings online from any computer or device. For more details about the membership levels and services, go to *www.creativecloud.com* in your browser. In order to sync program settings (**New!**) and access or download online content on Creative Cloud and Adobe.com, you'll need to sign in to the service with your Adobe ID, which you can do within an Adobe CC program. If you're not signed in when you start an Adobe CC program, you'll be asked to do so. If you synced program settings (**New!**) on Creative Cloud from another computer, you'll be asked if you want to sync settings to this computer on start up (**New!**).

Access Adobe Creative Cloud

1. Start your Adobe CC program.

2. To sign in to your Creative Cloud account, click the **Help** menu, click **Sign In**, click **Sign In Now**, create an account or enter your

   ◆ To sign out, click the **Help** menu, click **Sign Out (***account address***)**, and then click **Sign out**.

3. Click the **Edit** (Win) or *Adobe program name* (Mac) menu, point to *account address*, and then click **Manage Creative Cloud Account**.

   Your default web browser opens, displaying your Creative Cloud account.

4. Click the **Files**, **Apps** or **Upgrade** to access content and options.

5. Use the page options to work with files, view videos, and access Apps and services.

6. When you're done, click the **Close** button to exit your web browser.

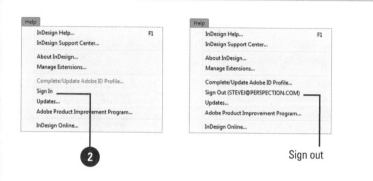

Sign out

New! Features

Adobe InDesign CC

Adobe InDesign CC means superior results faster with new features and enhancements that help you create and manage your images more easily and efficiently. The indispensable new and improved features help graphic web designers, photographers, and video professionals create the highest quality images, with the control, flexibility, and capabilities that you expect from the professional standard in desktop and mobile device digital imaging.

Each new release of InDesign brings with it new features, improvements, and added sophistication. This edition is aimed at the web designer, interactive media professional, or subject matter expert developing multimedia content, and the application developer.

Only New Features

If you're already familiar with InDesign CS6, you can access and download all the tasks in this book with Adobe InDesign CC New Features to help make your transition to the new version simple and smooth. The InDesign CC New Features as well as other InDesign CS6 to InDesign CC transition helpers are available on the web at *www.perspection.com.*

What's New

If you're searching for what's new in InDesign CC, just look for the icon: **New!**. The new icon appears in the table of contents and throughout this book, so you can quickly and easily identify a new or improved feature in InDesign CC. The following is a brief description of each new feature and its location in this book.

InDesign CC

◆ **Adobe Creative Cloud (p. 1, 2-5, 21, 421-422, 542)** Creative Cloud is a membership-based cloud solution that allows you to access and download Adobe software, personal files, tutorial videos, and sync Adobe CC program settings online from any computer or device. A free membership is available with entry level features. A monthly cost-based membership adds downloads and more features. You can go to *www.creativecloud.com* for more details.

- ◆ **64-bit Version of InDesign (p. 2, 4-5)** InDesign is available in a 64-bit version to leverage RAM beyond 3GB for both Mac and Windows computers. With support for 64-bit architecture, general processing is faster and more RAM can be made available to the application. This speeds up processes, and working on several large files at one time is easier. To take advantage of these features on Windows operating system, install on a 64-bit version of Windows, instead of a 32-bit version. The Mac version only comes in 64-bit.

- ◆ **Updated Interface (p. 4-5)** The user interface has been updated to match other Adobe apps, such as Illustrator, Photoshop, and Premier Pro.

- ◆ **HiDPI (p. 4-5)** InDesign comes with HiDPI, which enables the rendering process for an improved display on high resolution devices, such as a Macbook Pro with Retina display, where artwork, graphics, text, content, and UI elements appear crisper. You'll notice the improvement when you zoom, pan, copy paste, and drag elements.

- ◆ **Color Theme Interface (p. 6, 44, 234, 485)** In Interface preferences, you can change the appearance of the user interface by selecting a specific color theme from light gray to dark gray. You can also match the Pasteboard to the selected theme color.

- ◆ **InDesign CC File Format (p. 12-13, 24-25)** When you open an InDesign CS6 or earlier document, the document tab includes "[Converted]," which you can save to update it to the InDesign CC document file format.

- ◆ **New Document (p. 28-29, 32-33)** The New Document dialog box includes an option to show a preview of the new document. As you select new document options, you see the changes in the background at the same time. Two buttons—Save Document Preset and Delete Document Preset—have been added next to the Document Preset drop-down menu to save or delete presets.

- ◆ **Font Menu (p. 114)** When you display the font list from the Character or Control panel, the font families appear in groups with a triangle to their left, which you can click to expand/collapse the associated font family styles. A preview of the font appears next to the font name. You can browse the font list with the Arrow keys. On selection, the font is applied to the selected text for preview.

- ◆ **Find Fonts (p. 114)** You can search for the font you want from the Character or Control panel. You can perform the search based on the entire font name or first word only by using the Magnifying Glass icon in the Search box. You can clear a search by clicking the Close button or deleting the search in the Search box.

- ◆ **Favorite Fonts (p. 114)** You can add or remove a favorite font from the font list by clicking the Favorite icon (star) to the left of the font name. When the Favorite icon is highlighted, the font is marked as a favorite; when it's not (clear in the middle), the font is not marked as a favorite. You can select the Show Favorite Fonts Only check box to display only your favorite fonts. Adding or removing a font belonging to a family adds or removes the entire font family to the favorite font list.

- ◆ **QR Code (p. 379)** You can generate and edit high quality independent QR code graphics. You can select any one of the following data types for a QR code: Web Hyperlink, Plain Text, Text Message, Email, or Business Card. The default background of a QR code frame is transparent. However, you can change the

Frame's Fill and Stroke attributes such as the Color, Line Style, and Thickness using the traditional controls. The generated QR code element is a high-fidelity graphics object that behaves exactly like vector art in InDesign. You can move, resize or rotate the placed QR code object with the Selection tool. You can easily scale the code object and can fill it with colors. You can also apply effects, transparency, and printing attributes such as over printing, spot inks, and trappings to the code object. You can copy-paste the QR code graphics as a vector object into a standard graphics editor tool, such as Adobe Illustrator.

◆ **Language Support (p. 488)**   If you want to use a non-latin language, you need to enable options in Advanced Type preferences to use the Windows or Macintosh controls for language input, layout composition (Adobe composer for single-line or paragraph justification), and missing characters (glyphs). The Adobe composer option comes in three different variations for language support: World-Ready (middle-eastern or mixed), Japanese, and general (latin).

◆ **Adobe Exchange Panel (p. 522, 540, 541)**   With the Adobe Exchange panel, you can find, purchase, download, and install resources, extensions, and plug-ins for Adobe programs. You can access the Adobe Exchange panel from the Window menu under Extensions.

◆ **Adobe Camera Raw 8 (p. 526-529)**   Camera Raw 8 includes the Advanced Healing brush to touch up the shape of a region with the Spot Removal tool, the Radial Filter tool to apply adjustments to the outside or inside of an oval or circular area, and the Upright tool (under the Lens Correction tab, and the Manual tab) to automatically straighten horizons and apply perspective corrections without distorting the image. In addition, White Balance (under the Basic tab) includes added presets: Daylight, Cloudy, Shade, Tungsten, Fluorescent, and Flash.

EPUB Enhancements

◆ **Object Export Options for Object Styles (p. 316-317, 456)**   The Object Style Options dialog box includes Export Options for Alt Text, Tagged PDF, and EPUB and HTML. You can specify Rasterization settings and Custom Layout options. Objects with the applied style are handled based on the Export Options.

◆ **Emit CSS (p. 322, 451)**   An Emit CSS option has been added under Export Tagging in the Paragraph Style Options, Character Style Options, and Object Style Options dialog boxes, and under EPUB and HTML in the Edit All Export Tags dialog box. If you select the Emit CSS option while adding a class name for a particular style, the style takes precedence in case of a conflict and the CSS class is defined based on the style.

◆ **Object Style to Export Tag Mapping (p. 322, 451)**   The Object Style Options dialog box includes an Export Tagging category for mapping styles to classes and tags, similar to the one in the Paragraph Style Options and Character Style Options dialog boxes.

◆ **Multiple Class Names (p. 451-453)**   You can add multiple class names, which must be separated by one or more spaces and the first class name is used to generate the CSS for Style, if the Emit CSS option is enabled. This allows you to override or extend CSS properties with an additional CSS file in the Advanced category in the EPUB Export Options or HTML Export Options dialog boxes.

- **Style to Class Name Mapping (p. 451-455)** While generating a class name from a style name, InDesign generates a fully qualified class name: <style group name>_<style name>.

- **Style Class Ownership Conflict (p. 451-455)** If you map two styles to the same class name, it results in a conflict when you decide to generate CSS for the document. When exporting, InDesign flags a warning and displays a message about the conflict.

- **CSS Class Naming Override (p. 451-455)** When InDesign maps attributes with appropriate CSS properties, it is often necessary to generate a sort of "override class" to adjust the behavior of the CSS class generated from the style. When this happens, the generated class names reflect their purpose, which also reduces the confusion with user override class names from attribute overrides.

- **Export Without CSS (p. 452-456)** When you export an InDesign document or book to EPUB/HTML, you can specify whether to generate CSS. If you decide not to generate CSS, only the classes associated with the styles are marked in the HTML tags; no overriding classes are created.

- **Export Warning/Error Dialog Box (p. 452-455)** A dialog makes it easier to read multiple warning/error messages from an EPUB or HTML export.

- **Improved Markup for Ordered and Numbered Lists (p. 452-455)** The generated markup for "Map to Unordered List" and "Map to Ordered List" options for Bullets and Numbers in the EPUB Export and HTML Export dialog boxes no longer includes any extra classes. InDesign no longer inserts any characters or create any spans, and lets the browser be responsible for composing the lists.

- **Improved HTML Markup and CSS to Text Lists (p. 452-455)** The HTML markup and CSS of the "Convert To Text" options for Bullets and Numbers in the EPUB Export and HTML Export dialog boxes has been improved. InDesign inserts necessary bullet or number characters and override styling so that the overall look of the list option remains close to how it looks in InDesign.

- **Improved Bullet and Numbering Structure (p. 452-455)** For bullets, (1) InDesign treats two paragraphs which share all the same bullet related attributes, including left indent, as being part of the same list; and (2) a paragraph (not a bullet), which follows a bullet paragraph and has the same left indent is considered as a "nested" paragraph and becomes part of the list. For numbers, you can set the attribute for the "List," which has the highest priority relative to left indent or different number related attributes. Although InDesign supports setting the value attribute on the <li> tag, it is not possible to express a numbered list, which crosses Table and Story boundaries, in HTML. For correct numbering, export to EPUB 3.0.

- **Table of Contents (TOC) Stories (p. 452-453)** The TOC Story is exported like any other Story. If portions of the TOC Stories are copied and pasted elsewhere, the hyperlinks to the PDF and the source paragraphs (for an EPUB export) remain live. The NCX (navigation) file, required in the EPUB Package, cannot use an existing TOC and will be generated using the TOC Style as in CS6. If you don't want page numbers in the TOC, you need to remove them manually or generate the TOC without them. TOC stories generated in CS6 and before need to be regenerated in CC for the links to be live back to their source paragraphs.

- **Index Stories** Index stories are supported in the exported EPUB file. Live hyperlinks to indexed terms are displayed in the exported file. The terms retain their references to content at the paragraph level.

- **Version String Metadata** A version number has been added to the generator metadata: <meta name="generator" content="Adobe InDesign 9.0" />

- **Improved Naming Conventions to CSS Classes** InDesign generates a variety of extra classes for the purposes of improving the visual fidelity and conceptual mapping between InDesign and EPUB. The classes are renamed to match and clarify their purpose. The generated CSS classes include: *CharOverride-#*, *ParaOverride*, *TableOverride-#*, *CellOverride-#*, *ObjectOverride-3*, *_idGenParaOverride-#*, *_idGenCharOverride-#*, and *_idGenDropCap-#*.

- **CSS Generated for Japanese Ruby Tag** InDesign generates a separate CSS rule containing just the ruby related attributes.

- **Scripting Support for EPUB Book Export** The scripting support was not available in CS6, and the same is available now.

- **Improved Mapping of Bullet Character to List-Style Type** If any unicode value is found other than 0x2022 (bullet) for the "disc" CSS property, 0x25CB (white circle for the "circle" CSS property, and 0x25A0 (black square) for the "square" CSS property, the CSS will not specify it, leaving it to the browser or device default, which is typically "disc."

- **Paragraph Keep Option Property Mapping** The Keeps Option Paragraph options map to the following CSS properties: Keep With Previous to *page-break-before:avoid*, Keep All Lines together to *orphans: 99*, Keep first N to *orphans: #*, Keep Last N to *window: #*, and Keep With Next N to *page-break-after:avoid*. The Start Paragraph option maps to *page-break-before:avoid*. " If a conflict occurs between the Start Paragraph and the Keep With Paragraph option, the Start Paragraph takes precedence.

- **Improved CSS Generation for <li> Tags** As part of the HTML markup changes, all CSS properties which are defined as being relative to their parent (in HTML terms) need to generate override classes to behave as they did in InDesign.

- **Empty Tags Ranges Removed** InDesign looks for empty tag ranges and remove them. Empty paragraphs in InDesign are not really empty—they contain a carriage return and are composed with vertical height. InDesign maps paragraphs to <p> and <li> tags as appropriate and the carriage return is not part of the mapping that can lead to empty tags. Likewise there are certain transformations involving Anchored Objects and Tables that result in paragraphs which did contained content but no longer have any once in HTML.

- **Access to iBooks Reader Device Fonts** iBooks Reader supports a wide number of device fonts (*http://iosfonts.com*), and these fonts are not enabled by default when referenced via @font-face unless the special XML option file META-INF/com.apple.ibooks.display-options.xml is added to the package. The option file is added to both the EPUB2.0 and EPUB3.0 packages.

- **Font Embedding on iBooks Reader** EPUBCheck has been changed to accept the embedded font format as being acceptable for iBooks Reader.

What Happen To ...

◆ **Welcome Screen**   The Welcome screen that appears when you start InDesign or use the Help menu command has been removed.

◆ **HTML5 Pagination Options**   The HTML5 Pagination Options command on the layout Options menu in the Pages panel for alternate layouts has been removed.

◆ **EPUB 3.0 with Layout (p. 452-453)**   Since the DPS Reader has decided not to support this format, the EPUB 3.0 with Layout option from the EPUB Export dialog box has been removed.

◆ **Static Ordered List (p. 452-455)**   InDesign offers a true (stripped) markup to lists respecting the starting number values, so the "Map to Static Ordered List" option for Numbers from the EPUB Export and HTML Export dialog boxes has been removed.

◆ **Adobe Extension Manager (505, 540)**   The feature to Manage Sets from the Adobe Extension Manager CC program has been removed.

Adobe Certification

About the Adobe Certified Expert (ACE) Program

The Adobe Certified Expert (ACE) program is for graphic designers, web designers, systems integrators, value-added resellers, developers, and business professionals seeking official recognition of their expertise on Adobe products.

What Is an ACE?

An Adobe Certified Expert is an individual who has passed an Adobe Product Proficiency Exam for a specific Adobe software product. Adobe Certified Experts are eligible to promote themselves to clients or employers as highly skilled, expert-level users of Adobe software. ACE certification is a recognized worldwide standard for excellence in Adobe software knowledge. There are three levels of ACE certification: Single product certification, Specialist certification, and Master certification. To become an ACE, you must pass one or more product-specific proficiency exams and sign the ACE program agreement. When you become an ACE, you enjoy these special benefits:

- Professional recognition
- An ACE program certificate
- Use of the Adobe Certified Expert program logo

What Does This Logo Mean?

It means this book will prepare you fully for the Adobe Certified Expert exam for Adobe InDesign CC. The certification exam has a set of objectives, which are organized into broader skill sets. The Adobe Certified Expert objectives and the specific pages throughout this book that cover the objectives are available on the web at *www.perspection.com*.

 ID 3.1

Choosing a Certification Level

There are three levels of certification to become an Adobe Certified Expert.

◆ **Single product certification.** Recognizes your proficiency in a single Adobe product. To qualify as an ACE, you must pass one product-specific exam.

◆ **Specialist certification.** Recognizes your proficiency in multiple Adobe products with a specific medium: print, web, or video. To become certified as a Specialist, you must pass the exams on the required products. To review the requirements, go online to *http://www.adobe.com/support/certification/ace_certify.html*.

◆ **Master certification.** Recognizes your skills in terms of how they align with the Adobe product suites. To become certified as a Master, you must pass the exam for each of the products in the suite.

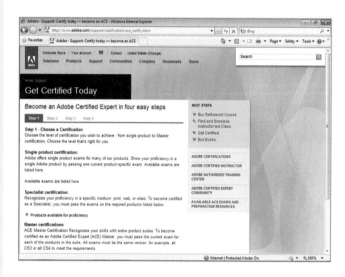

Preparing for an Adobe Certified Expert Exam

Every Adobe Certified Expert Exam is developed from a list of objectives, which are based on studies of how an Adobe program is actually used in the workplace. The list of objectives determine the scope of each exam, so they provide you with the information you need to prepare for ACE certification. Follow these steps to complete the ACE Exam requirement:

1 Review and perform each task identified with a Adobe Certified Expert objective to confirm that you can meet the requirements for the exam.

2 Identify the topic areas and objectives you need to study, and then prepare for the exam.

③ Review the Adobe Certified Expert Program Agreement. To review it, go online to *http://www.adobe.com/support/certification/ace_certify.html*.

You will be required to accept the ACE agreement when you take the Adobe Certified Exam at an authorized testing center.

④ Register for the Adobe Certified Expert Exam.

ACE testing is offered at more than a thousand authorized Pearson VUE and Thomson Prometric testing centers in many countries. To find the testing center nearest you, go online to *www.pearsonvue.com/adobe* (for Pearson VUE) or *www.2test.com* (for Prometric). The ACE exam fee is US$150 worldwide. When contacting an authorized training center, provide them with the Adobe Product Proficiency exam name and number you want to take, which is available online in the Exam Bulletin at *http://www.adobe.com/support/certification/ace_certify.html*.

⑤ Take the ACE exam.

Getting Recertified

For those with an ACE certification for a specific Adobe product, recertification is required of each ACE within 90 days of a designated ACE Exam release date. There are no restrictions on the number of times you may take the exam within a given period.

To get recertified, call Pearson VUE or Thomson Prometric. You will need to verify your previous certification for that product. If you are getting recertified, check with the authorized testing center for discounts.

Taking an Adobe Certified Expert Exam

The Adobe Certified Expert exams are computer-delivered, closed-book tests consisting of 60 to 90 multiple-choice questions. Each exam is approximately one to two hours long. A 15-minute tutorial will precede the test to familiarize you with the function of the Windows-based driver. The exams are currently available worldwide in English only. They are administered by Pearson VUE and Thomson Prometric, independent third-party testing companies.

Exam Results

At the end of the exam, a score report appears indicating whether you passed or failed the exam. Diagnostic information is included in your exam report. When you pass the exam, your score is electronically reported to Adobe. You will then be sent an ACE Welcome Kit and access to the ACE program logo in four to six weeks. You are also placed on the Adobe certification mailing list to receive special Adobe announcements and information about promotions and events that take place throughout the year.

When you pass the exam, you can get program information, check and update your profile, or download ACE program logos for your promotional materials online at:

http://www.adobe.com/support/certification/community.html

Getting More Information

To learn more about the Adobe Certified Expert program, read a list of frequently asked questions, and locate the nearest testing center, go online to:

http://www.adobe.com/support/certification/ace.html

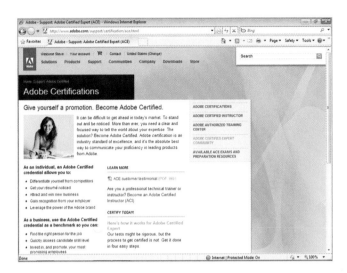

To learn more about other Adobe certification programs, go online to:

http://www.adobe.com/support/certification

Index

A

absolute colorimetric, specifying, 213
accessible PDF,
    Articles panel, ordering content, 446-447
    creating PDF, 448
    finishing in Acrobat Pro, 449
    tags, applying to, 450
Acrobat.com, Adobe.com
    DPS, folio publications, 388-396
    sign in and out, DPS, 388-389
Acrobat layers, Adobe PDF option for
    creating, 427
Acrobat Pro, 448-449
actions for buttons, editing or adding,
    372–373
activation of program, 2
Actual Size, viewing document in, 38
Add button, Pathfinder, 273
additive RGB. *See* RGB (Red, Green, Blue)
Adobe
    Acrobat, 427
    Creative Cloud, 1-5, 521-522, 542
        sign in and out, 2-5, 21, 542
    Dreamweaver, HTML format, exporting
        documents for, 454–455
    Exchange panel, 3, 522, 541
    exploring programs, 522
    Product Improvement Program, 23
    programs working with, 521–541
    web site
        plug-ins, availability of, 505
        updates and patches, checking for, 20
        Welcome screen links to, 4
Adobe Application Manager, 20
Adobe Application Manager Preferences
    dialog box, 20–21
Adobe Bridge, 1, 522
    automating tasks in, 535

Batch command in, 534
browsing
    documents, 14
    graphics, 148
camera raw plug-in, 1, 522
    working with, 510-511
color settings synchronizing, 211
copying and pasting settings in, 534
digital cameras preferences for Camera
    RAW, 526-527
DNG format, converting RAW files to,
    525
documents, inserting file information in,
    478–479
getting started with, 524
Home web site, 4
Image Processor command in, 534
images, working with, 532–533
JPEG files, opening, 530-531
labels to images, adding, 533
libraries, using, 399
linked graphics, locating, 148
Mini Bridge, 210, 536
modifying images in, 534
naming/renaming, 14
    automatically renaming files, 535
opening
    documents in, 12, 14–15
    graphics, 148
preferences
    camera raw files, 526-527
presets, applying, 534
previewing, 532–533
raw images
    importing, 527-529
    modifying, 527-529
    working with, 526–529
renaming files automatically in, 535

Adobe Bridge *(continued)*
   revealing documents in, 15
   screen, diagram of, 523
   searching in, 14, 532
   templates, accessing and selecting, 30
   thumbnails in, 532–533
   TIFF files, opening, 530-531
   Tools menu, automating tasks with, 535
   Web Photo Gallery, creating, 531
   working with files in, 15
   workspaces, 523
      customizing, 524
   XMP files in, 533
Adobe Certification, 533
Adobe Composer
   language options, 488
   using, 125, 140
Adobe Content Viewer, 388-391, 396
Adobe Creative Cloud, 1-5, 521-522, 542
   sign in and out, 2-5, 21, 542
Adobe Digital Editions, 452-453
Adobe Digital Publishing Suite (DPS)
   articles, importing, 394
   creating folio publication, 392-393
   designing, 391
   document setup, 28-29, 34-35
   getting started, 388-389
   HTML, inserting, 378
   interactivity, adding, 390-391
   preview, settings, 396
   properties, setting, 395
   sharing, 396
   sign in and out, 389
   viewing content, 388-389, 396
Adobe Edge Animate
   inserting, HTML, 378
Adobe Exchange
   panel, 3, 522, 541
Adobe ExtendScript Toolkit, 1, 522
   working with, 537
Adobe Extension Manager, 1, 522
   plug-ins and extensions, 505
   working with, 540
Adobe Flash, 422. *See also* SWF file format
   buttons in, 366-367
   export file formats, 423
   Flash movie, exporting document as, 442–443

FLA for Flash, exporting document as, 444–445
Kuler panel, accessing, 230
page transitions in, 365
XFL format, 444
Adobe Illustrator
   importing artwork from, 143, 144–145
   Kuler panel, accessing, 230
   placing graphic files saved in, 142
   specialty frames for graphics, importing, 158
Adobe InCopy, 512. *See also* assignments
   assignment files, creating, 514
   color of user, setting up, 513
   InDesign content, exporting, 514
   managed files, 512, 514
      notes, adding, 513
   Package for, 516
   screen, diagram of, 520
   updating content in, 519
   user identification, setting up, 513
   working with, 520
Adobe InCopy Document, 423
Adobe InDesign
   installing, 2–3
   32-bit and 64-bit, 5
   system requirements, 3
   tagged text, 423
   window, viewing, 6
Adobe InDesign Markup (IDML) file format, 12, 24, 422, 423
Adobe InDesign Template (INDT) file format, 30. *See also* templates
Adobe Media Encoder, 1, 522
   working with, 356-357, 538-539
Adobe PDF. *See* PDF file format
Adobe Photoshop
   Adobe Bridge, using commands in, 534
   automating tasks in, 535
   Batch command in Adobe Bridge, 534
   clipping paths, creating, 276
   Image Processor command in Adobe Bridge, 534
   importing images, selecting layers when, 143, 144–145
   Kuler panel, accessing, 230
   placing graphic files saved in, 142
   wrapping text, path for, 137

After-Blending Intent option, 212

AICB (Adobe Illustrator Clipboard), 158

Align and Distribute, 11

aligning. *See also* grids; Smart Guides
  bullets and numbering, 127
  Gap tool, 184-185
  objects, 184-185
  paragraphs, 121
  stroke on path, changing alignment of, 238
  table cells, content of, 291
  tabs, 128
  text frame options, setting, 132
  text on a path, 101
  Type tool option, 11

All Caps, styling text as, 114–115

alpha channels
  clipping path, selecting as, 277
  importing images with, 143, 144–145
  for wrapping text, 137

alt text
  for graphics, 168
  for exporting to PDF, 448
  for object styles, 316-317

alternate layouts,
  creating, 384-385
  HTML5 Pagination Options, 386
  split window to compare, 386
  viewing by, 56
  working with, 386

Amazon Kindle, creating for, 452-453

animation
  Animation panel, 360-363
  with Motion Presets, 360-363
    applying, 360-361
    editing, 360-361
  order changing, 364

anchor points
  adding, 264–265
  deleting, 265
  Direct Selection tool, selecting with, 177
  joining, 268
  moving, 260-261
  open path, adding to, 265
  with Pen tool, 258–259
  reshaping, 260-261
  selecting, 260-261
  Smooth tool, using, 269

splitting paths at, 266

anchors
  hyperlinks creating text anchors, 346
  for objects, 197-199

Android 10"
  creating for, 452-453
  document setup, 28-29, 34-35

ANPA color library, 224

anti-aliasing in Story Editor display, 498, 499

appearance
  Adobe InCopy, Appearance panel in, 520
  Black, preferences for appearance of, 497
  of conditional text, 406
  of graphic frames, 170
  hyperlinks, changing appearance of, 349
  ruler guides, changing appearance of, 44–45

Apple iPad, creating for, 452-453

AppleScripts, 414

Application bar, 6
  in Adobe InCopy, 520

Apply Effect, 11

Apply Photoshop Clipping Path Option, 276

Arabic typefaces, 140, 488

Arial font, 114

Arrange Documents menu, 18–19

artboards, importing, 143, 144–145

articles, for folio, DPS
  articles, importing, 394
  properties, setting, 395

Articles panel
  ordering content, 446-447

artwork. *See* graphics

assignments
  checking content out and in, 518
  creating, 516–517
  existing assignment, adding to, 517
  locked files, overriding, 519
  out-of-date content, checking for, 519
  packages, creating, 516
  same time, creating assignment and adding content at, 516–517
  updating content, 519

Assignments panel, 515. *See also* assignments

Assign Profile dialog box, 212–213

audio/sound
Media panel, inserting, 356-357
Autocorrect for text, 112
Auto-Fit, 160-161
autoflowing imported text, 105

B

backgrounds
guides in, 44
Smart Guides in back, showing, 47
Story Editor display, setting, 498
Background Tasks panel
in background, exporting PDF in, 434
Barnes & Noble Nook, creating for, 452-453
barcode, 379
base color, 225
baseline
characters, shifting, 117
for footnotes, 341
paragraph rule, setting for, 125
paragraphs to baseline, aligning, 121
printing options, 460
table sells, specifying option for, 291
for text frames, 133
baseline grids, 48
preferences, setting, 49
Basic Feather effect, 251
Batch command in Adobe Bridge, 14, 534
bevel effect, 250
with corner options, 252
rectangles, beveled, 254
strokes, bevel join on, 239
bibliographies, hanging indents for, 122
bicubic downsampling with Adobe PDF, 428
bitmaps
BMP file format, placing graphic files
saved in, 142
color profiles for, 212–213
fonts, creating, 116
print as bitmap option, 470
black. *See also* CMYK (Cyan, Magenta,
Yellow, Black)
tones, preferences for, 497
blank pages, printing, 460
bleed. *See* marks and bleed
Bleed view, 36
blend effect, creating, 246–247

blending mode
color space, selecting, 247
feather effects, 251
glow effects, 249
with shadow effects, 248
BMP file format, placing graphic files saved
in, 142
boldfacing, changing, 114
bookmarks
Adobe PDF option, 427
creating, 354–355
Bookmarks panel, 354-355
books
adding or deleting, 81
blank page, inserting, 83
eBook, EPUB, exporting document for,
452-453
existing book, opening, 80
new book, creating, 80
opening documents in, 81
Page Order options, 83
printing, 81
saving, 81
synchronizing, 82
updating page and section numbers in,
83
Books template, 30
Book workspace, 52–53
borders to tables, adding, 299
Bounding Box option, 136–137
Bridge. *See* Adobe Bridge
Bring Forward in object stack, 188
Bring to Front in object stack, 188
Brochures template, 30
browsing. *See also* Adobe Bridge
Kuler panel themes, 230
bullets and numbering
adding, 126
Adobe Dreamweaver, exporting HTML,
document for, 454-455
digital editions, EPUB, specifying
options for, 452-453
formatting, 127
paragraph styles, setting, 305
butt caps on strokes, 239
buttons
actions, adding or editing, 372–373
Buttons panel, working with, 366-367

button states, working with, 374

deleting, 366-367

events for button, setting, 372

objects to buttons, converting, 368-369

sample, creating from, 368

tab order, setting, 375

Buttons and Forms panel, 368-369

C

camera raw images. *See* Adobe Bridge; DNG file format

Canon CR2 format, 529

cap colors for paragraph rule, width of, 124

capitalization. *See also* case-sensitivity; drop caps; small caps

Autocorrect fixing, 112

changing case, 342

hyphenating capitalized words, 335

spell-checking preferences, 494

caps on strokes, changing, 238–239

captions

adding to graphics, 16, 158-159

static, 158

with variables, 159

case-sensitivity

Adobe PDF passwords, 432

changing case, 342

with Find/Change command, 331

of style names, 310

Catalogs template, 30

CD/DVD

contents of, 2

sets template, 30

Cell Options dialog box, Diagonal Lines tab, 298

cell phones and RGB color, 214

cells. *See* tables

centering

paragraphs, 121

with Smart Guides, 47

text on path, 101

Certificates template, 30

chapter numbers

adding to document, 76

text variable, 78

Character panel, InCopy, 520

characters. *See also* letters

advanced type settings for, 488

for bullets, 126–127

End Nested Style Here special character, 314–315

Find/Change command for, 330

Info panel, information in, 50

for leading text, 117

outlines, creating, 138

for page numbers, 74

spacing options, 337

special characters

Find/Change command for, 330

inserting, 130

character styles

attributes for, 307

creating, 306–307

deleting, 306

mapping styles to export tags, 307, 322, 451

nested styles, creating, 314–315

Character Styles panel, 302

check boxes, 126–127

Chinese typefaces, 140, 488

Chisel Hard option with bevel effect, 250

Choke effect

with feather effects, 251

with glow, 249

with shadows, 248

Classic System theme, 498

Clear Transformation command, 189

Clipboard

handling preferences, setting, 502

objects, copying, 180

Clip Content to Cell option, 291

clipping path

alpha path as clipping path, selecting, 277

editing on importing, 145

graphic, modifying from, 145, 276

importing images with, 143, 144–145

for wrapping text, 137

Close button, 18, 26

for panels, 8

closed path, opening, 266–267

closing documents, 26

CMYK (Cyan, Magenta, Yellow, Black), 214

Adobe PDF options, setting, 430

black tones, preferences for, 497

CMYK *(continued)*
    Color panel, selecting with, 218
    EPS file format options, 438
    preserving colors, 233
    Working Space controls, 210–211
code
    HTML, 378
    QR Code, 379
Collapse to Icons option for panels, 8
collapsing/expanding. *See* panels
Color blend mode, 246
Color guide panel, 236
Color Labels, 66
Color Management, 210–211
    printing options, 472
color modes, 214
    Color panel, selecting with, 218
Color panel, 174
    fill or stroke color, changing, 236
    selecting color modes with, 218
    working with, 219
Color Picker, 236, 237
color profiles
    for bitmap images, 212–213
    changing, 212–213
    deleting, 212–213
    document colors to other profile, con-
        verting, 212–213
    importing images with, 143, 144–145
    Info panel, information in, 50
    rendering intent, specifying, 213
colors. *See also* CMYK (Cyan, Magenta,
    Yellow, Black); color profiles; fills; gap
    color/tint; gradients; Lab color; marks
    and bleed; objects; paragraphs; print-
    ing; RGB (Red, Green, Blue); strokes;
    Swatches panel; tables
    Adobe InCopy, setting colors for, 513
    Adobe PDF output options, 430
    applying colors, 215
    assignments, association with, 516
    for baseline grids, 49
    blend effect, creating, 246–247
    for buttons, 374
    of camera raw images, 528-529
    changing settings, 210–211
    character styles, setting, 307
    color theme, interface, 6, 234, 485

    for commands, 504
    for conditional text, 406
    for cross-references, 352-353
    dashed/dotted lines, gap color for, 239
    for Document grids, 49
    EPS file format options, 438
    Eyedropper tool, using, 216–217
    frame for graphic, coloring, 165
    gradient swatches, creating, 226–227
    for guides, 44
    hidden text, changing colors of, 131
    for hyperlinks, 351
    Kuler panel, using colors from, 230–231
    layer colors, specifying, 202
    note colors, identifying, 509
    overprinting colors, 232
    for package files, 480
    proofing colors on screen, 233
    separations, previewing, 465
    soft proofing colors on screen, 233
    swatch libraries, adding colors from, 224
    synchronizing color settings, 211
    for text in Story Editor display, 498
    tint swatches, creating, 225
    for Web Photo Gallery, 531
Color Sampler tool with camera raw files,
    528-529
Color Settings dialog box, 210–211
color space
    for blending transparent objects, 247
    Info panel, information in, 50
color stops
    editing, 243
    with gradients, 226–227
color theme, interface, 6, 234, 485
    Match to Theme Color option, 44
columns and rows. *See also* guides; tables
    changing options, 34–35
    creating, multiple, 134-135
    for Data Merge, 416
    hyphenating across, 335
    for new documents, 29
    text frame options, setting, 132
Command Bar for InCopy, 520
commands, 6
    Adobe InCopy commands, 520
    Batch command in Adobe Bridge, 14,
        534

Community Help site, 22

Community resources, Welcome screen links to, 4

compatibility
    Adobe PDF options, setting, 426
    of assignments, 516

Composer, Adobe, 125, 140, 488

composition preferences, setting, 489

compound path, creating, 274–275

compression
    Adobe PDF options, 425, 428
    Flash movie, document exported as, 443

condensed style, changing, 114

conditional text, working with, 406–407

Conditional Text panel, 407

Configure Plug-ins dialog box, 505

configuring plug-ins, 505

consolidating all documents, 19

contact sheet, creating, 146–147

Content Collector tool, 408-409

Content Placer tool, 408-409

Content Grabber, 160-161

Content Viewer, 388-391, 396

continued text, adding page numbers to, 139

Control of Transform panel, 189, 191

Control panel, 6, 174
    Adobe Bridge, 523
    Customizing, 506
    resizing objects in, 178
    using, 11

Convert Direction Point Tool, 262-263

converting URLs to hyperlinks, 348-349

Conveyor, 408-409

copies
    printing option, 460
    saving copy of document, 25

Copyfit Info panel, Adobe InCopy, 520

copying. See also objects
    Adobe Bridge, settings in, 534
    Clipboard handling preferences, setting, 502
    master pages, 73
    paths, 159
    text, 113

corner object effects, 252
    Live corners, 253

Corner Options dialog box, 252

rectangle shapes using radius value in, 254

Create Outlines command, 138, 158–159

Creative Cloud. See Adobe Creative Cloud

creep for booklet pages, 475

cropping. See also positioning
    Adobe PDF setting options, 428
    camera raw files, 528-529
    fitting graphics in frames and, 163

Cross-Reference dialog box, 352-353

cross-references, creating, 352-353

CSS options
    Emit CSS option, 322, 451
    EPUB exporting, 452-453
    HTML exporting, 454-454

CSS styles
    Adobe Dreamweaver, exporting HTML document for, 454-455
    for eBook, EPUB, 452-453

CSV (comma-delimited) data fields, 416

cursors
    graphic preview cursor, 146
    Story Editor cursor options, setting, 499

curves, Pen tool for drawing, 258–259

custom-dashed stroke, applying, 240

custom page size, 29

cutting
    spacing, automatic adjustment of, 486
    text, 113

D

Darken blend mode, 246

dashes. See also strokes
    inserting, 130

Data Merge, 416–417
    template, 30

DCS file format, WMFgraphic files saved in, 142

Default Image Intent option, 212–213

Delete Workspace dialog box, 53

deleting. See also tables
    with Adobe Bridge, 14
    Adobe PDF preset, creating, 433
    anchor points, 265
    bookmarks, 354-355
    books, documents in, 81
    buttons, 366-367

deleting *(continued)*
>   button states, 374
>   character styles, 306
>   color profiles, 212–213
>   color swatch, 221, 222
>   combined object, 183
>   cross-references, 352-353
>   empty pages, 108, 487
>   guides, 43
>   hyperlinks, 345, 350
>   layers, 201
>   library items, 398–399
>   master pages, 72–73
>   moving, deleting pages after, 66-67
>   notes, 509
>   objects, 174-175
>   in Open dialog box, 13
>   pages in Pages panel, 65
>   paragraph styles, 304
>   plug-ins, 505
>   presets, 32–33, 459
>   in Save As dialog box, 13
>   script files, 414
>   segments, 265
>   styles, 319
>   tabs, 128
>   text on path, 100
>   text variables, 79
>   trap presets, 468
>   workspaces, 53
>   XML tags, 418

destination files
>   Adobe PDF options, setting, 430
>   for cross-references, 352-353
>   for hyperlinks, 344
>   for linked graphics, 153

detect edges and wrapping text, 137

diagonal lines in table cells, adding, 298

Diagonal Lines tab, Cell Options dialog box, 298

DIC color library, 224

dictionaries
>   Autocorrect dictionary, 112
>   custom dictionaries, using, 326
>   preferences, setting, 492–493

digital cameras. *See also* Adobe Bridge
>   documents, inserting file information in, 478–479

digital editions, EPUB, exporting documents for, 452–453

Digital Imaging and Communications in Medicine options, inserting, 479

digital publishing
>   document setup, 28-29, 34-35

Digital Publishing Suite. DPS. *See* Adobe Digital Publication Suite

Directional Feather effect, 251

Direct Selection tool. *See also* overflow text
>   anchor points, selecting, 177
>   frames and graphics, selecting and moving, 160
>   graphics, selecting, 160, 176
>   grayscale graphic, applying color to, 165
>   with grouped objects, 182–183
>   objects, selecting, 174-175, 177

display
>   bleed mode, 36
>   changing, 36
>   library display, changing, 402–403
>   normal mode, 36
>   output views, 36–37
>   preview mode, 36
>   presentation mode, 36
>   slug mode, 36
>   Story Editor display preferences, setting, 325, 498–499

Distribute Columns Evenly command, 288

Distribute Rows Evenly command, 288

distributing
>   columns, 288
>   objects, 186–187

DNG file format
>   converting raw images to, 525
>   description of, 529
>   saving raw images in, 527-529

docking/undocking
>   document windows, 19
>   panels, 8

Document grids, 48, 49

Document Presets dialog box, 32

documents. *See also* assignments; books; exporting documents; graphics; Microsoft Word; multiple documents; new documents; opening
>   Adobe Bridge, working with, 14
>   changing document options, 34
>   closing, 26

color profiles, converting, 212–213

display performance, setting, 167

file information, inserting, 478–479

fonts, 482

images, inserting, 16

object defaults, setting, 255

preview images with document, saving, 24–25

printing, 458

saving, 24–25

spell-checking, 324–325

swatches from other documents, importing, 224

tabs, open as, 485

text, inserting, 16

XML tags, placing, 418–419

zooming in/out view of, 38–39

Document Setup dialog box, 34-35

document windows, 6

    for Adobe InCopy, 520

    docking/undocking, 19

    working with, 18

double quotation marks, inserting, 130

downloading

    extensions with Adobe Extension Manager, 505, 540

    print option for downloading fonts, 464

downsampling with Adobe PDF, 428

DPS. *See* Adobe Digital Publication Suite

drag-and-drop

    graphics, 152

    pages, moving, 66–67

    paths, 159

    snippets, creating, 404–405

    text, 113

    text editing options, selecting, 487

    with Zoom tool, 38

drawing

    Live Screen Drawing, 208

drop caps

    creating, 123

    paragraph styles, setting, 305

Drop Shadow, 11, 248

DTBook format for eBooks, EPUB, selecting, 452-453

duplicating

    color stops, 243

    color swatch, 220

    layers, 200–201

    objects, 180–181

    pages, 58

    plug-ins, 505

DVD. *See* CD/DVD

dynamic spelling, 324, 325, 495

E

eBook, EPUB, exporting document for, 452–453

Edit Custom Dictionary dialog box, 326

editing. *See also* hyperlinks; Story Editor; text

    Adobe PDF editing preset, creating, 433

    button actions, 372

    clipping path on importing, 145

    color swatch, 221

    cross-reference formats, 352-353

    gradients, 242–243

    Kuler panel theme, 231

    linked graphics, 155, 156

    mixed ink groups, 229

    presets, 459

    QR Code, 379

    Quick Apply, styles with, 321

    scripts, 414

    Spread view content, 37

    styles with Quick Apply, 321

    tables, text in, 284–285

Edit With submenu, 156

effects. *See also* specific effects

    for text on a path, 101

elements in XML file format, 418

Ellipse Frame tool, 170

ellipses

    converting, 254

    creating elliptical shape, 170

Ellipse tool, 170

    text, adding, 96, 98

e-mail, hyperlinks to, 346

embedding

    Adobe PDF options, 427

    general preferences, setting, 484

    graphics, 152, 153

    preflight profiles, 476–477

emboss effect, 250

em dashes, inserting, 130

Emit CSS option, 316, 322, 451

empty pages, deleting, 108, 487

empty sounds or movie clip frames, 356

enabling/disabling
JavaScript, 484
Live Preflight, 476–477

en dashes, inserting, 130

End Nested Style Here special character, 314–315

endnotes. *See* footnotes

English typefaces, 488

envelopes with Data Merge, 416–417

EPS file format, 423
exporting document in, 438–439
inserting files in, 16
metadata to files, adding, 479
placing graphic files saved in, 142

EPUB format
Articles panel, 446-447
for eBooks, selecting, 452-453
mapping styles to export tags, 305, 307, 322, 451
object export options, setting, 456

erasing parts of paths, 272

errors. *See also* spell-checking
Preflight panel, options in, 477

Essentials workspace, 52–53

events for buttons, setting, 372

Excel. *See also* XLS file format
tables, importing, 282–283

Exclude Overlap button, Pathfinder, 273

EXIF file format for metadata, 533

existing document, opening, 12

Exit command, 26

exiting InDesign, 26

Expand Panels button, 8

exporting. *See* exporting documents; importing/exporting

exporting documents, 422. *See also* PDF file format
in background, exporting PDF, 434
for accessible PDF, 448-449
for Adobe Dreamweaver, HTML, 454–455
description of file formats, 423
for digital editions, EPUB, 452–453
as EPUB, 452-453
in EPS file format, 438–439

FLA for Flash, exporting document as, 444–445
in InDesign CS4 or CS5 with IDML, 24, 422, 423
as HTML, 454–455
for interactive PDF, 436-337
as JPEG files, 440-441
with object styles, 316-317, 451
as PNG files, 440-441
for print, 424-432
for tags (mapping) to EPUB/HTML or PDF, 316, 322, 451
with text styles, 322, 451

exporting objects, setting
alt text, 168, 316
EPUB and HTML, 316, 456
tagged PDF, 450

exporting tags, mapping styles, 305, 307, 316, 322, 451

Export PDF dialog box
interactive, 436-437
print, 424-432

ExtendScript Toolkit, 1, 522
working with, 537

Extension Manager. *See* Adobe Extension Manager

Extensions submenu for accessing Kuler panel, 230

Eyedropper tool
colors, using for, 216–217
fill or stroke color, changing, 236
options, changing, 217

F

F4V format, 356-358

facing pages
changing, 34
new documents, selecting for, 28
spreads, preserving, 487

Fancy corner options, 252

favorite fonts, 114

Favorites panel, Adobe Bridge, 523

feather effects, 251

fields for Data Merge, 416

file formats. *See also* exporting documents; specific types
opening document files in, 12
placing graphic files saved in, 142

File path, Adobe Bridge, 523

files. *See also* Adobe InCopy; assignments
documents, inserting file information in, 478–479
handling preferences, setting, 500–501
hyperlinks to, 346
package files, creating, 480–481
sidecar files, 533

fills. *See also* tables
adding, 294–295
applying fill colors, 215, 236–237
compound path, object's fill in, 275
default and switch for fill colors, 236–237
defaults, setting, 255
Eyedropper tool, using, 216–217

Filter panel, Adobe Bridge, 523

filters
with Adobe Bridge, 14, 523
Graduated Filter with camera raw files, 528-529

Find/Change command, 328–329
for glyphs, 328–329, 332
for GREPs, 328–329, 332
with objects, 328–329, 334
special characters, finding, 330

Find Font dialog box, 327

Fire/Nook
document setup, 28-29, 34-35

first-line indent
for bullets and numbering, 127
creating, 122

first page, navigating to, 63

Fit Page In Window option, 38

Fit Spread in Window option, 38

fitting
booklet pages, marks and bleed in, 475
Flash movie, document exported as, 442
FLA for Flash, document exported as, 444
graphics in frames, 163

FLA format, 356-358, 423, 444-445

Flash. *See* Adobe Flash

flattened artwork, printing, 471

Flattener Preview mode, 36–37

flatten transparency. *See* transparency

flipping, 11. *See also* objects
print orientation, 467
text on a path, 101

floating all windows, 19

floating tools panel options, 485

Focoltone color library, 224

Folders panel, Adobe Bridge, 523

folders with Adobe Bridge, 14

Folio Builder panel,
creating, folios, 392-393
getting, downloading, 388-389
importing, folios, 393
properties, setting, 395

Folio Overlays panel, 388-391
HTML, inserting, 378

folio publication
articles, importing, 394
creating, 392-393
designing, 391
getting started with DPS, 388-389
HTML, inserting, 378
interactivity, adding, 390-391
preview, settings, 396
properties, setting, 395
sharing, 396
sign in and out to DPS, 389
viewing content, 388-391, 396

Folio Producer tools, 388-389

Font Family option, Type tool, 11

fonts. *See also* glyphs; OpenType
Adobe PDF options, setting, 431
changing, 327
font family and style, 114
size of font, 116
digital editions, EPUB, specifying options for, 452-453
document, using, 482
favorite fonts, 114
Find/Change command, using, 328–329
finding fonts, 327
general preferences, setting, 484
graphics, options for, 464
package files including, 480–481
preferences, setting, 486–487
preview size, selecting, 487
printing options, 470
search for fonts, 114
size of font, changing, 116
Story Editor display, setting, 498
styles, changing, 114–115

Font Size option, Type tool, 11

Font Type option, Type tool, 11

Footnote Options dialog box, 340

footnotes

    adding, 340

    changing options, 341

    Find/Change command for searching, 329

    importing, 340

foreign characters, printing, 463

formatting. *See also* styles

    bullets and numbering, 127

    dragged text, inherited formatting for, 113

    footnotes, 341

    frames, graphics in, 165

    graphics in frames, 165

    JPEG files, documents exported as, 440-441

    PNG files, documents exported as, 440-441

    table of contents, 84–85

form

    adding controls, 371

    creating, PDF, 370-371

form letters with Data Merge, 416–417

Forms template, 30

45-degrees

    lines, drawing, 172

    objects, constraining movement of, 179

fractions. *See* glyphs

Frame Fitting Options dialog box, 162–163

frames. *See* graphic frames; text frames; unassigned frames

Frame tools for adding text, 96, 98

Free Transform tool, 191

French typefaces, 488

Fuji RAF format, 529

G

Gallery & Story panel, InCopy, 520

gamut colors. *See also* out of gamut

    identifying, 219

gap color/tint. *See also* tables

    for dashed/dotted lines, 239

    paragraph rule, width of, 124

Gap tool, 184-185

general preferences, setting, 484

Get Photos from Camera command, Adobe Bridge, 525

Getting Started, Welcome screen links to, 4

GIF file format

    EPUB and HTML, export, 451-456

    metadata to files, adding, 479

    placing graphic files saved in, 142

    WMFgraphic files saved in, 142

Global Light effect, 248

    with bevel effect, 248

    with emboss effect, 248

    setting, 250

    with shadows, 248

glow effects, 249

glyphs

    Find/Change command, using, 328–329, 333

    highlighting text with, 489

    inserting or replacing, 129

    spacing options, 337

Go Back option, 63

Go Forward option, 63

Google Maps

    inserting, HTML, 378

Go to Page option, 63

GPS (global positioning system) file format for metadata, 533

Gradient Feather tool, 245, 251

Gradient panel, 227. *See also* gradients

gradients. *See also* color stops

    applying gradient fill to object, 242

    editing, 242–243

    Gradient Feather tool, 245, 251

    Gradient tool, working with, 244

    swatches, creating, 226–227

Gradient tool, 244

Graduated Filter with camera raw files, 528-529

graphic frames. *See also* assignments

    appearance of, 170

    for bookmarks, 354-355

    captions

        adding to graphics, 158-159

        static, 158

        with variables, 159

    clipping path to frame, converting, 145, 276

coloring graphic frame, 165

compound path as frame, creating and releasing, 158

fitting graphics in, 162–163

formatting graphics in, 165

Frame Fitting Options dialog box, fitting graphics in frames with, 162–163

grayscale graphic, coloring, 165

moving frames and graphics, 160–161

nesting graphics in, 164

resizing, 161

    for fitting graphics in frames, 162

    graphics and frames, 161

searching for, 334

selecting frames and graphics, 160–161

specialty frames for graphics, creating, 158–159

type outlines as frames, creating, 159

graphic preview cursor, 146

graphics, 142. *See also* Adobe Photoshop; graphic frames; tables

Adobe Bridge, placing graphics from, 148–149

clipping path, modifying, 276

contact sheet, creating, 146–147

copying, 152

default display options, setting, 167

Direct Selection tool, selecting with, 160, 176

display

    changing display performance, 166

    default display options, setting, 167

documents

    file information, inserting, 478–479

    images, inserting, 16

drag-and-drop, 152

editing linked graphics, 155, 156

embedding, 152, 153

    changing graphic from linked to embedded, 155

existing frame with graphic, placing graphic in, 142

grayscale graphic, coloring, 165

high quality display, 166

InCopy, exporting content to, 514

Info panel, information in, 50

Info panel, viewing in, 51

inline graphic in object, placing, 197

linked graphics

    Adobe bridge, locating in, 148

    Conveyor, using, 408-409

    displaying information on, 153

    editing, 155, 156

    relinking, 153, 154, 155

    replacing, 154

    working with, 155

    XMP metadata, displaying, 157

locating graphics

    Adobe bridge, locating linked graphic in, 148

    Links panel, 154, 410-413

moving, 152

multiple graphics, placing, 146–147

nesting graphics in frames, 164

options, placing graphics with, 143

package files including, 480–481

pasting, 152

preview cursor, 146

print options, setting, 464

relinking, 154

    missing graphic, 153, 155

replacing linked graphic, 154, 410-411

resizing, 161

    allowing for, 387

    with Direct Selection tool, 176

    for fitting graphics in frames, 162

setting place import options, 144–145

sorting graphics in Links panel, 153

typical display setting, 166

updating links, 155, 410-411

XMP metadata, displaying, 157

zooming in/out view of, 38–39

grayscale

    with camera raw images, 528-529

    EPS file format options, 438

    graphics in grayscale, adding color to, 165

greeked text, 487

GREPs

    applying, 312–313

    creating, 308

    Find/Change command, using, 328–329, 332

    paragraph styles, setting, 305

    searching for, 332

GREP Styles dialog box, 332

grids. *See also* baseline grids
   Adobe PDF option, 427
   create multiple objects in, 173
   colors, specifying, 49
   preferences, changing, 48–49
   printing options, 460
   showing/hiding, 48
   Step and Repeat command, creating grid
     with, 181
   tiling documents in, 19
   working with, 48, 49
groups. *See also* objects
   mixed ink group, creating, 229
   style groups, creating, 309
guides. *See also* rulers; Smart Guides
   Adobe PDF option, 427
   changing guides, 44
   columns
     color, specifying, 44
     locking/unlocking, 43
   creating, 42
   deleting, 43
   moving, 42
   printing options, 460
   Smart Guides, 46–47
   working with, 43
gutters
   changing size of, 35
   new documents, selecting for, 29
   text frame options, setting, 132

H

H.290-encoded format, 356-357
Hand tool, moving with, 50
hanging indents, creating, 122
Hard Light blend mode, 246
harmony rule for colors, 231
headers and footers. *See also* tables
   for panels, 8
Hebrew typefaces, 140, 488
height, weight, width, 11. *See also* tables
   changing, 34
   for cross-references, 352-353
   Flash movie, document exported as, 442
   FLA for Flash, document exported as,
     444
   for hyperlinks, 349

for new documents, 28
   paragraph rule, width of, 124–125
   printing setup options, 461
   stroke, selecting weight of, 172, 174, 238
   text frame options, setting, 132
help information, 22–23
   searching for, 22–23
Help menu
   help information on, 22–23
   updates, checking for, 21
hidden lock files (IDLK), 518
hidden text
   in table of contents, 85
   working with, 131
hiding. *See* showing/hiding
Highlight Object under Selection Tool, 485
highlights
   composition preferences, setting, 489
   for conditional text, 421
   for cross-references, 352-353
   for hyperlinks, 349
HKS color library, 224
horizontal lines, converting, 254
horizontally tiling all documents, 19
horizontal text, leading applied to, 117
HTML document
   Articles panel, 446-447
   as Flash movie, exporting, 443
   exporting, 454-455
   HTML5, 454-455
   inserting HTML code, 378
   object export options, setting, 456
   mapping styles to export tags, 305,
     307, 316, 322, 451
hyperlinks
   Adobe PDF option, 427
   appearance, changing, 349
   creating, 346–347
   converting URLs and stylizing, 348-349
   cross-references, creating, 352–353
   defining destinations, 344
   deleting, 345, 350
   editing, 345
     from Hyperlinks panel, 351
   Flash movie, document exported as,
     443
   resetting, 350
   updating, 350

URLs
    creating hyperlink from, 346–347
    destination, setting URL as, 344
Hyperlinks panel, 350–351
  cross-references, creating, 352-353
hyphenation
  dictionary preferences, setting, 492
  inserting hyphens, 130
  options, changing, 335
  in package files, 481
  paragraph styles, setting, 305
Hyphenation dialog box, 335

I

ICMA files, 516
ICML files, 516
icons
  for linked graphics, 153
  Pages panel icons, 56–57
  showing/hiding, 504
IDML file format, 12, 24, 422, 423
  opening InDesign CS4 or CS5, 12
  exporting as, 420, 422-423
IDMS files. *See* snippets
Illustrator. *See* Adobe Illustrator
Image Processor command in Adobe
    Bridge, 52
images. *See* graphics
Images format, inserting files in, 16
importing/exporting, 512. *See also* export-
    ing documents; graphics; text
  Adobe PDF preset, creating, 433
  footnotes, 340
  plug-ins, 505
  presets, 459
  specialty frames for graphics, 158
  swatches from other documents, 224
  text variables, importing, 79
  XML tagged data, 418–419, 420
InCopy. *See* Adobe InCopy
INDD file format
  inserting files in, 16
  opening, 12
  saving as, 24
indenting. *See also* first-line indent;
    paragraphs
  bullets and numbering, 127

InDesign CS4 or CS5 with IDML, exporting,
    24, 422, 423
index
  entry
    creating, 88-89
    with keyboard shortcuts, 87
  creating, 90-91
  managing, 92-93
  starting, 86
  tips, 87
  topics, list of, 86
Indian typefaces, 140, 488
INDL file format. *See* libraries
INDT file format, 30
  saving as, 12
Info panel, 50–51
Ink Manager, 467
Ink on Paper theme, 498
inks
  Adobe PDF options, 430
  color separations, previewing, 465
  EPS file options, 439
  for printing, 467
inline object, creating, 197
Inner Glow effect, 249
Inner Shadow effect, 248
Insert Anchored Object dialog box, 198-199
inserting. *See also* pages
  Adobe Edge Animate, HTML, 378
  bookmarks, insertion point for, 354-355
  dashes, 130
  Google Maps, 378
  HTML code, 378
  QR Code, 379
  tabs, 128
  text variables, 79
  YouTube, 378
Insert Pages dialog box, 58–59
  multiple pages, inserting, 59
Inset corner options, 252
inside and outside margins. *See* margins
Inspector panel, Adobe Bridge, 523
installing
  extensions with Adobe Extension
    Manager, 505, 540
  Macintosh computers, InDesign in, 3
  Windows, InDesign in, 2

interactive documents. *See also* buttons; hyperlinks
   Adobe PDF options, 427
   Flash movie, interactivity options for, 443
interactive PDF, exporting, 436-437
   media options, 435
Interactivity workspace, 52–53
interface, color theme, 6, 234, 485
   Match to Theme Color option, 44
interface preferences, setting, 485
Internet
   North America Web/Internet color settings, 210
   updates, checking for, 20
   Web color library, 224
Intersect button, Pathfinder, 273
Inverse Rounded corner options, 252
inverted rounded rectangles, converting, 254
iOS, Apple
   creating for, 452-453
   document setup, 28-29, 34-35
iPad. *See* iOS, Apple
iPhone. *See* iOS, Apple
IPTC file format for metadata, 533
iRiver, creating for, 452-453
island spreads, 68
isolate blending, 246
italicizing, changing, 114

J

Japanese typefaces, 140, 488
JavaScript
Adobe Dreamweaver, exporting HTML document for, 454-455
   enabling or disabling, 484
   JDF File Using Acrobat checkbox with Adobe PDF, 431
Join or Close Path button, 268
joins on strokes, changing, 238–239
JPEG file format, 422, 423
   Adobe Bridge, opening with, 530-531
   EPUB and HTML, export, 452-456
   exporting documents in, 440-441
   importing images, options for, 143, 145
   metadata to files, adding, 479
   placing graphic files saved in, 142

raw images, saving, 527-529
   as recommended compression method, 428
Jump Object option, 136–137
Jump to Next Column option, 136–137
justification
   creating, multiple, 134-135
   options, changing, 337
   of paragraphs, 121
   paragraph styles, setting, 305
   table cells, content of, 291
   text frame options, setting, 132

K

Keep options for paragraphs, 336
kerning, 118
   highlighting text with, 489
   increments preferences, setting, 490–491
keyboard preferences, setting, 490–491
keyboard shortcuts
   defining, 503
   icons for starting InDesign, 4
   starting InDesign with, 5
   for tools, 10
   zooming in/out with, 39
Keywords panel, Adobe Bridge, 523
Kindle Fire, Amazon
   creating for, 452-453
   document setup, 28-29, 34-35
knockout group blending, 246
Kobo, creating for, 452-453
Korean typefaces, 140, 488
Kuler panel, using colors from, 230–231

L

lab color, 214
   Color panel, selecting with, 218
Labels and Stickers template, 30
labels for Adobe Bridge images, 533
landscape orientation
   changing, 34
   for new documents, 28
languages
   Adobe Composer options, 125, 140, 488
   advanced type settings for, 488
   for Autocorrect, 112
   changing, 140

last-line indent, creating, 122

last page, navigating to, 63

last saved version, reverting to, 24

Latin typefaces, 488

Layer Options dialog box, 202

layers

  Adobe InCopy, exporting to, 514

  Adobe PDF, creating Acrobat layers with, 427

  colors for layers, specifying, 202

  copying objects between, 206

  deleting, 201

  duplicating, 200–201

  Find/Change command, searching locked layers with, 329

  guides, options for, 202

  importing, 143, 144

  locking/unlocking, 202, 204

  merging layers, 205

  moving objects between, 206

    naming/renaming, 202

  new layer, renaming, 200

  new layer, creating, 200

  options, setting, 202

  pasting, creating new layer while, 200

  printing, 202

  printing options, 460

  reordering, 205, 206

  selecting layers, 206

  showing/hiding, 202, 203

    searching hidden layers, 329

  wrapping text, preventing, 202

Layers panel, showing/hiding objects and layers in, 203

Layout Adjustment options, 387

Layout menu

  pages, navigating between, 60–61

  table of contents, creating, 84–85

Layout view, drag-and-drop editing in, 113

LCD Optimized display for Story Editor, 499

leading

  Auto Leading option, 337

  entire paragraph, applying to, 486

  tabs, leaders with, 128

  text, 117

left-aligning paragraphs, 121

left indents

  for bullets and numbering, 127

  creating, 122

left side, dragging text to, 101

lens corrections with camera raw images, 528-529

letters

  half page size, 29

  page size, 29

  Quick Apply commands, 321

  spacing options, 337

libraries

  adding items in, 398–399

  Adobe Bridge libraries, using, 399

  changing item information, 401

  deleting items in, 398–399

  display, changing, 402–403

  existing library, opening, 398

  new library, creating, 398

  object types for items, changing, 401

  opening existing library, 398

  placing items on page, 400

  Samples button library, 368-369

  Samples form library, 370-371

  searching in, 402

  sorting items in, 402–403

  swatch libraries, adding colors from, 224

  updating items in, 400

ligatures. *See* glyphs

Lighten blend mode, 246

Linear gradients, 226

line breaks

  balancing, 336

  forcing, 110–111

lines. *See* strokes

Line tool, 172. *See also* strokes

links. *See also* graphics; hyperlinks

  Adobe Bridge, locating linked graphics with, 148

  Adobe PDF options, 427

  documents, across, 412

  Conveyer, using, 408-409

  missing link preferences, setting, 501

  in package files, 480

  objects, 410-411

  options, setting, 413

  preferences, setting, 501

  stories, 410-411

  styles, breaking links to, 312

Links panel. *See also* graphics
   sorting items in, 153
Liquid layout
   alternate layouts, 56, 384-386
   creating, 382-383
   Liquid Page Rules, 382-382
   panel, 382-383
List view, displaying library items in, 403
Live Corners, 253
Live Preflight, 476–477
Live Screen Drawing, 208
locating graphics. *See* graphics
locking/unlocking
   assignment files, overriding locked, 519
   guides, 43
   layers, 202, 204
   prevent selection, 484
   moving locked objects, 387
   object position, 196
Lock Position command, 196
lowercase text, creating, 342

M

Macintosh computers. *See also* PICT file
     format
   AppleScripts, 414
   installing InDesign in, 3
   starting InDesign in, 5
   System color library, 224
magnification. *See* zooming in/out
Make Compound Path command, 274–275
managing files. *See also* Adobe InCopy
   with Adobe Bridge, 14
mapping styles to export tags, 305, 307,
     316, 322, 451
margins. *See also* gutters
   changing options, 34–35
   guide color, specifying, 44
   new documents, options for, 29
   objects to margins, aligning, 186
   optical margin adjustment, setting, 337
markers, inserting, 130
marks and bleed
   with Adobe PDF, 429
   for booklet pages, 474
   changing bleed values, 34
   guide color, specifying, 44

for new documents, 28–29
   print options, setting, 462–463
master pages
   adding objects to, 70
   copying, 73
   creating, 70-71
   deleting, 72–73
   detaching, 72–73
   document page, applying to, 72
   existing page, creating master page
     from, 70–71
   Find/Change command for searching,
     329
   hiding master items, 73
   multiple pages, applying master to, 72
   overriding master element, 72–73
   page numbers, adding, 74–75
   page size, custom, 71
   printing options, 460
   scratch, creating master page from,
     70–71
   section numbers, adding, 74–75
   Start Page and Numbering At option, 75
   text variables, creating and using, 78–79
   unassigning masters, 72–73
master text frames
   changing, 34
   with imported text, 104
   new documents, selecting for, 28
   Smart Text Reflow for, 487
Match Pasteborad to Theme Color, 44, 234
Measure tool, 207
Media Encoder, 1, 522
   working with, 356-357, 538-539
Media Files format, inserting files in, 16
Media panel, 356-359
   adding a file, 356
   converting legacy files, 357
   setting media option, 356-359
menus, 6. *See also* specific menus
   colors for commands, 504
   customizing, 504
   InCopy menus, 520
   shortcuts for menus, creating, 503
Menus template, 30
Merge Layers command, 205
merging. *See also* Data Merge
   color swatches, 223

layers, 205
table cells, 286, 290
user dictionary into document, 493
metacharacters, 330
metadata. *See also* Adobe Bridge
description of, 533
documents, inserting file information
in, 478–479
Metadata panel, Adobe Bridge, 523
Microsoft Excel. *See also* XLS file format
tables, importing, 282–283
Microsoft Tablet PC. *See* Windows Tablet PC
Microsoft Word
importing text from, 102
inserting files in documents, 16
styles from Word document, importing,
310–311
tables, importing text into, 282–283
Mini Bridge, 210, 536
Minus Back button, Pathfinder, 273
missing link preferences, setting, 501
miter join on strokes, 239
mixed inks, 228–229
MOBI file format
Amazon Kindle, creating for, 452-453
monitors
colors, setting, 210
page size, setting, 29
More options for new documents, 29
Motion Presets, animation
applying, 260-261
converting objects to, 363
deleting, 362
duplicating, 362
editing, 363
importing, 362
options, settings, 260-261
saving, 362
Move Page command, 66–67
movies/videos
adding, 356–357
Media panel, 356-359
options, setting, 358–359
moving. *See also* objects
with Adobe Bridge, 14
anchor points, 260-261
books, documents in, 81

color swatches, 223
frames and graphics, 160–161
graphics, 152
guides, 42
with Hand tool, 50
help topics, moving between, 23
pages, 66–67
segments, 260-261
tabs, 128
text, 113
MP3 format, 356-359
MP4 format, 356-359
multiple documents
arranging, 19
working with, 18
multiple pages, inserting, 59
multi-state objects, creating, 376-377
Multi-State panel, 376-377

N

naming/renaming. *See also* Adobe Bridge;
layers
assignments, 516
bookmarks, 354–355
master page, 71
plug-ins, 505
styles, 310
navigating pages, 60–61
nesting
creating nested styles, 314–315
graphics in frames, 164
paragraph styles, setting, 305
tables, creating nested, 280
New Character Styles dialog box, 306
New Document dialog box, 32
new documents
presets, creating with, 32
template, creating from, 30
New Features, Welcome screen links to, 4
New Hyperlink From URL command,
346–347
New Paragraph Styles dialog box, 304
Newsletters template, 30
New Workspace dialog box, 52
next page, navigating to, 63
next spread, navigating to, 63
Nikon NEF format, 529

90-degree angles, drawing lines at, 172
Noise effect
    with feather effects, 251
    with glow, 249
    with shadows, 248
nonbreaking space, inserting, 130
non-Latin text, setting preferences for, 488
non-printing content
    Adobe PDF option, 427
    in package files, 481
    printing options for objects, 460
Nook, Barnes & Noble
    creating for, 452-453
    document setup, 28-29, 34-35
Normal view, 36
North American,
    Prepress 2 color settings, 210
    Purpose 2 color settings, 210
    Web/Internet color settings, 210
notes. *See also* footnotes
    to Adobe InCopy managed files, 513
    creating, 508
    Notes panel, working in, 509
    preferences, setting, 496
    tables, adding to, 508
    text to notes, converting, 508, 509
Notes panel, 509
No Wrap option, 136
Numbering and Section Options dialog box
    chapter numbers, adding, 76–77
    master pages, page and section numbers for, 74–75
number of pages
    changing, 34
    master spread, specifying for, 71
    new documents, selecting for, 28
numbers. *See also* bullets and numbering; chapter numbers; number of pages; page numbers
    footnotes, numbering, 341

O

objects. *See also* anchor points; gradients; graphics; layers
    aligning, 184-185
    anchored objects, creating, 198-199
    blend effect, creating, 246–247
    buttons, converting object to, 368–369

create multiple, in a grid, 173
colors
    applying, 215, 236
    Eyedropper tool, using, 216–217
    overprinting colors, 232
copying, 180–181
    layers, copying objects between, 206
    scaling and copying objects, 192
defaults, setting, 255
deleting, 174-175
deleting combined object, 183
Direct Selection tool
    grouped objects, working with, 182–183
    inline object, creating, 197
    selecting with, 174-175, 177
distances and angles, measuring, 207
duplicating, 180–181
export options
    Alt-text, 168
    EPUB and HTML, 451, 456
    tagged PDF, 450
Find/Change command, using, 328–329, 334
flipping objects, 194-195
Free Transform tool, transforming objects with, 191
Gap tool, 184-185
grouped objects, 182–183
    creating groups, 182
    selecting objects in group, 183
    ungrouping objects, 182
individual transformation, repeating, 190
inline object, creating, 197
library items, object types for, 401
locking/unlocking object position, 196
measuring distances and angles between, 207
moving, 179
    layers, moving objects between, 206
multiple objects, duplicating, 181
multi-state objects, creating, 376-377
overlapping objects, creating compound shapes from, 273
repeating transformations, 190
resizing, 178
rotating, 189, 194–195
    free rotating objects, 194-195

scaling, 178, 189–191, 192
searching for, 328–329, 334
Selection tool, 174-175
    inline object, moving, 197
    resizing objects with, 178
sequence of transformations, repeating, 190
shearing, 193
shortcuts for object editing, creating, 503
showing/hiding, 203
slipping objects, 192
Smart Guides for moving, 179
spacing, distributing objects with, 186–187
stack of objects, arranging, 188
styles
    creating, 316–317
    default object styles, modifying, 316
transformations, 189
    repeating transformations, 190
Object Shape option, 136–137
Object styles
    creating, 316-317
    exporting options, 316-317
OEBPS folder, 452-453
older versions, updating from, 2
On Blur event for buttons, 372
On Click event for buttons, 372
On Focus event for buttons, 372
online activation of program, 2
On release event for buttons, 372
On Roll Over event for buttons, 372
opacity, 11
    for Gradient Feather effect, 251
Open dialog box, 12
    deleting files in, 13
opening. See also Adobe Bridge
    books, documents in, 80
    closed paths, 266–267
    existing document, opening, 12
    IDML file format, InDesign CS4 or CS5, 12
    libraries, 398
    panels, 7
    recently opening document, 13
Open Package command, 516
Open Path button for splitting paths, 266

OpenType, 116
    character styles, setting, 307
    glyphs, inserting, 129
    highlighting text with, 489
    paragraph styles, setting, 305
Open With command with Adobe Bridge, 148
OPI options
    with Adobe PDF, 431
    print options, 470
optical margin adjustment, setting, 337
optical size of fonts, setting, 486
Options menu
    for panels, 8, 9
    for tools, 11
ordinals. See glyphs
ordering content, Articles panel, 446-447
orientation
    changing, 34
    flipping print orientation, 467
    for new documents, 28
    printing setup options, 461
Outer Glow effect, 249
outlines, creating, 138
out of gamut, 214
    converting out of gamut colors, 219
overflow text
    changing thread between frames, 107
    reshaping, 97
    text on a path, correcting, 101
    threading/unthreading, 106–107
overlapping objects, creating compound shapes from, 273
Overlay blend mode, 246
overprinting
    colors, 232
    paragraph rule, width of, 124
    simulating, 467
Overprint Preview mode, 36–37
overrides. See also styles
    Adobe PDF options, setting, 431
    assignment files, locked, 519
    print options, 470

P

Package for InCopy, 516
packages, creating, 480–481

PageMaker
    file format, 12
    Shortcuts for, 503
page numbers. *See also* number of pages
    books, options for, 82–83
    continued text, adding to, 139
    general preferences, setting, 484
    master pages, adding to, 74–75
    for table of contents, 85
pages. *See also* facing pages; master
        pages; Pages panel; spreads
    Adobe PDF options, setting, 426
    for bookmarks, 354-355
    Color Labels, adding, 66
    EPS file format options, 438
    Flash movie, exported as, 442
    FLA for Flash, exported as, 444
    hyperlinks to, 344
    inserting pages
        multiple pages, inserting, 59
        with Pages panel, 58–59
    JPEG files, documents exported as,
        440-441
    objects to page, aligning, 184-185
    PNG files, documents exported as,
        440-441
    Preflight panel options, 477
    size, changing, 28-29, 34-35, 62-64
    transitions, applying, 365
    trap preset, assigning, 468–469
page size options
    changing, 28-29, 34-35, 62-64
    list of, 29
    for new documents, 28
    printing, setup for, 461
Pages/Links panel, 8
Pages panel. *See also* master pages;
        spreads
    deleting pages, 65
    display, changing, 56
    duplicating pages, 58
    inserting pages with, 58–59
    multiple pages, inserting, 59
    navigating pages, 60–61
    showing/hiding icons, 57
    size, changing, 28-29, 34-35, 64
    target a page, navigating with, 60
    work on a page, navigating with, 60

Page tool
    changing the page size, 62-63, 382
    Liquid Page Rule, setting, 62
page transitions
    Flash movie, document exported as, 443
    for Pages panel icons, 57
Page Transitions dialog box, 365
panel groups, 6
    in Adobe InCopy, 520
panels, 6. *See also* Control panel; Pages
        panel; Tools panel
    in Adobe InCopy, 520
    collapsing/expanding, 7
        panel set between icons and panels, 9
    hidden panels, auto-showing, 485
    icons, auto-collapsing, 485
    Info panel, sizing object with, 51
    opening/closing, 7
    Options menu, using, 8, 9
    panels, 8
    shortcuts for panels, creating, 503
    showing/hiding, 7-8, 36, 52
Pantone color library, 224
Paragraph panel, InCopy, 520
paragraphs. *See also* bullets and number-
        ing
    Adobe Composer, 125, 140
    aligning, 121
    columns, creating multiple, 134-135
    colors
        rule, width of, 124
        styles, setting, 305
    creating, 110–111
    cross-references, creating, 352-353
    drop caps, creating, 123
    indenting, 122
        styles, setting, 305
    Info panel, information in, 50
    keeping lines together in, 336
    languages, work with, 140
    rules, applying, 124–125
    spacing, 122
    in table cells, 291
    table of contents, formatting for, 85
paragraph styles
    attributes, setting, 305
    basic paragraph style, changing, 303
    creating, 305

deleting, 304

existing text, creating from, 304

mapping styles to export tags, 305, 322, 451

for table of contents, 84

Paragraph Styles panel, 302

password options in Adobe PDF, 432

pasteboard. *See also* guides

match to theme color, 44, 234

Show Entire Pasteboard option, 38

Paste In command, 182–183

pasting

Adobe Bridge, settings in, 534

Clipboard handling preferences, 502

graphics, 152

layers while pasting, creating, 200

spacing, automatic adjustment of, 486

text, 113

patches, checking for, 20–21

Pathfinder command, 273

Pathfinder panel

Convert Shape buttons in, 254

Join or Close Path button, 268

Reverse button, 267

paths. *See also* clipping path; points; reshaping; strokes

closed path, opening, 266–267

closing open path, 268

compound path, creating, 274–275

erasing parts of, 272

frames, importing paths as, 159

Pencil tool, drawing with, 270–271

Pen tool, drawing with, 258–259

reversing direction of, 267

selecting path as clipping path, 277

Smooth tool, using, 269

splitting paths, 266

PDAs, RGB colors for, 214

PDF file format, 423

accessible PDF

Articles panel, ordering content, 446-447

creating PDF, 448

finishing in Acrobat Pro, 449

tags, applying to, 450

advanced options setting, 431

and bookmarks, 354–355

in background, exporting, 434

for buttons, 372–373

buttons in, 366-367

Clipboard handling preferences, 502

compression options, setting, 428

for data merged files, 416

exporting documents, 424

general options, setting, 426–427

graphic files saved in, 142

inserting files in, 16

for interactive, 435, 436-437

mapping styles to export tags, 305, 307, 322, 451

Marks and Bleeds option, setting, 429

media options, 435

metadata to files, adding, 479

output options, setting, 430

for page transitions, 365

placing, 144–145

Preflight panel, creating PDF report in, 477

presets, 425

exporting with, 433

for print, 424-432

security options, setting, 432

table of contents, PDF bookmarks for, 85

tagged PDF, 426, 450

PDF/X options with Adobe PDF, 424-427, 430

Pencil tool, 270–271

Pen tool, 258–259

perceptual colors, specifying, 213

Photoshop. *See* Adobe Photoshop

PICT file format

EPS file preview option, 439

WMFgraphic files saved in, 142

pirated versions, preventing, 2

Place and Link command, 410-412

Place command. *See also* graphics

with Adobe Bridge, 148

importing text with, 102–103

inserting artwork with, 16

multiple graphics, placing, 146–147

placing graphics. *See* graphics

plug-ins, configuring, 505

PNG file format, 423

EPUB and HTML, export, 452-456

exporting documents in, 440-441

metadata to files, adding, 479

placing graphic files saved in, 142

points. *See also* anchor points
Convert Direction Point Tool, using, 262-263
defined, 41
Direct Selection tool
converting points on path with, 262-263
moving, 266–267
and fonts, 116
ruler units preferences, setting, 490
Polygon Frame tool, 170
polygons
converting, 254
creating, 170–171
Pen tool, drawing with, 258
Polygon tool, 170
text, adding, 96, 98–99
portrait orientation
changing, 34
for new documents, 28
positioning
printing setup options, 461
poster images for sounds and movies, 358-359
PostScript
EPS file format options, 438
points preferences, setting, 490
preferences. *See also* type preferences
camera raw preferences, setting, 526-527
Clipboard handling preferences, setting, 502
composition preferences, setting, 489
dictionary preferences, setting, 492–493
file handling preferences, setting, 500–501
general preferences, setting, 484
grid preferences, changing, 48–49
interface preferences, setting, 485
links preferences, setting, 501
notes preferences, setting, 496
restoring, 501
ruler units preferences, setting, 490
spell-checking preferences, setting, 494–495
Story Editor preferences, setting, 498–499
Track Changes, 510
Units & Increments preferences, 490–491

prefixes for master pages, 71
Preflight panel, 476–477
Status bar, accessing from, 17
preflight profile
Status bar, accessing from, 17
using, 476–477
presentation mode, 36
presets. *See also* PDF file format
in Adobe Bridge, 534
deleting, 32–33, 459
printing with, 459
saving, 32
text variables, 78
transparency flattener preset, creating, 471
trapping preset, creating, 468
working with, 33
previewing. *See also* Adobe Bridge
color separations, 465
data merge data, 417
EPS file format options, 439
folio publication, 396
guide color for backgrounds, specifying, 44
images, saving, 24–25
overprinted colors, 232
page transitions, 365
save preferences, setting, 500
text frame options, 132
Preview view, 36
previous page, navigating to, 63
previous spread, navigating to, 63
Print command, 458
printers' marks options with Adobe PDF, 429
printing. *See also* overprinting; spreads; trapping
Adobe PDF print options, 425
advanced options, setting, 470–471
auto options, 461
booklet, spreads in, 474–475
books, 81
color handling options, 472
Color Management options, setting, 472
color separations, previewing, 465
data format options, 464
documents, 458
flattened artwork, 471

general options, setting, 460–461

graphics print options, setting, 464

Help topics, 23

keyboard shortcuts, list of, 503

layers, 202

marks and bleed print options, setting, 462–463

negative option, 466

output options, setting, 466–467

package files, print settings in, 480

preflight profile, using, 476–477

preserving color numbers, 472

with presets, 459

profile, setting, 472

sets, working with, 503

setup print options, setting, 460–461

simulating paper color option, 472

summary print options, 473

text as black, 466

transparency flattener preset, creating, 471

Printing and Proofing workspace, 52–53

Profile Inclusion Policy with Adobe PDF, setting, 430

projecting caps on strokes, 239

proofing colors on screen, 233

PSD file format

importing images, options for, 143, 144–145

metadata to files, adding, 479

placing graphic files saved in, 142

raw images, saving, 527-529

Q

QR Code, generating, 379

quality

Adobe PDF, setting image quality with, 428

JPEG files, documents exported as, 440–441

PNG files, documents exported as, 440–441

QuarkXPress

file format, 12

Shortcuts for, 503

Quick Apply, 11

for styles, 320–321

Quick Search, Adobe Bridge, 523

Quit InDesign command, 26

quotation marks

dictionary preferences, setting, 493

inserting, 130

typographer's quotes, using, 486

R

Radial Filter tool with camera raw files, 528-529

Radial gradients, 226

radius value in Corner Options dialog box, 254

range of page option for printing, 460

rasterizing

Flash movie, exported as, 443

FLA for Flash, exported as, 445

raw images. *See* Adobe Bridge; DNG file format

recently opening document, opening, 13

records for Data Merge, 416

Rectangle Frame tool, 170

rectangles

converting, 254

creating, 170

Rectangle tool, 170

text, adding, 96, 98

red-eye removal with camera raw files, 528-529

reference number for footnotes, 341

reference point

for fitting graphics in frames, 163

objects, transforming, 189

reflowing text, 487

Smart Text, 108–109

registration marks, printing, 463

relative colorimetric, specifying, 213

Release Compound Path command, 158–159

releasing compound paths, 158–159, 275

relinking. *See also* graphics

cross-references, 352-353

renaming. *See* naming/renaming

repeated words, spell-checking preferences, 494

replacing

books, documents in, 81

importing text, replacing item with, 102

table of contents, 85

reports for page files, creating, 480
resetting
all warning dialogs, 484
cross-references, 352-353
reshaping
anchor points or segments, 260-261
erasing to reshape paths, 272
Pencil tool, paths with, 270
resizing. *See* sizing/resizing
resolution
Adobe PDF setting options, 428
Info panel, information in, 50
JPEG files, exported as, 440-441
PNG files, exported as, 440-441
resource help, 22–23
restoring preferences, 501
retouching with camera raw files, 528-529
reusing linked text, 410-411
revealing documents
in Adobe Bridge, 15
in Status bar, 17
reverse order option for printing, 460
reversing fill in compound path, 275
RGB (Red, Green, Blue), 214
Adobe PDF options, setting, 430
Color panel, selecting with, 218
EPS file format options, 438
Working Space controls, 210–211
right-aligning paragraphs, 121
right indents
creating, 122
right side, dragging text to, 101
RIP (Raster Image Processing), 466, 468
rotating, 11. *See also* objects; spreads
with Adobe Bridge, 14
camera raw files, 528-529
Spread view, 37
tables, text in, 291
Rotation and Shear Angle, 11
round bullets, 126–127
round caps on strokes, 239
Rounded corner options, 252
round join on strokes, 239
RTF file format, 423
importing text from, 102
inserting files in, 16

rulers
changing ruler options, 40
guides
appearance, changing, 44–45
movement, allowing, 387
measurement units, changing, 41
origin, changing, 41
paragraph rule, applying, 124–125
showing/hiding, 41
units preferences, setting, 490
working with, 41
rules for paragraph styles, setting, 305
run-in style table of contents, 85
Running Header text variable, 78

S

sample, creating
buttons from, 368
forms from, 370
sampling options for Adobe PDF, 428
satin effect, 249
saturation, specifying, 213
Save As dialog box, 13
saving
in background, saving PDF, 24
books, 81
camera raw images, 527-529
color swatches, 223
copy of document, 25
documents, 24–25
file handling preferences, setting, 500
gradients, 227
in InDesign CS4 or CS5 with IDML, 24, 422, 423
presets, 32
print summary, 473
Web Photo Gallery, 531
Scale X and Y, 11
scaling
Flash movie, document exported as, 442
FLA for Flash, document exported as, 444
general preferences, setting, 484
Info panel, information in, 50
objects, 178, 189–191, 192
printing setup options, 461

shortcuts for scaling, creating, 503

text, 120

Scissor tool for splitting open paths, 266

screen fonts, 116

scripts

editing scripts, 414

general preferences, setting, 484

running scripts, 414–415

Scripts panel, 414–415

Script Label panel, 415

SCT file format, WMF graphic files saved in, 142

searching. *See also* Find/Change command

in Adobe Bridge, 14, 532

for fonts, 114, 327

for glyphs, 328–329, 332

for GREPs, 328–329, 332

for help information, 22–23

in libraries, 402

for objects, 328–329, 334

spell-check options, 325

Section 524 of the Rehabilitation Act of 1973, 450

sections

books, updating section numbers in, 83

master pages, adding numbers to, 74–75

security

Adobe PDF security options, setting, 432

JavaScript, enabling or disabling, 484

segments

deleting, 265

moving, 260-261

Pencil tool, drawing with, 270

reshaping, 260-261

selecting, 260-261

splitting paths in middle of, 266

selecting

anchor points, 260-261

frames and graphics, 160–161

segments, 260-261

text, 110–111

Selection tool. *See also* Direct Selection tool; objects

fitting frames in graphics with, 162

objects, selecting, 174-175

selecting and moving frames and graphics with, 160

with Smart Guides, 46

Send Backward in object stack, 188

Send to Back in object stack, 188

Sentence case, creating, 342

Separations Preview mode, 36–37

servers in Adobe InCopy, working with, 512

shadow effects, 248

Drop Shadow effect, 11, 248

shapes. *See also* reshaping; specific shapes

compound shapes, creating, 273

converting shapes, 254

creating, 170–171

with Smart Guides, 46

sharing. *See* Adobe InCopy; assignments; interactive documents

shearing objects, 189–191, 193

Shear tool, 193

shortcuts. *See also* keyboard shortcuts

Macintosh computers, creating shortcuts on, 5

showing/hiding. *See also* hidden text; layers; panels

grids, 48

guides, 43

icons, 504

master items, 73

notes, 509

objects, 203

Pages panel icons, 57

plug-ins, information on, 505

rulers, 41

separation inks, 464

Tools panel, 36

Show Text Threads command, 106–107

sidecar files, 533

signature for booklet pages, 475

sign in and out

Creative Cloud, 21, 542

simulating overprinting print option, 467

single quotation marks, inserting, 130

single word justification, 337

sizing/resizing. *See also* graphic frames; graphics; page size options

icon size for Pages and Masters, 56

Pages panel, 56

shortcuts for sizing, creating, 503

skewing text, 120

slug area
    Adobe PDF options, 429
    changing values, 34
    guide color, specifying, 44
    for new documents, 28–29
    page numbers in, 66
Slug view, 36
small caps, 488
    styling text as, 114–115
Smart Cursor, 179, 485
Smart Guides, 46–47
    objects, moving, 179
    with Pen tool, 258
    preferences, changing, 47
Smart Match Style Group synchronize
    options, 82
smart spacing, 47
Smart Text Reflow, 108–109
    options, selecting, 487
Smooth tool and preferences, 269
snapping options, adjusting, 387
Snap to Document Grid command, 49
Snap to Guides command, 42–43
Snap to Zone, 44, 47
snippets
    creating, 404–405
    dragging, creating by, 404–405
    import options, setting, 501
    using, 404–405
Soft Light blend mode, 246
soft proofing colors on screen, 233
Soft Proofs mode, 36–37
soft returns, forcing, 110–111
Solid Color Intent option, 212
Sony Reader, creating for, 452-453
sorting
    with Adobe Bridge, 14
    bookmarks, 354-355
sounds
    adding, 356–357
    Media panel, 356–359
    options, setting, 358–359
source files
    for cross-references, 352-353
    for hyperlinks, 344
    for linked graphics, 153
spacing
    automatic adjustment of, 486

    footnotes, 341
    glyph spacing, 337
    letter spacing options, 337
    objects with spacing, distributing, 186–187
    paragraphs, 122
    paragraph styles, setting, 305
    Story Editor display, setting, 498
    table columns and rows, evenly distributing spacing of, 288
    text on a path, 101
    word spacing options, 337
Spanish typefaces, 488
special characters. *See* characters
specialty frames for graphics, creating, 158–159
spell-checking. *See also* dictionaries
    Autocorrect fixing errors, 112
    documents, 324–325
    dynamic spelling, 324, 325, 495
    note content, 496
    options, 325
    preferences, setting, 494–495
spine, aligning paragraphs to, 121
splitting
    paths, 266
    table cells, 290
Split window to compare,
    Split Layout view, 18-19, 386
spot colors and mixed inks, 228–229
Spot Removal tool with camera raw images, 528-529
Spread effect
    with glow, 249
    with shadows, 248
spreads
    adding/removing pages from, 68
    EPS file format options, 438
    facing-page spreads, preserving, 487
    Flash movie, document exported as, 442
    FLA for Flash, document exported as, 444
    island spreads, 68
    JPEG files, documents exported as, 440-441
    object to spread, aligning, 184-185
    page transitions, applying, 365
    PNG files, documents exported as, 440-441

printing, 460
    booklet spreads, 474–475
rotating, 37, 69
    Pages panel icons, 57
spreadsheets, links preferences when
    placing, 501
stacking
    Adobe Bridge, images in, 14, 533
    object stack order, arranging, 188
StandardSoundPoster.jpg, 356
StandardMoviePoster.jpg, 358-359
star shape
    creating, 170–171
    frame for text, creating, 99
starting InDesign, 4–5
Start menu or screen, 4-5, 13
Start Page and Numbering At option, 75
Status bar
    pages, navigating between, 60–61
    working with, 17
Step and Repeat command
    grid, creating, 181
    objects, copying, 180
stories
    Adobe InCopy, exporting content to, 514
    Find/Change command, searching story
        layers with, 329
Story Editor
    background color for notes in, 496
    display preferences, setting, 325,
        498–499
    drag-and-drop editing in, 113
    show or hide elements, 339
    tables, editing text in, 284–285
    working with, 338-339
straightening camera raw files, 528-529
strikethrough options
    character styles, setting, 307
    paragraph styles, setting, 305
Strikethrough text, 114–115
Stroke panel, 8, 174
strokes. See also gap color/tint; tables
    alignment of stroke on path, 238
    applying strokes, 215, 236-237
    attributes, changing, 238–239
    caps, changing, 238–239
    converting, 254
    custom-dashed stroke, applying, 240

custom styles, creating, 240–241
dashed/dotted strokes
    applying, 240
    creating, 240–241
    gap color for, 239
defaults
    for colors, 236–237
    setting, 255
drawing, 174
Eyedropper tool, using, 216–217
Info panel, information in, 50
joins, changing, 238–239
styles, 239–241
    custom styles, creating, 240–241
    dashed stroke style, applying, 240
Structure pane for placing XML tags,
    418–420
styles. See also character styles; GREPs;
    objects; paragraph styles; strokes;
    tables
    applying, 312–313
    for bullets, 126–127
    case-sensitivity of names, 310
    cell styles, creating, 318
    Character Styles panel, 302
    clearing style overrides, 312–313
    for cross-references, 352-353
    deleting table and cell styles, 319
    editing with Quick Apply, 321
    End Nested Style Here special character,
        314–315
    font style, changing, 114–115
    groups, creating, 309
    for hyperlinks, 349
    importing styles, 310–311
    InDesign document, loading styles from,
        310
    letter commands with Quick Apply, 321
    links to style, breaking, 312
    loading styles, 310
    mapping to export tags, 316, 322, 451
    Microsoft Word document, importing
        styles from, 310–311
    nested styles, creating, 314–315
    overriding
        formatting, 312–313
        object style overrides, clearing, 317
    paragraph rule, width of, 124

styles *(continued)*
    with Paragraph Styles panel, 302
    Quick Apply, using, 320–321
    renaming styles, 310
    table styles, 318–319
Style Source setting for books, 82
subsampling with Adobe PDF, 428
subscript, 114–115
    advanced type settings for, 488
Subtract button, Pathfinder, 273
summary
    for booklet pages, 475
    print options, viewing summary of, 473
superscript, 114–115
    advanced type settings for, 488
swapping text on path, 101
swashes. *See glyphs*
Swatches panel. *See also gradients*
    adding color swatch, 221
    all unnamed colors, adding, 223
    for button colors, 374
    Color Picker, adding colors from, 237
    deleting color swatch, 221, 222
    display, changing, 220
    editing color swatch, 221
    fill or stroke color, changing, 236
    gradient swatches, creating, 226–227
    Kuler panel, adding, 230
    loading swatches, 223
    merging color swatches, 223
    mixed inks with, 228–229
    moving swatches, 223
    name of swatch, entering, 221
    saving swatches, 223
    selecting swatches, 223
    tint swatches, creating, 225
    working with swatches, 222–223
swatch libraries, adding colors from, 224
SWF file format, 356-359, 422, 423
    exporting document in, 442–443
SWF Preview panel, 378, 380
    Adobe Bridge, 523
switching between pages in Status bar, 17
symbols
    @ before field name, adding, 416
    Autocorrect, inserting with, 112
    inserting, 130

synchronizing
    books, 82
    camera raw images, 528-529
System color library, 224
system requirements, 3
    32-bit and 64-bit, 5

T

table of contents
    creating, 84–85
    for digital editions, EPUB, 452-453
Table Options dialog box, 299
tables
    adjusting options, 282
    aligning content in cells, 291
    alternating fills and strokes in, 296–297
    borders, adding, 299
    clipping for graphics, setting, 291
    colors
        for borders, 299
        for diagonal lines in cells, 298
        strokes and fills, setting for, 296–297
    columns and rows, inserting, 287
    Control panel, modifying tables with, 286
    converting
        tables to text, 281
        text to tables, 281
    defined, 279
    deleting
        cell contents, 284
        columns and rows, 287
        table and cell styles, 319
    diagonal lines in cells, adding, 298
    dimensions, specifying, 280
    editing text in tables, 284–285
    elements, selecting, 284
    fills
        adding, 294–295
        alternating fills, 296–297
    gap color/tint
        for borders, 299
        for diagonal lines in cells, 298
        tables, strokes in, 297
    graphics
        clipping for graphics, setting, 291
        importing graphics, 282

headers and footers, 292–293
    converting cells and, 293
height, weight, width
    adjustment options, 289
    for borders, 299
    elements, specifying, 286
importing
    graphics into tables, 282
    text into tables, 282–283
merging/unmerging cells, 286, 290
Microsoft Excel tables, importing, 282–283
Microsoft Word text, importing, 282–283
modifying, 286–287
navigating in tables, 284
nested tables, creating, 280
new table, creating, 280
notes, adding, 508
spacing of columns and rows, evenly distributing, 288
splitting cells, 290
Story Editor, using, 284–285
strokes
    adding, 294–295
    alternating strokes, 296–297
    cells, adding to, 294–295
    diagonal lines in table cells, adding, 298
    drawing order, setting, 294
    lines, 172
    style and weight, specifying, 286
styles, 318–319
Table panel, modifying tables with, 286
text
    converting tables and text, 281
    editing text in tables, 284–285
    entering text in tables, 284
    importing text, 282–283
    rotating, 291
    Story Editor, editing text with, 284–285
text frames, adjusting tables in, 300
tablets
    creating for, 452-453
    document setup, 28-29, 34-35
tabloid page size, 29
Tab Order dialog box, 375

tabs
    for bullets and numbering, 127
    button tab order, setting, 375
    paragraph styles, setting, 305
    setting, 128
    stops, defined, 128
tagged PDF options, 450
target a page, navigating with, 60
templates
    creating template document, 31
    new document, creating, 30
    saving document as, 25
    for Web Photo Gallery, 531
Terminal theme, 498
text. *See also* character styles; fonts; hidden text; kerning; overflow text; paragraphs; paragraph styles; Smart Text Reflow; Story Editor; tables; text frames; tracking; type preferences; wrapping text
    Autocorrect options, 112
    autoflowing imported text, 105
    baseline, shifting characters from, 117
    black, printing text as, 466
    for bookmarks, 354-355
    with bullets, 126–127
    for buttons, 374
    colors in Story Editor display, 498
    conditional text, working with, 406–407
    copying, 113
    cutting, 113
    documents, inserting text in, 16
    dragging text, 113
    Find/Change command, using, 328–329, 330
    Frame tools, adding with, 96, 98
    greeked text, 487
    importing text, 102–103
        autoflowing imported text, 105
        continued text, adding page numbers to, 139
        flowing imported text, 104–105
        with options, 102–103
    Info panel, viewing in, 51
    inherited formatting for text, 113
    leading text, 117
    linked text, reusing, 410-411
    links preferences when placing, 501

text *(continued)*
    notes, converting text to, 508, 509
    overflowing text, reshaping, 97
    pasting, 113
    reflowing, 108–109
    scaling text, 120
    searching, 328, 329–330
    selecting, 110–111
    skewing text, 120
    special text characters, inserting, 130
    track text changes, 510-511
    Type of a Path tool, using, 96
    typing text, 110
text breaks, inserting, 130
text frames. *See also* assignments; over-
    flow text
    baseline options, 133
    creating text in, 97
    elliptical frame, creating, 98
    ignoring text wrapping in, 133
    options, setting, 132–133
    outlines, creating, 138
    overflowing text, reshaping, 97
    polygon frame, creating, 99
    rectangle frame, creating, 98
    searching for, 334
    star frame, creating, 99
    tables, adjusting, 300
    wrapping text, 97, 137
        ignoring text wrap, 133
Text Only file format, 423
text variables
    defining, 78
    working with, 79
themes
    color theme, interface, 6, 44, 234, 485
    Kuler panel, using colors from, 230–231
    Story Editor display, setting, 498
threading/unthreading overflow text,
    106–107
3-D bevel effect, 250
threshold
    for grids, 49
    for guides, 45
thumbnails
    Adobe PDF options, setting, 426
    library items, displaying, 403
    options for showing, 485

    in Pages panel, 56
    printing setup options, 461
Timing panel, 364
TIFF file format
    Adobe Bridge, opening with, 530-531
    EPS file preview option, 439
    importing images, options for, 143, 145
    for metadata, 479, 533
    placing graphic files saved in, 142
    raw images, saving, 527-529
tiling documents, 19
Times New Roman font, 114
tints. *See also* gap color/tint
    dashed/dotted lines, tint color for, 239
    paragraph rule, width of, 124
    swatches, creating, 225
Title Case, creating, 342
tone curve for camera raw images, 528-529
tools. *See also* specific tools
    keyboard shortcuts for, 10
    shortcuts for tools, creating, 503
Tools panel, 6
    for InCopy, 520
    keyboard shortcuts, 10
    showing/hiding, 36
    using, 10–11
Tools Hints panel, 10-11
tooltips
    note tooltips, showing, 496
    options for showing, 485
top and bottom margins. *See* margins
Toyo color library, 224
track changes, 510-511
tracking, 119
    highlighting text with, 489
    increments preferences, setting, 490–491
Tracking and Indentation option, Type tool,
    11
Transform Again submenu, 189
transformation. *See also* objects
    values, showing, 485
transitions. *See* page transitions
transitions for pages, displaying, 365
transparency
    Adobe PDF options, setting, 431
    blend, create effect with, 247
    color space for blending transparent
        objects, 247

FLA for Flash, document exported as, 445

importing, 143, 144

for Pages panel icons, 57

print options, 470–471

trapping, 466

assigning trap presets to pages, 468–469

preset, creating, 468

Trap Presets panel, 468

triangles, converting, 254

triple-click, changing action of, 111

TrueType fonts, 116

Trumatch color library, 224

turning on/off

Smart Guides, 46

2-up perfect bound for booklet, printing, 474

2-up saddle stitch for booklet, printing, 474

TXT file format

data fields, 416

importing text from, 102

inserting files in, 16

Type on a Path tool, 96

creating text on path, 100

deleting text on path, 100

modifying text on path, 101

type outlines as frames, creating, 159

type preferences

advanced preference, setting, 488

general preferences, setting, 486–487

Type tools

options with, 11

text frame, creating text in, 97

using, 96

typing text, 110

typographer's quotes, using, 486

Typography workspace, 52–53

U

unassigned frames, 169, 170

searching for, 334

underlining, 114–115

character styles, setting, 307

conditional text, 406-407

paragraph styles, setting, 305

undoing/redoing, 53

updates and updating``

assignments, 519

data merge sources, 417

Help menu, checking on, 21

hyperlinks, 350

Internet, checking for updates on, 20

library items, 400

package files, 480

uploading Web Photo Gallery, 531

uppercase text, creating, 342

Upright tool with camera raw images, 528-529

URLs. *See* hyperlinks

user dictionary preferences, 492

V

vector-based images, inserting, 16

vertical lines, converting, 254

vertically tiling all documents, 19

vertical spacing in text, changing, 117

videos. *See* movies

views and viewing. *See also* display; rulers

InCopy views, 512

InDesign window, 6

object styles, 316

page transitions, 365

print summary, 473

Zoom tool, changing view with, 38–39

Visibility icon, 504

visibility settings

for cross-references, 352-353

for hyperlinks, 348-349

Visual Basic scripts, 414

visually impaired persons, PDF options for, 432

W

warning dialogs, resetting, 484

Web color library, 224

Web Photo Gallery, creating, 531

Web sites

hyperlinks to, 344

weight. *See* height, weight, width

Welcome screen

Open dialog box, 12

opening document from, 13

starting InDesign from, 4

What's New, finding, 23

White Balance with camera raw files, 528-529

white space, inserting, 130

width. *See* height, weight, width

Windows menu, 18–19

    System color library, 224

Windows Tablet PC

    creating for, 452-453

    document setup, 28-29, 34-35

WMF file format, graphic files saved in, 142

Word. *See* Microsoft Word

words

    Info panel, information in, 50

    spacing options, 337

Working Space color controls, 210–211

work on a page, navigating with, 60

workspaces. *See also* Adobe Bridge

    built-in workspaces, 52

    creating, 52

    deleting, 53

    displaying, 53

wrapping text. *See also* text frames

    composition preferences, setting, 489

    contour options, 137

    inside edges, including, 137

    layers, preventing wrapping in, 202

    objects, wrapping and unwrapping around, 136

    setting shape wrap options, 137

WYSIWYG font menu, 486–487

X

XFL file format, 444

XHTML format for eBooks, EPUB, selecting, 452-453

XLS file format

    importing text from, 102

    inserting files in, 16

XML file format, 423

    creating XML tags, 418

    document, placing XML tags in, 418–419

    elements in, 418

    exporting XML, 420

    importing XML tagged data, 418–419

    for motion presets, 360-361

XMP file format, 533

    alt text, adding to graphic, 168

documents, inserting file information in, 478–479

linked graphic, displaying information for, 157

XMP Software Development Kit, 479

Xoom

    document setup, 28-29, 34-35

Y

YouTube, inserting, HTML, 378

Z

zooming in/out

    in camera raw files, 528-529

    image view, 38–39

    shortcut keys for, 39